LAW AND SOCIAL T

There is a growing interest within law schools in the intersections between law and different areas of social theory. The second edition of this popular text introduces a wide range of traditions in sociology and the humanities that offer provocative, contextual views on law and legal institutions.

The book is organised into five sections, each with an introduction by the editors, on classical sociology of law, relating structure and action, critical approaches, postmodernism, and law in global society. Each chapter is written by a specialist who reviews the literature, and discusses how the approach can be used in researching different topics. New chapters include authoritative reviews of actor network theory, legal realism, critical race theory, postcolonial theories of law, and the sociology of the legal profession. Over half the chapters are new, and the rest include discussion of recent literature.

Law and Social Theory

Second Edition

Edited by

Reza Banakar

and

Max Travers

·HART·
PUBLISHING

OXFORD AND PORTLAND, OREGON
2013

Hart Publishing
An imprint of Bloomsbury Publishing Plc

Hart Publishing Ltd
Kemp House
Chawley Park
Cumnor Hill
Oxford OX2 9PH
UK

Bloomsbury Publishing Plc
50 Bedford Square
London
WC1B 3DP
UK

www.hartpub.co.uk
www.bloomsbury.com

Published in North America (US and Canada) by
Hart Publishing
c/o International Specialized Book Services
920 NE 58th Avenue, Suite 300
Portland, OR 97213-3786
USA

www.isbs.com

HART PUBLISHING, the Hart/Stag logo, BLOOMSBURY and the
Diana logo are trademarks of Bloomsbury Publishing Plc

Reprinted 2017

First published 2013

British Library Cataloguing-in-Publication Data
A catalogue record for this book is available from the British Library.

ISBN: HB: 978-1-84946-381-2

Typeset by Forewords, Oxon
Printed and bound in Great Britain by CPI Group (UK) Ltd, Croydon, CR0 4YY

To find out more about our authors and books visit www.hartpublishing.co.uk. Here you will find extracts,
author information, details of forthcoming events and the option to sign up for our newsletters.

Acknowledgements

We acknowledge permission from the *Annual Review of Law and Social Science* for granting us permission to publish from Yves Dezalay and Mikael R Madsen, 'The Force of Law and Lawyers: Pierre Bourdieu and the Reflexive Sociology of Law' 8 (2012) 433–452. We are also grateful to the *Journal of Legal Pluralism and Unofficial Law* for allowing us to publish material from A Griffiths, 'Pursuing Legal Pluralism: The Power of Paradigms in a Global World' 64 (2011) 173–202. We would like to thank the contributors who have given their time and energy to making the second edition of this book possible. We would also like to thank Hart Publishing for its support.

Acknowledgments

Contents

List of Contributors

Frédéric Audren, Senior Research Fellow, Centre National de Recherche Scientifique (CNRS) and Associate Research Professor, Sciences Po Law School and Centre d'étude européennes, Paris, France.

Reza Banakar, Professor of Legal Sociology, Lund University, Sweden and Professor of Socio-Legal Studies, School of Law, University of Westminster, London, UK.

Eve Darian-Smith, Professor of Global and International Studies, University of California, Santa Barbara, USA.

Mathieu Deflem, Professor of Sociology, University of South Carolina, USA.

Yves Dezalay, Directeur de Recherches Emeritus, Centre National de Recherche Scientifique (CNRS), Paris, France.

Robert Fine, Professor of Sociology, Department of Sociology, Warwick University, UK.

Anne Griffiths, Professor of Legal Anthropology, School of Law, University of Edinburgh, UK.

Ole Hammerslev, Professor of Sociology of Law, Department of Law, University of Southern Denmark, Denmark.

Angela P Harris, Professor of Law, University of California – Davis (King Hall), USA.

Alan Hunt, Chancellor's Professor in the Departments of Sociology and Legal Studies, Carleton University, Ottawa, Canada.

Michael King, Professor Emeritus, School of Law, University of Reading, UK.

Stewart Macaulay, Malcolm Pitman Sharp Professor Emeritus, University Wisconsin Law School, USA.

Elizabeth Mertz, John and Rylla Bosshard Professor of Law, University of Wisconsin, USA and Research Faculty, American Bar Foundation.

Mikael Rask Madsen, Professor of Law, Faculty of Law and Director of iCourts, the Danish National Research Foundation's Centre of Excellence for International Courts, University of Copenhagen, Denmark.

Shaun McVeigh Associate Professor, Melbourne Law School, University of Melbourne, Australia.

Ralf Michaels Arthur Larson Professor of Law, Duke University, Durham, North Carolina, USA.

Cédric Moreau de Bellaing, Assistant Professor in Political Science and Sociology of Law, Ecole Normale Supérieure, Paris, France.

David Nelken, Distinguished Professor of Legal Institutions and Social Change, University of Macerata, Italy, Distinguished Research Professor of Law, Cardiff University, UK and Visiting Professor of Criminology, Oxford Law Faculty, UK.

Harriet Samuels, Reader in Law, School of Law, University of Westminster, London, UK.

Max Travers, Senior Lecturer in Sociology, School of Social Sciences, University of Tasmania, Australia.

A Javier Treviño, Jane Oxford Keiter Professor of Sociology, Wheaton College, Massachusetts, USA.

Gary Wickham, Professor of Sociology, Murdoch University, Murdoch, Western Australia.

Introduction

REZA BANAKAR and MAX TRAVERS

I N 2002, WE were fortunate to obtain the support of Hart Publishing to edit an advanced introduction to law and social theory that we know has helped many postgraduates and those teaching contextual courses in law schools over the last ten years. Despite the title of the first edition, the book was not really introductory. It contained authoritative review essays by experts who were knowledgeable about different theorists or had the experience of working within different theoretical traditions. These essays were organised into sections that grouped together theorists with comparable epistemological assumptions, in a similar way to how these are presented in textbooks on sociological theory. In addition, there were section introductions in which we tried as editors to explain and clarify what the reviewers covered in their introductions. The aim was to present the theoretical diversity of the field of law and society, to demonstrate how various sociolegal theories were related to—or distinguished themselves from—each other and to explore how one could conduct empirical research about law through employing the ideas rooted in different sociological traditions. More generally, however, we hoped to convey the pleasures and challenges of engaging with difficult ideas that can lead in a variety of directions.

We are pleased, ten years later, to have the opportunity to edit a second edition that makes it possible to cover some new topics and to allow the authors of different chapters to discuss some of the new theoretical literature and research studies published in different fields. It seems important to say that we see this book as supplementing, rather than replacing, the first edition. Although sociological theory does change, in the sense that each generation has to make sense of its own times, the main approaches have been around for some time. Because some readers may only see this edition, we have reprinted some of the original chapters with minor revisions. We have, though, recruited several new authors to give a different slant on particular theorists and traditions. Some contributors to the first edition have supplied new chapters. We have also commissioned chapters on a few new theorists and traditions, as well as some essays that apply different theories to particular topics such as globalisation and the legal profession.

In the introduction to the first edition, we felt it was important to convey the diverse character of the sociology of law through reviewing some debates in sociological theory. We have therefore provided a similar overview here, since this background helps in making sense of the relationship between different theories and traditions. We should add that these debates are not always mentioned or seen as important in law and society texts, because the distinctions are not seen as important, or they are seen as too difficult for law students, or because the authors are committed to a particular viewpoint or perhaps have limited knowledge about other traditions. We will also explain the structure of this book and identify which chapters are new because they either address new topics or have different authors. Finally, we will make some general points about how to think about law sociologically, and we will also restate our views about the value of including contextual courses, particularly sociology of law, in the law school curriculum.

1. THE DIVERSE CHARACTER OF SOCIOLOGY OF LAW

The sociology of law, both as an academic discipline and an interdisciplinary field of research, embraces a host of disparate and seemingly irreconcilable perspectives and approaches to the study of law in society. This diverse character is celebrated by some scholars, who regard it as a source of theoretical pluralism and methodological innovation, and criticised by others, who see it as a cause of theoretical fragmentation, eclecticism and discontinuity in research.[1] Whether we approve of the theoretical diversity of the field of sociolegal research and view it as a source of innovation, or disapprove of it and describe it as 'an incoherent or inconclusive jumble of case studies', to borrow from Lawrence Freedman,[2] the fact remains that its diverse make-up entails a number of methodological challenges for students and researchers alike.[3] The present volume does not aim at resolving the problem of diversity and fragmentation in the field of sociolegal research, but instead hopes to offer insights into how various schools of thought, debate and discourse within the field have emerged. Although in the following we often refer to 'sociology of law' and borrow our main concepts and ideas from mainstream sociology, we nonetheless maintain that the thrust of our arguments is also applicable to sociolegal studies, law and society, or studies of law-in-society.

The sociology of law employs social theories and applies social scientific methods to the study of law, legal behaviour and legal institutions in order to describe and analyse legal phenomena in their social, cultural and historical contexts. It is therefore often considered as a subdiscipline of sociology or an interdisciplinary approach within academic law or legal studies. Whereas some sociolegal scholars, such as Mathieu Deflem, treat it as 'always and necessarily' belonging to the discipline of sociology,[4] others regard it as a field of research caught up in the disciplinary tensions and competitions between the two established disciplines of law and sociology.[5] Yet others regard it neither as a subdiscipline of sociology nor as a branch of legal studies, and instead present it as a field of research in its own right, within a broader social science tradition. For example, Roger Cotterrell describes the sociology of law, without reference

---

[1] Sociological studies of law have been criticised for being fragmented and theoretically undeveloped in relation to sociology. See A Hunt, *The Sociological Movement in Law* (London, Macmillan, 1978); M Travers, 'Putting Sociology Back into Sociology of Law' (1993) 20 *Journal of Law and Society* 438–51; R Banakar, *Merging Law and Sociology* (Berlin, Galda & Wilch, 2003).

[2] LM Friedman, 'The Law and Society Movement' (1986) 38 *Stanford Law Review* 779.

[3] For a discussion, see R Banakar and M Travers, 'Law and Sociology' in R Banakar and M Travers (eds) *Theory and Method in Socio-legal Research* (Oxford, Hart Publishing, 2005).

[4] M Deflem, *Sociology of Law: Visions of a Scholarly Tradition* (Cambridge, Cambridge University Press, 2008) 3; for a similar approach, see also M Travers *Understanding Law and Society* (London, Routledge, 2009).

[5] Banakar, above n 1.

to mainstream sociology, as 'the systematic, theoretically grounded, empirical study of law as a set of social practices or as an aspect or field of social experience'.[6] Cotterrell explains that academic lawyers interested in the study of law have often turned 'to sociology of law to escape the narrow disciplinary outlook of academic law',[7] which is why they do not wish to take refuge behind disciplinary walls, albeit those of legal studies or sociology. These researchers see the intellectual advancement in social studies as something which often occurs 'by ignoring disciplinary prerogatives, boundaries and distinctions'.[8] Similarly, Masaji Chiba avoided limiting his definition of the subject to the narrow conception of sociology and argued that the word 'sociology' referred to 'social sciences broadly' when it was used in combination with 'of law'.[9] Explicit in Cotterrell and Chiba's definitions is the desire to maintain sociology of law as an intellectually open and methodologically inclusive approach to the study of law. The intellectual openness flagged and practised by many sociolegal scholars has a number of implications for the development of the field. Admittedly, it safeguards the methodological diversity of the field by providing a 'space' for new and innovative thinking and approaches, but it also gives sociolegal research a non-cumulative, discursively scattered and theoretically eclectic appearance.[10] In the following, we shall adopt a broad and inclusive concept of sociology which acknowledges the relevance of other social sciences—in particular social and cultural anthropology and political science—for the development of sociology of law. We also refuse to make a sharp distinction between sociology of law's research interests and those of legal anthropology, law and politics, sociological jurisprudence, sociolegal studies, and the law and society movement in North America. Our argument is that an engagement with the central debates of social theory, in general, but with the theoretical concerns of mainstream sociology, in particular, is essential for the development of all social scientific studies of the law, irrespective of how 'law' and 'social' are conceptualised.

2. SOCIOLOGY OF LAW AND THE DEBATES WITHIN MAINSTREAM SOCIOLOGY

The starting point for sociology as a scientific discipline is the recognition that human beings are affected and shaped by—and yet at the same time influence—other people. Society exists before we are born and will be there after we die, so it was only natural for Durkheim to conceive it as having an independent existence, like the physical world, which could be studied using scientific methods. Moreover, the same can be said of the various organised and institutional groups that lay the foundations for social order in everyday life. The legal system consists, for example, of a set of institutions concerned with making and interpreting legal rules. Sociologists are interested in various groups

---

[6] R Cotterrell, 'Sociology of Law' in *Encyclopedia of Law and Society: American and Global Perspectives* (Thousand Oaks, CA, Sage, 2007) 1413.

[7] R Cotterrell, *Law, Culture and Society: Legal Ideas in the Mirror of Social Theory* (Aldershot, Ashgate, 2006) 6.

[8] Ibid.

[9] M Chiba, 'Introduction' in *Sociology of Law in Non-Western Countries* (Oñati Proceedings 15, Oñati IISL, 1993) 12.

[10] For a discussion, see Banakar, above n 1.

working in legal institutions (lawyers, judges, clerks, police officers, etc) and in how laws are made through the legislative process. One encounters legal institutions and rules at various points in everyday life, from calling the police to getting divorced, setting up a company, or buying a house, and will come into contact with the technical specialists who know the law and decide upon disputes. A sociological approach to law is concerned with how this institution works and the relationship between law and other areas of social life. However, once one begins to think about law in this way, matters quickly become complicated. One classical challenge is posed by the realisation that although law is an institution produced through a series of interactions and processes, which can only be described as *social* and understood in the broader context of the society in which it operates, it is at the same time also a *system* with its own operations, forms of communications and above all a claim to autonomy from the social forces which produced it in the same place.[11] Had there not been some truth to law's claim to system autonomy, some argue, we could not distinguish legal norms from social or moral norms. Matters become even more complicated once we realise that there are also sociolegal approaches which do not define law and legality in terms of the legal system alone and argue that forms of legality may also emerge independently of the formal mechanisms of lawmaking, such as parliament and courts. One such approach is 'living law', inspired by Eugen Ehrlich's sociology of law, which is discussed in Chapter 2.

If you read sociology textbooks, it will be apparent that there are numerous ways of understanding the social world and thus describing and analysing the law. There are all kinds of divisions and subdivisions within particular traditions. There are also three general debates or concerns that cut across the whole subject: the 'consensus-conflict', the 'action-structure' debate and the challenge posed by postmodernism to sociology.

The Consensus and Conflict Debate

Sociologists differ considerably in their political views or normative assumptions, which they might or might not articulate in political terms, but which nevertheless influence the way they understand society generally, view and describe social events and processes, and problematise and investigate social issues.[12] One influential body of social thought has argued that this must depend ultimately on maintaining a shared set of values. Law can be viewed along with education as a 'neutral framework' for holding society together.[13] If you take this view, then lawyers are not simply another occupational group—they are custodians of a cultural tradition that we take largely for granted.[14] Once law is explored from a consensus-oriented standpoint, it balances rights and obligations, protects us from crime and social harm, brings a degree of certitude to our collaborative and contractual relations, and facilitates the exchange

---

[11] The best modern proponent of this view is Niklas Luhmann, presented in Chapter 3.

[12] For a discussion, see R Banakar, 'Can Legal Sociology Account for the Normativity of Law' in M Baier, and K Åström (ed), *Social and Legal Norms* (Aldershot, Ashgate, 2013). E-copy at: http://ssrn.com/abstract=2140756.

[13] S Vago, *Law and Society* (Boston, Prentice Hall/Pearsons, 2012).

[14] See Chapter 18 on the legal profession.

of goods and services in a capitalist economy. Law also evolves over time in response to new social and economic circumstances,[15] although by definition it tends to lag behind social developments. Law's unwillingness to stay abreast of social developments demonstrates its inherent social conservatism; expressed differently, a law which adapts itself immediately to every large or small change in society would be, arguably, unable to preserve sociocultural values and norms and ensure continuity in social behaviour and relationships. Changes in family law, such as the recognition of partnership and same-sex marriage, and new legal concepts and ideas concerning civil rights and equal opportunity, to give a few examples, are often forced upon the law from without the legal system by social movements which engage in public political discourse.[16] However, the fact that the law allows new ideas and values to enter its internal domain of operations does not necessarily change the organisation of the law or modify the courts' practices, which creates a gap between legislation, or the intention of the legislature, and the practices of the courts. Hence, we find the classical distinction made by Roscoe Pound over a hundred years ago between 'law in the books' and 'law in action'.[17]

The most popular modern-day social theories take issue with the consensus-oriented view of society, arguing that it is not based on shared values but on the values and aspirations of culturally or economically dominant groups, which by imposing their own standards and worldviews on subordinate groups establish and legitimate their own power. Once law is viewed from this standpoint, it becomes ideological and an integral part of society's power structure. Marxist tradition, for example, saw the rule of law as a fraud imposed by force on the working classes. One can, however, use similar arguments in relation to any subordinate group, such as women (in traditional or early modernity), homosexuals or ethnic and religious minorities. The underlying assumption of conflict-oriented social theory is that these conflicts cannot be resolved without a major shift of economic and political power. Since the law is implicated in perpetuating hegemonic ideologies and subsequently social inequalities, it is part of the mechanisms generating social injustice. The solution to the problems of social injustice must therefore be sought outside the legal system.

Although one might assume that 'consensus' and 'conflict' theorists are forever talking past each other, or are engaged in bitter political arguments, the main trend in social theory in the past fifty years has been in fact towards a compromise or synthesis between the two traditions. Here one might note that in the 1960s and 1970s there seemed to exist greater opportunities to transform society through youthful protests, social movements and industrial militancy. Moreover, the Soviet Union was still a superpower committed to supporting socialist revolution across the world. Today, on the other hand, neither anticapitalist protests nor Islamic fundamentalism appear to pose much of a threat to the neoliberal ideology of Western countries. Furthermore, neither the Arab Spring of 2010 nor in fact the Islamic Revolution which took place

---

[15] See T Parsons, 'A Sociologist Looks at the Legal Profession' in *Talcott Parsons: Essays in Sociological Theory* (Toronto, Collier-Macmillan, 1964) 370–85.

[16] See M Antokolskaia, 'Comparative Family Law: Moving with the Times' in E Örücü and D Nelken (eds), *Comparative Law: A Handbook* (Oxford, Hart Publishing, 2007) 241–62, 241; and R Banakar, 'When Do Rights Matter?' in S Halliday and P Schmitt, *Human Rights Brought Home* (Oxford, Hart Publishing, 2004).

[17] R Pound, 'Law in Books and Law in Action' (1910) 44 *American Law Review* 12–36.

in Iran much earlier in 1979, and which for the first time established Islam as a state ideology and a basis for political action, were anticapitalist movements. They were, instead, social movements for democracy and a reaction against authoritarian rules, dictatorships, systematic human rights violations, political corruption and forms of neocolonialism.[18] Protest movements of various types have not died away and continue to make their voices heard, while the financial global crisis of 2007/08 has again demonstrated systemic flaws and fundamental internal contradictions, continuously threatening the integrity of the capitalist system from within. This does not mean that we are at the 'end of history', since we can still organise politically around all kinds of issues. However, it does mean that many contemporary theorists accept the values of liberal capitalism, whereas they were more critical towards established institutions, including the legal system, during the 1960s.

The Action–Structure Debate

Another reason why 'consensus' and 'conflict' traditions have tended to converge is because, despite their political differences, they are two sides of the same coin and, thus, adopt much the same approach to thinking about the social world. The key concepts one finds in liberal thinkers like Parsons and Luhmann, left-leaning liberals like Giddens, Bourdieu and Habermas, but also in hard-line Marxists like Althusser is that society can be understood as a system in which different elements can be related together. The terminology and the focus of analysis differ, so in Parsons and Luhmann one finds a focus on 'systems', whereas Bourdieu emphasises 'fields', Habermas 'communicative action' and Althusser 'practices'. The common objective, however, is to produce a grand, synoptic model of society that explains how different institutions fit together and how the whole changes over time.

The most systematic theory also addresses the relationship between the individual and society. Parsons offers the fullest and most explicit discussion, arguing that human beings acquire goals and values (eg a respect for the law) in the course of socialisation. The problem here is how to account or allow for 'free will' while at the same time retaining the notion of a social system. Anthony Giddens is one of the latest theorists to attempt to incorporate 'action' and 'structure' in the same theory, through his concept of the 'duality of structure'.[19] The basic idea is that social structures such as institutions are produced by people through their actions, but that these actions are constrained by the structural resources available to the actor (which can include cultural as well as material means).[20]

There are, however, difficult issues which are not resolved fully by attempts to solve

---

[18] The fact that they do not appear to have realised their democratic goals, however, is another matter, which cannot be explored here due to lack of space.

[19] The structure–action, or structure–agency, debate should not be confused with discussions on the possibility of micro–macro integration, which according to Randall Collins concerns if 'one type of explanation takes priority over the other, or whether the two types can be integrated into a combined theory. The question of agency and structure is not an explanatory question but an ideological one. It is an argument to show that human beings control their own destinies; it is a defence of free will.' R Collins, 'The Romanticism of Agency/Structure versus the Analysis of Micro/Macro' (1992) 40 *Current Sociology* 77.

[20] A Giddens, *The Constitution of Society: Outline of the Theory of Structuration* (Cambridge, Polity Press, 1986, reprint).

the action–structure problem. Twentieth-century critics, such as the ethnomethodologist Harold Garfinkel, have argued that systems theory seems to require human beings who are 'cultural dopes'. Besides the question of 'free will', this kind of theorising also offers an impoverished view of human action. It cannot address, for example, how people account for their actions by giving reasons, or how they make judgements about other people. From this perspective, the initial focus on structure prevents theorists from seeing what lawyers, judges or police officers are doing in their day-to-day activities, but there is also a deeper issue here which goes back to nineteenth century debates about the nature of sociology. Admirers, like Durkheim, of natural sciences argued that sociology should produce causal laws through observing patterned human conduct: there was no reason to investigate how people understood their own actions. By contrast, the hermeneutic tradition in Germany argued that this was an inappropriate way of studying human beings. Unlike the objects studied by natural scientists, human beings can think, experience emotions and have free will, which is why sociology has to be concerned with interpretation and meaning.

This nineteenth-century debate has never been resolved, despite many attempts by theorists such as Giddens and Habermas to combine or reconcile the two traditions. One can see that any systems theory must be based ultimately on a Durkheimian conception of sociology as a science, since it looks at human beings from the outside, but this can be contrasted with interpretive sociology, such as symbolic interactionism and ethnomethodology, which address how people understand and justify their own actions. There is no need in these traditions to make ironic contrasts between our superior knowledge, and the limited or imperfect understanding of the people we study as sociologists. Instead, the objective is to explicate and describe common-sense knowledge.

The Poststructuralist and Postmodern Challenge

Poststructuralism and postmodernism may in retrospect turn out to have represented only a short-lived, *fin-de-siècle* movement, one that can perhaps be explained best as the response of utopian left-wing intellectuals to the fall of communism. Nonetheless, it is important to recognise the immense difficulties that they have created for sociology. Just as systems theorists felt they had made some progress in producing a model of society that combined insights and ideas from the old consensus and conflict traditions and which solved the action–structure problem, the discipline came under attack from a different direction. A group of mainly French philosophers set out to trash the Enlightenment assumptions underpinning sociological inquiry, including the ideas that the application of reason and science can produce truth and progress (an idea which is widely shared in many academic disciplines) and that it is possible to produce objective or unproblematic descriptions through using social scientific methods.

Although poststructuralism does have implications for conducting empirical research, it is best understood as a philosophical critique that makes us question the authority and coherence of classic texts. Like other radical movements in the discipline, it has been absorbed and tamed largely by mainstream theorists, and subversive thinkers such as Foucault are most usually understood in law and society circles as saying something similar to Marx.[21] Both poststructuralism and postmodernism have exerted influence on the development of critical legal studies (CLS), feminism, theories of sexuality and legal pluralism, and more recently on parts of legal philosophy.

According to postmodernists, while modernity prolongs the aspirations of the Enlightenment and thus reproduces the values of universalism and reason, post-modernity denotes the dawn of a generically new age characterised by uncertainty, fragmentation and discontinuity. This marks a radical break from the totalising con-straints of the metanarrative of reason (totalising knowledge, truths and beliefs) which constitute classical modernism. These metanarratives make foundational claims, in that they provide a unifying system of thoughts into which all other ideas can be ordered and their truthfulness and historical direction assessed. Consequently, metanarratives provide a means of social control, manipulation, oppression and marginalisation, and therefore they should be *deconstructed*.[22]

In recent years, as noted above, postmodernism has spread among certain socio-legal and even legal researchers, who often engage in social critiques of the law at a normative level. These scholars either have little interest in empirical research or actively seek to undermine the truth claims of empirical methods which are linked to the metanarratives of sociology. For these scholars postmodernism provides a new understanding of the operations of the legal system in terms of law's discursive prac-tices and draws attention to the serious shortcomings of simplistic structuralist models which continue to dominate legal studies.[23] At the same time postmodernism has also been criticised; its critics question its transformative potential and its ability to offer an alternative practical vision of economy and polity.[24]

3. THE STRUCTURE OF THE BOOK

As in the first edition, there are numerous traditions that we have been unable to cover, and the reader will again notice some obvious omissions. There are still no chapters on Donald Black, on Talcott Parsons and structural functionalism.[25] There are also no chapters on legal consciousness or empirical legal studies, which have become influential movements in American law schools.[26] This may, of course, reflect our own theoretical bias and the company we keep, but the choice of theorists and topics is also constrained by the structure of the book. As in the first edition, we consider groups of

---

[21] For a recent study, see B Golder and P Fitzpatrick, *Foucault's Law* (London, Routledge, 2009).

[22] J Derrida, 'Force of Law: The "Mystical Foundation of Authority"' in D Cornell et al (eds), *Decon-struction and the Possibility of Justice* (London, Routledge, 1992) 2.

[23] Imaginative, albeit eclectic, postmodern theorising may be found in the works of Gunther Teubner and Andreas Philippopoulos-Mihalopoulos, both of whom conflate Luhmann's autopoiesis (which was developed theoretically and without empirical input) and postmodern theories. See G Teubner, 'Self-subversive Justice: Contingency or Transcendence Formula of Law?' (2009) 72 *Modern Law Review* 1–23, 9; A Philippopoulos-Mihalopoulos, 'Between Law and Justice: A Connection of No-Connection in Luhmann and Derrida' in KE Himma (ed), *Law, Morality, and Legal Positivism* (ARSP Beihefte, Stuttgart, Franz Steiner Verlag, 2004).

[24] JF Handler, 'Postmodernism, Protest, and the New Social Movements' (1992) 26 *Law and Society Review* 697–731, 727.

[25] For an example, see WM Evan, *Social Structure and Law: Theoretical and Empirical Perspectives* (New York, Sage, 1990).

[26] P Ewick and S Silbey, *The Common Place of Law: Stories From Everyday Life* (Chicago, University of Chicago Press, 1998).

theorists that have something in common and which align with contrasting traditions, rather than trying to do everything, or suggesting that it is desirable or possible to create a grand synthetic theory (although some sociologists, including Parsons, have tried to do this).

In this edition, we start with a section on the classical sociology of law which contains the challenging discussion of law in classical social theory by Alan Hunt, published in the first edition, but also a new review by Javier Treviño on the sociological jurists Pound, Ehrlich and Petrażycki. Then we have a section on systems theory. The last edition contained an interesting introduction to Niklas Luhmann by Klaus Ziegert, and in this edition we have an equally authoritative new review by Michael King, which represents a somewhat different presentation of Luhmann's systems theory. There is also a chapter on Jürgen Habermas by Mathieu Deflem (in the first edition this was authored by Bo Carlsson).

The next sections on critical approaches and postmodernism, which were also in the first edition, now include some new chapters and authors. In the section on critical theory, we have reprinted Robert Fine's review of Marxism. This is an example of an insightful and demanding review that would not be improved by, for example, discussing the global financial crisis or new theoretical work. We have included an abridged version of a previously published paper by Mikael Madsen and Yves Dezalay on Pierre Bourdieu, which in some ways develops the ideas presented in the first edition. Then, there is a new chapter on feminist legal theory by Harriet Samuel (Ruth Fletcher authored the chapter in the first edition), which provides an authoritative and up-to-date overview of the research and theoretical developments within law and feminism, as well as a new chapter on critical race theory by Angela Harris.

These theorists all have a structural bias, in that they start with a view of society as a whole and explain the actions of individuals within this framework. They can be contrasted with Bruno Latour's actor network theory and the interpretive tradition, which in different ways focus on individual actions and how they produce society. Max Travers supplies a review of symbolic interactionism and ethnomethodological research since the first edition. There is a new chapter on Latour written by Frédéric Audren and Cédric Moreau de Bellaing. To complicate matters further, the last chapter in this section by Stewart Macaulay and Elizabeth Mertz on the new legal realism, also new for this edition, attempts a synthesis or reconciliation of the different positions. For postmodernism, we have reprinted the chapter on Foucault by Gary Wickham and a revised version of Shaun McVeigh's chapter on postmodernism and common law which appeared in the first edition. We have, though, included a new chapter on postcolonial theories of law by Eve Darian-Smith.

The book concludes with a section in which we use law in the late modern world as a theme to bring together different traditions. We have printed a new chapter by Anne Griffiths on legal pluralism, which should be read alongside her introduction in the first edition of this text, and there is a new essay on globalisation by Ralf Michaels and a new chapter by Reza Banakar reviewing law in late modern society. Ole Hammerslev has supplied a new chapter considering different theoretical approaches to the legal profession. Finally, we have reprinted with minor revisions David Nelken's chapter from the first edition on comparative studies of law.

4. UNDERSTANDING LAW FROM A SOCIOLOGICAL PERSPECTIVE

In presenting these reviews, we should acknowledge that not all are written by sociologists—there are chapters by anthropologists (Darian-Smith, Nelken), by a legal theorist (Michaels) and by scholars interested in cultural studies and philosophy (Harris, McVeigh), which demonstrates that the boundaries between disciplines can be blurred in law and society studies, and some would argue that it should develop as an interdisciplinary field. However, our own interest in this collection lies in demonstrating and explaining the distinctive character of different sociological traditions and how they can be used to investigate law. Law is, of course, a complex social institution that is of central importance in modern societies. These chapters are worth reading because they show how a range of theorists and traditions approach law and understand the relationship between law and society. Further to the inclusion of contributors from different fields, it is also important to note that they do not simplify difficult ideas—there is nothing simple about the way in which Luhmann or Habermas understand law, or the ethnomethodologists, or Marxist and feminist theory, or postmodernism, so those who are new to the field have to spend some time getting to know these traditions to appreciate what they have achieved and to understand the differences between them.

Although there are significant differences, the different sociological approaches also have something important in common: they make it possible to investigate and understand law as a social institution, even as a form of reasoning. There are, of course, other ways of doing this in legal education, including offering courses in policy-oriented sociolegal studies, critical legal studies or disciplines in the humanities such as philosophy or cultural studies, and some of these courses can be quite political, in the sense of promoting different varieties of critical theory. By contrast, sociology asks students to reflect on the place of law in society through considering different theoretical traditions and perspectives. This in itself leads to students thinking about law critically (in our view a desirable educational outcome). Moreover, even if it has no direct practical value, sociological research makes one think about institutions and social processes in a way that is not possible through studying doctrinal (or black letter) subjects. Along with other contextualists influenced by Karl Llewellyn and Roscoe Pound, we would argue that studying sociology of law will make you a better lawyer.

In the first edition of this book we advanced this view in the introduction, and in the conclusion we even suggested that the law school curriculum should include courses on research methods and encourage students to conduct empirical research. Naturally, we were aware that nothing much would change, since there remain compelling institutional reasons why law schools should offer mainly doctrinal courses rather than looking critically at the nature of law and the place of lawyers in society.[27] What we could not have predicted is that law schools are facing profound challenges that might lead to even fewer contextual courses being offered. The legal profession

---

[27] We should hasten to add that a few textbooks have been published recently catering for multi-disciplinary research in law. But these remain few in number. See eg M McConville and WH Chui, *Research Methods for Law* (Edinburgh, Edinburgh University Press, 2010); R Cryer et al, *Research Methodologies in EU and International Law* (Oxford, Hart Publishing, 2011).

and courts also seem to be facing difficulties, partly because the state cannot properly fund legal services. Even corporate lawyers are affected by the uncertain economic outlook. Looked at more positively, social change often generates sociological reflection and eventually some kind of political response. In these circumstances, we would recommend sociology of law as a means of understanding changes in law as a social institution, even though none of the theorists or traditions reviewed in this book supplies definitive answers.

Section 1

Classical Sociology of Law

REZA BANAKAR and MAX TRAVERS

M OST UNDERGRADUATE COURSES on sociology of law begin with the three nineteenth-century 'founding fathers' of sociology: Karl Marx, Emile Durkheim and Max Weber. The two sides in the consensus–conflict debate we referred to in the general introduction take their lead from these theorists, who were writing about the massive social and economic changes that took place in nineteenth-century Europe which we now describe as the emergence of capitalism or modernity. Marx believed that the central dynamic of this new world would be a growing polarisation between rich and poor—between the minority who owned the means of production and the majority who had to sell their labour in order to make a living. The tension between these two opposing interests, Marx predicted, would result eventually in revolution. Weber offers a less deterministic view of human history, but one that places equal emphasis on the competition between different groups for wealth, power and status. Durkheim, on the other hand, believed that industrial unrest was simply a temporary symptom of adjustment and that political elites could re-establish a sense of order and wellbeing through fostering shared values.[1]

All three theorists were interested in law and legal institutions, although they regarded the subjects as only one constitutive element of society alongside the economy, political system and cultural institutions. For Marx, the idea of 'the rule of law', celebrated by British jurists, was a means of promoting the ideological idea that law benefits everyone, whereas in fact it only benefits the ruling class.[2] Durkheim took the opposing view that law embodies shared values, and he advanced his famous theory, expressed as a scientific law, on how laws change over time as society becomes more complex. Weber, on the other hand, was most interested in the development of law codes, as one example of a growing rationalisation of social life, and in contrast to both Marx and Durkheim he offered a pessimistic vision of modernity as a soulless 'iron cage' with no prospect of liberation through reason or science (since they were themselves partly responsible).

The first contribution by Alan Hunt to this collection contains a summary of Marx, Durkheim and Weber's ideas on law, but it does rather more than this and is

---

[1] For some useful introductions, see J Hughes et al, *Understanding Classical Sociology* (London, Sage, 1995); I Craib, *Classical Social Theory* (Oxford, Oxford University Press, 1997).

[2] This oversimplifies matters, since the few references to law in Marx can be interpreted in different ways. See H Collins, *Marxism and Law* (Oxford, Oxford University Press, 1982).

best read as a wide-ranging and provocative statement about the field of sociology of law as a whole. Hunt is provocative, in that he argues that the classical theorists have more in common than is generally realised: they each view law in a 'constructivist' way as a tool that can (and should) be used by the state in regulating human affairs. There was, Hunt suggests, a shift in the way intellectuals conceptualised law in the nineteenth century. Whereas in pre-modern times law was either viewed as a 'natural' phenomenon, deriving from tradition or ecclesiastical authority, or as representing the 'will of the sovereign', the new capitalist industrial economy required a different understanding thereof. Hunt argues that what has become dominant is 'legal constructivism' (which he contrasts to the idea of naturalism), the 'intentional deployment' of law 'to promote, secure or defend specific social interests'.

At the risk of oversimplifying a complex argument, Hunt implies that a common concern of these theorists (and also of the legal thinker Henry Maine) was the relationship between law and the state. Marx believed that law would eventually 'wither away' after a socialist revolution, but he recognised its importance for nineteenth-century governments as a means of controlling populations and securing the conditions for capitalist economic relationships. Similarly, a major theme in Weber's writings was the growth of 'professionalisation and bureaucratisation', which sustained 'the stability and security of the new capitalist order'. According to Hunt, Durkheim also saw 'modern law' and 'political democracy' as the only means of maintaining social solidarity in a complex, industrial society.

Hunt's chapter ends with some general reflections about law in the modern world, and about the sociology of law itself, which he argues still sees law 'as a manifestation of state sovereignty'. He contends that the relentless juridification that has occurred during the twentieth century (essentially the growth of the state) has solved many problems but created a reaction against the grip of law. However, initiatives intended to escape bureaucracy and law, such as the alternative dispute resolution movement or the rise of 'self-governance', end up promoting further juridification. Modern sociology of law should 'move beyond the state' and study 'new popular forms of engagement that reach out beyond ... the classical period of state, law and sovereignty'.

Those familiar with Hunt's recent work will know that this is very much a neo-Foucauldian argument, and he also draws on Habermas's idea of the system's colonisation of lifeworld.[3] It is worth adding, however, that each of these theorists can be understood as developing and elaborating a theme that was already present in the writings of Max Weber. Juridification is, after all, one part of what Weber viewed as a process of rationalisation through human history. There is arguably a moral ambiguity in all these writers towards the state, as they could imagine no alternative to liberal democracy, but they were aware that excessive regulation reduced human creativity and freedom.

One thing that will be apparent from the preceding discussion is that classical sociologists were all concerned with how the relationship between law and society was taking shape against the backdrop of the emerging new industrial capitalist society and its counterpart, the modern state. In our second chapter, Javier Treviño offers a different perspective on this issue by reviewing the ideas of three jurists—Roscoe

---

[3] See A Hunt and G Wickham, *Foucault and Law: Towards a Sociology of Governance* (London, Pluto, 1994) and Wickham's chapter in Section 5. Also, see Mathieu Deflem's chapter on Habermas in Section 2.

Pound (1870–1964), Eugen Ehrlich (1862–1922) and Leon Petrażycki (1867–1931)—who were also concerned with the role of the state but expressed their disquiet by attempting to develop a science of law. They all shared mistrust of legal formalism, and in the case of Ehrlich and Petrażycki highlighted the limited impact of state law on social relationships in their own countries.[4]

Petrażycki and Ehrlich worked independently of one another, and yet their theories came to overlap partially. Firstly, they regarded social sciences, rather than moral or analytical philosophy, as the foundation upon which a science of law could be built. Secondly, taking issue with the jurisprudence of their time, they refuted natural law theories and contested the assumption of legal positivism that a social norm became a legal rule only if it was posited by the state. The state could not be the primary source of law for the simple reason that its existence presupposed and was conditioned by law. Petrażycki and Ehrlich, each in his own way, argued for an empirically based concept of law which was broader than state law and existed independently of any outside authority. While Durkheim or Weber studied law as part of their concern with the rise of modernity, Petrażycki and Ehrlich explored it in an effort to improve the science of law.

Petrażycki and Ehrlich both lived and worked in the Continental Europe of the early 1900s. An anti-formalist movement, initiated by Oliver Wendell Holmes (1841–1935) and Roscoe Pound, was also taking shape under the banner of 'legal realism' during the same period in North America.[5] Holmes famously declared that the life of law was not logic but experience: '[T]he prophecies of what the courts … [did] in fact, and nothing more pretentious' constituted the law'.[6] This implied that we could not grasp the law through the exegesis of legal rules and doctrine, but we could do so by attending to how legal authorities interpret and enforce the law and decide upon cases. This sociological insight was elaborated further in the works of Pound, who distinguished between 'law in the books' and 'law in action'—a distinction that continues to inform sociolegal research concerning the discrepancies between the claims of the law and the intentions of the legislature, on the one hand, and the de facto regulatory impact of the law on social behaviour, on the other (this discrepancy is also known as the 'gap problem').

There were certain similarities between Ehrlich and Pound's antiformalism and their belief that social sciences should occupy a privileged position in the study of law, but there were also significant differences. It is worth emphasising that their concept of 'science' was rather narrow and, as Treviño emphasises, concerned with the 'implementation of empirical positivism and induction'. Pound did use Ehrlich's ideas, as he used many other theories to develop his eclectic approach to legal engineering, but as David Nelken explains, his 'programme and the conceptual tools designed to further it

---

[4] Georges Gurvitch should be mentioned in this context as heir to the tradition of sociolegal thought developed by Petrażycki. Gurvitch's notion of 'social law', elaborated in *L'idée du droit social* (Paris, Librairie de Recueil Sirey, 1932), is reminiscent of Petrażycki's 'intuitive law' and Ehrlich's 'living law'. See R Banakar, 'Integrating Reciprocal Perspectives: On Georges Gurvitch's Theory of Immediate Jural Experience' (2001) 16 *Canadian Journal of Law and Society* 67–91. An e-copy is available at: http://papers.ssrn.com/sol3/papers.cfm?abstract_id=1777167.

[5] See R Pound, 'Sociology of Law and Sociological Jurisprudence' (1943) 5 *University of Toronto Law Journal* 1–20.

[6] OW Holmes, 'The Path of Law' (1897) 10 *Harvard Law Review* 457–78.

were very different indeed from those of Ehrlich'.[7] Although Holmes and Pound were critical of legal formalism, their concept of law recognises state law (or official law) as the law proper, and in this respect it is in line with the ideology of legal positivism. In contrast, Ehrlich's concept of law is broader than state law and includes non-official law and forms of ordering. The broadness of his concept comes, however, at a price—he is often criticised for vagueness and, to borrow from Treviño again, 'for lack of scientific rigour'. Furthermore, his theory of 'living law' has been misrepresented as a conflation of 'is' and 'ought' by no less than Hans Kelsen.[8]

There are also similarities between the ideas developed by Petrażycki and Axel Hägerström, who is regarded as the founder of Scandinavian legal realism. Whereas Pound and Ehrlich, as Treviño explains, were familiar with each other's works and Ehrlich visited Pound in Harvard, Petrażycki and Hägerström appear not 'to have communicated or exchanged ideas'.[9] The similarities found between the works of Petrażycki and Hägerström, on the one hand, and Ehrlich and Pound, on the other, provide a key to the intellectual climate which prevailed at the end of the nineteenth century and the beginning of the twentieth century. Two of the central questions raised and deliberated at this time—one regarding the separation of facts and norms (or the distinction made between the facticity and the normativity of the law) and the other concerning the relationship between law and the state—remain with us and continue to inform much of the debate within legal theory.

The extent to which these classical models of law, state and society are compatible and relevant to the study of current social problems would be an interesting issue to consider on a law and society course (which would require some consideration of empirical examples). Naturally, there have been many anthropological studies about customary law and how this relates to state institutions which support Ehrlich's argument.[10] These studies often demonstrate that state law may only have a limited relevance to how people in developed, industrial societies conduct many aspects of their everyday lives. Interestingly, the concern with the role of law vis-à-vis law and society retains a central position in the more recent debates on the consequences of globalisation, which we shall discuss in Section 6. We see, for example, that the ideas of Ehrlich, on the one hand, and various forms of legal pluralism, on the other, are employed once again to describe and make sense of the transformation of the state and the development of transnational law.[11] It is to Ehrlich's credit that his theory of 'living law' has retained its relevancy despite the sustained criticism directed at it from the direction of legal positivism.

---

[7] D Nelken, 'Law in Action or Living Law: Back to the Beginning in Sociology of Law' (1984) 4 *Legal Studies* 157–82, 159.

[8] For a discussion, see B van Klink, *Facts and Norms: The Unfinished Debate between Eugen Ehrlich and Hans Kelsen* (2006). Available at SSRN: http://ssrn.com/abstract=980957.

[9] H McCoubrey and ND White, *Jurisprudence*, 2nd edn (London, Blackstone Press, 1996) 168.

[10] See M Hertogh, *Living Law: Reconsidering Eugen Ehrlich* (Oxford, Hart Publishing, 2009).

[11] See eg G Teubner (ed), *Global Law Without a State* (Aldershot, Dartmouth, 1997).

1

The Problematisation of Law in Classical Social Theory

ALAN HUNT

THIS CHAPTER EXPLORES the relationship between what will be termed the 'classical tradition' of social and legal theories of the nineteen and early twentieth centuries and contemporary trends in theoretically oriented studies in the fields of 'law and society' and 'sociology of law'.[1] A feature which the sociology of law shares with other subdisciplinary fields is an almost reverential acknowledgement of the 'founding fathers', in particular the familiar trinity of Marx, Durkheim and Weber. This chapter will focus on the trinity with some brief comments on Sir Henry Maine (1861–1905).

This undertaking will be approached by exploring the forms in which classical theory problematised law. For this purpose, I shall draw upon Foucault's reflections on problematisation as opening up a new and fruitful avenue for the historical study of the human sciences. While the key figures had very different intellectual and political agendas, it will be argued that there was an underlying shared problematisation about the configuration of economic, political and legal relations that was taking shape during the course of the nineteenth century. While the problematic of Weber and Durkheim was conceived within the perspective of liberal capitalist rule, Marx exemplified a break with the problems posed by this tradition. In that tradition the problematisation of law was preoccupied by the question of how to facilitate the possibility of an extension of the capacity of political institutions to govern the economic and social conditions of a nation and its population. The liberal tradition was concerned that the capacity to rule should be exercised without transgressing proper limits that preserved the expanded economic and political rights won in the transition from monarchical to parliamentary sovereignty.

The classical sociological interrogation of the legal field demarcates the period in which 'the social' had come to the fore as the central target for the governance of the population.[2] Marx had signalled, but did not complete, the separation of the fields

---

[1] For present purposes nothing hangs on the differences between these fields of inquiry.

[2] 'The social' came into being in the nineteenth century; it designated 'a certain region of society, a space between the economy and the state. It was an arena of collective needs, grievances and disruptions that were related to the transformations in the economic realm': G Steinmetz, *Regulating the Social: The Welfare State and Local Politics in Imperial Germany* (Princeton, Princeton University Press, 1993) 2.

of the economic, the political and the social. This separation and the emergence of the discipline which problematised 'the social' was furthered by Weber, but he was still concerned with the political problematic of liberalism, not posed in terms of the 'limits' of law, but rather in terms of the sphere of rational bureaucracy, the vehicle through which the state regulated the social. The separation and reification of the social, dissociated from the economic, was articulated in its most complete form by Durkheim for whom law was a major agent of 'moral governance' of the social totality. It is important to recognise that sociological reflection on law still remained heavily influenced by the political problematic of 'ruling too much' and the limits of legal infringement of personal autonomy. The emergent discipline of sociology was much less preoccupied with this question.

The influence of the way in which law was problematised that paralleled the emergent preoccupation with the 'social' is exemplified by 'social law', and the link between the welfarist regulation of the population as a whole was exemplified by the concern to grasp the connection between collectivist conceptions of welfare and social rights. This set of issues dominated sociologically inspired thought about law, more especially in Britain than in the United States, up until the emergence of 'law and society studies' in the 1960s.[3] This movement, without at first clearly defining its own problematic, was concerned with the limits of welfare and bureaucratic legal regula-tion.[4] With the eruption of the crisis of the welfare state in the late 1970s, the law and society movement, while still influential, has come under mounting criticism from both the Right, who have reinvigorated a concern with law as the guardian of individual liberty, and from the unstable radicalism of critical and postmodernist currents that have lost faith in the rational and bureaucratic potential of law.

The method to be pursued will seek to identify the problematisation of law present in theorisations of law. Problematisation serves to initiate a line of inquiry by drawing attention to the rudimentary organisation of phenomena which yields problems for investigation. I draw upon Foucault's reflections on problematisation but it should be stressed that Foucault's concept was far from completely developed. His historical method of study is a history of problematisations, that is, 'the history of the way in which things become a problem'.[5]

The trajectory of his own major works can be posed as the disarmingly simply questions: how did madness, health and sexuality come to be confronted as problems requiring intellectual work and political interventions? The present inquiry asks: how has law been problematised? Problematisation as a methodological strategy involves a commitment to challenging the 'taken-for-granted' nature of the 'problem' of law in different historical periods. One important implication of this approach is that it intentionally avoids any attempt to produce a chronological 'history' of the treatment of law in the social sciences.[6]

---

[3] See also: W Novak, *The People's Welfare: Law and Regulation in Nineteenth Century America* (Chapel Hill, University of North Carolina Press, 1996); J Handler, *Law and the Search for Community* (Philadelphia, University of Pennsylvania Press, 1990).

[4] Its most immediate concerns were the effectiveness of law as a means of securing social rights and welfare, policing discretion, and generally utilising law as an agent to promote social change.

[5] M Foucault, 'What Our Present Is' [1988] in S Lotringer and L Hohroth (eds), *The Politics of Truth* (New York, Semiotext(e), 1997) 164.

[6] This approach, which I now reject, informed my earlier discussion of the 'sociological movement in law' in A Hunt, *The Sociological Movement in Law* (London, Macmillan, 1978).

1. THE CLASSICAL PROBLEMATISATION OF LAW

How did classical social theory constitute law in relation to its object of inquiry? This question must be approached in a way that does not involve the implication that law necessarily formed a primary or even explicit focus of attention for the individual theorists. This is essential because, while Weber did devote self-consciously focused attention to law, with the 'sociology of law' forming an important component of his monumental *Wirtschaft und Gesellschaft*,[7] and though a similar sustained attention to the evolution of law was pursued by Sir Henry Maine, others did not accord law this centrality. In contrast, Durkheim devoted substantive attention to law primarily in the course of a study centred upon the transformation of the division of labour of which law served to provide convenient and accessible empirical evidence.[8] Nor did Marx ever take law as his immediate object of inquiry, although he and Engels had a great deal to say about law.

The impetus that causes human thought to shift has long been (but not always) a looming sense that something about life is new and different, and that things cannot or should not be discussed in the currently conventional terms. The prescient thinkers have been those able to encapsulate these shifts in ways that put together a narrative that makes sense of an array of symptoms and binds them together into a coherent account. The most popular narrative of our age has been that of 'modernity', a fact that is sustained, not controverted, by the recent extension of that storyline by the addendum effected by 'postmodernity'. I do not want to argue that the tropes of 'modern' and 'modernity' are wrong, but rather that they are dangerous. They are dangerous because a purely chronological label, one that distinguishes the past from the present, the traditional from the modern, is made the bearer of a whole complex of substantive dichotomous characterisations (agricultural–industrial, rural–urban, *Gemeinschaft–Gesellschaft* and the like) that have been the focus of early twentieth-century social thought.

The concept of modernity is especially precarious when applied to the phenomenon of law. Modernist theory conceives law as one of the important stars in the constellation of the modern. Yet it is usually remembered that law predates modernity, and the treatment of law thus becomes tarnished with an unexamined presentism in which the past of law is viewed as a long march towards modern rational law; the old pre-modern (irrational) elements are gradually sloughed off to reveal law in its glorious rational form. The great bulk of the writings on legal history, from Maine to the present, has been marked by the seductions of this presentism.

The issue of law comes to figure in the problematisation engaged with by classic social theory in so far as it becomes less and less feasible to treat law as a 'natural' phenomenon. The most obvious form of law as a natural phenomenon is that captured in both substance and in name by natural law theory. It was grounded on the presumption of a social order based on a taken-for-granted set of institutions and values constitutive of the social order. It makes little or no difference if these were articulated in theological form with a set of primary values stipulated in some principal religious

---

[7] M Weber, *Economy and Society: An Outline of Interpretive Sociology*, ed G Roth and C Wittich, 2 vols (Berkeley, University of California Press, 1978).

[8] E Durkheim, *The Division of Labour in Society* [1893], trans WD Hall (London, Macmillan, 1984).

text, or if theology was partially secularised through a process of reflection upon the human condition. Typically such reflections were expressed in terms of a generalised problem of social order—a set of questions most powerfully articulated by Thomas Hobbes in terms of a problem of order that could only be addressed through obedience to a vision of a political order grounded in a unitary conception of sovereign power.

This vision came increasingly into conflict with the challenges posed by the emergence of a capitalist economic order. Capitalism as used here involves the coexistence of the production of commodities, industrial forms of production and the mobilisation of mass wage-earning labour, with these elements being co-ordinated through markets. The most profound impact of these developments, even outstripping the social dislocations they caused, was the primacy of economic markets that required nothing less than the radical separation of an economic from a political sphere. But the self-regulating market could never achieve full self-regulation, and continued to require inputs from the political system to sustain and protect the market order. Law was the primary mechanism for this linkage of the economic and political orders. The crucial fact is that *laissez-faire* itself was enforced by the state and at the same time there was a major expansion of the state; the free market was sustained by an enormous increase in continuous, centrally organised and controlled interventionism.

The emergence of law as an object of sociological investigation rests on the implicit view that legal systems are essentially constructed, social creations (not natural orders) and thus presuppose an instrumental conception of law. In line with the Enlightenment vision of 'progress' understood as a project that gives effect to an ever-expanding realm of the human capacity to control its conditions of existence, law comes increasingly to be perceived as a primary steering mechanism for societies marked by complex interdependence, a task that can no longer be fulfilled by more traditional 'direct rule' through the political system. A persistent line of thought within legal theory has counterposed a divide between law as autonomous and law as dependent on society; this has in many accounts been presented as the core distinction between the internal perspective of legal positivism and the external perspective of the socially informed approach to law. While this distinction should not be ignored, it is important to recognise that these views of law are not antithetical; the rise of law as autonomous system increasingly separated from the political sphere is consistent with a view of law as dependent on society, in the sense of being an historical achievement, one that has wider ramifications embodied in the strange coexistent reality and mythology of the idea of the separation of powers and the rule of law.

The next step in my argument is decisive. It involves a profound reversal of Hayek's rejection of the dominant 'constructivist' vision of the dynamic of the intervention of the political order in the economic order or self-regulating market. Before attending to the reversal, however, some attention to Hayek's thesis is necessary.[9] Hayek has long been a controversial figure; despite the favour he has found by providing the theoretical grounding of modern neoliberal politics, he was one of the most important thinkers of the twentieth century.

---

[9] F Hayek's ideas were developed through a mass of published work; they are accessible in their most concentrated form in his three-volume, *Law, Legislation and Liberty* (London, Routledge & Kegan Paul, 1973–79).

Hayek set out to challenge what he viewed as the ruling myth of the twentieth century, shared by both welfare liberalism and social democracy, which he designated as 'constructivism'.[10] The 'constructivist fallacy' views social institutions as potentially amenable to intentional creation, reform and intervention by means of legislation and interventionist economic strategy. His objection is based on the contention that social planning is impossible; it is impossible because it is never feasible to accumulate systematic knowledge of the actions of individuals in pursuit of their interests exemplified in uncountable market transactions. Only the impersonal mechanism of 'the market' is capable of aggregating these actions to produce outcomes that are not reducible to the intentions of economic actors. To intervene in ways that impact on the market with imperfect knowledge can only result in the disruption and distortion of the market in ways that, far from rendering markets calculable and controllable, result in unintended consequences.

In other words, faced with the most profound implications of the commoditisation of labour and its products that constitutes capitalism, namely the radical disjunction of the economic and political realms, Hayek endorses the necessity of that separation and the corollary that the political realm must abstain from intervention in the functioning of the self-regulating market. Thus, it follows that for Hayek the ruling vision of modern law, particularly in the increasingly dominant form of statutory legislation as a mechanism of deliberative intervention, is fatally flawed. Law can and should do no more than give authoritative endorsement to the necessary conditions for the functioning of the self-regulating market such as the protection of the rights of property, free labour and capital.

This is not the occasion to engage in a critique of Hayek, but two important lines of inquiry can be indicated. While he is logically correct in claiming that full knowledge is unattainable, it is disputable whether it follows that such complete knowledge is a necessary precondition for purposive intervention; what forms and degree of knowledge are sufficient grounds for purposive intervention remain a matter of investigation. The second question is, given Hayek's radical separation between economic and political realms, where does the concept of 'society' fit into his schema; is it the mere aggregation of economics and politics or is it a field not reducible to the other constituents? What is at stake here is whether society is the passive reflex of economics and politics on everyday life, or an active arena in which through co-operation and conflict people 'construct' forms of life through which they seek to take control of their existence.[11]

The radical reversal of Hayek which I propose is that, whether we approve of its consequences, the constructivism of law, that is its intentional deployment to promote, secure or defend specific social interests, is precisely what was 'new' about the legal

---

[10] F Hayek, *Law, Legislation and Liberty*, vol 1: *Rules and Order* (London, Routledge & Kegan Paul, 1973).

[11] Hayek's position on the question of 'society' is complex. He views the evolutionary formation of human instincts as being formed when hominids lived in small co-operative bands that survived through solidarity. He rejects Hobbes's primitive individualism as a myth. 'The savage is not solitary, and his instinct is collectivist. There was never a "war of all against all"': F Hayek, *The Fatal Conceit: The Errors of Socialism*, vol 1: *The Collected Works of FA Hayek*, ed WW Bartley (London, Routledge, 1988) 12. What is significant about this argument is that it explicitly contends that social evolution runs counter to the 'instincts' formed through evolutionary processes; learned rules that promote the individualism of market relations have to overcome primitive collectivism.

orders that emerged in the late eighteenth century. Legal constructivism has continued to advance over the next two centuries; this fact is most simply attested to by rapid extension of constructivism into the international arena with the growth of international criminal law and human rights law. Constructivism is no aberration or accident; it is, quite simply, a social fact that law is one of the primary techniques of governance. It has displaced the two previous visions of law as either the expression of a natural social order or as the expression of the will of the sovereign. This has been a displacement, but not a disappearance. The quest for a general normative order still infuses our ongoing concerns with justice and human rights. And Foucault is right in noting that we still have not 'cut off the King's head',[12] that is law remains heavily imbricated with state sovereignty. My contention is that the problematisation of law in classic social theory was grounded in the challenges posed by the constructivist reality of law.

2. LEGAL CONSTRUCTIVISM IN CLASSICAL SOCIAL THEORY

While the substantive analyses, theoretical apparatuses and political commitments of Maine, Marx, Durkheim and Weber are radically different, nevertheless they can be understood as addressing questions that are posed by the rise of constructivist law. The issues they engage with are ones in which law is no longer the expression of the will of political authority (typical of monarchist or absolutist regimes) or a concretisation of shared religious-moral values.

Maine

Maine has not acquired the same status as the other theorists under consideration here. His canvas, though broad, was not as expansive as the others and his preoccupation with legal history has largely confined his reputation to this field. This fate is compounded by the fact that Maine's intellectual universe was, like so many others at the time, framed by one of the many variants of social Darwinism. For this reason I will have less to say about him than the other figures; but this does not detract from his significance. His best-remembered thesis is that the history of legal evolution can best be grasped as a transition from status to contract.[13] The ascribed status attached to individuals in pre-modern societies determined the law to which they were subject. Despite recognising the huge productivity of legislation, Maine insisted that it was the emergence of the consensual contract, by means of which individuals made their own law, that is the decisive, albeit prolonged and complex, line of development that endows the law of 'progressive societies' with the innovative capacity that allows law to keep pace with the increasing rapidity of social change.

What is significant for present purposes is the implication that individual contrac-

[12] M Foucault, *Power/Knowledge: Selected Interviews and Other Writings, 1972–1977* (New York, Pantheon, 1980) 121.
[13] H Maine, *Ancient Law: Its Connection with the Early History of Society and its Relation to Modern Ideas* (London, John Murray, 1861).

tual activity effects a decisive shift in the location of law within social life. It marks a radical break with the identification of law with sovereignty; and this is evident in Maine's sharp and telling criticism of the 'imperative theory of law', associated with Jeremy Bentham and John Austin, who reduced all law to commands of the sovereign. What Maine advances in contrast is a model in which law is attributed a distinctively liberal role as an autonomous entity that serves, as it were, the role of neutral umpire, determining the boundaries of the relations between contracting individuals. However, Maine never took the decisive step that could complete the liberal model which would have posited a separation between law and state such that courts could mediate the relations between individuals and the state.

Marx

Marx's relationship to the emerging liberal model of law was far more complex. Most obvious is the fact that law never presented itself as his primary object of inquiry.[14] Marx's primary concern was with the 'critique' of capitalist society. This critique involved the analysis of the mechanisms through which capitalism reproduced itself and in so doing revolutionised all social relations. It also concerned the political question of how the gross inequalities instituted through the very freedoms which capitalism promoted in overcoming pre-capitalist forms of social organisation could be superseded by the revolutionary transformation of society. His primary answer is well known; it is that one of the most important creations of capitalism, the conversion of the great majority of the population into wage-labourers, the proletariat, was the only force whose potential revolutionary action could conquer capitalism and institute a realm of equality based on the collective ownership of society's productive capacity.

Marx's treatment of law exhibits two very different emphases. While he viewed capitalism as a self-reproducing economic system, he also emphasised that capitalist economic relations secure dominance over all other major fields of social and political life. In particular, he emphasised the intimate connection between law and the state. Law in this manifestation is first and foremost a mechanism of state power giving effect to the state's monopoly of the legitimate means of violence and its capacity to use legally sanctioned coercion to advance and protect the interests of capital. Indeed, he argued that 'the bloody expropriation of the peasantry' effected by laws of enclosure and vagrancy law was a primary mechanism by which the rural population was driven to accept the necessity of submitting themselves to work in the mines and factories. Marx stressed the repressive character of law in order to redress the blindness of most liberal thought which played down the role of legal repression. But in reacting against the omissions of liberal theory Marx came perilously close simply to reversing liberalism's error by equating law with repression.

Marx's account of law exhibits a second line of analysis. Capitalist relations exhibit a powerful self-reproducing tendency, one that effects the general subsump-

---

[14] Because of the scattered character of Marx's engagement with law individual texts will not be cited. For general compilations and discussions of Marx's treatment of law, see: M Cain and A Hunt, *Marx and Engels on Law* (London, Academic Press, 1979); H Collins, *Marxism and Law* (Oxford, Oxford University Press, 1982); P Hirst, *On Law and Ideology* (London, Macmillan, 1979) and R Phillips, *Marx and Engels on Law and Laws* (Oxford, Martin Robertson, 1980).

tion of wider social and economic relations under the logic of commodity relations; consumption, leisure and family relations all succumb to a greater extent to the logic of the market. But Marx stressed the instability of capitalist societies, their tendency to crisis. It is in this context that he drew attention to the significant degree of law's autonomy and separation from the state. Most importantly law provides and guarantees a regime of property and of contractual exchange. The expansion of the forms of capital and their circulation require a regime that protects the multiple forms in which capital circulates as legal interests. Legal relations have distinctive effects. The most important of these is the extent to which legal relations actually constitute economic relations, as witnessed in the formation of corporations with limited liability; these are legal creations in that it is the ability to confer a legal status which determines the liability of participants and thus makes the corporation a viable vehicle for the co-operation of diverse capitals.

Just as important was that legal rules and procedures make provision for regulating the interrelations of capital, through commercial law, insurance, banking and other financial services. For Marx, these mechanisms function as background conditions which constitute the framework within which economic relations are conducted. Law also provides the central conceptual apparatus of property rights, contract and other legal relations that play the double role of both constituting a coherent framework for economic activity and providing important components of the ideological conceptions of rights, duties and responsibilities. Legal relations share important features of capitalist economic relations in that they abstract from real-life relations, and in so doing, they fetishise relations, viewing them as having an existence, such as ownership or liability, disconnected from their concrete conditions. It is in this respect that Marx's critique is at its most acute. The primary way in which law participates in securing the conditions of existence for capitalist social relations takes the form of endowing legal subjects with actionable rights. Marx scathingly denounced 'the so-called rights of man' and 'the rights of egoistic man', and called talk of equal rights, 'obsolete verbal rubbish'.[15]

Marx's problematisation of law shares with Weber, in particular, the pervasive concern with law as a mechanism of rule at a distance, as if the rules were abstracted from specific economic or political interests. He gives this problematisation his own distinctive inflection by focusing on the implications of this new proximity of law and capitalist economic relations by considering its implications for the forms of rule to be envisaged in a future communist society. Marx was adamant in his refusal to speculate on utopian models of future society. But it is clear that his critique of rights is not only a criticism of the fetishism of legal rules, but is asserting the proposition that since industrial capitalism operates increasingly through the medium of law, such a mechanism can play no significant role in the construction of egalitarian relations. This line of thought was taken to its logical derivation by the early Soviet legal theorist Evgeny Pashukanis who extrapolated from Marx to arrive at the conclusion that, under socialism, law would necessarily wither away.[16]

---

[15] K Marx, 'On the Jewish Question' [1843] in *Karl Marx, Frederick Engels: Collected Works*, vol III (London, Lawrence & Wishart, 1975) 150, 165; K Marx, 'Critique of the Gotha Programme' [1875] in *Karl Marx: Selected Writings*, ed D McLellan (Oxford, Oxford University Press, 1977) 565.

[16] E Pashukanis, *Pashukanis: Selected Writings on Marxism and Law*, ed P Beirne and R Sharlet (London, Academic Press, 1980).

Weber

There are strong lines of filiation between Weber's treatment of law and that embedded in Marx's writings. This connection is certainly not an identity, not least because Weber was always conscious, however much common ground he might cover, of a concern to distinguish his position from Marx's in what has come to be referred to as 'the debate with the ghost of Marx'. Another crucial difference is that Weber's treatment of law is far more systematic. With Marx, we have pithy pronouncements that are left hanging, tantalising suggestions that remained undeveloped. Weber meets just about all the hallmarks of a rigorous general theory of law. Thus in drawing attention to continuities between Weber and Marx, I will attend to the differences by pointing to the way in which a problematisation of law which exhibits continuity is inflected in different directions with respect to his substantive lines of inquiry.

Weber's problematisation of law derives from his central concern to understand 'the uniqueness of the West'; how it was that in Western Europe the extraordinary economic transformation of capitalism took place. It was this question that led him into his extensive explorations of the world's great civilisations. Underlying this concern was an anxiety about the long-term viability of industrial capitalism, the continued economic advance of which seemed to depend on an increasingly militant and organised working class. Weber did not share the almost religious faith in the evolutionary guarantee of progress which was still such a powerful influence into the opening years of the twentieth century. Nor did he have any great enthusiasm about the advance of mass political democracy, for this was endangered, particularly in the German context, by the advance of socialist parties.

Thus, the core problematic of Weber's social and political theory addressed the question of how the stability and security of the capitalist order could be sustained. The substance of this problem is readily apparent from a consideration of his tripartite model of the forms of authority.[17] Traditional authority was readily understandable; it was the force of habit, rationalised as tradition and surrounded by religious and other legitimations, that secured its authority; but an authority that was always vulnerable to conditions that could more or less rapidly undermine its legitimacy as was the fate of most of the *ancien regimes* of Europe and beyond. Nor could such a system take full advantage of the economic potential of nascent capitalism. Similarly, the legitimacy of the intermediate or transitional form of political authority that he termed charismatic was readily understandable. It was the response to the attributes of the charismatic leader that endowed the leader with legitimate authority; the personal nature of such authority is attested to by the primary difficulty encountered by charismatic regimes, namely that of securing succession or, as Weber called it, the routinisation of charisma.

In important respects the rational or rational-legal authority that Weber identified as the key characteristic of modern forms of political authority has none of the advantages of the other forms in that it lacks a readily available symbolic figurehead; rather it was, by its very nature, a faceless impersonal order. From the Enlightenment onwards, political authority systematically shifted its claims to legitimacy from tradition, emotion and religion to rational, bureaucratic and professional sources.

---

[17] Weber's writings on law from various sections of *Wirtschaft und Gesellschaft* are collected in an English translation in M Rheinstein (ed), *Max Weber on Law in Economy and Society* (Cambridge, MA, Harvard University Press, 1954).

Rational authority had to supply its own legitimacy by making a merit out of professionalisation and bureaucratisation; by no means an easy task. Such a legitimation might prove acceptable on pragmatic grounds such as its fairness or impartiality, but it starts out as a 'weak' legitimation unlikely to command strong allegiance until such ideals as the separation of powers and due process of law can be articulated as strong constitutional doctrines. Significantly, Weber himself barely made appeal to such ideals. Rational authority as he conceived it relied largely on the capacity of rational law to generate its own legitimation, requiring obedience to law in and of itself to provide the grounds for citizen compliance. The major functional attribute which Weber saw as inhering in rational law was that it facilitated predictability. While undoubtedly significant in the self-interested calculus of the market, predictability is unlikely to provide anything more than a weak legitimation. The three substantive features of rational law that he identified were a professional judiciary (always likely to be distant from popular sentiment), a bureaucratic public service following 'the rules laid down' (also distant and impersonal) and the codification of rules (only compelling when associated with democratic legitimation).

One important feature of Weber's version of rational authority is frequently overlooked, namely that he makes only minimal appeal to democratic legitimation. The significant strength of appeal to democracy is that it has the capacity to go a long way to bind citizens of a democratic regime by invoking the collective responsibility of the citizenry. In its simplest form, democratic legitimation derives from the assertion that one's fellow citizens have chosen a system of rule or a law to be implemented, and such a decision is binding on all by virtue of their shared status as citizens.

Weber's vision of modernity draws attention to a tension between individual autonomy and formal legal rationality. He saw the consequence of the rise of legal rationality as manifesting itself in what Habermas was later to term 'juridification processes' through which not only expanding realms of social relations become subject to legal regulation, but in a wider sense law-like processes, rules and procedures are adopted in many fields of social life. Weber saw the peculiarity of the West as centred in its legalistic rationality in which rational self-control and rational economic calculation form a unity. Rationality exhibits two dimensions, one impersonal and connected to control and mastery, and the other normative linked to choice and freedom. Legal rationality contributes to 'freedom' via purposeful self-regarding conduct. This is the root of the tension that Weber perceived between rationalisation and disenchantment.

Weber's project of solving the problem of articulating a political order for modern capitalist society capable of sustaining legitimacy is rendered more difficult by the tension which he recognised as built into the form of justice generated by rational law. There is an inescapable friction between formal and substantive justice. Formal justice generates its claim to realise justice from the impersonality of its decisions that arises solely from being the result of following the rules laid down such that any similar case would be decided in the same way. On the other hand, the claim of substantive justice requires not merely that the rules are followed, but that the results can be morally just by reference to some criteria external to the rules. Formal justice may fail to realise substantive justice, just as securing substantive justice may require the breach of the requirements of formal justice. Thus Weber tends to conflate 'law' with 'legality' and identifies 'law as order' with 'law as justice'. The 'paradox' at the heart of Weber's position is that the institutionalisation of Western rationalism raises the very possibility of its extinction in the form of a domination of means over ends that characterises the pursuit of capitalist interests.

Weber was aware of these and related problems. Its most distinctive manifestation is in his much discussed remarks about the 'iron cage' in his conclusion to *The Protestant Ethic*:

> [T]he pursuit of wealth, stripped of its religious and ethical meaning, tends to become associated with purely mundane passions, which often actually give it the character of sport. No one knows who will live in this cage in the future.[18]

It is undoubtedly true that Weber exhibited a certain pessimism or lack of hope about the long-term viability of the framework of rational law and bureaucratic organisation as a stable and sustainable set of supports for rationality and capitalism. It is also evident that Weber, perhaps more than other social theorists, articulated a constructivist view of law as a conscious and intentional means of governing complex social and economic relations. And the constructivist task is firmly located in the hands of the state. Here, as will be seen, there is an important link with Durkheim, for both identified the basis of social cohesion in modernity in the primacy of the imagined community of the nation-state; it is this which goes a long way towards explaining Weber's unproblematic nationalist politics.

Durkheim

While Marx and Weber directly confronted the problem of the legitimacy of capitalist social relations (Marx) and capitalist political order (Weber), Durkheim rarely used the term capitalism. Yet his problematic was in one important respect similar to those of Marx and Weber. Durkheim's abiding question was: How is it possible that modern society, lacking a cohesive religion or spontaneous morality, can sustain social bonds sufficient to offset the fragmenting tendencies associated with industrial societies? Durkheim sought to establish that the complexity of industrial society and the individualism that it fosters does not have to lead to fragmentation and class conflict. In modern society, individuals, whilst becoming more autonomous, also become increasingly interdependent and—here is his crucial step—interdependence between individuals results in their depending more closely on society. One element of this rejection of Marx was the insistence that there could be no turning back from individualism which 'is henceforth the only system of beliefs which can ensure the moral unity of the country'.[19] Durkheim's problematic asked how social cohesion could be rendered compatible with advancing individualism.[20]

---

[18] M Weber, *The Protestant Ethic and the Spirit of Capitalism*, trans T Parsons (London, George Allen & Unwin, 1930) 181–82.

[19] E Durkheim, 'Individualism and the Intellectuals' [1898] in WSF Pickering (ed), *Durkheim on Religion: A Selection of Readings with Bibliographies*, trans J Redding and WSF Pickering (London, Routledge & Kegan Paul, 1975) 66.

[20] An illustration of this line of inquiry is found in Durkheim's account of the changing forms of punishment. With advancing individualism the deprivation of liberty alone becomes the normal means of social control. He identifies an historical shift from 'religious criminality' (crimes directed at 'collective things') to 'human criminality' (crimes which injure only individuals, such as homicide and theft): E Durkheim, 'Two Laws of Penal Evolution' [1900] (1973) 2 *Economy and Society* 285–308.

For Durkheim the task confronting sociology is to:

> discover those moral forces that men, down to the present time, have conceived of only under the form of religious allegories. We must disengage them from their symbols, present them in their rational nakedness, so to speak, and find a way to make the child feel their reality without recourse to any mythological intermediary.[21]

As Durkheim expressed it in one of his best-known formulations: 'The old gods are growing older or already dead, and others are not yet born.'[22] The task is to elaborate a secular morality as the source of social cohesion, and in this task law plays a significant role.

Durkheim had an ambivalent attitude towards industrialism and capitalism. He rejected Marx's strategy for the revolutionary overthrow of capitalism; but he recognised that the pursuit of self-interest produced adverse effects and generated conflict.

> Man's passions are stayed only by a moral presence they respect. If all authority of this kind is lacking, it is the law of the strongest that rules, and a state of warfare, either latent or acute, is necessarily endemic.[23]

This led him to argue that economic life must be regulated in order to 'have its morals raised, so that the conflicts that disturb it may have an end'.[24]

In his early work, *The Division of Labour*, Durkheim's interest in law was peripheral; the tabulation of different types of laws provided a useful measure of the prevalence of two primary forms of social solidarity, the mechanical solidarity of simple societies and the organic solidarity of complex societies. When he ceased to make use of the mechanical–organic distinction, what emerged was a more sophisticated view of the intertwining of law, morals and politics.[25] His problem was to discover a secular morality to serve as a substitute for religion; hence his interest to understand law as a moral phenomenon. His primary claim was that law expresses what is fundamental in any society's morality; thus to understand law sociologically it is necessary to explore how law articulates the basic characteristics of the society. He makes the fundamental claim that human desires must be constrained and channelled through internalised self-discipline. Law is the most visible, formalised element in processes of social regulation. Most significantly, law gives authoritative voice to morality conceived as a system of rules and sanctions that stipulate how people should act, and to behave properly they must obey conscientiously. While he recognised that law may be insensitive and oppressive, Durkheim perceived in the essential nature of law the roots of social cohesion, the ties that bind the individual to the group and its collective aspirations.

---

[21] E Durkheim, *Moral Education: A Study in the Theory and Application of the Sociology of Education*, trans EK Wilson and H Schnurer (New York Free Press 1961) 11.

[22] E Durkheim, *The Elementary Forms of Religious Life* [1912] (New York, Collier Books, 1961) 427. There is a significant parallel between Durkheim's formulation and Gramsci's thesis that the crisis of capitalism 'consists precisely in the fact the old is dying and the new cannot be born; in this interregnum a great variety of morbid symptoms appear'. See A Gramsci, *Selection from the Prison Notebooks of Antonio Gramsci* (London, Lawrence & Wishart, 1971) 276.

[23] Durkheim, above n 22, xxxiii.

[24] E Durkheim, *Professional Ethics and Civic Morals*, trans C Brookfield (London, Routledge & Kegan Paul, 1957) 12.

[25] For a detailed examination of the relationship between law and morality, see R Cotterrell, *Emile Durkheim: Law in a Moral Domain* (Edinburgh, Edinburgh University Press, 1999).

This vision of the law as the embodiment of commitment to society is somewhat naïve, for it grants no effectivity to the play of power, politics or even the autonomy of the formation of the substantive content of law. I suggest that the root deficiency is that, without stating the thesis explicitly, he views law as the modern substitute for religion which is the concentrated expression of the whole collective life, since in worshipping the divine, society unwittingly worships and celebrates itself. Law is the vehicle through which modern society worships itself. Durkheim, however, emphasised the necessity of incorporating individualism as the moral basis for modern law. Individualism is not necessarily egoism (a distorted form, manifesting itself in *anomie* and other negative manifestations), but rather individualism expresses sympathy for fellow humans by demanding respect for the liberty of each. Here, more clearly than elsewhere, Durkheim is closest to liberalism. The 'cult of the individual' provided modern law with its moral basis, but this humanist vision depends on the dubious assumption that social divisions are non-antagonistic.

It is in this context that Durkheim's views on law come into contact with his account of the state and democracy. His conception of the modern state exhibits compatibility with Weber's rational bureaucracy, but as a paternalistic organisation of disinterested specialists supervising the 'cult of individualism'. Moral leadership, governmental skill and diligent administration are needed to translate the morality of complex societies into law. He had no perception of the state as a site of conflict; politicians and experts are treated as benign agents trying to decide what is best for society.

Durkheim proposed that sectional interests and immediate forms of participation be provided through expanding the role of intermediate occupational bodies (such as guilds and trade associations, but not trade unions) as a moral force capable of curbing individual egoism by invigorating feeling of common solidarity. His key idea was that only occupational groups, guilds or corporations could carry out this function because they included all who worked in the same economic field.

His question is, can a governmental morality express the conditions of solidarity in complex societies? How does it maintain authority when collective beliefs no longer unify society? Durkheim's theory of democracy sought to provide an answer to these questions. Under representative democracy, the authority of the state not only depends upon, but encourages, the attachment of citizens to society. Thus political democracy is a necessary basis for government in modern individualist societies. Modern law is the form in which the results of these communicative processes are expressed in impersonal rules in a form capable of uniting the citizens. The element which has a largely unspoken but decisive place in the solution that Durkheim proposes to the general problematisation, which holds his inquiries together, is that the nation-state and the concomitant nationalism which it stimulates function as the glue that binds the imagined community of republican France into a governable entity.[26]

---

[26] Much of Durkheim's work is concerned with the role of education as the governmental training of citizens into a civilized nationalism: E Durkheim, *Education and Sociology* [1925] (New York, Free Press, 1956); Durkheim, above n 24.

3. CONCLUSION

Despite the manifest differences between their projects, their conceptual apparatus and their political agendas, there is a common core to the problematisations that underlie the work of Maine, Marx, Weber and Durkheim. There is a certain linear advance in a recognition and commitment to a constructivist vision of law and one of the primary strategies and techniques of law; Marx opposed this line of development, but Weber and Durkheim were deeply committed to this strategic vision.

I conclude with a few brief conjectures on the extent to which the problematisation of law has changed over the last century. During this period there has been an academic institutionalisation of inquiries that take law as their immediate object of inquiry. There has been a demarcation into a set of overlapping subdisciplinary fields, each with their own institutional apparatuses of departments, research institutes, conferences and journals. Jurisprudence, sociology of law and sociolegal studies each have their own distinguishing marks. For present purposes I ignore these, but a fuller treatment would need to take account of the differing lines of development of these disciplinary specialisms.

The primary trajectory of social studies of law has been to carry forward a variety of versions of the constructivist project in such a way as to resonate with the dominant politics of the twentieth century, namely the social democratic or liberal welfarist model. But over time there has been an increasing realisation of the contradictory nature of the unintended consequences of the juridification tendencies inherent in deployment of law as a mechanism of conscious social change. My suggestion is that the history of the post-classical sociology of law and sociolegal studies can be understood as a range of responses to the crisis of juridification.

The theme of a crisis of juridification has been expressed in its most developed theoretical form by Habermas.[27] The most important phase of juridification manifests an inescapable side effect of the welfare state project. The web of welfare norms were intended to cushion the effects of capitalist relations (social insurance, etc) but, in so doing, these measures, designed as means of guaranteeing freedom, operate in such as way as to endanger the freedom of the recipients of benefits. The price paid has been a bureaucratisation that undermines the independence and self-image of welfare recipients. Thus, 'while the welfare state guarantees are intended to serve the goal of social integration, they nevertheless promote the disintegration of life relations'.[28]

Within the predominantly empiricist and policy-oriented field of sociolegal studies there is little explicit consciousness of the crisis of juridification; but its presence is evident in the continuation of the long-standing realist preoccupation with the effectiveness of law which embodies the implicit project of making legal interventions more effective at reducing popular dissatisfaction with the legal enterprise. There is also evident a newer concern which I designate as a preoccupation with legal citizenship whose self-awareness is generally articulated as a concern with 'participation' or 'inclusion/exclusion'. In its most straightforward form the concern is to make law accessible

---

[27] J Habermas, 'Law as Medium and Law and Institution' in G Teubner (ed), *Dilemmas of Law in the Welfare State* (Berlin, de Gruyter, 1986) and 'Tendencies Toward Juridification' in *The Theory of Communicative Action*, vol II: *Lifeworld and System* (Boston, Beacon Press, 1987).

[28] Habermas, ibid (1986), 364.

to previously excluded, disadvantaged or marginalised groups. One of the more active trends has been the alternative dispute resolution movement, which in promoting its vision of 'user-friendly' alternatives to litigation has been largely unaware that rather than promoting an escape from juridification, it is an active agent of juridification promulgating law-like interventions in ever wider social fields. So whether the specific topic is legal aid and resources for the poor or with advancing gay-lesbian rights, the feature that unites these projects is a vision of law as a strategy for an inclusive citizenship through legal rights and their delivery.

There is a deep tension at the root of this style of work. On the one hand, it grapples with many important dimensions of the reformist project of legal constructivism, that is the use of law as a means of directed social change. Yet its strategy is unambiguously one of juridification. While it resists hierarchical and bureaucratic forms of juridification, it furthers an increasing legalisation of expanded fields of social life. In this respect, it exemplifies the problem which Habermas's discussion of juridification tendencies has highlighted. The problem in its simplest form is that law is both part of the problem and part of the solution. Welfarist interventions participate in the 'colonisation of the lifeworld' but the expansion and deepening of legal rights consolidates advances in the promotion of normative values arrived at through democratic political dialogue. In some of his earlier formulations Habermas seemed to suggest a tension, even an opposition, between the positivity of law and its promotion of values. In subsequent moves away from this suggestion he advances the view that law 'functions as a hinge between system and lifeworld'.[29] While this aspiration is attractive it seems to ignore the likelihood that in each specific context legal intervention may be skewed in one direction or the other.

There has been a marked tendency for the gap between sociology of law and sociolegal studies to widen and for there to be more open hostility or, perhaps worse, a tendency to ignore developments on the other side of the intellectual fence. This gulf may, however, be more a matter of style than of substance; the language of metatheory has become more arcane such that the texts of postmodernism verge on the incomprehensible for all but those that have pored over the privileged texts; while empirical studies become more mundane as they rework ever smaller questions about the functioning of legal institutions and processes. It does not follow that the substantive topics addressed have necessarily diverged: certain currents pursued by theoretically informed sociology of law manifest some degree of continuity with the general trajectory of sociolegal studies as described above.

Sociology of law, like so many other areas of the humanities and social sciences, has undergone a decisive 'cultural turn'.[30] This major current has promoted concern with sets of issues variously termed informalism, legal pluralism, law in everyday life and community law. It is important to recognise that such interests are by no means 'new'. As discussed above, Maine's metahistory of law gives prominent place to deep-seated shifts in the ordering of social relations that only subsequently leave their mark

---

[29] J Habermas, *Between Facts and Norms: Contributions to a Discourse Theory of Law and Democracy*, trans W Rehg (Cambridge, MA, MIT Press, 1996) 56.

[30] D Chaney, *The Cultural Turn: Scene-Setting Essays on Contemporary Cultural History* (London Routledge 1994); V Bonnell and L Hunt (eds), *Beyond the Cultural Turn: New Directions in the Study of Society and Culture* (Berkeley University of California Press 1999); F Jameson, *The Cultural Turn: Selected Writings on the Postmodern, 1983–1998* (London, Verso, 1998).

on state law. Eugen Ehrlich could well have been singled out for recognition as a classical founder of law and society studies;[31] he perhaps more than anyone else pressed the claim for the cultural roots of legal ordering. Thus, it might be more accurate to speak of a 'cultural return'.

My concern is not to engage in an extended discussion of contemporary scholarship, but rather to situate it. Foucault perceptively grasped that current discussion of law still starts out from a deeply engrained assumption that law is located as a manifestation of state sovereignty. He challenges us by chiding us about our failure 'to cut off the King's head'. Nevertheless, the sociology of law has tended to focus on the modernisation of state law as a major 'steering mechanism'. The alternative proposed by the cultural turn is that a sociology of law that has freed itself from a preoccupation with state-law can discover and elaborate 'alternative legalities' and provide a source of resistance to hegemonic state projects.[32]

The shift of attention towards an informalism and community ordering that is either beyond state legality or, more cautiously, a parallel mechanism of social ordering interest, has been the dominant focus of the sociology of law for more than a decade.[33] It is part of a much wider concern with the transformation of modern liberalism into a form conventionally styled 'neoliberalism'. This concept has the merit of avoiding the debate which has become somewhat sterile as to whether our present is still modern or is now postmodern, or that we may indeed 'have never been modern'.[34]

Neoliberal forms of social ordering are characterised by a complex and shifting deployment of forms of state-law regulation which seek to stimulate the self-governing capacity of increasingly individualised citizens.[35] This account of neoliberal forms of governance has been most fully developed by the Foucauldian governmentality tradition.[36] This rigorous interrogation of the changing forms of liberal rule has yet to have realised its potential in work specifically focused on the changing forms of legal ordering. However, a particularly promising avenue is suggested by O'Malley's identification of the rise of a new 'prudentialism'.[37]

In welcoming the cultural turn in the sociology of law, I end with a cautionary observation. The rise of self-governance and enterprising individualism does not herald either the death of the state or of 'the social'. We have not been witnessing the demise of the state or of state-law, but its transformation into new configurations with other modes of ordering. The task, having celebrated the cultural turn, is

---

[31] Indeed Ehrlich was only omitted on the grounds that to have included substantive discussion would have opened up the field to other claimants and resulted in transforming this essay into an encyclopaedia entry.

[32] S Silbey and A Sarat, 'Reconstituting the Sociology of Law: Beyond Science and the State' in D Silverman and J Gubrium (eds), *The Politics of Field Research: Beyond Enlightenment* (Beverly Hills, Sage, 1989) 162; see also B Santos, *Toward a New Common Sense: Law, Science and Politics in the Paradigmatic Transition* (New York, Routledge, 1995).

[33] The concept 'social ordering' is employed to contrast with 'social order'. Social ordering is a process of attempts that are never complete, that frequently fail or produce unintended consequences. Its incompleteness and failures only prompt renewed attempts at ordering.

[34] B Latour, *We Have Never Been Modern* (Hemel Hempstead, Harvester-Wheatsheaf, 1993).

[35] Those people who are unwilling, unable or lack the resources and capacities to engage in self-governing are either excluded and left to eke out a liminal existence or encounter elevated levels of disciplinary control.

[36] N Rose, 'The Death of the Social? Re-figuring the Territory of Government' (1996) 25 *Economy and Society* 327–56; M Dean, *Governmentality: Power and Rule in Modern Society* (London, Sage, 1999).

[37] P O'Malley, 'Risk, Power and Crime Prevention' (1992) 21 *Economy and Society* 252–75

therefore to 'bring the state back in'. The task is to grapple with the changing forms in which state law is imbricated with other forms of legal ordering. This provides a problematisation that is no longer, as in the classical tradition, essentially confined to the relationship between state sovereignty and the law, but now reaches out to new connections between forms of ordering. These new prospects are at one and the same time dangerous and exciting. They are dangerous because they herald a globalisation of power without responsibility and accountability whose primary agents are giant corporations and unelected international institution; yet they also create the possibility of envisaging new popular forms of engagement that reach out beyond the classical electoral forms of politics of the classical period of state, law and sovereignty. Marx, Weber and Durkheim, despite the obvious differences between them, all problematised law with respect to sovereignty. Modern sociology of law can and should stimulate the problematisation of law in its relation to democracy.

2

Sociological Jurisprudence

A JAVIER TREVIÑO

T HE CHIEF GOAL of Marx, Weber and Durkheim was to analyse formal, rational, centralised law as a way of understanding the structures of modern society. Each of them saw law as a coercive mechanism sanctioned by large-scale social forces—capitalist economic relations, bureaucratic organisation, civic solidarity—that have little bearing on people's experiences in their everyday lives. Although Marx and Weber had acquired university training in law, neither made legal practice their lifelong career. Weber and Durkheim were professors of economics, political science, education and sociology, while Marx's early jobs were in journalism. Their contributions to the sociological theory of law were made from *outside* the legal profession.

In this chapter I examine the work of three jurists whose contributions to the sociology of law came from *within* jurisprudence: Eugen Ehrlich (1862–1922), the Austro-Hungarian legal theorist who taught at the University of Czernowitz in the Bukovina (now part of Ukraine); Roscoe Pound (1870–1964), the American legal scholar and long-time Dean of the Harvard Law School; and Leon Petrażycki (1867–1931), the Polish-Russian jurist who held the first Chair of Sociology at the Law Faculty of the University of Warsaw. While a significant feature of these three scholars' agendas was a trenchant critique of formalist legal doctrine, their main objective, and that which distinguished them from Marx, Weber and Durkheim, was to study the social nature of law by paying attention to its living and working aspects.

In aggregating the ideas of Ehrlich, Pound and Petrażycki under the rubric of *sociological jurisprudence* I do not wish to suggest that they were in complete agreement with each other; they were not. To take only two significant examples of their differences: Pound always held fast to a state-centred notion of law, whereas Ehrlich and Petrażycki built their legal theories in opposition to it; in addition, Pound's jurisprudence was more reformist than Ehrlich's and Petrażycki's whose interest in law was mainly academic. Nonetheless, all three shared several important objectives that went far beyond the orientation of most jurists of their time. First, they sought to shift the central focus of legal science from official doctrine and statutes to social experience. Second, they proposed that the methods and insights of empirically oriented sociology (and social psychology) be employed as a counter, and corrective, to formalist jurisprudence. Finally, they, each in their own way, analysed law sociologically and in the process, revealed its significance in social life.

In what follows I introduce the sociolegal ideas of Ehrlich, Pound and Petrażycki by comparing and contrasting them with each other. In so doing, I focus on their scientific approach to law; the role of sociology and social psychology in their work; their pluralistic view of law, politics and society; and their ideas about the nature of law. I close with an assessment of the inheritance that they have bequeathed to today's legal sociologists.

1. SCIENTIFIC APPROACH TO LAW

Pound's scientific background and sympathies with the principles of American Pragmatism led him to view law in terms of its empirical purpose. As befitting this philosophy, he approached law instrumentally: as a tool for responding to the exigencies of societal conditions. Pound advocated for a scientific law and, indeed, deemed formalist jurisprudence to be scientific, but only in the *conceptual* sense; as a deductive system of law it reduced judges' biases, ignorance and possibility of corruption, preventing their departure from clearly articulated, predetermined rules. Pound, however, favoured the notion of scientific law in its *pragmatic* sense. Thus, he revealed the shortcomings of a jurisprudence that was abstractly scientific as concerned the logical processes of its internal structure but not concerning the practical results it achieved. According to Pound, inasmuch as formalist jurisprudence treated law not as a means to achieving an empirical end but as a means in itself, it had become overly 'mechanical', turning lawmaking and judicial adjudication into a technical and artificial enterprise.[1] Along these lines, he noted that jurists, in regarding science as something to be pursued for its own sake, tended to forget the true purpose of law, which is to be responsive to society's needs, wants, and interests.

As an undergraduate at the University of Nebraska, Pound studied botany, eventually earning a PhD in that field, and acquired a thorough grounding in the method of the natural sciences. The importance that he gave to empirical investigation was to influence his jurisprudence throughout his long career. Employing a taxonomic approach he engaged in the scientific ordering, the 'botanisation' as it were, of minutely detailed judicial terms.[2] Indeed, much as a botanist would collect and classify various species of flora Pound had a penchant for doing the same with legal ideas.

Pound advocated as a first step the method of cataloguing—of surveying and inventorying—in order to infer those social interests that have pressed upon lawmakers, judges and jurists for recognition and satisfaction.[3] Through a laborious and comprehensive analysis of hundreds of legal and extra-legal documents he culled the *social interests*, which is to say, the prevalent de facto claims, demands or desires that people collectively seek to satisfy and that society must recognise and protect through law.

Pound identified sixteen such interests that he fitted into six categories. Generally, the social interests consist of claims that ensure against behaviours that threaten a society's security, institutions, morals, resources, progress and freedom of self-assertion. Pound's analytic dissections notwithstanding, they in no way compromised his

---

[1] R Pound, 'Mechanical Jurisprudence' (1908) 8 *Columbia Law Review* 605–15.
[2] See eg R Pound, *Outline of Lectures on Jurisprudence* (Lincoln, NE, Jacob North & Co, 1903).
[3] R Pound, 'A Survey of Social Interests' (1943) 57 *Harvard Law Review* 1–39, 17.

conception of law as an organic 'living' entity. Sounding much like the biologist he had been trained to be, Pound wrote: 'Law is a living developing thing and when studied as such must be intensely interesting to one who can get interested in a living thing.'[4]

Relative to Pound's fastidious taxonomies, Ehrlich's attempts at identifying normative phenomena were notoriously vague and abstruse. Indeed, his efforts in this direction contained numerous subtle distinctions and partial overlaps that make it 'difficult to arrange Ehrlich's key concepts systematically and almost impossible to draw neat boundaries'.[5] As one example of the confusing nomenclature that confounded Ehrlich's conceptualisations is his explanation that 'legal propositions' that contain 'legal norms', and that serve as the basis for judicial decisions, are 'norms for decision'.[6]

Pound extolled Ehrlich for renouncing 'the metaphysical-analytical-historical jurisprudence of the last century'[7] and considering instead 'relations and groups and associations, rather than abstract individuals'.[8] Nevertheless, in a somewhat backhanded compliment Pound commended Ehrlich for providing '*only* the beginnings'[9] of a technique for ascertaining the patterned sociolegal actions that make up the living law. But what exactly was Ehrlich's technique and why did Pound regard it as an inchoate attempt?

Ehrlich, in fact, advocated for not one, but two, general techniques or methodologies for obtaining knowledge and understanding of the living law. He regarded both of them as scientific in that they arrived 'at general findings through the collection of individual data and their systematization'.[10] The first, which is for Ehrlich the most significant and chronologically prior method, involves the close scrutiny of 'the modern legal document'.[11] A legal document, such as, for example, the report of a judicial decision, must be examined, not for its statutory interpretations and juristic constructions, but for what it has to say about legal relations and life. Doubtless Pound would have readily accepted the textual examination method as he had himself employed it heavily when he combed through dozens of statutes, legal proceedings, court opinions, administrative rulings, legislative proposals, and a wide array of works in legal history, sociology and social psychology in his attempt at deducing the social interests.[12]

It was, however, the second methodological technique that Ehrlich utilised that was the most avant-garde for the formalist orthodoxy that, at the time, dominated the continental and Anglo-American legal world. In order to study the living law of

---

[4] As quoted in NEH Hull, *Roscoe Pound and Karl Llewellyn: Searching for an American Jurisprudence* (Chicago, University of Chicago Press, 1997) 45.

[5] S Nimaga 'Pounding on Ehrlich, Again?' in M Hertogh (ed), *Living Law: Reconsidering Eugen Ehrlich* (Oxford, Hart Publishing, 2009) 162–63.

[6] E Ehrlich, *Fundamental Principles of the Sociology of Law* [1936] (New Brunswick, NJ, Transaction Publishers, 2002) 171.

[7] R Pound, 'Introduction' to Ehrlich, *Fundamental Principles*, ibid, xxx.

[8] Ibid, xxi.

[9] R Pound, 'Fifty Years of Jurisprudence' (1938) 51 *Harvard Law Review* 777–812, 805 (emphasis added).

[10] KA Ziegert, 'The Sociology behind Eugen Ehrlich's Sociology of Law' (1979) 7 *International Journal of the Sociology of Law* 225–73, 239. Ziegert identifies Ehrlich's two main methods as the historiographical method and the questionnaire method. I see Ehrlich's methods as slightly different from the ones named by Ziegert.

[11] Ehrlich, above n 6, 493.

[12] Pound, above n 3.

the diverse peoples of Bukovina, he advocated for the 'direct observation of life, of commerce, of customs and usages, and of all associations not only of those that the law has recognized but also of those that it has overlooked or passed by, indeed of those that it has disapproved'.[13]

Ehrlich intended legal ethnography to be a detailed record required for lawyers and judges to learn what people are actually doing. Indeed, in his famous Seminar in Living Law, which he taught at the University of Czernowitz in 1909–10, Ehrlich proposed to teach law students how to collect empirical data on the social practices and usages of the vastly different ethnic populations of Bukovina, in order to understand the details of real life and enlist them in their investigations.[14] He did this through his own observations in the field of customary law coupled with the use of questionnaires.[15] Making the 'household and how it organizes its social relations by norms the research-unit of his studies',[16] Ehrlich collected data on such questions as: What does a man think his rights are with reference to his wife? How is a contract of lease entered into? When does the contract begin and how long does it last? Can a peasant drive cattle on the pasture land if he has mowed the meadow and harvested the crop?[17]

But to return to the question of why Pound found Ehrlich's techniques for understanding the living law to be wanting, we need to re-examine their slightly, but significantly, different orientations to the scientific. For both men, legal science meant the implementation of empirical positivism and induction. As we have seen, however, Pound's pragmatism and categorisation always informed his scientific endeavours. These influences lead ultimately to a higher purpose for his jurisprudence, a purpose defined by an activist agenda: the systematic classification of the diverse social interests that would have practical utility for engineering society. Ehrlich, on the other hand, was neither interested in social reform nor in developing conceptual typologies. Instead, he was mainly concerned with what Pound the progressive pragmatist would have regarded as a more prosaic (though not unimportant) goal: the reform of the study and teaching of law for the purpose of harmonising living law and 'official' law, and making decision-making more fair and efficient.

It is worth noting briefly that while Ehrlich was quite likely the first jurist to advocate the coupling of textual and ethnographic approaches, Petrażycki proposed combining textual analysis, not with direct observation of cultural and economic life, but with the more atomistic scrutiny of people's *moral emotions* and *physical reactions*. In Petrażycki's view, the external observation of people's 'speech, facial expressions, body movements'[18] allows for the direct study of their concrete social behaviour as they are engaged in legal relationships. But given that for Petrażycki legal phenomena have their origins not in the inner order of associations, but in the inner order people's *consciousness*, he goes further than Ehrlich, inward and deeper, in fact, with his advocacy of 'introspection' which requires understanding people's psychic world and their

[13] Ehrlich, above n 6, 493.

[14] See M Eppinger, 'Governing in the Vernacular: Eugen Ehrlich and Late Habsburg Ethnography' in Hertogh, above n 5, 41. Also KA Ziegert, 'World Society, Nation State and Living Law in the Twenty-first Century' in Hertogh, above n 5, 232.

[15] Ziegert, above n 10, 227.

[16] Ibid, 238.

[17] See A Likhovski, 'Czernowitz, Lincoln, Jerusalem, and the Comparative History of American Jurisprudence' (2003) 4 *Theoretical Inquires in Law* 621–57, 642.

[18] R Sadruska, 'Jurisprudence of Leon Petrażycki' (1987) 32 *American Journal of Jurisprudence* 63–98, 66.

specific experiences in the context of legal relationships. A self-referential technique, *introspection* involves the 'observation of one's own mental processes and body movements resulting from them; and inferring contents of the mental processes of others, by analogy, from their body movements'.[19]

Ehrlich and Pound both attempted to reform legal education and they equated its improvement with bringing a scientific understanding of the relations of law and society. Pound implored law teachers to supplement the abstract study of legal doctrine and include a practical consideration of the needs and interests of modern industrial life. As for the student, Pound believed that he or she must enter law school 'with a foundation in history, in economics, in politics, and in sociology which general college training alone can supply'.[20] For his part, Ehrlich directed his efforts at providing young lawyers with a portfolio of methodology and research techniques on how to observe social life and, understanding it, to produce better decisions and better law.[21] 'It is the business of legal science', Ehrlich stated tersely, 'to teach law as it actually works.'[22]

2. SOCIOLOGY AND SOCIAL PSYCHOLOGY

'In the past fifty years', wrote Pound in 1927, 'the development of jurisprudence has been affected profoundly by sociology.'[23] Twenty years earlier, he had noted that with the rise and growth of the social sciences, but particularly sociology, the time was ripe for a new tendency in legal scholarship that would take into account the practical relations of law to society.[24] This new tendency, called 'sociological jurisprudence', was to be an applied science in the tradition of positivism. Indeed, Pound admits to this tradition's early influence on him, acknowledging that he had been educated on the positivist sociology of Auguste Comte.[25] For Pound it was essential for the jurist to use sociology, and its empirical investigations, to ascertain the social interests articulated by people over a span of time and that had to be procured for the maintenance of a well-ordered society.

It was from the early American sociologists Lester F Ward, Albion W Small, and most especially EA Ross, a colleague of Pound's at the University of Nebraska, that Pound drew the assertion that law should be studied as a social institution.[26] He presented a picture of law as a social institution, a legal order, which allowed him to reflect upon its structural functions within the context of a changing society. As for his notion that law is a 'highly specialized form of social control'[27] (a notion derived from

[19] J Górecki (ed), *Sociology and Jurisprudence of Leon Petrażycki* (Urbana, IL, University of Illinois Press, 1975) 4.

[20] As quoted in Hull, above n 4, 53.

[21] KA Ziegert, 'Introduction' in Ehrlich, above n 6, xxi.

[22] E Ehrlich, 'Judicial Freedom of Decision: Its Principles and Objects' in Association of American Law Schools (ed), *Science of Legal Method* (Boston, The Boston Book Co, 1917) 47–84, 77.

[23] R Pound, 'Sociology and Law', in WF Ogburn and A Goldenweiser (eds), *The Social Sciences and Their Interrelations* (New York, Houghton Mifflin, 1927) 319–28, 327.

[24] R Pound, 'The Need of a Sociological Jurisprudence' (1907) 19 *The Green Bag* 607–15.

[25] R Pound, 'Philosophy of Law and Comparative Law' (1951) 100 *University of Pennsylvania Law Review* 1–19, 17.

[26] See G Geis, 'Sociology and Sociological Jurisprudence: Admixture of Lore and Law' (1964) 52 *Kentucky Law Journal* 267–93.

[27] R Pound, *Social Control through Law* [1942] (New Brunswick, NJ, Transaction Publishers, 1997) 41.

Ross's hopelessly incoherent exposition of that concept),[28] its fuller expression would have to await Talcott Parsons's[29] consideration of law's sanctions and its functional regulation of social relationships.

In short, then, Pound's jurisprudence is sociological precisely because it is unconcerned with law as rigid dogma, and instead approaches it as an institution operating within a larger societal context with the objective of securing and protecting society's interests.

Whereas Pound purposefully cultivated personal relationships with many of the prominent sociologists of his time, it appears that Ehrlich had no contact with academic sociology. Nowhere in his work does he cite his contemporaries Emile Durkheim, Max Weber or Georg Simmel. In *Fundamental Principles of the Sociology of Law* Ehrlich did make passing mention of Auguste Comte, Herbert Spencer and Gabriel Tarde, but only in reference to their general ideas about the development of societies and their organisations.[30] However this may be, Ehrlich is today recognised as one of the undisputed founders of legal sociology and an early theorist of the sociological causation of law. It was, in fact, around the time that Ross was tutoring Pound in a sociological view of the operation of the courts that Ehrlich was also explicitly using his homespun sociology to explain a variety of everyday social relations that were outside the purview of formalist legal doctrine. These explanations revolved around his famous concept of *living law*, 'the law that dominates life itself, even though it has not been printed in legal propositions'.[31]

But having rejected the statist theory of law, Ehrlich needed an alternative for distinguishing the legal norms of the living law from other types of non-legal norms, such as those having to do with morality, ethical custom and decorum; and for this he relied on what he called the *opinio necessitatis* approach.

Opinio necessitatis, in essence, constitutes an index of emotions: 'The various classes of norms release various overtones of feeling', explained Ehrlich, 'and we react to the transgression of different norms with different feelings.'[32] The legal norm of living law was unique in that the emotive reaction it evoked in people for its violation is *revolt*.

While Ehrlich's *opinio necessitatis* has rightly been criticised for its imprecision and lack of scientific rigour,[33] it must nonetheless be allowed that inasmuch as he explicitly considered *reactive* (social) emotions, his was a valid social-psychological approach.

If by 'revolt' Ehrlich meant the response of aversion, a turning away from the transgression and transgressor, it is a socially emotional reaction for two reasons. The first is that it is social in the reflective, reflexive and relational sense: people contemplate the legal norm in relation to the offender, in relation to how they think they should react to the offender. The second reason is that the reaction of turning away from

---

[28] EA Ross, *Social Control: A Survey of the Foundations of Order* [1901] (New Brunswick, NJ, Transaction Publishers, 2009).

[29] T Parsons, 'Law and Social Control' in WM Evan (ed), *Law and Society* (New York, Macmillan, 1962) 56–72.

[30] Ziegert, above n 10, 227.

[31] Ehrlich, above n 6, 493.

[32] Ibid, 165.

[33] See D Nelken, 'Law in Action or Living Law? Back to the Beginning in Sociology of Law' (1984) 4 *Legal Studies* 157–74; M Hertough, 'From "Men of Files" to "Men of the Senses": A Brief Characterisation of Eugen Ehrlich's Sociology of Law' in Hertogh, above n 5.

actions that are considered to be 'beyond the pale' demonstrates social rejection on the basis that these deviant actions threaten the association's social bonds.

Revolt, and for that matter the other overtones of feeling that Ehrlich identified with the violation of non-legal norms—eg indignation, disgust, disapproval, ridicule and critical feeling of superiority—are behaviour-tendencies and therefore not social emotions in the manner of Charles Horton Cooley,[34] who gave primacy to their correspondence with empathy and self-consciousness. But Ehrlich's feeling of revolt is certainly close enough to GH Mead's[35] recognition of people's emotional reactions of 'hostility' toward the lawbreaker (and its attendant attitudes of retribution, repression and exclusion), to put Ehrlich's effort squarely within the venerable tradition of contemporaneous American social psychology. Notwithstanding this fact, however, Ehrlich's social-psychological orientation does not add rigour or precision to his *opinio necessitatis* approach for defining law.

If anyone was able to offer a convincing conceptual distinction between law and morality, without reference to state authority and dispute resolution, it was Petrażycki. He went further than Ehrlich in distinguishing, and also correlating, more clearly and precisely the tripartite dimensions of the human condition: legal consciousness, emotions and behaviour-tendencies.

As will be more fully explained presently, Petrażycki conceived of law as a psychological phenomenon, having its real existence only in the human psyche or *consciousness*, where it takes the form of legal emotions. These latter are then projected outward and in the process give law its 'objective' character. Once externalised, however, conduct that violates law, in turn, affects people's emotions, invoking in them the feeling of 'repulsion'.[36] Further, it is emotions, not external sanctions, declared Petrażycki, that chiefly motivate people to realise their rights and fulfil their duties in the legal relationship. That is to say, people obey law because they *feel* committed to each other; they are bound by obligation.[37]

As concerns *behaviour-tendencies*, Petrażycki began with the premise that people's subjective experiences are constituted of psychic drives or 'impulsions'. *Impulsions* are behaviour-tendencies that motivate a person to act, or to refrain from acting, in a given situation. *Legal impulsions* consist of the action ideas of right and duty that guide social relationships between people, and it is on this basis that he distinguished law from morality.

Petrażycki defined morality as those norms that 'establish obligations free in respect to others: these authoritatively prescribe certain conduct for us but give others no claim or rights of any kind to fulfilment by us'.[38] Morality, therefore, is one-sided; it is not attributive but only imperative—urging or recommending a given form of conduct. Morality stipulates the conduct that should be shown toward others but does not recognise our entitlement to demand the same conduct from others. In contradistinction

---

[34] CH Cooley, *Human Nature and the Social Order* (New York, Scribners, 1902).

[35] GH Mead, 'The Psychology of Punitive Justice' (1918) 23 *American Journal of Sociology* 577–602.

[36] If Ehrlich's 'revolt' refers to the reaction of 'turning away from', Petrażycki's 'repulsion' refers to the act of 'driving back'. In either case, the two emotions involve rejection.

[37] This sentiment approximates Ehrlich's *opinio necessitatis* that refers to the feeling of obeying a social necessity. See R Cotterrell, 'Ehrlich at the Edge of Empire: Centres and Peripheries in Legal Studies' in Hertogh, above n 5. See also A Cassese, 'A Follow-Up: Forcible Humanitarian Countermeasures and *Opinio Necessitatis*' (1999) 10 *European Journal of International Law* 797, quoting Georges Scelle.

[38] L Petrażycki, *Law and Morality* [1955] (New Brunswick, NJ, Transaction Publishers, 2011) 46.

to morality, law is imperative *and* attributive and, thus, fundamentally based on the idea of quid pro quo. In short, for Petrażycki law has its origins in the human psyche, which gives rise to feelings of obligations, and inclines people to interact in reference to a consideration of reciprocal rights and duties.

With this discussion of the sociological, and social-psychological, influences on Pound, Ehrlich and Petrażycki, I now turn to their views of law, politics and society.

3. LAW, POLITICS AND SOCIETY

In this section I examine how Pound and Ehrlich each took a pluralistic view of law, politics and society, but in different ways and for different reasons. According to Likhovski,[39] it was precisely the frontier conditions of Pound's Nebraska and Ehrlich's Bukovina that compelled them to take into account legal and social heterogeneity.

At the time that Ehrlich began writing about the living law in 1910, the population of Bukovina consisted of Ruthenians, Romanians, Jews, Armenians, Gipsies, Hungarians, Poles, Russians and Slovaks. What is more, each of these populations 'obeyed totally different legal rules in all the legal relations of their daily lives',[40] in spite of these rules coexisting alongside the statutes of the Austro-Hungarian Empire.

Although the majority of the inhabitants of Pound's town of Lincoln, in the early twentieth century, were of English background, there were also many Germans, Russians, Swedes and Danes. In fact, in 1910, nearly half of the population of Nebraska was foreign-born or had foreign parents. These settlers had come from several countries including, Ireland, Norway, France, Bohemia and even from Ehrlich's Bukovina. These demographically heterogeneous and culturally diverse conditions of life created an amalgam of nationalities in the Great Plains.

However, Pound was decidedly not interested in the living law of various cultural communities. Instead, his preoccupation was, as he pointedly put it, with 'the legal order of a politically organized society instead of with the order implicit in all groups and associations and relations'.[41] This meant that his jurisprudence compelled him to deal with society administratively, as politically constituted, and thus, for him, law comes from only one source: the bureaucratic state. Although Pound was not concerned with the harmonious arrangement of various social networks that was Ehrlich's province, he was nonetheless much intrigued by the *political operations* of the many interest groups that compose a pluralistic society, and, significantly, with their competition for scarce resources. So whereas Ehrlich looked first to the normative structure of social associations—whose natural state he considered to be not 'an order of war, but of peace'[42]—and regarded central legislation as a last resort for dealing with discord, Pound turned first to politicised society and lauded the capacity of the courts, as state agencies, to reconcile conflicting claims and demands between different interest groups.

Although much influenced by American pragmatist philosopher William James's

---

[39] Likhovski, above n 17.
[40] Ziegert, above n 10, 229.
[41] R Pound, *Jurisprudence*, vol 1 (St Paul, MN, West Publishing Co, 1959) 345.
[42] Ehrlich, above n 6, 127.

social-ethical principal that the end of ends is the goal for satisfying at all times as many demands as possible,[43] Pound extended it in two significant ways. First, he allocated—specifically to law—the task of satisfying as much of the total amount of demands (or interests) as possible, for as many demands as possible. For Pound, law is a mechanism of social control that 'makes it possible to do the most that can be done for the most people'.[44] However, since all desired resources are limited, people's demands for goods and objects will inevitably conflict with or overlap those of their neighbours. As a result, in dealing with specific situations, Pound always considered the totality of interests that matter most in society as a whole. Second, he argued that the balancing of social interests and the stabilising of pluralistic community gives rise to the 'fundamental problem of jurisprudence' which is the question of how best to measure or weigh discordant social interests.[45] While the general, and rather vague, guiding principle of sociological jurisprudence was to push to its results the greatest amount of immediately pressing interests, Pound conceded that '[m]anifestly one cannot speak with assurance as to how we are in the end to value competing and overlapping interests'.[46] The challenge and task for judges and other lawyers, acting as social engineers, was to formulate a reasoned scheme for valuing conflicting interests and arrive at social consensus through compromise.

In today's environment of heightened cynicism toward legislative and judicial processes, coupled with extreme hardline partisanship, Pound's attempt at consensus in the face of social pluralism is seen as naïve at best, and wrong at worst. His assumption that law is the broker of the demands of competing interests has become an anachronism. The pluralistic-consensual conception of politics has yielded to the more critical notion that the legal order actively supports some (powerful) interests at the expense of others as well as to the general proposition of critical legal studies that 'all law is politics'.

As we have seen, Pound's *state legal pluralism* means that he considered the diversity of interests among various political action groups as they vie for recognition in a liberal democracy. Ehrlich, however, was more focused on *cultural legal pluralism*, which made him particularly keen to investigate the legal order of a multitude of mutually related communities of an ethnically diverse society. Thus, for him, society consisted of the sum total of diverse coexisting social associations with a legal order that, in most cases, is free from the state's coercive powers. For Ehrlich *social associations* are comprised of

> a plurality of human beings who, in their relations with one another, recognize certain rules of conduct as binding, and generally at least, actually regulate their conduct according to them.[47]

What Ehrlich referred to as the associations' 'inner order' is determined by these *rules of conduct*, or 'legal norms' (not to be confused with *legal propositions* which are the statutes that make up 'official' law). This means that law, by definition, is a part

---

[43] W James, 'The Moral Philosopher and the Moral Life' in H Hall (ed), *Readings in Jurisprudence* (New York, The Bobs-Merrill Co, 1938) 236–37.
[44] Pound, above n 27, 64.
[45] R Pound, 'Law and the Science of Law in Recent Theories' (1934) 43 *Yale Law Journal* 525–36, 534.
[46] Pound, above n 27, 126.
[47] Ehrlich, above n 6, 39.

of the many different kinds of association in which people interrelate and that legal pluralism is an inherent quality of society.[48]

Social associations—whether formal or informal, enduring or transient—include an impossibly wide variety of relatively stable patterns or networks of social relations, from contractual relationships, families, churches, political parties, corporations, social classes and professions to cities, states, nations, and even international groupings of nations. Whatever their kind or scope, however, they are all organised by legal norms that assign to members their relative positions and roles in the association. This normative ordering ensures that 'most affairs work themselves out without any dispute', and that 'only a very few matters come before the court'.[49]

But more than just demonstrating a functional process, Ziegert[50] sees the associations' internal means of regulation as possessing a degree of *reflexivity*. He explains that the legal norms provide the individual members with a relational 'reference point' that tells them not only what conduct is expected of them, but that also tells them, in relative terms, what they can expect from others. These prescribed actions and anticipated reactions among the members of an association form its inner order—what Ziegert describes as the 'reflexive web of normative expectations'—which constitutes the domain of law.[51]

Recently, Nelken[52] has contended that by interpreting Ehrlich's associations in systemic (autopoietic) terms (note the 'reflexive web' denotation), Ziegert aims to depict Ehrlich as a forerunner of Luhmannian thinking. A circularity, or mutuality, of expectations and communications exists in all normatively ordered interchanges; what Parsons,[53] and also Luhmann,[54] have referred to as a situation of 'double contingency', or the idea that ego and alter must conform with one another's expectations of each other.

Based on the foregoing, we may see two crucial parallels between Ehrlich's and Petrażycki's notions of law. The first is that, for Petrażycki, what he called 'intuitive' law, like Ehrlich's 'living' law, emerges spontaneously from people's actions and reactions. But in the case of Petrażycki these actions and reactions take place, not in the context of associations generally, but within the *imperative-attributive* structure of bilateral relationships. These relationships are legal inasmuch as it is imperative that the interacting parties fulfil their duties, and in the process they are attributed certain rights corresponding to those duties.

For Petrażycki, all legal phenomena, whether of a civil, criminal, administrative or constitutional nature, are reducible to imperative-attributive (right- and duty-oriented) legal relationships. He identified three types of such relationships based on the imperative-attributive parings articulated through the Latin verbs *facere* (to act), *non facere* (not do act), *pati* (to allow), *non pati* (not to allow) and *accipere* (to receive):

---

[48] Eppinger, above n 14, 38–39.

[49] E Ehrlich, 'The Sociology of Law' (1922) 35 *Harvard Law Review* 130–45, 141.

[50] Ziegert, above n 21, xl.

[51] *Ibid.*

[52] D Nelken, 'Ehrlich's Legacies: Back to the Future in the Sociology of Law?' in M Hertogh (ed), *Living Law: Reconsidering Eugen Ehrlich* (Oxford, Hart Publishing, 2009), 237–72, 261.

[53] T Parsons and EA Shils (eds), *Toward a General Theory of Action* (Cambridge, MA, Harvard University Press, 1951).

[54] N Luhmann, *Social Systems* (Stanford, CA, Stanford University Press, 1995).

(1) The duty of the obligor may consist in doing something (paying a sum of money, delivering a merchandise, performing a service, or working) for the obligee; ie for the rightful claimant (*facere*). The corresponding right of the claimant consists in getting those goods or services (*accipere*). Or, on the contrary, (2) the duty of the obligor may consist in refraining from doing certain things; eg, not to attack the life, health, liberty, property or civil rights of another person or persons (*non facere*) and the other person or persons have the right not to tolerate such attacks (*non pati*). Finally, (3) the duty of the obligor may consist in tolerating certain rightful activities of a person or persons entitled to them (*pati*). The latter person or persons have a right to do certain things, they have certain areas of freedom—freedom of speech, press, assembly and so forth (*facere*).[55]

The second point of agreement between Petrażycki and Ehrlich is that for them the actual norms governing the daily lives of people have no connection with external authority or coercion. Petrażycki's *intuitive law* (which he posited in opposition to positive law) consists of 'those legal experiences which contain no references to outside authorities and are independent thereof'.[56] As is typically the case with intuitive law, 'there are neither commands emanating from authorities nor normative facts of any kind'.[57] For example, it may be said that a husband's impulsions are imperative if he 'experiences his duty and his wife's right to fidelity without even thinking about family code, religious command, or any other source establishing the obligation'.[58]

Having now examined Pound's, Ehrlich's and Petrażycki's legal and social pluralism, it is time to turn to their ideas about the character and purpose of law.

4. CONCEPTIONS OF LAW

Two of Pound's key ideas concerning law were derived, in part, from the nineteenth-century neo-Hegelian jurist Josef Kohler. First, the notion of historical relativity took form in Kohler as he looked at law, not as a fixed and permanent entity suitable for all time, but as a dynamic phenomenon of human civilisation. Given that civilisation is constantly developing and changing, so too must law evolve and adapt to its fluctuating needs and demands. It follows, then, that law that is appropriate for one period of civilisation is not so for another.

Picking up on this theme, Pound delighted in pointing out, time and again, the inability of legal formalism to keep up with social progress and excoriated it for being rigid and unyielding. Indeed, because it had become unable to accommodate changing social and economic conditions it had failed abjectly in what Pound believed to be law's pragmatic purpose: to accomplish socially worthwhile purposes. This disconnect between formal law and social reality, between the abstract and actual events, led

---

[55] A Rudzinski, 'Petrażycki's Significance in Contemporary Legal and Moral Theory' (1976) 21 *American Journal of Jurisprudence* 107–30, 117. A fourth legal relationship, not discussed by Petrażycki, involves the *pati* and *non facere* pairing. In this case, the duty of the obligor may consist in tolerating certain rightful activities of a person or persons entitled to them (*pati*). The latter person or persons have a right to refrain from doing certain things; eg a soldier who is wounded has the right not to perform his service (*non facere*). See E Fittipaldi, *Everyday Legal Ontology: A Psychological and Linguistic Investigation Within the Framework of Leon Petrażycki's Theory of Law* (Milan, LED, 2012) 186–97.

[56] Petrażycki, above n 38, 57.

[57] Ibid, 155.

[58] Górecki, above n 19, 7–8.

Pound to declare his famous distinction between *law in books*, the official rules and procedures, and *law in action*, the implementation of these rules and procedures in practice.[59] As he put it, law 'falls short of what is expected of it, especially in dealing with the many new questions and endeavors to secure newly pressing interests'.[60]

Pound announced the need for a sociological jurisprudence that treated law pragmatically, as an institution that regulates social processes with the object of securing and protecting society's interests. It was therefore necessary that written law respond conscientiously and adequately to the practical needs of society or else risk its effectiveness and good name. And the simplest procedure for doing so was to bridge the gap between 'law in the books' and 'law in action'.

The other notion that Pound borrowed from Kohler was that of the *jural postulates*—ideals of right and justice that the civilisation of a given period must identify for guiding lawmaking and judicial decision-making.[61] But whereas Kohler never specified how the jural postulates are determined and derived, Pound conceived of them as de facto claims, demands or interests that are procured, inductively, from various branches of law including criminal law, tort law, property law, contract law and the law of restitution.

As fundamental principles of human conduct, the jural postulates have a practical threefold purpose. First, they are meant to identify and explain the substantial totality of actual human claims, demands or interests of a particular social order. Second, they express what the majority of individuals in a given society want law to do. Third, and related, the jural postulates are meant to guide the courts in applying law. Pound asserted that the jural postulates are not eternal, immutable or exhaustive. Indeed, he regarded them as principles that overlap, conflict and are in continuous dynamic transition. His position toward the jural postulates was therefore one of relativity, for upon being recognised, the postulates are legally protected only until the empirical facts of a changing society make them outmoded and obsolete. In the meantime, they are employed in the practical work of bringing a particular society's legal institutions into accord with the jural postulates, and, concomitantly, into a condition of harmony with the de facto claims made by the majority of persons in a specific society at a certain time.

Just as Pound believed that the jural postulates formed the basis of all law, so Ehrlich regarded the 'facts of law' as fundamental to the emergence of legal norms. The *facts of law* are those organisational rules that assign to each individual their positions and duties in a social association. There are, Ehrlich claimed, four such facts of law: (i) usage; (ii) relations of domination and subjection; (iii) possession; and (iv) declarations of will.[62] The jural postulates and the facts of law are both foundational to social and legal relationships.

But whereas Pound saw the jural postulates as emanating from legal sources, and thus the state, Ehrlich regarded the facts of law as originating directly from a matrix of human relationships. This demonstrated to him that social relations, from which the great mass of law is derived, precede the state (which in its earliest form is purely

[59] R Pound, 'Law in Books and Law in Action' (1910) 44 *American Law Review* 12–36.
[60] Pound, above n 27, 14.
[61] R Pound, *Interpretations of Legal History* (Cambridge, Cambridge University Press, 1923).
[62] Ehrlich, above n 6, ch 5.

a military centre of might, unconcerned with law or courts), which precedes state law (law created through legislation).[63] Thus, in their endeavours at developing a socio-logical jurisprudence we see that Pound gave primacy of fact to the jurisprudential or *administrative* aspect, and Ehrlich to the sociological or *associational* aspect, of the science of law.

As for Petrażycki, he understood legal facts—eg obligation, right, property, contract—to exist only in the human psyche. In his view, law's origins lie in people's 'psychical experiences'; for it is not in social relations, but through a series of mental pictures that legal behaviours are first identified. Petrażycki also flatly rejected the fun-damental notion of formalist jurisprudence that law is a concrete, external entity to be found in the legal codes, court opinions, law books and other objective sources. Indeed, he regarded these extraneous manifestations of law as nothing more than 'phantasmata', naïve projections of individuals' states of consciousness.[64] Thus, in Petrażycki's view, law stands above, or has its origins conceptually prior to, the state, and for that matter, the social association.

Ehrlich's conceptualisation of law, by contrast, was first and foremost a sociological phenomenon. Taking an expansive, and therefore scientific, view of its social reality, he considered law in the context of 'that which lives and is operative in human society'.[65] For Ehrlich, it was typically the case that people in communal relations voluntarily perform their duties and in the process create their own rules. Indeed, it is because people are generally engaged in the practical affairs of life that they desire to relate to others amicably. This means that legal norms are the primary normative order that make social associations 'predominantly communicative, peaceful, stable and predictable';[66] they neither require verbal expression nor do they depend on compul-sion by a state apparatus. They are the 'living law', those norms that 'tie participants to a network of expectations, which are dependent on each other'.[67]

This is not to say that Ehrlich considered legal propositions (precepts) to be irrele-vant or unnecessary. However, their main task is not to order society; it is to reproduce *norms for decision*, which are the technical rules that impersonally instruct bureaucrat judges and government officials on how to administer cases of dispute and litigation. Legal propositions are not, primarily at least, for people who are the doers in life, but for those 'who sit in judgment upon the doers'.[68]

In the end, it has been observed that Pound's law-in-action conception posed as its central question: *how* do people experience law? Conversely, for Ehrlich (as well as for Petrażycki, both of whom treated law as a *dependent* variable), the pertinent question was: *what* do people experience as 'law'?[69]

---

[63] Ehrlich, above n 49.

[64] It is entirely appropriate to ask if Petrażycki's ideas belong in a discussion of *sociological* jurisprudence given that 'the quintessential feature of Petrażycki's theory of law in general, and his concept of law in particular, is psychologism': K Motyka, 'Law and Sociology: The Petrażyckian Perspective' in M Freeman (ed), *Law and Sociology* (Oxford, Oxford University Press, 2006) 126. Most commentators on his work have placed him in the sociological camp.

[65] Ehrlich above n 6, 10.

[66] Ziegert, above n 14, 228.

[67] Ziegert, above n 21, xxx.

[68] Ehrlich, above n 6, 122.

[69] M Hertogh, 'A "European" Conception of Legal Consciousness: Rediscovering Eugen Ehrlich' (2004) 31 *Journal of Law and Society* 457–81.

5. HERITAGE

It may be said that, ultimately, both Pound and Ehrlich perceived legal life as harmonious. For Pound this was to be *achieved though consensus* arrived at by the judicial, and judicious, valuing of social interests. Similarly, for Ehrlich, harmony was to be *maintained through agreement* in social relationships where discord is often settled in a friendly manner, without resort to the courts. But how has the sociological jurisprudence of these two jurists, and that of Petrażycki, fared since their deaths? In this section I assess the continuing merit of their ideas.

Pound's Legacy

In her magisterial book, which consists of twin intellectual biographies of Karl Llewellyn and Roscoe Pound, Hull[70] makes it clear at the outset that 'Pound has slipped into semi-obscurity'. This unfortunate state of affairs for Pound is not only true in jurisprudence (where he is usually given only 'footnote' credit for his contributions to American legal realism and critical legal studies), but also in sociolegal inquiry and the sociology of law. Indeed, insofar as Pound is today discussed by legal sociologists, it is invariably in comparison with someone else, most notably Ehrlich.[71] In what follows I briefly examine Pound's influential, if somewhat limited and frequently obscured, legacy, in two conceptual areas.

The Politicisation of Interests

In the year of Pound's death, 1964, it was observed that sociologists had 'paid virtually no attention to Pound's doctrine, either in terms of rejecting it, refining it for their purposes, or supplementing it with sociological material of more recent vintage'.[72] That situation is still true today. While Pound's conjectures are now widely accepted by sociologists and jurists, there have been few attempts to revise his famous theory of interests to reflect sociological developments. One outstanding exception has been the criminologist Richard Quinney,[73] who attempted to construct a sociological theory of criminal law by reformulating and extending Pound's pluralistic-consensus approach. As such, Quinney makes certain assumptions about law and society that constitute a radical reconceptualisation of Pound's premises.

First, Quinney sees society as characterised by diversity, conflict, coercion and change, rather than by consensus and stability. Second, he considers law to be the *creation* of interests, rather than an *instrument* which functions outside of particular interests. Third, he maintains that law incorporates the special interests of specific persons and groups in society, instead of representing the compromise of the diverse interests of all members of society.[74]

These assumptions lead Quinney to the following conclusions that, although made

---

[70] Hull, above n 4, 2.
[71] See Nelken, above n 33; Likhovski, above n 17; Hertogh, above n 69; Nimaga, above n 5.
[72] Geis, above n 26, 292.
[73] R Quinney, *Crime and Justice in Society* (Boston, Little, Brown and Co, 1969).
[74] Ibid, 25–56.

within the general tradition of Pound's interest theory of jurisprudence, also depart significantly from that tradition: law is created and interpreted in the context of a politically organised society. Politically organised society is based on the different institutional concerns of the various interest groups. Some interest groups have more power than others. Those interest groups that have the power to realise their concerns in public policy formulate and administer law. Finally, in formulating law, some interest groups are able to control others to their own advantage. Thus, in stark contrast to Pound's *pluralistic-consensus* conception of society, Quinney's *conflict-power* model sees law as resulting from the differential distribution of power and conflict between political action groups.

The Fundamental Problem

And what of Pound's 'fundamental problem', the empirical problem of values, of finding a criterion for balancing competing interests? Quite simply, it has either been ignored or inadequately accounted for in sociological jurisprudence. No doubt this has been due largely to the fact that, as Pound pointed out, 'contemporary sociology, pursuing a strict methodology, while it recognizes values, rigidly excludes all valuings as subjective and unscientific'.[75]

Particularly thorny in regard to the question of values has been the issue of the diverse and complex interests involved in the sharing of water supplies. Indeed, Pound admitted that in 'our western states, where there was abundant opportunity for free judicial development, judicial law making proved inadequate to adjust water rights'.[76] When the demand for any resource, including water, exceeds the supply, some adjustments must be made.[77] One type of adjustment is the 'engineering solution' which involves taking concrete measures such as building a dam, storing and importing water, or seeking a new source. However, it was the 'economic solution', based on the principle of efficiency, that was the facilitation that Pound favoured for ordering 'the activities of men in their endeavour to satisfy their demands so as to enable satisfaction of the whole scheme of demands with the least friction and waste'.[78] Most telling perhaps is that in James Willard Hurst's[79] description of the adjustment scheme involved in people's use of forest streams in nineteenth-century Wisconsin, 'the father of modern American legal history' makes no mention whatsoever of Pound or his fundamental problem of values.

Ehrlich's Legacy

As for Ehrlich, his legacy has fared less well. Aside from occasional analyses of his work, Ehrlich has been largely neglected in the general literature in the sociological study of law.

---

[75] Pound, above 41, 329.
[76] Pound, above n 59, 23.
[77] FJ Trelease, 'Climatic Change and Water Law' in National Research Council (ed), *Climate, Climatic Change, and Water Supply* (Washington, DC, National Academy of Sciences, 1977) 70–84.
[78] As quoted in ibid, 71.
[79] JW Hurst, *Law and Economic Growth: The Legal History of the Lumber Industry in Wisconsin, 1836–1915* (Cambridge, MA, Harvard University Press, 1964).

Moreover, what was previously said about Pound being regarded largely in comparison with Ehrlich also holds true of Ehrlich—effectively denying his work its own signal relevance. Ziegert himself has admitted that '[m]any, if not most, sociologists of law today would be hard pressed if asked how their work was related to Ehrlich's foundation of the sociology of law'.[80] A recently published collection of essays, aptly titled *Living Law*,[81] is the first edited volume in the English language dedicated entirely to Ehrlich's ideas. It remains to be seen whether it will incite further reading, writing and discussion about this important pioneer in the sociology of law.

It is clearly Klaus A Ziegert[82] who has, for over three decades, done the most to champion Ehrlich's ideas and make them available to an English-speaking public. Roger Cotterrell[83] has also consistently kept Ehrlich's work relevant and fresh. Moreover, it is particularly in discussions about legal pluralism, to which Cotterrell has greatly contributed, that 'often refer to Ehrlich's writings and current debates continue to make explicit reference to his ideas'.[84]

Legal Pluralism and Moral Diversity

According to Cotterrell,[85] Ehrlich's enduring contribution lies in his advocacy of a legal pluralist approach, particularly as applied to contemporary Europe's cultural and legal heterogeneity. In this regard, his work can today serve as a guide to issues of legal regulation that bear directly on the European project's attempts at political, economic and social integration.

Cotterrell reasserts that Ehrlich's distinction between living law and state law was formulated in a specifically European context, that of the old Austro-Hungarian Empire, which consisted of a number of nationalities and diverse ethnic populations. Moreover, it was Ehrlich's geographical placement in multicultural Bukovina—located on the edge of the dying empire, far from the legal centre of Vienna—that made him aware that modern European law must address the varied regulatory expectations of different populations.

In addition, Cotterrell contends that Ehrlich's experiences with the legal centre and periphery gave him the unique perspective of an *insider–outsider*, of the expert who well understands official law (state and juristic), but who is also sensitive to the infinite varieties of living law that regulate different types and networks of community.

Further, Cotterrell maintains that Ehrlich was one of the first modern writers to study empirically the moral distance between regulators and regulated. Law that is remote from the moral conditions of existence appears inflexible and absolutist and denies to centralised authority a sophisticated understanding of and sympathy for a regulated citizenry. Finally, Cotterrell states that it was the prevailing ambition that was implied in Ehrlich's conception of living law a century ago, that is just as relevant

---

[80] Ziegert, above n 21, xix.

[81] M Hertogh (ed) *Living Law: Reconsidering Eugen Ehrlich* (Oxford, Hart Publishing, 2009).

[82] Ziegert, above n 10, 14, 21. Also KA Ziegert, 'A Note on Eugen Ehrlich and the Production of Legal Knowledge' (1998) 20 *Sydney Law Review* 108.

[83] R Cotterrell, *Law's Community: Legal Ideas in Sociological Perspective* (Oxford, Clarendon Press, 1995); id, *Law in Social Theory* (Aldershot, Ashgate, 2006); id, *Living Law: Studies in Legal and Social Theory* (Aldershot, Ashgate, 2008).

[84] Nelken, above n 52, 248.

[85] Cotterrell, above n 83 (2008) 45–163.

for sociolegal research today: 'to require state law to cooperate pluralistically with other forms of regulation precisely in order to respect and regulate moral diversity and so preserve and enhance law's own regulatory authority'.[86]

Petrażycki's Legacy

While Petrażycki's significance to sociological jurisprudence is incontrovertible, he nonetheless remains, as the title of an article by his proponent, Adam Podgórecki,[87] has said, an 'unrecognized father of sociology of law'.

Limited Reception and Influence

Petrażycki's work is relatively well known in his native Poland, where scholars have access to his unified works. But he has had limited reception in the West, not only because of the language barrier, but also because those few of his writings that have been translated into English are all contained in one volume only, the generally neglected *Law and Morality.*

Petrażycki, who wrote in Polish, Russian and German, was first introduced to the Anglophone world, and particularly to American audiences, in the late 1930s in a couple of articles by Hugh W Babb,[88] who later translated, from the Russian, *Law and Morality*. The book is an abridgement of two of Petrażycki's fundamental works: it consists of seven chapters taken from his *Introduction to the Study of Law and Morality*, published in 1905, and twenty-two chapters from his *Theory of Law and State in Connection with a Theory of Morality*, published in 1907. Given this jumbled and abbreviated compilation of excerpts, the volume 'did not allow for a full insight into the core of Petrażycki's views and did not display their coherence, implications, and significance'.[89]

Of particular significance is the English-language volume, *Sociology and Jurisprudence of Leon Petrażycki*, edited by Jan Górecki,[90] which contains essays offering a concise and critical presentation of Petrażycki's work. The collection, however, has had minimal influence on the sociology of law and is today seldom cited in the literature.

Edoardo Fittipaldi has given due consideration to Petrażycki (mainly in Italian), analysing his work from psychological, sociological and philosophical points of view. Most recently Fittipaldi[91] has conducted a linguistic-ontological investigation in which he endeavours to complete and correct Petrażycki's conceptions concerning the objectification and shared nature of psycholegal illusions, using 'debts' as the illustrative case par excellence.

---

[86] Ibid, 70.

[87] A Pódgorecki, 'Unrecognized Father of Sociology of Law: Leon Petrażycki' (1980–81) 15 *Law and Society Review* 183–202.

[88] HW Babb, 'Petrazhitskii: Science of Legal Policy and Theory of Law' (1937) 17 *Boston University Law Review* 793–829; id, 'Petrazhitskii: Theory of Law' (1938) 18 *Boston University Law Review* 511–78.

[89] A Kojder, 'Leon Petrażycki's Socio-legal Ideas and their Contemporary Continuation' (2006) 6 *Journal of Classical Sociology* 333–58, 347.

[90] Górecki, above n 19.

[91] Fittipaldi, above n 55.

Section 2

Systems Theory

REZA BANAKAR and MAX TRAVERS

OUR OBJECTIVE IN this introduction is to give some background on how law is understood by Niklas Luhmann and Jürgen Habermas, which may in turn help in understanding the advanced introductions by Michael King and Mathieu Deflem in this section. These are first-rate essays that explain highly difficult ideas authoritatively (meaning that these commentators have spent years on this intellectual task) and are also bold in offering a critical view of their significance and taking others to task for misunderstanding or misrepresenting their ideas. One argument advanced by Deflem is that these major twentieth-century theorists cannot be compared easily, except at a superficial level, because they were pursuing distinctive intellectual projects of great complexity. Nevertheless, at the risk of oversimplifying, but also because we believe that comparison is necessary when trying to understand the ideas of any theorist, we would like to suggest that they did have something in common. Each of these European thinkers can be understood as engaging with, yet at the same time making a radical departure from, the systems theory that Talcott Parsons developed at Harvard during the 1940s, in which law was viewed positively as an integrative mechanism (although Parsons would have approved of Habermas's last book on law).

There is unfortunately no chapter on Parsons in this reader, which partly reflects the fact that very few modern-day academics draw explicitly on structural functionalism as a research paradigm.[1] There has, of course, been a reaction against the idea that sociology can aspire to become a science since Parsons was writing in the 1940s. The interpretivists (see Section 4) have always been a minority group protesting on the sidelines, but many supporters of the Durkheimian project were taken aback by the extent to which poststructuralists' ideas were taken up in the 1980s and 1990s (see Section 5). A generation of radical scholars has also turned against Parsons, unhappy with his endorsement of capitalism and his inability to address social conflict. Nevertheless, if one sides with those who see sociology as a science, Parsons is the key macrotheorist after Durkheim, and systems theory remains the only means of thinking deeply, and systematically, about the relationship between the individual and society and how different institutions in society fit together.[2]

---

[1] Although see AJ Traviño (ed), *Talcott Parsons Today: His Theory and Legacy in Contemporary Sociology* (Lanham, MD, Rowan & Littlefield, 2011).

[2] J Holmwood, *Founding Sociology? Talcott Parsons and the Idea of General Theory* (London, Longman, 1996).

In simple terms, Parsons presents society as a smoothly functioning system, capable of meeting the four functional needs which any society (or biological organism) has to satisfy. These needs are:

(A) *Adaptation* to the physical environment;

(G) *Goal attainment*, which means finding ways to organise the system's resources to achieve its gaols and obtain gratification;

(I) *Integration*, which concerns how the system manages internal tensions and conflicts and co-ordinates its different parts; and

(L) *Latency or Pattern maintenance*, which is how the system maintains and reproduces itself over time.

Four subsystems enable society to survive. The economy adapts the system to its environment by extracting resources from the natural world (Adaptation). The political system sets goals for the system through the legislative process (Goals). The educational system and the mass media ensure that the population is socialised into shared values, such as respect for law, and a desire to consume economic goods (Latency). Finally, the legal system binds everything together[3] and acts as a safety net by punishing deviants who have not been properly socialised (Integration). For this reason, Parsons was a great admirer of the legal profession and praised lawyers for fulfilling important 'latent functions' for society, such as persuading clients to settle disputes without going to court.[4]

Parsons was criticised roundly by conflict theorists for offering a conservative and uncritical view of American society in the postwar period.[5] It is, however, important to recognise that the model did acknowledge the existence of tension between, and conflict created by, inadequate socialisation and also by poor integration between subsystems. The theme in Parsons' writing was that the economy was evolving faster than the rest of the system. Institutions and practices lagged behind economic needs, and new laws often ran into opposition from individuals and groups socialised with traditional values. Parsons in fact acknowledged the existence of strains and conflicts inside each subsystem and within individuals trying to meet conflicting role expectations. However, unlike conflict theorists, he supported the core values of American society and was optimistic about the prospect for securing greater equality, democracy and economic growth.[6]

The systems theorists who came after Parsons all retained the basic framework of society as an evolving social system, but they placed much greater emphasis on strains and conflicts between and within subsystems. Jeffery Alexander's neofunctionalism is probably the closest in spirit to Parsons, in that it still regards society as something that can be steered and managed by enlightened government. Luhmann and Habermas

---

[3] In 'The Law and Social Control' in WM Evan (ed), *The Law and Society* (New York, The Free Press, 1962) 56–72, Parsons describes the legal system in highly differentiated societies as a 'generalised mechanism of social control' operating through the economy, polity and pattern maintenance to integrate society.

[4] T Parsons, 'A Sociologist Looks at the Legal Profession' in *Essays in Sociological Theory* (New York, The Free Press, 1964)

[5] See eg CW Mills, *The Sociological Imagination* (Oxford, Oxford University Press, 1961).

[6] Researchers in this tradition have often employed quantitative methods to measure outputs and inputs between different systems, conceptualised as 'feedback-loops', an example of which can be found in WM Evan, *Social Structure and Law: Theoretical and Empirical Perspectives* (Newbury Park, Sage, 1990). It was assumed that the analyst can act like a scientist or a physician in identifying faults and correcting them.

offer a rather more sober assessment, one better suited to a contemporary world where we can see no alternatives to the present system but are increasingly aware of the massive economic equalities, environmental problems and psychological anxieties generated by capitalism.

In the first edition, we were fortunate to have an introduction to the ideas of Luhmann from Klaus Ziegert, who knew him personally and provided what some readers might find a daunting exposition of the main concepts and arguments, perhaps because it is remorselessly clear and precise. In this edition, we are equally fortunate to have an introduction by Michael King, which goes further in explaining the ideas but also presents a different and perhaps controversial interpretation. King asks sociolegal researchers to read Luhmann in a way that appreciates and respects his objectives as a 'non-interventionist' sociologist. Many sociologists have believed that they can change the world for the better through developing a scientific understanding of society, placing their faith in rationality and establishing rational ways of ordering human affairs, including through law and regulation. However, Luhmann saw this as 'self-deception practised by human beings on themselves'. King argues that Luhmann is worth reading because he challenges assumptions that many academic lawyers and sociologists take for granted—about the inevitability of progress, the ability to obtain sound scientific knowledge and the effectiveness of regulation.

Luhmann studied with Parsons at Harvard for a year (1960–61) and shared his ambition to devise a grand theory of social systems. He viewed Parsons' theory as a suitable starting point for devloping his own systems theory (also known as *autopoiesis*, ie self-(re)producing), which soon went beyond Parsons' initial project and transcended the classical understanding of object/subject. In Luhmann's system theory, communication (and not social action) serves as the basic element of the social system. It also means that Luhmann, controversially, does not consider human beings as the element of his social systems, a point which has caused a great deal of misunderstanding. This radical move marked a break from traditional systems theory, not only bringing Luhmann closer to what he regarded as the solution to the problem of the humanised subject, but also paving the way for a paradigm shift from the mechanical descriptions based on the classical cybernetic feedback loop and structural understandings of self-organisation which constituted influential approaches within sociology during the 1960s. One of Luhmann's achievements in this regard was his ability to illustrate that systems theory and hermeneutics could be integrated with the help of the concept of 'meaning'.[7] In the context of autopoiesis, 'meaning' is the medium through which observers can fix and dissolve forms and observe other observers' attempts to form and distinguish what they see.[8]

According to Luhmann, the increased complexity of modern society necessitates the differentiation of subsystems such as law, economics, politics and science. These subsystems are operationally closed—ie their mode of operation is not regulated by normative factors external to them—and function recursively, or self-referentially, in accordance with their own internal logic or binary codes (each system has its own binary code: that of law is legal/illegal), thus reproducing their constituent elements

---

[7] See N Luhmann, 'Meaning as Sociology's Basic Concept' in *Essays on Self-reference* (New York, Colombia University Press, 1990).

[8] See 'An Interview with Niklas Luhmann' (1994) 11 *Theory, Culture & Society* 37–68.

by referring to themselves. They are, however, cognitively open in the sense that they absorb information selectively from their environment, which enables the systems to learn and evolve over time, making them socially dynamic. Nevertheless, it should be pointed out that what is regarded ultimately as relevant information and learning is determined by the internal logic of the system itself. Law's learning operations are carried out through (self-)reference to law and not by references to the environment. As Ziegert explains, even 'the facts of the case' are internally constructed:

> Without doubt, however, facts are also constructions of the legal system (legal operations) and not a materialisation of the environment in the legal system, as any external scientific observation of court proceedings and their treatment of evidence can demonstrate. Also, the observation of the environment—the facts of the case—is an operation of the legal system in the legal system.[9]

Expressed differently, the key idea in Luhmann is that the systems (including law, politics, economy, art and mass media, to name a few) that constitute society (which in turn is a *meanings* system itself) are not integrated in the way Parsons believed. Even worse, social systems cannot even communicate with each other, although they can observe each other's operations. However, as with everything else in Luhmann's theory, this is hardly a straightforward event, as systems can only construct what they observe internally by employing their own binary codes to interpret observations. This is why King notes that we can see 'all these areas of activity [law, politics, economy, etc] as systems which understand the external world and their place within that world in their own unique terms and only within those terms'. But King goes further in identifying what the modernist might see as an even more disturbing side to Luhmann. According to King, Luhmann also contested the view that 'scientific disciplines' can 'identify absolute truth and reality in the social world' and that 'sociology is capable of producing factual knowledge'. This means that in describing the operation of the legal system we should not simply acknowledge that law cannot control the future; rather, we should also recognise that we cannot understand or produce a theory of law other than examining how actions are given meaning retrospectively within legal relevancies. Put in these terms, we have a 'radical' Luhmann that seems to have leanings towards ethnomethodology, actor-network theory and even postmodernism (as mentioned in the Introduction, Luhmann's systems theory has been embraced by some postmodernist theorists). Conversely, his ideas can be interpreted in a way that is closer to Parsons and more friendly to sociolegal research that seeks to improve society. In the Introduction we published in the first edition, Ziegert saw the function of law more positively in terms of stabilising normative expectations, which enabled it to operate as an 'immune system', and he suggested that the 'irritations' caused through misunderstanding were productive for different systems.[10]

Habermas can also be interpreted in a variety of ways, which is made possible partly because he has changed his position considerably, not least in relation to law. Habermas, started as a critical theorist and, during the 1970s, published an influential

---

[9] KA Ziegert, 'The Thick Description of Law: An Introduction to Niklas Luhmann's Theory of Operatively Closed Systems' in R Banakar and M Travers (eds) *An Introduction to Law and Social Theory*, 1st edn (Oxford, Hart Publishing, 2002) 55–76, 66.

[10] Ibid.

popular text principally directed at Parsons, entitled *Legitimation Crisis*,[11] in which he also began to interrogate the limits of the Weberian concept of rationality and explore the limits of law as a rational instrument of bureaucratic intervention and regulation. Deflem takes us through Habermas's career and interests in more detail and does justice to the way he has engaged with, and been influenced by, many sociological theorists in developing what in the first edition we described as 'an awesome synthesis which owes as much to Marx and Weber as to Parsons'. This itself oversimplifies, and it would be hard to do justice in any introduction to all the intellectual influences. It is worth emphasising, though, that in common with many sociological theorists, Habermas became particularly interested in the foundational problem of the relationship between action and structure.[12] Deflem notes that, in the two-volume *Theory of Communicative Action*,[13] he 'moved from philosophy to the very centre of debates in sociological theory, specifically by relying on the dichotomies between, on the one hand, action-theory, communicative action, and lifeworld and, on the other hand, systems theory, strategic action and system'.[14]

Parsons saw modern societies as becoming more complex and individualistic, all without great strains in the system or at personal cost. By contrast, Habermas at this stage in his thinking seems to bring from Marx, Durkheim and Weber the insight that there are tremendous economic, social and psychological problems during this process of modernisation. A central term used by Habermas in drawing out these issues was the 'colonisation of the lifeworld'. The lifeworld, a concept from phenomenology, is used by Habermas to refer to the 'micro' level of society—what happens in face-to-face interaction.[15] He also uses the term to advance an argument about change in the modern world. In this sense, the lifeworld is the kind of small-scale society (or community) in which people used to live, but it is now threatened by the growth of massive, impersonal forces such as the market and state. For Habermas, 'modern-day social ills, such as a loss of meaning, anomie and alienation, exist as a result of a colonization of the lifeworld'.

The argument is considerably more complex than this, and we are grateful to Deflem for explaining this in relation to law. Using a 'a dual concept of law', Habermas distinguished between law in the lifeworld and in the system—in the latter law functions as 'an institution', reflecting morality and guaranteeing basic rights in trying to achieve social integration, whereas in the former it works as a 'steering medium' that 'operates in the political and economic systems on the basis of functional needs'. Law in this second sense has expanded in the modern world, and there is now more need for 'legal regulations' that 'operate effectively by means of a specified procedure, such as in the case of business and administrative law'. There is also both the formalisation of law in 'bureaucratic intervention and judicial control' and an expansion of regulation ('juridification'). This was understood by Habermas as an undesirable 'internal colonization of the lifeworld by means of law as a medium', one that had resulted

---

[11] J Habermas, *Legitimation Crisis* (London, Heinemann, 1976).

[12] For discussion, see our introduction to Sections 3 and 5.

[13] J Habermas, *Theory of Communicative Action*, vol I (Cambridge, Polity, 1984); *Theory of Communicative Action*, vol II (Cambridge, MA, MIT Press, 1989).

[14] 'Lifeworld' refers to the sphere of spontaneously generated intersubjectively shared values, norms and worldviews, which are taken for granted by social actors, and out of which 'system' is born.

[15] Also see above n 12.

in a legitimation crisis.[16] He also advanced the hope, as a critical theorist, that we could achieve a better future based on a form of non-instrumental communication (not contaminated through the influence exerted by the imperatives of systems such as the economy or mass media) aimed at enhancing mutual understanding and respect.[17]

As Deflem explains, Habermas came to view law more positively during the 1990s. He abandoned the distinction between law as belonging to the system and lifeworld and instead 'reformulated his legal theory to conceptualize law entirely as an institution of the lifeworld'. This seems to suggest that we no longer experience bureaucracy and regulation as oppressive or even irritating, and that he was mistaken that there had been excessive formalisation. Instead, Habermas believes that regulation has a moral justification and law offers the best means of preserving a democratic, pluralist society. Colonisation of law by 'the systems of economy and politics', in such a way that 'legal norms and practices are redefined and implemented on the basis of standards of instrumental efficiency', is no longer viewed as something sinister, but this does not bring him any closer to Luhmann, who is pessimistic about the modern world and also sees law and morality as two separate entities, whereas Habermas has always seen them as interrelated in complex ways. However, you could argue that Habermas in his later work has something in common with Parsons. Law is understood positively as having an integrative function in a smoothly functioning industrial society. But this summary hardly does justice to how Habermas arrived at this position, or the way he combines sociology and philosophy in advancing a theory of modern law.

---

[16] See above n 2.
[17] As is often the case in the writings of critical theorists, the remedy was not entirely clear. Deflem notes in his chapter that Habermas has never, for example, advocated the abolition of prisons.

3

The Radical Sociology of Niklas Luhmann

MICHAEL KING

T HE LAST DECADE has seen an increasing number of scholars from a multitude of disciplines turning to systems or autopoietic theory as a framework
for their research. These have included researchers into the operation of the
legal system and its relations with other systems, such as politics and science.[1] Among
sociolegal scholars the results have been somewhat mixed, due mainly to the mismatch
(which these researchers often fail to recognise) between a critical stance which seeks
to expose, explain and offer remedies for the failures of the legal system—the aim
of many sociolegal projects on the one hand—and the overriding aim of Niklas
Luhmann (1927–69)—the theory's creator—to reconstruct and develop sociology as
a science capable of describing modern society and how it came about and analysing
the way in which it operates. For this reason we need to start this chapter with a very
basic question—one that often appears on the first page of introductory sociology
textbooks, but which nevertheless sets the scene for the intellectual problems that
Luhmann tackles in a fascinating and original way: what do we mean by sociology?

If we contrast Anthony Giddens's definition 'Sociology is the study of human social
life, groups and societies'[2] with that which appears in Wikipedia under the name of
Auguste Comte (1798–1857)—'the scientific study of society'—two differences stand
out. Firstly, Giddens's version omits the term 'scientific'; secondly, Comte does not
include any reference to 'humans' or 'life'. Comte is recognised as the founding father
of what has become known as positivism, the belief that social phenomena could be
studied scientifically in much the same way as physical phenomena. By the time that
Giddens was lecturing his students at Cambridge and LSE on the meaning of soci-

---

[1] See eg the extensive research carried out by Richard Nobles and David Schiff on various aspects of the
criminal justice system, including R Nobles and D Schiff, 'Miscarriages of Justice: A Systems Approach'
(1995) 58 *MLR* 299–320. See also J Paterson and G Teubner, 'Changing Maps: Empirical Legal Autopoiesis'
(1998) 4 *Social and Legal Studies* 7, 451; M King and D King, 'How the Law Defines the Special Educational Needs of Autistic Children' (2006) 1 *Child and Family Law Quarterly* 18; E Esposito, *The Future
of Futures. The Time of Money in Financing and Society* (Cheltenham, Edward Elgar, 2011; M Neves,
'From the Autopoiesis to the Allopoiesis of Law' (2001) 28 *Journal of Law and Society* 242; D Tosini, 'The
Autonomy of Law in the War on Terror: A Contribution from Social Systems Theory' (2012) 2 *International
Journal of Law, Crime and Justice* 40.

[2] A Giddens, *Sociology*, 5th edn (Cambridge, Polity Press, 2006) 4.

ology, ethnomethodologists and the constructivists (among others) had already raised serious questions about sociology's scientific credentials. They taught us to beware of imposing our own interpretations of social events and calling the results 'scientific'. If what constitutes truth becomes dependent upon the constructions and interpretations of the observer, this makes a mockery of those wishing to create a science of society where hypotheses can be verified through such scientific methods as empirical testing and the replication of findings. Observers starting with different beliefs will see things differently.

Given this fundamental problem, it may seem surprising that, by the time that Luhmann began publishing his early works on social theory in the 1960s, not only sociology, but all the other human and social sciences—anthropology, psychology, psychoanalysis, economics, etc—had been embraced by many influential politicians and administrators throughout the West. After the desolation of two world wars, where humanity appeared to have lost its way, there was ample reason to seize on the knowledge now offered by social sciences as offering the key to a bright future and to turn a blind eye to their limitations. It is not surprising that 'human sciences' in particular, with their emphasis on humanity and human rationality and critiques of human frailty, should have been seen as a providing a reliable combination for uncovering the 'facts' about society and social behaviour through their theories and research methods.

This idea of humane, human science providing scientific legitimacy for policies and programmes for reform and rebuilding was especially attractive to those charged with implementing the massive social changes associated with the emerging welfare state in Europe. In this context sociology stood out not just because of the belief that, as *the science of society*, it could play a crucial role in building a new social order, but also because it could be also deployed in highly critical ways to expose all the inequalities, injustices and abuses of power that stood in the way of the construction of a brave new world. Moreover, several sociologists, such as Sir Ralph Dahrendorf and Anthony Giddens himself, eventually found themselves appointed to high positions where they were able to apply their scientific knowledge to real-life decision-making and advise others on how to do so, while others became actively engaged in social movements, charged with observing the failures and inadequacies of society from the outside and advocating radical or not-so-radical reforms.

Niklas Luhmann and Jürgen Habermas (b 1929; see Chapter 4) may be seen as representing two very different breeds of twentieth-entury European sociologists— Luhmann, the detached and non-interventionalist; Habermas, the critical theorist of the Frankfurt School, advocating social action through truly democratic decisions and taking the view that any social scientist who was not actively engaged in attempting to transform society was shirking his or her responsibility towards humanity. Both belonged to that generation of Germans which had witnessed the devastation of their homeland and disruption to their personal lives following the rise of totalitarianism under the National Socialists. Both had a stake in the sociological enterprise of opening the eyes of future generations to the disasters that can result from sociological 'misreadings'. Yet, to see both Habermas's theory of communicative action and Luhmann's theory of functionally differentiated social systems simply as reactions to the events that had taken place during their childhood and adolescence is to oversimplify. In Luhmann's case, it is true that he was highly sceptical about claims that society

could be ordered and controlled through political planning,[3] but he was equally sceptical about the critical theories of Habermas and other members of the Frankfurt
School, and their claims to be capable of observing society from the outside and so
revealing its inequalities, its injustices, its contradictions, its abuses of power and then
to apply their critical analyses in finding solutions to society's problems.[4] Luhmann
(like Habermas) belonged to that strong tradition of European intellectual scholarship
that revered learning as an end in itself and sought to build on the foundations, laid
down by Greek and Roman scholars and rediscovered during the Enlightenment, in
ways that made them relevant to their own time. The ends to which each of them
deployed this intellectual tradition were, however, very different.

Luhmann was one of those young German scholars who benefited from the postwar
opportunities offered for European academics to visit the United States. He chose to
spend a year studying with the Harvard sociologist Talcott Parsons (1902–79) and in
1967 wrote an article defending Parsonian systems theory against its many critics.[5]
Parsons had himself adopted and developed the concept of the social system from
the theory of open systems proposed by Bertalanffy (1901–72), an Austrian-Canadian
biologist. In direct contrast to the critical sociologists, he, Parsons, had sought to
explain how societies (and, more specifically, American society) were able to achieve
both equilibrium and dynamism through the integration and control of the behaviour
of its members.[6]

However, while the model of society that Luhmann himself developed on his return
to Germany did contain some elements of the Parsonian scheme, it was far from a
blueprint for the integration of individuals into a stable collective enterprise. Nor did
it take the form of a critique of the failures and shortcomings of modern society
that Habermas, and his critical-theoretical colleagues, claimed to identify. Uniquely,
Luhmann saw society's existence rather as a highly improbable event presenting a
series of theoretical problems that needed solving. What were these problems?

The first problem was the very idea that people refer to as 'society'. Luhmann set
about tracing the effects of the European Enlightenment upon the way in which the
notion of society had become conceptualised and then analysed on the assumption
that it had some factual existence. His approach went beyond that of a historian of
ideas in that he saw his task as the formulation of a grand theory, a *theory of theories*—a theory which demonstrated how a conceptual world could have been created a
way that allowed what we accept as reality to exist and ideas about causes and effects
to flourish.

For Luhmann, Enlightenment-inspired sociology had taken a fundamental misdirec-
tion in regarding humanity, human rationality and human consciousness as the driving
forces in society, If the study of people was to be central focus of sociology, then
which of the more than five billion individual conscious beings living in the world

---

[3] N Luhmann, *Politische Planung. Aufsätze zur Soziologie von Politik und Verwaltung* (Opladen, Westdeutscher Verlag, 1971).

[4] N Luhmann, 'Wahrheit und Ideologie: Vorschläge zur Wiederaufnahme der Diskussion' in *Soziologische
Aufklärung*, vol. I: *Aufsätze zur Theorie sozialer Systeme* (Cologne, Westdeutscher Verlag, 1970).

[5] N Luhmann, 'Soziologie als Theorie sozialer Systeme' (1967) 19 *Kölner Zeitschrift für Soziologie und
Socialpsychologie* 615.

[6] G Verschraegen, 'Institutionalised Individualism. Parsons and Luhmann on American Society' in
H Bergthaller and C Shinko (eds), *Addressing Modernity. Social Systems Theory and US Cultures*
(Amsterdam and New York, Rodopi, 2011).

at that time was the one which was selected by social theory as offering that unique knowledge and power of observation which could be relied upon as valid and true?[7] If sociology was to exist as a truly scientific enterprise, and not as just as an academic discipline built on a combination of research methods and untested and untestable assumptions about human nature, then society, as a concept, had to be seen as quite separate and distinct from the people who existed in that society.

This rejection of 'people' or conscious beings as the appropriate unit for studying society was not, as some critics of Luhmann have suggested, anti-humanist in the sense of a denial on his part of the importance of humanity, human values and human ideals.[8] Rather, it was simply an attempt to distinguish what he regarded as 'individualised', 'psychologised' or 'anthopologised' accounts of what happens in the world from what he regarded as uniquely and distinctively 'sociological', which, as we shall see later in this chapter, he defined in a highly original and idiosyncratic way.

A related problem for Luhmann, which was also a legacy of those Enlightenment beliefs from which he wished to escape, was that presented by 'ideology'. He regarded much of what are passed off as sociological accounts of society as *ideological* not merely in the sense that they derive from specific political, moral or religious positions, but more widely, in that they all originate in pre-existing beliefs about the basic nature of humankind, which could be neither proved nor disproved through evidence. As such, this was not a direct criticism of any of these beliefs; nor, as we shall see, was it a plea for total objectivity. The issue for Luhmann was rather that, once again, these accounts of the world and issues within that world interfered with or even blocked the way entirely to what he regarded as a genuine sociological understanding. There were two reasons for this. The first, which we have already touched upon, is that the foundation of such ideologies lies in a belief in a particular version of *human nature*. Not only is it assumed that an objective description of human nature is possible, but also that the description of human nature selected by the specific ideological approach actually corresponds to truth or reality.

Luhmann even included here the idea that *human rationality* was an incontrovertible aspect of human nature that could be deployed as a reliable method for accessing truth and knowledge. This, for Luhmann, was also ideological in the sense that it relied upon a constructed notion which was elevated to the status of a having universal and timeless application. In his critique of rationality Luhmann exposed what he saw as the self-deception practised by human beings on themselves. We shall see later how his disillusionment with attempts to unravel social problems by applying highly optimistic and unrealistic notions of human nature and the capacity of human beings based on rationality led him to rethink entirely the way the role that law played in society.

For Luhmann, a sociology based on ideology (of any kind) leads almost inevitably to the self-deluding belief that purposeful human action in the direction in which ideological beliefs point will invariably result in the kinds of social change desired by holders of that ideology. Luhmann sees all belief systems essentially as *ways of giving meaning* to the unchartered morass that constitutes the social environment in which

---

[7] See N Luhmann, 'The Cognitive Program of Constructivism and a Reality that Remains Unknown' in W Krohn, G Kuppers and H Nowotny (eds), *Self-organization, Portrait of a Scientific Revolution. Sociology of the Sciences Yearbook* (Dordrecht, Kluwer, 1990).

[8] See Z Bankowski, 'How Does it Feel to Be on Your Own? The Person in the Sight of Autopoiesis' in D Nelken (ed), *Law as Communication* (Aldershot, Dartmouth, 1996).

we all live. The proper task of sociology is to observe these attempts, based on such theories of human action, to endow the world and human action with meaning. In his observations of the ideological he includes religious convictions and political creeds, such as socialism, conservatism, liberalism and the various forms of nationalism. Nor does he make an exception of those strongly held beliefs that the objectives that many hold as necessary for a healthy society, such as humanism, feminism, anti-racism, ecologism, and multiculturalism.[9] This is hardly good news for lawyers, many of whom would subscribe to at least one of these '-isms'. However, the news for lawyers gets even worse when it becomes apparent that Luhmann includes human rights in his list of ideologies.[10]

For Luhmann, as we have seen, all of these beliefs are in one way or another always based on selective observations derived from particular assumptions (often unacknowledged) about human nature and about society as a collection of attributions of different human natures. Only a sociology which observes these attempts to generate meaning for what they are, rather than adopting them as a presenting the truth or reality, can possibly begin to call itself scientific, since only such a sociology is able to free itself from unchanging and uncontrollable ties to a pre-given nature'... It 'forces [sociology] to take responsibility for itself'.[11]

Luhmann's hallmark irony is at its most scathing when he is observing social scientific theories based on ideologies that not only provide highly selective descriptions of social events and call them truth or reality but also use empirical methods to mimic the predictive powers of the natural sciences. He is highly critical of those theories that turn themselves into predictive tools by claiming that they are able to provide the know-how necessary to pave the way to a better, fairer, more just, more equal, happier, safer, wealthier future—provided always that people accept the assumptions and the agendas for change that they promote. The only way that they are able to make these claims, he explains, is by simplifying and reducing complexity in ways that make it appear possible both to identify definitive causes of past events and to use this 'knowledge' in the quest to change the future in predictable ways.

Yet we need to be clear just what Luhmann is saying here. Unlike neo-Marixst and critical scholars, he does not take issue directly with these ideologies which are deceiving and, at the same time, self-deceptive both to those who produce and disseminate them and those who accept them. Nor does he rebuke their adherents by telling them they or their convictions are inadequate or misguided or by exposing them as fraudulent or exploitative. On the contrary, he accepts that these ideologies may well be functional for the stability and continuity of society and for the recruitment and retention of people in co-operative ventures (in the case of politics) and in maintaining norms (in the case of law). He does not in any way condemn the good intentions or those who subscribe to these beliefs, but he is disputing they can ever form the basis of a sociology capable of describing what society is and how it works. His argument rather is with those social scientists who promote ideologies to the status of scientific theories and then proceed to construct whole scientific disciplines in the conviction

---

[9] For a discussion of these ideologies, see A Heywood, *Political Ideologies*, 4th edn (London, Palgrave Macmillan, 2007).

[10] N Luhmann, 'Are There Still Indispensable Norms in Our Society?' (2008) 1 *Soziale Systeme* 18.

[11] Ibid.

that they are able to identify absolute truth and reality in the social world and make accurate predictions based on their observations.

Luhmann's critique of what he sees as this legacy of the Enlightenment is particularly pertinent today when so many of the 'truths' identified by twentieth-century social scientists, particularly economists and political scientists, seem to have led only to disappointment and disillusionment, not only with the economy and politics but also with social science and its predictive powers. For Luhmann such disappointments and disillusionment are the inevitable result of sociology misdirecting itself in the way that it describes society and the role of human consciousness in society.

From 1967 to 1995 Luhmann wrote a series of articles in a collection of six volumes entitled *Soziologische Aufklärung (Sociological Enlightenment)*. This title reflects the full extent of his ambitions for sociology. It looks back to the radical intellectual achievements of the seventeenth and eighteenth centuries in liberating knowledge and understanding from religious dogmas and superstition and placing human reason at the heart of quests for the truth in any field of intellectual endeavour. At the same time, it implies that sociology was not included in this transformation, because it has continued to base its knowledge on outdated metaphysical beliefs, though this time in the centrality of human consciousness. Only now, according to Luhmann, with the development of a *theory of autopoietic or self-referring systems* is sociology able to cast off the shackles of the past and offer a scientific way of understanding society which does justice to the legacy of the Enlightenment.

This, for Luhmann, involved returning to the very basic question of the way in which meaning is constructed. His answer is anything that has meaning for society has to be generated by communications and it is the sum of all possible meanings (everything that makes sense, everything that can be communicated) which constitutes *society*. Communications are necessarily organised into systems, because, if this were not the case, there would be no way of attributing any communication to any particular semantic context and no way of excluding irrelevant and inappropriate meanings, so that it would not be possible to know what was being referred to. In other words, without the existence of systems communications—the creation and transmission of information could not take place. It would thus be impossible for society to come into being, evolve and continue to exist. Society, therefore, consists not just of everything that has meaning, but also of *all systems of communication* that make meaning possible.

This notion of society again creates enormous difficulties for those searching after and believing in the existence of absolute truths. Not only is it possible for very different versions of human nature to coexist, as we have seen, without any way of determining which one is true and valid. It also means that any event, any action or inaction is subject to any particular interpretation which emerges from the system observing it. Agency then exists only in so far as it is possible to attribute causality to events and causality is a matter of interpretation, to apply the repertoire of motives and interests that make sense to the particular observing system.

One cannot begin to appreciate the full implications of Luhmann's social systems theory without being aware of what it was that Luhmann sought to achieve for the science of sociology, what he saw as his intellectual task. In a similar vein, one cannot begin to appreciate the full implications of Luhmann's writings *on law* without being aware of the place of the legal system in his account of social systems. It is to this that we shall now turn.

WHAT DID LUHMANN MEAN BY SOCIETY'S LAW?

Luhmann wrote two major books devoted to law, both of which apply his unique approach to sociology in order to describe how the legal system operates as a self-referring social system. The first, *Rechtsziologie*,[12] published in English in 1985 as *A Sociological Theory of Law*[13] and more recently *Das Recht der Gesellschaft*,[14] which translates literally as 'Society's Law' but which was published in English in 1993 as *Law as a Social System*.[15] He also wrote many articles and book chapters on the subject of the legal system.

As indicated, the problems facing sociology, as Luhmann saw it, were firstly how to conceptualise society itself, and secondly how to escape from a sociology which insisted that the only way to understand society was to study human consciousness. His solution was to make a clear distinction between consciousness and society which, in his terms, becomes a separation of thoughts from communications. Both use meaning as their way of transmitting information, but what individuals think does not become part of society until and unless it is communicated, and what is not communicated remains as thoughts and, as such inaccessible to society.

Social systems, as we have seen, are systems that have evolved as distinct ways of communicating meaning about their environment and events within that environment. In Luhmann's terms the evolution of social systems made it possible to deny all possible meanings other than those specifically transmitted by the system. Admittedly, this is very abstract and its relevance to, say, law, politics and science is not immediately obvious. However, if we put it another way by seeing all these areas of social activity as systems which understand the external world and their place within that world in their own unique terms, and only within those terms, things may start to become a little clearer. When people communicate about the application of the law to, say, a person's state of mind when they caused someone's death, they exclude from their mutual understanding of what is at stake all references to class or racial differences, jealousy, mental states, *except* (and this is the crucial point) *in so far as these are relevant to or have meaning for what is recognised as the legal issue.* If this were not the case, and each time a non-natural death occurred and people had to try and work out from scratch the significance of the information being conveyed simply from the words being spoken in response to the event, it would be virtually impossible for them to engage together in order to make an decision which would appear anything other than arbitrary. All interpretations of the event would be equally possible and equally valid with the result that any 'communication'—meaning utterance, transmission and understanding—would be highly unlikely. The legal system, therefore, has evolved and exists as a framework for communication, which gives a particular meaning—a legal meaning—to events.

To take another example, if you switch on a video clip in the middle and see a person turn towards the camera and speak the words 'But they shook hands and nodded their heads', there is no way of knowing what the significance of these words could be.

---

[12] N Luhmann, *Rechtssoziologie* (Reinbek, Rowolt, 1972).
[13] N Luhmann, *A Sociological Theory of Law* (London, Routledge, 1985).
[14] N Luhmann, *Das Recht der Gesellshaft* (Frankfurt, Suhrkamp, 1993).
[15] N Luhmann, *Law as a Social System* (Oxford, Oxford University Press, 2004).

But suppose you then rewound the video and found out these words were spoken in answer to the question 'In fact, there was no actual agreement, was there?' Not only do you have information which allows you to make sense of it by putting it in the context of some pre-existing framework with which you may be familiar, but there is a very good chance that the framework or system concerned is law. How do you know this? Simply because the words 'actual agreement' do not really have any resonance for other possible frameworks or systems. Certainly not for science which is concerned with facts or scientific truths or for economy (money and property), medicine (health and illness) or politics (power). You can be fairly sure, then, that it involves the issue of whether something was lawful or unlawful—perhaps it concerns a breach of the alleged agreement or perhaps someone is being accused of being involved in a drug deal. Either way, you know that the relevant framework is law and that consequently not only can we exclude at this stage any other information concerning these two people who shook hands and nodded their heads (eg concerning their health or love lives), but you also now know what to expect, at least in respect of the legal process, even if the final outcome is uncertain.

At this point we come upon another stumbling block in the understanding of what Luhmann was seeking to achieve. Many commentators take Luhmann's theory as an attempt at a factual account of what actually happens in the world. However, Luhmann, as we have seen, makes it quite clear that the belief that sociology is capable of producing factual knowledge, that there are facts or concepts out there 'which need only be unearthed and cleaned up a little', is based on a naïve 'assumption that the real world has already been decided upon and that all that remains is to determine the facts with the help of suitable concepts'.[16] For Luhmann society is in a constant state of flux, where facts exist only so long as they are communicated and accepted as such. A sociology which claims direct access to some objective reality, therefore, is no longer viable, as reality exists in society only in so far as it is accepted as valid information in communications. What was a law yesterday may no longer be law today. Yet Luhmann goes even further in regarding as unsustainable and as self-deceptive claims by social researchers that the adherence to sociological methods necessarily results in superior or more reliable social knowledge. This is the case even where the researcher admits that access to absolute reality is an illusion. To put it in a nutshell, he would be highly sceptical of the current demand for 'evidence-based policies' and claims that such policies are likely to anticipate accurately future trends or events.

For Luhmann, the world is chaotic and events in that world are contingent. Both the world and events in that world can be made to make sense at any particular time only through those necessarily selective and reductionist representations generated by social systems. It is in this context that Luhmann presents law as one of several *function systems*—that is systems that are necessary for the successful operation of modern society, systems of communication that allow society to take on a form which is both meaningful to itself and to those individuals who participate in its operations.

What, then, is the function of law for society and how does the law perform its function? In simple terms law (meaning legal communications) presents society with a kind of certainty which allow other systems (including people) to rely upon its decisions. If my laptop is stolen from my office, this may be in line with my cognitive

---

[16] N Luhmann, *Essays on Self Reference* (New York, Columbia University Press, 1990) 21.

expectations based on my knowledge of the poor security in the building, but does not change my normative expectations that this will be regarded as an unlawful act, that the police should be called in and, that, if the thief is caught, my laptop will be returned to me and that wrongdoer will be punished. Law's function, in Luhmann's terms, is *to stabilise normative expectations over time and so avoid reliance on experience*. In this example, if my experience that belongings are always being stolen from offices and the thieves are never caught to was operate as a general social norm, this would give encouragement to a state of lawlessness whereby ordinary citizens would be entirely responsible for protecting their own property, thieves would prosper and there would be no point in calling the police. The normative expectations associated with thefts from offices may be entirely counterfactual, but they are necessary for the stability of society 'and law's function is to ensure that societal communications operate according to expectations formulated on the basis of norms, that is on how things *ought to be*'.[17]

It is not solely a matter of normative expectations displacing those based on experience; they also have to be stabilised. These expectations also have to be established in a form that allows them to resist and survive their own disappointment. According to Luhmann, they need to be sufficiently general in nature to allow conflicts to be 'decided in advance without knowing who will be involved in them' and in what ways they will be involved.[18] They also need to be 'time-bound', that is resistant to changes in expectations experienced through the passage of time. The fact that many violent offenders and thieves demonstrate by their actions that they have not learnt to change their ways, despite having been deprived of their liberty, does not invalidate laws which lay down the sentences that should be imposed. Nor does the fact that faulty goods are rarely replaced by retailers invalidate implied terms that they should be of satisfactory quality. The law remains in place, untroubled by this knowledge. Only changes within the legal system itself, either through legislation or court decisions, can alter the normative expectations generated by legal communications. Of course, there is a social price to pay for this imposed stability in that outdated laws can still generate expectations which bear no relation to knowledge gained through experience. This applies even where the moral climate has changed, as it has in the case of cannabis use, for example. Disregard for the law and protests about its injustice have no effect directly upon those normative expectations produced by the legal system. These expectations continue to provide a bridge between the past, the present and the future, making it safe and certain for all other systems to assume that the present differs from the past only to the extent that the law itself recognises 'any differences and also that the future will *normatively* be no different from the present ... The same distinctions marking what conduct is legal and illegal will exist tomorrow as they exist today' (unless, of course, the law itself changes).[19]

---

[17] M King and C Thornhill, *Niklas Luhmann's Theory of Politics and Law*, (Basingstoke, Palgrave Macmillan, 2003).

[18] Luhmann, above n 15, 146.

[19] See King and Thorhhill, above n 17, 54.

LAW'S ENVIRONMENT

An essential feature of Luhmann's account of social systems, including the legal system, and one that leads to some confusion and misunderstanding, is the idea of a system existing in an environment. For Luhmann, the best way of describing the operation of any system is in terms of the relationship between system and environment. He starts from the premise that systems, in general, exist only in so far as they can be distinguished from their environment; otherwise everything would be system or everything would be environment. However, in the case of social systems, the environment for the system is not external to and independent of the system as it is for biological systems. We cannot talk of law surviving in its environment in the same way as we speak of a species of butterfly continuing to exist in the natural world. For social systems (and conscious systems) '*the environment*' meaning 'reality'—the world as it actually is—is accessible only through the medium of these systems themselves. Put the other way round, reality for each system becomes whatever is accessible to that system, that is whatever it is able to observe, whatever it selects and recognises *as real*.[20] This means that system and environment are independent of one another only from the perspective of *the system itself* and not in the eyes of an observer who, unlike the system, is able to present the possibility that the system is operating in an environment which does not necessarily constitute reality and may even be a gross distortion of the reality that the observer recognises. Moreover, the system, unlike the observer, cannot see that the environment is *its own creation*. To a Luhmannian observer, therefore, when lawyers argue a case in court or when judges give their decisions, they do not, therefore, present the external world *as it really is*, but rather a filtered, selected image of that world which both responds to and reinforces the operations of the legal system. Furthermore, when lawyers and judges in their formal communications (pleadings, submissions, speeches and judgments) communicate about politicians, sex offenders, dysfunctional families or illegal loggers, these become not flesh-and-blood beings, but artefacts of the legal system.[21] And when they communicate about the role of the law in regulating and controlling such people, they do not speak or write of the legal system as it *really* impacts on, but again of a filtered, selected self-image of law and the ways that it operates in a society as constructed by the legal system for its own purposes.

How is all this achieved, given that law and all other social systems do not have the capacity to see, touch or hear and are not endowed with consciousness which would allow them actively to construct their own environments, to select and exclude anything that did not fit in with their vision of the external world? The answer lies in the system's coding, that is in its unique way of giving meaning or reducing to manageable proportions what would otherwise appear as total (meaningless) complexity. The system's code is its sole means of 'observing' its environment and by doing so making available its own interpretation of that environment. In the case of the legal system, its unique code is that of *lawful/unlawful* and, in applying this code, everything that

---

[20] See M King, *Systems, Not People Make Society Happen* (Edinburgh, Holcombe Publishing, 2009) 72–73.

[21] G Teubner, 'How the Law Thinks: Toward a Constructivist Epistomology of Law' (1989) 5 *Law and Society Review* 727.

lies within the scope of legal communications becomes part of law's environment. Conversely, anything that is not amenable to a lawful/unlawful resolution is invisible to law as it exists outside its environment.

Law's environment is not static, but is constantly changing. What was once regarded as outside the scope of or invisible to the legal system may enter its environment and present itself as a matter for legal decision-making, available to be given meaning through law's lawful/unlawful code, for example the corporal punishment of children. What was once regarded by law as beyond its horizon is now seen as falling within law's compass. The reverse may also occur as in breaches of promise which were once a possible cause of action by victims of a broken engagement to marry.

If we move up the scale of human affairs from private behaviour that affects only a few individuals to the conduct of national leaders, which can have catastrophic consequences for many thousands of people, we can see the same process at work. The introduction of the International Criminal Court and War Crimes Tribunals transformed conduct which was once regarded as outside law's environment, and, as such, immune from lawful/unlawful decision-making, into evidence justifying arrest warrants, prosecutions, trials and punishment. This was done entirely through law's own (in this case international law's) operations. In both instances, once the conduct in question becomes visible as 'a legal issue', law's coding filters out all information that is not strictly relevant to legal communications, that is to the court's or tribunal's lawful/unlawful decision-making process, and allows law's operations to concentrate on whether the conduct in question meets the legal criteria.

There are two important points here. The first is to re-emphasise the one already made, relating to law's function. The legal system, through its binary coding, creates for itself an environment that not only gives the impression of a world amenable to law's normative control, but also of a well-ordered, well-managed evolution. Within the legal system, that is, both law and law's environment change only in legal ways, that is in ways that law itself recognises. The environment for law is, therefore, far removed from an image of the social world as disorganised, chaotic and events in that world as contingent and totally unpredictable. We are presented instead with a version of reality in which behaviour, whether of individuals, corporations or nation-states, may be definitively classified as either legal or illegal by laws the legitimacy of which may be challenged only within the legal system itself. History, as observed through the code of the legal system (rather than historians), gives not the slightest hint of the mêlée of complex interacting factors, political, religious technological, moral or economic, etc, which accounted for changes from lawful to unlawful or from unlawful to lawful. In legal communications these transitions appear rather as part of the rational progress of evolution brought about in a well-ordered manner through legislation and court decisions.

Secondly, just as law constructs its environment from its own elements using its unique code, so do other social systems, such as politics, science or the mass media. There is not just one social environment and one social reality but a multitude, each depending on which social system is 'doing the observing'. Politics using its code, governing/governed or government/opposition, will select its environment in these terms and, in doing so, will see law and the operation of the legal system as a forum for the interplay of political forces. The recent claim by some conservative voices in the United Kingdom's coalition government that the powers of European Court of Human

Rights 'interfere' with national sovereignty is an example of this.[22] Law, for politics, is also an important a way of implementing and giving legitimacy to the implementation of power. Science, applying its scientifically true/scientifically false code regards the legal process as a search for the truth—that is a truth that is amenable to identification through systematic observations and experiments. For the mass media the code is information/non-information, where once having been communicated, information immediately becomes non-information. Courts, of course, provide an endless and readily accessible supply of information for the media, but everything which does not enhance the 'news value' of the story is excluded from its observations.[23]

LAW'S AUTOPOIESIS

Some of Luhmann's fiercest critics are those who have seized upon the notion of self-reference under the misapprehension that each social system works in total isolation, as insulated, autonomous entities, totally disconnected either from people or from one another.[24] They refer (often in derisory terms) to Luhmann's adoption of the biological term 'autopoiesis', with organs reproducing themselves from their own elements, as encapsulating this autonomy and isolation, which they see as the defining features of his theory. How, they ask, can systems possibly be independent of the people who operate them? Needless to state, Luhmann does not deny that people have their parts to play in the legal system. What he proposes rather is that law exists as a system of communications, distinct from the individual judges, advocates, jurors and so on who are engaged in its operations. Not only must law as a social system be treated as separate from human consciousness, as we saw in his critique of Enlightenment-based sociology, but, correspondingly, *there cannot be any direct interaction* between people and society, when the one transmits through thoughts and the other through communications. It is certainly not suggested that the legal system and people are totally independent of one another. On the contrary, law may very well influence the way that people think and behave, in a general way, by making available to all conscious beings a particular way of making sense of the world in which they exist and individually by providing a framework for individual decision-making: 'Should I risk using my mobile phone while driving, knowing that it is against the law?' Likewise, the way that people think may very well influence law. During the 2012 UK city centre riots a number of people acted on the belief that the risk of being caught looting had been greatly reduced by the police being overstretched. The law responded by imposing severe sentences for relatively minor crimes. In both cases, one cannot say that one event directly *caused* the other, but there was certainly indirect influence.

The other related 'absurdity' that certain of Luhmann's critics identify in the notion of autopoiesis is the idea that law is somehow autonomous, that is totally immune from other social forces such as politics, technology or economics. The often-quoted

[22] See www.bbc.co.uk/news/uk-politics-17748035 (accessed 31May 2012).
[23] N Luhmann, *The Reality of the Mass Media* (Cambridge, Polity, 2000) ch 3.
[24] See eg A Wolfe, 'Sociological Theory in the Absence of People: The Limits of Luhmann's System's Theory' (1992) 13 *Cardozo Law Review* 1729; M Rosenfeld, 'Justice According to Law, Justice Beyond Law, and Autopoiesis' (1992) 13 *Cardozo Law Review* 1681; G Frankenberg, 'Down by Law: Irony, Seriousness and Reason' (1989) 83 *Northwestern University Law Review* 360.

description of the legal system as 'normatively closed, but cognitively open' can be misleading[25] here as it suggests, firstly, that law is receptive simply to knowledge or information, but to nothing else, and, secondly, that this information or knowledge comes from *outside* the legal system. Yet, as Luhmann points out 'In theoretical terms, the ultimate problem always consists of combining internal and external references, and the real operations which produce and reproduce such combinations are always internal operations. *Nothing else is meant by closure.*'[26] Law is open to whatever the legal system itself is able to observe but to nothing else, and what it observes is observable only in 'legal' terms. Law, along with politics, economics and science may all be communicative systems, but what makes them closed and self-referring as social systems has nothing to do with autonomy in the sense of independence, self-sufficiency or sovereignty, but with the fact that they construct *both themselves and their environment*, including other systems, that is other forms of communication, through their coding, from their own internal elements. This means that the formula 'cognitively open' need not refer just to solid facts gathered from law's environment, but to anything which the legal system itself through its internal operations regards as requiring a lawful/unlawful pronouncement, that is anything which it 'sees' as relevant to the decision rather than being part of the mechanics of the decision-making process—in law's eyes 'facts' rather than law.[27]

SYSTEM AND ENVIRONMENT

Whether one is observing the relationship between conscious beings and social systems or between different social systems, Luhmann's key formula for understanding what is going on, as we have seen, is always system/environment. Although it is impossible for thoughts to become communications or for political or scientific communications to become legal communication without their reformulation by the observing system, this does not prevent mutual influence and even interdependence between these different spheres. The term that Luhmann uses to describe the process by which different systems are able to form such relationships is *structural coupling*. He makes it quite clear that this is not a 'causal chain with systems serving as the connecting part linking inputs and outputs',[28] so that an event in one system triggers a reaction in the other. Nor is it even one system reconstructing the actual communicative outputs of the other system in its own terms (a common misconception), since there is no way that one system may gain direct access to the outputs of another. Rather the image is

---

[25] It is taken from N Luhmann, 'Operational Closure and Structural Coupling: The Differentiation of the Legal System' (1992) 13 *Cardozo Law Review* 1419. What in fact Luhmann wrote was:

> Legal reasoning uses the distinction between norms and facts, between normative and cognitive expectations. It has to know in which respects it is supposed to learn (did somebody kill another woman?). Legal reasoning would not get along very well by confusing these questions. *In this sense, the system is normatively closed and cognitively open at the same time.* (1427, emphasis added)

His footnote expresses his reservations to this 'highly reduced formula'.

[26] Ibid, 1431.

[27] If this were not the case, there would be no possibility of law making lawful/unlawful pronouncements on its own decisions, as in appeals to a higher court. Here the decision-making process becomes in effect 'information for law'.

[28] Luhmann, above n 25, 1432.

of one system *becoming the environment* for the other and vice versa. For each system, the other exists only in 'the world' constructed by that system, as an artefact of that system. In the relationship between law and people, therefore, law becomes part of people's (consciousness's) environment in the sense that people present themselves with the restraints, duties and responsibilities that they observe as legal requirements and then respond to in a variety of ways. Law, for its part, is able to observe conscious beings only as legal artefacts. This applies both in terms of the specific roles that they may play in the legal process—claimant, defendant, third party, advocate, victim, judge—and, equally importantly, in terms of its reduction of the complexities of people as conscious beings to concepts that make sense within the legal system, such as malice, provocation, diminished responsibility, indirect discrimination, dishonesty, undue influence. No matter what actually went on in the black box of the individual's consciousness, he or she will be judged by the law applying the categories and by considering the 'evidence' that is recognised by the legal system. Law, as a system of communications, does not become personified or anthropomorphised. Law does not become transformed in Luhmann's hands into a conscious entity capable of observing human complexities from a number of different angles, weighing them up and then arriving at a decision. It remains a social system, with all the limitations of social systems, observing only what exists in its environment, namely other systems and their communications—an environment is entirely the product of its unique lawful/unlawful coding. Of course, in order to apply this raw coding to its increasingly complex, self-made environment, law requires internal programmes, that is all those subsystems of law which transform its environment into specialist categories—commercial law, equity, criminal law, the law of evidence, family law, etc. In this way issues as far removed as assessing the best interests of a child and determining the priority among creditors of a liquidated company may be made amenable to a lawful/unlawful decision.

LAW IN SOCIETY

If we turn finally to that specific concept of structural coupling between social systems, we find that this holds the key to Luhmann's highly distinctive account of law in modern society. It explains both the endless inventiveness of the legal system in creating from the overwhelming maelstrom of complexities that characterises today's world the impression of order based on rational principles. At the same time, it draws attention to the limits of law as an instrument for social engineering, whether in the hands of judges, politicians or administrators.

Once one abandons the notion idea that there can be direct intervention between different systems and substitutes in its place the image of each system constructing both itself and all other systems in a world of its own making, one also has to discard any belief that any one system can dominate or control others. Far from one system, whether economics, law or politics, governing or dictating to the other, we are presented with a vision of multiple systems each constructing its own world, reacting to its own interpretations of the outputs of other systems, and producing communications based on these interpretations. Other systems then respond in a similar manner to these communications. As such, systems can only relate to each other indirectly by producing their own unique communications (based on their unique and specific code) which reflect only a partial and limited 'understanding' of how these other systems operate. When these communications become part of society there is always the risk that they will not be seen by other systems as relevant to their operations or interpreted by those systems in a different way to that intended—often a matter of serious concern for the legal system.

This polycentric world and the absence of any overall control are for Luhmann defining characteristics of modern society which distinguish it from traditional societies or totalitarian states. They allow each system to evolve in ways that allow unprecedented dynamism and inventiveness. In law and politics, for example, it has, on the one hand, generated ever more elaborate methods of regulation of everything that is seen as a threat to stability and well-being—from drug trafficking to environmental damage, from rogue traders to paedophiles—and an endless proliferation of organisations charged with enforcing such regulation. One the other hand, Luhmann sees all this creativity occurring at the level of second-order observation—that is through law and politics, as observing systems, giving meaning and order to a world that is essentially fluid and contingent and unpredictable. The ultimate in self-deception, one may think. But again Luhmann observes, without condemning, this massive growth in the regulatory mechanisms. What he questions is not their right to exist or even the possibility that they may have some beneficial effects, but rather the pretence that they are able to contain risks or control the future or indeed that it is possible to foresee the unintended impact of these mechanisms on the regulated, the regulators or on other of society's systems.

It is very tempting for both practising lawyers and legal academics intent on improving the world through law to regard Luhmann as the high priest of scepticism, preaching against all those who are engaged in the ongoing search for solutions to society's many problem. Yet to dismiss Luhmann as a sceptical conservative is to ignore his importance as a social theorist who offers an a unique and unrivalled description of how the whole of modern society operates. The questions that Luhmann's social theory poses for lawyers and students of law are both profound and disturbing. Is it not time for academic lawyers in particular, whose specific task it is to observe and criticise various aspects of the legal system, to recognise that the long catalogue of regulatory failures—financial, penal, political, technological and ecological—makes it impossible for them to continue in the belief that the way forward for society and humanity lies simply in persuading individuals, organisations and governments to embrace and disseminate globally the principles of equality, justice, democracy and respect for human rights? Is it not also time for those academic lawyers who choose to adopt a sociolegal approach in their attempts to improve the world to abandon the cherished notion that this belief in progress is founded on sound scientific[29] knowledge? While they all may invoke a different version of sociology in support of their criticisms and proposals, it is in Luhmann's eyes, likely to be a version that owes more to an idealised belief in the power of human rationality and Enlightenment ideals than to the realities of the world as it is today. This is why Luhmann has rightly been described as radical.

---

[29] H-G Moeller, *The Radical Luhmann* (New York, Columbia University Press, 2011).

4

The Legal Theory of Jürgen Habermas: Between the Philosophy and the Sociology of Law

MATHIEU DEFLEM

The work of the German philosopher and sociologist Jürgen Habermas counts among the most significant achievements in social theory of the past several decades. Since Habermas's writings have reached the public from the early 1960s onwards, his work has essentially combined philosophical aspirations with sociological interests in developing a theory of societies in the modern and late-modern age while also retaining a critical attitude towards the problems those societies face. This dual ambition of Habermas's work is at once one of its most appealing characteristics and one of its central difficulties, especially in terms of its adequate reception, as the sciences have developed such that increasing specialisation, even within delineated fields of inquiry, has become the order of the day. Further, it is now a truism to note that the work of Habermas is not only ambitious in scope and its reliance on and relevance to a multitude of intellectual traditions, but also that it is, as a result, complex and not always easy to understand. This characteristic is somewhat ironic given that mutual understanding is one of the most critical objectives of Habermas's work, yet it should also not be considered an insurmountable obstacle towards the analysis and application of his thought. This chapter hopes to fulfil a critical task by laying bare the essential elements of Habermas's theories on law and thereby guide the reader towards a more detailed and comprehensive study of Habermas's thought as it is relevant to the interests of students of law working in various disciplinary traditions.

It is fortunate for scholars interested in the role of law in modern society that Habermas has devoted several of his writings explicitly to the study of law and the problems associated with law in contemporary society. Rather than having to construct a Habermasian theory of law congruent with his writings on society, therefore, a specific perspective on law can be uncovered in the work itself. Nevertheless, the task is not entirely straightforward as there has been an evolution in Habermas's thinking, both in terms of the aspirations and direction of his work, in general, as well as in terms of his thought on law, in particular. This chapter will situate Habermas's ideas on law within the background of his broader work in social theory and philosophy. Given its prominence in contemporary social science, the humanities and philosophy,

Habermas's work has been greeted with numerous secondary analyses and commentaries, of varying degrees of usefulness, a literature that I will briefly discuss at the end of this chapter. More importantly, this contribution will focus on explicating the ideas Habermas has introduced with respect to the study of law. In keeping with the objectives of this volume to provide an introduction into the role of social theory in the study of law, a critique of Habermas's ideas is beyond the scope of this chapter. Adequately situating the legal theory of Habermas in the broader contest of his sociology and philosophy is the central objective of this chapter.

1. CRITICAL THEORY

Jürgen Habermas was born in Düsseldorf, Germany, on 18 June 1922 and spent most of his childhood in nearby Gummersbach.[1] Upon his graduation from high school (*Gymnasium*) after the end of World War II, he studied at universities in Göttingen, Zürich and Bonn from 1949 until 1954 when he earned a doctorate in philosophy on a dissertation about the German philosopher Friedrich Schelling. After a two-year period of work as a freelance journalist, Habermas recommenced his academic career by joining the Institute for Social Research (Institut für Sozialforschung) at the Johan Wolfgang Goethe University in Frankfurt.

The Institute for Social Research had been privately founded by Felix Weil, the son of a wealthy industrialist, in 1923, with the aim of providing an intellectual home to a multidisciplinary group of social scientists and philosophers working in the tradition of Karl Marx.[2] Shortly after the Nazi seizure of power in 1933, the Institute was shut down by the Gestapo. Several Institute members (some of whom were also Jewish) moved abroad, especially to New York City, where they continued their activities. After the war, the Institute was refounded in Frankfurt in 1951 and again became the central home to the intellectual tradition now commonly known as critical theory. The perspective is represented by Max Horkheimer, Theodor Adorno, Erich Fromm, Otto Kirchheimer and Herbert Marcuse, amongst others, followed by a younger generation of scholars, among whom Habermas became a key figure after he had initially taken up an assistantship with Adorno.

The perspective of critical theory that was represented by the Frankfurt School, as the Institute's members came to be collectively known, was originally introduced by Horkheimer in 1937 as a counterpart to so-called traditional theory.[3] Striving towards a reinterpretation of Marxian thought and the application of its central tenets to the social-scientific analysis of modern society, Horkheimer defined critical theory as an intellectual bridge between theory and praxis, between knowledge and action. The perspective thus rejected a simple view of value-freedom in social science and instead sought to establish intimate connections between knowledge and science, on the one hand, and emancipation and democracy, on the other.

Habermas's position in the tradition of critical theory is more than interesting to

---

[1] On Habermas's life and work, see MB Matuštík, *Jürgen Habermas: A Philosophical-Political Profile* (Lanham, MD, Rowman & Littlefield, 2001).

[2] M Jay, *The Dialectical Imagination: A History of the Frankfurt School and the Institute of Social Research, 1923–1950* (Berkeley, CA, University of California Press, 1996).

[3] M Horkheimer, 'Traditionelle und Kritische Theorie' (1937) 6 *Zeitschrift fur Sozialforschung* 245.

note because it betrays some of the enduring aspirations and tensions in his work. When Habermas was developing the ideas for his *Habilitationsschrift* (the post-doctoral dissertation required of academics in Germany), he met with resistance from his supervisors at Frankfurt, especially Horkheimer. Rather than revise his work, Habermas decided to take it elsewhere and defended the dissertation successfully at the University of Marburg under the direction of the political scientist Wolfgang Abendroth. In this study, which remains to date one of Habermas's most distinctly sociologically oriented empirical works, Habermas argues for the role of democracy in the development of modern Western societies.[4] Specifically, he traces the eighteenth-century development of a bourgeois public sphere in which debates were held concerning important matters of politics and culture, both in face-to-face meetings in cafés and coffee houses as well as through the medium of print. During the twentieth century, Habermas argues, the critical potentials of the public sphere were gradually eroded by its commercialisation into a mass society of public opinion.

The theme of democracy that is central to the transformation of the public sphere is one that has stayed with Habermas throughout his career. After two years of teaching at Marburg and Heidelberg, he returned to the Goethe University at Frankfurt in 1964 as professor of philosophy and sociology. Between 1971 and 1983, he was co-director of one of Germany's Max Planck Institutes, a series of government-funded but otherwise independent research institutes, in Starnberg. Thereupon he returned to Frankfurt as a philosophy professor until his retirement in 1994, since when he has continued to be a prolific writer and participant in various public and academic debates.

Although distinctly placed in the tradition of critical theory and Marxism, Habermas's work has come to enjoy a reputation that also stands by itself.[5] Aside from his work on the public sphere, Habermas made an impact early on in his career through his epistemological writings on the relationship between theory and praxis.[6] Most famous in this respect is his conceptualisation of various scientific traditions on the basis of three knowledge-interests: (i) the technical interest of the empirical sciences oriented at an effective manipulation of the natural environment; (ii) the practical interest of the hermeneutical tradition oriented at the proper interpretation of meaning; and (iii) the emancipatory interest of the critical social and human sciences oriented at analysis as well as critique and social change. Habermas situates his work within the latter tradition, as can be expected from a neo-Marxist scholar. Equally significant is that his work immediately took on, besides a deeply embedded philosophical component, also a distinctly sociological interest in the analysis of society.

Focusing attention towards Habermas's construction of a systematic theory of society from the late 1960s onwards and especially during the 1970s, what is most striking is that Habermas gradually begins to diverge from the Marxian preoccupa-

[4] The study was originally published in 1962 and translated into English in 1989. See J Habermas, *Strukturwandel der Öffentlichkeit. Untersuchungen zu einer Kategorie der bürgerlichen Gesellschaft* (Neuwied/Berlin, Luchterhand, 1962); J Habermas, *The Structural Transformation of the Public Sphere: An Inquiry into a Category of Bourgeois Society* (Cambridge, MA, MIT Press, 1989).

[5] There are many overviews of the work of Habermas available that can be helpful to introduce his own writings. See eg D Ingram, *Habermas: Introduction and Analysis* (Ithaca, NY, Cornell University Press, 2010); T McCarthy, *The Critical Theory of Jürgen Habermas* (Cambridge, MA, MIT Press, 1978).

[6] J Habermas, *Technik und Wissenschaft als 'Ideologie'* (Frankfurt, Suhrkamp, 1968); English translation: J Habermas, *Theory and Practice* (Boston, Beacon Press, 1973). See also J Habermas, *Knowledge and Human Interests* (Cambridge, Polity Press, 1987).

tion with labour and economy towards the inclusion of the categories of interaction, language and democracy.[7] In other words, what Habermas complements to an orthodox Marxism focused on the control over nature (as a subject–object relationship) is an expanded view that also considers social interactions (among subjects). This interest towards the interactional dimension of social life was already present, in embryonic form, in Habermas's work on the public sphere, but it would now be gradually yet resolutely pursued in a direction that took Habermas not only away from a more narrowly conceived neo-Marxism but also from an epistemologically preoccupied philosophy towards linguistic theories of communication. Even more interesting in the present context is that Habermas moved from philosophy to the very centre of debates in sociological theory, specifically by relying on the dichotomies between, on the one hand, action-theory, communicative action and lifeworld, and, on the other hand, systems theory, strategic action and system.[8]

Before explaining the systematics of where this intellectual development would ultimately take Habermas, it can be recognised from the outset that Habermas's relationship to Marx and the Marxists has remained a matter of continued contention just as much as has been his relative distance and closeness vis-à-vis the traditions of (continental) philosophy and (theoretical) sociology. What is important for the purposes of this chapter is that Habermas not only moves from a theory of science via an inquiry on the logic of the social sciences to a theory of society, but also from an initial and somewhat uncertain and unsystematically developed interest in interaction and language to a comprehensive theory of society that is partially grounded in a theory of speech. Having clarified the epistemology of critical theory in connection with an emancipatory interest and subsequently a methodological interest in the language-theoretical foundation of the social sciences, Habermas thus accomplished a move towards the development of a sociological and philosophical perspective that he judged useful for both the study and critique of society.

2. THE THEORY OF COMMUNICATIVE ACTION

Habermas's work towards a new social theory culminated in his impressive magnum opus, *The Theory of Communicative Action*, which was originally published in German in 1981 as a two-volume work.[9] In the formal construction of this work, Habermas relies on the model presented by Talcott Parsons in his 1937 *The Structure of Social Action*[10] to systematically develop a theory of society with reference to a

---

[7] Habermas, above n 6 (1973) 142.

[8] J Habermas, *Zur Rekonstruktion des historischen Materialismus* (Frankfurt, Suhrkamp, 1976); English translation: J Habermas, *Communication and the Evolution of Society* (London, Heinemann, 1979); J Habermas, *Legitimationsprobleme im Spätkapitalismus* (Frankfurt, Suhrkamp, 1973); English translation: J Habermas, *Legitimation Crisis* (Cambridge, Polity Press, 1988). The methodological implications of the turn towards social theory are addressed in J Habermas, *Zur Logik der Sozialwissenschaften* (Frankfurt, Suhrkamp, 1970); English translation: J Habermas, *On the Logic of the Social Sciences* (Cambridge, Polity Press, 1988).

[9] J Habermas, *Theorie des kommunikativen Handelns*, 2 vols (Frankfurt, Suhrkamp, 1981); English translations: J Habermas, *The Theory of Communicative Action*, vol 1: *Reason and the Rationalization of Society* (Boston, Beacon Press, 1984); J Habermas, *The Theory of Communicative Action*, vol. 2: *System and Lifeworld: A Critique of Functionalist Reason* (Boston, Beacon Press, 1987).

[10] T Parsons, *The Structure of Social Action* (New York, McGraw-Hill, 1937).

group of more and less recent writers in social theory. Since the resulting theory of communicative action has remained central to Habermas's writings until this day and also contains an important contribution to the study of law in modern society, it is worthwhile to devote some time to explaining the basic contours of this aspect of Habermas's sociological theory on the basis of a brief summary of *The Theory of Communicative Action*.

Habermas begins the exposition of his theory by postulating the problem of the rationality of action or the rationalisation of society as the central subject matter in sociological theory, going back to the great works of the sociological classics. Sociology's special place is in this respect secured because the discipline has retained an interest in society as a whole, even when the differentiation of society is a central aspect of the development to modernity, bringing about a specialization within sociology to focus on the various institutional components of differentiation (economy, polity, law, culture). This comprehensive perspective is informative, of course, of a proper understanding of the very foundation of the sociology of law, approached from whichever theoretical tradition, as the scientific study of law *in* society, rather than a jurisprudential misreading of law *and* society.[11]

Habermas differentiates between two concepts of rationality: (i) cognitive-instrumental rationality pertains to conduct that is oriented at the successful realization of certain goals; and (ii) communicative rationality is applicable to interactions whereby the actors are oriented towards mutual understanding. Importantly, Habermas argues that social action cannot be curtailed towards either conceptualisation of rationality, but that the two forms of rationality must be ideal-typically understood and can thus be variably applicable to various social formations at different stages of development.

Habermas considers it an exclusive characteristic of human interactions that they are symbolically mediated on the basis of the use of language through speech. Forgoing a more detailed presentation of some of the involved issues of linguistic theory, Habermas focuses on the claims that are implied in the actual use of language or speech-acts among actors as they are oriented towards reaching understanding. Even though consensus is not a necessary outcome of communicative action, Habermas suggests that speech-acts, which are sufficiently well-formed so that they are comprehensible, inevitably imply claims on three levels: (i) a claim that the speech-act is true as corresponding to or otherwise harmonising with a state of affairs; (ii) that the speech-act is right with respect to a specified or implied normative context; and (iii) that the speech-act is expressed truthfully by the speaker. Habermas argues that communicative actions—which are expressed either verbally or by means of an equivalent such as by means of gestures or in writing—imply that all the claims are accepted or, conversely, that any one or more of the claims will be brought into question and thus become the subject matter of additional communications concerning the validity of implied claims. Habermas refers to this order of communication as discourse and thereby differentiates: (i) the theoretical discourse concerning truth; (ii) the practical discourse on rightness; and (iii) the expressive and evaluative discourse concerning authenticity and sincerity.

Habermas notes that the validity of speech-acts is not routinely questioned because

---

[11] M Deflem, *Sociology of Law: Visions of a Scholarly Tradition* (Cambridge, Cambridge University Press, 2008).

they take place within the given context of what he calls the lifeworld (*Lebenswelt*). Extending from established phenomenological traditions of German philosophy, the concept of lifeworld is defined by Habermas as referring to the whole of cultural values, social norms and socialisation patterns that often remain unquestioned among actors and that, in fact, enable interactions to take place. To explain the specific development or rationalisation of modern societies, Habermas makes two important observations. First, the rationalisation of the lifeworld has brought about an internal differentiation around three central functions: (i) cultural reproduction for the transmission of values; (ii) social integration for the co-ordination of interactions through norms; and (iii) socialisation for the formation of personal identity. Second, an additional level of societal differentiation has to be introduced because certain domains of social life have 'uncoupled' from the lifeworld on the basis of non-communicative or 'delinguistified' media of interaction. To conceptualise these relations, the interactionist perspective of the lifeworld needs to be complemented with a systems-perspective that focuses on the cognitive-instrumental rationality orientation at a successful realisation of specified objectives. Specifically, Habermas argues, in the context of Western societies an economic system of capitalism and a political system of a bureaucratic state have developed which function, respectively, on the basis of money and power. The rationality of monetary transactions in the capitalist economy is such that only productivity criteria are considered, whereas power in the bureaucratic state is oriented at effectiveness in political processes of decision-making.

Similar to the role of communicative action in the lifeworld, Habermas argues that cognitive-instrumental action in the economic and political system need not necessarily bring about problematic consequences. However, social problems do ensue when the lifeworld is intruded upon by society's systems resulting in communicative actions being redefined in instrumental terms. Actions oriented at mutual understanding are then perverted into conduct instrumentally aimed at success. Habermas argues that the central problems of late-modern societies are precisely of this kind. Modern-day social ills, such as a loss of meaning, anomie and alienation, exist as a result of a colonisation of the lifeworld by economic and political systems.

Understood from the viewpoint of sociological theory, Habermas's perspective of communicative action and the dual nature of modern society in terms of lifeworld and system merges insights from interactionist perspectives, on the one hand, with systems-theoretical theories, on the other. As such, Habermas can rely on the great works of otherwise seemingly very diverging authors, such as Max Weber and Emile Durkheim as well as Talcott Parsons and Karl Marx. Especially from the viewpoint of a critical theory, Habermas's two-level perspective of society should be able to demonstrate its value, beyond its theoretical consistency, as a theory of modernity that can be fruitfully applied in the analysis of concrete social formations. In *The Theory of Communicative Action*, Habermas indeed undertakes such an analysis and thereby also specifies a sociological theory of law.

3. LAW AS AN INSTITUTION AND LAW AS A MEDIUM

The theory of communicative action is by any standard complex as well as complicated, especially so in view of its abstract orientation and reliance on multiple traditions of social theory. It is interesting to note in this respect that Habermas suggests in his preface to *The Theory of Communicative Action* that the reader who wonders about the empirical relevance of his work could first read the concluding chapter of the book, the chapter in which Habermas applies his theory to a concrete analysis and introduces a sociological perspective of law.[12] Interestingly, Habermas prefaces this discussion by stating that the area of law presents no special methodological problems because, he writes, 'The development of law belongs to the undisputed and, since Durkheim and Weber, classical research areas of sociology.'[13]

Habermas's concept of law refers at the most general level to an institutionalisation of norms.[14] Thus, on a philosophical level, Habermas posits an intimate connection between law and morality, whereby he maintains that law, even in highly rationalised societies, retains a critical normative dimension. Despite a trend towards technocratisation on the basis of instrumental criteria of efficiency, modern law retains a need for moral justification, more specifically on the basis of procedural criteria that allow only for the force of the better argument through communication and debate. In other words, Habermas argues that the modern rationalisation of law in purposive-rational terms, such as Max Weber already formulated it, implies only a displacement, but not an elimination, of moral questions. Modern law is characterised by conditions of both legality and legitimacy and the latter is not exhausted by the former. In simple terms, it is not because something is legal that it is accepted as just. As such, Habermas's work on law opens the way for an important philosophical component to determine the rational foundation of just law or the connection between law and rights.

Additionally, Habermas argues that law in modern societies functions and develops in ways that need to be sociologically uncovered. In the differentiation of system and lifeworld, law fulfils a central function by legally institutionalising the independent functioning of money and power in, respectively, the economic and administrative systems. This function is fulfilled, more specifically, in private and public law. The significance of the role of law is additionally shown from the fact that political authority has historically evolved from judicial offices. In a lasting sense relevant to contemporary societies, the special connection between law and politics is confirmed by the fact that legislation is a political function and that political authority, as Weber already argued, is legal-rational.

In the concluding chapter of *The Theory of Communicative Action*, Habermas conducts a rather detailed historical investigation of the development of law, which enables him to show the empirical value of his theory and in the course of which he develops a more comprehensive sociology of law.[15] Specifically, Habermas relies on the concept of juridification (*Verrechtligung*) to suggest the development of the welfare state. In general terms, juridification refers to an increase in formal or written law, either in the form of an expansion of law of hitherto unregulated conduct or in the

---

[12] Habermas, above n 9 (1984) xli.

[13] Habermas, above n 9 (1987) 356.

[14] Habermas, above n 9 (1984) 243–71; above n 9 (1987) 172–79. For overviews, see A Brand, 'Ethical Rationalization and "Juridification": Habermas' Critical Legal Theory' (1987) 4 *Australian Journal of Law and Society* 103; M Deflem, 'La Notion de Droit dans la Théorie de l'Agir Communicationnel de Jürgen Habermas' (1994) 18 *Déviance et Société* 95.

[15] Habermas, above n 9 (1987) 356–73.

form of a densification of law in the form of a more detailed regulation of conduct that was already legally regulated.

Habermas analyses juridification processes in the development towards the welfare state in the history of the European state system and suggests four waves of juridification.[16] First, in the period of the bourgeois state that developed in pre-nineteenth-century Europe, a capitalist economy begins to evolve whereby a new class of industrialists can gradually secure legal rights to conduct business in the market, while leaving the absolute powers of the sovereign ruler in the political sphere untouched. Civil law in this period thus guarantees freedom rights and obligations in the economic market to regulate contractual relations. Second, during the nineteenth-century development of the constitutional state, the private rights of citizens to life, liberty and property are secured over and against the rights of the political sovereign. In other words, freedom rights are now legally guaranteed against the intrusion of political rulers, who are held to economic *laissez-faire* policies. Third, as the democratic-constitutional state system develops under influence of the ideas of the French Revolution, citizens can legally ascertain rights also to participate in the shaping of their government by means of the institutionalisation of a democratic election process. Thus, juridification entails a legal institutionalisation of social rights in the political system. Fourth, with the development of the democratic welfare state during the twentieth century, welfare laws are passed to secure that certain problems brought about in capitalist society are responded to on the basis of principles of fairness and equity to guarantee that certain basic needs are met. In this final stage, in other words, legally guaranteed social rights react against an unrestrained functioning of the market.

Habermas outlines this history of juridification to show how welfare laws can be interpreted in terms of the institutionalisation of rights of the lifeworld vis-à-vis the economic and political systems. Welfare laws originate from increasing demands of the lifeworld to act within and react to the independent workings of media-controlled systems. Both individual as well as social rights are thereby to be guaranteed on the basis of a balance of the principles of freedom and equality. The development of welfare law, however, Habermas notes, brings about certain unintended effects.[17] While welfare law is aimed at alleviating social ills created by the functioning of the capitalist economy, the manner in which these problems are legally responded to are framed in terms that accommodate the economic and administrative systems. The legal form in which rights are secured in itself thus endangers some of those rights. Habermas specifies four problems in particular: (i) welfare laws guarantee entitlements that are understood as individualised claims even when the problems addressed are of a collective nature; (ii) claims need to be successfully petitioned under formally specified conditions; (iii) claims are implemented in ways that suit the needs of large bureaucratic organisations rather than the people involved; and (iv) entitlements often take on the form of monetary compensation. In other words, the rights that welfare laws guarantee are defined and implemented in terms of the media of money and power.

In the original formulation of his sociology of law in *The Theory of Communicative Action*, Habermas interprets the ambivalent implications of the development

---

[16] Ibid, 358–61.
[17] Ibid, 361–64.

of welfare law on the basis of a dual concept of law.[18] On the one hand, law as an institution refers to legal norms that remain in need of justification on the basis of the intimate connection of law to morality. Habermas in this case mentions certain areas of law that are closely related to deeply held belief systems, such as criminal law. On the other hand, Habermas argues that law can also function as a medium, in which case it suffices that legal regulations operate effectively by means of a specified procedure, such as in the case of business and administrative law. Whereas law as an institution belongs to the lifeworld, law as a steering medium is relieved of substantive justification because it operates in the political and economic systems on the basis of functional needs.

As the case of welfare law shows, law as a medium can also concern areas of society that properly belong to the lifeworld. For example, the collective problems of structural unemployment and of old age are in welfare laws redefined as individualised claims to be met by monetary settlements. Habermas discusses similar problems in (German) family and school law.[19] In these areas, basic rights are guaranteed on the basis of principles of the welfare of the child and the equal opportunity for all concerned (student, teacher, husband, wife, parent, child). However, to secure these rights legally, family and school have to be redefined and formalised in terms that allow for bureaucratic intervention and judicial control. Family and school law can supplement the informal relations that exist in these lifeworld areas of social life, but they can at times also go further and intrude upon family and schools by means of law as a medium. A child, for instance, can legally be subjected to removal from the home on the basis of a judge's decision to protect the physical well-being of the child, while not considering that a different approach may be in order on the basis of a more holistic viewpoint that also considers other important dimensions of the child–parent relationship. In such cases, there is an internal colonisation of the lifeworld by means of law as a medium.

4. LAW BETWEEN FACTS AND NORMS

Habermas's perspective of law and morality opens the way for an important philosophical component in his work to specify how modern societies can secure the legitimacy of legality. At the same time, however, Habermas also introduces a concept of law as a medium that would be relieved from normative discussions. Within the contours of Habermas's own theoretical ambitions, this dual conceptualisation in his legal theory reveals an insurmountable problem for it could only be sustained if various areas of law can be categorised either as law as an institution or as law as a medium. Yet, as Habermas himself introduced the terminology in *The Theory of Communicative Action*, this is not the case in the areas of welfare policy and school and family law. In these instances, legal regulations intrude into lifeworld dimensions on the basis of systems needs and thereby produce certain problems, which are addressed in discussions on deregulation, debureaucratisation, and other morally justified terms. The

[18] Ibid, 366–68.
[19] Ibid, 368–73.

concept of law as a medium and the related notion of an internal colonisation of the lifeworld are not conceptually meaningful in the context of Habermas's own theory.

Habermas soon realised the rather straightforward mistake he had made in his original formulation. In response to critics of his work,[20] he wrote that his theses on juridification were 'perhaps over-presumptuous'[21] and that he could not maintain the distinction between law as an institution and law as a medium.[22] The error may have resulted from the fact that Habermas in his original 1981 book treated the lifeworld somewhat one-sidedly from the perspective of the potentially damaging effects of systems and the colonisation of the lifeworld. Possibly in a rush to show the critical potential of his theory, Habermas's book is in fact as much a theory and study of strategic action and system as it is of communicative action and lifeworld.

The intellectually consistent consequence is that Habermas has in the meantime reformulated his legal theory to conceptualise law entirely as an institution of the lifeworld. In 1992, Habermas systematically addressed his rethinking on law in his book *Faktizität und Geltung*, translated in 1996 as *Between Facts and Norms*.[23] The study was the result of a five-year grant project that was awarded to Habermas in the mid-1980s on a subject matter of his own choosing. Habermas then formed a research group on legal theory in which several legal philosophers, sociologists of law, and jurists participated, resulting in multiple publications on the role of law in modern society.

Habermas's work addresses most extensively the way in which modern law can be justified rationally on the basis of a system of rights. This conceptualisation implies that law is intimately related to morality and, more specifically, that both moral and legal norms are oriented at resolving social integration problems in the lifeworld. Moral and legal norms are differentiated by their different levels of institutionalisation and formalisation. Moral norms have the advantage of being deeply embedded in the lifeworlds of different communities, but they miss the coercive power and enforceability of law. To ensure the authority of legal norms, law also remains connected to the political system, which oversees a proper and ideally effective administration and enforcement of law. The characteristic of modern law to combine a claim to legiti-

---

[20] See eg K Eder, 'Critique of Habermas' Contribution to the Sociology of Law' (1988) 22 *Law and Society* 931; K Raes, 'Legalisation, Communication and Strategy: A Critique of Habermas' Approach to Law' (1986) 13 *Journal of Law and Society* 183; W van der Burg, 'Jurgen Habermas on Law and Morality: Some Critical Comments' (1990) 7 *Theory, Culture and Society* 105.

[21] J Habermas, 'A Reply' in A Honneth and H Joas (eds), *Communicative Action* (Cambridge, MA: MIT Press, 1990). See also J Habermas, 'Law and Morality' in SM McMurrin (ed), *The Tanner Lectures on Human Values* (Salt Lake City, University of Utah Press, 1988).

[22] J Habermas, 'Remarks on the Discussion' (1990) 7 *Theory, Culture and Society* 127.

[23] J Habermas, *Faktizität und Geltung: Beiträge zur Diskurstheorie des Rechts und des demokratischen Rechtsstaats* (Frankfurt, Suhrkamp, 1992); English translation: J Habermas, *Between Facts and Norms: Contributions to a Discourse Theory of Law and Democracy* (Cambridge, MA, MIT Press, 1996). For overviews and discussions, see H Baxter, *Habermas: The Discourse Theory of Law and Democracy* (Stanford, CA, Stanford Law Books, 2011); M Deflem (ed), *Habermas, Modernity and Law* (London, Sage, 1996); M Deflem, 'Théorie du Discours, Droit Pénal, et Criminologie' (1995) 19 *Déviance et Société* 325; M Rosenfeld and A Arato (eds), *Habermas on Law and Democracy: Critical Exchanges* (Berkeley, University of California Press, 1998); CL Orjiako, *Jurisprudence of Jürgen Habermas: In Defence of Human Rights and a Search for Legitimacy, Truth and Validity* (Milton Keynes, Authorhouse, 2009); C Ungureanu, K Günther and C Joerges (eds), *Jürgen Habermas*, vol 1: *The Discourse Theory of Law and Democracy* (Aldershot, Ashgate, 2011).

macy and a guarantee of legality accords law its societal relevance and sociotheoretical centrality.

On the basis of Habermas's new perspective of law, his legal theory in *The Theory of Communicative Action* can briefly be reformulated. The regulation of money and power can then indeed be conceived as a normative anchoring in the lifeworld. Business and administrative law do not only regulate the workings of the economic and administrative systems efficiently or functionally but they do so authoritatively as well with reference to norms of justification. Additionally, and even more importantly, the earlier specified thesis on the internal colonisation of the lifeworld can now be reconceptualised as a colonisation of law itself. In other words, modern law can be colonised by the systems of economy and politics in such a way that legal norms and practices are redefined and implemented on the basis of standards of instrumental efficiency.

In view of law's dual characteristics of legitimacy and legality, Habermas's central objective in *Between Facts and Norms* is to elaborate a legal theory that bridges a (normative) philosophy of law with an (empirical) sociology of law, combining insights derived from both traditions. Specifically, Habermas posits that law, on the one hand, must rely on the coercive force of the state to be properly administered but must, on the other hand, also be grounded in intersubjectively recognised claims of rights. At the level of adjudication where legal statutes are applied and interpreted, legal norms are appropriately measured in terms of their suitability to specific cases or to constitutional principles without the legitimacy of legal norms themselves being at issue.

Besides seeking to reconstruct modern law in terms of its relationship to morality and rights, Habermas spends much time contemplating the connection between law and politics under conditions of democratic regimes. Habermas's work thus becomes not only a philosophy of law in addition to a sociology of law, but also a political theory, albeit with important implications for law. Specifically, Habermas defends a deliberative concept of democracy that focuses on the procedures that exist, or should exist, whereby the ideas and ideals that inform democratic debate as well as the decisions that are brought about in democratic regimes remain open to debate. An important function for law thereby is to establish procedures that ensure that legal norms enable a peaceful coexistence of a plurality of ethical traditions. In other words, democratic law is needed to guarantee that norms can co-ordinate social action and secure integration in view of the preservation of a diversity of values in a plurality of lifeworlds. A central problem in Habermas's work is thus the relationship between law (norms) and culture (values), an especially poignant problem in view of an increasing drift towards multiculturalism.

5. RECEPTION AND CRITIQUE

This chapter is primarily oriented at providing a helpful exposition of the ideas of Habermas on law in the context of his broader theoretical project, but it will also be useful to have a brief look at the influence his work has enjoyed in the realm of legal and sociolegal studies. As noted, Habermas's legal theory involves both distinctly philosophical and sociological components. His work has consequently also been discussed across disciplinary fields, although in a less integrated manner than Habermas achieved in his own work. It must also be observed that Habermas's writings on law have involved a shift from the sociology of law, which is most comprehensively articulated in *The Theory of Communicative Action*, to questions of legal (and political) philosophy, which he especially addressed in *Between Facts and Norms*.

As a result of the shift in Habermas's legal theory, certain distinct and sometimes problematic consequences can be noted in the reception of his work in the academic fields interested in the study of law. In the secondary literature, philosophical debates far outweigh sociological writings, and theoretical discussions are much more prevalent than empirical investigations. Also, the majority of secondary sources on Habermas's legal theory were published in the 1980s and 1990s, and his work has attracted less explicit attention since. A contributing factor to this relative decline is that Habermas has in more recent years written about topics that have no direct relationship to law, with most of his efforts being devoted the integration of the European Union, international politics (especially since the events of 9/11) and the changing role of religion in the world.[24]

Reviewing the debate and criticisms that have been published on Habermas's legal theory, several currents can be detected of variable degrees of theoretical sophistication and empirical usefulness. Following the original publication of *The Theory of Communicative Action*, several papers were devoted from within jurisprudence and sociolegal studies to an exposition and internal critique of Habermas's formulation of law as an institution and law as a medium. Theoretically, it is thereby interesting to observe that some sociolegal scholars readily observed the internal contradiction in the theory, which Habermas was also quick to acknowledge and which he would gradually, during the 1980s, explore in more detailed by developing a systematic philosophy of rights, law and morality under the heading of 'discourse ethics' (*Diskursethik*).[25]

As a specification of the procedural conditions under which legal question and other lifeworld debates can be legitimately conducted, the perspective of discourse ethics suggests that norms can only be legitimate when they meet or could meet with the approval of all those who are affected. Such a determination presupposes the conditions of a so-called ideal-speech situation, whereby nobody who is competent to speak would be denied from bringing up any argument or question deemed relevant and would not be excluded from debate. These conditions are, according to Habermas, not utopian because they are presupposed in communicative action, as is revealed, most sharply, when they turn out to have been violated. The key implication of discourse ethics for Habermas's legal philosophy, as he explained in *Between Facts and Norms*,

---

[24] See eg J Habermas, *Der Gespaltene Westen* (Frankfurt, Suhrkamp, 2004), English translation: J Habermas, *The Divided West* (Cambridge, Polity Press, 2006); J Habermas, *Zwischen Naturalismus und Religion* (Frankfurt, Suhrkamp, 2005); English translation: J Habermas, *Between Naturalism and Religion* (Cambridge, Polity Press, 2008); J Habermas, *Ach, Europa* (Frankfurt, Suhrkamp, 2008): English translation: J Habermas, *Europe: The Faltering Project* (Cambridge, Polity Press, 2009); J Habermas, *Zur Verfassung Europas* (Frankfurt, Suhrkamp, 2011); English translation: J Habermas, *The Crisis of the European Union: A Response* (Cambridge, Polity Press, 2012).

[25] J Habermas, *Moralbewußtsein und kommunikatives Handeln* (Frankfurt, Suhrkamp, 1983); English translation: J Habermas, *Moral Consciousness and Communicative Action* (Cambridge, MA, MIT Press, 1990); J Habermas, *Erläuterungen zur Diskursethik* (Frankfurt, Suhrkamp, 1991); English translation: J Habermas, *Justification and Application: Remarks on Discourse Ethics* (Cambridge, MA, MIT Press, 1993).

is an emphasis on the procedural conditions of argumentation at various levels of law, ranging from legislation over adjudication to law enforcement.

Tailored towards the needs of empirically oriented legal and social science, some scholars have applied insights from Habermas's theory to their investigations. Given the ambivalence of Habermas's original perspective of law, the results present a mixed bag. Some scholars working in a critical tradition of social science, especially in the areas of criminal justice and criminology, relied on Habermas's social theory to contemplate the systemic qualities of law, especially in the area of criminal law. Specifically, the so-called abolitionist perspective that has been developed in the European tradition of critical criminology undertook this effort to argue that the modern criminal justice system deals with issues of deviance and crime in such a way that the manner in which these problems are experienced by the participants themselves are done no justice, but instead are treated on the basis of the requirements of legal and political administrators and other professional expert cultures.[26] Some abolitionist scholars reformulated this theoretical orientation in conceptual terms derived from the theory of communicative action to argue that the criminal justice system is indeed to be conceived as a system in the sense in which Habermas uses the term. Needless to say, this unsystematic appropriation of Habermas's ideas involves a serious misreading of his work.[27] Relying on a conception of the administration of criminal law as a system in the Habermasian sense, the abolitionist perspective completely overlooks the possibility of procedurally legitimated law and the place of law in the lifeworld. Habermas's social and legal theory simply does not lend itself to support the abolitionist quest to abolish the criminal justice system, but would instead be useful to work towards a procedurally guaranteed democratisation of criminal law.

The charge of a conceptually unjustified reliance on Habermas's work in abolitionist perspectives of criminal law, which is largely a European-continental tradition, is also applicable to currents in the so-called critical legal studies movement.[28] Especially as it has been developed and practised in the United States and the United Kingdom, critical legal studies represents a diverse group of legal scholars who basically argue that law is essentially characterised by an indeterminacy that is rooted in arbitrary decision-making on the basis of contradictory legal principles. Developed within the professional boundaries of jurisprudence, scholars working in the critical legal studies tradition have relied upon a variety of thinkers in philosophy and social theory to justify their programmes. At times, the name of Habermas and selected aspects of his thought have thereby also popped up.[29] Yet, in the wide and diverse literature of critical legal studies, the work of Habermas has been mostly appropriated in a form that mixes it, ostensibly without realising the theoretical and philosophical inconsistencies involved, with many other scholars and traditions as varied as Marxism, feminism and, most troublesome from the Habermasian viewpoint, poststructuralism and post-

[26] JR Blad, H Van Mastrigt and NA Uildriks (eds), *The Criminal Justice System as a Social Problem: An Abolitionist Perspective* (Rotterdam, Erasmus Universiteit, 1987); H Bianchi and R Van Swaaningen (eds), *Abolitionism: Towards a Non-repressive Approach to Crime* (Amsterdam, Free University Press, 1986).

[27] M Deflem, 'Jürgen Habermas: Pflegevater oder Sorgenkind der abolitionistischen Perspektive?' (1992) 24 *Kriminologisches Journal* 82.

[28] See P Fitzpatrick and A Hunt, *Critical Legal Studies* (Oxford, Basil Blackwell, 1987); RM Unger, *The Critical Legal Studies Movement* (Cambridge, MA, Harvard University Press, 1986).

[29] See eg F Munger and C Seron, 'Critical Legal Studies versus Critical Legal Theory: A Comment on Method' (1984) 6 *Law & Policy* 257.

modernism.[30] Perhaps this assemblage can itself be assumed to be a postmodern pose, but it is of course entirely contrary to the thought of Habermas, one of the staunchest proponents of the modernist tradition originating from the Enlightenment.[31]

The comparison of the legal theory of Habermas with the theories of law of other sociolegal scientists has formed another area of debate in the secondary literature. To some extent, these writings involve actual discussions between Habermas and other scholars. In the national tradition in which Habermas is situated, the debate with the German sociologist Niklas Luhmann stands out.[32] As explained more elaborated by Michael King elsewhere in this volume, Luhmann develops an autopoietic theory of law that conceives of all of society and its constituent parts in systemic terms as being operationally closed. In response, it will cause no surprise, Habermas fundamentally argues against Luhmann's theory because it does not acknowledge the specificity of the lifeworld in action-theoretical terms. With respect to the study of law, Habermas consequently rejects the notion of operational closure to suggest that law fulfils an important mediating function between lifeworld and system by negotiating between the demands of everyday communicative actions, on the one hand, and the functional needs of the economic and administrative systems, on the other.[33] These capacities of modern law, under conditions of democratic politics and procedurally justified legitimacy, precisely account for its centrality in contemporary society. The connection between law and morality, which Luhmann conceives as two separate closed systems, remains central to Habermas.

Additional comparisons of Habermas with other sociolegal scholars or social theorists with implied or explicit relevance to the study of law have been conducted by commentators independently of any actual debates Habermas has engaged in.[34] In this respect, the so-called debate between Habermas and Michel Foucault is of special significance because both intellectuals have greatly inspired legal and sociolegal work.[35] Yet, such comparisons are at best modestly supported by writings in which the two authors have explicitly discussed the value of each others' contributions.[36] The results of these and other such interpretive exercises remain tenuous at best to the extent that the theoretical comparisons could be judged unwarranted as the original scholars were not exposed to their respective ideas or, at the very least, did not judge them useful to be entertained.

The apparent scholarly obsession to attempt to think about, for or against,

---

[30] D Ingram, 'Dworkin, Habermas, and the CLS Movement on Moral Criticism in Law' (1990) 16 *Philosophy and Social Criticism* 237.

[31] J Habermas, *Der philosophische Diskurs der Moderne: Zwölf Vorlesungen* (Frankfurt, Suhrkamp, 1985); English translation: J Habermas, *The Philosophical Discourse of Modernity: Twelve Lectures* (Cambridge, Polity Press, 1987).

[32] N Luhmann, *A Sociological Theory of Law* (London, Routledge & Kegan Paul, 1985); N Luhmann, 'Operational Closure and Structural Coupling: The Differentiation of the Legal System' (1992) 13 *Cardozo Law Review* 1419.

[33] Habermas, above n 23 (1996), 47–54. In response, see N Luhmann, 'Quod Omnes Tangit ...: Anmerkungen zur Rechtstheorie von Jürgen Habermas' (1993) 12 *Rechtshistorisches Journal* 36.

[34] Eg JP McCormick, 'Three Ways of Thinking "Critically" about the Law' (1999) 93 *American Political Science Review* 413; A Lefebvre, 'Habermas and Deleuze on Law and Adjudication' (2006) 17 *Law and Critique* 389; DM Rasmussen, 'Communication Theory and the Critique of the Law: Habermas and Unger on the Law' (1988) 8 *Praxis International* 155.

[35] See Gary Wickham's chapter on Foucault in this volume (Chap 12).

[36] Habermas devoted two chapters to the work of Foucault, but the French philosopher died before a true debate could begin; see J Habermas, above n 31 (1987) 238–93.

Habermas has not been complemented by an equally enthusiastic curiosity to conduct empirical investigations on the basis of his theories. This unfortunate limitation in the secondary literature applies to the entire reception of the oeuvre of Habermas and its many substantive themes, but it has been especially pronounced in the areas of political and legal theory. The development in Habermas's legal theory towards a philosophy of law, rights and deliberative politics with the publication of *Between Facts and Norms*, at the expense of a more systematic sociological investigation, has additionally fuelled a direction towards commentaries and expositions of a predominantly theoretical nature.[37] And among the latter, the objectives of legal philosophy have been much better served than those of sociology of law and, more broadly, socio-legal studies.

Among the relatively few available empirical applications of Habermas's legal theory are the present author's study in the field of the sociology of law that applied propositions derived from Habermas's theory to an analysis of the history of US abortion law.[38] Related work concerned the development of a perspective of social control on the basis of Habermas's theory of system and lifeworld and its application to selected contemporary forms of surveillance.[39] In view of the sparse use of Habermas's work in sociology of law (and sociolegal studies more broadly), it is striking that the most sustained efforts to develop empirical applications of Habermas's legal theory have been contributions by authors in the field of jurisprudence. To some extent this applies to strands in American professional jurisprudence where concepts of Habermas have occasionally informed analyses of specific aspects of legal policy.[40] Yet, the influence of Habermas's legal work is especially strong in the more academically oriented tradition of German jurisprudence, which has greatly contributed to a Habermasian-inspired understanding of law in concrete sociohistorical settings.[41] Attuned to the needs of the empirically minded student of law, Habermas's discourse model is applied to the

---

[37] See eg B Honig, 'Between Decision and Deliberation: Political Paradox in Democratic Theory' (2007) 101 *American Political Science Review* 1; S Grodnick, 'Rediscovering Radical Democracy in Habermas's Between Facts and Norms' (2005) 12 *Constellations* 392; J Mahoney, 'Rights without Dignity? Some Critical Reflections on Habermas's Procedural Model of Law and Democracy' (2001) 27 *Philosophy and Social Criticism* 21; JL Marsh, *Unjust Legality: A Critique of Habermas's Philosophy of Law* (Lanham, MD, Rowman & Littlefield Publishers, 2001); T Hedrick, *Rawls and Habermas: Reason, Pluralism, and the Claims of Political Philosophy* (Stanford, Stanford University Press, 2010); MC Modak-Truran, 'Secularization, Legal Indeterminacy, and Habermas's Discourse Theory of Law' (2007) 35 *Florida State University Law Review* 73.

[38] M Deflem, 'The Boundaries of Abortion Law: Systems Theory from Parsons to Luhmann and Habermas' (1998) 76 *Social Forces* 775.

[39] M Deflem, 'Social Control and the Theory of Communicative Action' (1994) 22 *International Journal of the Sociology of Law* 355; JR Lilly and M Deflem, 'Profit and Penality: An Analysis of the Corrections–Commercial Complex' (1996) 42 *Crime and Delinquency* 3.

[40] See eg AA Felts and CB Fields, 'Technical and Symbolic Reasoning: An Application of Habermas' Ideological Analysis to the Legal Arena' (1988) 12 *Quarterly Journal of Ideology* 1; D von Daniels, *The Concept of Law from a Transnational Perspective* (Burlington, VT, Ashgate, 2010); A Bächtiger and J Steiner (eds), 'Empirical Approaches to Deliberative Democracy' (2005) 40 *Acta Politica* 153; WE Scheuerman, *Frankfurt School Perspectives on Globalization, Democracy, and the Law* (New York, Routledge, 2008).

[41] Most instructive for the influence of Habermas's thought in jurisprudence is the discussion between Robert Alexy and Klaus Günther. See R Alexy, 'A Discourse-Theoretical Conception of Practical Reason' (1992) 5 *Ratio Juris* 1; R Alexy, 'Justification and Application of Norms' (1993) 6 *Ratio Juris* 157; K Günther, *Der Sinn für Angemessenheit: Anwendungsdiskurse in Moral und Recht* (Frankfurt, Suhrkamp, 1988); K Günther, 'A Normative Conception of Coherence for a Discursive Theory of Legal Justification' (1989) 2 *Ratio Juris* 155; K Günther, 'Criticial Remarks on Robert Alexy's Special-Case Thesis' (1993) 6 *Ratio Juris* 143.

analysis of juridical discourse on the basis of the principle that legal debates (ranging from legislative discussions to judicial decisions) rely upon linguistic means to arrive at rational conclusions that are oriented at meeting the consensus of all who are involved. From the viewpoint of a practically minded legal policy, such work can lead the way to develop legal regulations in the form of a juridification that is not systematically distorted and instead democratically accountable.

Regardless of the strength and limitations of the debates on the merits of Habermas's legal theory in the realm of legal and sociolegal studies, such secondary works demonstrate the potential relevance of Habermas to the study of modern law. Conceptually, they provide clarification within the context of Habermas's broader theoretical project as well as relative to other, competing and complementary theories. Empirical applications in social science and legal research additionally show that it is possible to use rather than merely discuss Habermas. This chapter, likewise, hopes to have explained some of the key elements of Habermas's legal theory which can and should be further investigated by means of consultation of the primary sources, a reading that can and ideally will also pave the way towards the elaboration of a Habermasian tradition of empirical work on law.

Section 3

Critical Approaches

REZA BANAKAR and MAX TRAVERS

THE LARGEST AND most influential tradition in studies of law in society, at least in the English-speaking world, is critical theory. The chapters in this section cover Marxism, Bourdieu's sociology, feminism and critical race theory, within which, as we shall see, many debates are taking place. They all emphasise the role of conflict, rather than consensus, in the development of society, view social life in terms of a power struggle between dominant and subordinate groups, and see law as implicated fully in economic exploitation and upholding social relations which generate inequality. As a result, critical approaches to the study of law tend to explore justice by focusing on the social conditions of 'marginalised groups, peripheral institutions, deviant behavior',[1] fostering what their critics describe as a partisan understanding of the law.[2] From the standpoint of critical scholars this is hardly a problem; the field of sociolegal studies (or the law and society movement)[3] offers a home not only to those who seek refuge from the methodological constraints of the discipline of law,[4] but also to those who question its hegemony and paradigmatic focus, which takes the power and authority of law for granted.[5]

The best place to start in understanding the critical tradition is with the ideas of Karl Marx, and so the first chapter in this section by Robert Fine provides a thoughtful and authoritative introduction to the views of a range of Marxist theorists on law. His central theme is the debate between those who view law as irredeemably bad—as implicated in relations of power and domination and in the capitalist system of commodity production—and those who believe that law is necessary for a good

---

[1] R Abel, 'Redirecting Social Studies of Law' (1987) 14 *Law & Society Review* 805–29, 827.

[2] The critics argue that the sociolegal research has abandoned the canons of social scientific inquiry in favour of preaching left-wing values. See B Tamanaha, *Realistic Socio-legal Theory: Pragmatic and Social Theory of Law* (Oxford, Clarendon Press, 1997).

[3] 'Sociolegal' is used here to refer to all social scientific approaches to the study of law including the law and society movement and the sociology of law. There are, however, significant differences between these approaches, which are in the first place defined in terms of their engagement with social theory, generally, and sociological methodology, in particular. For a discussion, see R Banakar, 'Law Through Sociology's Looking Glass' in A Denis and D Kalekin-Fishman (eds), *The New Handbook in Contemporary International Sociology: Conflict, Competition and Cooperation* (London, Sage, 2009).

[4] For a discussion on the challenges of interdisciplinarity, see R Banakar and M Travers, 'Law and Sociology' in R Banakar and M Travers (eds), *Theory and Method in Socio-legal Research* (Oxford, Hart Publishing, 2005).

[5] See eg A Sarat, 'Pain, Powerlessness, and the promises of Interdisciplinary Legal Scholarship' (2000) *Windsor Year Book of Access to Justice* 187–212, 194.

society, and he finds himself siding with humanistic Marxists such as György Lukács and EP Thompson, who see law as essential for the protection of individual liberties. From this perspective, the 'abstract and utopian' view that law will 'wither away' under communism 'ultimately [points] in a lawless and even totalitarian direction'. The problem with taking this view, however, is that it involves accepting and even celebrating liberalism, which follows once you accept that no radical transformation of society is either morally desirable or politically possible.[6]

We particularly like this piece because it acknowledges the difficulties facing Marxism, but it also makes one think about the problems facing its liberal and postmodern critics. Fine argues that those motivated by 'the rightful desire to construct a relation to law that has no kinship with totalitarianism' are usually also suspicious of '*social* theory' (his italics). The strength of Marxism is that it does address 'social questions' about the relationship between law and society. As a result, it is more difficult to assimilate Marxism into the 'dominant positivistic and natural law traditions in Western legal thought', although one might also argue that when Marxists start accepting and celebrating the rule of law, they are also vulnerable to the charge of sliding into liberalism.

The Marxist insight that law reflects and maintains the position of dominant economic groups was taken up in law schools, mainly by left-leaning law professors, who formed the critical legal studies (CSL) movement in the United States in the 1970s.[7] The followers of CLS (or 'Crits' as they are also known) shared 'an abiding distrust of institutional authority (born of the Vietnam War); a rejection of the orthodox forms of legal scholarship (which were viewed as intellectually sterile); and a certain countercultural sensibility (reflecting the values of the 1960s)'.[8] Intellectually, Pierre Schlag writes, they were highly eclectic and drew on the Marxism of Lukács and Weberian social theory as well as American legal realism, structuralism and postmodernism. The Crits might have appeared, Schlag argues, as a monolithic group to outsiders, but they were viewed from within the CLS movement as consisting of both liberal- and radical-minded scholars, who were united by a belief in the political nature of the law. The leading Crits, such as Duncan Kennedy and Roberto Unger, regarded the law as inherently political and contradictory (oppositional)—and thus indeterminate.[9] According to Angela Harris, CLS, echoing its predecessor, ie American legal realism from the 1930s, 'took the position that the internal logic of legal doctrine did not play any real role in deciding cases'.[10] This is what is known as the 'indeterminacy thesis'. Not only was law indeterminate (or contingent on its social context), but also the legal reasoning was driven ideologically in order to legitimise the prevailing political and economic relations. This also meant that law's claims to objectivity, coherence and neutrality were myths.

[6] For a more comprehensive discussion on the impact of neoliberal ideology, see Chapter 17 on late modernity.

[7] In Chapter 8 on critical race theory, Angela Harris provides an overview of the central ideas and concerns of the followers of CLS. For a more comprehensive review of CLS, see Jiří Přibáň's chapter in the first edition.

[8] P Schlag, 'Critical Legal Studies' in SN Katz (ed), *The Oxford International Encyclopaedia of Legal History*.(Oxford, Oxford University Press, 2009) 295.

[9] According to Alan Norrie, for example, 'Western Liberal law is essentially contradictory and antinomial, so that legal concepts, troubled and oppositional, generally hunt in pairs.' A Norrie, *Law and the Beautiful Soul* (London, Glasshouse Press, 2005) ix.

[10] See Chapter 8.

Although Crits incorporated ideas from legal realism and various branches of social theory, they saw no need for empirical research of the type developed within social sciences, thus distinguishing their work from the critical branches of legal sociology and the law and society movement.[11] The CLS's lack of interest in empirically informed arguments explains why Crits treat Derrida's 'Force of Law', which claims famously that 'deconstruction is justice',[12] as a central text, while they ignore Bourdieu's 'The Force of Law', which from a sociological standpoint explores the symbolic power of law and questions its claim to objectivity.[13] Madsen and Dezalay's review of Bourdieu's sociology of law in Chapter 6 shows that although Bourdieu's conceptualisation of the law has a great deal in common with how Crits understand law, it nonetheless has a sociological concern with reconciling dualisms such as the structure/agency divide and subjectivity and objectivity. It also demonstrates Bourdieu's attempt to go beyond the conflict theories of Marx and Weber by developing ideas such as *forms of capital*, *habitus* and *the field*. Madsen and Dezalay introduce Bourdieu's sociology of law by focusing on the role of the legal profession in the context of the internationalisation and globalisation of the law as a field of practice. They are at pains to distinguish their approach from 'both Marxists and normative functionalist accounts', and they write that the 'Bourdieusian perspective is not normative in its approach but focused on how law is constructed out of power and regardless of who is in power'. Notwithstanding Madsen and Dezalay's attempts to distance their analysis from Marxists, Bourdieu's general theory and his concept of 'cultural capital' remain indebted to Marx's social theory.

The two other critical approaches presented in this section include feminism and critical race theory (CRT), both of which are linked to, and influenced by, CLS. Adherents of these two approaches have systematically explored forms of discrimination and oppression not directly (or necessarily) based on social class, but on gender, sexuality, race or ethnicity. These critical scholars, nevertheless, usually recognise—in the same way as Marxists—a tension between 'radical' and 'reformist' approaches to law. Many of them also engage with the postmodern concept of difference. In the first edition we included a chapter on feminism by Ruth Fletcher, which showed how the feminist movement came under attack during the 1970s and 1980s from black and working-class women who felt that their voices and experiences were not being represented. This chapter also discussed the political and epistemological problems that followed once one accepted that there are women with all kinds of identities and experiences. The review of feminism in Chapter 7 by Harriet Samuels considers these questions. For example, does the category of woman provide an appropriate constituency for feminism, and should feminism take a break from its primary focus and instead apply its intellectual labours to exploring sexuality? One of the new debates introduced by

---

[11] The various studies which constitute the field of sociology of law, or law and society, are 'brought together by a common epistemology that views law as a social construct and argues that law and all its manifestations should be studied empirically and contextually. See R Banakar, 'Sociology of Law' (2011) *Sociopedia.isa*, www.isa-sociology.org/publ/sociopedia-isa/.

[12] J Derrida, '*Force of Law: The "Mythical Conditions of Authority"*', trans M Quaintance (1990) 11 *Cardozo Law Review* 920–1045, 945.

[13] Bourdieu maintains that law's 'symbolic power' extends itself beyond the circle of 'believers', ie jurists, law officials, law professors and others, who have internalised the values of the legal system, such as law's objectivity and autonomy, not to mention its ability to deliver 'social goods'. P Bourdieu, 'The Force of Law: Toward a Sociology of the Juridical Field' (1987) 38 *Hastings Law Journal* 814–53, 843–44.

Samuels concentrates on the theme of 'exclusion', coined by DG Reaume, which offers a methodological tool to examine 'how law directly and indirectly excludes women ... by its competing versions of how women's inclusion may be achieved'. In her chapter, Samuels refuses to abandon hope in law as an instrument that can establish gender equality, and stresses the significant role that feminist lawyers and the feminist critique of law continue to play in reforming it. Moreover, in spite of its many shortcomings, Samuels write, 'the use of the legal apparatus has clear normative and tactical advantages'.

Finally, in Chapter 8, Angela Harris tells the story of how CRT grew out of the disenchantment of some lawyers and scholars of colour with the CLS in the 1980s. The problem highlighted by the CRT was that although race as 'the grammar of governance' had been denounced by all Western nations, it was nonetheless employed—albeit in a disguised form and without direct reference to the discredited concept of race—as a criterion for organising social relations. Harris's focus is on race relations in the United States, but much of what she writes in regard to 'sedimented inequality' and the effects of racist discourse (to spread racist ideas in terms of the Other's culture and religion, without referring to the concept of race) is relevant to understanding all Western countries. More importantly, Western liberal law (at the level of legislation and legal policy) and legal reasoning (at the level of the everyday practices of legal authorities and officers of the law) continue to be implicated in this racist discourse.

It is also important to point out that the body of research on the interaction between law, race, ethnicity and culture suggests an ambiguous picture—a picture which finds its reflection in the misgivings expressed by radical feminists in the ability and willingness of the law to mediate social change. On the one hand, law provides a forum for fighting against various forms of injustice and changing public policy. It is therefore employed to combat racial discrimination and to promote equal opportunity, civil rights and so on. At the same time, law is criticised for its institutional and normative shortcomings, for its unwillingness to facilitate social change and for perpetuating prejudiced and harmful attitudes towards immigrants, demonising and criminalising ethnic minorities, and perhaps most crucially refusing to acknowledge the possibility of racism in law and disregarding the significance of race and ethnicity in legal doctrine and legal education.[14]

Although CLS, schools of feminism and critical race theory highlight various forms of domination—at the risk of oversimplification, they focus on class domination, gender/sexuality and race—they nonetheless overlap on several points. This overlap is captured by the concept of 'intersectionality' coined by Crenshaw.[15] However, as Harris points out in Chapter 8, intersectionality should be understood as much more than 'the imbrication of race with other axes of subordination and identity, such as gender, sexuality, disability, and class. It should be taken as a methodological warning to those who engage in social theorising that 'no given set of finite categories can capture the complexity of the social world'.

---

[14] See A Sarat (ed), *Race, Law, and Culture* (Oxford, Oxford University Press, 1997); P Tuitt, *Race, Law, Resistance* (London, Glasshouse Press, 2004); R Banakar, 'Law, Race and Ethnicity' in *Encyclopaedia of Law and Society: American and Global Perspectives* (Thousand Oaks, CA, Sage, 2006).

[15] KW Crenshaw, 'Demarginalizing the Intersection of Race and Sex: A Black Feminist Critique of Antidiscrimination Doctrine, Feminist Theory and Antiracist Politics' (1989) *University of Chicago Legal Forum* 139, 141.

5

Marxism and the Social Theory of Law

ROBERT FINE

MARXIST THEORY OF law remains relatively undeveloped in comparison with Marxist critiques of political economy. One reason is that Marx himself never returned to the project he set himself in his youth: to complement his critique of political economy with a critique of jurisprudence.[1] There are, however, asides in Marx's scientific works, the *Grundrisse* and *Capital*, where he raises juridical issues of right and law and provides clues as to how the method of his critique of political economy might be transposed to the field of jurisprudence.[2]

There are also political texts in which Marx reveals something of his practical approach to questions of law,[3] and there are texts by Engels in which he summarises his and Marx's approaches.[4] That said, there is no possibility of discovering a *theory* of law and legal relations ready-made in Marx's works.

Learning from Marx is also made difficult by equivocations in Marx's own analysis of law. In some texts Marx appears to offer a negative criticism of legal rights as mere forms without substantive content, and an antinomian view of communism as a political order superseding all constitutional limits. In other passages Marx shows an appreciation of the value and durability of legal forms whose contradictions he analyses without normative preconception of what ought to replace them. He writes of the 'positive supersession' of bourgeois law, as opposed to its 'abstract negation', but he does not give this much content.[5] Even in early texts such as *On the Jewish Question*, where Marx at first sight appears unequivocally critical of civil rights as icons of egoism and separation, the thrust of his work is to defend the rights of Jews against a form of radicalism which declared that Jews ought not to be granted equal

---

[1] Marx wrote: 'I shall therefore publish the critique of law, morals, politics, etc in a series of separate independent pamphlets and finally attempt in a special work to present them once again as a connected whole, to show the relationship between the parts', preface to the 'Economic and Philosophical Manuscripts' in L Colletti (ed), *Karl Marx: Early Writings* (Harmondsworth, Penguin, 1992) 281.

[2] See R Fine, *Democracy and the Rule of Law: Marx's Critique of the Legal Form* (Caldwell, NJ, The Blackburn Press, 2002) ch. 4 'Law, State and Capital'.

[3] See M Cain and A Hunt, *Marx and Engels on Law* (London, Academic Press, 1979); A Hunt, 'Marxism, Law, Legal Theory and Jurisprudence' in P Fitzpatrick (ed), *Dangerous Supplements: Resistance and Renewal in Jurisprudence* (London, Pluto, 1991).

[4] F Engels, *Anti-Dühring* (London, Lawrence & Wishart, 1943).

[5] The terms are drawn from Marx 'Economic and Philosophic Manuscripts of 1844' in R Tucker (ed), *The Marx–Engels Reader* (New York, Norton, 1978).

rights unless and until they abandon their Judaism.[6] Perhaps the one thing we can say about Marx's conception of modern legality is that he never abandoned the desire to look more closely into the matter. Critics of Marx have often displayed a rather crude and stereotyped view of what Marx wrote about jurisprudence, and there is no denying that some forms of Marxism, especially those once connected with the state power of Stalin and his successors, have lived up to these images. But to identify Marx as a precursor of a totalitarian destruction of law, as some critics do, would be no less of a travesty than to identify as such any of the other great nineteenth- and early twentieth-century rebels against tradition—be they Hegel, Nietzsche or even Weber.[7]

What makes Marx's *Grundrisse* and *Capital* 'classics' is that when we read them we find original and unexpected elements that surpass all our previous conceptions of what they contained and that force us to question the images we have of them. The texts themselves never seem to exhaust what they have to say to us and common use of terms such as 'Marxist' always seems inadequate in relation to what we read. To discover what animated Marx and what makes him significant for our own times, we need to shake off what Italo Calvino has called 'the pulviscular cloud of critical discourse' that so often surrounds his works.[8] For me, the key to understanding Marx's critique of jurisprudence is to see that his task was not to posit communism as an abstract ideal built on the ruins of law, redeeming past injuries and violence through the prospect of future reconciliation, but rather to resist all forms of historicism, dispel all teleologies of progress—in short, to criticise all claims to perfect harmony which conceal real social antagonisms beneath sanctified juridical categories.

The contribution of Marxism to our understanding of law lies in its determination to uncover the social relations between human beings expressed, mediated and obscured in legal categories such as private property or state property, constitutional government or the workers' state, representative government or the people's will, individual right or national interest. The term Marxism indicates a commitment to a *social* theory of law, which investigates why and with what consequence certain social relations assume legal form. Conversely, the contemporary repudiation of Marxism may signify a move away not just from socialism but from any idea of the social. In opposition to both natural law theory and legal positivism, Marxism is a declaration that the idea of right is not a natural attribute of individuals, nor a mere product of sovereign legislation, but a social form of the subject which emerges under given historical conditions. Marxism does not make an 'ism' of the social in the sense that it stands for the abolition of legal forms in the name of social transparency, but it traces the immanent development of the forms and shapes of law—from the simplest forms of abstract right to the most complex and concrete forms of state and international law—as a radically incomplete system open at every point to human agency and political action. Marxism names the perception that if there is one thing worse than the idealisation of law and its absolution from critical inquiry, it is hatred or contempt for law whether or not hatred is expressed in the name of 'the people'.

---

[6] Marx rejected the spurious reasoning of some young Hegelians that Jews were only concerned with the acquisition of money, lacked any wider sense of national loyalty, and were undeserving of civil and political rights. His argument was that modern society is a money society in which self-interest trumps wider social concerns. Why then pick on the Jews? See Marx, 'On the Jewish Question' in Colletti, above n 1

[7] See H Arendt, *Between Past and Future* (Harmondsworth, Penguin, 1977) 26–27.

[8] I Calvino, *Why Read the Classics*, trans M McLaughlin (London, Jonathan Cape, 1999) 6.

1. MARX 'S CRITIQUE OF RIGHT

Marx's most important insights into law are to be found in his marginal comments on the idea of 'right' in works focusing on the critique of economic forms.[9] In these asides Marx argued that the kind of society which gives rise to the commodity form, money relations and capital also gives rise to modern forms of right, law and state. They are two sides of the same coin. His argument may be reconstructed thus.

In a society based on production by *independent* producers, whose contact with one another is mediated through the exchange of products, producers are *free* to produce what and how much they wish, *equal* in that no producer can force others to produce or expropriate their products against their will, and *self-interested* in that they are entitled to pursue their own private interests. Relations with other producers take the form of free and equal exchanges in which individuals alienate their own property in return for the property of another for the *mutual benefit* of each party. Exchange relations make no reference to the circumstances in which individuals seek to exchange or to the characteristics of the commodities offered for exchange. They appear as self-sufficient relations, divorced from any particular mode of production and enjoyed by free and equal property owners who enter a *voluntary contract* in pursuit of their own mutual self-interests.[10] The parties to the exchange must place themselves in relation to one another as *persons* whose will resides in those objects and must behave in such a way that each does not appropriate the commodity of the other and alienate his own, except through an act to which both parties consent.[11]

Marx's claim is that the form of law is rooted in commodity exchange. The presupposition of exchange, however, is an organisation of production which *forces* producers to exchange their products. Their *interdependence* means that they cannot survive except by exchanging the products of their labour. Both the form of their relations, that of a contract between two private parties based on the exchange of property, and the content, the terms on which such contracts are made, are beyond the will of individuals and become a power over them. Individuals are *formally* independent but the

[9] JD Balbus 'Commodity Form and Legal Form' (1977) 2 *Law and Society Review* 571–88; G Kay and J Mott, *Political Order and the Law of Labour* (London, Macmillan, 1982); D Sayer, *The Violence of Abstraction: Analytical Foundations of Historical Materialism* (Oxford, Blackwell, 1987).

[10] In exchange relations, Marx writes:

[E]ach confronts the other as owner of the object of the other's need, this proves that each of them reaches beyond his own particular need ... as a human being and that they relate to each other as human beings ... there enters in addition to the quality of equality, that of freedom. Although individual A feels a need for the commodity of individual B, he does not appropriate it by force, nor vice versa, but rather they recognise one another reciprocally as proprietors, as persons whose will penetrates their commodities. Accordingly, the juridical moment of the *Person* enters here ... all inherent contradictions of bourgeois society appear extinguished ... and bourgeois democracy even more than the bourgeois economists takes refuge in this aspect. (K Marx, *Grundrisse* (Harmondsworth, Penguin, 1973) 243 and 251)

[11] Marx writes:

The sphere of circulation of commodity exchange, within whose boundaries the sale and purchase of labour power goes on, is in fact a very Eden of the innate rights of man. It is the exclusive realm of Freedom, Equality, Property and Bentham. Freedom because both buyer and seller of a commodity, let us say labour-power, are determined only by their own free will . . . Equality because each enters into relations with the other as with a simple owner of commodities and they exchange equivalent with equivalent. Property because each disposes only what is his own. And Bentham because each looks only to his own advantage. The only force bringing them together is the selfishness, the gain and the private interest of each. (K Marx, *Capital*, vol 1 (Harmondsworth, Penguin, 1976) 280).

relations they enter, far from being an abolition of relations of dependency, are rather the 'dissolution of these relations in a general form. ... *Individuals are now ruled by abstractions*, whereas earlier they depended upon one another.'[12]

The illusion of a free and equal relationship is dissolved once we explore the *content* of exchange. Where commodity production is sporadic or peripheral and exchange takes the form of an occasional barter between communities, the terms of the exchange are determined by the producers and each party has a right to defend its property by force of arms. With the generalisation of commodity production, competition between producers ensures that commodities exchange at or around their values, according to the socially necessary labour time that enters their production. Since there is no guarantee that the actual labour time taken by the producer corresponds to the socially necessary labour time for the goods in question, equal right in these circumstances entails that some producers exchange their commodities for more than their particular costs and some for less. This leads to extremes of impoverishment on one side and enrichment on the other, but if one party grows impoverished and the other grows wealthier, then this is, as it were, of their own free will. Under these circumstances producers are, as Rousseau once put it, forced to be free, that is to observe the rules governing the exchange of commodities.

Relations between capitalists and wage-labourers continue to take the form of free and equal exchanges, but the form and content of these exchanges now change.[13] On the surface relations between capitalist and worker still look like a simple exchange, but they are distinguished by the entry into the market of a new commodity, labour-power, whose historical presupposition lies in the double freedom of individuals—their freedom to own their own body, mind and capacity to work, and their freedom from other means of subsistence or production than their labour-power. The buyer of labour-power is no longer a simple buyer who wishes to use it as an object of personal consumption but a capitalist who uses it specifically for the production of surplus value. The secret behind the exchange between capital and labour is that workers receive in the form of wages a value equivalent to the value of their labour-power (ie the labour time socially necessary for the reproduction of the labourer) and not equivalent to the value of the products they produce on behalf of the capitalist. In this context, the unequal appropriation of unpaid surplus labour becomes the *substance* of equal right.

Turning to the reproduction of capitalist society, Marx argues that the social content of the exchange between capital and labour changes once more. Looked at individually, the exchange between capital and labour consists of the expropriation of part of the product of the workers' labour by the capitalist. The capitalist says that the capital he exchanges with labour-power is his own property—perhaps because he worked hard for it or because it is the product of his own earlier labour. This may be true of primitive accumulation but ignores the role of violence and international pillage. In any event after several cycles of production the entire capital owned by the capitalist will consist only of capitalised surplus value, that is of the product of the

[12] Marx, above n 10, a 164.

[13] Marx writes: '[A] worker who buys a loaf of bread and a millionaire who does the same appear in this act as simple buyers ... all other aspects are extinguished ... the content of these purchases appears as completely irrelevant compared with the formal aspect' (Marx, above n 10, 251).

labour of workers expropriated by the capitalist and turned into capital. It is now revealed that the exchange between capital and labour is no exchange at all, since the total capital is but a transmuted form of the expropriated product of workers from a previous period. On the surface, free and equal exchange carries on as before. Beneath the surface there is the appropriation of the property of one class by another without equivalent.[14] The law that presupposes that we own the products of our labour 'turns ... through a necessary dialectic into an absolute divorce of property and appropriation of alien labour without exchange'.[15]

Marx's argument reaches its climax in the conclusion that *in this context* abstract right becomes a 'mere semblance', a 'mere form ... alien to the content of the transaction', a 'mystification', 'only a semblance and a deceptive semblance'.[16] Perhaps the most original proposition in this account of Marx's social theory of right is that the social relations of production which give rise to the commodity or value form of the products of human labour also give rise to the 'right' or 'person' form of the producers. Both economic and juridical categories, as well as the split between them, are revealed as the results of determinate social relations of production. We might say that Marx's theory of *modernity* is a theory of the separation of subject and object, person and thing, right and value. Yet the difficulty Engels alluded to, that he and Marx 'neglected the formal side of political, juridical and other ideological notions— the way in which these notions come about—for the sake of their inner content', was not addressed.[17] For all the sophistication of the analysis, we are left with a potentially negative presentation of right as a mere form, a semblance, an empty illusion, a *mirror* of economic relations. While the forms of value are understood by Marx as *real* appearances, the forms of right are trapped within a *logic of illusion* from which it seems that Marx did not escape. Yet if the surface form of a thing is as real as its social content, as Marx recognised in his analysis of the value form, there is no reason to think that the appearance of a subject—as a person, a possessor of right, a human being—is not also as practical in its effects as its social content.

In short, Marx left a rich but incomplete legacy of juridical criticism. The task of developing his critique of jurisprudence was left for others to fulfil. It has not proven easy.

2. SPLITS WITHIN MARXISM AND THEIR EFFECTS ON LEGAL THEORY

With the historical split of Marxism into social democratic and bolshevik wings, Marxist legal theory was also torn apart. On the revolutionary side, the writings of

---

[14] Marx writes:

Originally, the rights of property seemed to us to be grounded in man's own labour. ... Now, however, property turns out to be the right on the part of the capitalist to appropriate the unpaid labour of others or its product and the impossibility of the worker of appropriating his own product. The separation of property from labour thus becomes the necessary consequence of a law that apparently originated in their identity. (Marx, above n 11, 729)

[15] Marx, above n 10, 514.

[16] Marx, above n 11, 729–30.

[17] Engels, 'Letter to Mehring' [1893], in K Marx and F Engels, *Letters on Capital*, trans E Drummond (London, New Park, 1983).

the Soviet legal theorist Evgeni Pashukanis represented a rich attempt in the 1920s to apply the method of Marx's critique of political economy to jurisprudence.[18] Pashukanis was one of the first to draw upon the systematic connections Marx observed between the commodity form and the juridical subject, and on this basis generated a Marxist theory of law in opposition to both a formalism that abstracts the legal form from social relations, and to a reductionism that ignores legal form in favour of political interests or economic functions. Pashukanis argued that law is a historically determinate social form, which signifies relations of mutual competition between juridical subjects who affirm their private rights against one another and are otherwise indifferent to the needs of others. He argued that the legal form arose in the modern bourgeois era, was indelibly marked by its origins and would wither away under socialism.

Pashukanis's commodity form theory of law represented a productive step forward in reconstructing Marx's critique of right, but the result was a one-sided critique of law as a power that operates on the basis of atomistic social relations and is disinterested in the rights and freedoms of individuals. This theory of law played into the hands of the evolving Stalinist regime and its thesis concerning the withering away of law under socialism served to justify the Soviet regime's disregard for legal procedure. Like many intellectuals, Pashukanis was useful for a totalitarian movement in the period of its ascendancy. Once the Stalinist regime sought to legitimise terror legally, as it did in the 1936 constitution, then Pashukanis and his work were soon dispatched. A productive reconstruction of Pashukanis's theory was attempted in the 1970s by new left critics of law in an attempt to revive the revolutionary tradition of Marxist legal criticism, but the theoretical and political limitations of his work have become increasingly apparent.[19]

On the other side of the Marxist divide, social democratic legal theorists, such as Karl Renner in Austria, were not interested in overcoming the legal form but in actualising it and giving it a socialist content. For Renner, legality is like a bottle in which different social contents can be poured. The stronger version of his argument is that *only* under socialism can the rule of law be realised, while under capitalism private interests necessarily corrupt the rule of law. The transition to socialism is premised on the extension of legal regulation into previously considered private spheres—for example, through legislation on health and safety, minimum wages, trade union rights, unemployment benefits, or the nationalisation of privately owned services—and the democratisation of legislative representation and procedure.[20] This idea of the progressive socialisation of law was historically buried under the weight of intensified class conflicts and then of totalitarian forces, but its main internal weakness was a failure to recognise the justified revulsion that can arise at the gulf between legal ideals and the sea of human misery to which they fail to respond—a revulsion which totalitarian

---

[18] E Pashukanis, *Law and Marxism* (London, Pluto, 1983); id, *Selected Writings on Marxism and Law* (London, Academic Press, 1980).

[19] C Arthur, 'Toward a Materialist Theory of Law' (1966–67) 7 *Critique* 31–46; R Fine, above n 2, 155–69; A Norrie 'Between Structure and Difference: Law's Relationality' in M Archer et al (eds), *Critical Realism: Essential Readings* (London, Routledge, 1998); R Warrington, 'Pashukanis and the Commodity Form Theory' (1981) 9 *International Journal of the Sociology of Law* i, Feb.

[20] K Renner, *The Institutions of Private Law and their Social Functions* (London, Routledge & Kegan Paul, 1949).

movements were quick to exploit. When social democracy resurfaced after the war, its legal theory became largely independent of Marxist underpinning.

A more direct confrontation with the rise of fascism and Stalinism in the 1930s was to be found among critical theorists of the Frankfurt School. Critical theory was transfixed by the 'consummate negativity' of the system of right: a world of chained and defeated figures walking through social life as in a prison yard; a world that represents total domination under the guise of human freedom. This image of the totally administered society was drawn from Hegel's *Philosophy of Right*, which was read as a rationalisation of a social order in which autonomy had declined into mass conformity. Following Marx, critical theory maintained that 'freedom ... is a histor-ical category par excellence' and that the system of right had turned into a 'torture instrument'.[21] The increasing philosophical authoritarianism of natural law was, according to critical theorists, but a mirror of the proclivity of liberalism, faced with worsening class inequalities and conflicts, to turn the state into an independent power. In the face of the crisis besetting the system of rights, Herbert Marcuse argued in this vein that Hegel betrayed his philosophy of freedom because he conceived the system of right in the manner of natural law—as a closed ontological system identical with the end of history.[22] Marcuse maintained that we must move beyond Hegel's 'abstract, logical, speculative expression of the movement of history' and rediscover the 'pos-sibility and truth' immanent within the modern state: that humankind can become the conscious subject of its own development. He stood for an historical materialism that would foster new forms of individualism beyond abstract right, new forms of association beyond civil society, new forms of command beyond law, new forms of self-determination beyond the state.

Franz Neumann also read Hegel's *Philosophy of Right* as an 'inexcusable paean' to the Prussian state, 'the state of broken promises', and explained the decline of rational law as the result of the transition from competitive to monopoly stages of capitalism.[23] While rational law was necessary for the predictability of market exchanges in a com-petitive capitalist economy, it was less needed in the era of monopoly capital when planning and control substitute for free exchange. If the major social functions of law are to secure the dominance of capital, make economic processes calculable, and guarantee the individual a minimum of freedom, the decline of the first two functions still left the third intact. While capital lost interest in maintaining rational law (fascism being one expression of this), the defence of rational law became all the more neces-sary for labour. Neumann sought to integrate Marx and Weber by linking Weber's opposition to the introduction of substantive legal principles to Marx's analysis of

[21] T Adorno *Negative Dialectics* (New York, Continuum, 1981) 345.

[22] H Marcuse, *Reason and Revolution: Hegel and the Rise of Social Theory* (Boston, Beacon Press, 1979) 294–315. For a critical assessment of readings of Hegel, see R Fine, *Political Investigations: Hegel, Marx, Arendt* (London, Routledge, 2001) ch 1.

[23] Social democracy's reliance on the constitution which no longer had real guarantees behind it had the ambiguous effect of legalising class struggles and allowing a hostile judiciary to determine their outcomes. See F Neumann, *The Democratic and Authoritarian State* (London, Macmillan, 1957); id, *The Rule of Law* (Oxford, Berg, 1986); id, *Behemoth: The Structure and Practice of National Socialism* (London, Gollanz, 1942). See also W Scheuerman (ed), *The Rule of Law under Siege: Selected Essays of Franz L Neumann and Otto Kirchheimer* (Berkeley, University of California Press, 1996); M Salter 'The Visibility of the Holocaust: Franz Neumann and the Nuremberg Trials' in R Fine and C Turner (eds), *Social Theory after the Holocaust* (Liverpool, Liverpool University Press, 2000); W Scheuerman *Between the Norms and the Exception: The Frankfurt School and the Rule of Law* (Cambridge, MA, MIT Press, 1994).

the changing character of capital. His conclusion was not to surrender to doctrines that divorce justice from legality but to fuse the idea of socialism with that of rational law—while supporting the use of extra-legal methods to defend legality. Arguing that rational law possesses certain formal qualities of generality, specificity, non-retroactivity, etc, and contains certain substantive freedoms of speech, movement, religion and association, Neumann attacked tendencies to subordinate *ratio* to the *voluntas* of state sovereignty. While totalitarian movements opposed positive law in their exercise of terror, Neumann argued that Marxism could not be blind to the fact that rational law was not merely a 'lesser evil' but a genuine repository of democratic values.

Theodor Adorno went further in contrasting his own approach to the 'entire dialectical tradition of Hegel and Marx' when he maintained the necessity of preserving the 'permanent component' of freedom.[24] He acknowledged the historicity of freedom, highlighting, for instance, the limited scope of freedom possible in the Spartacus uprising or in Babeuf's conspiracy, but his core suggestion was that the concrete possibilities of freedom could be found at every moment of history, that is whenever individuality genuinely asserts itself. Adorno argued there was no way of jumping over the system of rights. We may struggle against positive law in the name of a higher justice, but such utopian projects would inevitably be marked by worse distortions than those they were intended to overcome.[25] In the face of this impasse Adorno kept returning to Kant's philosophy of right, since it at least offered 'recognition of the bourgeois equality of all subjects' and confronted 'the allegedly *a priori* differences that are supposed to exist between people according to fascist principles'.[26]

In opposition to the hatred and contempt for law expressed in totalitarian movements, Adorno sought accordingly to relate critical theory to the natural law tradition. He argued that natural law and Nazism were impossible bedfellows since the former stood for legality, individual rights and rational norms and the latter for ethnic claims of belonging and non-belonging. Although Adorno criticised Kant's philosophy of right for imposing fixed standards of legality on subjects irrespective of their will or welfare and for neglecting class inequalities contained within an apparently egalitarian legal framework, he insisted that Kant's idea of right should not be treated as merely false as it was by 'those who adopted the fascist practice of making ... men's membership or non-membership in a designated race ... the criteria of who was to be killed'.[27] Adorno acknowledged the abstract character of equal rights but reaffirmed the efficacy of rights in countering the fetishised forms of capitalist society: '[D]espite and because of its abstractness, there survives ... something of substance: the egalitarian idea'.[28]

3. THE POST-WAR RESURGENCE OF MARXIST CRITICISM

A resurgence of Marxist criticism of law took off in the latter half of the 1950s, gathered strength with the rise of the new left in the 1960s and became linked to new social movements in the 1970s. This critique was diverse but shared a more or less

[24] T Adorno, *History and Freedom: Lectures 1964–65* (Cambridge, Polity, 2006) 180–81.
[25] S Jarvis, *Adorno: A Critical Introduction* (Cambridge, Polity, 1998) 169
[26] Adorno, above n 24, 252–53.
[27] Adorno, above n 21, 237.
[28] Ibid, 236.

anti-authoritarian radicalism directed East at the party-state, West at cold war militarism and everywhere at imperial domination. It was driven by a sense of profound disillusionment at the gulf between what law ought to be and what it actually is. One expression of this feeling was to be found in the then influential works of Louis Althusser and Nicos Poulantzas who formed the school of *structural Marxism*. They focused on the manifold functions which law plays in the reproduction of capitalist relations of production: functions of repression and violence, legitimation of the existing order, organisation of dominant classes, fragmentation of subordinate classes, depoliticisation of social movements, institutionalisation of class relations, and individuation of collective struggles. Marxism combined forces at first with sociological structural functionalism and then with the poststructuralism of Michel Foucault.[29] There was an in-built equivocation in this critique of law—whether emphasis was put on the determination of law in the last instance by economic forces or on the relative autonomy of law—and part of its appeal was predicated on its ideological flexibility. It provided a conceptual framework in which legal processes could be examined for their effects on the wider social order—albeit from a top-down, functionalist standpoint.

In *State, Socialism, Power* Poulantzas argued that in the modern political order law *appears* as a limitation on the violence of the state, but this appearance gives rise to an *illusory* opposition between law and terror—illusory according to Poulantzas because the bloodiest of empires have historically been founded on constituent rules and even Stalin's terror was paraded as the most democratic in the world in the Soviet Union's 1936 constitution. Poulantzas opined that 'nothing could be more mistaken than to counterpose the rule of law to arbitrariness' and that such a vision corresponded to a 'juridical-legalistic view of the state'. It was allegedly mistaken because the modern state 'holds a monopoly of violence and ultimate terror' and law is 'an integral part of the repressive order' which 'organises the conditions for physical repression'.[30]

Poulantzas granted that direct violence is not practised within the core capitalist societies as much as it once was, and attributed this in part to the functions law plays in constituting individuals as juridical subjects. Since law fragments and individualises the ruled, cements the social formation under the aegis of the rulers, and organises the apparatuses of administrative and judicial power, the direct employment of violence is no longer so urgently required. Poulantzas insisted, however, that the connection between law and terror is not severed, even when law 'organises and sanctions certain *real rights* of the dominated classes' and even when formal liberties are secured as 'conquests of the popular masses'.[31]

Under the title of *state-derivation* and *capital-state* theories, some Marxists focused on the place of law in the dynamics of capital accumulation in a less functional mode.[32]

---

[29] Althusser located law within the repressive and ideological superstructure of the state, determined in the last instance by the economic base and functioning to secure the reproduction of capitalist relations of production. See L Althusser, *Lenin and Philosophy and Other Essays* (London, Monthly Review Press, 1971) 134–58. In *Fascism and Dictatorship* (London, NLB, 1974) 320–22, N Poulantzas modified this functionalist account of law, arguing that law perpetuates and sanctions class rule by regulating political power through a system of general norms, which impose limits on the exercise of state power. While he denied that the fascist state is the antithesis of the liberal state, he acknowledged that in the former arbitrariness reigns.

[30] N Poulantzas, *State, Power, Socialism* (London, Verso, 1980) 76.

[31] Ibid, 92.

[32] J Holloway and S Picciotto (eds), *State and Capital* (London, Edward Arnold, 1978); W Bonefeld, 'Social Constitution and the Form of the Capitalist State' in W Bonefeld, R Gunn and K Psychopedis (eds),

They recognised that class relations should be seen as relations of production in a wider sense than economic determinism allows and that capitalist relations of production necessarily present themselves in mediated forms that are at once economic and juridical. They reread Marx's critique of capital not just as a theory of the exploitation of labour by capital but as a theory of capitalist society as a whole, including the juridical forms in which class relations between labour and capital are reproduced.[33] The problem of the isolation of law from productive relations was addressed by seeing capital not merely as an economic category but as a more general principle of explanation. The core proposition here is that in a capitalist society the commodity is not only the general form of the product but the fundamental social form that structures social life as a whole—including the state, law, rights and even legal philosophy.

A more radical critique of the structuralist approach came from Marxists who focused on popular struggles from the bottom up and gave their approach the name of *Marxist humanism*. Their critique was directed at a 'Marxism' which considered human beings merely as units in a chain of determined circumstances and which denied the creative agency of human beings. It was this denial that the Marxist historian, EP Thompson, called a 'heresy against man' and identified with official Communism and structural Marxism. Workers are not mere 'bearers of capitalist relations of production', he wrote, and 'contrary to the view of some theoretical practitioners, no worker known to historians ever had surplus value taken out of his hide without finding some way of fighting back'.[34] Thompson's approach to law was brimming with 'bloody-minded distrust' of power and dismissive of an authoritarian legalism that equates law with the will of government. He urged Marxists to recover their moral imagination from the numbing language of a 'party-speak' that had also entered into academe.

Thompson emphasised the *social* character of Marx's critique of political economy, but argued that even Marx was trapped within the circuits of capital and only partly sprung that trap in *Capital*. While Marx could not be blamed for the deformations of Marxism, Thompson acknowledged that there was no 'virgin untouchable purity of original Marxism to which Stalinism owes no kinship'.[35] Thompson rejected a model of modern society that forcibly isolates law as part of the superstructure from the

Open Marxism, vol 1 (London Pluto 1992) 93–132; R Gunn, 'Marxism and Mediation' (1987) 2 *Common Sense* 57–66; R Gunn 'Rights' (1987) 77 *Edinburgh Review*, availavle at http://richard-gunn.com/pdf/rights. pdf (accessed on 10 June 2013); M Postone, *Time, Labour and Social Domination: A Re-interpretation of Marx's Critical Theory* (Cambridge, Cambridge University Press, 1996).

[33] W Bonefeld comments on the social constitution of the capitalist state: 'the relation of the state to society' implies that

> private individuals exist as abstract individuals endowed with standardised rights and as such treated as abstract citizens. This treatment complements politically the processing of class as wage labour. This reassertion of the right of property denies the existence of class. ... The formal safeguarding of rights inverts into the substantive guarantee of exploitation. ... The attempt of the state (and capital) to harness class conflict into bourgeois forms of legality ... implies not only the legalisation of social relations ... it denies the existence of the working class as class. ... The historical composition of the state during fascism cannot be seen as an 'exceptional' form of state. ... Rather the coercive character of the state exists as presupposition, premise and result of the social reproduction of the class antagonism. (see Bonefeld et al, above n 32, 116–20)

[34] EP Thompson, 'Poverty of Theory', in *The Poverty of Theory and Other Essays* (London, Merlin, 1978) 345.

[35] Cited in R Fine 'The Rule of Law and Muggletonian Marxism: The Perplexities of Edward Thompson' (1994) 21 *Journal of Law and Society* 197.

economic relations, which make up the base, and the 'age-old academic procedures of isolation which are abjectly disintegrative of the enterprise of historical materialism, the understanding of the full historical process'. Referring to his own eighteenth-century historical studies, he wrote:

> I found that law did not keep politely to a 'level' but was at *every* bloody level; it was imbricated within the mode of production and productive relations themselves (as property rights, definitions of agrarian practice) ... it contributed to the self-identity both of rulers and of ruled; it afforded an arena for class struggle within which alternative notions of law were fought out.[36]

Class relations are at once legal, political and cultural as well as economic, so that if the base-superstructure metaphor is to be retained at all, it should be recognised that the base is not economic but social—human relationships involuntarily entered into in productive processes. The problem with orthodox Marxism is that it inverts the spirit of Marx's critique of capitalist society: instead of confronting the inhumanity of a society that preaches economic determinism, it postulated economic determinism as its own doctrine.

Thompson's approach to law was driven by the conviction that capitalist society offers an inhuman form of political community and that this inhumanity was mirrored in existing socialist states. This conviction led him along a variety of theoretical and empirical paths at different stages of his writing. In his historical writings he sought to recapture the moral community of eighteenth-century plebeian movements committed to upholding traditional use rights against modern laws of private property, seeing them as 'a last desperate effort of the people to re-impose the older moral economy as against the economy of the free market'.[37] In other writings Thompson defended the rule of law as an 'unqualified human good' and as a crucial 'inhibition on power'.[38] He thought it essential for Marxism to put its own house in order: this meant above all abandoning its dismissal of law as a mere instrument of class rule. He commented with some acerbity on how in the twentieth century even the most exalted thinker ought to be able to tell the difference between a state based on the rule of law and one based on arbitrary, extra-legal authority, and he attacked the essentialism of Marxist critiques of law which substituted a Platonic notion of the true, ideal capitalist state for actual capitalist states, and turned law into no more than a confirmation of existing property relations. Here Thompson presented law as a *mediation* which imposes effective inhibitions on power and defends the citizen from power's all-inclusive claims. In yet other phases of his journey Thompson looked for inspiration to the antinomian communities of love upheld by certain radical Protestant sects in opposition to the violence of law. This attitude was expressed in his Spring 1968 lecture at Columbia University, in which he declared himself a 'Muggletonian Marxist'. The Muggletonians were a Protestant sect which maintained that legality or the 'moral law', as exemplified in the Ten Commandments, is a code of repression and that its prohibitions are not binding on Christians committed to the gospel of forgiveness, love and mercy. Law may discover sin but it cannot remove it, for 'it changeth

---

[36] Thompson, above n 34, 286–88.
[37] EP Thompson, *The Making of the English Working Class* (Harmondsworth, Penguin, 1986) 73.
[38] EP Thompson, 'The Rule of Law', in *Whigs and Hunters* (London, Penguin, 1990) 268.

not the heart' and its principle is 'envy'. The gospel of love was to usher in the New Jerusalem after the fall of Rome. Where God lives in the heart, laws are relegated to mere ordinances. Thompson saw in this antinomian tradition a challenge to 'the authority of the ruling ideology and the cultural hegemony of Church, Schools, Law and even of "common-sense" Morality'.[39]

Taken as a whole, the strength of Thompson's alliance of Marxism and humanism was to face up to the burden of history without proclaiming the innocence of Marxism, to hear the voices of the oppressed in all their inconsistency, and to address historically the equivocations of law.[40] Perhaps the main limitation of his approach is that, despite itself, it too sometimes ended up dissociating law from productive relations and treating law and economics as belonging to opposed logics.

The dissociation of law from productive relations has been the unresolved thematic of contemporary Marxism. The central contention of critical theory, that the commodity form should be seen as the structuring principle of capitalist society as a whole, including its legal aspects, may be traced back to Lukács's judgements in *History and Class Consciousness* that the chapter in *Capital* dealing with the fetish character of the commodity 'contains within itself the whole of historical materialism'; that at this stage in the history of humankind 'there is no problem that does not ultimately lead back to that question'; that 'there is no solution that could not be found in the solution to the riddle of the commodity structure'.[41] Lukács presented the commodity as the *universal category* that determines the world in all its dimensions, and proceeded from the notion that workers can only become conscious of their actual existence in capitalist society when they become aware of themselves as commodities, not as individual bearers of rights. He treated the possession of 'right' as in essence a right over things: an expression of the instrumental domination of 'man' over 'nature'.

We might say that Marxist theory has followed a difficult path between Lukács and Thompson. Most Marxists present their own particular resolutions as a recovery of the authentic Marx from traditional Marxism, but the important part of Marx's argument (at least after 1848) is that the modern *subject* is neither a commodity nor a human being in the abstract, but an owner of commodities, a possessor of at least his or her labour power, and in this respect a subject of right, a person, a human being in the substantial sense of the term. For Marx, this quality of personality marks the beginning of the long and arduous journey in the development of self-consciousness, one that takes producers beyond their status merely as workers to their human emancipation.

[39] EP Thompson, *Witness against the Beast: William Blake and the Moral Law* (Cambridge, Cambridge University Press 1993) 5, 19 and 225.

[40] I discuss the equivocations of law in B Fine and R Millar (eds), *Policing the Miners' Strike* (London, Lawrence & Wishart, 1985); and R Fine, F de Clercq and D Innes, 'Trade Unions and the State in South Africa' (1981) 15 *Capital and Class* 79–114.

[41] G Lukács, *History and Class Consciousness: Studies in Marxist Dialectics* (London, Merlin, 1971) 83 and 170.

4. MARXIST LEGAL THEORY TODAY

Confronted with the difficult task of comprehending new forms of terror and counter-terror, Marxism has generally remained a marginal force in contemporary legal criticism. This has never been a desirable outcome, since Marxism has been a rich source of social theorising about law, and there are signs that in the face of renewed and severe crises of capital accumulation, Marxist theories of law have a new-found importance. Behind the will to declare Marxism dead we find the desire to construct a relation to law that has no kinship with totalitarianism, but the rejection of Marxism not only misrecognises the origins of totalitarianism, it may also express a deeper distrust of *social* theory—whether from the standpoint of natural right or legal positivism or a deconstruction that goes beyond law's social underpinnings to an elusive moment of alterity and justice.

A proclivity of modern thought Marxists have shared is to construct 'ism's—be it functionalism, instrumentalism, humanism, formalism or critical realism—every one of which is presented as the royal road to the truth. There is nothing wrong in exploring, say, the functions of law for capital accumulation, or the social interests and backgrounds of those who enforce the law, or popular conceptions of law held by the labouring classes, or the inhibitions on economic and political power imposed by the law, or the connections that tie the form of law to that of the commodity, or indeed the immaturity expressed when individuals relate to one another exclusively on the basis of their rights. There is every reason to examine these issues and the strength of Marxism has been to take up the social questions that others have neglected. A weakness of Marxists, however, has been to turn particular concerns into exclusive concerns and devalue those of others. It may be more appropriate to abandon the 'ism' of Marxism itself, whose unity is in any event illusory, and see Marx alongside the great nineteenth-century critics of tradition as one source of critical thinking among others.

Critical legal theory with a Marxist accent has taken off in numerous sites and from numerous standpoints. It has attached itself to the struggle for a democracy in which human rights have pride of place. And from very different standpoints it has immersed itself in reading legal texts. For example, in *Toward a New Common Sense* Boaventura de Sousa Santos explores the plurality of legal forms as a basis for his critique of the dominant positivistic and natural law traditions in Western legal thought. He identifies different forms of law relating to different structural sites—the household, the workplace, the marketplace, the community, the citizenplace, the worldplace—and argues that by prioritising the citizenplace over all other sites, Western legal thought loses sight of the connections which constitute the whole. Defining the citizenplace as 'the set of social relations that constitute the "public sphere", the vertical political obligation between citizens and the state', de Sousa Santos acknowledges that in the core capitalist societies it tends to be a place of formal legal freedoms and democratic procedures.[42] However, he argues that the restriction of democratic rights to this single site 'allowed for the shifting of the global emancipatory promises of modernity to the promise of state democratisation'—a narrower ambition that left despotic forms

---

[42] B de Sousa Santos, *Towards a New Common Sense: Law, Science and Politics in the Paradigmatic Transition* (London, Routledge, 1995) 421.

of *social* power in other sites unhindered. According to the broader conception of human emancipation de Sousa Santos identifies with Rousseau and Marx—a conception involving the affirmation of *social* equality and the delegitimation of class differences—we must raise the question of links between the functioning of law in the citizenplace and the forms of social power exercised in other sites. He speaks of *interlaw* to express a sense of the connectedness of the whole, the incompatibility of capitalism with the radical democratic claims of modernity, and an expanded, ultimately anticapitalist conception of human rights to embrace the forgotten spheres of the social.[43]

To take another example, in *Empire* and other writings Michael Hardt and Antonio Negri have argued that the social constitutions of the late modern period were founded on a recognition of labour and premised on a conflictual model of political life whose juridical expression was that of legal realism: a theory of law which holds that those who command over society secure their hegemony by means of law in such a way that the law is continually modified, open to conflict and reformed in line with changes in social life. According to Negri, the presupposition of legal realism is that law is a living part of the superstructure, but he argues that this has now imploded. The increasing integration of the economic and the legal has radically transformed this context of constitutional reference. A revolution from above has destroyed not only the pre-existing structures of social democracy but also the working class as one of the subjects of this relationship. It has resulted in what Negri calls, following Foucault, a 'biopolitical' model of disciplinary arrangements that differs from that outlined by Foucault only in that it is now marked by the 'imperial hierarchies' of a global system. For Negri the impact of this social revolution from above on legal studies is not only to render legal realism redundant, but also those open, anti-authoritarian Marxist tendencies whose beliefs in a strong reformism and in the alternative uses of law were predicated on a social and political situation that is now ended. For Negri, the postmodern claim that the dynamics of law and the dialectic of enlightenment are over is basically correct. There is no outside—no other place from which to base the overcoming of what is now going to rack and ruin. Negri attaches Marxism to the conceptual framework of poststructuralism to argue that in contemporary capitalism law has lost whatever normative autonomy it might once have possessed. It has become identical with the regulated and disciplined sphere of the social.

In this new social situation Negri maintains that the subject of change is no longer the working class but the multiplicity of immaterial workers (defined by their plasticity), intellectuals, temporary labourers, female workers, immigrant workers, etc. He calls them a 'multiplicity' (a term drawn from Spinoza) to express the manifold desires that set them in opposition to capitalist biopower, and argues that this multiplicity no longer mediates its activity through the democratic system of political representation, a system which no longer works at any level, but through a plurality of movements and sites of struggle, against a plurality of forms of exploitation and oppression,

---

[43] This approach has met with criticism from within the Marxist tradition that de Sousa Santos does not penetrate the law of the citizen place itself, or question its positivistic self-understanding, or acknowledge the forces of denial, suppression, conflict and confrontation which operate *within*. Norrie argues that de Sousa Santos's pluralistic conception of sites of law lacks 'structural depth' and does not enable us to understand the articulation of structures which constitute these sites as a capitalist totality. See Norrie, above n 19, 729–30.

according to a plurality of ideas of life and freedom. The challenge Negri poses to lawyers and politicians is the construction of a new 'constitution of liberty'—one that no longer starts from the enigma of political representation and no longer separates politics from the whole of social life, but recognises the right of all citizens to a social wage adequate for their reproduction, legitimates the exercise of counterpower, guarantees the right of mobility and welcomes foreigners. Marxism is linked here to the poststructuralism of Foucault, Deleuze and Guatarri, and to a radicalised struggle for universal human rights outside the conventional system of democratic representation. Negri is sometimes presented as an organic intellectual of the anticapitalist movement.[44]

These radicalised views of the struggle for human rights constitute a rich strand in contemporary Marxism. Many other critical writers have reassessed relations between Marxism and the law. Jürgen Habermas has addressed what he sees as the intimate connections linking the legal rights championed within modern natural law, the radical democracy championed within Marxism, and the rise of new forms of global justice and cosmopolitan rights.[45] Some Marxists address the legal regulation of international capital in the context of globalised and financialised capital accumulation.[46] Some develop the more directly social rather than political aspects of Marxist legal theory, in particular by relating it to feminist social critiques of law.[47] Some re-examine philosophically relations between Marx and the liberal tradition of jurisprudence.[48] Some have traced the turn of international law to human rights in terms of its functions for American hegemony.[49] Many are now exploring relations between Marxism and global social movements. The legacy of Marx is alive in all these investigations but it is increasingly difficult to demarcate the boundaries of what Marxism is and is not. In recompense, we now have a rich engagement between critique, crisis theory and social theories of law that promises much for the future.

---

[44] This account is drawn from M Hardt and A Negri, *Labor of Dionysus: A Critique of the State Form* (Minneapolis, University of Minnesota Press, 1994). Criticism has focused on inconsistency between critique of law and reaffirmation of constitution and human rights. If all law contains objective and subjective dimensions—regulation, authority and sovereignty on one side and rights, freedoms and agency on the other—Negri splits this unity in claiming that in the present law has become purely objective and that in the future it can become purely subjective.

[45] See R Fine *Cosmopolitanism* (London, Routledge, 2007).

[46] See eg S Picciotto and J McCahery (eds), *Corporate Control and Accountability: Changing Structures and Dynamics* (Oxford, Clarendon Press, 1993).

[47] See eg C MacKinnon, *Toward a Feminist Theory of the State* (Cambridge, MA, Harvard University Press, 1989); id, *Feminism Unmodified: Discourses on Life and Law* (Cambridge, MA, Harvard University Press, 1987).

[48] See G Rose, *Mourning Becomes the Law: Philosophy and Representation* (Cambridge, Cambridge University Press, 1996).

[49] See eg B Bowring, *The Degradation of the International Legal Order? The Rehabilitation of Law and the Possibility of Politics* (London, Glasshouse, 2008); C Douzinas, *Human Rights and Empire: The Political Philosophy of Cosmopolitanism* (London, Glasshouse, 2007); V Miélville, *Between Equal Rights: A Marxist Theory of International Law* (London, Haymarket Books, 2006).

6

Pierre Bourdieu's Sociology of Law: From the Genesis of the State to the Globalisation of Law[*]

MIKAEL RASK MADSEN and YVES DEZALAY

P IERRE BOURDIEU'S MOST direct attempt at developing a sociological analysis of law is found in his seminal article 'The Force of Law: Toward a Sociology of the Juridical Field' (FoL).[1] As indicated by the interplay of its title and subtitle, Bourdieu's scientific aim and interest in law is twofold. He is concerned, first, with law as a discourse of power, which is part of the construction of the state as it contributes to its legitimacy—that is, how the force of law is both legally and socially constructed. Second, he is concerned with law as a historical and social construction produced in part by legal agents in competition with other agents—that is, the emergence of the juridical field. With regard to the former, FoL provides an important analysis of the inner workings of law, particularly legal form and language and how it contributes to the force of law. This original analysis evolves around the double construction of law as both a practical applied science and a discourse of universality and how this compels law perpetually to seek to conceal itself in order to avoid falling victim to politics. Bourdieu points to the appropriation effect of legal language in terms of the ways in which legal discourse transforms elements of common language into specialised legal terms.[2] Law thereby produces a rhetoric of universality and neutrality. On the one hand, universality is expressed by the generality of the law in reference to trans-subjective values that presuppose the existence of an ethical consensus and by the use of formulas that leave little room for individual variation; on the other hand, neutrality is expressed by the use of passive and impersonal grammatical constructions, helping normative expressions to appear neutral. The outcome of these deeply intertwined linguistic processes is the symbolic power of law as a tool for ordering

[*] Most of this chapter has previously been published as Y Dezalay and MR Madsen, 'The Force of Law and Lawyers: Pierre Bourdieu and the Reflexive Sociology of Law' (2012) 8 *Annual Review of Law and Social Science* 433–52. Permission to reprint granted by the publisher.
[1] P Bourdieu, 'The Force of Law: Toward a Sociology of the Juridical Field' (1987) 38 *Hastings Law Journal* 805–53.
[2] Ibid.

politics without necessarily doing politics. Moreover, it is a specific juridical capital possessed only by those in the position to exercise the symbolic power of law.

What is, however, less developed in FoL is the corresponding analysis of those different historical conditions under which the relative force of law and legal language is made possible—that is, the analysis of the juridical field. To be fair, FoL was mainly a programmatic article seeking to set a new research agenda and less so empirically grounded.[3] It is clearly based on a particular view of law and the state in which formalised law and legal doctrine play a major role. Bourdieu's subsequent writings, however, reveal a far more complex picture, opening for rethinking the genesis of law, jurists and the state in terms of a plurality of models emerging even within Europe since the thirteenth century.[4] In particular, his posthumously published Collège de France lectures from the period 1989–92[5] offer almost exactly what is absent in FoL.[6] In these lectures, the role of lawyers in the autonomisation of politics and state is highlighted but with an emphasis on the empirical contingencies of the actual outcomes. He explores the change from early law to modern politics as a long historical process in which the jurists not only change camp between church and early state but also turn the church against the church to construct the state in Europe.[7] In this process, the jurists rely on their symbolic resources of 'words and concepts',[8] which in combination with their unique ability to blend universality and private interest help them gradually conquer an increasingly autonomous space in state and society and, thereby, rationalise the state in their own image. And that increasingly autonomous space is precisely what Bourdieu terms the juridical or legal field.

The legal field itself is marked by a division of juridical labour that reflects its varying ties to other fields—state power, academia, the business world, etc. It also has broad commonalities, notably a set of mental and institutional structures, that influence all legal agents in the ongoing struggles over defining and dividing the terrain of law, struggles that are hardly discernible due to the collective interest in publicly presenting law as a more fixed and coherent profession. There is, however, an important twist to this analysis which is often overlooked. Although law can in principle be studied in terms of a legal (or juridical) field, this approach insists on situating law, its institutions and its agents in the broader context of law's interrelationship with social forces other than those immediately at stake only in the microcosm of law. Hence, what in practice becomes the *field* of inquiry following a Bourdieusian research logic is not what is most often presented simply as the legal system but typically more specific and specialised areas of practice—human rights, international commercial arbitration,

---

[3] In practice, at his research centre in Paris, the sociological work on law was outsourced to younger, more specialised researchers, including the authors of this article.

[4] We develop this part further in Y Dezalay and MR Madsen, 'La construction européenne au carrefour du national et de l'international' in A Cohen, B Lacroix and P Riutort, *Les formes de l'activité politique: Èlements d'analyse sociologique XVIIIè–XXè siècle* (Paris, Presses Universitaires de France, 2006) 277–95.

[5] P Bourdieu, *Sur l'État: Cours au Collège de France* (Paris, Seuil, 2012).

[6] Prior to the publication of these lectures, the main analyses were found in the many articles published around the research project of the state nobility and the bureaucratic field, eg P Bourdieu, *Raisons pratiques. Sur la théorie de l'action* (Paris, Seuil, 1994); id, *The State Nobility: Elite Schools in the Field of Power* (Stanford, CA, Stanford University Press, 1996).

[7] Bourdieu, above n 5.

[8] Ibid, 512–24.

European legal integration, international criminal law, etc.[9] Moreover, following the same logic of inquiry, fields are not contained or closed entities but rather spaces of practices that remain in competition with other fields.[10]

Bourdieu's insistence on the constitution of the legal field in its relationship with other social fields has two reasons. The first is a combination of actual empirical observation and an underlying ontological idea in Bourdieusian sociology, namely that social reality does not exist in and of itself but only relationally—the real is relational.[11] The other, though closely linked, is a question of research strategy. If law is as powerful in demasking itself as suggested by Bourdieu's analysis, any sociological inquiry into law that is situated too close to the orthodoxy of law runs the risk of being trapped by law's logic of domination and, thus, becoming legally biased. This is also the backdrop for why Bourdieu throughout his oeuvre argues for the need for a reflexive sociology. His aim is to construct a more scientifically autonomous object of research in the social sciences as opposed to an object of inquiry that is essentially based on the 'intuitive readings and spontaneous classifications'.[12] This search for objectivisation is not restricted, however, to the research object as such but also implies a critical examination of the dominant academic preconstructions of the specific subject area in question (ie a critical analysis of the research tradition and the application of that tradition by the researcher). This double scepticism—or double historicisation—is what Bourdieu initially termed 'double rupture' and later 'reflexive sociology' in the context of the notion of field.

Considering this logic of inquiry, it is our claim that the most significant contribution that Bourdieusian sociology can make to the sociology of law is not by selective transplantation of concepts (field, habitus, etc) but by the deployment of these concepts as research tools in combination with an understanding of the notion—and indeed practice—of a reflexive sociology. For the same reason, this chapter is organised around the application of the Bourdieusian idea of sociology to law in empirical research.[13] Drawing mainly on our own empirical work on international and transnational legal fields, we describe the possibility of turning the general analytical scheme of Bourdieu into a sociological practice in the sociology of law, meanwhile introducing key concepts and their application. Throughout the chapter, we will moreover underline the double-take on law that is the starting point of FoL in terms of an analysis

---

[9] A Cohen, 'Legal Professionals or Political Entrepreneurs? Constitution Making as a Process of Social Construction and Political Mobilization' (2010) 4 *International Political Sociology* 107–23; Y Dezalay and BG Garth, *Dealing in Virtue. International Commercial Arbitration and the Construction of a Transnational Legal Order* (Chicago, University of Chicago Press, 1996); J Hagan and R Levi, 'Crimes of War and the Force of Law' (2005) 83 *Social Forces* 1499–534; MR Madsen, *La genèse de l'Europe des droits de l'homme: Enjeux juridiques et stratégies d'Etat (France, Grande-Bretagne et pays scandinaves, 1945–1970)* (Strasbourg, Presses Universitaires de Strasbourg, 2010); A Vauchez, 'The Transnational Politics of Judicialization. Van Gend en Loos and the Making of EU polity' (2010) 16 *European Law Journal* 1–28.

[10] P Bourdieu and L Wacquant, *An Invitation to Reflexive Sociology* (Chicago, University of Chicago Press, 1992).

[11] This is further developed in MR Madsen, 'Reflexivity and the Construction of the International Object: The Case of Human Rights' (2011) 5 *International Political Sociology* 259–75.

[12] P Bourdieu, J-C Chamboredon and J-C Passeron, *The Craft of Sociology. Epistemological Preliminaries* (Berlin, Walter de Gruyter, 1991).

[13] We have in previous publications outlined Bourdieu's sociology of law on a more conceptual level. See eg MR Madsen and Y Dezalay, 'The Power of the Legal Field: Pierre Bourdieu and the Law' in R Banakar and M Travers, *An Introduction to Law and Social Theory* (Oxford, Hart Publishing, 2002) 189–204.

of those different historical conditions under which the relative force of law and legal language is made possible.

1. THE GLOBALISATION OF LAW AS FIELDS OF PRACTICE

As already suggested, a Bourdieusian approach to law can provide an understanding of the many different paths followed by lawyers in the formation of modern society, ranging from defenders of public virtue to clerks of an advanced bureaucracy. It is thus different from both Marxist and normative functionalist accounts, which operate under the assumption that law is either instrumentalised political ideology or modern society's substitution of morality with a liberal ideology of rights as a device for social coherence. This is also where Bourdieusian reflexive sociology of law most fundamentally differs from mainstream law and society scholarship: the Bourdieusian perspective is not normative in its approach but is focused on how law is constructed out of power and regardless of who is in power.[14] In this chapter, we do not attempt to provide substantial empirical analysis of a cross-section of the processes of law, jurists and state formation around the world.[15] Instead, we limit our focus to the sociology of the internationalisation and globalisation of law, as this allows for an analysis of the frontier of law, a frontier where the geneses of law are once again unfolding.

The concept of 'the field' developed by Bourdieu offers a number of heuristic advantages for the study of new and open objects such as those encountered in the context of the globalisation of law.[16] The relatively open-ended definition of a field as a network of objective relations provides a broad conceptual ground for analysing both the social continuities and the construction of new practices. Moreover, this approach emphasises what is often downplayed in the context of weakly institutionalised international legal practices, namely social interests and class. The field approach also underscores the generally adversarial nature of social practices and the political and institutional effects of sociolegal struggles over domination. What makes the return to such basic sociological issues seem further justified in the context of the internationalisation of law is the observation that international strategies are often directly related to national processes of social and legal reproduction. More specifically, such strategies often correspond with national social hierarchies to the extent that they are intertwined with an attempt to revalorise the capital of national, often cosmopolitan, elites as a way of maintaining their elite positions. The continuous reconstruction of international or European legal practices is influenced, among other things, by such a system of reproduction, because of the ways in which it offers the means for securing and converting social positions in a continuously evolving class structure that extends to the international level.

As concerns law and lawyers, this has a particular interest. Owing to the interdependence of the emergence of modern law and the construction of the modern

---

[14] Madsen, above n 9.

[15] Ibid; Y Dezalay and B Garth, *The Internationalization of Palace Wars: Lawyers, Economists, and the Contest to Transform Latin American States* (Chicago, University of Chicago Press, 2002); Y Dezalay and BG Garth, *Asian Legal Revivals: Lawyers in the Shadow of Empire* (Chicago, University of Chicago Press, 2010).

[16] The notion is defined below.

state, jurists have inherently been agents of state expertise.[17] This embeddedness of jurists in the modern state also allowed them to play central parts in the international import and export of state knowledge and institutions, first as medieval mediators and diplomats between city states[18] and much later as actual international lawyers.[19] In practice, this entailed a very long historical process of both institutionalisation and legitimisation, in which the actual force of international law well into the late nineteenth century was very much subject to the interaction and clashes of imperial European societies.[20] In other words, the idea of an autonomous practice of international law and a corresponding profession of international lawyers was very far from accomplished. Instead, a group of internationalist lawyer-politicians with significant social and political resources shared the business of international relations with a similarly exclusive group of cosmopolitan state notables trading in state expertise. This small cosmopolitan elite enjoyed the privilege of typically being members of not only a national higher class but also an international cosmopolitan class.

This exclusive practice—and club—was eventually transformed by the intensification in both legal and political interaction during the twentieth century, which eventually led to significant investments in international and, perhaps particularly, European supra- and international institutions. Thus, international law and relations went from being the dominion of a small club to starting to attract a far broader group of agents, who competitively sought to construct new international and European venues configured around their own specific expertises. Although the histories of both the League of Nations and the United Nations over the past century exhibit the cumbersome progress of international institutions,[21] international and European law nevertheless went from being an affair between legal gentlemen, conducted in closed elite networks, to eventually becoming part of increasingly differentiated fields of practice during the period. Yet, this does not imply, as is nevertheless often assumed, that transnational elites vanished from international affairs and were replaced by a social segment of professionals.[22] The area of international commercial arbitration provides a telling example of how the domination of the field by a traditional European internationalist elite of grand professors was challenged by the arrival of a Wall Street law firm-based practice of arbitration. However, the outcome was not a complete collapse of the European business but a general restructuring of the field, integrating this new line of opposition.[23] Recent

---

[17] E Kantorowitz, 'Kingship under the Impact of Scientific Jurisprudence' in M Clagett, G Post and R Reynolds, *Twelfth-century Europe and the Foundation of Modern Society* (Madison, University of Wisconsin Press, 1961) 89–111.

[18] JA Brundage, *The Medieval Origins of the Legal Profession: Canonists, Civilians, and Courts* (Chicago, University of Chicago Press, 2008); L Martines, *Lawyers and Statecraft in Renaissance Florence* (Princeton, Princeton University Press, 1968).

[19] M Koskenniemi, *The Gentle Civilizer of Nations: The Rise and Fall of International Law 1870–1960* (Cambridge, Cambridge University Press, 2001); G Sacriste and A Vauchez, 'Les "bons offices" du droit international: la constitution d'une autorité politique dans le concert diplomatique des années 20' (2005) 26 *Critique Internationale* 101–18.

[20] Madsen and Dezalay, above n 13; MR Madsen and A Vauchez, 'European Constitutionalism at the Craddle. Law and Lawyers in the Construction of a European Political Order (1920–1960)' (2004) 25 *Recht der Werkelijkheid* 15–36.

[21] M Mazower, *No Enchanted Palace: The End of Empire and the Ideological Origins of the United Nations* (Princeton, Princeton University Press, 2009).

[22] Dezalay and Garth, above n 9

[23] Ibid.

research, some of it inspired by the renewed interest in notions of hegemony and empire, also points to the often overlooked but nevertheless very central role played by elites in globalisation. Examples include Huntington's 'Davos Man', Rothkopf's 'global superclass', Sklair's 'transnational capitalist class', and even Jackson's 'globalisers', the international community of development workers.[24] Most of this literature, however, has a different objective, namely to denounce the denationalising effects of global elites. We suggest instead examining legal agents as 'transnational power elites',[25] that is as social groups rooted in society, national and international, and with the goal of exploring the battles over the structuration of transnational fields of law.

This is linked to observations of the structural effects of changes in international practices over the past decades. Generally, by the twentieth century transformation of international law and legal practice, the very distinction between the international and the national—traditionally based upon the legal dichotomy between inter-state and domestic affairs—was itself challenged. In more conceptual terms, one can observe a certain transnationalisation of the notion of the international[26] via the emergence of increasingly autonomous legal fields in specific subject areas at the crossroads of national and international law. The latter is what a number of researchers have now labelled the functional differentiation of international law, assuming a perhaps overly legalist view of the actual differentiation of international law.[27] Yet, what is certain is that these processes of internationalisation and transnationalisation, both in terms of international transformations of national practices and the proliferation of international law and institutions, pose a challenge to the conventional understandings of law; that is, they call for research methods that can comprehend the complexity of interdependent social fields that, at face value, claim to be autonomous beyond the state but nevertheless are deeply embedded in a national configuration of law and power.[28] It is our claim that the Bourdieusian concept of field provides a particularly suitable theoretical starting point for studying what in practice is a growing number of differentiated and increasingly institutionalised fields of transnational legal practice.

Conceptually, a field is a place for struggle between different agents where different positions are held based on the amount and forms of capital. In Bourdieu's own words, it is a network, or a configuration, of objective relations between positions. These positions are objectively defined, in their existence and in the determinations they impose upon their occupants, agents or institutions, by their present and potential situation (*situs*) in the structure of the distribution of species of power (or capital) whose possession commands access to the specific profits that are at stake in the field,

[24] SP Huntington, *Who Are We? America's Great Debate* (New York, Free Press, 2005); D Rothkopf, *Superclass: The Global Power Elite and the World They Are Making* (New York, Farrar, Straus and Giroux, 2008); L Sklair, *The Transnational Capitalist Class* (Oxford, Blackwell, 2001); JT Jackson, *The Globalizers: Development Workers in Action* (Baltimore, The Johns Hopkins University Press, 2005).

[25] N Kauppi and MR Madsen, *Transnational Power Elites: The New Professionals of Governance, Law and Security* (Abingdon, Routledge, forthcoming 2013).

[26] A-M Slaughter, 'Breaking Out: The Proliferation of Actors in the International System' in Y Dezalay and BG Garth, *Global Prescriptions: The Production, Exportation, and Importation of a New Legal Orthodoxy* (Ann Arbor, Michigan University Press, 2002) 12–36.

[27] M Koskenniemi and P Leino, 'Fragmentation of International Law? Postmodern Anxieties' (2002) 15 *Leiden Journal of International Law* 553–79.

[28] S Sassen, *Territory, Authority, Rights: From Medieval to Global Assemblages* (Princeton, Princeton University Press, 2006).

as well as by their objective relation to other positions (domination, subordination, homology, etc).[29]

In more operative terms, the emergence of a field implies a degree of structural consistency and autonomy, meaning a set of objective and symbolic relations between agents and institutions around increasingly specific issues. Through this process, a field constructs its own particular symbolic economy in terms of the valorisation of specific combinations and forms of capital (social, economic, political, legal, etc). The process of capitalisation results from the struggle between the agents over gaining dominant positions in this social space, a process fuelled by interest, dedication, belief, etc, in the issues at stake. But, above all, it is a struggle concerning the dominant visions and divisions of the field itself, which conversely help create not only the field's logic and taken for granted limits (*doxa*) but also its consecration mechanisms, enabling the translation of the external world into the specific code and issues of the field. Thus, a field is a social space composed of competing positions. It has a more structured centre of gravity where the effects of the field are most strongly felt, while the effects eventually diminish at its outskirts. Consequently, and essentially different from a systems-theoretical conception of law, there are no fixed boundaries of fields. This conversely allows for studying the crossroads of fields (eg how neighbouring fields are mutually influential or how the evolution of transnational legal fields is taking place interdependently of national legal transformations).

Because the emergence of a new field almost always has its roots in other fields and, in the case of transnational legal fields, in more national modes of producing law, the import–export of different social logics to transnational fields becomes an issue of particular sociological interest for understanding these processes of structuration. In this light, exploring basic sociological issues, such as doctrines, modes of education and reproduction, paths to access, and definitions of competences, becomes central for understanding institutional processes of autonomisation and legitimisation. As the discussion above suggests, a key component and dynamic of the field is found in the practices of the agents. They are the authors of the performative acts providing for the circulation of ideas and concepts between fields, as agents by definition always operate in more fields.[30] In order to examine these crucial relations between agents and social structures, Bourdieusian research tools such as the notions of habitus and symbolic power are deployed with the goal of exploring this more subjective level (ie the structuring level of agency) of the field in combination with an analysis of the structures of the field. This is also the point at which Bourdieusian social theory potentially violates the basic premises of Bourdieusian reflexive sociology. The notion of habitus poses a double challenge in this regard. On one hand, even if its intellectual origins are more complex, the notion is infused by a long series of empirical studies of French society[31] and has, for many, come to reflect a specific and nationally informed social reality. On the other hand, but closely connected, the notion seems to work best in highly structured national fields. Needless to say, both aspects are problematic with regard to applying habitus to transnational fields that are neither French nor particularly stable.

---

[29] Bourdieu and Wacquant, above n 10.

[30] P Bourdieu, 'Les conditions sociales de la circulation internationale des idées' (2002) 145 *Actes de la recherche en sciences sociales* 3–8.

[31] Bourdieu, above n 6; P Bourdieu, *Distinction: A Social Critique of the Judgement of Taste* (Cambridge, MA, Harvard University Press, 1984).

The solution is both conceptual and empirical—that is, with respect to the former, to accept that transnational or international fields are rarely structured in ways that entirely mimic national fields and in practice encompass much greater diversity and, with respect to latter, to avoid imposing too nationally defined preunderstandings of transnational fields by carefully exploring the actual dynamics at play.

Habitus is generally defined as the internalised schemes guiding the behavior of agents. It is a practical sense of reality that is acquired throughout the agent's particular and individual trajectory.[32] Yet, as demonstrated in a number of previous studies of transnational fields, leading international players typically pursue both international and national careers.[33] This enables them to valorise their capital and knowledge in more places, even to shift identity and ultimately exercise double (or even triple) strategies from their multiple—national and international—social positions.[34] Contributing to the structuration of transnational fields, these multiple strategies are important to the import–export between fields. But with regard to understanding the habitus of these agents, the notion can be applied only with the understanding that the agents are somehow more schizophrenic on the international than on the national level. In other words, the notion of habitus can be employed in the analysis but only in a more indicative and flexible fashion. Law degrees from two different top universities, known nationally as well as internationally, for example Harvard and Oxford, have different values nationally than internationally. Moreover, the socialisation the agent has gone through at the specific law school produces different outlooks on the national and international levels. Yet, what nevertheless restructures and reorganises these behavioural schemes is the fact that agents on the international level also tend to organise around professional identities—even if these are relatively different if compared nationally. The challenge is therefore both methodological and empirical—namely to capture how international and transnational fields at a single point in time present both a relatively autonomous structure and an unsettled mélange of different outlooks and ideas on the very same issue. This only underscores the need to avoid deploying the notion of habitus as a freestanding concept and instead apply it in combination with the concept of field, which allows for a double observation of social practice as both stable and adversarial.

The other key notion from the Bourdieusian toolbox, symbolic power, provides a further key to uncovering the complex symbolic economy of transnational legal fields at the crossroads of the national and the international levels of law.[35] As demonstrated in Bourdieu's work on the emergence of the state, retracing the various battles and processes of defining the state provides a view into the laboratory of what might now be taken for granted: the law, the state agencies, etc.[36] A good example of similar processes of naturalisation (via neutralisation) and universalisation is the construction of European integration. Europe generally tends to naturalise and universalise its social constructions and does so to such an extent that the researcher entering this space of 'symbolic violence' is practically compelled to rephrase Bourdieu's fun-

---

[32] P Bourdieu, *Outline of a Theory of Practice* (Cambridge, Cambridge University Press, 1977).
[33] Dezalay and Garth, above n 9; Madsen, above n 9.
[34] Dezalay and Garth, above n 9.
[35] Dezalay and Madsen, above n 4.
[36] P Bourdieu, *Raisons pratiques. Sur la théorie de l'action* (Paris, Seuil, 1994).

damental research question—what is the state?—to: what is Europe?[37] Regardless of the rhetoric deployed with respect to the European Union—constitution, justice and home affairs, etc—there is obviously no European state. Yet, there is a unique social construction that bears resemblance to the state because of the way it has been built using state knowledge and models imported from Member States and third-party countries, in particular US models of federalism.[38] Hence, Europe is, if anything, a hybrid, made up of the competitive forces of the involved states as well as its histori-cally specific position vis-à-vis other states, notably the United States during the cold war.[39] Moreover, contemporary processes of economic and financial globalisation have made Europe even more of a market state—something in between a market and a state—where the disaggregating European nation-states compete over the definition of the terrain and the institutions. The European Union is thus increasingly being made into a prolongation of the European state, whereas individual nation-states are, as a result, reforming themselves into market-states. Hence, the state in the national context is in some ways not the same as the state in the European setting, even if they are in many ways converging.

The same is also particularly true for both law and lawyers having different charac-teristics depending on the social universe in which they intervene or act. The notion of symbolic power becomes, in this regard, a tool for understanding how the exchanges and competition between different national and international models are key to the structuration of transnational legal fields. Conceptually, symbolic power is the power to transform the world 'by transforming the words for naming it, by producing new categories of perception and judgment, and by dictating a new vision of social divi-sions and distributions'.[40] More specifically, the emergence of any new field functions both internally and externally as a way of questioning and redefining social hierarchies and power. This can be observed in the social mechanisms that produce nomencla-tures, métiers, modes of education and generally other paths to power. One of the key social mechanisms behind the production of new structures is symbolic power. That fact raises the pivotal question of how symbolic power is distributed within a given field. There is obviously no simple answer except to examine the structuration of the field in question in light of the processes of capitalisations that have helped create the dominant positions. This brings us back to the argument presented throughout the previous sections—namely that the actual configuration of any legal field is histori-cally contingent and, thus, a social product that needs to be analysed in light of its historical process of construction. It is the underlying claim of Bourdieusian sociology of law that the application of the notions of field, capital, habitus and symbolic power, in combination with a reflexive posture, provides the sociological tools for precisely such an empirical analysis.

---

[37] Bourdieu and Wacquant, above n 10.

[38] A Cohen, 'Constitutionalism without Constitution: Transnational Elites between Political Mobilization and Legal Expertise in the Making of a Constitution for Europe (1940s–1960s)' (2007) 32 *Law & Social Inquiry* 109–35.

[39] G Lundestad, *The United States and Western Europe Since 1945: From 'Empire' by Invitation to Trans-atlantic Drift* (Oxford, Oxford University Press, 2005).

[40] Bourdieu, above n 1.

2. LAWYERS AS GLOBAL ENTREPRENEURS

Exploring the transnational developments of law provides a particularly salient empirical terrain for conducting this form of critical and structural analysis of law. Not only is the transnationalisation of law an interesting empirical development in itself, but it also offers a unique sociological viewpoint for reconsidering the production of both national and international law. Using a transnational starting point, which invariably also involves elements of comparative analysis, in many ways facilitates the outlined processes of deciphering law and legal practices, as it helps to repose and reframe a whole series of key questions related to the foundational issues of law, politics, the state, etc. Basically, it provides a way to break with the historically ingrained structures of law in national culture, language and the state. As Bourdieu points out at length in FoL,[41] the very operation of law is based on a high degree of social concealment: the formalist separation between law and politics (and thus social context) and the corresponding notion of judges as simply '*la bouche de la loi*', a notion reproduced in the handy opposition between the rule of law and the rule of man. At the transnational level, however, law appears much more open and multilinguistic than it does at the national level. It thereby provides a more transparent account of the social processes of producing and reproducing the force of law, which also take place at the national level but in a far more camouflaged manner. Thus, a central objective of this specific international sociology of law is to devise research strategies that help the research avoid and even evade the strongly prescriptive discourses inevitably involved in the production of law, both nationally and internationally. One way to attain this objective is to break with the functionalist view of law permeating great parts of the sociology of law. We suggest instead to study the actual agents of law, not simply as the operators of transnational law but also, and specifically, as the entrepreneurs building transnational legal fields. Making the empirical object of inquiry legal agents, as opposed to a self-describing and self-referencing legal system, further allows for posing actual sociological questions about legal agency, which by definition are always downplayed in national contexts of law by the double concealment of law described above. These concealed sociological issues include, for example, social capital, the multipositioning of legal agents both within and outside the law, and other key social traits of any given societal elite. The goal is not a prolongation of conventional studies of the legal profession but rather an analysis of the involvement of legal agents in the fabrication of specific fields and the formation of new transnational legal groupings.

Considering the history of international relations and law, it is of course not surprising that the transnationalisation of law is deeply influenced by the import–export of national and international ideas and strategies. It is at the level of agency, however, that it becomes transparent how the 'courtiers of the international'[42] act on both national and international levels of law and, thus, facilitate these processes of exchange. They are basically the entrepreneurs of these developments. To give an example, two of the most central agents of European integration with respect to the European Coal and Steel Community and the European Convention on Human

---

[41] B Latour, *La fabrique du droit: Une ethnographie du Conseil d'État* (Paris, La Découverte, 2002).

[42] Y Dezalay, 'Les courtiers de l'international: Héritiers cosmopolites, mercenaires de l'impérialisme et missionnaires de l'universel' (2004) 151–52 *Actes de la recherche en sciences sociales* 5–34.

Rights, Robert Schuman and Pierre-Henri Teitgen, very clearly pursued double careers on both the national and European levels.[43] Using their unique positions and multiple specialisations in politics and law, they became both the couriers of the idea of European integration and the middlemen of the import–export between the multiple political levels involved, helping to circulate both national and foreign ideals, models and interests. A number of studies have also underscored the political, social and legal importance of the lack of clear boundaries between the ideology of European integration—politically or scientifically—and the basic national diplomatic interests in the building of Europe.[44] From the outset, the very definition of the boundaries of Europe became an essential part of the strategy of institutionalising this uncharted legal and political landscape. For exactly these reasons, studying legal entrepreneurs provides a tangible, empirical object for examining these processes of definition and ultimately structuration, as well as for understanding how these more international processes and struggles are interdependent with national politics and legal ideas.

The heuristic value of making legal entrepreneurs the object of inquiry is that it facilitates an understanding not only of emerging fields but also of the dynamics of more established fields. It is self-evident that deeply structured fields, for example certain subfields of European law, leave less space for entrepreneurs, as they operate with more differentiated legal knowledge and professional career patterns than what was the case at their initial stages. Nevertheless, the perspective is not thereby inapt. In-depth empirical analysis demonstrates that professional–ideological and national–international double strategies are pervasive not only in new emergent transnational fields but also in established ones. Particularly as concerns the latter, this focus on legal entrepreneurs allows for understanding the dynamics of change that would otherwise be entirely unattainable if institutions were too narrowly perceived as once-and-for-all settled autonomous entities. One striking example in this regard is the area of European environmental law. Deeply influenced by the import–export between national and European ideas and models, the history of the field of European environmental practices illustrates how national players contributed to the Europeanisation of environmental policy and law by using European venues to challenge national practices and vice versa.[45] Like many other activists of the British left of the 1980s, British environmentalists utilised the European level to bypass, but also to challenge, the national environmental policies of Prime Minister Margaret Thatcher. The main agents relied on both national and European resources in the pursuit of these strategies, which effectively enabled them to reconstruct their positions both nationally and on the European level. And at the end of the day, not only English policy but also European policy and law were changed. A very similar account of change can be found in the area of European human rights in which British lawyers who were involved in

[43] A Cohen and MR Madsen, 'Cold War Law: Legal Entrepreneurs and the Emergence of a European Legal Field (1945–1965)' in V Gessner and D Nelken, *European Ways of Law: Towards a European Sociology of Law* (Oxford, Hart Publishing, 2007) 175–202.

[44] A Cohen, 'Le plan Schuman de Paul Reuter. Entre communauté nationale et fédération européenne' (1998) 48 *Revue française de science politique* 645–63; A Cohen and A Vauchez, 'Introduction: Law, Lawyers, and Transnational Politics in the Production of Europe' (2007) 32 *Law & Social Inquiry* 75–82; N Kauppi and MR Madsen, 'European Integration: Scientific Object or Political Agenda?' (2007) 1 *Praktiske Grunde* 28–46.

[45] Y Dezalay, 'From a Symbolic Boom to a Marketing Bust: Genesis and Reconstruction of a Field of Legal and Political Expertise at the Crossroads of a Europe Opening to the Atlantic' (2007) 32 *Law & Social Inquiry* 161–81.

the battle with Thatcherism during the 1980s, in this case over civil rights and trade unionism, also started using international—and particularly European—forums to relaunch and revalorise their national strategies. As a byproduct, the integration and institutionalisation of European human rights were accelerated.[46]

These different cases related to the law and politics of Europeanisation more broadly highlight the multiple identities of the key players and how they utilise their positions in multiple—national and international—social fields. Moreover, these findings suggest that international and transnational legal and political constructions such as Europe, to an extent, always remain in the process of reconstruction vis-à-vis the national levels. It is our claim that the many and different processes of European integration are intertwined with these various interests and strategies; in fact, they are very much the by-products of these strategies as well.[47] This argument is both empirical and methodological. It is apparent that such double strategies are less easily played out at the national level where agents, for a number of reasons, are far less mobile in the social structure. International and transnational terrains seem to offer much more versatile social arenas for bypassing both social hierarchies and categories, even after a relatively comprehensive institutionalisation has taken place. Analytically, this offers a unique possibility for examining both the internal and external construction of transnational legal fields by following the practices of key agents of change. Conceptually, it also means that the evolution of international and transnational fields should not be limited simply to the story of the building of institutions and the political interaction of states and increasingly other agents but perhaps instead the story of a particular set of political and legal opportunities, which in some cases eventually resulted in institutions and law.[48]

This particular and obviously deeply sociological view of institutions generally suggests a dynamic approach to transnational fields. It highlights how international and transnational fields from time to time function as catalysts for significant change, changes that would often be entirely politically unachievable on the national level where such strategies are much more constrained by formalised politics and institutional frameworks. However, because of the way in which the entrepreneurs of globalisation tactically pursue the international level, they can occasionally accelerate social changes with great impact on national politics and social configurations. We have mentioned the two examples of European environmental and human rights law and politics. Both provide telling examples of the instigation of such radical shifts through European strategies. The original orthodoxy of environmental regulation of the 1970s and 1980s in terms of control and command was emblematically turned into a very different market regulation of the environment during the 1990s, with the help of industrious agents tactically using the European opportunity; the area of European human rights, in a somewhat comparable way, was used to transform the national legal fields from

---

[46] MR Madsen, 'France, the UK and "Boomerang" of the Internationalization of Human Rights (1945–2000)' in S Halliday and P Schmidt, *Human Rights Brought Home: Socio-Legal Perspectives on Human Rights in the National Context* (Oxford, Hart Publishing, 2004).

[47] See also A Cohen, Y Dezalay and D Marchetti, 'Esprits d'État, entrepreneurs d'Europe' (2007) 166–67 *Actes de la recherche en sciences sociales* 5–13.

[48] The argument is further developed in MR Madsen, 'Sociological Approaches to International Courts' in K Alter, CPR Romano and Y Shany, *Oxford University Press Handbook of International Adjudication* (Oxford, Oxford University Press, forthcoming 2013).

the mid-1980s, with entrepreneurial lawyers and European judges inventing a new European doctrine of human rights that considerably redefined national conceptions of justice in the Member States.[49] This should not be viewed as a phenomenon specific to these two fields of practice but rather as a generalisable feature of transnational fields, which both sets them apart from national fields and explains their salience in contemporary law and politics.

3. IN THE FIELD

As argued above, applying the Bourdieusian conceptual tools—or 'thinking tools'[50]—in many ways requires deploying the underlying idea of reflexive sociology. In practice, this calls for devising actual research strategies that use the insights of the conceptual tools in an actual sociological practice. Thus, very different from the common usage of Bourdieusian sociology in law and society research, which employs a few concepts or uses Bourdieu's work only to theorise on a more general level, we suggest that the real strength of the approach is in its empirical application. This, of course, alludes to a long-standing debate with regard to the general reception of Bourdieu in American sociology,[51] as well as other great French thinkers, notably Michel Foucault. What is certainly lost in translation is the relative uniqueness of French human and social science and its trademark of a combination of heavy theory and extensive empirical research. This does not travel all that well, particularly when it has to fit into pre-existing departmental features of academic life, in which the relative oppositions of quantitative and qualitative research or empirical and theoretical sociology set the boundaries. In view of the approach presented here, these are of course only false dichotomies and institutional limits to genuine scientific inquiry. Bourdieusian reflexive sociology cannot be adequately deployed if it has to fit into such predetermined categories. Instead, it calls for a sociological engagement that is both conceptual and empirical at the very same time—that is, a reflexive engagement with theory, method and empirical data collection as not only interdependent but also mutually constitutive elements of sociological practice. So far we have deployed the approach to discuss theory and empirical findings. In what follows, we resume this analysis of transnational fields with a particular focus on the third element, the actual conduct of such an analysis and its methods.

The previous section generally highlighted how transnational fields, when compared with highly structured national fields, are structurally more ambiguous. This relative ambiguity is the background to the so-called double games in terms of the agents' usage of international or transnational venues to advance national interests—and vice versa. And because of the strategic opportunities offered by international fields

---

[49] MR Madsen, 'The Protracted Institutionalisation of the Strasbourg Court: From Legal Diplomacy to Integrationist Jurisprudence' in MR Madsen and J Christoffersen, *The European Court of Human Rights between Law and Politics* (Oxford, Oxford University Press, 2011) 43–60.

[50] A Leander, 'Thinking Tools: Analyzing Symbolic Power and Violence. Qualitative Methods' in A Klotz and D Prakash (eds), *International Relations: A Pluralist Guide* (Basingstoke, Palgrave Macmillan, 2008) 11–28

[51] M Lamont, 'How Has Bourdieu Been Good to Think With? The Case of the United States' (2012) 27 *Sociological Forum* 228–37.

and institutions, partly the effect of their tendency towards perpetual transformation, the boundaries between law and politics tend to be less strict. This is also central to developing research strategies that can help the researcher gain access to the deeper sociolegal dynamics of the globalisation of law. As the agents in question here often rely on a number of double games, as well as multiple identities, the researcher—if not very carefully tracing these multiple movements—is capable neither of going beyond the very symbolic discourses produced in these interactions nor of escaping them. In the specific case of the sociology of law, there is moreover often an explicit interest in integrating the work of the researcher in these symbolic practices, as many of the entrepreneurs of legal globalisation rely on academic and quasi-academic resources for legitimising their practices. In these social contexts in which the distinctions between political and legal practices are at best vague, the sociologist of law, when seen from the point of view of the agents, provides a perfect object for legitimising weakly institutionalized or legalised practices. This is probably particularly exacerbated in the case of the sociology of law, as the researcher is potentially a catalyst for providing, if not law, then learned legal discourse on these emerging legal structures. In many studies of the globalisation of law, this risk of adapting to discourses of power and legitimacy is not seen as a problem, however. Particularly in the more activist forms of inquiry, the choice of empirical terrain is directly informed by the convergence of scientific and political agendas. Yet, in the sort of approach propounded in this chapter, such a choice poses a real problem, as it essentially conflicts with the underlying aim of establishing a more objectively defined object of inquiry.

The response to this dilemma, which can be drawn from Bourdieu's work, is for the researcher both to follow the agents and their actions in order to empirically document actual movements and to seek to impose a different and scientifically guided agenda. Basically, the researcher has to follow the agents in order to observe what is the alleged core of the game, but at the very same time he or she must also examine and reframe the issues at play by, for example, relating them to the agents' multiple national and international interests. In this reflexive engagement, the sociologist has the advantage that he or she has far greater mobility within the field than the actual agents who by definition are more trapped by their specific position in the field. Closely connected, the sociologist also has the advantage over the agents that he or she can more objectively contrast the positions within the field. The agents' perceptions of the field and its structures are based upon subjective experiences, and they only rarely share the global, structural view of the field that is the sociologist's starting point and ultimate scientific objective. Yet, the many and different accounts being presented throughout the research process provide critical data for interrogating the agents and escaping their neutralizing and naturalizing discourses. But to do so, the sociologist necessarily must take full advantage of his or her mobility in the field. In practice, and very different from the agents' manoeuvring capabilities, the researcher can interview the opposing camps, if not at the same time, then immediately after each other, following a research logic that breaks with the logic of the practices of the respective agents. In fact, it is by following such a zigzag course inside the field that the researcher can fully benefit from the information gained in previous stages of the research process, including knowledge of personal bonds and enmities. What we suggest here is basically to turn the logic of field inside out as a means for deconstructing social practices and reconstructing them in terms of fields.

This more qualitative form of field analysis has been applied in numerous international and transnational settings. A guiding line of inquiry in these studies of transnational fields has been to study the relational networks and personal trajectories of the agents of the fields in question. Yet, these background social structures are used not only to conduct prosopographical analysis but also to explore the underlying battles forming the structures of the field, using agents as the starting point: how are the agents situated in more fields than the ones with which they are immediately identified, and how do they mobilise different capital in each of these different social spheres? These more hidden lines, which are revealed by analysis of the agents' multiple specialisations, provide guidance for moving beyond the dominant—and often naturalised—institutional and categorical structures of the field in question. Take, for example, the fabrication of new legal expertise: notwithstanding the way in which legal expertise is by definition presented as highly differentiated knowledge, its transformation takes place in the margin of official categories or on the frontiers of disciplines. This means that the data needed for understanding such processes of conversion are available only if one challenges the social categories—which are often uncritically applied by the agents themselves—with the goal of reconstructing the socioprofessional battles that have formed them. Such an analysis is feasible only if the researcher has multiple points of departure for retracing and understanding the new social categories as the outcome of both antagonistic positions and subjective bonds. In other words, the described mobility of the researcher within the field is absolutely key to conducting an analysis that is formed both by the oppositions of positions and by their subjective links, such as alliances and networks.

The different research strategies we have briefly outlined all come down to the basic problem of ensuring a scientific autonomy in the engagement with normative discourses—that is, avoiding the sociologist being turned into yet another double agent of globalisation, playing multilevel games. These strategies are all building on the problem we discussed in the opening section of this chapter concerning what Bourdieu framed as the necessity of a 'double rupture'.[52] This scientific ideal, which we refer to here as reflexivity, concerns, as noted, both the subject and the researcher and is, at the end of the day, related to the scientific process of uncovering the agents' (and the researcher's) orientations and predispositions and how these shape their habits vis-à-vis other positions in the field.[53] It thus implies two very closely related actions: first, a critical reflection on the preconstructions that dominate a given subject area; and, second, a self-critique as the means to considering one's own scientific and social assumptions of the subject area. This is not an operation that is done once and for all but is instead an ongoing measure for questioning findings and the way they are gathered. In our research, we have generally used qualitative interview methods for mapping transnational fields. More specifically, we have applied a relational biographical method as a measure for comparing elements of individual trajectories with the aim of bridging them in terms of a field. The approach has enabled us to assess the various resources—forms of networks, competences and capital—that have been critical for creating positions within specific fields. Basically, by following the course by which

---

[52] Bourdieu, Chamboredon and Passeron, above n 12.
[53] P Champagne, R Lenoir, D Merllié and L Pinto, *Initiation á la pratique sociologique* (Paris, Dunod, 1999).

a disputed subject area has been established as a field, these studies have attempted to identify the key points of transformation and how these changes are reflected in the practices and trajectories of the agents: the way the agents have oriented themselves vis-à-vis new opportunities, strategic challenges or simply the increased structuration of a given field. Moreover, the biographies of the players suggest which capital and resources have been brought into play at the different stages of structuration.[54]

It might sound almost like a contradiction in terms, but this approach of assembling the collective relational biographies of a given field is used as a means to examine the field's structural transformations, but as documented in the agents' actual practices. Hence, the agents' practices are studied with regard to their ability to influence the general structuration process of the field. Yet, at the same time, to bridge micro- and macrolevels of analysis, this analysis also explores the flipside of the question— namely how the general social structures of the field are inscribed in the agents' practices. Above all, this empirical usage of agents' trajectories offers a means of decoding the different struggles that have existed at different stages of the historical structuration of the field.[55] This implies a certain emphasis of agents over institutions, as the assumption is that the agents' trajectories provide concrete empirical examples of the different battles related to the build-up of the field and its institutions. Put differently, the agents embody the development of the field: what the agents say and how they say it, to an extent, reveal their position both within and outside the field in terms of social class, political affiliations, etc. However, the method performs not by individual cases but by assembling a cumulative story that can be established by comparing a large number of trajectories within a particular field. It thereby provides the intellectual means for constructing an objectively different account of the field that is not limited by the self-representations of institutions, professions, social movements, etc. Indeed, rather than taking the legal definitions of, for example, institutions as the starting point for their understanding, this approach explores how legal institutions and practices emerged on the basis of the legitimacy of collective entities of agents and their common capital and ideas within broader constraining social structures.[56]

To identify the dynamics of a field by, among other things, mapping it by the means of its collective and relational biography is, in practice, an ongoing attempt at sociological reconstruction and objectivisation. Our emphasis of structures and relations, as revealed through the practices of the agents, has turned out to be particularly useful when analysing fields in which the stakes are very political but typically presented in very different ways by the agents, and perhaps notably legal agents. The more or less fixed standpoints presented by agents involved in many forms of human rights politics are often a real hindrance to a deeper understanding of the field. This is exactly where the outlined methods serve a very clear purpose in terms of addressing the agents' involvement in and around the particular subject, as well as in terms of their multiple identities. By interviewing the agents about their personal trajectories rather than their legal or political involvement, the researcher can assess how they pursue multiple

---

[54] With the term trajectories, we underscore the difference between our approach, which highlights how individual action is greatly constrained and informed by the more objective and structural ordering of fields, and biographic methods, which tend to place more emphasis on specific actions of individuals. cf Bourdieu, above n 36.

[55] Dezalay and Garth, above n 15.

[56] Madsen, above n 11.

strategies, even if they often prefer to present themselves as associated only with a particular stance. This form of analysis cannot be based on singular or individual cases but naturally requires multiple points of entrance to the field if the goal is to challenge the 'officialised' discourses, which for the agents themselves often appear completely naturalised. Our approach basically provides for breaking up the discourse into its many overlapping and even opposing texts and for identifying its cowriters. This echoes the very definition of 'field', as these conflicting narratives reflect the stakes in the field and the agents' positions in the field. The analysis of the field is then carried out by examining the correspondence between the positions (the agents) and the position-takings (the stakes). For the same reasons, the approach is not limited to more politicised spheres of social life but applies across all fields and agents, literally ranging from mercenaries of imperialism to missionaries of the universal.

4. CONCLUSION

As may already be clear, the approach we outline here provides neither empirical nor theoretical shortcuts to understanding transnational fields. Quite on the contrary, it typically implies a very substantial number of interviews if the objective of linking agency and structuration through qualitative interviews in terms of collective relational biographies is to be fulfilled. The major research projects on transnational fields evoked in this chapter have all been rather large in scope and involved between 200 and 400 interviews conducted in numerous international and national settings around the world. In addition, a variety of primary and secondary sources have been used to inform the interviews and provide cross-checking of information. This is, of course, not the only way to apply reflexive sociology in the area of law. Smaller and more contained objects can also be studied using these insights,[57] and more quantitative methods can be deployed.[58] We would nevertheless maintain that the greatest impact of Bourdieusian relational and reflexive thinking is generated when it is deployed to understand complex and dynamic fields that, for instance, involve national and international interplays and exchanges. Transnational legal fields are, as we have argued, almost by nature complex, dynamic and obviously transnational. They simply pose a methodological and theoretical challenge, which most conventional sociolegal research methods fail to meet as they remain constrained by a set of predetermined categories that rest on increasingly inadequate ideas of the national and international. By its non-essentialist search for sociological truth, Bourdieusian reflexive sociology seems, on the contrary, uniquely well suited for conducting such analysis.

Bourdieusian sociology, on a more general level, also seems particularly appropriate for conducting sociological studies of law. Indeed, many of the examples we have introduced by drawing on our studies of transnational fields can equally be applied across a range of subjects in the sociology of law. Because of the powerful socio-

---

[57] Hagan and Levi, above n 9; S Parikh and B Garth, 'Philip Corboy and the Construction of the Plaintiffs' Personal Injury Bar' (2005) 30 *Law & Social Inquiry* 269–304; O Hammerslev, 'The European Union and the United States in Eastern Europe: Two Ways of Exporting Law, Expertise and State Power' in Y Dezalay and B Garth, *Lawyers and the Rule of Law in an Era of Globalization* (London, Routledge, 2011) 134–55.

[58] M Börjesson and D Broady, 'The Social Profile of Swedish Law Students. National Divisions and Transnational Educational Strategies' (2006) 29 *Retfær—Nordic Journal of Law* 80–107.

linguistic mechanisms of law, any attempt at sociological inquiry needs to reflect upon how the officialising and objectivising discourses of law can be challenged. One way to break with legal discourse and the closely related powerful positioning of legal agents that benefit from this sociolegal machinery is through an analysis of the specific historical geneses of law and power. As we have argued, this can be accomplished by inquiring into agendas and games of power as dispositions that reflect positions of power, politics, social class, etc. Considering the generally ambiguous position of the sociology of law in regard to law as both an opponent and a protagonist of legal discourse, we note a particular need for these measures of sociological reflexivity in this area of study. It is easy to point to how the sociology of law has occasionally been the victim of a certain legal bias because of its proximity to legal discourse. Whether this is a result of the institutional set-up of the sociology of law vis-à-vis law faculties and law schools or a path dependence due to the training of sociologists of law remains in itself a key question for sociolegal inquiry. Needless to say, to study the effect of the force of law and lawyers on the sociology of law is an object of study that calls for not only sociological reflexivity but also a sociological framework that has some of the qualities as the one developed by Pierre Bourdieu.

7

Feminist Legal Theory

HARRIET SAMUELS

F EMINIST LEGAL THEORY has absorbed and produced a multiplicity of contradictory and challenging ideas that have subjected feminism and law to an excruciating self-examination. This scrutiny has raised a series of troubling issues including reservations as to whether the category of woman provides an appropriate constituency for feminism.[1] Popular culture has represented feminist activism as redundant, portraying the current era as 'post-feminist', because equality has already been achieved.[2] More recently legal scholars, such as Halley, have suggested that it is time to take a break from feminism in order to explore other theories of sexuality, realities and different political goals.[3] Nevertheless, distinctly feminist critiques of the existing political and legal order have persisted. Feminists disagree on many issues, but as Walby states, 'In spite of differences in emphasis, there is remarkable consensus on the areas of concern to feminists, even at the ostensibly disparate locations of the UN, EU, UK and US.'[4] Doubts about the use of law as a vehicle for change have also been a long-standing theme of feminist legal theory. Smart famously urged feminists to resist the 'siren call of law'.[5] She accused the law of having an over-inflated view of itself, and cautioned against an excessive reliance on legal solutions. Whilst Smart was right to urge feminists to contain their enthusiasm for law reform, this does not diminish the necessity to engage fully with law and its institutions. To neglect law would be to miss the opportunity to develop legal modalities that respond to the needs of women and other marginalised groups. Feminist encounters with law are valuable because they hold it to account for the consequences of its adjudicatory and other processes. Notwithstanding Smart's influence, there is a body of feminist legal scholarship and activism around law reform which has led to the emergence of a set of methodological and conceptual tools that have been used both to critique, and to deploy law to progress feminist aims.[6]

---

[1] J Butler, *Gender Trouble: Feminism and the Subversion of Identity* (London, Routledge, 1990).

[2] Y Tasker and D Negra (eds), *Interrogating Post-Feminism: Gender and the Politics of Popular Culture* (Durham, NC, Duke University Press, 2007).

[3] J Halley, *Split Decisions: How and Why to Take a Break from Feminism* (Princeton, Princeton University Press, 2006) 10.

[4] S Walby, *The Future of Feminism* (Cambridge, Polity, 2011).

[5] C Smart, *Feminism and the Power of Law* (London, Routledge, 1989).

[6] For a recent assesment of the impact of Smart's work on legal feminism, see R Auchmuty and K Van Marle, 'Special Issue: Carol Smart's *Feminism and the Power of Law*' (2012) 20 *Feminist Legal Studies* 65–69.

It is difficult to pin down what makes feminist analysis distinctive. Rather than responding to this task by identifying a common concept of 'woman', or a set of shared experiences or beliefs, Reaume adopts a conceptual approach that concentrates on the theme of exclusion.[7] Her aim in attempting to 'systematize feminist legal scholarship' is to highlight the theoretical connections between a diverse set of feminist critiques, and to explain feminism to those on the outside.[8] Exclusion is used as the 'overarching conceptual frame', because, in her view, feminist jurisprudence is united by its focus on how law directly and indirectly excludes women, and by its competing versions of how women's inclusion might be achieved.[9] Critiques of feminism also tend to centre on its exclusion of groups of women, for example on the basis of race, class and sexuality.[10] This chapter will adopt exclusion as its organising structure to examine feminism's most important methodological tools, which are equalities theory, the private/public binary and the gendering of legal method. Contrary to Halley's call to take a break from feminism, and Smart's over-cautious approach to law, this chapter will stress the significant role feminist lawyers play in providing an ongoing critique of law, and it will take the position that, despite the law's sometimes lacklustre performance in righting gendered harms and progressing equality agendas, the use of the legal apparatus has clear normative and tactical advantages. The contemporary examples, from UK domestic law, will make the empirical case for continued feminist engagement with law by demonstrating that feminist analysis and method can be used simultaneously to uncover exclusion and to struggle for inclusion within the legal frame.

1. ENGAGING WITH EQUALITY

First-wave feminists were understandably preoccupied by their direct exclusion from personhood, and, particularly their inability to vote, stand for Parliament or enter the professions.[11] Their attempts to use the courts to progress their claims were unsuccessful, and the common law failed to realise the potential of the equality principle.[12] The courts maintained women's incapacity by reinforcing assumptions about their nature, citing respect and the need to 'protect' the 'delicate' woman from the burden of public duties such as voting.[13] Most famously Lord Atkinson, in *Roberts v Hopwood*, ridiculed a council's decision to pay men and women an equal minimum wage as based on, 'eccentric principles of socialistic philanthropy, or by a feminist ambition

---

[7] DG Reaume, 'What Is Distinctive about Feminist Analysis (1986) 2 *Legal Theory* 265–99.

[8] Ibid, 269.

[9] Ibid, 279.

[10] Ibid, 273.

[11] The periodic bursts of feminist activism that occurred from the nineteenth century onwards are referred to as waves. This conveys the notion that feminist ideas have vacillated in popularity, but have come to be accepted through a process of slow but persistent progress. See generally R Strachey, *The Cause: A Short History of the Women's Movement in Great Britain* (London, Virago, 1978); C Law, *Suffrage and Power: The Women's Movement 1918–1928* (London, IB Tauris, 1997).

[12] See generally J Jowell, 'Is Equality a Constitutional Principle?' (1994) *Current Legal Problems* 1. For a discussion of the suffragists use of the courts, see generally C Harlow and R Rawlings, *Pressure through Law*, (London, Routledge, 1992) 22.

[13] Per Willes J, *Chorlton v Lings* (1868–69) LR 4 CP 374, 392. See also A Sachs and J Hoff Wilson, *Sexism and the Law: A Study of Male Beliefs and Judicial Bias* (Oxford, Martin Roberstson, 1978) 3.

to secure the equality of the sexes in the matter of wages in the world of labour'.[14] Most legal disabilities were removed incrementally by legislation, in what Fredman has described as a 'slow and conflictual process'.[15]

The use of equality, despite it being a frustratingly contradictory and contrary idea, has been fundamental to the removal of legal disqualifications against women both in domestic and international law.[16] But its usefulness has been limited by conceptual and mechanical constraints. First, equality is premised on the assumption of comparing like with like, and liberal feminists have made extensive use of the *sameness* of women to men to argue for equal treatment. However, finding a relevant male comparator is not always straightforward as is shown by the case law on pregnancy and childbirth.[17] Fitting pregnancy, a state unique to women, within discrimination law epitomises the difficulties of the equalities frame.[18] Second, gender differences rooted in structural factors, such as the burden of family responsibilities and childbirth, raise issues of substantive equality, which have traditionally been poorly addressed by legislation and the courts.[19] Thirdly, implementing equality laws can result in a levelling down, leading to the loss of a benefit or advantageous social conditions counter to the central tenets of feminism, which is to improve the lives of subjects.[20] Feminist thinking on equality has varied, with some feminists attempting to reformulate or strategise equality norms, whilst others have embraced alternative conceptual tools such as capabilities theory. This debate between feminists has provided a rich source of experiential knowledge that has made a vital contribution to the wider debate on equality, and has ensured that women's lived realities are encompassed by any legal reformulations or deployment of the equality principle.

Revising or Rejecting Equality?

In an effort to overcome the difficulties that equality presents, some feminists have rejected the idea of equality as sameness, and instead stressed women's different qualities to men. The debate regarding difference and sameness has preoccupied at least one generation of feminists.[21] Difference feminism is premised on the work of Gilligan whose research led her to the conclusion that women had a 'different voice' to men.[22]

---

[14] Per Lord Atkinson in *Roberts v Hopwood* [1925] AC 578, 592.

[15] S Fredman, *Women and the Law* (Oxford, Oxford University Press, 1997) 95.

[16] See key domestic laws such as the Equal Pay Act 1970 and the Sex Discrimination Act 1975, and international instruments such as the Convention on the Elimination of All Forms of Discrimination against Women (CEDAW) that are grounded in the principles of equality and non-discrimination.

[17] The lack of a male comparator meant that pregnancy was initially excluded as a form of discrimination (*Turley v Allders* [1980] ICR 66), then seen as comparable with sickness (*Hayes v Malleable Working Men's Club* [1985] ICR 703), and finally declared, by the European Court of Justice, to be sex discrimination (*Webb v EMO Air Cargo (UK) Ltd* [1994] ECR I-3567). Pregnancy is now considered a protected characteristic in accordance with s 149 of the Equalities Act 2010. See generally G James, *The Legal Regulation of Pregnancy and Parenting in the Labour Market* (London, Routledge, 2009).

[18] CA MacKinnon, *Sexual Harassment of Working Women* (New Haven, Yale University Press, 1979) 104.

[19] See generally Fredman, above n 15, 283.

[20] Ibid, 357.

[21] For an overview of the sameness/difference debate, see H Barnett, *Sourcebook on Feminist Jurisprudence* (London, Cavendish, 1997) 161–274; DW Weisberg (ed), *Feminist Legal Theory* (Philadelphia, Temple University Press, 1993) 121–320.

[22] C Gilligan, *In a Different Voice* (Cambridge, MA, Harvard University Press, 1982).

Her psychological experiments, which tested children's responses to moral dilemmas, led her to challenge the then prevailing orthodoxy that boys had a superior capacity for reason.[23] She found that female decision-making was more likely to be based on an 'ethic of care' characterised by context, and the importance of preserving relationships.[24] This was juxtaposed with the 'ethic of justice' used by the boys, whose reasoning was based on autonomy, hierarchy and a more absolute sense of right and wrong. [25] Her research was a springboard, for some feminists, to highlight women's difference from men rather than their sameness.[26] However, there is a rich literature analysing Gilligan's work. The main criticisms are that the 'ethic of care' simply reflects cultural constructions rather than innate differences, reinforces stereotypes of women, as in need of protection, and exaggerates the uniformity of the female experience and voice.[27] Despite the flaws in difference feminism it remains an important school of feminist thought challenging the existing order, and acting as a reminder that that there are alternative methods of reasoning.[28] It also draws attention to many traditional female activities, and demands that they are made visible and appropriately valued.[29]

Mackinnon is particularly scathing about the utility of both the difference and sameness equality frames, believing that neither disrupts the gender order. She argues that it is impossible to know the extent of women's sameness or difference in a world that is dominated by men.[30] In an oft-quoted passage she states that:

> [M]an has become the measure of all things. Under the sameness rubric, women are measured according to correspondence with man, their equality judged by proximity to his measure. Under the difference rubric, women are measured according to their lack of correspondence from man.'[31]

Using what she calls the dominance theory, she argues that inequalities must be seen from the standpoint of women, the subordinate group, and that the purpose of equalities law should be to bring about a change in the gender hierarchy.[32] For her the route out of the sameness/difference trap is through the 'inequality approach' whereby,

> [a] rule or practice is discriminatory ... if it participates in the systemic social deprivation of one sex because of sex. The only question for litigation is whether the policy or practice in question integrally contributes to the maintenance of an underclass or a deprived position because of gender status.[33]

---

[23] Ibid, 19.

[24] Ibid, 19.

[25] Ibid, 171–74.

[26] R West, 'Jurisprudence and Gender' (1988) *University of Chicago Law Review* 1. See also M Drakopoulou, 'The Ethic of Care, Female Subjectivity and Feminist Legal Scholarship' (2000) 8 *Feminist Legal Studies* 199

[27] CA MacKinnon, *Feminism Unmodified: Discourses on Life and Law* (Cambridge, MA, Harvard University Press, 1987) 39; L Segal, *Is the Future Female* (London, Virago, 1987) 148.

[28] See eg M Minow, *Making All the Difference: Inclusion, Exclusion and American Law* (Ithaca, NY, Cornell University Press, 1990).

[29] See eg M Waring, *Counting for Nothing: What Men Value and What Women Are Worth* (Wellington, Allen & Unwin, 1986).

[30] CA MacKinnon, *Towards a Feminist Theory of the State* (Cambridge, MA, Harvard University Press, 1989) 51.

[31] Ibid, 220.

[32] Mackinnon, above n 27, 43.

[33] CA MacKinnon, *Sexual Harassment of Working Women* (New Haven, Yale University Press 1979) 117.

So being deprived of a benefit because of pregnancy, for instance, is discrimination not because a woman is being treated less favourably than a man. It is because there is no justification for a practice that systematically disadvantages women. For MacKinnon equality must work to remedy domination and hierarchy, and so discrimination exists if there are 'comparatively unequal results'. [34]

MacKinnon's dominance theory has been widely critiqued for its essentialism. She is accused of presenting women as having a universally fixed essence or innate character.[35] Her location of women's commonality in a set of shared experiences of oppression is regarded as deeply problematic.[36] As Harris explains, this means that, 'in the description of the experiences of "women" issues of race, class and sexual orientation can therefore be safely ignored or relegated to footnotes'.[37]

One way of understanding the complexities of multiple forms of discrimination is through the notion of intersectionality.[38] This was posited, by Crenshaw, as a method with the potential to address the marginalisation of minority women whose intersectional identities, as women of colour, mean they are failed by the discourses of race and sex discrimination.[39] Intersectionality scrutinises the interaction of the category of sex with other grounds of discrimination such as race, sexuality, age, etc. For feminists this approach appears a useful antidote to the problem of essentialism. It draws attention to the law's insistence that discrimination is read through predetermined categories, which sometimes fail to capture the experience of certain types of discrimination.[40] The increase in the number of, and conflicts between, the grounds of discrimination, and the creation of a single equalities commission has made the concept of intersectionality particularly prescient.[41] However, Conaghan in her analysis of intersectionality and the feminist project concludes that, although intersectionality does valuable analytical work, it fails to get to grips with a more material analysis of what generates inequalities, and the systems that produce them.[42] Ultimately, it does not provide a means of challenging inequality and thus fails to measure up to the larger feminist project of engendering social transformation.

Nussbaum's theory of capability moves further away from equality as a goal for feminists and instead uses the measure of human capability. Drawing on economist Amartya Sen's theory, she refocuses feminist energies on developing a set of 'human functional capabilities' that are necessary to lead a dignified life as a human being.[43]

---

[34] Ibid, 118.

[35] See generally on essentialism, J Conaghan, 'Reassessing the Feminist Theoretical Project in Law' (2000) *JLS* 27

[36] W Brown, *States of Injury; Power and Freedom in Late Modernity* (Princeton, Princeton University Press, 1995) 131.

[37] A Harris, 'Race and Essentialism in Feminist Theory' in AK Wing (ed), *Critical Race Feminism: A Reader* (New York, New York University Press, 1997) 11–18, 13.

[38] J Conaghan, 'Intersectionality and the Feminist Project in Law' in E Grabham, DCooper, J Krishnadas and D Herman (eds), *Intersectionality and Beyond: Law, Power and the Politics of Location* (Oxford, Glasshouse, 2009) 21–48.

[39] K Crenshaw, 'Mapping the Margins: Intersectionality, Identity Politics, and Violence against Women of Color' (1991) 43 *Stanford Law Review* 1241, 1244.

[40] S Hannett, 'Equality at the Intersections: The Legislative and Judicial Failure to Tackle Multiple Discrimination' (2003) 23 *Oxford Journal of Legal Studies* 65.

[41] For a discussion of intersectionality in the context of the UK, see J Conaghan, 'Intersectionality and UK Equality Initiatives' (2007) 23 *South African Journal of Human Rights* 316.

[42] Conaghan, above n 38

[43] MC Nussbaum, *Sex and Social Justice* (Oxford, Oxford University Press, 1999) 42.

These go beyond identifying the necessary elements for human functioning, and are requirements for human flourishing without which there cannot be a 'good human life'. Ensuring these basic capabilities provides women with the autonomy to make choices about how they live. Human capabilities exert a moral claim on policymakers who must concentrate on ensuring that as many people as possible achieve these thresholds.[44] According to Nussbaum, the definition of human capabilities is such that it is much harder to deny women personhood, or basic capabilities, on the grounds of stereotypical characteristics. There are many varied analysis of Nussbaum's theory, but perhaps the most important feminist repost comes from Phillips.[45] She acknowledges that capability theory may be an effective way to 'eliminate global poverty' and that 'focusing on a minimum is good practical politics'.[46] But she is disturbed by the move away from the equality discourse.[47] Although inequality will often be counted as a capability failure its elimination is no longer a priority, and there is no relational measure. Once the capability threshold has been achieved there may still be remaining inequalities of power and resources based on sex.[48]

There are numerous feminist theories on equality, and capability theory is not the only attempt to suggest a different aim for feminists. Munro, for example, maintains that equality should only be regarded as a first step towards feminist success, and that respect should provide an alternative, moral idea that focuses on individual realities, needs and interests.[49] By contrast, Cooper regards equality as a 'foundational political principle', but she suggests that the objective should be equality of power. This would ensure that everyone had equal power, to exert pressure across society, through discourse, use of resources and within institutions.[50] This lack of consensus between feminists on the meaning of equality, and its value as an organising principle, has not deterred activists and policymakers from relying on it as a mechanism to produce social inclusion. This is particularly apparent in the development of the practice of gender mainstreaming that will be considered below.

Strategising Equality?

Mainstreaming represents an attempt to advance an equalities agenda without a commitment to any one type of equality. It is a strategy that has been adopted at domestic, European and international levels. Mainstreaming requires the 'analysis of

---

[44] MC Nussbaum, 'Human Capabilities, Female Human Beings' in MC Nussbaum and J Glover (eds), *Women, Culture and Development: A Study of Human Capability* (Oxford, Oxford University Press, 1995) 60–104, 88.

[45] A Phillips, 'Feminism and Liberalism Revisited: Has Martha Nussbaum got it Right?' (2001) 8 *Constellations* 249.

[46] Ibid, 259.

[47] For other feminist discussions of capability theory, see S Mullally, *Gender, Culture and Human Rights: Reclaiming Universalism* (Oxford, Hart Publishing, 2006) 59–68; K Van Marle '"The Capabilities Approach", "The Imaginary Domain" and "Asymmetrical Reciprocity" Feminist Perspectives on Equality and Justice' (2003) *Feminist Legal Studies* 255.

[48] Van Marle, ibid, 264.

[49] V Munro, *Law and Politics at the Perimeter: Re-evaluating Key Debates in Feminist Theory* (Oxford, Hart Publishing, 2007) 141.

[50] D Cooper, '"And You Can't Find Me Nowhere": Relocating Identity and Structure with Equality Jurisprudence' (2000) 77 *Journal of Legal Studies* 249, 255.

all policies for their gender impacts, and … calls for nothing short of the wholesale transformation of the institutions and processes of government'.[51] There are various models of mainstreaming reflecting different views of governance. However, all modes adopt a broad view of inequality and its causes, and are not limited by the legal language of discrimination. Mainstreaming does not resolve the sameness/difference or the substantive/formal equality debate, but renders it less urgent. This is because it emphasises empirical knowledge, and stresses the impact of policies on the everyday lives of individuals and communities rather than a concern with the type of equality in question.[52] It has also been suggested that mainstreaming makes 'equality a value to be represented at all times and in all activities', but it does not regard equality as 'an end in itself'.[53] It also represents a shift from individualistic and fault-based discrimination laws towards an attempt to embed equality in institutions and processes.[54] One of the most significant legal manifestations of mainstreaming has been the introduction of the equalities duty, which imposes positive obligations on public authorities to eliminate discrimination and advance equality.[55] The Equalities Act 2010, an initiative of the New Labour government, consolidated the equalities duties in the various antidiscrimination statutes, and extended its remit to all the protected characteristics covered by the legislation.[56] Fredman has described the equalities duties as changing 'the whole landscape of discrimination law. The focus is no longer on the perpetrator of a discriminatory act. Instead the spotlight is on the body in the best position to promote equality. Individual fault becomes irrelevant.'[57] However, although the equalities duty is a welcome measure it has significant drawbacks. The legislation requires only that the public authority pay 'due regard' to the need to promote equality in carrying out its functions. This is a relatively weak formulation compared with alternatives that would have required the authority to take all proportionate steps, or to achieve particular results.[58] There are some indications, from the case law, that the equalities duty is in danger of becoming a procedural requirement fulfilled by box-ticking, with the courts adopting a light-touch approach in judicial review cases. [59]

Walby has described the introduction of institutional structures within government,

---

[51] F Beveridge and S Nott, 'Mainstreaming: A Case for Optimism and Cynicism' (2002) *Feminist Legal Studies* 299, 302. See also T Rees, 'Mainstreaming Equality' in S Watson and L Doyal (eds), *Engendering Social Policy* (Buckingham, Open University Press, 1999) 165–83.

[52] Beveridge and Nott, ibid, 306.

[53] F Beveridge, S Nott and K Stephen, 'Moving Forward with Mainstreaming' in F Beveridge, S Nott and K Stephen (eds), *Making Women Count: Integrating Gender into Law and Policy Making* (Aldershot, Ashgate, 2000) 277–85, 278.

[54] Ibid, 277.

[55] The first equalities duty in the UK was s 71 of the Race Relations Act 1976. The aim was to tackle 'institutional racism' of the kind that was identified in the police force by the Macpherson Inquiry. This was set up to investigate the failures of the criminal justice system in the racist murder of Stephen Lawrence (Home Office, *Report of the Macpherson Inquiry*, Cmnd 4262, 24 February 1999). It was followed by the gender and disability equalities duties in s 76 of the Sex Discrimination Act 1975 and the Disability Discrimination Act 1995.

[56] S 149 of the Equalities Act 2010. The protected characteristics are age, disability, gender reassignment, marriage and civil partnership, pregnancy and maternity, race, religion or belief, sex and sexual orientation.

[57] S Fredman, *Discrimination Law* (Oxford, Oxford University Press, 2011) 302.

[58] S Fredman, 'The Public Sector Equality Duty' (2011) 40 *Industrial Law Journal* 405, 405.

[59] See generally M Bell, 'Judicial Enforcement of the Duties on Public Authorities to Promote Equality' (2010) *PL* 672, 685; H Mountfield, 'Public Sector Equality Duties: The Case Law' (2012) 225 *Equal Opportunities Review* 7, 9.

as installing feminist machinery or architecture.[60] She includes, as examples, the establishment of national bodies such as the Equality and Human Rights Commission.[61] The equalities duties can be similarly conceptualised as a type of legal architecture or machinery that provides a structure to progress equality. It has been used as a tool by feminists, and others, to try to prevent cuts in public expenditure, and has more recently been used to challenge the UK coalition government's austerity agenda.[62] Prior to the introduction of the Equalities Act 2010, Southall Black Sisters (SBS), a feminist group providing services to Asian and Afro-Caribbean women suffering domestic violence, mounted a successful challenge using one of the precursors to the current equalities duty, section 71 of the Race Relations Act 1976.[63] SBS disputed a policy change by Ealing Council, which terminated SBS's funding because the authority had decided to provide for a single service provider to help victims of domestic violence throughout the borough. The authority's failure to conduct an impact assessment on black and minority women before making this decision was held to breach the race equality duty. The case is noteworthy for several reasons. First, it demonstrates how the equality duty can be used to ensure that equality issues are considered when policy is formulated in line with the principles of mainstreaming. Second, SBS's strategy was to deploy an intersectional approach, which required the Council to acknowledge the specific experience of minority women when seeking help for domestic violence. Hence SBS contended that, '[I]ssues of racism, culture, language and immigration status ... make the task of accessing services much harder ... for black and minority women.'[64] Third, the court adopted a flexible view of equality, and rejected the proposition that community cohesion required providing a uniform service to the whole area. Moses LJ agreed with SBS that 'specialist services are more effective in empowering minority women so that they can take their place in the wider society'.[65]

By contrast, the unsuccessful attempt of the Fawcett Society to challenge the budget demonstrates the limitations of the equalities duty.[66] The backdrop for the decision was the austerity budget introduced, by the UK coalition government, in 2010. The cuts in public expenditure, intended to reduce the deficit, were said to have disproportionately disadvantaged women.[67] The Fawcett Society's argument was that, in drafting the budget, there had been a failure to have due regard to the gender equality duty and that the government should have conducted an equality audit.[68] The dispute centred on the procedures by which the duty was dealt with. The court declined to accept arguments based on statistical methods, the timing of the gender impact assessment,

---

[60] Walby, above n 4, 58.

[61] Ibid, 59.

[62] C Annesley, 'Campaigning against the Cuts: Gender Equality Movements in Tough Times' (2012) 83 *Political Quarterly* 19.

[63] *R (on the application of Kaur and Shah) v London Borough of Ealing* [2008] EWHC 2062.

[64] Ibid, para 34.

[65] Ibid, para 54.

[66] *R (on the application of the Fawcett Society) v Chancellor of the Exchequer* CO/8217/2010 (unreported). The Fawcett Society (www.fawcettsociety.org.uk) describes itself as a leading campaign group for equality between men and women. It traces its origins back to 1868 and the work of the suffragist Millicent Garrett Fawcett.

[67] Fawcett Society, *The Impact of Austerity on Women* (Fawcett Society, March 2012); MA Stephenson, *Women and the Cuts Toolkit: How to Carry Out a Human Rights and Equality Impact Assessment of the Spending Cuts on Women* (Trades Union Congress, 2011).

[68] S 76A Sex Discrimination Act 1975 inserted a gender equalities duty into the sex discrimination legislation. This duty is now contained in s 149 Equalities Act 2010. See above n 56.

and the failure to consider the overall effect of the budget on women. In refusing the Fawcett Society permission to proceed with the judicial review the judge highlighted that parts of the budget had been implemented and that any remedy would now be academic. Although the case demonstrates the boundaries of the equalities duty and its procedural character it did establish that the gender equality duty does apply to 'government action such as the preparation and presentation of the budget, including public expenditure limits'.[69] At a minimum the equalities duty has the potential to ensure that equalities issues are mainstreamed into policy at a high level of government decision-making. Whilst it would be wrong to claim too much for the legislation, it does at least require authorities to explain what consideration they have given to equality, and thus include it as part of the decision-making process. However, the coalition government has announced a review of the duty as part of its 'red tape challenge' to reduce 'unnecessary bureaucracy'.[70] This discourse depicts antidiscrimination measures in conflict with the aims of efficiency in government and business, and thus as impediments to swift decision-making and growth. Despite its defects, the repeal of the duty would be a retrograde step and would turn the clock back on the progress that has been made in mainstreaming equality.[71]

Equality continues to be a key conceptual mechanism for progressive politics and remains an important mechanism for highlighting exclusion. Whilst feminism, as a social movement, may elicit opposition notions of equality are central to public discourse and have political purchase.[72] However, there is little public consensus on the meaning of equality, the extent to which it has been achieved and what is required of the law to attain social inclusion. There is much at stake here for feminists as a conclusion that gender equality has been achieved runs the risk that progress will be stultified. Feminists need to participate fully in the political and legal conversations on equality to influence the debate, and prevent the dismantling of the equalities architecture. In practice, feminists, despite their divergent views, have adopted a pragmatic stance towards equality, and have wisely used whatever version of equality is most likely to ensure women are included in the legal and political frame.[73]

2. THE PUBLIC/PRIVATE DICHOTOMY

Feminists have identified law's separation of the private and the public as a significant cause of the exclusion of many of women's interests from the law. There is a prolific feminist legal literature that documents how this binary served to dismiss whole areas of female life from the ambit of law.[74] The public sphere was traditionally perceived

---

[69] Per Ouseley J. Above n 56, para 6.

[70] See the statement of the Home Secretary, Theresa May, in the House of Commons, 15 May 2012, Hansard 29WS.

[71] For the terms of reference for the review see www.homeoffice.gov.uk/equalities/equality-act/equality-duty/equality-duty-review/terms-of-reference/

[72] K Aune and C Redfern, *Reclaiming the F Word: The New Feminist Movement* (London, Zed Books, 2010) 5.

[73] J Squires, 'Is Mainstreaming Transformative? Theorising Mainstreaming in the Context of Diversity and Deliberation' (2005) 12 *Social Policy* 366.

[74] See the account given by K O'Donovan, *Sexual Divisions in the Law* (London, Weidenfeld & Nicolson, 1985).

as peopled by men, whereas the domestic sphere was the domain of women. As Thornton states, the public sphere is 'represented as the sphere of rationality, culture and intellectual endeavour, whereas the domestic sphere has been represented as the sphere of nature, nurture, and non rationality'.[75] Second-wave feminist activity focused not only on women's unequal treatment in the public spheres of work and politics, but also on the failure of the law to intervene in the private sphere of home and family, and thus on its failure to prevent or redress harms perpetrated against women. The lack of redress against violence in the home, and the fact that rape in marriage was not criminalised until 1991, exemplified the disadvantages that arose from the public/private binary.[76] Similarly the assumption that employees would enter the public world of work devoid of responsibility for the care of children or the elderly has also been attributed to liberalism's public/private divide. However, there are limitations to this analysis. It over-emphasises the power of the state, the division between the two spheres is blurred and analytical accounts tend to reinforce rather than transcend the binary.[77] In addition, the private sphere can, on some occasions, provide an important space for privacy and autonomy, which have been helpful conceptual tools in the forging of principles, protecting sexual and bodily self-determination.[78] However, the public/private dichotomy has been a staple of feminist method, and still does important work, in a wide range of areas, in drawing attention to the relationship between different spheres and how they are formed. It has helped to shift rigid mind-sets, and ensured that caring responsibilities for children, the elderly and the disabled have entered the political agenda—for example in workplace settings it has become more difficult to 'hide the family from the market'.[79] To this extent the analysis of the public/private binary complements notions of substantive equality, which demand that structural obstacles to discrimination are acknowledged. As the contemporary examples given below show, it continues to be an important frame of analysis when conceptualised as a space with shifting and temporal boundaries.

Forced Marriage

The debate on legal responses to violence against women, such as forced marriage and so-called 'honour killings' within minority communities, have reflected feminist ambivalence towards the role of law.[80] Relying on a second-wave feminist analysis of violence against women, the state's initial failure to acknowledge such wrongs, mainly affecting women, can be depicted as the reluctance, typical of the liberal state, to take

---

[75] M Thornton, 'The Cartography of Public and Private' in M Thornton (ed), *Public and Private: Feminist Legal Debates* (Melbourne, Oxford University Press, 1995) 2–16, 13.

[76] *R v R* [1991] 4 All ER 481. For a discussion of the debate on criminalising marital rape, see S Atkins and B Hoggett, *Women and the Law* (Oxford, Basil Blackwell, 1984) 72–74.

[77] See especially N Lacey, *Unspeakable Subjects: Feminist Essays in Legal and Social Theory* (Oxford, Hart Publishing, 1998) 82–86.

[78] K Engle, 'After the collapse of the Public/Private Distinction: Strategizing Women's Rights' in D Dallmeyer (ed), *Reconceiving Reality: Women and International Law* (Washington DC, American Society of International Law, 1993).

[79] Fredman, above n 15, 17.

[80] A forced marriage is a marriage into which one party enters not only without her or his free and full consent, but also as a result of force including coercion by threats or by other psychological means: s 63A(4) of the Family Law Act 1996 as amended by the Forced Marriage Civil Protection Act 2007.

seriously a form of violence that occurs within the family home. Grafted onto this there is alleged to be a hesitation, by law enforcement agencies, to intervene for fear of being perceived as racist, and showing disrespect to religious groups or minority cultures.[81] One reaction to this problem has been to lobby the state to identify such wrongs, and the feminist movement has been instrumental in pressing national governments and international bodies to adopt strategies to tackle violence against women. Such approaches are not without criticism. Postcolonial feminists have questioned the focus on violence against women, arguing that it reinforces gender and cultural stereotypes of women as victims of their own culture, and invites unhelpful reactionary interventions by the state.[82] Razak relies on this analysis to disapprove of the introduction of coercive laws to deal with forced marriage, arguing that such laws make minority women hypervisible.[83] For Razak, the use of the law is intrusive and mired in racist beliefs that reinforce notions of Western cultural superiority vis-à-vis supposed primitive medieval-style communities. From this perspective, laws on forced marriage are a means of regulation of minority families by a state that is intent on surveying and disciplining them, making it more difficult for women to challenge patriarchal violence.[84] Initially, in the United Kingdom, feminists took a cautious stance towards law reform on forced marriage, and laws were introduced that provided civil remedies, such as injunctions, rather than the introduction of criminal sanctions.[85] Activists welcomed the 'victim-centred' approach, which made forced marriage a civil wrong and made it easier to obtain preventative civil protection orders. But there were still concerns that the law tended to characterise forced marriage as a cultural issue rather than perceiving it as a form of domestic violence.[86] Razak's warnings that the state's interest in minority communities is not benign continue to resonate. There are plans to criminalise forced marriage despite long-standing reservations that this will not improve the situation of victims.[87] And there have also been attempts by government to use immigration laws to restrict the granting of marriage visas where one of the parties to the marriage is under 21 on the grounds that this would deter marriages that were not genuine.[88]

The forced marriage debate demonstrates that the private/public frame has the potential to reveal inequalities and hidden harms. The problem identified is that the private space of family and culture can combine together to create an area where

---

[81] H Siddique '"There Is No Honour in Domestic Violence Only Shame!" Women's Struggles against "Honour" Crimes in the UK' in L Welchman and S Hossein (eds), *Honour: Crimes, Paradigms, and Violence against Women* (London, Zed Books, 2005) 263–81, 270.

[82] R Kapur, 'The Tragedy of Victimization Rhetoric: Resurrecting the "Native" Subject in International/Post-colonial Feminist Legal Politics' (2003) *Harvard Human Rights Journal* 1.

[83] S Razack, 'Imperilled Muslim Women, Dangerous Muslim Men and Civilised Europeans' (2004) 12 *Feminist Legal Studies* 129.

[84] Ibid, 167.

[85] See the Forced Marriage Civil Protection Act 2007.

[86] S Anitha and A Gill, 'Coercion, Consent and the Forced Marriage Debate in the UK' (2009) 17 *Feminist Legal Studies* 165, 168.

[87] Home Office, *Forced Marriage—A Consultation: Summary of Responses*, June 2012, Statement of the Prime Minister on Forced Marriage, 8 June 2012. See also the critique by N Pearce and A Gill, 'Criminalising Forced Marriage through Stand-alone Legislation: Will it Work?' (2012) *Family Law* 534.

[88] But see *R (on the application of Quila) v Secretary of State for the Home Department* [2011] UKSC 45. The Supreme Court granted a declaration of incompatibility under s 4 of the Human Rights Act holding that raising the age for marriage migration from 18 to 21 was a disproportionate interference with the right to a family life in Art 8 of the Convention.

violence may be perpetrated with impunity. But the danger in advocating legal intervention is that the state's motive for intrusion, in this space, is not solely to provide
protection against violence. It co-opts feminist concerns for its own ends, which are
not necessarily beneficial to women. Feminists have been willing to support some legal
measures, but other approaches, especially those involving criminal sanctions and
immigration controls, have produced a more mixed reaction.[89] Any feminist response
to issues of forced marriage must be contextual, recognising that in some circumstances legal intervention is necessary, but that the state has its own agenda and that
regulation may end up hurting those it is intended to benefit.

Privatisation

The public/private divide has also been sufficiently pliable to contribute to an analysis
of the gendered impact of the privatisation of public services. Here the binary has been
used to designate the market as a 'private' place free of the regulation and bureaucracy
of the state. Once issues and interests are labelled as private they become matters for
economics and the market, and must, according to the logic of neoliberalism, be less
encumbered by the kind of regulation and obligation that governs the state and its
organs.[90] This accounts for some of the resistance towards equality legislation, which
is seen as an unnecessary fetter on the market. Scrutiny of the public/private boundary
has become more pressing, as the liberal state has been reconfigured to divest itself
of many of its functions. As it transfers responsibility for the provision of services
to the private sector, there has been a recasting of the relationship between the state,
the family and the market.[91] Feminist method is well placed to probe the changes, in
the gendered order, brought about by this restructuring.[92] The law has been instrumental in bringing about this transition whilst simultaneously being a site of conflict
between different interests. One example of this is the dispute that has occurred over
the definition of a public authority in section 6(3)(b) of the Human Rights Act 1998.
The courts' delineation of the boundary between a public and private authority is
crucial in determining whether an individual can claim the protection of the European
Convention on Human Rights in domestic law. A feminist analysis of the landmark
decision of the House of Lords in *YL v Birmingham City Council* demonstrates how
the court's reasoning prioritised the interests of the market over those of the vulnerable
claimant.[93] Here the majority decided that the care home, a private company looking
after residents under a contract with the local authority, was not a public authority
even though the latter had a statutory responsibility to provide care. The court drew

---

[89] Opinions amongst women's groups diverge as to whether forcing someone to marry should become
a criminal offence. Most feminist groups are against criminalisation. See A Gill, 'Exploring the Vability
of Creating a Specific Offence of Forced Marriage in England and Wales, Report of Findings', July 2011,
University of Roehampton, www.avaproject.org.uk/media/68857/forced-marriage-legislation-survey-report-
of-findings_gill_13july_final.pdf, 30.

[90] N Fraser, *Justice Interruptus: Critical Reflections on the 'PostSocialist' Condition* (New York, Routledge, 1997) 88.

[91] B Crossman and J Fudge (eds), *Privatization, Law and the Challenge to Feminism* (Toronto, University
of Toronto Press, 2002) 4.

[92] Ibid, 5

[93] *YL v Birmingham City Council* [2007] UKHL 27.

the boundary in a way that distinguished between the responsibility to provide care (a public function of the local authority) and the provision of care (a private function). It failed to consider the purpose of the Human Rights Act in protecting rights, used the floodgates argument, and fretted about the burden that compliance with the Human Rights Act would have on the commercial entity. The consequence was that the claimant, an 84-year-old woman who suffered from Alzheimer's disease, could not argue that the termination of her lease by the care home was a breach of her rights under Article 8 of the European Convention on Human Rights.[94] The feminist scrutiny of the judgment highlights how the interest of commercial contractors were privileged over those of YL and her family, and underscores how demarcating the boundary so narrowly relegated the claimant's interests to the periphery.[95]

To sum up, the public/private binary remains a useful analytical tool. It has the capacity to identify areas of exclusion, even when its boundaries are in a state of flux or have acquired new dimensions. It has, more generally, been pivotal in alerting feminists to the value-laden nature of legal categories. The profoundly political distinction as to which matters are public and which are private is still masked by law's claim to objectivity. The benefit of a feminist analysis is that it constantly precipitates a series of inquiries that encourages a critical examination of who participates in the drawing of the boundaries, who are disadvantaged by them and how far they reinscribe gendered or other hierarchies?

3. FEMINIST LEGAL METHOD

One strand of feminist scholarship has turned its attention to the legal process by which issues are defined, facts selected as pertinent, and principles, precedents and ideas deemed relevant or irrelevant by the courts.[96] It has exposed the gendered and partial nature of legal method as historically shaped, and administered by male lawyers and judges. Mossman's seminal article on legal method stresses that it is not sufficient to include women's experience in law or to discuss feminist approaches to legal problems. She writes that 'legal method is structured in such a way that it is impervious to a feminist perspective'.[97] She exhorts feminists to confront and question the barriers posed by legal method. Feminist lawyers have responded to this by trying to cultivate alternative legal techniques, and by working within the norms of traditional legal adjudication, they have suggested how the law might resolve legal disputes by the use of feminist principles. The benefit of this type of feminist engagement is that it fosters change from inside the legal domain by revising the legal apparatus to ensure that it takes account of gender and other categories.

---

[94] Lord Scott, paras 27–32, Lord Neuberger, paras 145–70 and Lord Mance, paras 111–23. Lord Bingham and Lady Hale dissented, holding that the care home was a public authority. Parliament subsequently reversed the decision in relation to care homes in s 141(1) of the Health and Social Care Act 2008. But the principles in YL are still good authority for interpreting s 6(3)b of the Human Rights Act.

[95] See H Carr and C Hunter, 'YL v Birmingham City Council and Others' in R Hunter, C McGlynn and E Rackley (eds), *Feminist Judgments: From Theory to Practice* (Oxford, Hart Publishing, 2010) 311–28; M McDermont, 'YL v Birmingham City Council-Commentary' in Hunter et al, ibid, 311–17, 313.

[96] MJ Mossman, 'Feminism and Legal Method: The Difference it Makes' (1987) 147 *Wisconsin Women's Law Journal* 147, 149.

[97] Ibid, 165.

Bartlett's work provides the starting point for any discussion of feminist legal method. She includes asking the woman question and feminist practical reasoning as part of her methodology. Asking the woman question involves striving to understand the gendered meaning of rules, their nuances and implications.[98] It also includes feminist practical reasoning, which requires that principles be applied in context and that the impacts of decisions, particularly on the marginalised, are considered carefully. Judges are encouraged to do justice to the parties in the case before them rather than abdicate responsibility by applying abstract rules. As Bartlett states, it focuses on 'real life dilemmas posed by human conflict … that more abstract forms of legal reasoning often tend to gloss over'.[99] In attempting to contextualise decisions judges should be open to reasoning from other disciplines beyond law and to feminist legal scholarship.[100] They should also be receptive to the evolving equality and human rights norms of international law and other jurisdictions. The feminist emphasis on equality endorses doctrines that emphasise 'looking to the bottom' or the 'antidisadvantage principle' whereby the court takes on the task of safeguarding the interests of the disadvantaged.[101] There is an understanding that decision-making can never be totally free of politics, or moral considerations, and that to achieve greater transparency judges must be explicit in their reasoning, giving the real reasons for their decision.[102] The application of feminist legal method has been explored, in depth, by the feminist judgments project. Feminist scholars rewrote key judgments in order to demonstrate the existence of alternative judicial paradigms. Rather than engage in critical commentary the purpose was to illustrate that within the boundaries of current legal reasoning alternative conclusions, which were more gender sensitive, could have been achieved.[103]

Although the majority of the judges, in the higher courts, are male, there have been a number of significant female appointments to the bench including, in the United Kingdom, Lady Hale to the Supreme Court.[104] She has applied some of the techniques, discussed above, in her judgments, producing outcomes that are more egalitarian and contextual.[105] There has been no empirical study of the case law in which she has been involved, but there are two recent cases that provide pertinent instances of a feminist style of judgment writing. In *Yemshaw v London Borough of Hounslow*[106] the Supreme Court had to decide whether the word 'violence' in section 177(1) of the Housing Act 1996 meant physical contact, or whether it included other

[98] KT Bartlett, 'Feminist Legal Methods' (1990) 103 *Harvard Law Review* 829.
[99] Ibid, 850.
[100] M Minow, 'Justice Engendered' in P Smith (ed), *Feminist Jurisprudence* (Oxford, Oxford University Press, (1993) 217–42, 238.
[101] R Colker, 'Section 1, Contextuality and the the Anti Disadvantage Principle' (1992) 42 *University of Toronto Law Journal* 77, 86; MJ Matsuda, 'Looking to the Bottom: Critical Legal Studies and Reparations," (1987) 22 *Harvard Civil Rights–Civil Liberties Law Review* 323.
[102] A Scales, *Legal Feminism, Lawyering and Legal Theory* (New York, New York Press, 2006) 103.
[103] Hunter et al, above n 95, 4.
[104] For information on judicial diversity in the UK, see the judicial diversity statistics on the website of the judiciary of England and Wales (www.judiciary.gov.uk/publications-and-reports/statistics/diversity-stats-and-gen-overview). For the significance of Lady Hale's appointment to the House of Lords, see E Rackley, 'Difference in the House of Lords' (2006) 15 *Social and Legal Studies* 163.
[105] Lady Hale has described herself as a feminist, and discussed how she has reconciled this with her duty, as a judge, to act impartially. See Lady Hale, 'A Minority Opinion? Maccabaean Lecture in Jurisprudence' (2008) 154 *Proceedings of the British Academy* 319–36.
[106] *Yemshaw v London Borough of Hounslow* [2011] UKSC 3. See further CJS Knight, 'Doing Linguistic Violence to Prevent (Domestic) Violence? Yemshaw v Hounslow LBC in the Supreme Court' (2012) 24 *Child and Family Law Quarterly* 95.

forms of conduct. If the claimant was compelled to leave the family home because she had been subject to violence, from her husband, she would *not* be considered intentionally homeless, and would therefore be entitled to be rehoused by the local authority. Lady Hale held that the conduct of the claimant's husband, falling short of physical violence but consisting of shouting, withholding of housekeeping and threats to take away the children, could come within the definition of violence. She stated that violence is a term that needs to be interpreted by the courts as developing and changing over time.[107] She referenced the key international instruments on violence against women, which were drawn to the court's attention by the interveners including the Women's Aid Federation, that define violence as embracing both physical and psychological harm. She considered the general statutory framework, and took the view that the meaning adopted must be consistent with the statutory purpose, which in this case meant that 'a victim of domestic violence has a real choice between remaining in her home and seeking protection from the criminal or civil law and leaving to begin a new life elsewhere'.[108] Lady Hale homed in on the practical consequences of the interpretation, for the victim, showing an understanding that domestic violence often involves a pattern of behaviour that may include trivial acts of physical violence that may escalate, or non-physical acts such as locking up a person at home or depriving them of food. She acknowledged that whether violence has occurred may be an intrinsically difficult question, but it is to be judged objectively based on the 'particular facts, circumstances and personalities of the people involved'.[109]

Lady Hale also drew on feminist legal method in another landmark case, *Granatino v Radmacher*, where her dissenting judgment provides a telling contrast to that of the majority.[110] The court had to decide on the weight to be given to an agreement made by the parties before they got married on what should happen to their assets if they divorced.[111] Such agreements had previously been deemed to be contrary to public policy, and unenforceable in England and Wales, although the court could take them into account when deciding on the distribution of assets on divorce. The majority of the court decided that, in the case before it, the parties should be bound, and that the general principle was that an agreement freely entered into with a full appreciation of its implications should be given effect unless, in the circumstances prevailing, it would not be fair to do so.[112] The majority decision was underpinned by an emphasis on the value of autonomy with the court regarding it as patronising to ignore an agreement the parties had voluntarily entered into.[113] Lady Hale, in her dissent, gave less weight to issues of autonomy, stating that 'others may wonder whether people who are typically … in love can be expected to make rational choices in the same way businessmen can'.[114] She reflected that the purpose of such agreements is to deprive the economically weaker partner of financial provision and she showed a greater understanding

---

[107] *Yemshaw*, para 27.

[108] *Yemshaw*, para 27.

[109] *Yemshaw*, para 36.

[110] *Granatino v Radmacher* [2010] UKSC 42. For an analysis of the broader issues raised in the case, see PG Harris, R George, and J Herring, 'With this Ring I Thee Wed (Terms and Conditions Apply)' (2011) 41 *Family Law* 367.

[111] These are usually referred to as pre nuptial (pre nups) or ante nuptial agreements.

[112] *Granatino*, para 75. Lord Mance agreed with the majority on the outcome, and most of the issues, but wrote a separate judgment where he agreed on some points with Lady Hale.

[113] Ibid, para 78.

[114] Ibid, para 136.

than the majority of the interconnectedness and messiness of people's lives. She discussed the difficulties a court faces in deciding whether one of the parties should be compensated on divorce for the loss of opportunities during the marriage. These might include moving to a different location or giving up a well-paid job to pursue a more satisfying career. She stated that choices are often made 'for the sake of the overall happiness of the family'.[115] Her judgment shows insight into the complexities of family life and recognises that compromises and decisions made by the parties may be governed by emotion and notions of self-sacrifice that cannot easily be captured by conceptions of autonomy. This attempt to understand that decision-making is often relational and concerned with the preservation of relationships echoes Gilligan's 'ethic of care' theory.[116] Lady Hale was also aware of the gender dimension of the decision, which she says makes it 'ill suited to decision by a court consisting of eight men and one woman'.[117]

The judgments of Lady Hale demonstrate how feminist legal method can be used within the confines of existing legal precepts. The techniques used try to ensure that the court is attentive to different forms of gender, and other kinds of discrimination. There is a reflexive and contextual approach to judging that shows a determination to understand human experiences and dilemmas rather than to focus on abstractions. For feminists, legal method is a critical site of inquiry, providing the opportunity to confront legal orthodoxies.

4. CONCLUSION

Feminist legal theory destabilises and dispels law's vision of itself as a neutral and objective force implemented by dispassionate judges. It provides an analysis of law that is rooted in women's exclusion from the legal process that has alternately dissected and reconstituted law's liberal values. Its critique of law's methods yields important observations on the way in which power is exercised by the use of legal norms and categories. It attempts to break down the boundaries of law and insists it must be enacted and administered to encompass a broader set of experiences. Feminist encounters with law have historically gone beyond a critique of its shortcomings. As Conaghan has observed, feminist legal engagement is a 'practical activity', and as a consequence law's strategic potential as a vehicle for change has been irresistible.[118] Feminists have used the political and legal processes to bring issues as varied as rape, abortion, domestic violence and childcare into the public arena, and have made them the business of law.[119] But as feminist legal scholarship and activism has evolved, the use of law has been problematised and its ineptitudes highlighted. Legal regulation is often an inadequate response, and the danger of law being used regressively in a harmful manner has rightly made many feminists wary of an over-emphasis on legal

---

[115] Ibid, para 188.
[116] Gilligan, above n 22.
[117] *Granatino*, para 137.
[118] Conaghan, above n 38, 40.
[119] See generally on feminist activism on rape C McGlynn, 'Feminist Activism and Rape Law Reform in England and Wales: A Sisyphean Struggle' in C McGlynn and V Munro (eds), *Rethinking Rape Law: International and Comparative Perspectives* (Oxford, Glasshouse, 2010) 139–53.

solutions. Nevertheless, feminists have continued to work within the legal frame. It is difficult to abandon law. It is a powerful force governing most aspects of everyday life, and to relinquish legal engagement would be to leave law to those who may have little understanding or sympathy of gender issues.[120] Feminist legal method has been shown to be sufficiently contextual to reject or invest in law depending on the circumstances. The different strands of feminist thought are not limited to providing observations on the character of law but have also provided very specific techniques that can be used as part of the adjudicatory process. In short, feminist legal theory and method have proved to be powerful tools to scrutinise and rejuvenate law, and it is predicted that they will continue to adapt and develop to deal with new problems and priorities.

---

[120] Munro, above n 49, 84.

8

Critical Race Theory

ANGELA P HARRIS

1. CRITICAL ORIGINS

I began to scribble down words associated with our objectives, identities, and perspectives, drawing arrows and boxes around them to capture various aspects of who 'we' were and what we were doing. The list included: progressive/critical, CLS, race, civil rights, racism, law, jurisprudence, theory, doctrine, and so on. Mixing them up and throwing them together in various combinations, one proposed combination came together in a way that seemed to capture the possibility we were aiming to create. Sometime toward the end of the interminable winter of 1989, we settled on what seemed to be the most telling marker for this peculiar subject. We would signify the specific political and intellectual location of the project through 'critical,' the substantive focus through 'race,' and the desire to develop a coherent account of race and law through the term 'theory'.[1]

S O BEGINS ONE first-person account of the origins of critical race theory by one of its central figures, Kimberlé Crenshaw. As Crenshaw has explained elsewhere, critical race theory was developed first by a small group of mostly junior legal scholars of colour, and inspired and nurtured by the fledgling critical legal studies movement and by iconoclastic civil rights scholars such as Derrick Bell and Richard Delgado.[2] Structurally speaking, the movement's proximate cause was race-conscious admission to US higher education from the late 1970s to the mid-1980s, a set of policies that transformed the demographics of undergraduate institutions and eventually the professional schools. The newcomers to the legal academy—children of colour for whom the civil rights battles of the 1960s had been fought—found the tides of racial integration receding just as they arrived, and dedicated themselves to understanding why and how the US civil rights movement had failed to achieve its goal of social transformation.

Crenshaw, like others in this group, had been a student of Derrick Bell. A professor at Harvard Law School, dean of the University of Oregon Law School, and then professor at Harvard Law School again (before his decision to withhold his labour until

---

[1] KW Crenshaw, 'The First Decade: Critical Reflections or "A Foot in the Closing Door"' (2002) 49 *University of California, Los Angeles Law Review* 1343, 1360–61.

[2] KW Crenshaw, N Gotanda and G Peller, *Critical Race Theory: The Key Writings that Formed the Movement* (New York, New Press, 1966) xvi.

Harvard invited a woman of colour to its tenure track—a decision that eventually resulted in his departure), Bell had begun to teach his students that the conventional liberal narrative of halting yet steady progress toward racial equality was wrong. In his pioneering casebook *Race, Racism, and American Law* (first published in 1973), Bell argued instead that white supremacy was too crucial to America's institutions and traditions to be fully uprooted. Just as the country's economic wealth had been built on the backs of slaves, its sense of solidarity and purpose continued to rely on the ideological 'wages of whiteness'. Rather than embark upon widespread social upheaval and the political and economic shifts necessary to establish true racial equality, post-civil rights law and policy—even civil rights doctrine itself—would stretch as necessary to preserve white supremacy.

Twenty years later, Bell's pessimism seemed amply justified. The 1954 decision in *Brown v Board of Education*, which was followed by a torrent of new federal antidiscrimination protections crafted by Congress, the executive branch and the administrative state under presidents Kennedy, Johnson and Nixon, had encouraged civil rights attorneys to pursue racial justice in court. But by the 1980s, the 'Colored Only' signs had been taken down and the political, economic and judicial environment had grown chilly toward further change. Real wages were falling, manufacturing jobs were leaving the United States and the white working class was hurting, a pain that easily became resentment toward blacks. The infamous 'Southern Strategy' had begun to take shape, delivering the white South to the politicians who could most effectively denounce black people while still paying lip service to the moral ideal of racial equality. Ronald Reagan's promises of 'morning in America', for example, came along with words of contempt for 'welfare queens' having too many babies and driving Cadillacs with taxpayer money. Affirmative action policies served as a public flashpoint for this emerging backlash against the civil rights era. In a move that infuriated civil rights progressives, in the Reagan era a new cadre of black conservatives ascended to the public stage and vigorously attacked race-based affirmative action, denouncing it as stigmatising and as undermining the national commitment to meritocracy.[3] The ultimate symbol of their ascent was the 1991 nomination of Clarence Thomas to the Supreme Court.

In 1987, Bell mused of the civil rights movement, '[Q]uestions arise from the ashes of our expectations: How have we failed—and why? What does this failure mean—for black people and for whites? Where do we go from here?'[4] Reflecting on these words in an article published two years later, Frances Ansley wrote:

> It is almost eerie to read these words of Derrick Bell's now, and my ensuing talk of crisis and crossroads, knowing that they were written before not only *City of Richmond v JA Croson Co*, 109 SCt 706 (1989), but also the baleful litter of cases birthed by the Court in the summer of 1989. These cases include *Jett v Dallas Indep School Dist*, 109 SCt 2702 (1989) (municipal and state governments not liable for discriminatory practices performed as part of an employee's official duties); *Patterson v McLean Credit Union*, 109 SCt 2363 (1989) (§ 1981 does not cover conditions of racial harrassment on the job, but only activities more narrowly confined to 'making' contracts); *Lorance v AT&T*, 109 SCt 2269 (1989) (statute of

---

[3] See eg S Steele, *The Content of Our Character* (New York, Harper Perennial, 1991) 118–19; SL Carter, *Reflections of an Affirmative Action Baby* (New York, Basic Books, 1991) 25–27; see generally ML Ondaatje, *Black Conservative Intellectuals in Modern America* (Philadelphia, University of Pennsylvania Press, 2012).

[4] DA Bell, *And We Are Not Saved: The Elusive Quest For Racial Justice* (New York, Basic Books, 1989) 3.

limitations restrictively applied to Title VII claimants); *Martin v Wilks*, 109 SCt 2180 (1989) (disaffected, nonconsenting white males given great latitude in when and how to attack affirmative action consent decree); *Wards Cove Packing Co v Atonio*, 109 SCt 2115 (1989) (burden of proof significantly stiffened for Title VII plaintiffs and disparate impact theory significantly weakened). Suffice it to say that the sense of crisis has deepened and intensified.[5]

The founders of critical race theory were thus disenchanted not only with the political results of the civil rights movement and the prospects for further change; they were disenchanted with lawyering and law itself. As early as the mid-1970s, Bell had charged that National Association for the Advancement of Colored People (NAACP) lawyers bringing school desegregation litigation ended up prioritising their own ideological concerns over their clients' desire for a good education for their children.[6] Twenty years later, Bell's expression of scepticism would be reinforced by the publication of Gerald Rosenberg's *The Hollow Hope* (1991), which made the sweeping claim that contrary to the beliefs of a generation of civil rights lawyers inspired by the story of the road to *Brown*, courts were ineffective at bringing about social change.

The disappointment of critical race theorists extended to legal scholarship. In 1984, Richard Delgado, like Bell one of the very few people of colour (outside Puerto Rico and historically black institutions) with a tenure-track position in the US legal academy, published a bombshell article attacking white liberal civil rights and constitutional law scholars for establishing a whites-only club. Wrote Delgado:

> I knew that there are about one hundred Black, twenty-five Hispanic, and ten Native American law professors teaching at American law schools. Many of them are writing in areas about which they care deeply: antidiscrimination law, the equality principle, and affirmative action. Much of that scholarship, however, seems to have been consigned to oblivion.
>
> My assistant and I prepared an informal sociogram, a pictorial representation of who-cites-whom in the civil rights literature. It is fascinating. Paul Brest cites Laurence Tribe. Laurence Tribe cites Paul Brest and Owen Fiss. Owen Fiss cites Bruce Ackerman, who cites Paul Brest and Frank Michelman, who cites Owen Fiss and Laurence Tribe and Kenneth Karst. ...
>
> It does not matter where one enters this universe; one comes to the same result: an inner circle of about a dozen white, male writers who comment on, take polite issue with, extol, criticize, and expand on each other's ideas. It is something like an elaborate minuet.[7]

Finally, the young architects of critical race theory were deeply influenced by critical legal studies and its portrayal of legal reasoning as a similarly elaborate minuet. Many of the scholars who would later establish critical race theory first met at the 'summer camps' held by the Critical Legal Studies group (CLS). Critical legal studies offered a method of taking apart liberal and doctrinal pieties from the inside out. The movement—like its predecessor from the 1930s, American legal realism—took the position that the internal logic of legal doctrine did not play any real role in deciding cases (the 'indeterminacy thesis'). Rather, legal reasoning's primary function was ideological—the legitimation of political, economic and social relations. More pointedly,

---

[5] F Ansley, 'Stirring the Ashes: Race, Class and the Future of Civil Rights Scholarship' (1989) 74 *Cornell Law Review* 993, 994.

[6] DA Bell, 'Serving Two Masters: Integration Ideals and Client Interests in School Desegregation Litigation' (1976) 85 *Yale Law Journal* 470, 480.

[7] R Delgado, 'The Imperial Scholar: Reflections on a Review of Civil Rights Literature' (1984) 132 *University of Pennsylvania Law Review* 561, 563.

CLS took aim at the liberal legal faith in neutrality, objectivity and process that characterized mainstream constitutional scholarship. In the 1950s and 1960s, reflecting on the recent global cataclysms of fascism and totalitarianism and the new Cold War, legal process scholars had concluded that American democracy was superior to its alternatives because of its commitment to procedural values. Americans could enjoy the benefits of freedom and live in harmony despite substantive disagreements about the good life because they could agree on fair, objective and neutral ways to settle their conflicts. Like the Realists before them, the 'Crits' attacked this faith in objectivity and 'neutral principles' as a sham. They also brought something new to the table: methods of reading texts that were sweeping in from structuralist and poststructuralist 'theory' in the humanities. Crits borrowed from Derrida's notion of textual 'deconstruction', for example, in order to locate 'fundamental contradictions' within legal doctrines which rendered doctrine incapable of resolving genuinely hard cases. The Crits also took a different path than the Realists by placing their faith in a reconstructed politics rather than in social science. Some Crits, like Roberto Unger, aspired to rethink governance from the ground up, painstakingly re-imagining basic social institutions. Others, like Peter Gabel, looked to the power of critical writing itself and argued that total critique, or 'trashing', of legal doctrine and legal reasoning could lead the reader to an existential 'intersubjective zap', clearing the way for true, authentic human relations. Still others, like Mark Tushnet, questioned the language of 'rights' as mystification and argued that doctrine and policy should focus instead directly on human needs.

One result of these wayward intellectual and organising energies was a symposium issue published in 1987 in the *Harvard Civil Rights–Civil Liberties Law Review* called 'Minority Critique of the Critical Legal Studies Movement'.[8] Some of the authors published in that symposium were writers who would later become important figures in critical race theory, such as Patricia Williams and Mari Matsuda. These authors were generally sympathetic to the critical legal studies critique, but argued that racism had to be understood as a central category for understanding American law, and that racism made talk of rights indispensable.

The 1989 workshop on critical race theory at the St Benedict Center outside Madison, Wisconsin signalled a definitive break with critical legal studies as well as traditional civil rights scholarship. Missing from the meeting were not only the well-credentialled white men Delgado had excoriated, but also the 'young turks' of critical legal studies. The organisers of the workshop were all people of colour, and the elders present were Bell, Delgado and other relatively well-established legal scholars of colour such as Charles Lawrence III and Elizabeth Patterson. Critical race theory's young turks were women of colour, notably Crenshaw and Matsuda. Their aim was to show how law, including civil rights law, had taken on the task of rehabilitating white supremacy for a post-civil rights era.

Critical race theory and feminist legal theory, its conjoined twin, have outlived critical legal studies, remaining vibrant into the twenty-first century. Their survival is no doubt due in part to their personal relevance to many scholars. Critical race theorists continue to be predominantly people of colour, trying to understand the impact of racism on their personal and professional lives while they analyse racism on

---

[8] 'Minority Critique of the Critical Legal Studies Movement' (1987) 2 *Harvard Civil Rights–Civil Liberties Law Review*.

a societal level. We will return to the benefits of this reflexivity later. In the meantime, a closer examination of the themes and methods of critical race theory is in order.

2. CRITICAL CONTRADICTIONS

Critical race theory is founded on a series of contradictions which (ideally) function as productive tensions. Like other intellectual movements linked with identity-based social movements, critical race theorists simultaneously work to reveal group identity as a means of domination and to champion it—demystified—as a path to liberation. A central contradiction from which critical race theory emerged is its commitment to the concept of 'race' itself.

Emerging in the eighteenth century and reaching the apex of its influence in the late nineteenth and early twentieth century, race was a central grammar of governance in state institutions and in civil society in the New World and the African and Asian colonies of the Old World. The idea of race resolved a contradiction that became acute as nations such as France and the United States announced revolutionary commitments to democracy: how can human unfreedom and inequality be justified in societies devoted to freedom and equality?[9]

Race, along with and through gender and sexuality, answered this question by drawing a line between politics and nature. Racial difference justified political domination, economic exploitation and social–sexual misrecognition by placing inequality outside politics, on the side of the natural. If inequality is not the result of politics but of natural endowments, then the free and equal can govern the unfree and unequal with clean hands. Indeed, the assertion of racial difference as a fundamental, natural reality not only permitted but encouraged governance projects of exploitation, exclusion, forced assimilation (at best) or extermination (at worst), by insisting that governance must take account of natural differences between groups and that the higher had a responsibility to govern the lower. This formulation, as others have noted, links the invention of race with the birth of the sciences of man and with the modern state—the state which, in Foucauldian terms, attends to and intervenes in the health of its constituent population.[10] In the terms through which modern political theory understands its own origins, the 'racial-sexual contract' undergirded the 'social contract';[11] only those humans 'civilised' enough to be capable of democratic self-government were parties to the social contract.

American colonial law, and later the law of the new nation, reflected this *Herrenvolk* democracy and its justification in terms of natural difference. African slaves in the United States were deemed incapable of self-government, and so were ruled by their masters; indigenous tribes were accorded a partial sovereignty but denied crucial elements of full political equality with whites, such as the right to hold title in land.[12]

---

[9] See G Frederickson, *Race, A Short History* (Princeton, Princeton University Press, 2003) 68–69.

[10] See P Rabinow and N Rose, 'Biopower Today' (2006) 1 *Biosocieties* 195–217 (doi:10.1017/S1745855206040014).

[11] See generally C Pateman and C Mills, *The Contract and Domination* (Cambridge, Polity, 2007).

[12] A crucial move from a political to a natural conception of 'race' was taken by the Supreme Court in the *Dred Scott* decision. In his opinion, Justice Taney stated definitively that the American nation had been founded not only for free people, but for white free people: 'We think they are not, and that they are not

The first federal naturalisation act, passed in 1791, restricted the right to become a naturalised citizen to 'white' persons. And as many scholars have pointed out, Virginia conflated the political condition of enslavement with the natural condition of heredity as early as 1662, when that state enacted the rule of *partus sequitur ventrem*, providing that a child would be enslaved if born to a slave mother.

The North's victory in the Civil War changed the legal administration of white supremacy. The congressional architects of Reconstruction passed the Fourteenth Amendment, providing that African Americans would henceforth be considered citizens of the several states and of the United States, and they began to give content to 'national citizenship' with a concurrent expansion of the federal government, granting all citizens political rights such as the right to vote, civil rights such as the right to own and alienate property and enter into contracts on the same terms as whites, and rights of federal enforcement such as the right to due process and the right to the equal protection of the laws. With this shift away from direct racial domination through law and the rise of racial equality as a legal ideal, however, the idea of 'race' as a natural, pre-political difference ironically intensified, as Walter Benn Michaels has argued.[13] As race no longer stood simply for relations of inferiority and superiority, those who defended racial governance had to emphasise even more strongly the idea of inherent, natural 'difference'. Racial equality under the law coexisted with social inequality, and the law could buttress white supremacy in the social realm by insisting that the races were legally equal—but also, by reason of culture, civilisation, custom, preference and biology—stubbornly and perhaps forever socially 'different'.

In American law, this resolution is exemplified by the Supreme Court's decision in *Plessy v Ferguson* (1896), permitting states to segregate the races in the name of custom. The rule of *Plessy*, which came to be known as 'separate but equal', built on earlier postbellum decisions such as that in the *Civil Rights Cases* and the *Slaughter-House* cases by asserting that the government retained power to treat the races differently despite the new commitment to legal equality. As the Court insisted in its opinion, racial segregation had no implication of inequality other than what blacks 'put on it'.[14] The races were equal; they were simply different, and 'reasonable' measures to accommodate this difference, such as segregation, did not violate the equal protection clause.

The terms of the racial contract shifted again in the period known as the Second Reconstruction (from the late 1940s to roughly 1980), during which litigants for black rights successfully pressed the courts to acknowledge that in the world of Jim Crow, racial equality did not exist and that the natural and customary 'differences' asserted by state and local governments claiming the right to segregate the races were really only a cover for white supremacy. The decision in *Brown v Board of Education* held,

included, and were not intended to be included, under the word "citizens" in the Constitution, and can therefore claim none of the rights and privileges which that instrument provides for and secures to citizens of the United States.' *Dred Scott v Sanford* (1857) 60 US 393, 404.

[13] WB Michaels, *Our America: Nativism, Modernism, and Pluralism* (Durham, NC, Duke University Press, 1995) 64–67.

[14] 'We consider the underlying fallacy of the plaintiff's argument to consist in the assumption that the enforced separation of the two races stamps the colored race with a badge of inferiority. If this be so, it is not by reason of anything found in the act, but solely because the colored race chooses to put that construction upon it.' *Plessy v Ferguson* (1896) 163 US 537, 551.

for instance, that racial segregation in elementary education was inherently unequal, stamping the hearts and minds of black children with a sense of inferiority, and thus violated the equal protection clause.[15] In a series of subsequent decisions issued per curiam (without a published opinion), moreover, the Court applied the rule of *Brown* to all instances of government de jure racial segregation that came before it. Congress extended this dismantling of racial segregation by moving activities that had formerly been considered 'private'—and thus not subject to the strictures of equality law at all—into the 'public' sphere; these included employment, public accommodations, housing and transactions involving interstate commerce. In this expanded public sphere, different treatment according to race was no longer considered a reasonable way to govern social relations. American law was now in line with the new global consensus, which emerged after World War II and the racial extermination policies of the Nazi regime, viewing race as not only meaningless as an objective, quasi-scientific category but pernicious as a tool of governance.

Once again, however, white supremacy did not vanish. The new ban on race-conscious governance required enforcement, and in 1965 President Johnson signed Executive Order 11246, requiring federal contractors not only to stop discriminating against racial minorities, but to take 'affirmative action' in all aspects of minority employment. Twenty years later, as critical race theory emerged, critics of affirmative action policies argued that such policies were racist. In the courts, conservatives argued that there was no such thing as a 'benign' use of race (or that courts were unable to distinguish the benign from the malign). Any government use of racial categories should therefore receive the strictest judicial scrutiny and should be considered presumptively unconstitutional. The Court steadily moved toward accepting this position, and with it, the idea that the state should be 'colour blind'. As civil rights scholars of the time observed, this shift rewrote the Equal Protection Clause as a ban on racial classification, rather than a ban on racial subordination. Nonetheless, 'colour-blind constitutionalism' began to look like the moral high ground of civil rights.

Critical race theorists set about defending race-conscious affirmative action as necessary to a substantive commitment to equality. They argued that since the founding of the United States, whites had engaged in 'opportunity hoarding', reserving for themselves the lion's share of political, economic and cultural power. The move to refrain from race-conscious redistribution came at a time when African Americans had already been subject to many generations of what Melvin Oliver and Thomas Shapiro call 'sedimented inequality': owning only a fraction of the wealth that whites controlled, lacking political power as a 'discrete and insular' group subject to continued discrimination, and locked out of the country's elite institutions and professions.[16] The decision at this point that race-conscious affirmative action constituted 'reverse discrimination' meant that market mechanisms, social networks and 'private' discrimination would keep blacks out of power as effectively as government had in a prior era. Critical race theorists thus attacked the Court's turn to colour-blind constitutionalism as an attempt to maintain 'whiteness as property'.[17] From their perspective, the rule of

---

[15] *Brown v Board of Education of Topeka* (1954) 347 US 483.

[16] M Oliver and T Shapiro, *Black Wealth/White Wealth: A New Perspective on Racial Inequality* (London, Routledge, 2006) 52–54.

[17] CI Harris, 'Whiteness as Property' (1993) 106 *Harvard Law Review* 1707, 1768.

Plessy—accepting extralegal inequality while extolling formal legal equality—seemed still to be in force.

Nevertheless, as the twenty-first century began, the critical race theorists' position that race-conscious government action was an indispensable tool for justice continued to lose ground as economic contraction, a continuing decrease in real wages, and the rise of neoliberal ideology and policy further weakened American tolerance (episodic at best) for large-scale structural redistribution. Criticisms of state race-consciousness mounted with the election of President Barack Obama as the first African American to hold that office. Now, many pundits asserted, the United States was finally 'post-racial'. The continued insistence by critical race theorists that racial subordination was alive and well began to seem increasingly out of the step with the new social mobility of affluent people of colour, even while the prisons were disproportionately filled with black and Latino men. Critical race theory could be, and was, attacked as 'divisive' and a form of spoils politics at best, or anti-white racism at worst. Affirmative action policies in employment and education were subjected to increased scrutiny in the federal courts, and eliminated by legislative or popular action in many states.

In defending race-conscious affirmative action policies and, more broadly, a continued commitment to understanding economic, political and social relations through racial categories, critical race theorists have had to struggle with this contradiction: 'race' is a concept both essential and inadequate to understanding racial subordination. It is essential because, as historians and social scientists have repeatedly demonstrated, American inequality continues to follow racial patterns and because interpersonal racism—in conscious and 'implicit' forms—continues to shape decision-making in employment, education, healthcare, family formation and criminal justice.[18] It is also inadequate, for many reasons.

First, 'race' continues to be understood in popular discourse as a 'natural', quasi-biological difference; painstaking academic efforts to explain it as a social fact rather than a natural one have not transformed lay understandings of the term. Those who defend race-consciousness as a policy tool are thus liable to be misunderstood as defending race as a biological fact. Second, perhaps because 'race' emerged as a deliberate obfuscation (misrepresenting political domination as natural difference), the language of race is impoverished, running together different dynamics of identity and different levels of explanation. Racial identity as ascribed by others operates differently than racial identity as claimed from within; self-proclaimed 'white' identity functions primarily as a claim to privilege, while non-white racialised identity categories tend to be bound up with ethnicity; and race as ancestry, as physiognomy, and as custom, civilisation or 'culture' are frequently conflated in both academic and popular discourse. Much of the work of critical race theory has been devoted to trying to tease out and compensate for these inadequacies. The slipperiness and ubiquity of race talk, however, ensures that critical race theorists are constantly struggling with how to articulate the legacy of the civil rights movement and the meaning of basic terms such as 'racism'.[19] Meanwhile, the policy contradiction remains: as Justice Harry

---

[18] See JR Feagin, *Racist America: Roots, Current Realities, and Future Reparations* (London, Routledge, 2010) 17–19.

[19] For instance, some on the political right have taken up again the notion of pre-political difference under the banner of 'culture' or 'civilization' rather than 'race'. The insistence that such formulations are not 'racist' because they do not rely on scientific racism ignores the fact that nineteenth-century racism

Blackmun put it: 'In order to get beyond racism, we must first take account of race. There is no other way.'[20] As racism is increasingly understood as 'employing racial categories' rather than 'hoarding opportunity for racialised groups', the attachment of critical race theorists to racialisation looks increasingly suspect.

A second contradiction on which critical race theory was founded involves the fact that law, too, is both essential to and inadequate for the project of racial liberation— a contradiction which Crenshaw has identified as an indissoluble tension between 'reform' and 'revolution'.[21] Law is essential to the critical race theory project as a practical matter because rules of law serve as the architecture for social institutions in mass societies: there can be no corrective justice for structural inequality, for example, in a large-scale society without state law. Because law takes as its ideological reference ideas of justice and of rights, law is also indispensable as a symbolic touchstone for ethical behaviour at the level of social and institutional relations.[22] From a critical race theory perspective, however, law is also inadequate to the task of reparation. Drawing on the critical legal studies critique, critical race theorists have argued that the law always serves power first and foremost. At the pragmatic level, as Bell argued with respect to the NAACP, lawyers and legal process tend to derail or dissolve grassroots movements. At the substantive level, private legal rules of property, contract and procedure, as well as public legal rules from constitutional law, treaty law and the law of nations, make corrective justice for large-scale racial wrongs such as slavery and Indian conquest all but impossible, even unthinkable.

Indeed, critical race theorists have argued that late twentieth-century and early twenty-first century antidiscrimination law has operated paradoxically to protect certain forms of white supremacy. The Supreme Court's treatment of the American Equal Protection Clause of the Constitution provides an example. Since the 1980s, the Supreme Court has held that the Equal Protection Clause prohibits only governmental actions taken with the conscious intent to harm an individual or a group on the basis of race. This 'intent requirement', later imported into the jurisprudence of Title VII of the 1964 Civil Rights Act (which covers, among other things, discrimination in employment), makes unconscious and institutional racism invisible to the law. It also, as many have pointed out, even makes a great deal of conscious and intentional racism invisible, since in the post-*Brown* era very few decision-makers are foolish enough to be caught on the record explicitly linking their decisions to racist logic or racial identity. Most perniciously, this narrow legal understanding of intent reinforces a social understanding of racism as the sole province of hateful people spouting racial epithets, and obscures the role of social norms and market mechanisms in preserving white supremacy. Critical race theorists have thus looked for concepts, such as 'implicit

was as much 'cultural' as 'biological'. Without a shared commitment to the concept of race as a social construction, however, the right's evasion of charges of racism succeeds. See L Volpp, 'Blaming Culture for Bad Behavior' (2000) 12 *Yale Journal of Law & the Humanities* 89, 89.

[20] *Regents of the University of California v Bakke* (1978) 438 US 265, 407 (opinion of Justice Blackmun).
[21] KW Crenshaw, 'Race, Reform and Retrenchment: Transformation and Legitimation in Antidiscrimination Law' (1988) 101 *Harvard Law Review* 1331, 1368.
[22] See generally P Williams, 'Alchemical Notes: Reconstructing Ideals from Deconstructed Rights' (1987) 22 *Harvard Civil Rights–Civil Liberties Law Review* 401, 432–33 (discussing the ideological framework of rights).

bias', 'institutional racism' and 'locked-in discrimination', that challenge the restriction of racism to intentional action.[23]

A second way in which law is inadequate to the liberatory desires of critical race theory involves the notorious 'public–private' split in American law. As several generations of scholars have explained, under American law the doctrine of 'state action' protects existing distributions of wealth and power, by ignoring the way in which the state creates those distributions in the first place.[24] Under the doctrine of state action, the 'sedimented inequality' of wealth between whites and blacks, for instance, is inaccessible to antidiscrimination law; it represents mere 'social inequality' that the law is powerless to disturb.[25]

The public–private distinction interacts with another obstacle to racial liberation: the absence of positive economic rights in the United States. Without such rights, a crucial source of reparations for slavery and segregation is lacking. The absence of economic rights as a means of legal remedy for racial subordination also fosters what left critics have decried as a politics of suffering at the heart of civil rights movement. In Nancy Fraser's terms, because American law bestows primarily symbolic 'recognition' rights rather than material 'redistribution' rights, civil rights remedies similarly tend toward the symbolic.[26] Moreover, the logic of the Equal Protection Clause—the primary surviving constitutional tool for racial justice—pushes claimants to articulate suffering and victimisation as the basis for legal action (as in *Brown*'s vision of scarred hearts and minds) rather than a demand for institutional accounting. In this way as well, a jurisprudence ostensibly designed to foster equality subtly undermines those who seek to use it for that purpose.

Finally, the lack of general economic rights in American law encourages a politics of division between poor whites and people of colour. To the extent that affirmative action programmes in education and employment have served as a kind of economic redistribution, they are available only to racialised minorities, fostering resentment on the part of poor whites and encouraging their continued reliance on what WEB DuBois called 'a sort of public and psychological wage' associated with white identity.[27] The lack of general economic rights also pushes people of colour using the civil rights model into a cramped version of racial liberation that focuses on 'equal opportunity' going forward (much like the 'free labour' championed by mainstream Republicans after the Civil War) rather than changing the structures of advantage and disadvantage inherited from a racist past and maintained in the present.[28]

The limitations of equality discourse point to a third way in which law has proved inadequate to the hopes of critical race theorists: the Supreme Court's truncation

---

[23] Implicit bias: see C Lawrence III, 'The Id, the Ego, and Equal Protection' (1987) 39 *Stanford Law Review* 317, 322; LH Krieger, 'The Content of Our Categories: A Cognitive Bias Approach to Discrimination and Equal Employment Opportunity' (1995) 47 *Stanford Law Review* 1161, 1239. Institutional racism: see I Haney-Lopez 'Institutional Racism: Judicial Conduct and a New Theory of Racial Discrimination' (1999) 109 *Yale Law Journal* 1717, 1806–08. 'Locked-in segregation': see D Roithmayr, 'Locked in Inequality: The Persistence of Discrimination' (2003) 9 *Michigan Journal of Race & Law* 31, 31.

[24] CR Sunstein, *The Partial Constitution* (Cambridge, MA, Harvard University Press, 1998) 51–52.

[25] See *Croson v City of Richmond* (1989) 488 US 469, 490.

[26] N Fraser, *Justice Interruptus: Critical Reflections on the 'Postsocialist' Condition"* (London, Routledge, 1997) 24–25.

[27] WEB DuBois, *Black Reconstruction in America, 1860–1880* [1935] (New York: Free Press, 1995) 700–01.

[28] See RL Goluboff, *The Lost Promise of Civil Rights* (Cambridge, MA, Harvard University Press, 2010) 72.

of the Reconstruction Constitution. For example, although the architects of Reconstruction granted federal protection to the 'privileges and immunities of national citizenship' alongside the right to the equal protection of the laws, potentially creating a charter of broadly conceived positive and negative human rights, the Court early on defined these privileges and immunities narrowly, rendering them useless for racial justice purposes.[29] Similarly, critical race theorists have argued that the Thirteenth Amendment, abolishing slavery, could have formed the basis for a vibrant jurisprudence of antisubordination, but the Court has read this amendment narrowly as well, to abolish only forced labour itself and not slavery's 'badges and incidents'.[30] The lack of these broader tools has left civil rights movements with only 'equality' as a viable basis for legal intervention. By limiting the horizons of race-based social movements to 'inclusion' rather than fundamental transformation, however, equality jurisprudence has had a taming effect on movements for racial liberation. The limitation to equality claims has obscured the way in which racism has linked the fates of racialised minorities and indigenous peoples, who do have a limited right of political sovereignty and self-determination.[31] Indeed, current constitutional jurisprudence increasingly pits the two groups against one another, because colour-blind constitutionalism has been used to attack the political rights of Indian tribes.[32]

Finally, critical race theorists' reliance on law has meant that critical race theory, born in the United States and identified with American legal doctrine, has been slow to make connections with racial justice initiatives in other countries, despite the transnational character of race and racism. This isolation may be coming to an end as critical race theory migrates past borders; an understanding of racism as a global project—intimately connected with colonialism—is long overdue. We will return to this possibility at the end of the chapter.

At an abstract level, the tension between critical race theorists' 'reformist' goals and their 'revolutionary' critical stance expresses a tension between the movement's philosophical and professional commitments. Critical race theorists draw from the postmodernist 'hermeneutics of suspicion' in insisting that racism and race are fundamental to American society, including American law; for example, Bell famously asserted that racism was 'permanent'.[33] Their insistence on analysing antidiscrimination law as a tool of white supremacy similarly installs suspicion, doubt and even cynicism at the heart of the theory. At the same time, critical race theory was founded by lawyers, well aware of law's symbolic and material power, and by people of colour, well aware of the recent victories and continuing dreams of movements for racial liberation. And critical race theory, as a form of legal scholarship, demands that legal

---

[29] See AP Harris and R Hall, 'Hidden Histories, Racialized Gender, and the Legacy of Reconstruction: The Story of United States v Cruikshank' in EM Schneider and SM Wildman (eds), *Women and the Law Stories* (New York, Thomas Reuters/Foundation Press, 2011) 21, 24.

[30] See B Azmy, 'Unshackling the Thirteenth Amendment: Modern Slavery and a Reconstructed Civil Rights Agenda' (2002–03) 71 *Fordham Law Journal* 981, 983–94.

[31] See BR Berger, 'Red: Racism and the American Indian' (2009) 56 *University of California, Los Angeles Law Review* 591, 654–55.

[32] See C Goldberg-Ambrose, 'Descent into Race' (2002) 49 *University of California, Los Angeles Law Review* 1372, 1390–93.

[33] See DA Bell, *Faces at the Bottom of the Well: The Permanence of Racism* (New York, Basic Books, 1993) 92.

remedies be proposed for social problems.[34] Critical race theorists thus simultaneously condemn law and state power as fundamentally invested in white supremacy, and take up the tools of law and state power to challenge white supremacy. To borrow a phrase from Audre Lorde, their quixotic mission is to dismantle the master's house using the master's tools.

3. CRITICAL CONTRIBUTIONS

Despite, or perhaps through conscious attention to, these contradictions, critical race theory has offered legal theory a viable model of postmodern jurisprudence. Critical race theorists have exhibited a willingness to incorporate the exacting reflexiveness demanded by postmodernism without taking on that movement's tendency to enervation through an inability to ground itself on any commitment other than critique. Its reflexivity—reflected in a commitment to self-examination and a humility about law as a tool for liberation—is a resource for other movements, inside and outside the law.

Mustafa Emirbayer and Matthew Desmond, writing to an audience of sociologists of race, identify three levels of scholarly reflexivity: the social, the disciplinary and the scholastic.[35] By social reflexivity, Emirbayer and Desmond mean the recognition that all views of the world are partial, meaning that scholarship on race will inevitably be limited by the scholar's own identity and knowledge. Emirbayer and Desmond argue in particular for recognition of what they call 'the social unconscious', by which they mean the idea that the social positionings of the scholar that are the least visible are the most important because most potentially destructive.

Critical race theorists have pressed for, and exhibited, social reflexivity in their writing despite legal scholarship's commitment to 'objectivity' and 'neutrality'. For example, Patricia Williams's book *The Alchemy of Race and Rights* attacked this commitment head on, calling attention to how an insistence on objectivity and neutrality masked the epistemological gaps between white and non-white experiences of the world. Williams employed first-person narratives to disrupt legal analysis, while Bell and Delgado used fables and stories about fictional characters to do the same. Their controversial introduction of 'storytelling' as a method of legal scholarship focused critical race theory directly on the problem of knowledge and insisted on social reflexivity as a critique of traditional legal scholarship's belief in a 'view from nowhere'.

A second analytical tool emerging from critical race theory that exhibits its commitment to social reflexivity is the concept of 'intersectionality'. Coined early on by Crenshaw, this concept marks the imbrication of race with other axes of subordination and identity, such as gender, sexuality, disability and class.[36] The embrace of intersectionality has encouraged critical race theorists and those who draw on critical race theory to make their critiques reflexive, by recognising that no given set of finite categories can capture the complexity of the social world.

---

[34] For a CLS-influenced critique of this relentless 'normativity' in legal scholarship, see generally P Schlag, 'Normative and Nowhere To Go' (1990) 43 *Stanford Law Review* 167.

[35] M Emirbayer and M Desmond, 'Race and Reflexivity' (2012) 35 *Journal of Ethnic and Racial Studies* 574, 578.

[36] KW Crenshaw, 'Demarginalizing the Intersection of Race and Sex: A Black Feminist Critique of Antidiscrimination Doctrine, Feminist Theory and Antiracist Politics' (1989) *University of Chicago Legal Forum* 139, 141.

Finally, critical race theory has given rise to a literature on the invisibility of whiteness and the need to investigate white privilege.[37] This interest in recognising unmarked social positions as unstated norms is another reflection of social reflexivity.

The second form of reflexivity Emirbayer and Desmond advocate is what they call disciplinary reflexivity: a willingness to identify the limitations that disciplinary training places on a scholar's ability to identify issues and problems. Critical race theorists' candid acknowledgement of the necessity and the inadequacy of legal responses to racial subordination is an example of disciplinary reflexivity. Critical race theory's embrace of this contradiction has, moreover, influenced both scholars and practitioners. Within the realm of legal theory, for instance, 'trans' legal scholars have found inspiration in critical race theory's open admission of law's limitations, and built on critical race theorists' critique of equality discourse, accepting the importance of equality as a tool while simultaneously seeking to transcend it.[38] A new generation of lawyers inspired by critical race theory, similarly committed to disciplinary reflexivity, recognises the limits of law and does not equate legal victories with social liberation.[39]

The third form of reflexivity Emirbayer and Desmond advocate is 'scholastic reflexivity', meaning awareness of how being an intellectual and an academic itself frames and limits the ability to think and talk about the subject of race. Critical race theory's intellectual roots in Third World feminist scholarship, and the counterdisciplinary energies that produced ethnic studies departments around the country and ethnic studies as a discipline, have imbued it with a commitment to scholastic reflexivity. Law's position as a profession—with only one foot in academia and the other in action in the world on behalf of clients—has also provided critical race scholars with a vantage point from which to examine academia critically. Less benignly, scholastic reflexivity has been, to some extent, forced upon critical race theory by critics of the movement who have attacked it as insufficiently scholarly and, in response to the high proportion of faculty of colour who write in this area, as devoted to a politics of racial divisiveness and racial victimhood. Particularly for those scholars defending affirmative action policies, scholastic reflexivity has thus been an inescapable condition of employment. In this sense, as Wendy Leo Moore has written in a response to Emirbayer and Desmond, academics of colour writing about race have no choice but to be reflexive, if only in the negative sense of self-consciousness about the fact that one's performance of doing the work, as well as the work itself, are always under scrutiny.[40]

Although occasionally the product of coercion, one of the most important accomplishments of critical race theory is the movement's thoroughgoing embrace of its critical contradictions in the service of a rigorous reflexivity—social, disciplinary, and

---

[37] B Flagg, '"Was Blind But Now I See": White Race Consciousness and the Requirement of Discriminatory Intent' (1993) 91 *Michigan Law Review* 953, 969–70. See generally SM Wildman, *Privilege Revealed: How Invisible Preference Undermines America* (New York, New York University Press, 1996).

[38] See D Spade, *Normal Life: Administrative Violence, Critical Trans Politics, and the Limits of Law* (New York, South End Press, 2011).

[39] See EK Yamamoto, 'Critical Race Praxis: Race Theory and Political Lawyering Practice in Post-Civil Rights America' (1997) 95 *Michigan Law Review* 821,824; GP Lopez, *Rebellious Lawyering: One Chicano's Vision of Progressive Law Practice (New Perspectives on Law, Culture, and Society)* (Boulder, CO, Westview Press, 1992).

[40] WL Moore, 'Reflexivity, Power, and Systemic Racism' (2012) 35 *Journal of Ethnic and Racial Studies* 618–19.

scholastic. As the field expands beyond law to take up residence in education, law and society studies, philosophy, and elsewhere, it is to be hoped that its example will be followed.

4. A CRITICAL CONCLUSION

Race as a grammar of governance has been central to the prosperity, dominance and sometimes founding of the Western nations, and race remains a powerful folk category that makes sense of group differences and secures social and political hierarchies. Yet, today every Western nation has formally renounced race as a grammar of governance and prohibited racist behaviour in labour and educational settings as a matter of civil and/or criminal law. One of the most important forward directions for critical race theory is the transcendence of its American roots and the development of transnational perspectives on law and racial subordination.

There are a number of obstacles to this movement beyond boundaries. Mathias Moeschel, exploring the value of critical race theory to European law and policy, identifies several, including a less sociological and more technical understanding of law in Europe; the differences between common law and civil law systems; and, perhaps not least, a widespread view that racism is unique to the United States, or at least more pernicious in the United States than anywhere else.[41] There is also an issue of language; in Latin America and in Europe, as within American 'colour-blind constitutionalism', the conviction that to use racial categories is itself racist makes it difficult even to discuss racism. Finally, racism takes different forms in different societies; the entanglement of race with religion, nation and postcolonial struggle makes any simple 'application' of American critical race theory to other countries or regions ill-advised at best. Yet the fundamental insight of critical race theory—that contemporary societies both explicitly deplore racism and covertly uphold racial hierarchies—is applicable far beyond the United States. The roots of race are to be found in European settler colonialism, imperialism and Atlantic slavery, all global phenomena. The future of critical race theory lies in comparative and international studies.

---

[41] M Moeschel, 'The Relevance of Critical Race Theory to Europe', PhD dissertation, European University Institute Department of Law, 2011.

Section 4

Law in Action

REZA BANAKAR and MAX TRAVERS

T HE PHRASE 'LAW in action' is fairly central in law and society scholarship. It originates from Roscoe Pound, who invited American jurists to look beyond legal texts and examine how the law was applied.[1] It became something of a rallying call for the realist movement in jurisprudence during the 1930s and 1940s. The Law and Society Association, founded in the early 1960s, has also understood law in action in this general sense. This interdisciplinary movement has examined how laws are made, what lawyers do, how the courts work and how citizens relate to the legal system, using a variety of empirical methods. There is also, however, a different way of understanding the term—as reflecting or leading into theoretical debates in sociology about the relationship between action and structure. There is, arguably, a natural affinity among many American law and society researchers with the action tradition, in the sense that they have a preference for conducting empirical research about specific social processes rather than engaging in abstract theorising. But there are also significant differences, in that sociologists, even when they appear to be conducting empirical research, are often also engaged in making philosophically driven claims about the nature of society and how to study this phenomenon.

We explained why the action–structure debate was important in sociology in the main introduction. Many of these debates originate in the different conceptions of sociology as a science advanced by Durkheim and Weber. Durkheim saw sociology as being akin to natural science, explaining patterns and relationships from the outside, which makes it possible to see society as having 'macro' and 'micro' levels and to identify social structures that shape and constrain (even produce) individuals. The structural sociologist, even when describing actions at the 'micro' level, is always concerned to explain these activities or understand them in the context of the structure of society conceived as a whole. Moreover, the structural sociologist always makes the claim, explicitly or implicitly, that he or she knows more than those being studied in particular institutions or social settings.

There is, however, no agreement on how to establish sociology as a scientific discipline. This is not simply manifest in occasional eruptions of dissent such as postmodernism (see Section 5), as many thinkers have argued against the view that sociology is, or should become, like natural science, seeing this as a fundamentally

---

[1] R Pound 'Law in Books and Law in Action' (1910) 44 *American Law Review* 12.

mistaken notion. The most influential sociologist who has advanced this dissenting view is Weber, who argues at the start of *Economy and Society* that sociology as an academic discipline had to be concerned with the meaningful character of human group life. In contrast to Durkheim (the founder with Auguste Comte of systems theory), Weber was insistent that society was no more than a collection of interacting individuals:

> Interpretative sociology considers the individual and his action as the basic unit, as its 'atom'—if the disputable comparison for once may be permitted. In this approach the individual is also the upper limit and the sole carrier of meaningful conduct. ... In general, for sociology, such concepts as 'state', 'association', 'feudalism' and the like, designate certain categories of human interaction. Hence, it is the task of sociology to reduce these concepts to 'understandable' action, that is, without exception, to the actions of participating individual men.[2]

Weber believed that meaning was impossible to study with the precision of natural science (like other interpretive thinkers he viewed physics as an inappropriate model for sociology), but it was possible to write generally about the world using the device of the 'ideal type'. This is how he can talk about what we might call 'macro-phenomena', such as 'capitalism', 'bureaucracy' and 'law', and how these develop through history. This was, however, the closest one could get to addressing meaning on the ground: what people understand they are doing in any area of social life.

This broadly characterises the approach to law adopted by the 'interpretive' sociological traditions of symbolic interactionism, ethnomethodology and conversation analysis, although none of these was directly influenced by Weber.[3] In our first edition, we provided separate introductions to symbolic interactionism, by Max Travers, and to ethnomethodology and conversation analysis, by Robert Dingwall. In this edition, Travers provides a review of work published in each tradition relating to law since 2002. This also contains some discussion on the philosophical foundations and the implications for legal theory and practice.

Over the years, mainstream structural traditions have tried with varying degrees of success to incorporate a tamed version of interpretive sociologies, by conceptualising them as 'micro' approaches. They have had most success with interactionism, in which some influential figures (most notably Norman Denzin) have welcomed incorporation and hybridisation.[4] Ethnomethodology and conversation analysis have proved more difficult to assimilate, partly because the philosophical assumptions of Alfred Schutz and Ludwig Wittgenstein differ considerably from those informing Durkheimian social science. Travers notes that researchers are drawn to interpretivism 'because they are dissatisfied with the idealisations and abstractions offered by other sociological litera-

---

[2] H Gerth and CW Mills (eds), *From Max Weber: Essays in Sociology* (London, Routledge, 1991) 55. Weber was, arguably, more favourable to the feminist movement than many contemporaries. See J Radkau, *Max Weber: A Biography* (Cambridge, Polity, 2009). But he still appears to view men as the only people who matter in this theoretical statement.

[3] Ethnomethodologists see the term 'interpretive' as misleading, not least because people are not constantly interpreting the meaning of people and objects in the world around them. For discussion, see W Sharrock and G Button 'Ethnomethodology and Constructionist Studies of Technology' in M Rouncefield and P Tolmie (eds), *Ethnomethodology at Work* (Aldershot, Ashgate 2012).

[4] N Denzin, *Symbolic Interactionism and Cultural Studies: The Politics of Interpretation* (New York, Wiley-Blackwell, 2007).

tures'. Furthermore, they have no interest in 'identifying hidden causes', and they do not believe that 'sociology offers a way to look behind appearances'.

Presenting this as a clash between paradigms understates the way in which foundational differences are productive in sociology,[5] and how theorists are inventive in combining approaches. In the main introduction, we noted that most significant modern theorists, such as Parsons, Luhmann, Habermas, Bourdieu and Giddens, have each recognised the importance of the action–structure debate. They are each familiar, at more than a superficial level, with the arguments, ideas and research studies in different interpretive traditions. Moreover, a traditional route to becoming a major theorist is to offer a new framework that relates action and structure. A good example, at the present time, is Bruno Latour's actor–network theory.

Latour is perhaps best known for advancing the controversial philosophical and methodological argument that non-humans should be viewed as having agency. But he has been arguably most influenced by Gabriel Tarde, who was a critic of Durkheim and viewed society as the outcome of associative social processes. What is not usually noted is that he also explicitly acknowledges the influence of the interactionist Howard Becker and the ethnomethodologist Harold Garfinkel.[6] He also criticises structural traditions for looking for hidden causes, and he makes fun of theorists such as Bourdieu and Foucault for not examining social actions or experiences too closely. It is therefore unsurprising that, in an insightful review, Ron Levi and Mariana Valverde wrote in positive terms as theorists sympathetic to the structural tradition on Latour's achievements in addressing the practices that produce law, while displaying some discomfort towards his 'studied apoliticism'.[7] The same criticism can be made of Garfinkel, who recommended a policy of 'ethnomethodological indifference' towards moral and political questions.

We are pleased to include an introduction to Latour's anthropological writings on law by two of his associates, Frédéric Audren and Cédric Moreau de Bellaing. This demonstrates the subtle and insightful view of law and its relationship to other social institutions that becomes possible through being analytically sensitive to association. They note that, in his ethnography of a French administrative appeals court, the Conseil d'Etat, Latour has not simply described the workings of a particular institution but has attempted to capture non-reductively the practices involved in making law. In addition, he is concerned with exploring law 'as a mode of enunciation, the cosmological quality of which is equivalent to that of science, technology, religion or politics'. We learn from this chapter that Latour has a positive view of law that might be contrasted with Luhmann as much as with the critical tradition. He sees a principal element as 'hesitation', or slowness. Audren and De Bellaing draw our attention to his observations on the scales of justice. Latour reminds us that 'the scales, that are made up of two pans suspended from a beam, and understood as a classical representation of justice, express the horizon of equality less than the imperative of hesitation'.

The different philosophical foundations and methodological commitments of interactionism, ethnomethodology and actor–network theory do not interest most

---

[5] A Abbott, *Chaos of Disciplines* (Chicago, University of Chicago Press, 2001).

[6] See B Latour *Reassembling the Social: An Introduction to Actor–Network Theory* (Oxford, Clarendon Press, 2005).

[7] R Levi and M Valverde 'Studying Law by Association: Bruno Latour Goes to the Conseil d'Etat' (2008) 26 *Law and Social Inquiry* 805.

researchers in the field of law and society studies. Nor are they greatly interested in the relationship between action and structure as a theoretical problem in developing a scientific understanding of society. This should be evident from reading the third chapter in this section by Stewart Macaulay and Beth Mertz, who provide an overview of legal realism and current developments in empirical research within American law schools. As one might expect, researchers in this field tend to be drawn to the middle ground of the action–structure debate. Contemporary realists 'in one sense … share ethnomethodology's preference for allowing the research process to guide theory-building', but they also want to incorporate 'the insights of more structuralist theories'. Most of the studies reviewed as examples of realist research seem to have much in common with interactionist research, but with more attention given to the content of law that one finds in the sociological and criminological literatures. Writing in this pragmatist tradition, Macauley and Mertz defend 'empiricism' as valuable in combating the excesses of theorising, or what is sometimes termed 'theoreticism'.[8]

It might be expected that, through editing a collection of this kind, we must be advocating the value of theory over empirical research. A better way of putting this is that we see an understanding of theory as beneficial for conducting empirical research, in that it helps to know why you are pursuing an approach and the alternatives even if, as in some varieties of interactionist and ethnomethodological research, you are most concerned with conducting empirical research. Nonetheless, we would agree that there are dangers, and it is possible for theory to lose connection with the empirical world or to become an indulgent, self-referential exercise. Similarly, it is possible for research to become completely empiricist. Macauley and Mertz report on the growth of empirical legal studies in American law schools. The economists and psychologists in this movement seek to test hypotheses using scientific (mainly statistical) methods, in a way that seems to leave little room for speculative theorising or qualitative research unless this is conceptualised in narrow terms. We would not, however, see this necessarily as empiricism, since any research programme has a theoretical rationale and competes with other theoretical traditions for students and resources. As Macauley and Mertz suggest, the challenge for realists based in law schools lies in conducting empirical research that avoids the traps of empiricism or theoreticism and remains relevant to 'doctrinal scholarship'.

---

[8] For a discussion of theoreticism, see F Crews, *Skeptical Engagements* (Oxford, Oxford University Press, 1986).

9

Interpretive Sociologists and Law

MAX TRAVERS

I N THE FIRST edition of this collection, there was a separate section on interpretive approaches in sociology that contained a chapter that I authored on
symbolic interactionism, and a chapter on ethnomethodology and conversation
analysis by Robert Dingwall. In this second edition, these approaches have been
combined or reduced into one chapter, which may reflect their minority status in
social science, or even the normative perception that they should be absorbed into
the mainstream. These traditions are, after all, associated with the 'action' side of
the action–structure debate, which some readers may feel is outdated, given that every
sensible social scientist now recognises that actions take place and reproduce social
structures. It is, however, just this lack of interest in how people act, and the tendency
for this to disappear from view beneath generalisations and idealisations, that these
interpretive approaches are still seeking to challenge by demonstrating that there is an
alternative way of doing social science.

There have been many authoritative introductions to each of these research traditions.[1] The most recent advanced introduction considering ethnomethodological and
conversation analytic research on law can be found in chapter 3 of a recent study
by Baudouin Dupret that looks at judicial decision-making, drawing on documents
(judgments, witness statements and academic commentary) collected during fieldwork in the Egyptian criminal courts.[2] There have also been simpler introductions,
including some chapters in textbooks.[3] Since there are many introductions, I will not
summarise the findings of earlier, classic studies (an example would be Garfinkel's

---

[1] See, for example, on symbolic interactionism, H Blumer, *Symbolic Interactionism: Perspective and Method* (Berkeley, University of California Press, 1969); R Prus, *Symbolic Interaction and Ethnographic Research* (New York, State University of New York Press, 1996); L Reynolds and N Herman-Kinney (eds), *Handbook of Symbolic Interactionism* (Lanham, MD, Altamira, 2003); on ethnomethodology, E Livingston, *Making Sense of Ethnomethodology* (London, Routledge, 1987); S Hester and D Francis, *An Invitation to Ethnomethodology* (London, Sage, 2004); W Sharrock, *Ethnomethodology* (London, Sage, 2012); and on conversation analysis, P ten Have, *Doing Conversation Analysis*, 2nd edn (London, Sage, 2007); E Schegloff, *Sequence Organization in Interaction* (Cambridge, Cambridge University Press, 2007).

[2] B Dupret, *Adjudication in Action* (Aldershot, Ashgate, 2011). For older introductions, see M Travers, 'Ethnomethodology, Conversation Analysis and Law' (1999) 48 *Droit et Société* 349; M Travers and J Manzo (eds), *Law in Action* (Ashgate, Aldershot, 1997).

[3] See the chapters on symbolic interactionism and ethnomethodology in E Cuff, W Sharrock and D Francis, *Perspectives in Sociology*, 5th edn (London, Routledge, 2006) and the introduction to the interpretive tradition in M Travers, *Understanding Law and Society* (London, Routledge, 2009).

research on jurors[4]), but instead focus on what recent studies reveal about law as a social institution.

The term 'interpretive sociology' is potentially misleading given that there are a number of distinct approaches, informed by different philosophical assumptions.[5] Max Weber made a forceful early statement about the importance of addressing meaning, which he advanced against those in his own time who wanted the discipline to become more like natural science.[6] However, the influence of Weber on either symbolic interactionism or ethnomethodology is at best indirect. It should also be noted that ethnomethodologists do not even see themselves as belonging to the interpretive tradition, partly because this implies that they accept the terms of the structure–action debate as established by theorists such as Giddens or Bourdieu who claim to have achieved a synthesis.[7] There are also all kinds of approaches and debates that take place within ethnomethodology, particularly in recent years as the legacy of Harold Garfinkel (1917–2011) is being assimilated and debated.[8]

This review starts by considering the distinctive philosophical assumptions informing interpretive research, and then discusses research by symbolic interactionists, and in three research traditions within ethnomethodology, focusing on studies published since 2002. The three traditions are studies of work, conversation analysis and membership categorisation, each of which could be considered complementary or overlapping parts of one field, ethnomethodology/conversational analysis, although there has been some fragmentation and institutionalisation into distinct traditions.[9] The remaining part of the chapter draws out some implications for legal theory, legal practice and social justice (three aspects of law and society studies), and then offers some thoughts on future directions.

1. INTERPRETIVISM AS A PHILOSOPHY OF SOCIAL SCIENCE

Interpretive sociologies are informed by a variety of philosophical positions. Many prominent symbolic interactionists have been influenced by Pragmatism, an American intellectual movement that reacted against the abstractions and idealisations in nineteenth-century European philosophy. By contrast, ethnomethodology developed through Garfinkel engaging with the ideas of the phenomenological theorist Alfred

[4] H Garfinkel, 'Some Rules of Correct Decisions that Jurors Respect', in H Garfinkel, *Studies in Ethnomethodology* (Cambridge, Polity Press, 1984).

[5] For a review, see M Travers, 'The Philosophical Assumptions of Constructionism' in K Jacobs, T Manzi and J Kemeney (eds), *Social Constructionism and Housing Studies* (Aldershot, Ashgate, 2004).

[6] M Weber, *Economy and Society* (Berkeley, University of California Press, 1979).

[7] A Giddens, *New Rules of Sociological Method* (London, Hutchinson, 1976); P Bourdieu, *Outline of a Theory of Practice* (Cambridge, Cambridge University Press, 1977). For critical views by interpretive sociologists on the action–structure debate, see P Martin and A Dennis (eds), *Human Agents and Social Structures* (Manchester, Manchester University Press, 2010).

[8] See eg M Pollner, 'The End(s) of Ethnomethodology' (2012) 43 *American Sociologist* 7; E Livingston, 'Games, Pastimes, and Leisure Pursuits' (2012) 43 *American Sociologist* 109.

[9] For criticisms of conversation analysis by ethnomethdologists, see M Lynch, *Scientific Practice and Ordinary Action* (Cambridge, Cambridge University Press, 1993); M Travers, 'Understanding Talk in Legal Settings: What Law and Society Studies Can Learn from a Conversation Analyst', with replies by J Conley and D Maynard (2006) 31 *Law and Social Inquiry* 447.

Schutz.[10] Other ethnomethodologists, particularly those associated with Wes Sharrock in the United Kingdom, have pursued a programme of research informed by Ludwig Wittgenstein's ordinary language philosophy.[11] In each case, the philosophical ideas are presented as offering a means of seeing and appreciating ordinary aspects of social life that are concealed or distorted by other philosophical traditions, because these have a preference for idealisation.

To give one example of how this argument has been advanced, consider the claim made by the British philosopher Peter Winch that most of social science is 'misbegotten epistemology'.[12] According to Winch, who was influenced by Wittgenstein's ordinary language philosophy and asks us to investigate the language games that constitute different social practices, most of the time researchers are not simply making empirical findings, but advancing or buying into different ways of thinking about the world that originate in philosophy. His main target was the widespread assumption that human conduct must be explained using positivist theories modelled on natural science. But it could equally well be applied to realist types of explanation. In each case, it is assumed that social life cannot be understood without identifying hidden causes, and that sociology offers a way to look behind appearances.

Hutchinson et al portray this dominant tradition in sociological theorising as the pursuit of a seductive illusion that arises from overgeneralising:

> Since what people have in mind is a general theory, it is all too easy to suppose that the idea that something makes us do the things we do identifies the explanatory form for actions— actions result from causes. From that springs the idea that everything we do we are made to do. For some people, this though brings a frisson, or is somewhat uncanny—we never really know what we are doing, our actions are the mere effects of unknown causes.[13]

This criticism is not only directed against sociologists in their search for hidden structural causes. Cognitive scientists in psychology and those who seek to explain human conduct in terms of genetic factors (both large academic fields) also make what the interpretivist views as a philosophical mistake in believing that abstract models have value in explaining human actions. Hutchinson et al complain, for example, that sociobiology 'tends towards crudity in its portrayal of the practices it would explain' and 'to leave us less clear about many social phenomena than we were before we started'.[14]

Whether or not you agree with this viewpoint, it would be hard fully to understand or appreciate empirical research on law by interpretive sociologists without realising that they are advancing a philosophically driven critique of how other sociologists represent social reality and explain human actions. Wittgenstein presents his own investigations as a long journey, something you have to struggle with in ridding yourself of errors you have learnt through becoming a philosopher, so that finally you can see the world as it is without being troubled by false problems.[15] For sociologists, perhaps this

---

[10] See the first two chapters in J Heritage, *Garfinkel and Ethnomethdology* (Cambridge, Polity Press, 1984).

[11] See, for example, the chapter on ethnomethodology in P Hutchinson, R Read and W Sharrock, *There Is No Such Thing as Social Science: In Defence of Peter Winch* (Aldershot, Ashgate, 2008).

[12] P Winch *The Idea of a Social Science and its Relation to Philosophy*, 2nd edn (London, Routledge, 2007) 8–9.

[13] Hutchinson et al, above n 11, 21.

[14] Ibid, 3.

[15] L Wittgenstein, *Philosophical Investigations* (Oxford, Blackwell, 1958).

means giving up the false comfort that scientific explanation might offer any answers to social and political problems. Having made this point, it also seems important to recognise that many researchers are drawn to symbolic interactionism and ethnomethodology because they are dissatisfied with the idealisations and abstractions offered by other sociological literatures. The philosophical literature is helpful in providing a clearer grasp on action and meaning, and in providing a theoretical rationale for conducting naturalistic research.

2. SYMBOLIC INTERACTIONISM: LAW AS A SOCIAL PROCESS

Symbolic interactionism originates with the ethnographic research conducted by the first Chicago School in the 1920s and second Chicago School in the 1950s, but has diversified into several traditions. There are, for example, lively internal debates between realist and postmodernist ethnographers, and between those who understand it as a distinct oppositional voice within sociology and others who believe that it should be hybridised with mainstream structural traditions.[16] The central thinker for classical interactionism was George Herbert Mead, who advanced a theory of individuals and groups producing society through a process of shared definition and interpretation, while working within and reproducing existing social structures.[17]

In an insightful review, published after the first edition of this book, Peter Manning argued that symbolic interactionism results in a distinctive way of viewing legal institutions:

> [This] argument that holds for the legal institution as for any other, means that the acting, interpreting unit, be it an organization, collectivity, or individuals, responds to situations as they are interpolated and interpreted. The law is a filter or matrix of cliches, ideologies, rules of thumb, rules, and regulations that preshape the matters brought to legal deciders. ... Rather than seeing [a legal] institution as a system of determinant, functional parts, interactionists focus on the interpreting, defining, and choosing that results from situationally defined contingencies.[18]

What, though, should be recognised as an interactionist contribution to law and society studies? Manning's review might confuse some readers in that, after considering the deficiencies of legal realism, and the distinction between law in the books and law in action (each of which see law as a process of definition), he praises the work of Donald Black,[19] often viewed as a positivist with little interest in interaction or meaning, for providing a 'structural map ... within which to fill in and fill out social processes of definition, deciding and "producing" law'.[20] One way to understand these apparent contradictions is that Manning, like other sociologists, believes that the law and society movement cannot advance unless it frees itself from 'the common-sense lawyer view of the institution'.[21] Black makes it possible to take this step, but he

---

[16] For discussion, see K Sandstrom and G Fine, 'Triumphs, Emerging Voices, and the Future' in Reynolds and Herman-Kinney, above n 1; P Atkinson and W Housley, *Interactionism* (London, Sage, 2003).

[17] G Mead, *Mind, Self and Society* (Chicago, University of Chicago Press, 1934).

[18] P Manning, 'The Legal Institution' in Reynolds and Herman-Kinney, above n 1, 607.

[19] D Black, *The Social Behavior of Law* (New York, Academic Press, 1970).

[20] Manning, above n 18, 605.

[21] Ibid, 602.

still sees law as an independent or dependent variable rather than an object of analysis in its own right. Manning complains that, as in medical sociology, 'secondhand' concepts that originated within the sponsoring field (law or medicine) were adopted uncritically: 'black box, medical or legal processes, meanings and interpretations, were simply taken or accepted rather than deeply questioned'.[22]

Manning's answer to the question posed above is that interactionist research is concerned with the 'naturalistic' study of legal decision-making. The best research studies 'look at deciding as seen by the participants, through their culturally shaped perspectives, over time, and in an organizational context'.[23] One might add that to do this well requires a commitment to participant observation, and an interest in describing different occupational perspectives and the content of day-to-day work, represented by the best interactionist studies on medicine. This is missing in, for example, the legal realist literature, which employs quantitative methods to examine the impact of social factors on judicial decision-making.

There are not many interactionist studies about law, at least if interactionism is defined narrowly as a theoretically driven research programme directly influenced by the first and second Chicago Schools. Fortunately, a wider definition is possible since key figures, such as Everett Hughes,[24] were anthropologists, and many qualitative researchers have been influenced by this tradition without seeing themselves as interactionists. In my own graduate training, studies such as William Foote Whyte's *Street Corner Society*[25] and Elliot Liebow's *Tally's Corner*[26] were used as examples, alongside interactionist studies, of what could be achieved through naturalistic observation.

Although there are relatively few in-depth ethnographies published about legal settings, at least four major studies have been published since the first edition of this book that investigate meaning and describe legal work in some depth. Although there is a lot of theorising in addition to ethnographic description, Thomas Scheffer's ethnography of English criminal lawyers[27] can be appreciated as sharing many of the objectives discussed by Manning. This study looks closely at the processes involved in preparing cases, such as obtaining, interpreting and shaping witness statements at different stages of the pre-trial process and during trials. In theorising this ethnographic account, Scheffer draws on several theorists and theoretical traditions including Luhmann, Bourdieu and ethnomethodology. Whether combining approaches that have such different assumptions and objectives works is a matter for debate, but it is certainly a way of making interactionism attractive to mainstream sociologists.

Another study that seems interactionist in spirit is Bruno Latour's ethnography of the collaborative work of judges, lawyers and administrators in a French administrative appeals court.[28] Latour himself acknowledges that his work is heavily influenced by interactionism (and also ethnomethodology), in seeing society as a social process ('disassembling the social').[29] Consider, for example, this summary of his findings:

---

[22] Ibid, 604.
[23] Ibid, 613.
[24] E Hughes, *The Sociological Eye* (New Brunswick, Transaction, 1993).
[25] W Whyte, *Street Corner Society* (Chicago, University of Chicago Press, 1943).
[26] E Liebow, *Tally's Corner* (Boston, Little Brown, 1967).
[27] T Scheffer *Adversarial Case-Making* (Leiden, Brill, 2010).
[28] B Latour, *The Making of Law: An Ethnography of the Conseil D'Etat* (Cambridge, Polity Press, 2002).
[29] B Latour, *Reassembling the Social* (Oxford, Oxford University Press, 2005).

In this book, I have tried to provide evidence of that by capturing law in the ceaseless movement of documents that, in case of dispute, serve to constitute a sound case, provided that other texts have offered a procedure of resolution which, if attacked, makes it possible to go through right to the end by following the process step by step, from court to court and text to text, including all the links established prior to that, which other agents ... endeavour to make coherent through a continuous process of reparation, updating, forgetting, rectification, codification, comments and interpretations, so that nothing is lost and nothing is created, everything that inexorably passes by—time, humans, places, good, decisions—remains attached by a continuous thread, so that legal stability serves as a net for all potential applicants, and humans may live in the house of law. ... The sentence is long, and cannot be shortened, but does it not contain the essential features of what should be entrusted to the particular vehicle of law?[30]

Latour seems as much interested as an anthropologist in talking up the exotic character of law through making fun of the 'ceaseless movement' of files in this extract, or making comparisons between law courts and scientific laboratories, than carefully documenting legal work in this setting (although he does both). Nevertheless, this ethnography is in many respects a classic interactionist study that examines the collaborative work involved in producing legal outcomes as this happens through the deliberately slow workings of the various committees, as they consider precedents and arcane points of law. Interactionists have also described social processes and perspectives impressionistically or used literary devices, such as metaphors or the perspective by incongruity, to reveal differences and similarities between social settings.

It is worth mentioning two additional qualitative studies published since the first edition of this book, each of which make a major contribution to understanding legal practice. Susan Shapiro interviewed 100 lawyers in Chicago about conflicts of interest that arise when a firm cannot take on work because it already represents the other party to a legal dispute.[31] It is an interesting and revealing study that demonstrates the scale of the problem, but also describes in considerable detail different responses, including the elaborate measures taken to build 'Chinese walls', that themselves have unintended consequences. It takes you inside legal practice, and the nature of professionalism, in a way that is not available from looking at newspaper reports or court cases. In a similar way, Annalise Riles described the work of lawyers and regulators in the financial services industry. She worked in a Japanese bank for several years, and describes in some detail the technical issues that concern regulators.[32]

One criticism of these ethnographies, which returns to the observations made by Manning about law and society studies more generally, is that despite offering insights into the nature of legal work, and law as a process, they still reflect the lawyer's point of view. Shapiro views the efforts of lawyers to avoid conflicts of interest as illustrating the virtues of professional self-regulation. Riles offers what many readers might consider an highly optimistic view of the effectiveness of regulation in the financial sector, given that her book was written following the 2008–09 financial crisis. These positive accounts might be contrasted with the sceptical, debunking character of interactionist research conducted during the 1960s which did not take professional claims at face value. Interactionism does not require you to address every viewpoint:

---

[30] Latour, above n 28, 277.
[31] S Shapiro, *Tangled Loyalties* (Ann Arbor, University of Michigan Press, 2002).
[32] A Riles, *Collateral Knowledge* (Chicago, University of Chicago Press, 2011).

the ethnographer can choose which side to support,[33] or attempt to present a variety of perspectives with objectivity and balance.

3. ETHNOMETHODOLOGY: THREE RESEARCH TRADITIONS

Ethnomethodology is still not well understood as a theoretical tradition, and is often confused or conflated with interactionism, despite there being many significant differences, not least that it cannot easily be absorbed or integrated into mainstream sociology as a 'micro' approach that complements the insights supplied by 'macro' traditions. Nevertheless, this summary by Baudouin Dupret on his objectives in studying how a court deals with issues of moral conduct as an ethnomethodologist sounds similar to the statements by Manning and Latour in viewing law as a social process:

> This book's goal is to observe the contextualised deployment of various practices, and the activities of very diverse people who, in different capacities, found themselves involved in or faced with institutional judicial space. More specifically, the objective is to observe and describe, in an empirically documented and detailed manner, the moral dimension of judicial activity, and the judicial approach to questions of morality.[34]

In the next paragraph Dupret identifies a few 'fundamental axes' of ethnomethodology that inform his description of judicial work: 'the respecification of sociological objects; the attention paid to the practical grammar of actions, notably acts of language; [and] the rejection of sociological irony and overhanging stance vis-a-vis the people and actions they undertake'.[35] A central objective is to appreciate and explicate how those being studied understand their actions, instead of claiming superior knowledge. Put in more pointed terms, there are no hidden causes or structures, and you will not obtain much insight into how society works from reading theorists such as Marx, Foucault, Luhmann or Bourdieu (other than as an idealisation or politically driven distortion of what people already know). There are only the practices ('the practical grammar of actions' in Wittgenstein's terms) that constitute social life.

There are a variety of ways of researching law and legal institutions within this framework. The most distinctive sub-traditions are the studies-of-work programme, conversation analysis and membership categorisation.

Studies of Work

Perhaps the most important ethnomethodological study published since 2002 is Garfinkel's *Ethnomethodology's Program*.[36] Although most of the work and ideas had been available for some time, as unpublished papers or in specialist edited collections,[37] this was inevitably viewed as a programmatic statement that invited discussion about the difference between his early and later work. *Studies in Ethnomethodology* is mostly

---

[33] H Becker, 'Whose Side Are We On?' (1967) 14 *Social Problems* 239.
[34] Dupret, above n 2, 1.
[35] Ibid.
[36] H Garfinkel, *Ethnomethodology's Program* (Lanham, MD, Rowman and Littlefield, 2002).
[37] G Watson and R Seiler (eds), *Text in Context* (London, Sage, 1992).

concerned with identifying interpretive methods, shared within our whole culture, such as the documentary method of interpretation, that are used in making and producing sense, retrospectively and prospectively, in different social settings.[38] By contrast, some essays in the 2002 collection recommend that researchers acquire competence in different technical pursuits and then write about these as insiders (what Garfinkel calls the 'unique adequacy requirement').

Similar ideas have been advanced by Eric Livingston in a remarkable study about the practices in different 'domains' which include games, such as chequers and bridge, but also the work of solving simple mathematical puzzles.[39] Livingston has argued, pedagogically, in a similar way to Garfinkel on scientific experiments, that the only way to understand the practice is to acquire a competence in this specific form of reasoning through working through simple examples. The objective expressed in phenomenological language is that 'in the midst of those doings', say working out a move in chequers, the researcher will come to see, or perhaps cannot fail to see despite an academic training that constantly tells us to do otherwise, 'the observability of those doings as the ordinary, practical things that they are for their practitioners'.[40]

This raises the question as to whether law is such a 'domain' and, if so, how to investigate it experientially, in a way that satisfies the 'unique adequacy requirement'. Some caution is necessary, in my view, before making too much of this shift in the research agenda. This is, partly, because Livingston only recommends the study of practices that can be learnt quickly. You can learn how to play chequers, and even appreciate the play of grand masters in an hour, but you cannot become a competent surgeon or judicial officer without years of professional training.[41] Only a few students supervised by Garfinkel have pursued research that attempts to describe and explicate this kind of specialist knowledge.

A good example of such a study, published since 2002, is Stacy Burns's analysis of the work of judges mediating in civil disputes in the United States.[42] The procedure employed in this court was for the judge to meet with each party and ask difficult questions, with the aim of getting them to modify their negotiating position and reach a settlement. This is achieved partly through drawing on technical knowledge, sometimes relating to how precedents are followed in that particular court. Burns argues that in order to understand judicial mediation there is no substitute to examining how these were made relevant through the skilful work of competent judges and attorneys in each case. The extracts (which cannot be included here) show that a range of issues emerged in the discussions:

> These became (and were made) relevant to concession-seeking and included such things as the litigants' negotiating stances, settlement positions and volition to settle; the parties specific factual and legal claims, contentions, interpretations and arguments (including the

---

[38] H Garfinkel, *Studies in Ethnomethodology* (Cambridge, Polity Press, 1984).

[39] E Livingston, *Ethnographies of Reason* (Aldershot, Ashgate, 2002).

[40] Livingston, above n 8, 258.

[41] Latour, above n 28, 255 makes this point about his experiences as an ethnographer in the Conseil D'Etat: '[I]t was impossible ... even after several years of familiarisation, to get gradually closer to the legal utterance. To speak the law, he lacked not only words and concepts, but everything, absolutely everything. To legally state something, he would have to become a State counsellor.'

[42] S Burns, '"Think Your Blackest Thoughts and Darken Them": Judicial Mediation of Large Money Damage Dispute' (2001) 3(24) *Human Studies*, 227.

substantial strengths and weaknesses of each); the ways in which favourable (or harmful) legal and local precedent and authority were being asserted; and the course of progress in the negotiations up to that point.[43]

One feature of law as a 'domain' of practice which is evident from this study is that it involves both technical knowledge (eg being able to interpret how a judge would interpret a precedent), but also lay skills such as the ability to negotiate by calculating the odds of a jury finding sympathy for a particular litigant.[44] In my own research on sentencing in children's courts, I describe the considerations involved in sentencing young offenders.[45] There were not many legal options available to magistrates. A defendant could be given a good behaviour bond, made subject to a supervision order or sent to a detention centre. An ethnomethodological question would be what makes a minor or major offence? How is the seriousness of the offence, and what should happen, understood both by magistrates, but also by anyone observing the hearing?

One consideration is the circumstances of the case. For example, many offences involved assaults on other youths, incidents involving the police or spontaneous breaches of the law (an example would be going out on a bicycle to get an ice-cream without wearing a helmet). These offenders may have committed many such offences before appearing in court, and normally received a reprimand or a good behaviour bond. There were also, however, what magistrates described as 'serious' or 'repeat' offenders. These continued offending through various orders, and committed burglaries and offences involving violence. In her sentencing remarks, one magistrate summarised the offences committed, and their seriousness, concluding that 'the only appropriate sentence is a detention order'.[46] For other defendants, there were mitigating factors, such as psychological difficulties, or social circumstances arising from poverty and disadvantage, that were seen as relevant by magistrates.

My study describes how these considerations were applied on a case-by-case basis in detail. It is not, though, concerned with technical discussions about law or procedure. These come up in the lower courts from time to time, and a discussion about whether charges were legally correct is described as this happened in real time. But as Garkinkel recognised in his early research on jurors, 95 per cent of legal work involves common-sense skills and knowledge. One challenge is to obtain a greater analytic purchase on legal reasoning as 'domain-specific' knowledge. This can be examined in first-year law tutorials, so it is not necessarily esoteric or hidden from view in the chambers of senior judges.

Conversation Analysis

Conversation analysis originated in, and remains centrally concerned with, the methods used in ordinary conversation, but which are also used in different occu-

---

[43] Ibid, 243.

[44] For a similar study, see J Bilmes, 'Truth and Proof in a Lawyer's Story' (2012) 44 *Journal of Pragmatics* 1626. This is one of a number of papers from an ethnographic study of a division of the US Federal Trade Commission in the late 1970s and early 1980s during which Jack Bilmes obtained permission to record meetings between lawyers negotiating penalties after violations of laws regulating business practice.

[45] M Travers, *The Sentencing of Children* (Washington, DC, New Academia, 2012).

[46] Ibid, 112.

pational settings. It is interested in, for example, the sequences of conversational actions through which questions are followed by answers, that can be shown happening in elaborate, patterned ways. A central method is the careful transcription of audio-recordings in numbered lines using a set of symbols that captures details of the talk, such as the length of pauses or the timing of utterances in cases of overlapping speech. When studying interaction in occupational or institutional settings, conversation analysts employ the same methodology, but focus on the distinctive character of different speech exchange systems. There is usually, for example, an asymmetry of conversational actions in professional–client interviews, and in courtrooms only lawyer and judges have the right to ask questions.

One development since the 1980s and 1990s has been the analysis of video-recordings to examine how judges use new technology as part of their publicly visible work during hearings, and how gestures are employed in advocacy.[47] As Martha Komter notes, there is tremendous scope for investigating courtroom talk beyond 'the sequential organization of cross-examinations':

> [T]here are many different kinds of courtroom talk, and many different actions accomplished through courtroom talk that could also be investigated: jury deliberations, jury selections, objections, sidebars, summings up, jury instructions and so on. All these actions will exhibit different kinds of sequential organization, depending on the length of the turns (eg monologues and question answer sequences) and on the institutional identities of the speakers and recipients (judge, juror, attorney, defendant etc).[48]

There has also been some recent conversation analytic research on police interrogations,[49] and lawyer–client interviews.[50] Derek Edwards and Elizabeth Stokoe, for example, identify the occasions when the lawyer is required or allowed to speak in a police interrogation, and 'the features that make for success in objecting to a line of questioning'.[51] These researchers do not claim to have access to a domain of technical knowledge. Instead, they believe that their own technical knowledge makes it possible to understand police interrogations as a speech exchange system, and that this can can assist lawyers in developing better communication skills.

Membership Categorisation Analysis

A third strand or sub-tradition in ethnomethodology examines the organised cultural knowledge used in making sense of people and their actions. Harvey Sacks noted in

---

[47] See eg C Licoppe and L Dumoulin, 'The "Curious Case" of an Unspoken Opening Speech Act: A Video-ethnography of the Use of Video Communication in Courtroom Activities' (2010) 43 *Research on Language and Social Interaction* 211; G Matoesian, 'Role Conflict as an Interactional Resource in the Multimodal Emergence of Expert Identity' (2008) 171 *Semiotica* 15.

[48] M Komter, 'Conversation Analysis in the Courtroom' in J Sidnell and T Stivers (eds), *The Handbook of Conversation Analysis* (Oxford, Wiley-Blackwell, 2013) 628.

[49] D Edwards and L Stokoe, '"You Don't Have to Answer": Lawyers' Contributions in Police Interrogations of Suspects' (2011) 44 *Research on Language and Social Interaction* 21; M Komter, 'From Talk to Text: The Interactional Construction of a Police Record' (2009) 39 *Research on Language and Social Interaction* 201.

[50] I Halldorsdotir, 'Orientations to Law, Guidelines and Codes in Lawyer–Client Interaction' (2009) 39 *Research on Language and Social Interaction* 263.

[51] Edwards and Stokoe, above n 49, 21.

one of his lectures that it was interesting that, when hearing the opening of a children's story, 'The baby cried. The mommy picked it up', we immediately know that this is about a mother and her baby.[52] Everyone knows that babies cry, and mothers pick them up. But we also know that mothers have a moral obligation to pick up crying babies. Sacks is not, though, suggesting as a conventional sociologist that people simply acquire this knowledge through socialisation. Instead, they use it in complex ways both in understanding other people's actions, and descriptions of these actions, but also in making our own actions understandable.

Although Sacks was one of the founders of conversation analysis, these ideas have not been taken up by this tradition, partly because they are still viewed as a loose or permissive form of analysis that diverts efforts away from establishing sequential analysis as a science.[53] Nevertheless, those conversation analysts who have studied courtrooms have always been interested in how categories are used in sequences of cross-examination.[54] These studies show that the lawyer has a significant structural advantage over a witness in being able to ask chains of questions. But they can also draw on cultural knowledge about what everyone knows to discredit or undermine testimony. Greg Matoesian has, for example, examined how what might be termed categorical knowledge (how someone might be expected to behave after being raped) was used by a skilled advocate to demolish the credibility of a witness.[55]

Perhaps the most important ethnomethodological study of law in the last ten years (certainly if assessed in terms of its level of engagement with legal theory) has been conducted by Baudouin Dupret.[56] While based in Egypt, he collected a number of law cases relating to sexual conduct, in addition to conducting observational research and interviewing practitioners about their work. Most of the study is, however, based on the analysis of documents such as judgments and records of interviews with defendants by prosecutors. There is a certain 'exotic' flavour for readers in Western societies in that he conducted the study in Egypt where having a sex-change operation, or engaging in consensual homosexual sex is a criminal offence.[57] In the *Queen's Boat* case, a group of men were sentenced to prison sentences involving hard labour for homosexual acts in a law that criminalises debauchery and prostitution. The category 'homosexual' is not recognised in the Egyptian penal code. Nevertheless, their actions were presented by the prosecution as examples of debauchery and perversion. Although there were no victims, the judicial ruling implies that society is a victim that needs protecting from this criminal offence. There is a common-sense morality built into the police questioning and inevitable judgment organised around categorical pairs:

To say of someone that 'he was arrested' implies that 'representatives of the social order'

---

[52] H Sacks, 'On the Analysability of Stories by Children' in R Turner (ed), *Ethnomethodology* (Harmondsworth, Penguin, 1974) 216.

[53] The handbook on conversation analysis edited by Sidnell and Stivers, above n 48, does not discuss membership categorisation analysis.

[54] See eg P Drew, 'Contested Evidence in Courtroom Cross-examination: The Case of a Trial for Rape' in Travers and Manzo (eds), above n 2, 51.

[55] G Matoesian, '"I'm Sorry We had to Meet under these Circumstances": Verbal Artistry (and Wizardry) in the Kennedy Smith Rape Trial' in Travers and Manzo (eds), above n 2, 137.

[56] Dupret, above n 2.

[57] The focus of the study is not on the distinctive beliefs or system of law in Egypt or the Islamic world, but in documenting and understanding the nature of adjudication, through publicly accountable legal procedures, in a court of law.

did so, and this in turn implies that the person belongs to the category of 'offender'. To say that someone is 'sexually depraved' implies that he breached 'the social order', which in turn implies that he belongs to the legal category of 'perverts'. The many activities linked to the different categorization pairs are also linked to each other: 'arresting', 'interrogating', 'accusing', 'judging', which are activities linked to the category 'law and order officials', are paired with, respectively, 'committing a crime', 'breaching public order', and 'acting against morality'—activities linked to the category of 'perverts'.[58]

This may sound overdeterministic for an ethnomethodological study, but Dupret does not refer to some transcendental entity, such as heteronormativity, in explaining this judgment.[59] Instead, he explicates the reasoning and assumptions in this corpus of documents about a particular case. Sacks himself believed that political change resulted from people inventing new categories, or contesting stereotypical assumptions. It would appear from the *Queen's Boat* case that there is little possibility of this happening in the Egyptian legal system, even if there is a successful transition to democracy. Like any other ethnomethodological study, however, this is snapshot, taken in this case of a whole court system, at a particular moment in time. It may be that, through broadening the corpus of documentary data, one could analyse many cultural changes taking place in Egypt, resulting in conflict between religious conservatives and progressives.

4. IMPLICATIONS FOR LAW AND SOCIETY STUDIES

Each of these interpretive approaches offers a distinctive way of understanding law as a social institution, through examining everyday actions and experiences that are usually overlooked, or seen as having little importance by other academic traditions. The next section will consider specific implications for legal theory, legal practice and social justice.

Legal Theory

Although interpretive approaches ask us to look at ordinary actions and experiences, and many of the empirical studies are aimed at a general readership, there is the paradox that their programmatic statements are part of intellectual debates in sociology and other academic disciplines, and tend to develop a technical vocabulary. This is perhaps less true of symbolic interactionism during the 1950s in which training consisted of doing fieldwork, or in contemporary conversation analysis, which takes place within a particular set of theoretical assumptions but is driven by data analysis. Nevertheless, it is hard to be taken seriously by academic readerships unless there is a technical language and some theorisation.

We have already seen how symbolic interactionists, such as Manning, have con-

---

[58] Dupret, above n 2, 314.
[59] This approach might be compared to G Matoesian, *Reproducing Rape* (Cambridge, Polity, 1993). Matoesian uses the concept of patriarchy, while examining the practices through which it is reproduced in cross-examination during rape trials.

trasted the view of law as a social process with the dominant view in law and society studies. Manning argues that conventional 'law in action' studies do not address or describe what happens in legal practice. Similarly, Dupret is critical towards legal philosophy. Dupret believes that 'it is difficult to perceive the entire value of the praxeological approach without bearing in mind the background and the counterpoint of the traditional way of dealing with relations with law and morality'.[60] This is true in the sense that, if you are interested in legal philosophy, it may seem strange that the large literatures on legal rules in the positivist tradition, or law and morality in the natural law tradition, have little interest in the actual work of lawyers and judges.

In advancing this critique, Dupret draws upon some ideas advanced by Garfinkel during the 1990s about phenomenological pairs[61] in making a distinction between 'a legal rule and its uses':

> The legal rule and its uses make up a pair endowed with phenomenologial properties. By focusing exclusively on the first segment of the pair, to wit [legal stipulations], formal/classical analysis loses sight of the work that makes up legal reasoning and is concerned only with bringing the finished product to light. In this way it neglects the elements that constitute the workplace. It paraphrases legal rules, but ignores the effective reasoning carried out by real people in real places and circumstances.[62]

There is also, though, the implication that conventional philosophers and social scientists are guilty of some kind of moral failing, in accepting idealised accounts at face value, and in having no interest in the skilful production by human beings. Although Garfinkel explicitly warns against this kind of political reading,[63] there are similarities to the arguments made by some antimodernist thinkers concerned about the activities of the state.[64] This may also explain the success of Dorothy Smith in establishing a programe of critical ethnographic research about what she calls the 'relations of ruling' that combines humanist Marxism and ethnomethodology.[65]

There seems to be an ambiguity in Garfinkel's writings on whether ethnomethodology is intended to critique formal methods of representation, or simply point to an alternative domain of practices that could be investigated. It seems unclear why either jurists or sociologists should be blamed for writing about human activities using generalisations and idealisations. One argument might be that this way of viewing law may have some political or ideological value to law schools. It maintains the fiction that there is a knowledge base, and a set of distinctive skills, that are taught in law schools and used in professional practice. It also makes it possible to retain a transcendental view of law as something reliable, coherent and independent from moral or political considerations, while accepting that individual decision-makers and actual courts do not meet these standards.

---

[60] Dupret, above n 2, 10.

[61] Garfinkel uses this device in *Ethomethodology's Program* to reveal the practices concealed by, or not available to, mainstream social science. One slogan that is, perhaps, easier to understand than phenomenological pairs is that 'phenomena of order are identical with procedures for their local endogenous production and accountability' (Garfinkel, above n 36, 72).

[62] Dupret, above n 2, 296.

[63] Ibid.

[64] For example, J Scott, *Seeing Like a State* (New Haven, Yale University Press, 1998); Z Bauman *Modernity and the Holocaust* (Cambridge, Polity Press, 1991).

[65] See eg D Smith, *Institutional Ethnography* (Lanham, MD, Altamira Press, 2005).

Legal Practice

The law school is centrally concerned with training lawyers, and preparing them for professional practice. It is, therefore, possible to view any literature about law in social science instrumentally, as contributing to the knowledge or skills needed by lawyers. One argument made in support of teaching sociology of law is that it gives students a broader knowledge, and makes it possible for them to think critically about the role of law in society. Whether or not this could also be acquired through reading novels, or makes a difference when establishing a relationship with clients, is unclear. Each of these traditions has made a stronger claim for usefulness.

In advocating the value of interactionism over grand theories, Blumer argued that the precondition for doing applied research was to develop a close familiarity with the social world being studied.[66] Earlier in this review, I summarised the work of Shapiro and Riles, who, though not interactionists, are pursuing research that employs similar methods. They work, respectively, in interdisciplinary legal research institutes and law schools, and have contributed to debates within law and regulation as professional fields, admittedly by advancing arguments congenial (and, because of this, useful) to those being researched.

Ethnomethodology has been successful as an applied field both in assisting technology companies to design and evaluate new products, in which researchers have mainly employed ethnographic methods,[67] and in teaching communication skills. Conversation analysts have received considerable funding and support from medical schools for programmes to investigate the medical interview as a speech exchange system. According to one review:

> [R]ecognition is growing that [conversational analysis] is a crucial resource for medical educators, practitioners and others whose aim is to improve the quality of medical care and relationships among participants in medical encounters. Because recordings and transcripts make it possible to focus in on the interactional detail of interactional sequences, subtle variations in behavior can be compared—for instance, different ways doctors solicit patients' presenting concerns, which can convey that they are more or less willing to listen.[68]

Despite the recognised benefits of legal clinics as a means of teaching practical skills, no law school, at least to my knowledge, has invested in a systematic programme of training that could incorporate these techniques. One problem is that law firms are understandably reluctant to allow researchers to record confidential lawyer–client interviews, whereas doctors and hospitals are used to facilitating clinical research. But perhaps the major hurdle is that no one really believes that teaching communication skills will improve legal practice. Will watching a video of a skilled advocate, with an expert instructor, teach you how to conduct an effective cross-examination? Perhaps it may help, just as, say, reading a manual may help you pass a driving test, or taking a course on ethics may make you more ethical. But it is not exactly a substitute for learning by doing, and learning what is competence for all practical purposes (you would look foolish trying to be Perry Mason in your local magistrates' court).

---

[66] Blumer, above n 1.

[67] See M Rouncefield and P Tolmie (eds), *Ethnomethodology at Work* (Aldershot, Ashgate, 2011); M Szymanski and J Whalen (eds), *Making Work Visible* (Cambridge, Cambridge University Press, 2011).

[68] V Gill and F Roberts, 'Conversation Analysis in Medicine' in Sidnell and Stivers, above n 48, 589.

Whether or not teaching doctors and lawyers communication skills improves their performance, it seems important to recognise that this is only one aspect of professional practice. This was nicely dramatised in the television series *House* based on the idea that a brilliant doctor could routinely, and deliberately, be rude to patients. It is not necessarily the ability to communicate that makes you a good doctor, but your understanding of medicine. Interactionist and ethnomethodological studies about medical and legal practice have demonstrated that there is no agreement among professionals on what constitutes good work, irrespective of how this knowledge is communicated.[69] The practical or educational value of such studies may lie in making law students aware of the dilemmas they will face in practice, although they will learn about this for real soon enough.

Social Justice

Interpretive traditions have been much criticised by critical sociologists for their conservatism or political quietism, and this also explains their marginal position in the discipline given that most people have progressive political views. During the 1960s, interactionists stood up for subordinate groups such as drug-users and young offenders. But this was criticised by progressives as a naïve or romantic political programme, not based on a structural analysis.[70] Ethnomethodologists were viewed with even more disdain. They deliberately pursued a policy of 'indifference' towards the moral and political questions that interest mainstream sociologists.[71]

It is easier to defend interpretivism today than during the 1960s since most intellectuals are disillusioned with what Lyotard called the 'grand narratives' of modernity,[72] and accept that there are no easy solutions to establish a better world, certainly one free from economic inequality. This is more or less the position of Max Weber, who realised that this would be a problem if the discipline turned away from natural science. The best interpretive studies, for example those by the first Chicago School, have arguably provided a more complex view of moral and political questions through examining social processes in some depth. A recent example, which has probably been influenced indirectly by interactionism, is Kathleen Hull's study of the movement in the United States campaigning for gay marriage.[73] Hull showed through interviewing gay couples that there were a variety of views. It suggests that political activists have to simplify issues and to some extent misrepresent the people they are representing in order to advance a political argument for law reform.

To give another example, most studies of juvenile offenders by critical criminologists portray these offenders as victims, and invariably suggest that they are frightened

---

[69] This was a central theme in my ethnographic study about a firm of 'radical' lawyers. There is a detailed description of an episode in which the owner of the firm, pseudonymously called Jane Gregson, persuaded a client to plead guilty. Gregson believed that she was acting in a more moral and competent fashion than those who were in law 'for the money'. However, critics of the firm disagreed entirely with this assessment. See M Travers, *The Reality of Law* (Aldershot, Ashgate, 1997).

[70] For example, A Gouldner, 'The Sociologist as Partisan: Sociology and the Welfare State' (1968) 3 *American Sociologist* 103.

[71] For a restatement, see Garfinkel, above n 36.

[72] J Lyotard, *The Postmodern Condition* (Manchester, Manchester University Press, 1984).

[73] K Hull, *Same-Sex Marriage* (Cambridge, Cambridge University Press, 2006).

by the proceedings. However, I noticed in my study of Australian children's courts that many defendants had quite a relaxed posture. At midday, after most of the court business had concluded, it was common to see groups of youngsters congregating outside the court and welfare offices engaging in social activities. There is nothing especially ethnomethodological about such an observation: other than that it is an obvious feature of this social setting that is not mentioned by other studies. Nor does it necessarily have any implications for political debates about juvenile justice. It is possible to view detention centres as punitive and potentially damaging, even if some young people are quite comfortable there, and view the court order as a 'badge of honour'. But nevertheless it seems to undermine a political case on behalf of disadvantaged groups if young people are portrayed as victims, even when they do not see their own lives in these terms.

5. FUTURE DIRECTIONS

In a review published some years ago, I predicted that there would be a trickle of ethnomethodological and conversation studies about law by researchers trained in American departments of sociology.[74] This considerably understated the amount of work that has been produced by these traditions, and also by symbolic interactionists if you accept the broader definition of interactionist research employed in this chapter. It also overstated the importance of the United States as providing an institutional base. Arguably, the most interesting study in the last ten years, at least in the sense of engaging with broader questions raised by legal theory, and again demonstrating the value of membership categorisation analysis, is based on research conducted by a French sociologist in Egypt.

Because they are few in number, but also due to the well-known difficulties of getting access to legal settings, interpretive sociologists have so far only looked at a limited range of topics. Most researchers have obtained access to the work of practitioners concerned with determining matters of fact or sentencing in the lower courts. We do not know much about how judges use precedents in making law which would make possible a greater engagement with legal theory (although Latour, who is not normally considered an interactionist or ethnomethodologist, has made an important contribution in his ethnography of the Conseil d'Etat). Only a small number of courts, and types of legal work have been studied. There has been little attention to the experiences of litigants or defendants. There has not been much research on how laws are made through the parliamentary process. Aside from Burns's paper based on her experiences at Yale Law School,[75] there has been little research within these traditions on legal pedagogy. Perhaps it will be possible to address more aspects of legal practice in the next decade.

[74] Travers, above n 2.
[75] S Burns, 'Practicing Law: A Study of Pedagogic Interchange in a Law School Classroom' in Travers and Manzo (eds), above n 2, 265.

10

Bruno Latour's Legal Anthropology

FRÉDÉRIC AUDREN and CÉDRIC MOREAU DE BELLAING

MANY WERE SURPRISED when Bruno Latour, a philosopher and anthropologist and currently a professor at Sciences Po (Paris), and who is first and foremost well known for his work in the sociology of science, published a book on a French administrative jurisdiction, the Conseil d'État (Council of State).[1] Having dedicated so many years to the study of scientists, from California's neuroendocrinology laboratories[2] to the pedologists who work on Amazonia,[3] why had Latour changed directions and taken an interest in law? The author himself offered a disarmingly simple answer: he had not changed direction at all—on the contrary, this was the obstinate continuation of the very programme he had followed for forty years, namely identifying the 'modes of existence' that are characteristic of our societies.[4] In many respects, though, because of law's capacity to preserve its specific form of reasoning over time, it could even prove to be the purest case study of the empirical philosophy that Latour seeks to develop.[5] As he has observed, 'What is most surprising is that we are still today so very Roman in the rulings we hand down'![6]

What is an empirical philosophy? It is an approach that conjoins the rethinking of the ontological question within a rigorous ethnographic approach on the one hand, with an attempt to outline the forms that are characteristic of the cosmology of the Western world, the 'modes of existence' (as the philosopher Etienne Souriau called them),[7] on the other. In fact, if Bruno Latour's ethnography is exacting, it is because it provides an underpinning for two symmetrical operations: (i) reconstituting the list of elements, of the heterogeneous beings that form a network (to use the terms of art associated with *actor-network-theory* (ANT)), which render it possible, prolong

---

[1] B Latour, *The Making of Law—An Ethnography of the Conseil d'État* (Cambridge, Polity Press, 2002).

[2] B Latour and S Woolgar, *Laboratory Life: The Social Construction of Scientific Facts* (Princeton, Princeton University Press, 1979).

[3] B Latour, 'The "Topofil" of Boa Vista. A Photo-Philosophical Montage', in *Pandora's Hope. Essays on the Reality of Siences Studies* (Cambridge, MA, Harvard University Press, 1999).

[4] B Latour, *Enquête sur les modes d'existence. Une anthropologie des Modernes* (Paris, La découverte, 2012).

[5] B Karsenti, 'Tenir au monde, le faire tenir. Linéaments pour une philosophie de l'attention' (2012) 75 *Archives de philosophie* 574–75.

[6] Latour, above n 4, 366.

[7] E Souriau, *Les différents modes d'existence*. Présentation d'Isabelle Stengers et Bruno Latour (Paris, Presses Universitaires de France, 2009).

it, sustain its activity and extend it;[8] and (ii) capturing, in each network, the specific mode of existence that is being put to the test, and discerning the value that it reveals. Thus, legal, political, scientific or religious institutions all have in common the fact that they are made up of a multiplicity of actors, monuments, books, files or even computers that the ethnographer undertakes to explore.[9] However, the latter also tries to highlight how, beyond such a shared heterogeneity, and in a given situation, there is something that is at this moment specifically 'legal', or now 'political', or now 'religious', etc. Each of these domains is irreducible to the others. From this point of view, ethnography is indispensable, and, at the same time, it is never self-sufficient. It is decisive, because describing the beings that make up a network as precisely as possible is the only way to understand of what and by whom the world in which we live is composed. Ethnography is also unmistakably a space for anthropological explicitation, for rendering the values to which we hold explicitly.

Recapitulating this way allows us to underscore what the ethnography carried out by Latour at the Conseil d'État is *not*, and at the same time to indicate how some commentaries fail to characterise his work accurately, indeed how sterile some of the criticisms of his book prove to be, because they have been levelled at arguments that Latour never intended to defend. Contrary to a widespread idea, Latour's work on the Conseil d'État is neither a sociological study of the Conseil d'État, nor even a legal sociology. First, it is not a sociological study of the Conseil d'État, since Latour never intended to carry out a monographic study that would give a thorough account of the activity of that institution. That is why he has not addressed many of its dimensions. The social characteristics of the counsellors are not his focus, nor are the organisation of their work, the forms of socialisation at play in that institution, or the function that the Conseil d'État has within the French political and administrative structure. In that respect, *The Making of Law* does not aim at contributing to the elaboration of the sociology of legal institutions, nor to the sociology of jurists. The book does not offer a sociological study of the state in which the Conseil d'État would offer a vantage point for the understanding of the state machinery either.

Secondly, Latour's work is not part of a legal sociology. Admittedly, law is at the heart of the book, but the author does not try to carry out a study of the relations between law and society, as legal sociology will traditionally do. Latour, for that matter, distances himself from such an approach from the very first lines of his book. For him, it is meaningless to study law through the relations it would have with society since the two of them are not separate entities. There exist only networks that articulate legal elements to other elements, to other actors.[10] Such connections are societies, or, as one could say, make societies, but their building up is not strictly speaking 'social'. Indeed, the 'social' dimension does not explain anything; on the contrary, it is explained by the description of associations:[11]

---

[8] Latour, above n 4.

[9] L de Sutter and S Gutwirth, 'Droit et cosmopolitique. Notes sur la contribution de Bruno Latour à la pensée du droit' (2004) 56 *Droit et Société* 259–89.

[10] B Latour, *Reassembling the Social—An Introduction to Actor-Network-Theory*, (Oxford, Oxford University Press, 2005).

[11] R Levi and M Valverde, 'Studying Law by Association: Bruno Latour Goes to the Conseil d'État' (2008) 33 *Law & Social Inquiry* 805–25.

One of the main research programmes of the sociology of law, according to which a relationship has to be established between the corpus of rules on the one hand and society on the other, does not withstand examination: law is already of the social, of association; alone it processes more of the social than the notion of society from which it is in no way distinct since it works on it, kneads it, arranges it, designates it, imputes it, makes it responsible, envelops it.[12]

From that point of view, Latour's work may be compared with ethnomethodology,[13] legal praxeology or with the perspective developed in the wake of Patricia Ewick and Susan Silbey's work.[14] However, Latour's perspective in its double ambition is different from those two approaches. He wants to explore at the same time law in its development and law's specific 'mode of existence', that is, the proper truth which, by contrast, makes it different from politics, science, morals etc. Therefore, Latour's anthropological approach is an endeavour of the 'empirical philosophy' we have already referred to which is in line with the work of Alfred North Whitehead, Gilles Deleuze and the American pragmatists John Dewey and William James.[15] That philosophy claims that it starts from fieldwork and never breaks from it, even when it is elaborating concepts. Trying to capture the mode of veridiction of law, Latour is consequently quite far from a legal sociology, so doggedly does he refuse to explain that kind of law with social factors.

Bruno Latour's approach is therefore that of an *empirical metaphysics* (those two words being absolutely equal), which leads the reader much closer to social theory than legal sociology. The following pages try to explain that ambition. The first part is devoted to the ethnography Latour carried out at the Conseil d'État and shows that his approach was quite close to that of one of his former works, *Laboratory Life*. The second part focuses on some of the conclusions he drew from that inquiry, more specifically on the idea of hesitation and even more importantly on that of means—two notions that are at the heart not only of law, but also of Latour's approach. They are essential to understanding what Latour, in a determining chapter of *The Making of Law*, calls the 'passage of law'. The third part shows that it is impossible to separate that ethnography from a larger ambition: identifying and describing a specific *mode of existence*, which is that of law. This will be the occasion for clarifying what Latour means by that expression. Last, the fourth part is a conclusion which comes back on some of the criticisms levelled at Latour's work and shows that they are indeed erroneous, since they interpret *The Making of Law* as a contribution to legal sociology, while in fact it is part of a work that has, in an exemplary way, pursued an anthropological inquiry into the regimes of enunciation in the modern world that was started forty years ago.

---

[12] Latour, above n 1, 262.

[13] Bruno Latour regularly pays tribute to Harold Garfinkel, and the work he did with Woolgar in *Laboratory Life* was clearly in line with ethnomethodology.

[14] S Silbey and P Ewick, *The Common Place of Law. Stories from Everyday Life* (Chicago, University of Chicago Press, 1998).

[15] B Latour, 'Biographie d'une enquête—à propos d'un livre sur les modes d'existence' (2012) 75 *Archives de philosophie* 549–66.

1. AN ETHNOGRAPHIC STANDARD: FROM THE NEUROENDOCRINOLOGY LABORATORY TO THE CONSEIL D'ÉTAT

In *Laboratory Life*, Bruno Latour and Steve Woolgar studied the work of a neuro-endocrinology laboratory, following the daily activity of the researchers as close to their practices as possible.[16] Their idea was the following: researchers must be studied as if they were a remote tribe, whose rites, customs, ways of life and practises one, as a good anthropologist, wanted to discover. This is the principle of 'symmetrical anthropology'[17] that Latour created very early in his work, in a radical reinterpretation of David Bloor's Strong Programme.[18] This means that the two authors were not only interested in the laboratory workers' research protocols and in the moments when they carried out experiments, but also in their active seeking of funding, in the creation of files, in the thorny problems linked to publications, in the scientific, political, personal and possibly moral problems implied in those stages of the work of a researcher, etc. Through that inquiry, the two social scientists were then led to describe scientific work from the countless *inscriptions* it produces.[19]

The ethnographer, who is not a member of the laboratory, indeed notices that laboratory workers spend their time writing, coding, correcting, reading, marking, etc—in short, producing inscriptions. Those are the only daily and concrete *products* of the laboratory: inscriptions in books of protocol, inscriptions on the printouts, inscription-diagrams, inscriptions on the blackboard, and inscriptions in the form of articles, of research projects, of applications for funding, etc. *Laboratory Life* is consequently made up of the thousands of operations that aim at producing inscriptions that will make sense of the network of scientific texts. Thus, Latour and Woolgar described the production of a scientific fact, holding together the scientific operations carried out on a peptide, the activity of the researchers around the experiment, the texts and the necessary writings that weigh upon those researchers, etc, as a summation of inscriptions resulting in successive transformations (also called 'translations'),[20] which, step by step, lead to a 'scientific discovery'. Such a set of inscriptions then constitutes a *network* at the heart of which scientific truth develops. The more the network undergoes stress tests (eg the test of an experimental set-up or the criticisms levelled at an article in a scientific journal),[21] the wider and more real the network becomes. That is the reason why a scientific fact is indeed *made*, but it is all the more real as it is built.[22]

---

[16] Latour and Woolgar, above n 2.

[17] Latour proposed a systematisation of it in *We Never Have Been Modern* (Cambridge, MA, Harvard University Press, 1993).

[18] D Bloor, *Knowledge and Social Imagery* (Chicago, Chicago University Press, 1976).

[19] Latour uses the notion of 'inscription' but does not reduce it to the language or symbolical dimension it may suggest, thus avoiding the dangers of the *linguistic turn*. Inscriptions in Latour's work therefore have meaning only insofar as they are inscribed in communities. Consequently, the scientific truth that moves along the chain of inscriptions and is formulated once the network has been covered is not a symbolic or language truth, for it comes at the end of the network, carried by all the inscriptions that allow its circulation. The inscription is therefore what is most empirical, in the same way as scientific truth, which holds only through the connection of all those inscriptions.

[20] M Akrich, M Callon and B Latour, *Sociologie de la traduction* (Paris, Presses de l'École des Mines, 2006).

[21] That notion of *ordeal* was jointly created by the new anthropology of science (B Latour, *The Pasteurization of France* (Cambridge, MA, Harvard University Press, 1984)) and French pragmatic sociology (L Boltanski and L Thévenot, *On Justification: Economies of Worth* (Princeton, Princeton University Press, 2006)).

[22] Latour, above n 3.

The ethnographic approach Latour adopted in his work on the Conseil d'État was exactly the same as the one he developed twenty years earlier in his inquiry on the neuroendocrinology laboratory. Latour spent several months intensively attending the meetings and activities of the Conseil d'État. That institution is the highest French administrative court (as in other countries, there are two sorts of jurisdiction in France, an administrative and a judicial one), the mission of which is at the same time to advise the government on the preparation of bills and to rule on the disputes related to the activities of the administrations. Immersed in that legal matter, Latour devoted the same attention to the inscriptions that were produced there (even though he did not insist on that notion as much) in his inquiry. After studying science 'in action',[23] he decided to study law through the most material of its traces: the first inscriptions of law that are visible to the ethnographer as he arrives at the Conseil d'État, the *files* that are being examined.

> If the ethnographer wants to achieve this unstable mix of proximity (that only a field study can obtain) and detachment (which allows him to avoid immediately attaching himself to concepts that have been worn out by much prolonged usage) then it is sufficient for him to substitute the grand talk about Law, Justice and Norms with a meticulous inquiry about files—grey, beige or yellow, thin or thick, easy or complex, old or new—and to see where they lead him. Yes, let us begin law at the beginning, that is to say at the stamps, elastic bands, paper clips and other office paraphernalia which are the indispensable tools of cases.[24]

Thus, law is embodied and takes shape, materially and narratively, in and through the files. The legal experiment eventually consists in

> watching a very particular fluid, which will be materially recognised through the successive *files* (the content, thickness and composition of which will vary based on the stage of the dispute), proceed from one step to the following one. Those files are related, by one of their extremities, to multiform complaints that are more or less well articulated by claimants who feel they are under attack. ... But by the other extremity, they are related to case law which, one way or another, gradually calls up the whole law.[25]

Following law therefore means following its traces, its supports, through an obstinate tracking of cardboard files, through the observation of how files are filled, how they circulate and through which office they go. Such a tracking work reveals that those files are made up of links that are progressively established by the interlocking of the facts that are stated and of the considerations to which the files refer. Latour thus asserts that one will understand nothing about law if one tries to go directly from the norm to the fact, and vice versa, without taking seriously the modest but central accumulation of papers of various origins, the successive translations the result of which is that law proceeds step by step. Similarly, scientific discoveries cannot be understood unless the successive layers of inscriptions that are produced through the activity of the laboratory workers are accounted for. That is why all the stages of the flux of the files are important, and all the transformations, all the circulations must be described. The power of law, Latour writes, is comparable to that of a chain, 'exactly as strong

---

[23] B Latour, *Science in Action: How to Follow Scientists and Engineers through Society* (Cambridge, MA, Harvard University Press, 1987).

[24] Latour, above n 1, 71.

[25] Latour, above n 4, 353.

as its feeblest link, which could not possibly be detected if one did not follow the whole chain, link after link, without forgetting even one of them'.[26]

From the study of the files he followed, Latour isolated what, quoting semiotics, he called the 'value objects', through which the files go, and which mark the *passage* of law. Those ten value objects (see Table 1) may be understood as specific types of transformations, which are necessary for law to *pass*. They are the means to 'know whether a given fact corresponds to a definition that would allow it to be assessed or not'.[27]

Table 1. Value objects that are modified through testing

1.   Authority of the members participating in the ruling
2.   Progress of the case as it overcomes obstacles
3.   Organisation of the disputes that allow the logistics of complaints to be respected
4.   Interest of the disputes measuring the difficulty of the cases
5.   Weight of texts which create an increasingly contrasted landscape and story
6.   Quality control that reflexively assesses the conditions of felicity of the whole process
7.   Hesitation that allows the production of some freedom of judgement through a de-bonding before a re-bonding
8.   Legal means that make it necessary to link case law and disputes
9.   Consistency of law itself which modifies its inner structure and quality
10. Limits of law that make it possible to start or to suspend the beginning of the process.[28]

2. THE PASSAGE OF LAW

Those value objects are the transformations that give law its force.[29] They make up the network through which law flows without being limited to their summation. As such, it must be noted that they are neither purely social nor purely legal. In Bruno Latour's work, there is a complete and assumed rupture with the two main modes of understanding law developed in social sciences. On the one hand, in a reading of Pierre Bourdieu's work that rather lacks charity, Latour refuses to see law as a tool for domination, for the disguise of power. Reading law as a simple instrument of the legitimacy of force would be the best way to miss its inherent logic.[30] On the other hand, law as formalism, described as an autonomous subsocial system in an essentially procedural version, must be left aside. Because it is focused only on 'legal reasoning', such a conception conceals all the moments of hesitation, of negotiation or compromise that nonetheless mark the practice of jurists. Latour thinks that what is legal can only be captured in itself, and that it is therefore in its development that it must be understood, by following the *traces*[31] it leaves behind. This is the condition

---

[26] Ibid.

[27] Ibid, 353.

[28] Latour, above n 1, 140.

[29] K McGee, 'The Fragile Force of Law: Mediation, Stratification, and Law's Material Life' (2012) *Law, Culture and the Humanities* 6–7 (published online, 12 June 2012, doi: 10.1177/1743872112447144).

[30] Latour referred in particular to economist Olivier Favereau's reading of Bourdieu's approach of rules of law in 'L'économie du sociologue ou penser (l'orthodoxie) à partir de Pierre Bourdieu' in B Lahire (dir), *Le travail sociologique de Pierre Bourdieu. Dettes et critiques* (Paris, La découverte, 2001) 255–314.

[31] More generally speaking, one can notice that *The Making of Law* keeps clear of a wider division between internalism and externalism. Internalism postulates an absolute autonomy of law from social

for the understanding of its strange autonomy to become possible, even though it is dependent on the political, the economy or passions.

Its different transformations will not be detailed here, except for two of them, which are essential to the analysis of Latour's work. The first is about the *hesitation* of the counsellors. It is a fundamental hesitation, as if those who declare the law measure the accomplishment of their performances by their own capacity to have properly, considerably and sufficiently hesitated:

> Crushing and grinding the content of the files, by having enough case law react to them. … A case which produces many hesitations is a case in which the relationship between the case and the usual formulation of the norm has not been considered self-obvious. Hesitating is indeed knowing that the norm is abstract, not in the sense of the power of abstraction on concrete cases, but in the sense that none of its particular formulations is authoritative, that it can always be further unfolded and receive formulations the meaning of which would not have been noticed before the case which makes the occasion arise.[32]

> Have we judged well? Yes, provided we have hesitated well and long enough.[33]

To a large extent, the Conseil d'État can successfully complete its jurisdictional task only if it founds itself, for each of the cases that are examined, on a collective and uninterrupted work of hesitation. The latter thus makes it possible for other solutions to be found, other case law to apply, other objections to overcome. Latour reminds us that the scales that are made up of two pans suspended from a beam, understood as a classical representation of justice, express less the horizon of equality than the imperative of hesitation.

The second value object that we wish to highlight here has an even more important role in the network that we are studying, even though, once more, law cannot pass if one of the transformations that have been referred to above is missing. It is the *means*. Jurists, for example, refer to 'legal means' (matters of law), 'factual means' (matters of fact) or 'purely legal means' (pure matters of law). What is at stake each time is the motive or the reason upon which a legal claim or a ruling could be founded. As a word used by the counsellors perfectly echoing ANT, it is fundamental in two ways. First, the means is the empirical moment when Latour notices the most distinctive passage of law, 'Either there is a legal means and *it passes* (law is sometimes said to be "a living tree") or there is no legal means and the case "*stops there*".'[34] If you are not 'standing to act', if the limitation period during which it is possible to act has expired, or if you do not bring the requisite evidence of a fact or an act, all the goodwill in the world will not be enough to have the legal system start working or your right recognised. To put it more mundanely, the means is the tool that links a fact and its phenomenological richness to the legal texts drawn upon by the Conseil d'État, which allows a 'fractional distillation':

---

forces. Law and the social are radically opposed, the juridical depending only on the decisions founded on the rule of law. Externalism, for its part, consists in assuming that law is only the result of social forces, which is the same as denying any autonomy from the social to law. Externalism then presupposes a society which exists outside law and therefore considers the latter a simple covering of power relations most of the time, of relations of domination.

[32] I Stengers, 'Une politique cosmopolitique du droit est-elle possible ?' (2004) 8 *Cosmopolitiques* 24.
[33] Latour, above n 4, 356.
[34] Ibid, 354.

> By isolating the notion of means, the ethnographer of law clearly sees what allows to overcome the successive gaps between the case which is full of noise, blood and emotions, and the stable, strict principles it must progressively lead to. Following the cases, she understands through what kind of 'fractional distillation' a huge and complex file comes down to a single sentence submitted to a jury or a court.[35]

Secondly, the means is fundamental, for, to use Bruno Karsenti's words, it is upon it that Latour's whole philosophical inquiry has been founded for so many years. The ethnographic case of law may be that which best manages to isolate it, but one of Latour's constant standards[36] is to stay at the level of means so as to

> understand the means themselves, account for their own weight, acknowledge the status of that transitional materiality without transfering it to another level. ... The means is an alteration, and, in that sense, it is a contruction of the singular reality that it makes happen. It is the medium for the constitution of the being *as other*.[37]

In other words, the means exemplarily reproduces the movement that is at the foundation of the network ontology, for it ensures the passage from one statement to another, from one entity to another (without the first one disappearing in favour of the second), while always adding a slight difference.[38] It therefore operates a translation that is always at the same time a betrayal and an enrichment. Consequently, it is fundamentally what enables law to *pass*.

The succession of value objects identified by Latour enables him to understand how law *passes*. For law only exists as it circulates through and thanks to a series of entities, which, together, make up a network. 'In legal reasoning, everything counts',[39] he asserts, including the most insignificant links, including what does not first belong to the legal domain. On the contrary, he adds, it is essential to the quality of law that law is not only made up of law. In that description,

> the dynamic of the judgement does not alternate between fact and law, nor does it seek to reconcile them by means of some unstable compromise ... but it picks out the elements which will allow the file to be made to progress according to a particular thought process that we can only call 'legal'.[40]

What matters here is the manner in which the elements that are unconnected when the file is opened are joined together when it is closed.[41] This joining movement is what enables law to be possible. The movement that is law's, its passage, therefore becomes describable through the reconstitution of the reasoning of the actors in a non-formal version, which accounts for what they have recourse to.

However, let us say it again: the means occupies a very specific position in that passage of law. It is similar to the legal qualification of the case among several pos-

---

[35] Ibid, 357.
[36] Eg B Latour, 'Moral and Technology. The End of the Means' (2002) 19 *Theory, Culture and Society* 247–60.
[37] Karsenti, above n 5, 576.
[38] Here the influence of Deleuze and Tarde on Latour is noticeable. B Latour, 'Gabriel Tarde and the End of Social' in P Joyce (ed.) *The Social in Question. New Bearings in History and the Social Sciences* (Routledge, London, 2002) 117–32.
[39] Latour, above n 1, 141.
[40] Ibid, 150.
[41] Note here the influence of J Dewey's theory of inquiry on Latour. J Dewey, *Logique. Une théorie de l'enquête* (Paris, Presses Universitaires de France, 1993) 169ff.

sibilities upon which it is decided whether or not the claim is admissible. The passage of law is that so particular movement that is similar to

> a process of transformations, translations, transmutations and transubstantiation which, through successive degrees, and the cost (sometimes quite considerable) of the participation of a very great number of court clerks, commentators, specialised professors, progressively modifies the relation between what may be called the *quantity* of fact, of emotion, of passion, and the *quantity* of principle, of texts upon which it will be possible to rule. It is that proportion of relative quantities that are admirably called legal *qualification*.[42]

Here can be identified another specificity of law: the issue of what is transported (be it morals, truth or objectivity) never comes to define what is at stake in the very possibility of *passage*.

3. LAW AS A MODE OF EXISTENCE

> If you ask how the European Convention on Human Rights can be transported to the expulsion case of the foreigner Mr Farouk, the answer is simple: it is there, in foreigners' rights, since the decision was taken on such-and-such a date, authorising Article 6 to be invoked against the prefects' decisions. Making the connection, linking up these elements, weaving the social: all this is law itself.[43]

Law is therefore at the same time what evolves along a chain made up of value objects identified by the ethnographic method and what, once the operation has been made, makes it possible to 'characterise the type of values that seem to be circulating in a given network and to give it its specific tone'.[44] Law is a way of making connections and giving them a *legal characterisation* or *quality*. Such a capacity to make connections, to create links between entities of all kinds, as well as the fact that law refers to a very specific *texture* must therefore be apprehended at the same time. That texture is wrongly described as 'formal'—it is better characterised as superficial (without this term being derogatory). The jurist does not waste time looking for founding principles (the question of appearances and reality that is so very central in sciences is of no importance in legal issues). He obstinately tries to link a tiny case to the Constitution, to establish a connection between Mr So-and-So's claims and such article of the Napoleonic Code or the Penal Code, to create case law out of a modest case. In legal cases, form is everything, while content is nothing. This does not mean that law is useless, on the contrary. This amounts to insisting on the fact that law is at the same time strong and weak. It is weak because it is nothing else than a 'fragile bridge of texts'.[45] It is strong because, as long as they have access to the judicial institution and follow its conditions of felicity, claimants can assert their claims, modest though they may be, and stand in the way of people that are more powerful than them. Bruno Latour also likes to refer to the example, analysed by historian Alain Boureau, of an English monk, who, in the thirteenth century, armed with law, won his humble case against the appetites of powerful lords. To understand what a legal

---

[42] Latour, above n 4, 353.
[43] Latour, above n 1, 260–61.
[44] Latour, above n 4.
[45] Ibid, 86.

operation is, there is therefore no need to plunge into the depths of the social domain or to look *behind* law for some hidden interests. Law is in itself its own explanation (according to Latour, law remains in perfect homeostasis).[46] There is no need to draw on ethology, zoology or biology to define what an animal is. In a legal case, an animal may be 'furniture by its nature' or 'immovable by its intended purpose'. The specific autonomy of law is therefore not subject to a demand of clarification, which explains why its definitions are so often tautological. Courts *legally* determine what is true and what is false. The animal that is of interest to the jurist is that which is defined *according to the meaning* it has in such legislative measure or such precedent. Law is what law is. What characterises it is less its autonomy from the social domain than that strange tautology that moves it in any circumstance.

Such self-reference can only be correctly understood provided one notes that Latour makes an important difference between two registers that are linked but nonetheless different: law as an institution and law as enunciation (or *mode of existence*).[47] Law, he says, is made of law no more than a gas pipe is made of gas! The legal world is not law. Under certain conditions, it allows its development, and it takes on meaning only because law as a mode of existence allows it.

> The Conseil d'État is not made 'of law' but consists of walls, corridors, frescoes, files, a body of members, texts, careers, publications, controversies. If there is law in it, if it is capable of saying the law, it is surely not because it belongs to a system distinct from the rest of the social world, but because it stirs it in its entirety *in a certain mode*.[48]

Although the elements the activity of the Conseil d'État is made of are necessary to its making, law cannot be reduced to them. That is why Latour is not satisfied with an ethnography of that *institution*. He associates it with the exploration of a specific mode, of a *mode of enunciation* the cosmological quality of which is equivalent to that of science, technology, religion or politics.[49] Each of these practices determines the criteria of the true and the false *in their own way*. If you wait for law to give some objective truth on the world, to alleviate your psychological pains, or to side with morals all the time, then you will be disappointed. From that point of view, law, as science, or religion, must be understood as a 'preposition'.[50] Making science or making law means starting an activity in such a way that jurists or scientists will acknowledge it as one of their own and as respecting some conditions of felicity. Although the criteria of the veridiction of science or religion are not the same as those of law, one must nonetheless learn to acknowledge that here, now, in this context, one *talks in a legal way* and not objectively or religiously. Understanding law as an enunciation, a preposition or an adverb (Latour uses those three words) is therefore giving oneself a reading key on the way one must interpret, talk of and understand *what follows*.[51] By way of contrast, Latour refers to the example of fiction:

---

[46] Ibid, 234.

[47] That distinction is strongly specified in B Latour, 'Note brève sur l'écologie du droit saisie comme énonciation' (2004) 8 *Cosmopolitiques* 34–40.

[48] Latour, above n 1, 263–64.

[49] Latour also talks of 'mode of veridiction', of 'adverb' or 'link'.

[50] Latour, above n 4, 66–77.

[51] Latour, above n 47, 37.

If you read a novel, you will not find it difficult to distinguish the story, what happens to the characters, the sudden developments of the plot. ... In other words, for you to understand and read, there must be a reading key, a particular form of directing movement, which accompanies you all along the story and which enables you to constantly adjust the type of veridiction that is being used.[52]

The fiction enunciation establishes a certain kind of truth that nobody would mistake for reality. In the same way, you will understand nothing of the activity of the juridical institution 'if this reading key is not added: beware, what you are going to read or to hear is Law, not fiction or politics, etc'.[53]

The modes of existence are therefore not an umpteenth set of categories or criteria the aim of which is to compartmentalise elements of the social domain. It is a means to acknowledge *at the same time* that networks are always associations that cannot be reduced only to legal, political, economic or scientific matters *and* that those networks are nonetheless pervaded with values that are those of a specific domain of our Western cosmology. Those domains are less compartments than harmonics that reveal 'a certain tone of the experiment, felicitous or unfelicitous conditions that are each time specific, and, above all, and that is where it becomes dangerous, a particular ontology'.[54] In other words, the modes of existence are those specific regimes in which singular truths, which are attached to values and to forms of computation that are inseparable and compose them, are developed. They are, to use Bruno Karsenti's words, 'modes of commitment, but only in the sense that, at their level, distinct beings are likely to be established, as long as our active attention is given to that differentiated establishment of each mode of being'.[55] Although there is a legal anthropology in Latour's work, it is not because he is looking for legal invariants, but because law must be understood as a *way of being* in the world which is different from other ways of being that are of equivalent dignity.

In order to account for their own activities, jurists often resort to epistemology, for the elaboration of scientific facts is supposed to give the best vantage point for the understanding of the making of law. A biology or neuroscience laboratory would be a model to understand legal work. However, nothing is more different from an expert piece of information than a legal qualification.[56] Both are distinct modes of enunciation. In a scientific laboratory, objectivity is folded *within* the object (be it a peptide, a mouse or a frog that is subjected to terrible ordeals), and the scientist works, through a series of successive transformations, to transport such or such a phenomenon in the laboratory, in a pipette or under a microscope, in order to produce a new piece of information. Science thus reveals chains of references that allow circulation from a phenomenon to its expert translations and vice versa. Besides the fact that legal objectivity does not have any object strictly speaking, law presents different features. It is characterised by its capacity to keep the trace of *all* the courses of action, of *all* the disengagements (this word must be understood in its semiotic meaning),

---

[52] Ibid.
[53] Ibid.
[54] Latour, above n 15, 549.
[55] Karsenti, above n 5, 583.
[56] Latour, above n 1, ch 5.

provided only the possible *minimum* is kept. ... Everything happens as if law (that regime which allows to link speakers and statements with invisible threads) managed to *go into the direction opposite to that which the increasing number of directing movements and flights of enunciation ceaselessly take.*[57]

What is to be understood? A very simple thing in fact: if you act, if you don't act, if you behave as a criminal, if you promise something, if you sign a contract, law is that operation that keeps a trace of a past action or of a statement to link it, to impute it, to assign it to an author or to a speaker. Through a strange historicity, it joins what a constant movement detaches, distributes and buries. Even though you no longer keep up the old house you inherited twenty years ago, you are still responsible for the damage a falling tile causes to a passer-by. Although you committed a crime two years ago, you cannot that easily, through the mechanism of a limitation period, escape the rigour of justice if your crime is discovered later on. The signature you appended at the bottom of that contract obliges you to your co-contracting party, even when the terms of that contract no longer suit you. There is no search for a foundation, no production of new pieces of information, but only a patient work of attribution or assignment. Thus Latour asserts that he has 'extracted (tried to extract) a form of veridiction unusual and unjustly treated (even by the jurists who are too accustomed to it) which gives all its sense to all the acts, case law, institutions that are called "juridical"'.[58] His inquiry undoubtedly pays attention to how two modes of existence both overlap and complicate one another. But more than anything else, it indeed tries correctly to refer to what is important to them, to the jurists themselves, while respecting law's specific form of truth.

4. A FEW ISSUES OF INTERPRETATION

Bruno Latour's work has found some critical echo in the world of legal social sciences. His methodological principles, as well as the conclusions of his inquiry, have been the object of discussions and controversies. His book has been fairly well received by the Counsellors of State, who have nonetheless reproached him for not granting enough importance to the issue of the reciprocal effects of legal theory and legal practice. This was a criticism that some jurists may also have shared. Among the latter, those who sought to promote an open conception of the legal dogma hoped that they would find in Latour's work some arguments against legal internalism. In fact, their hope was disappointed. Although Latour announced that he would above all oppose externalism, it seems quite difficult when one reads his book to assert that his approach reinforced internalism, for did not he assert several times that law was not only made up of law? The kind of linking that makes the passage of law possible does not associate only legal beings, far from it.

Other jurists worried, among other things, about the fact that the perspective that was developed in *The Making of Law*, by granting a fundamental importance to the judge in the handling of a case, would paradoxically reinforce the doctrinal approach (if not its power). In fact, it would justify the role that the doctrine gives itself. As the

---

[57] Latour, above n 4, 359–60.
[58] Latour, above n 47, 37.

judge makes law but does not know the law he makes, the doctrine, that is, the community of professors, is there to tell him what it is. In order to reach its objective, such a criticism needs to truncate Latour's arguments, which, in reality, hardly deal with the power of the judges and of the professors. Although the judge indeed plays a part at several moments in the circulation of the files, reducing the passage of law to those precise moments conflicts with Latour's argument that law may pass only on the one condition that it reviews all the value objects that the empirical inquiry has allowed to reveal. From that point of view, the role of the judge is essential, but it is so only as it is part of a chain, each link of which is important.

Those criticisms have, in fact, more largely asked the question of the empirical place chosen by Latour to study the question of law. Thus, some reproached him with studying the Conseil d'État to account for the passage of law, although it is a very specific institution which produces a no less very specific kind of law, administrative law. What would have happened if Latour had, for example, decided to work on the Parliament or on a civil court? Would he have accounted for the same chain allowing the passage of law? By focusing on the Conseil d'État's case law, does not the inquiry enlighten the production of *administrative law* rather than provide an analysis of the production of *law*? Such a criticism is not illegitimate, for it quite rightly points out that the work Latour did in the sociology of science to explain how the passing from *sciences* to science is made was only partly done for law. Chapter 5 in *The Making of Law* is the only chapter to sketch a similar question, through a confrontation between the forms of objectivity produced by law and science. However, those different objections to Latour forget, or feign to forget, that his work is not a legal sociology, and purely and simply mistake law as an institution for law as a mode of existence.

It must be repeated: what Bruno Latour is interested in is not the real truth on the institutional balances between codified law and jurisprudential law, but the correct understanding of the specific passage of law, its texture and the network that allows it. Latour tries to describe the associations that make up our societies based on what exists and what holds the world together. In order to achieve that, one must adopt a vantage point, and the Conseil d'État reveals itself to be paradigmatic for the understanding of one of the values (law) that are so fundamental to the modern. Moreover, the confusion that is made between law as an institution and/or a mode of existence is at the heart of a series of other reproaches which have pointed out the absence of a critical stance of the author on what the counsellors do and say, the omission of the public function of the Conseil d'État and its effects on decisions, the silence of the inquiry on the media status of the institution or on the social properties of the counsellors, whose categories of thought Latour used without questioning them because they had been elaborated by the state. Such criticisms could have been justified, if, once again, Latour had produced a legal sociology or a sociology of the Conseil d'État. But this would omit a fundamental stage of *The Making of Law*: the ethnographic identification of the passage of law is mechanically linked to the description of law as a mode of existence. One may wish that Latour were a legal sociologist, but it is not possible to reproach him with a legal sociology that is not part of his project.

Bruno Latour: caution, slow down! His anthropological endeavour to identify the modes of existence is one of the most ambitious and original ever attempted. It is also one of the most disconcerting, both because of the project itself and because of the semiotic universe it conveys. No doubt, Latour's project, and more particularly his empirical metaphysics, will somewhat unnerve the reader, and the jurist in particular. What is to be done, once the mode of existence law (the [LAW] mode in Latour's language) has been extracted and given its specific coloration? Whether it fascinates or irritates, Latour's book requires of the reader a certain *slowness* that will provide the capacity to learn from it, to better think our modernity, and to create new types of relations between law and the other values we cherish.*

---

* Translation by Solène Semichon.

11

New Legal Realism and the Empirical Turn in Law

STEWART MACAULAY and ELIZABETH MERTZ

THIS CHAPTER EXAMINES contemporary debates over realist and empirical approaches to studying law, situating them in terms of both doctrinal scholarship and social theory.[1] Current empirical work on law embraces a variety of social theories, epistemologies and methodologies. This eclecticism makes it difficult to present one overarching approach as canonical. At the same time, some scholars stress the benefits of using multiple methods and synthesizing diverse theories. In one sense, they share ethnomethodology's preference for allowing the research process to guide theory-building. On the other hand, unlike ethnomethodologists, many new legal realists want to move beyond close study of local legal phenomena also to examine connections with wider social structures and/or cultures—incorporating the insights of more structuralist theories. To do this requires some theoretical grasp of the 'macro'-levels within which micro-level human interaction is situated, pushing today's legal realists and empiricists toward a reconsideration of social theory. It is for this reason that the interdisciplinary study of law offers perhaps one of the most promising places for developing a synthesis of theory and empiricism which could cross old divides and stumbling blocks.

We begin with a brief exploration of today's turn to empiricism among legal scholars. We then consider emerging debates among current scholars in the area. A third section presents examples of how, as they explore law empirically, some contemporary realist scholars also address classic questions in social and legal theory. We conclude by considering how new forms of translation between empirical and theoretical studies of law might follow from a new legal realism.

1. TODAY'S REALIST AND EMPIRICAL APPROACHES TO LAW

Despite their many differences, proponents of empirical approaches generally share a distaste for purely theoretical research lacking any reference to studies of human

---

[1] In keeping with the editors' charge that we write accessibly, and at a relatively introductory level, we have simplified a number of much more complicated issues. We hope that these sketches will serve as invitations to read further.

life 'in action'. They also tend to reject purely doctrinal research, which occupies itself only with statements of formal law 'in books'. For example, sociologists and anthropologists studying law would expect to perform fieldwork, interviews and/or surveys before they would conclude anything about how law works in reality. Like legal theorists, they might begin with a formally stated rule of law—take, for example, the '*Miranda* rule' in the United States that requires police officers to read suspects their rights. However, social scientists would then proceed to examine what actually happens when officers take a suspect into custody (and they would ideally study this in different places, not assuming that all police operate in the same way). They might find that even if the same rule 'in the books' is *supposed* to apply across many different places, in practice police officers act in a variety of ways.[2] For these scholars, what makes the research 'social' is that it examines how a stated rule actually works in practice, using established social science methods of data collection, based on actual observations. This is quite different from focusing only on what courts have officially said that police should do.

The venerable insight that 'law in action' differs from 'law in books' is by now thought to be old hat in legal scholarship, although there is good reason to question whether it has actually been incorporated into the mainstream.[3] Empirical research on law has a long history; we will not waste time here arguing over where that history starts. Social scientists might point to Maine, Morgan, Durkheim or Weber;[4] legal scholars to Ehrlich, Pound or Clark.[5] Suffice it to say that scholars in multiple fields have long recognised the need to look outside of legal doctrine if we are to grasp what law actually means and does in people's lives. Yet despite this early recognition of the importance of empirical work, much of Western legal scholarship and law teaching has proceeded primarily on the basis of analysing legal doctrine.[6]

For most of the twentieth century, the focus of mainstream legal scholarship was on judges and logical systems of rules. Marc Galanter has pointed out that the standard model of legal thought simply *assumes* that the behaviour of legal actors will generally conform to the rules; it then follows that the 'authoritative normative learning generated at the higher reaches of the [legal] system provides a map for understanding [all that is important]'.[7] Nonetheless, we can point to many instances during the last century when scholars turned to empirical work to gain a picture of the law in action. For example, noted legal realist Karl Llewellyn ran a study of divorce in New

---

[2] See, for example, the overview of some such studies provided in R Leo, 'Questioning the Relevance of Miranda in the Twenty-first Century' (2001) 99 *Michigan Law Review* 1000–29.

[3] While the stark distinction between law-in-action and law-in-books is in some ways oversimplistic, it is difficult to consider the subtleties involved when so many scholars have yet to consider the most basic questions that follow from recognizing that formal rules as stated do not automatically translate into practice.

[4] HS Maine, *Ancient Law* (London, John Murray, 1861); LH Morgan, *Ancient Society* (New York, Henry Holt, 1877); see also E Durkheim, *The Division of Labor in Society* [1893] (New York, Free Press, 1947); M Weber, *Economy and Society: An Outline of Interpretive Sociology* [1922] (Berkeley, University of California Press, 1978).

[5] E Ehrlich, *Fundamental Principles of the Sociology of Law* (Cambridge, MA, Harvard University Press, 1936; see also R Pound, 'Law in Books and Law in Action' (1910) 44 *American Law Review* 12–36.

[6] E Mertz, *The Language of Law School: Learning to 'Think Like a Lawyer'* (New York, Oxford University Press, 1997); S Macaulay, 'Introduction' to K Llewellyn, *The Bramble Bush* (New Orleans, Quid Pro Quo, 2012) i–xxi; W Sullivan et al, *Educating Lawyers: Preparation for the Profession of Law* (San Francisco, Jossey-Bass, 2007).

[7] M Galanter, 'Notes on the Future of Social Research in Law' in S Macaulay, L Friedman and J Stookey, (eds), *Law & Society: Readings on the Social Study of Law* (New York, Norton, 1995) 25–27.

York and coauthored research on the legal practices of the Cheyenne.[8] Charles Clark studied delay and overcrowding in the court system.[9] Roscoe Pound undertook a study of the criminal justice system with Felix Frankfurter.[10] The University of Chicago jury project studied the jury in many ways.[11] Willard Hurst created a whole new form of legal history that asked what the historical record showed about the functions played by lawyers and the legal system in the economic development of the United States.[12] These foundational realists pushed legal scholars to consider the way formal laws worked out in practice.

However, legal realism in the United States waned, and the legal process school which rose to prominence in the 1950s and 1960s insisted that normative choices in law should be made by legislatures; the proper role of judges was to apply the law, conceived as a set of rules and underlying principles.[13] While empirical research could uncover the consequences of those rules after they had been put into action by courts and other legal institutions, it was the legislatures' job to track what was happening and to decide if something needed to be changed. The task of legal academics was thus to analyse how the courts conceptualised and applied rules, and to theorise about how courts could work with other governmental institutions to best effectuate partic-ular kinds of goals; following this line of reasoning, empirical research became largely irrelevant to legal scholars. Legal process scholars did attempt to find a middle road between extremes of formalist and realist approaches, but they did not help to foster any further development of empiricism within law schools.

During this time, the US Supreme Court made a series of decisions that seemed to demand major changes in American society, and American law was impacted by the burgeoning civil rights, antiwar and feminist movements. Subsequently within the legal academy during the 1970s, critical legal scholars drew on social theory to question courts' significance in effecting real social change.[14] This work echoed the realists' in

---

[8] K Llewellyn, 'Behind the Law of Divorce', pts I and II (1932) 32 *Columbia Law Review* 1281–308 and (1933) 33 *Columbia Law Review* 249–94; W Twining, *Karl Llewellyn and the Realist Movement* (Norman, University of Oklahoma Press, 1973) 195; K Llewellyn and EA Hoebel, *The Cheyenne Way: Conflict and Case Law in Primitive Jurisprudence* (Norman, University of Oklahoma Press, 1941); J Conley and W O'Barr, 'A Classic in Spite of Itself: The Cheyenne Way and the Case Method in Legal Anthropology' (2004) 29 *Law & Social Inquiry* 179–217.

[9] J Schlegel, *American Legal Realism & Empirical Social Science* (Chapel Hill, University of North Carolina Press, 1995); J Schlegel and D Trubek, 'Charles E Clark and the Reform of Legal Education' in P Petruck (ed), *Judge Charles Edward Clark* (New York, Oceana Publications, 1991) 81–113.

[10] R Pound and F Frankfurter, *Criminal Justice in Cleveland* (Cleveland, OH, The Cleveland Foundation, 1922).

[11] H Kalven Jr and H Zeisel, *The American Jury* (Boston, Little, Brown & Company 1966).

[12] JW Hurst, *Law and Economic Growth: The Legal History of the Lumber Industry in Wisconsin 1836–1915* (Cambridge, MA, Harvard University Press, 1964); JW Hurst, *Law and the Conditions of Freedom in the Nineteenth-century United States* (Madison, University of Wisconsin, 1956).

[13] The legal process school did realise that judges at times make law and exercise creative judgment, but argued that this creativity should be limited to reasoning from aspects of legal texts, processes and institu-tions. K Greenawalt, 'The Enduring Significance of Neutral Principles' (1978) 78 *Columbia Law Review* 982–1021; H Wechsler, 'Toward Neutral Principles of Constitutional Law' (1959) 73 *Harvard Law Review* 1–35.

[14] Kalman has recounted the story of the Yale Law School's retreat from realism and law-and-society scholarship in the early 1970s. L Kalman, 'The Dark Ages' in A Kronman (ed), *History of the Yale Law School: The Tercentennial Lectures* (New Haven, Yale University Press, 2004) 154–257. For discussions of CLS in relation to empirical research on law, see D Trubek, 'Where the Action Is: Critical Legal Studies and Empiricism' (1984) 36 *Stanford Law Review* 575–622; see also S Macaulay, 'Law and Behavioral Science: Is There Any There There?' (1984) 6 *Law & Policy* 149–87.

its scepticism about how neutral or rule-governed law could be, and in pushing legal scholarship to consider the role of law's social contexts. The 'crits' were particularly dubious about the degree to which law helps underprivileged people, arguing that the legal system generally serves the wealthy. While many of the critical legal studies arguments aimed attention at the social surroundings of law, the scholarship itself did not generally take much of an empirical turn. Indeed, some critical legal studies scholars were hostile to empirical work, seeing its claim to objectivity as deceptive. From the 1970s onward, US law schools were swept by a form of law-and-economics scholarship that looked at classic legal problems and offered relatively definite solutions in the name of efficiency, generally taking a somewhat conservative political stance. This could have demanded empirical research into the actual consequences of legal decisions aimed at achieving efficiency. But although a small group of law-and-economics scholars performed empirical research that took social context into account, the standard research performed by legal academics in this area tended to theorise and model how law should work based on assumptions about how a rational actor would behave.

On a parallel track with these developments in US law schools, the Law and Society Association (LSA) was formed in 1964 by a group that included both social scientists and legal academics. It sought to provide a journal and academic meetings for scholars from all of the social sciences who were interested in the functioning of the legal system and its place in society. While a small group of law professors played a key role in the development of LSA, the law-and-society movement never occupied a major place in most law schools. One likely reason for this is the fact that the majority of its work did not engage directly with the central concern of most law professors: very little of it focused on how cases should be decided. Moreover, few law professors had the necessary training, resources or time to undertake scientific empirical work. Finally, some would argue that there were political reasons why some kinds of scholarship took hold in the legal academy rather than others.[15]

2. NEW LEGAL REALISM, EMPIRICAL LEGAL STUDIES AND MORE

Matters changed remarkably in the first decade of the twenty-first century. More law faculties began to hire professors who held postgraduate degrees in both law and social sciences. Law faculty members became associated with three groups devoted to fostering empirical work on law—empirical legal studies (ELS), new legal realism (NLR) and a miscellaneous collection of other efforts that have been identified as realist. [16]

Empirical Legal Studies

Theodore Eisenberg, one of the founders of ELS, has written about the group's

---

[15] See eg M McCluskey, 'How Money for Legal Theory Disadvantages Feminism' in K Abrams (ed), *Issues in Legal Scholarship: Legal Feminism Now* (Berkeley, Bepress Online, 2011).

[16] Nourse and Shaffer provide some examples of this additional category of NLR research. V Nourse and G Shaffer, 'Varieties of New Legal Realism: Can a New World Order Prompt a New Legal Theory?' (2009) 96 *Cornell Law Review* 61–137, 75–90.

origins.[17] According to his account, there were a number of scholars who held appointments at law schools and who had training in statistics who were not totally at home in the LSA. Part of the problem purportedly involved questions of method; the ELS scholars advocated statistical analysis of large databases rather than the more qualitative approaches often (although far from exclusively) found at LSA meetings and in the Association's journal, the *Law & Society Review*.[18] Another part of the difficulty involved the challenge of bringing together competing social sciences with inconsistent theories and vocabularies. He argues that LSA, to a large extent, reflected sociology and anthropology and neglected economics and experimental psychology. (As there were LSA members from both of these fields, there is some room for disagreement on this point—especially as regards psychology.[19]) Yet another contributing factor may have resulted from differing attitudes toward business, markets and politics.[20]

As Eisenberg goes on to explain, Lee Teitelbaum, late Dean of the Cornell Law School, pressed him to start a journal, during a discussion at the Budapest meeting of the LSA in 2003. As a result, the *Journal of Empirical Legal Studies* (*JELS*) appeared in 2004. The editors' introduction to the first issue tells us:

> *JELS* seeks to encourage, promote, and provide an impetus for the careful collection of empirical data and the dispassionate, rigorous testing of empirical hypotheses. The central purpose of *JELS* is to add to knowledge of the legal system based on observation or empirical analysis, including experimental analysis.[21]

Professor Bernard Black staged the first ELS conference at the University of Texas Law School in 2006, and these conferences are now regular events staged at various law schools. In addition, those involved in ELS have offered various programmes to teach social science methods to law professors.

ELS is largely a creature of the law schools; many of those who identify with ELS have an appointment on a law faculty and are centrally concerned with reaching a legal audience for their scholarship. A recent review article in the *Annual Review of Law & Social Science* by Suchman and Mertz asserts that 'ELS is currently unified more by its institutional focus (legal) and its methodological proclivities (quantitative) than by any specific substantive or theoretical focus.'[22] A brief look at the types of questions addressed by papers in *JELS* illustrates the point; some examples include: (1) Have the amounts of damages awarded by juries increased over the last forty years? (2) Are there common clusters of problems that go to court, and, if so, what are the social and demographic indicators? (3) Why has there been a sharp decline in the number of trials in the United States, and what are the consequences?

ELS has been remarkably successful. One could argue that this is partly because

---

[17] T Eisenberg, 'The Origins, Nature, and Promise of Empirical Legal Studies and a Response to Concerns' (2011) *University of Illinois Law Review* 1713–38.

[18] This perception on the part of ELS scholars is contestable, as the Law & Society Association had always included work from a broad range of disciplines using a variety of methods. It is true that quantitative work did not dominate, but it was always a part of the LSA package.

[19] For example, psychologists Tom Tyler, Allan Lind and Shari Diamond have all won the highest prize given by the Law & Society Association, the Kalven Prize.

[20] Eisenberg, above n 17, 1719.

[21] T Eisenberg, J Rachlinski, S Schwab and M Wells, 'Editors' Introduction' (2004) 1 *Journal of Empirical Legal Studies* v–vi.

[22] M Suchman and E Mertz, 'Toward a New Legal Empiricism: Empirical Legal Studies and New Legal Realism' (2010) 6 *Annual Review of Law and Social Science* 555–793, 559.

there are now many public data sets related to legal questions, and there are user-friendly statistical programmes for personal computers. Eisenberg sees ELS as serving to lead to fairness by the 'promotion of legal rules that better reflect reality'.[23] Suchman and Mertz add: 'And rather than demanding that legal scholars engage more directly with the social world, ELS emphasizes the ease with which statistically skilled law professors can pluck low-hanging fruit in the comfort of their campus offices.'[24] Work with already-assembled large data sets does not require the arduous and slow work of original data gathering; this fits with the legal academy's preference for research that can be conducted solely in libraries.

Despite these advantages, Eisenberg says that ELS growth likely has at least one important limit that will be difficult to overcome: most mainstream law professors and virtually all law students remain uninterested in performing (or sometimes even reading) quantitative or qualitative empirical analyses. Their primary training and expertise continues to centre on the analysis of legal doctrine, with policy and social science added in on the sides. We suspect that course enrolments in ELS-related courses will remain modest, that law school graduates entering academia and the profession will have had little opportunity for ELS training, and that the path of least resistance for most will not involve ELS scholarship.

New Legal Realism

Those who follow the approach of NLR also seek to bring social science into the legal academy to a greater extent than in the past. As with the old legal realism, there are a number of different strands of NLR scholarship. Some focus on judicial decision-making. For example, Tom Miles and Cass Sunstein tell us about what they call 'the' new legal realism; in their view, this work is 'an effort to understand the sources of judicial decisions on the basis of testable hypotheses and large data sets'.[25] In one study, Sunstein and his colleagues looked at published opinions of the US Courts of Appeal and votes of individual judges from 1995 to 2004 in areas where ideology might matter.[26] In eight kinds of cases involving contentious issues in American political life, the authors found that they could predict the outcomes if they knew the political party of the president who had appointed the three judges on the panels that heard the cases.[27] The authors caution that ideology is clearly not the only factor operating here, since the votes of Republican and Democratic appointees overlap substantially. Moreover, the votes of the judges were not related to the politics of the appointing president in many of the less politically salient areas.

Research focused on judicial voting within courts toward the top of the legal hierarchy is not the only type of work done under the aegis of NLR. Many other scholars involved in NLR stress the importance of the interplay between 'top-down' and

---

[23] Eisenberg, above n 17, 1738.
[24] Suchman and Mertz, above n 22, 560. This may, however, underestimate how challenging it is to formulate questions, apply appropriate statistical analyses and draw well-grounded conclusions, even when all materials are obtainable without original data gathering.
[25] T Miles and C Sunstein, 'The New Legal Realism' (2008) 75 *University of Chicago Law Review* 831–51.
[26] C Sunstein, D Schkade and L Ellman, 'Ideological Voting on Federal Courts of Appeal: A Preliminary Investigation' (2004) 90 *Virginia Law Review* 301–54, 311.
[27] D Schkade and C Sunstein, 'Judging by Where You Sit', *New York Times* 11 June 2003, A31.

'bottom-up' approaches to the law in action.[28] Legal rules and the actions generated by a small number of elites heading up the legal system may have great importance, but whether and to what extent their contributions have effect in the world is an empirical question. People cope with the law in many ways, and other-than-legal normative and sanction systems often compete with cases, statutes, police, judges and the rest of the state legal system. The kinds of factors emphasised by NLR include, for example: (1) organisations can be expected to create structures to minimise burdens imposed by the formal legal system;[29] (2) profitable, but illegal, enterprise always exists, evading the commands of the law;[30] (3) people can use contract, trusts and the law of property to create private policing and dispute resolution that may rival or undercut that provided by the state;[31] (4) much commerce exists in multinational trade where the jurisdiction of state legal systems is uncertain or clearly inapplicable; nevertheless, transactions involving large sums take place;[32] (5) lawyers engage in instrumental and symbolic action to reassure those involved in many types of transactions that they face no more than manageable risks.[33] Contrary to some of the judicial politics scholars, most of the other researchers associated with NLR pride themselves on a 'big tent' approach that includes the study of law outside of appellate courts—indeed, outside of courts altogether (interactions between lawyers and clients, administrative agencies, legislatures, prisons, police behaviour, etc).

In this regard, then, the 'big tent' legal realists are part of the broader law-and-society tradition, but with more of an emphasis on addressing legal scholars and legal questions. Thus new legal realists are likely to incorporate social theory into their research—albeit in hybrid and mixed forms. One overview of various strands of NLR can be found in the work of Victoria Nourse and Gregory Shaffer, whose very creative synthesis grounds NLR in a recursive linking of method and theory, with four distinctive features: '(i) an emphasis on empiricism; (ii) a focus on institutions of which markets are only one form; (iii) a grounding in philosophical pragmatism; and (iv) critical scrutiny and ambitions'.[34] They describe a core method for NLR: '[S]cholars study a real problem in the world (they do not start with a theory or a normative agenda), and as they encounter the problem, scholars emerge with different ideas and new strategies.'[35]

---

[28] See eg H Erlanger, B Garth, J Larson, E Mertz, V Nourse and D Wilkins, 'Is it Time for a New Legal Realism?' (2005) 2005 *Wisconsin Law Review* 335–63.

[29] See LB Edelman, 'Legal Environments and Organizational Governance: The Expansion of Due Process in the American Workplace' (1990) 95 *American Journal of Sociology* 1401–39; LB Edelman, SE Abraham and HS Erlanger, 'Professional Construction of Law: The Inflated Threat of Wrongful Discharge' (1992) 26 *Law & Society Review* 47–83.

[30] See eg PR Keefe, 'The Snow Kings of Mexico', *New York Times Sunday Magazine* 17 June 2102, 36 ('It is no accident that the world's biggest supplier of narcotics and the world's biggest consumer of narcotics just happen to be neighbors').

[31] See S Macaulay, 'Private Government' in L Lipson and S Wheeler (eds), *Law and the Social Sciences* (New York, Russell Sage Foundation, 1986) 445–518; M Galanter, 'Justice in Many Rooms: Courts, Private Ordering, and Indigenous Law' (1981) 19 *Journal of Legal Pluralism* 1–47.

[32] See eg T Dietz, 'Contract Law, Relational Contracts, and Reputational Networks in International Trade' (2012) 37 *Law and Social Inquiry* 25–57; G Calliess and P Zumbansen, *Rough Consensus and Running Code: A Theory of Transnational Private Law* (Oxford, Hart Publishing, 2010).

[33] J Flood, 'Lawyers as Sanctifiers: The Role of Elite Law Firms in International Business Transactions' (2007) 14 *Indiana Journal of Global Legal Studies* 35–66.

[34] Nourse and Shaffer, above n 16, 112.

[35] Ibid, 84–85.

NLR scholars, then, are eclectic in their choice of methods, and they embrace both quantitative and qualitative work. Most of those allied with NLR want to promote research that draws on the full range of social science learning. They accept the value of quantitative research, but also note that—as with all social science methods—numerical data and statistics have limitations. Some tables of data have been collected in ways that undercut their validity. Police departments, for example, too often have recorded crime statistics in such a way as to make themselves look good.[36] Sometimes you cannot get the random sample required for a statistical test. Some questions can be answered only by talking directly with informants; to get access, a researcher may have to promise anonymity.[37] If the question is important and this situation pertains, one uses the information cautiously with full disclosure of the limits of the data.

The Empirical Turn

How do ELS and NLR relate one to the other? There are some statements suggesting conflict or claiming that one offers hard clear thought as opposed to softer and less precise analysis. Suchman and Mertz conclude, however, that these two movements could be viewed as expressions of a common impulse: 'Quantitative and qualitative methods can coexist peacefully and even symbiotically, as long as researchers remain open-minded and sensitive to the strengths and weaknesses of each. ... They are united by their preferences for observation over ratiocination.'[38] These groups also share a respect for the doctrinal categories and language in which law is couched, understanding that this is a part of the reality that must be considered in order to grasp how legal systems operate. However, for empirically oriented legal scholars, this is just a starting point for the analysis rather than the last word.

3. THE CONTRIBUTION OF TODAY'S REALISM TO LEGAL KNOWLEDGE

As the new legal empiricists develop their evolving tradition, there is both an interesting potential and the risk that much energy could be dissipated in extended squabbling over academic territory. The rest of this chapter considers what sorts of substantive advances might flow from serious consideration of a new generation of legal realist scholarship. Some NLR scholars have called for careful attention to the process of interdisciplinary translation itself, noting that legal scholars and social scientists do not really speak the same language. How, then, can the perspectives gained from good empirical research be made relevant to law in its own terms?

---

[36] Compare J Eterno and E Silverman, *The Crime Numbers Game: Management by Manipulation* (Boca Raton, FL, CRC Press, 2012) with F Zimring, *The City That Became Safe* (Oxford, Oxford University Press, 2012). See also C Bialik, 'Fuzzy Facts Can Make Crime Rankings Suspect', *Wall Street Journal* 28 January 2012, A2; B Poston, 'Hundreds of Assault Cases Misreported by Milwaukee Police Department: City's Violent Crime Rate Lowered Based on Faulty Data', *Milwaukee Journal-Sentinel* 22 May 2012, 1. (This also appears at: www.jsonline.com/watchdog/watchdogreports/hundreds-of-assault-cases-misreported-by-milwaukee-police-department-v44ce4p-152862135.html.)

[37] See, for example, the important work of Sudhir Venkatesh on gangs in Chicago. S Venkatesh, *Off the Books: The Underground Economy of the Urban Poor* (Cambridge, MA, Harvard University Press, 2006).

[38] Suchman and Mertz, above n 22, 564.

Example #1: The 'Rule of Law'

Kathryn Hendley's work on 'the rule of law' in Russia serves as a good example of how new legal realist research can contribute to legal and social theory. The rule of law has occupied many scholars, including those campaigning for social change as well as members of international organisations. However, the concept is imprecise.[39] More recently, John Ohnesorge reviewed various publications of international organisations, political leaders and scholars dealing with the concept.[40] Those who are not lawyers tend to assume that the rule of law is a condition of a society which is governed by a complete and functioning legal system. According to this view, society is either characterised by the rule of law or it is not. These writers assumed that legal rules are 'not subject to significant indeterminacy, and that these are sufficient to provide single correct solutions without resorting to principles, policies or purposes'.[41] They did not consider such things as police and prosecutorial discretion, cost barriers, delays and other similar parts of the law in action commonly found in any society. Legal scholars tend to see the rule of law as an aspiration; a society honours the rule of law when a large number of its characteristics are met a high percentage of the time. Similarly, Hendley asserts: 'No country has ever fully realized "the rule of law." Rather ... countries move back and forth on a continuum from legal systems labeled repressive to those that embody the "rule of law".'[42]

Hendley's research provides empirical insight into this problem. A number of organisations have sought to rank the legal systems of various nations according to indices of the rule of law. Russia does very poorly on these indices, but Hendley argues that the reason for this is that the indices too often rest on the opinions of supposed experts rather than on studies of what is actually going on in today's Russia: 'Nowhere in this myriad of indicators can I find any effort to incorporate the rise or fall in cases brought in the courts or any effort to document empirically the level of enforcement of judicial decisions.'[43] Instead, commonly accepted accounts focus on high-profile cases that reveal admittedly corrupt practices in the Russian system.[44] Hendley warns against generalising from cases involving those who have provoked the ire of the Kremlin. They are but a tiny percentage of all the disputes in the society.

While acknowledging that there are very valid concerns about corruption in the Russian legal system, Hendley notes that since the 1980s the government has taken many steps to improve its legal system, at least as a formal matter.[45] Efforts have been made to reduce corruption, including paying higher salaries to legal officials so that they will be less likely to succumb to bribes. Moreover, from 1997 to 2007, the number of civil cases decided by the Russian courts of general jurisdiction more than doubled.

---

[39] L Fuller, *The Morality of Law*, rev edn (New Haven, Yale University Press, 1969).

[40] J Ohnesorge, 'The Rule of Law, Economic Development, and the Developmental States of Northeast Asia' in C Antons (ed), *Law and Development in East and Southeast Asia* (London, Routledge, 2003).

[41] Ibid, fn 9.

[42] K Hendley, 'Assessing the Rule of Law in Russia' (2006) 14 *Cardozo Journal of International and Comparative Law* 347–391 .

[43] Ibid, 373.

[44] K Hendley, '"Telephone Law" and the "Rule of Law": The Russian Case' (2009) 1 *Hague Journal on the Rule of Law* 241–49, 241.

[45] Hendley, above n 42, 352–63.

This raised the question of why Russians are willing to use a system that seems to the experts so deeply flawed.

Hendley addressed this question using empirical research, and discovered a dualism within Russian law.[46] On the one hand, throughout Russian history, law has served as a tool for the powerful. Kremlin officials used show trials to defend state interests in unusual situations. At the same time, legal officials also applied the 'rule of law' in ordinary situations. Although many of the study's subjects pointed to shortcomings in the Russian legal system, they also might consider going to court if the dispute involved ordinary citizens:

> Many of the objections to litigating I heard could just as easily have come from litigants in countries generally thought to have strong judicial systems. ... [T]he most common concerns were the time, money, and the emotional energy required to see a lawsuit through to its conclusion.[47]

Like many others around the world, the Russians with whom Hendley spoke dislike conflict.[48] Many did not see taking a dispute to court as proper. People were likely still to have to deal with an ex-spouse, an employer or a neighbour after litigation was over, and one usually had reason to preserve relationships.

Hendley also found that some Russians were willing to assert legal rights against the state in non-litigation settings.[49] To be sure, this research did not produce a picture anything like an idealised rule of law in Russia. Instead, Hendley draws on Llewellyn's idea of 'reckonability':[50] in this system, citizens have some predictability as to when they can use courts versus when these institutions are likely to be compromised. In Russia, just as elsewhere, a bottom-up empirical view of people handling problems shows law to be but one possible tool to try to cope with trouble. While it may be a far better tool in other nations (at least for some purposes), social science research shows that it also plays a role in Russia.

Hendley's work exemplifies the 'big tent' approach championed by NLR. She queries a representative sample of Russians and analyses the results statistically. She examines caseload data collected by Russian courts, and does not limit her research to Moscow where it is easier to work. She fashions many focus groups with an attempt to include people likely to have different ideas, and she selects them from various regions of a very large country. She followed this by interviewing many of the participants and letting them control the interaction. She is sceptical of 'what everyone knows' as found in elite media and academic writing. Most importantly, while she is familiar with what is broadcast from the top, she focuses on her problem from the bottom up,

---

[46] The research included conducting 29 focus groups that met during the summers of 2007 and 2008 in five different locations in Russia. The members of the groups varied in age, gender, educational background and work experience. The discussions focused on people's problem-solving strategies and when, if ever, law was relevant. In addition, Hendley conducted follow-up interviews with 79 of the people who had participated in the focus groups.

[47] Hendley, above n 44, 241–49.

[48] See eg C Greenhouse, *Praying for Justice* (Ithaca, NY, Cornell University Press, 1986); see also S Merry, *Getting Justice and Getting Even* (Chicago, University of Chicago Press, 1990); S Macaulay 'Non-Contractual Relations in Business: A Preliminary Study' (1963) 28 *American Sociological Review* 55–69, 61.

[49] K Hendley, 'Varieties of Legal Dualism: Making Sense of the Role of Law in Contemporary Russia' (2012) *Wisconsin International Law Journal* (forthcoming).

[50] K Llewellyn, *The Common Law Tradition: Deciding Appeals* (Chicago, University of Chicago Press, 1960) 17–18.

seeking what various types of Russians understand and have done. She is appropriately cautious about generalising when she lacks a representative sample, but she seeks to explore in depth what law looks like to those subject to it.

This empirical research sheds light on a core issue debated in legal theory: how to conceptualise 'the rule of law' as well as the rules of law. Hendley's sort of work shares with ethnomethodology a primary commitment to building theories of how social and legal interactions work from close observations of those interactions, with an emphasis on grasping how individuals understand law. However, she also examines larger social forces shaping the legal system with which individuals interact.[51] Hendley characterises her work on rule-of-law issues as broadly rooted in Max Weber's form of social theory, although her particular findings on rationality and rule of law do not support some of his specific assertions.[52] She also draws on what she, along with other social scientists, would call 'mid-level theory'—in her case drawn from sociolegal scholarship such as the well-known strand of research on stages of dispute processing, and another on social distance as a predictor of legal behaviour.[53] Hendley's work provides an example of the integrative potential of new legal realist research with roots in the social sciences and law-and-society.

Example #2: Easy Cases as Well as Hard Cases

In a recent essay, Frederick Schauer argues that mainstream legal scholarship may have overshot the mark in its 'taming' of legal realism.[54] By 'taming' he means marginalising the realists' insights by consigning them to the margins of law, allowing only for the possibility that on relatively rare occasions 'paper rules' might not be all-controlling (as in the unusual 'hard cases'). But in the vast centre of law, in this view, 'easy cases' predominate and law as it is written in books translates relatively transparently into practice. This 'tamed' view assumes a functionalist model in which 'paper rules' govern in unproblematic ways through most of the legal system, and through most of how law works in everyday life. That such a view could be taken seriously may leave many social scientists amazed, shocked that any group of scholars could have ignored the substantial findings to the contrary through multiple generations of social science research. Nevertheless, Schauer's article in a sense explains how this might be the case, and may actually open up another option for conversation.

---

[51] See K Hendley, *Trying to Make Law Matter: Legal Reform and Labor Law in the Soviet Union* (Ann Arbor, University of Michigan Press, 1996) 178–80 (discussing Weber).

[52] Hendley, ibid; see also Hendley, above n 44:

> For those who subscribe to the Weberian view that societal dissatisfaction with authoritarianism can give rise to a rational legal order, the spillover argument is compelling. In my early work on the legal reforms in Russia, I was seduced by its siren call. I have since come to rethink my position. ... A review of the evolution of the state-society relationship in Russia suggests that waiting for a Weberian rational legal system to evolve is likely to be futile. Instead, Russia's legal system is better seen as an equilibrium that somehow balances 'rule by law' and 'rule of law'.

[53] K Hendley, e-mail to authors, 8 August 2012 (on file with authors). Turning to legal theorists, Hendley names Fuller as another touchstone for her thinking about the rule of law. On 'naming/blaming/claiming', see W Felstiner, R Abel and A Sarat, 'The Emergence and Transformation of Disputes: Naming, Blaming, Claiming' (1981) 15 *Law & Society Review* 631–49; on social distance and law, see Merry, above n 48, and also the work of David Engel.

[54] Frederick Schauer, 'Legal Realism Untamed' (2013) 91 *Texas Law Review* 749–80.

Schauer suggests the possibility of untaming realism in mainstream legal scholarship by turning attention back to the question of how 'real rules' might differ from 'paper rules' at the centre of law's functioning. Following Llewellyn, Schauer frames this inquiry in terms of the division between paper rules and real rules:[55]

> These examples suggest that departures from paper rules are common, and that American law contains ample resources permitting judges to avoid paper rules while still appearing faithfully to be applying the law. This conclusion does not address the question of just how often judges in fact do so, or the extent to which such escape routes are routinely available, but it does suggest that judicial avoidance of the most immediately applicable paper rule is hardly unusual, that there are multiple methods of accomplishing this end, and that the existence of paper rule-real rule gaps is a significant part of the American legal environment.[56]

On the one hand, sociolegal scholars might rightfully respond to this observation with much irritation, given that the insight here announced as 'news' is in fact well-established 'old news' in many fields. On the other hand, from our proposed new legal realist perspective, Schauer's formulation could make an important contribution, serving as a translation highlighting the potential relevance of large amounts of empirical research to mainstream legal scholarship.

Schauer poses a challenge, suggesting that whether departures from paper rules are common needs to be tested empirically. How, then, could sociolegal scholars answer Schauer's challenge? One translation issue that immediately leaps into mind is the possibility that those studying law in action might tend not to focus on the paper rules or formal legal reasoning. Thus, although they have produced a large number of studies demonstrating that law in action responds to social forces in patterned ways, they have not necessarily made it easy for scholars who are concerned about the formal or paper laws to translate those empirical findings into the language of legal theory. (On the other hand, it must be said that the circle of scholars involved in jurisprudence appears to maintain a very closed discourse, one which until now has not opened many doors to other disciplinary perspectives or interlocutors.) If sociolegal scholars have already shown that everyday legal outcomes are shaped by sociological and cultural factors, then it might seem obvious to them that 'paper rules' cannot be governing the central operations of the legal system. After all, it would be hard to find a 'paper rule' that says, 'Rich people should win more than poor people in court', or 'People of color should generally be barred from succeeding with valid claims of discrimination in court', or even 'The average person should be penalised for attempting to use the legal system to enforce clearly stated "paper-rule" rights.' Thus it seems fairly obvious, from this perspective, that the central operations of our system of justice are governed by social forces distant from stated ideals in 'paper laws.'

Through the years, the law-and-society movement and its journals have brought law professors, social scientists and law reformers together in a common conversation on this issue, despite disciplinary differences. Much empirical support for a gap between 'paper' and 'real' rules can be found in articles that have appeared in the *Law &*

---

[55] Ibid, 766–69. As he considers 'real rules' outside of a courtroom context—eg police officers deciding which speed limits to enforce—he seems to be moving beyond the narrower realm of judges' rules to the wider (and more sociolegally satisfactory) realm of law in society. (This obviously also includes judges and courts.)

[56] Ibid, 776.

Society Review, the *Annual Review of Law and Social Science* and other sociolegal journals. A brief survey of the articles in these journals does reveal some potential seeds of the Schauer translation problem in that many do not take legal doctrinal categories or 'paper laws' as their central points of departure. Nevertheless, although the research is often framed in terms of social science theories and questions, it frequently empirically investigates some aspect of 'real law' that does not map neatly onto 'paper rules.'

For example, in 1987, Wheeler, Cartwright, Kagan and Friedman tested a canonical sociolegal 'mid-range' theory[57] which held that powerful people in a society will tend to be advantaged in court 'either because the normative structure of the American legal system has favored "the haves," or because judges' attitudes do, or because stronger parties have strategic and representational advantages in litigation'.[58] Wheeler and his co-authors concluded that there was a small but significant advantage for more powerful parties—but also that this varied according to historical time period and other factors. Their nuanced finding recognised that there were many cases in which money and power did not determine outcomes, but also pointed out that

> if one starts out with an idealist image of the court system as providing a law-guided, neutral forum ... our discovery of a consistent margin of victory for stronger parties is hard to explain or dismiss, and represents a significant blow to that concept.[59]

Among a number of other follow-up articles, a 2001 study by Brace and Hall similarly found that contextual factors made a large difference in shaping whether the 'haves' came out in state Supreme Court cases. [60] These sorts of studies do not necessarily refer to doctrine explicitly, but they are part of a by-now well-established, empirically documented, persistent difference in legal outcomes for the 'haves' and 'have nots.'

One could protest that this is all very well and good, but it says nothing about what judges are doing or how they reason. (On the other hand, someone could also respond that it makes little difference to litigants if the unfairness in legal outcomes derives from appellate court judges' reasoning or from the way the overall system winds up working; surely if the 'paper law' as envisioned by courts does not map onto reality in significant and predictable ways, there is a serious problem with which judges and legal scholars ought to be grappling.) So let us move on to an example from the sociolegal literature in which the authors specifically focus on 'paper rules'. In their 2005 article in the first *Annual Review of Law and Social Science*, Michael Saks and David Faigman reviewed the state of sociolegal research on the *Daubert* cases, which are judge-made law on the admissibility of scientific evidence.[61] Their article reviews the doctrinal history and analyses the jurisprudence of expert evidence. It then asks the (realist) question of what difference the *Daubert* cases have actually made in court practices, contrasting 'admissibility on the books versus admissibility

---

[57] See M Galanter, 'Why the "Haves" Come Out Ahead' (1974) 9 *Law & Society Review* 95.

[58] S Wheeler, B Cartwright, R Kagan and L Friedman, 'Do the Haves Come Out Ahead—Winning and Losing in State Supreme Courts, 1870–1970' (1987) 21 *Law & Society Review* 403–46.

[59] Wheeler et al, ibid, 443–44.

[60] P Brace and MG Hall '"Haves" versus "Have Nots" in State Supreme Courts: Allocating Docket Space and Wins in Power Asymmetric Cases' (2001) 35 *Law & Society Review* 393–413.

[61] M Saks and D Faigman, 'Expert Evidence after *Daubert*' (2005) 1 *Annual Review of Law and Social Science* 105–30, 105.

in action'.[62] The research cited by Saks and Faigman demonstrates that judges do not follow the *Daubert* guidelines even in straightforward cases; for example, judges continue to admit highly dubious forensic 'science' for which there is no systematic empirical support.[63] The authors conclude that '*Daubert* has precipitated a pattern of gatekeeping that is impossible to explain in terms of *Daubert*'s doctrinal elements or the relative quality of underlying science presented for review.'[64]

4. CONCLUSION: MID-LEVEL THEORY AND RESEARCH ON LAW IN ACTION

We have cited just a few examples from a vast pool of available research that could be used to shed light on classic jurisprudential questions: the rule of law, the indeterminacy of 'paper rules' and the relevance of sociological factors to legal outcomes in run-of-the-mill cases. We conclude by considering how legal scholars could make better use of existing empirical research, and how a new legal realism could generate exciting combinations of legal theory, social theory and empirical research on law. In so doing, it could also open up new syntheses and conversations for social theories of law.

Both NLR and ELS call for legal scholars to deal with social science, whether to perform empirical research themselves or merely to become more sophisticated consumers of that research. ELS tends to advocate for law professors to perform their own social science research. This will be very challenging for the majority of law professors who do not have training in both law and social science; while undoubtedly there are excellent short courses, it seems unlikely that most will attain professional levels of competency in statistics or qualitative research in short periods of time—and oversimplification of complicated matters could simply lead to faulty conclusions.

Translating Basics for Legal and Sociolegal Scholarship

It seems more likely that many legal scholars participating in this new 'turn' will want to draw on empirical work without trying to become experts at a professional level. Here the need for interdisciplinary translation becomes very evident. We may need courses designed to help a legally trained person use the work of professional social scientists without undue distortion. Law professors may need to do or draw upon qualitative and/or quantitative research in appropriate ways—or to engage in new forms of collaboration with social science researchers. Social scientists studying law may need better understandings of how it works from the inside.

The task of conceptualising this translation process is, we argue, an important step for those who wish to incorporate new realist perspectives into legal education. We here offer just a few examples of the sorts of instruction that might be included

---

[62] Ibid, 120 ('That the law in action can sometimes be quite different from the law on the books is something legal realists noted decades ago. The implementation of the *Daubert* trilogy can be viewed as an immense case study of this phenomenon').

[63] Ibid, 124.

[64] Ibid, 125.

in such a course. Along with learning how empirical methods can be useful, legal scholars could consider the limitations of social science knowledge. For example, despite impressive tables and statistics, many quantitative studies are snapshots. The study may have been done at a most unusual moment. The world may have changed since the subjects were questioned. The subjects may not be representative in some way. Furthermore, we must ask whether the data really tested the theoretical question under consideration, and whether the researchers gathering the data had a stake in the outcome. And, as Eisenberg says:

> Nearly all data and results are limited by time and place, by techniques for gathering and analysing data that change, and by reinterpreting old results in light of additional evidence. The humbling truth is that probably nearly all ... scholars ... make mistakes or may be shown to be incorrect by subsequent research.[65]

Qualitative studies present a different set of problems. On the one hand, they have fewer validity problems in terms of how realistic they are; participant observation, for example, places researchers right in the actual places and situations about which they seek information. However, these studies also have their limitations. For example, interview subjects can distort or misremember events. Sometimes subjects do not want to admit what they do not know, or have an agenda—whether this is pleasing the interviewer or making an organisation look good. Participant observers may be able to avoid some of these problems by steeping themselves in a particular setting for a long period of time, but then they have to ask how far they can generalise from one in-depth set of observations. Thus, legal scholars who turn to social science must handle it with appropriate caution. As we have noted, the most obvious error to avoid is failing to notice the qualifications in an empirical study.

New Legal Realism and Social Theories of Law

We close by considering the intersection of empirical research, social theory and legal theory. We here build on Nourse and Shaffer's suggestion that new legal realists' work fits with pragmatist philosophy and with 'mid-range' social science approaches.[66] The idea of pursuing a middle-range research programme that combines social theory and empirical research is ubiquitous in the social sciences and sociolegal studies. Noted sociologist Robert Merton characterised this as 'theories of the middle range', which operate in-between larger theories of how society works and detailed empirical findings.[67] This general approach is evident in recent calls within the field of sociology for 'bridging the unfortunate gap between theoretical and empirical work'.[68] Within anthropology, current research commonly combines larger social theoretic constructs with microlevel ethnographic observation. And sociolegal studies has similarly produced a great deal of mid-range research.

---

[65] Eisenberg, above n 17, 1730–31.
[66] See also A McEvoy, 'A New Realism for Legal Studies' (2005) 2005 *Wisconsin Law Review* 433–54.
[67] RK Merton, *Social Theory and Social Structure* (New York, Free Press, 1968) 39–72 (distinguishing middle range theories from comprehensive political philosophies such as Marxism).
[68] P Hedstrom and P Ylikoski, 'Causal Mechanisms in the Social Sciences' (2010) 36 *Annual Review of Sociology* 49–67, 65.

Because law-and-society as a field has embraced multiple social science approaches, it is uniquely situated to aid in integrating social theory and social science for the study of law. Social theories are often conceptualised as being in competition, with the resulting conversation more an argument over who is right than a shared investigation of when, how and under what circumstances one theoretical tradition might help to shed light on empirical questions. Against this antagonistic approach to scholarly inquiry, new legal empiricism offers the possibility of a collaborative conversation in which the insights of multiple social theoretic traditions are available along with ongoing iterative feedback from empirical researchers examining law in action—and from legal researchers skilled in the intricacies of the language and practice of law as it is understood by insiders. There are many scholarly models for this integrative approach. For example, after generations of debate over whether 'nature' or 'nurture' was more important in general in shaping human beings, many contemporary researchers have turned to more 'middle-range' investigations, examining how genetic and environmental factors might interact to shape specific kinds of outcomes. Could NLR afford a similar meeting ground for different views of law?

Our examples have illustrated just such a potential, both in Hendley's description of the 'rule of law' in Russia, and in research that has explored how law favours the 'haves.' As mid-range theories evolve in conversation with growing empirical evidence, some parts of the grander social theories can help to guide the conversation but in turn are altered or developed further.

This open conversation may not seem satisfactory to those who seek to champion one tradition or theorist as 'the answer'. But the more pragmatist synthesis now emerging may actually provide a way for hitherto competing scholarly traditions to enter into a more productive dialogue about how particular theories contribute to parts of a larger puzzle: the ongoing realist struggle to understand law in action.

Section 5

Postmodernism

REZA BANAKAR and MAX TRAVERS

Postmodernism is an intellectual movement that became popular during the 1970s and 1980s. It was originally used to describe a trend within art, architecture and literature, but it soon grew into an entire worldview that broke radically with, and urged its followers to move beyond, the totalising constraints of the 'metanarratives' of reason that constituted modernism.[1] Somewhat oversimplified, postmodernism means that the world, as it was described by theorists such as Karl Marx, has ended. As a result, we are ushered into a qualitatively new age which is best captured by *post*modernity (not to be confused with 'late modernity' discussed in Section 6, which does not assume a radical break with modernity). This is partly a claim about the unfolding of modernity and the social consequences of the many changes which have transformed the face of industrial societies of the nineteenth and twentieth centuries.

In this section, we shall also discuss poststructuralism. Poststructuralist thinkers, such as Michel Foucault, have much in common with postmodernists, but they do not always use the term 'postmodern', or think that we have entered a new area of human history. They too, however, challenge the central modernist assumption that one can arrive at 'the truth' through the exercise of reason, and then construct a better world. In our view, poststructuralism—like theories of 'late modernity'—is best understood as making a point about modernity. It does not necessarily ask us to give up science, nor does it argue that sociology as an empirical discipline is no longer possible or should be abandoned as an attempt to produce a better society. Nor does it have any political implications, since one can hold liberal or conservative views as a poststructuralist.

The philosophical objective of someone such as Jacques Derrida, who is among the most influential postmodern scholars (even though he 'dissociated himself from the term postmodernism'[2]), is to make us question the received ideas that we take for granted from the Enlightenment. More importantly, Derrida (like Foucault) makes this point by drawing attention to the use of language and critiquing *meaning* which is imposed on our perceptions of reality and which amounts to an act of violence against language.[3]

---

[1] Deconstruction is a technique associated with Jacques Derrida, who viewed it as a form of humanism. See J Derrida, *A Derrida Reader: Between the Blinds* (New York, Harvest Wheatsheaf, 1991).

[2] M Deflem, *Sociology of Law: Visions of a Scholarly Tradition* (Cambridge, Cambridge University Press, 2009) 204.

[3] For a discussion on this point, see EC Cuff et al, *Perspectives in Sociology* (London, Routledge, 1990) 282.

Derrida's idea of 'deconstruction' aims at exposing the repressive dimensions of the way language is employed in Western traditions to mediate thoughts and ideas. In line with structuralists, such as Saussure and his followers, he rejects the central place assigned to the author (or the speaker) in constructing the meaning of a text, thus 'decentring' the subject, that is, rejecting the individual author or speaker as the originator or 'the source of meaning'.[4] In other words, the presence of the author does not secure the meaning of a text, and taking this argument to its final conclusion, the essence of a thing (like the meaning of a text) is not, as commonly assumed, a function of its origin (or the author). It should be noted that 'deconstruction' is not a method applied to the text but a self-contradictory occurrence generated by ambiguities inherent in the text's key ideas and concepts which allow internal inconsistencies and equivocal or oppositional interpretations. In 'Force of Law', for example, Derrida contrasts justice with law, maintaining that law claims to do justice while hindering, negating and concealing justice at the same time. This is neither a purely negative act, in the sense that law *only* negates justice, nor a dialectical relationship, in a Hegelian sense of the word, aimed at generating a synthesis. Instead, to borrow from Marianne Valverde, it is a permanent process involving 'fruitful tension and mutual reinforcement'.[5] Law 'echoes' paradoxically, explains Philippopoulos-Mihalopoulos, as it 'oscillates in the movement away from the law and towards justice'.[6]

Derrida challenges the assumption that a text has 'a' meaning or that there can be 'an' authentic reading of a text, which may be redeemed through the application of certain hermeneutic techniques, such as those developed by theologians and used as a basis for legal methods to interpret legal texts. Deconstructionism thus denies the interpretative primacy attributed to the author as the source of meaning. The key to the understanding of any text is to be found in the text itself, for example in how it excludes other alternative interpretations, and not in the author, because meaning is not encapsulated in language (by the author). It also means that a text does not have one meaning but many, some of which subvert the conscious intentions of the author and the very order that brings unity to the text. Attempts to determine the meaning of a text by, for example, examining the biographical circumstances of the author or interviewing him/her to ascertain her opinions, life experiences, etc, is, according to Derrida, an interpretative operation which attempts to determine 'the meaning of one text by reference to other texts', some of which are written, some spoken.[7] This actually amounts to constructing meanings through 'intertextuality' and the decentring of texts. As regards the law, because of its dependency on text and documentation, and the fact that it is founded on layers of 'interpretable and transformable textual strata',[8] it is prone to deconstruction as any other text. The deconstructibility of law is hampered by the dominant legal discourse, which in its search for the truth of the law reduces the meanings interpreted in a text and conceals the open-ended nature of legal texts.

---

[4] Ibid, 283.
[5] M Valverde, 'Derrida's Justice and Foucault's Freedom: Ethics, History and Social Movements' (1999) *Law and Social Inquiry* 655–76, 656 and 659.
[6] A Philippopoulos-Mihalopoulos, *Niklas Luhmann: Law, Justice, Society* (London, Routledge, 2010) 3.
[7] Cuff et al, above n 3, 287.
[8] S Ahmed, 'Deconstruction and Law's Other: Towards a Feminist Theory of Embodied Legal Rights' (1995) 4 *Social and Legal Studies* 55–73, 61.

Postmodernism defies attempts to create systems, questions all urges for unity, and challenges all drives towards homogeneity and totalising conditions. Instead, it highlights flux, diffusion, fragmentation, plurality and localism by exploring the marginal, the different and the 'Other'. Moreover, it provides an understanding of the hegemony of law, in terms of its discursive practices, and draws attention to the serious shortcomings of simplistic structuralist or functionalistic models of law and the legal system. However, postmodernism is criticised for being a nihilistic and relativistic philosophy and for 'reacting' against the supremacy of dominant discourses. Its critics argue that it lacks transformative potential, a weakness which, to borrow from Joel Handler, is related to its inability to 'come up with an alternative vision, a vision of the economy and of the polity that will complement its vision of community'.[9] Similarly, Marianne Valverde indicates that 'the rejection of universal norms shared by all poststructuralist thinkers gives us a negative starting point' and deconstruction is a critical but 'relentlessly negative method' which does not appear at first sight to allow us to engage in normative evaluation.[10]

The poststructuralist philosopher who had the greatest impact on social science is undoubtedly Michel Foucault. Before his death from AIDS in 1984, Foucault advanced a sustained critique of Enlightenment through a series of historical studies. *Discipline and Punish* was, for example, intended to show that modern rational methods of punishment, such as imprisonment, are not necessarily morally superior to the tortures inflicted on criminals in the Middle Ages.[11] The book has a Weberian theme, in that the use of reason has resulted in a soulless world, in which governments classify populations using statistical methods, and we have given up our freedom to experts such as doctors, social workers and psychiatrists.

In this section, Gary Wickham starts his chapter by acknowledging that Foucault 'rarely wrote at any length about law' (the same observation should be made about Marx). Wickham, nonetheless, has managed to find a number of characteristically provocative comments and asides made by Foucault about the relationship between law and the 'disciplines' that 'characterise, classify [and] specialise' human populations.[12] In most of these comments, law is portrayed as the surface of a secondary phenomenon that prevents us from understanding the real nature of power. He observes, for example, that the 'system of rights', which was 'egalitarian in principle' and created by the nineteenth-century bourgeoisie, was 'supported by all those systems of micro-power that are essentially non-egalitarian ... that we call the disciplines'.[13] Similarly, when Foucault developed an interest in 'governmentality' in the 1970s, he was not interested primarily in law, but rather in the 'national forms' and 'technical procedures' through which governments exercise power over populations or encourage them to govern themselves.[14]

How, then, can one employ a Foucauldian approach in studying law? Wickham suggests that one way would be to employ 'archaeological' and 'genealogical'

---

[9] JF Handler, 'Postmodernism, Protest, and the New Social Movements' (1992) 26 *Law and Society Review* 697–731, 727.

[10] Valverde, above n 5, 657.

[11] M Foucault, *Discipline and Punish: The Birth of the Prison* (London, Alan Lane, 1977).

[12] Ibid, 223.

[13] Ibid, 222.

[14] M Foucault, *The Foucault Reader*, ed P Rabinow (New York, Pantheon, 1984) 337–38.

approaches to investigating how law features in any area of society, such as gambling, and how this is implicated in relation to power. It should be clear from this section that Wickham is not interested in making a political point about gambling, and instead he presents it in almost neutral terms as a set of discourses and practices. A critical theorist such as Herbert Marcuse would have viewed this as a device used by economically dominant groups to control and pacify the masses, along with horoscopes and television soaps.[15] What Foucault himself would have made of this topic must remain a matter for conjecture, although he would probably have used it to say something provocative about modernity, with his usual philosophical bite.

Shaun McVeigh is a legal philosopher, rather than a social scientist, and so this chapter, like many papers published in journals such as *Social and Legal Studies* or *Law and Critique*, is not concerned with collecting and analysing empirical data. It should be read alongside, and is helpful in understanding, the philosophical position he advanced in relation to common law in the first edition of this book through considering the ideas of different poststructuralist thinkers. The central argument is that human beings have lost their freedom, or even their souls, in a society run by experts and dominated by technology and the media. Postmodernism is presented both as an intellectual critique of modernity and as 'an exuberant (or despairing) rebellion aimed at re-peopling and re-placing forms of modern life'. But as a form of rebellion, it hardly offers a straightforward means of challenging inequality or injustice, or in telling us how to obtain fulfilment or happiness. For Derrida, 'the question of the conduct of law and justice is shaped around the responsibility for the other'. However, justice is only a 'promise' or 'possibility', and there are no firm philosophical foundations to any political or moral position.

McVeigh might be looking for something compatible with critical theory, and, as we explained in Section 3, postmodernism has had a lasting impact on the development of CLS. There is, however, always the potential for points of contention and debate between mainstream critical legal theorists, who have stayed true to the conflict theories of neo-Marxists, and postmodernists. One such point of contention was raised by critical race theory, which we discussed in Section 3. Another may be found in Eve Darian-Smith's chapter reviewing postcolonial theories of law. The central argument is that many ex-colonies and indigenous peoples are subject to 'oppression' and 'subordination' relating to neocolonialism (although some theorists see '99% of white people living within wealthy Western nations' as also experiencing some form of oppression). The task for critical legal scholars is to expose the contribution of law. One influential body of scholarship has sought to contest 'the underlying orientalist assumptions in national and international law'. Here, however, there is a potential tension between poststructuralists and critical theorists. Edward Said, in his seminal book *Orientalism*,[16] looked critically at Western explorers and colonial officialdom's stereotypical representations of non-Western societies as backward. But not all the poststructuralists who took up these ideas have advanced a straightforward political viewpoint (see, for example, Homi Bhabha on identity[17]) or would agree that one can always easily identify 'oppressed' and 'oppressors', either historically or at present.

---

[15] H Marcuse, *One Dimensional Man* (London, Routledge, 1974).
[16] E Said, *Orientalism* (Penguin, London, 1978).
[17] H Bhabha, *The Location of Culture* (London and New York, Routledge, 1994).

Darian-Smith concludes by expressing the modernist hope that we can build 'a legal future that is more responsible, equitable, and inclusive of humanity however defined', whereas McVeigh concludes that 'the postmoderns have sought ways to dispute and judge with law on grounds that are not altogether there, in the name of a justice that remains as yet undetermined, singular—and to come'.

12

Foucault and Law

GARY WICKHAM

T HIS CHAPTER HAS three main aims: to offer a summary and discussion
of what Foucault had to say about law, to offer an introduction to some
of Foucault's methods for those interested in learning to use Foucault as a
resource for the study of law in society, and to offer a discussion of what Foucault's
notion of governmentality might mean for this study.

The first section deals with the fact that Foucault had little directly to say about
law and suggests he thought the category less useful than those of discipline and
norms. The second section provides a brief introduction to the tools of archaeology,
genealogy, discourse and power-knowledge, and indicates how they may be employed
in the study of law in society. The third section extends this methodological discussion
to cover the later notion of governmentality, which has spawned a new and distinct
approach within the world of Foucault scholarship.

1. FOUCAULT, LAW, DISCIPLINE AND NORMS[1]

Foucault rarely wrote at any length about law. Admittedly, in *Discipline and Punish*[2]
and in a lecture published (at least in English) as the second of 'Two Lectures'[3] there
are extensive discussions and in the first volume of the *History of Sexuality*[4] project,

---

[1] Much of the shape and content of this section relies on A Hunt and G Wickham, *Foucault and Law:
Towards a Sociology of Law as Governance* (London, Pluto Press, 1994) 39–40; and A Hunt, 'Foucault's
Expulsion of Law: Toward a Retrieval' (1992) 17 *Law and Social Inquiry* 1. It should be noted that the
argument, expressed in these places, that Foucault concentrates on the notions of disciplines and norms
at the expense of law—an argument followed, at least to some extent, here—has been challenged by some
scholars. The most detailed counter-argument is provided by V Tadros, 'Between Governance and Discipline—The Law and Michel Foucault' (1998) 18 *Oxford Journal of Legal Studies* 75; but see also R Mackie,
'Review of A Hunt and G Wickham *Foucault and Law: Towards a Sociology of Law as Governance* and
D Caudill and S Gold (eds) *Radical Philosophy of Law*' (1997) 2 *Newcastle Law Review* 121; N Rose and
M Valverde, 'Governed by Law?' (1997) 7 *Social and Legal Studies* 541.
[2] M Foucault, *Discipline and Punish: The Birth of the Prison* (London, Allen Lane, 1977).
[3] M Foucault, 'Two Lectures' in C Gordon (ed), *Michel Foucault. Power/Knowledge: Selected Interviews
and Other Writings 1972–1977* (Brighton, Harvester, 1980).
[4] M Foucault, *The History of Sexuality*, vol I: *An Introduction* (New York, Pantheon, 1978).

law occasionally features, as it does in a number of his interviews,[5] especially those given after 1975. However, there is not much more; no one would ever seriously apply to Foucault any label such as legal scholar, legal theorist, sociologist of law or critical legal thinker. In this sense, then, it is hardly surprising that the worlds of legal and sociolegal scholarship have been slow to recognise the potential of his insights and remain somewhat wary of the speculation necessary to draw them out.

At the centre of Foucault's treatment of law lies his treatment of power. Indeed, it might be said that Foucault is only interested in law to the point that it helps him propose his very particular understanding of power. 'Instead of seeking the explanation in a general conception of the Law, in the evolving modes of industrial production ... it seemed to me far wiser to look at the workings of Power.'[6]

For Foucault, while law is crucially about power, the power of law is very limited, very one-sided (simultaneously 'complex and partial'). This is perhaps why he spends so little time on law. He tries throughout much of his work (as I discuss in more detail in the next section) to study power as a positive as well as a negative phenomenon— power as productive, as producing social relations, producing subjects and institutions. If we view power only as a negative force— that is, as a force that says 'no, thou shalt not', that works by prohibitions— Foucault believes we will miss much, even most, of what power does. For Foucault, law seems to be largely about negative power, sometimes only about sovereignty and its capacity to guarantee truth, and he is keen to change this, to move law aside in favour of a broader conception of power:

> In short, it is a question of orienting ourselves to a conception of power that replaces the privilege of the law with the viewpoint of the objective, the privilege of prohibition with the viewpoint of tactical efficacy, the privilege of sovereignty with the analysis of a multiple and mobile field of force relations, wherein far-reaching, but never completely stable, effects of domination are produced. The strategical model rather than the model based on law.[7]

During the nineteenth century, Foucault proposes, the 'psy' sciences (psychiatry, psychology, etc) added another dimension to the law's capacity to guarantee truth. In this way, the law, both supported by and under the influence of these sciences, turned particularly towards a certain sort of individual. The law here is still about negative power, but its focus is more particular. The negative control of individuals and society expresses itself through the category of 'the dangerous individual':

> by bringing to the fore not only the criminal as author of the act, but also the dangerous individual as potential source of acts, does one not give society rights over the individual based on what he is? [—] a foreboding of the dreadful dangers inherent in authorizing the law to intervene against individuals because of what they are; a horrifying society could emerge from that.[8]

Returning to law-as-sovereignty, Foucault insists that this form of law became 'the monarchic system's mode of manifestation', its very way of ruling, in other words, not simply a tool it used:

---

[5] See especially Gordon (ed), above n 3; L Kritzman (ed), *Michel Foucault. Politics, Philosophy, Culture: Interviews and Other Writings of Michel Foucault, 1977–1984* (New York, Routledge, 1988).
[6] M Foucault, *The Foucault Reader*, ed P Rabinow (New York, Pantheon, 1984) 337–38.
[7] Foucault, above n 3, 102.
[8] M Foucault, 'The Dangerous Individual', in Kritzman (ed), above n 5, 151.

Law was not simply a weapon skilfully wielded by monarchs: it was the monarchic system's mode of manifestation and the form of its acceptability. In Western societies since the Middle Ages, the exercise of power has always been formulated in terms of law.[9]

For Foucault, this way of thinking about power—monarchy as negative law and negative truth—has been so persistent, and so persistently problematic, that he minted a dramatic metaphor to try to breach its dominance:

> At bottom, despite the differences in epochs and objectives, the representation of power has remained under the spell of monarchy. In political thought and analysis we still have not cut off the head of the king.[10]

Foucault's treatment of law-as-sovereignty leads him to a particular treatment of rights. For Foucault, 'right'—that is, the sovereign right of the king to command—slides easily into 'rights', such that the rights that are at the heart of modern legal and political discourse are simply another means for negative power to operate.[11] In making this move, Foucault subtly introduces the notion of the subject into the picture. The subjects that emerge are definitely negative—subjects in the sense of being subjected, subjected to power—but they are subjects nonetheless. They are the vehicles by which law as negative power operates. Crudely put, subjects have rights, but they only have rights so that negative power can operate through law, and they are only subjects inasmuch as this negative power operates. Seen in this bleak way, Foucault's account of law and rights is not a long way from some Marxist accounts. As Foucault notoriously opposed Marxist accounts, we should not be surprised that at this point he wants to move away from law and rights and introduce the more subtle notions of disciplines and norms:

> The problem for me is how to avoid this question, central to the theme of right, regarding sovereignty and the obedience of individual subjects in order that I may substitute the problem of domination and subjugation for that of sovereignty and obedience.[12]

Foucault says disciplines are 'to be found on the underside of law', as they make their way from prisons and asylums to factories, schools, hospitals and other modern institutions. Indeed, disciplines are the characteristic forms of modern power:

> disciplines characterize, classify, specialize … effect[ing] a suspension of the law that is never total. … Regular and institutional as it may be, the discipline, in its mechanism, is a 'counter-law'.[13]

This suggests that while he sometimes contrasts law and discipline, more fundamentally Foucault sees them as interdependent—law is 'colonised' by the disciplines.[14]

> Historically, the process by which the bourgeoisie became in the course of the eighteenth century the politically dominant class was masked by the establishment of an explicit,

[9] Foucault, above n 4, 87.
[10] Ibid, 88–89.
[11] Foucault, above n 3, 95–96.
[12] Ibid, 96.
[13] Foucault, above n 2, 223.
[14] Ibid, 170.

coded and formally egalitarian juridical framework, made possible by the organization of a parliamentary, representative regime. But the development and generalization of disciplinary mechanisms constituted the other, dark side of these processes. The general juridical form that guaranteed a system of rights that were egalitarian in principle was supported by these tiny, everyday, physical mechanisms, by all those systems of micro-power that are essentially non-egalitarian and asymmetrical that we call the disciplines. ... The real, corporal disciplines constituted the foundation of the formal, juridical liberties.[15]

While this has the disciplines dominating law, it is slightly misleading. It is not all one-way traffic, by any means. Law tries to recode disciplines as a form of itself and has some success. Many aspects of the daily work of the disciplines in the modern institutions upon which Foucault concentrates (the prisons, hospitals, asylums, schools, factories, etc) are given a quasi-legal form.

Even when we turn to what Foucault considers the core of disciplinary power—techniques of surveillance (Foucault's provocative histories of some of these techniques of surveillance at work in the asylum, the prison, the hospital, etc, are now almost legendary)—we see law and disciplines weaving an intricate web. The asylum, for instance, Foucault tells us, was a 'juridical microcosm':

> The asylum as a juridical instance recognized no other. It judged immediately and without appeal. It possessed its own instruments of punishment, and used them as it saw fit.[16]

As I have indicated, this already complex picture is made more complex by Foucault's insistence on a separate role for norms. The law/discipline nexus outlined above, this is to say, has an even more particular operational character. While quasi-legal forms of discipline may be the order of the day, the limits to the law's role mean that very little reaches the stage of formal legal proceedings, of offences actually being prosecuted. Far more commonplace is the use of norms or standards. He even speaks of the 'growing importance assumed by the action of the norm, at the expense of the juridical system of the law'.[17]

Foucault's treatment of 'normalisation' involves, as is to be expected, his very particular understanding of power. In the everyday work of the disciplines (more correctly the discipline/norm nexus) power functions more as a power 'whose task is to take charge of life needs continuous regulatory and corrective mechanisms ... to qualify, measure, appraise, and hierarchise, rather than display itself in its murderous splendor'.[18] In other words, power-through-disciplines/norms is more positive, more productive, than power-through-law-alone.

In marking out some differences between law, on the one hand, and disciplines and norms, on the other, Foucault discusses the expansion of the reach of judges and judging, arguing that we have moved 'from an age of "inquisitorial" justice to an age of "examinatory justice"':

---

[15] Ibid, 222.
[16] M Foucault, *Madness and Civilization: A History of Insanity in the Age of Reason* (New York, Harper & Row, 1965) 265–66.
[17] Foucault, above n 4, 144.
[18] Ibid.

[J]udging has increased precisely to the extent that the normalising power has spread. ... The judges of normality are present everywhere. We are in the society of the teacher-judge, the doctor-judge, the educator-judge, the 'social worker'-judge.[19]

Crucially Foucault eventually shifts his focus from both the law/discipline nexus and the discipline/norms nexus to the relationship between law and governmentality. We return to this matter in a later section, after our introduction of some of Foucault's methodological tools.

2. FOUCAULT'S TOOLS AND THE STUDY OF LAW IN SOCIETY [20]

As noted in the introduction, this section considers archaeology, genealogy, discourse and power-knowledge—four research tools (perhaps 'philosophical tools' is not too strong a term) Foucault developed. He developed them in ways that mark them out very much as 'Foucaultian' tools, but this is not to say, of course, that he invented them as if in a vacuum. Far from it; they are, taken as a group or singly, the products of his diligent study of the work of the many thinkers who influenced him. For now, it is enough to mention just a handful: negatively, he was strongly influenced by his desire to rid himself (and his followers) of the effects of phenomenology (particularly as espoused by Sartre) and a certain type of hermeneutics, on the one hand, and of Marxism, on the other (in the 1950s in France these two poles seemed to define the outer limits of what was possible); in achieving this, among his positive influences were the French historians of sciences around Canguilhem, the German philosophers Nietzsche and Heidegger, and some French thinkers who straddled literature and philosophy, such as Blanchot and Bataille.[21] I offer a brief summary of the main features of each of these four tools in turn before offering an example to demonstrate how, together, they might be used in sociolegal studies.

Archaeology

Archaeology's main task is to describe statements in the archive,[22] statements covering the sayable and the visible (as, for example, in the invention and maintenance of prisons). This is no simple matter. Even if we understand 'statement' in its most basic sense, accept Foucault's basic definition of 'archive'—'the general system of the formation and transformation of statements'[23]—and allow that his concern to develop a particular type of French history as a defence against 'totalisation'—'the archaeological description of discourses is deployed in the dimension of a general history'[24]—

---

[19] Foucault, above n 2, 304–05.
[20] Much of the shape and content of this section relies on G Kendall and G Wickham, *Using Foucault's Methods* (London, Sage, 1999) 24–56.
[21] M Gane 'Introduction: Michel Foucault' in M Gane (ed), *Towards a Critique of Foucault* (London, Routledge & Kegan Paul, 1986).
[22] M Foucault *The Archaeology of Knowledge* (London, Tavistock, 1972) 131.
[23] Ibid, 130.
[24] Ibid, 164.

is not necessarily relevant to our present task, we still must come to grips with the complexities of what is involved in the task of description. To give some idea of these complexities, consider the following facts about archaeology:

— archaeology describes regularities of statements in a non-interpretive manner (content to remain at the level of appearances, eschewing any quest to go 'beyond' this level to find 'deeper meanings');
— archaeology describes statements in a non-anthropological manner, as a means of avoiding the search for authors (again remaining at the level of appearances—the appearances of statements—to avoid the habit of seeking to source meaning in human beings);
— archaeology describes the relation between one statement and other statements;
— archaeology describes 'surfaces of emergence'—or places within which objects are made objects in discourse;
— archaeology describes the institutions that acquire authority and provide limits within which discursive objects may act;
— archaeology describes the 'forms of specification' in which discursive objects are targeted.

In performing these complex tasks of description, it must also be said that archaeology formulates rules for the repeatability of statements—that which allows certain statements to recur—and analyses the positions that are established between subjects in regard to statements.[25]

Genealogy

Foucault developed the tool of genealogy well after he had developed that of archaeology, as he realised the importance of the notion of power to his thinking (archaeology in the 1960s, genealogy mainly in the 1970s; he seems to have borrowed the term 'genealogy' from Nietzsche, but, as always with Foucault, used it in his own special way). I suggest the two are complementary, inasmuch as genealogy still concentrates on statements in the archive. As Foucault puts it:

> If we were to characterise it in two terms, then 'archaeology' would be the appropriate methodology of this analysis of local discursivities, and 'genealogy' would be the tactics whereby, on the basis of the descriptions of these local discursivities, the subjected knowledges which were thus released would be brought into play.[26]

Indeed, I see no evidence against supposing that Foucault meant all the tools in his toolkit to be used alongside one another.[27] It is this spirit that I add four to our list of summary points about the methodological tools of Foucault:

---

[25] For more on the complexities of archaeology, see especially: P Bevis, M Cohen and G Kendall 'Archaeologizing Genealogy: Michel Foucault and the Economy of Austerity' (1989) 18 *Economy and Society* 323; B Brown and M Cousins 'The Linguistic Fault: The Case of Foucault's Archaeology' in Gane (ed), above n 21.
[26] Foucault, above n 3, 85.
[27] I am grateful to Gavin Kendall for this point.

— genealogy describes statements but with an emphasis on power;

— genealogy introduces power through a 'history of the present', concerned with 'disreputable origins and unpalatable functions';[28] for example, with regard to psychiatry, Foucault says, 'Couldn't the interweaving of effects of power and knowledge be grasped with greater certainty in the case of a science as "dubious" as psychiatry?';[29]

— genealogy describes statements, as an ongoing process, rather than as a snapshot of the web of discourse;[30]

— in this way, genealogy concentrates on the strategic use of archaeology to answer problems about the present.

Discourse

This term should be marked 'Danger'. The tool of discourse is undoubtedly crucial in Foucault's work, but it is crucial in ways that are in fact not necessarily related to, indeed sometimes opposed to, what is, perhaps, the standard meaning of the term in English. Where the English word suggests the dominance of the linguistic, Foucault means language as only one component among several. We might add English words such as 'institution', 'procedure' and 'practice', perhaps among others, into the mix, were we to try to pin down Foucault's 'discourse' in this way. But better, I think, to tackle the problem of how to make wise use of this multifaceted tool by first offering some examples of Foucault's own use of it, showing in doing so that he never meant it as a totalising tool, and by grasping as its two key features that it has no 'inside' and no 'outside'.

In Foucault's hands, a discourse is primarily about production. In this way, certain discourses on sex produce sexuality and types of person such as 'homosexual', 'heterosexual', 'deviant', etc, certain medical discourses produce asylums and mental patients, and certain penological discourses produce prisons and prisoners. This does not mean, of course, that Foucault is proposing that before the existence of these discourses none of these things existed.

For example, the discourses on sexuality on which he focuses his attention emerged in the eighteenth and nineteenth centuries not out of thin air, but as more and less dramatic refinements of certain kinship ties, certain Christian 'sins of the flesh', certain ancient but long-lasting techniques of 'self-mastery', etc.[31] However, care is also needed at the other end of this dilemma—Foucault is certainly not suggesting, therefore, that sex 'itself' exists in some 'pure' non-discursive space and time. While we might reasonably think of the 'raw materials' of Foucault's discourses—bodies, sex, death, etc—as non-discursive, we must not think we can gain access to this realm without discourse.

---

[28] N Rose 'The Formation of the Psychology of the Individual in England 1870–1939', unpublished PhD thesis, University of London, 1984.

[29] Foucault, above n 3, 109.

[30] M Foucault, 'The Order of Discourse' in R Young (ed), *Untying the Text: A Post-Structuralist Reader* (London, Routledge & Kegan Paul, 1981) 70–71.

[31] Foucault, above n 4.

Foucault weaves an intricate web here, but it is one that would be familiar to many philosophers, especially those concerned with epistemology. The relationship of the discursive to the non-discursive is pretty much that portrayed in those sophisticated philosophical accounts of knowledge that recognise the dangers of both extreme scepticism and extreme dogmatism (that is, those that are aware that we cannot successfully argue that knowledge of the external world is impossible or that it is straightforwardly possible either—knowledge is something in between). Exponents of various forms of this position—best known as mitigated or constructive scepticism—include Mersenne and Gassendi in the seventeenth century, Hume and perhaps Kant in the eighteenth, Quine, Wittgenstein and Davidson in the twentieth.[32] To flesh out just one aspect of just one of these thinker's work in the area, consider Quine's use of Neurath's ship metaphor. This suggests that producing knowledge is not at all the same as building a wooden ship under perfect conditions, perhaps in a dry dock (new materials, good tools, plenty of time, etc). Rather, it is like repairing such a ship at sea: one has to work a plank or two at a time, often in difficult conditions and with whatever tools one has to hand, and, crucially, the other planks must remain in place while one is working.[33] Such is Foucault's way of handling the relationship between the discursive and the non-discursive: the non-discursive might be thought of as the 'pure' sailing space within the ship, but the operation of discourses—the planks working together as a ship—define it, such that while we know its existence is important, this existence is dubious or even meaningless without the ship; and we can only ever deal with the ship a few planks at a time.

By insisting that discourses have 'no inside',[34] Foucault is insisting that there is no hidden mechanism that makes discourses work, nothing we should be digging for beyond or behind the use of words and symbols that make their use possible. What we need for Foucaultian discourse analysis is there in front of us. Remembering that when Foucault was invited to name his Chair at the Collège de France he chose 'Professor of the History of Systems of Thought', we should be especially keen to understand discourses in terms of visible 'systems of thought'. This involves being vigilant against the possibility that 'thought' is seen as something special, as the product of some higher order called 'thinking'. For Foucault, it is much better to understand 'thought' as simply the name given to 'surfaces of appearance' involved in the operation of various institutions, procedures, apparatuses, etc, all of them quite public and visible. So, to give a preview of the example which is to conclude this section, the legal discourses involved in the regulation of gambling involve much thought, but we do not and should not look for the 'source' of the thinking 'inside' some head or heads. We are presented with the surfaces of appearance of this thinking in written judgments and regulations, in the design of casinos and other gambling venues, in the com-

---

[32] See especially RJ Hankinson, *The Sceptics* (London, Routledge, 1994); C Hookway, *Scepticism* (London, Routledge, 1990); J Malpas, *Place and Experience: A Philosophical Topography* (Cambridge, Cambridge University Press, 1999); RH Popkin, *The History of Scepticism from Erasmus to Descartes* (New York, Harper Torchbooks, 1968).

[33] Hookway, ibid, 222–24.

[34] I owe much of the discussion of the relationship between Foucault's discourse and its 'inside' and 'outside' to I Hunter, 'Michel Foucault: Discourse versus Language', unpublished MS thesis, Brisbane Griffith University, 1984.

portment and conversations of the gamblers and the staff at the venues, in policing arrangements and practices, and so on. This is discourse—quotidian not mysterious.

By saying that discourses have no 'outside', Foucault is, in an important sense, simply expanding his argument that discourses have no 'inside'. In accepting that surfaces are what we have to work with and that we need no more—there is nothing 'inside' or 'behind' discourses making them 'tick'—we are accepting that there is, neither, nothing 'outside' them, nothing that somehow guarantees their existence and operation. This is to say, we should not trouble ourselves by trying to anchor discourses to 'the world', or some other such supposedly fixed point of reference. Points of reference for Foucault are never fixed, they are always fragmented. Before attempting to cement this point in place by expanding the above example, I should stress that we are again on the ground of mitigated or constructive scepticism. Inasmuch as we cannot say either that knowledge of the external world is impossible or that it is straightforwardly possible, we must recognise that both extremes of the 'inside' and 'outside' positions—'pure thinking' and the 'independent world'—are wrapped up in the same package. There is no way to separate either or both of them such that it or they function as some sort of bedrock on which our investigations might rest when needed.

The legal discourses involved in the regulation of gambling involve many references to things supposedly 'outside' gambling. But we do not and should not look for the 'source' of the things in some supposedly fixed 'world' or other external 'reality'. Again I must stress that we are presented with the surfaces of appearance of these things—in written judgments and regulations, in the design of casinos and other gambling venues, in the comportment and conversations of the gamblers and the staff at the venues, in policing arrangements and practices, and so on. Discourses do not produce the 'external world', in some crude sense, just as they do not crudely produce thoughts, but it is not possible to separate 'internal thinking', 'external world' and discourses from one another; in Foucault's discourse analysis, they are all parts of the one package and cannot meaningfully be taken as separate entities, just as 'ship', 'space inside ship' and 'sailing' cannot meaningfully be taken as separate entities when one analyses a sailing ship at sea.

A final note about the tool of discourse is called for, to deal briefly with the notion of episteme. The simplest way to understand this notion—and this is simple without being simplistic—is to think of an episteme as a large, loose collection of discourses built up over time and space. Epistemes are not in any way determinate of discourses, rather the term is used by Foucault to allow us to occasionally consider the vaguely co-ordinated (co-ordinated without a co-ordinator, of course) operation of discourses over certain time periods and certain spaces. As McHoul and Grace put it:

> Sometimes he treats the discourses separately; at other times, he looks at their contribution to the possibility of each period having an overall view of the world (which he calls 'the Western episteme').[35]

---

[35] A McHoul and W Grace, *A Foucault Primer: Discourse, Power and the Subject* (Melbourne, Melbourne University Press, 1992) 32.

Power-knowledge

I introduced Foucault's treatment of power in the previous section. I have so far said nothing directly about its complex relationship with knowledge. I will allow my discussion of this relationship to emerge from the following summary of power-knowledge. It almost goes without saying that Foucault uses the tool of power-knowledge alongside the others I have been at pains to outline. It is definitely one tool in his toolkit, not a super-tool that might be used in place of the others. Bearing this in mind, the main points about power-knowledge are:

— power-knowledge helps in the use of the tools of archaeology, genealogy and discourse, as part of Foucault's approach to history;
— power-knowledge starts with discourse—discursive relations are power relations, connecting the visible and the sayable; but remember, Foucault does not want us to conflate power and discourse;
— 'power', in Foucault's 'power-knowledge' formulation, is best thought of in technical terms, in the mundane sense of making things work;
— 'power', in Foucault's 'power-knowledge' formulation, is a strategy focusing on relations between the visible and the sayable, one that prevents the exhaustion of the visible. Remember, for Foucault, power is productive, not repressive and not a possession;
— 'power', in Foucault's 'power-knowledge' formulation, involves resistance to power, but this too is a technical component of power, part of the way it operates;
— 'power', in Foucault's 'power-knowledge' formulation, is a relation of forces while knowledge is a relation of forms, yet the two relate to each other as different— power is non-stratified, local, unstable and flexible, while knowledge is stratified, stable and segmented;
— 'power', in Foucault's 'power-knowledge' formulation, is 'microphysical', inasmuch as Foucault positions it in the relationship with knowledge as having a slight primacy;
— this is to say that 'power', in Foucault's 'power-knowledge' formulation, would exist without knowledge, but knowledge could not exist without power;
— in other words, knowledge supports power in action;
— 'power', in Foucault's 'power-knowledge' formulation, produces subjects;
— these subjects are not the same as individuals, in the way they are commonly understood;
— for Foucault, the category of individuals is an invented category, not a natural one;
— 'power', in Foucault's 'power-knowledge' formulation, is involved in subjectivity, via discourse, so we can say that subjects form some of the conditions for knowledge.

A Detailed Example

Our example, introduced already, concerns the regulation of gambling. It will be remembered that discourses of gambling regulation have no 'inside' and no 'outside', but this does not tell us much about how a Foucaultian analysis of these discourses would work in full. First stop is archaeology.

An archaeology of gambling regulation would describe regularities of statements concerned with gambling and its regulation—formal documents produced by governments, courts, lobby groups, etc, and informal statements that might find their way into an archive, such as newspaper reports and transcripts or copies of broadcasts—in a non-interpretive manner. Such descriptions would not, this is to say, go 'beyond' these archival traces in a bid to find 'deeper meanings'. As well, such descriptions would be 'non-anthropological'—not looking for the authors of the statements (even if the name of some leading politician or judge of the time and place is prominent among the statements; Foucaultian analysis does not, of course, completely eschew reference to the names of prominent authors of statements, rather, it does not grant them special status). In this way, Foucaultian analysis seeks to avoid the supposed need to determine some 'human meaning' in statements, in favour of remaining at the level of appearances (it should be clear by now that this is one of the keys to good Foucaultian analysis).

In doing all this, an archaeology of gambling regulation would also describe the relation between one statement and other statements. For instance, it would describe the ways in which statements about the need for fewer gambling outlets must, at least in most jurisdictions in the Western world, confront statements about the attractions of gambling as a source of taxation revenue (though it would remain silent on the political morality battles involved, unless of course such battles surface as statements of their own; its silence covers only supposedly implicit meanings).

In addition, an archaeology of the regulation of gambling would describe the institutions which acquire authority and provide limits within which discursive objects may act and would describe the 'forms of specification' in which these discursive objects are targeted. By this I mean such an analysis would describe courts, police, casinos, legal and illegal betting operations—in short, any institutions actively involved in defining the discursive objects of gambling and its regulation in any given jurisdiction—and describe the ways in which such institutions limit what is to count as gambling and its regulation (by legislation, commercial competition, police operational procedures, possibly even organised criminal violence and intimidation, etc). And it would, in doing this, describe the exact nature of such legislation, competition, procedures, violence, etc, as the forms of specification in which gambling and its regulation are targeted.

The tool of genealogy would enhance the descriptive work of archaeology by describing the 'disreputable origins and unpalatable functions' of the ways gambling and its regulation are conducted—undermining any attempts to hide the sordid aspects behind the cloak of any formal 'scientific' studies of the industries involved. In this way, the genealogical component seeks to add an ongoing strategic dimension to the snapshot picture made available through archaeology.

Having said enough above about the use of discourse concerning this example, I move straight on to power-knowledge.

The discursive relations involved in this example are power relations, connecting the visible and the sayable—the visible of casinos, legal and illegal betting shops, police officers and their uniforms, etc, and the sayable of politicians, judges, gambling advocates and opponents, etc, and prevents the exhaustion of the visible. Of course, inasmuch as Foucault does not want us to conflate power and discourse, we must not think that the power involved in these discourses is the only power involved in the regulation of gambling. Power is also involved in the mundane sense of making the acts of gambling and its regulation work—power produces the types of person to be investigated here (gamblers, judges, officials, police officers, criminals, etc) and the institutions to be investigated (casinos, courts, even the law, etc), power is productive, not repressive and not a possession. Clearly there is resistance to the power here, but this is part of the way it operates—the resistance (formal organised opposition to gambling, attempts by operators to bribe or coerce regulators, even the sheer grinding nature of the legislative and bureaucratic procedure, etc) is much more a part of the operation of power than it is a threat to its existence.

These power relations are relations of forces, but of course in being discursive relations they also involve knowledge, as a relation of forms. Power and knowledge relate to each other in the following manner: the power that produces the gambling persons and institutions is non-stratified, local, unstable and flexible (the judges, courts, gambling houses, laws, gambling, criminals, families, money, governments, taxes, etc, form a jumble of shifting alliances and hierarchies, the reach of which varies and the effects of which are never certain), while knowledge is stratified, stable and segmented (the knowledge of gambling and its regulation, whether formal or informal, is slower to shift in these ways and hence provides the continuity to this particular power-knowledge relationship). Yet it must be remembered that this gambling and regulation 'power jumble' has a slight primacy—it would exist without the gambling-regulation knowledge, but the knowledge could not exist without it. The gambling-regulation knowledge supports the gambling-regulation power in action (and here we can see that the production of particular types of subjects through power forms some of the conditions for knowledge).

3. GOVERNMENTALITY AND LAW[36]

The word 'governmentality', a neologism of Foucault's, is an amalgam of 'government' and 'mentality' (literally, mentalities of government). A useful way to begin to think about what Foucault means by it is to see it as a development of his various tools examined above. In this way, governmentality, too, is not a radical departure for Foucault, it is another stage in his long-term project to understand and analyse the complexities of the relationship between power and knowledge, a project that includes his development of archaeology, genealogy and discourse as tools. Nonetheless, it is certainly the case that Foucault's thinking about governmentality appears to have accelerated in the late 1970s and it is at this time that he wrote his suggestive essay 'On Governmentality'.[37]

I will return to this essay shortly, after some necessary definitional discussion.

Mitchell Dean says Foucault's 'study of governmentality is continuous with' at least some approaches to the study of the state—it, like these approaches, 'regards the exercise of power and authority as anything but self-evident'.[38]

Differences between the two, Dean argues, emerge at the point where Foucault

---

[36] Some of the shape and content of this section relies on Hunt and Wickham, above n 1.
[37] M Foucault, 'On Governmentality' (1979) 6 *Ideology and Consciousness* 5.
[38] M Dean, *Governmentality* (London, Sage, 1999) 9.

breaks with 'the characteristic assumptions of theories of the state' in order to think about government as the 'the conduct of conduct'.[39] Dean then offers two related definitions of 'governmentality'. By the first,

> It deals with how we think about governing, with the different mentalities of government. ... The notions of collective mentalities and the idea of a history of mentalities have long been used by sociologists (such as Emile Durkheim and Marcel Mauss) and by the *Annales* school of history in France. ... For such thinkers, a mentality is a collective, relatively bounded unity, and is not readily examined by those who inhabit it. ... The idea of mentalities of government, then, emphasizes the way in which the thought involved in practices of government is collective and relatively taken for granted ... the way we think about exercising authority draws upon the theories, ideas, philosophies and forms of knowledge that are part of our social and cultural products.[40]

By Dean's second definition,

> 'governmentality' marks the emergence of a distinctly new form of thinking about and exercising of power in certain societies ... bound up with the discovery of a new reality, the economy, and concerned with a new object, the population. Governmentality emerges in Western European societies in the 'early modern period' when the art of government of the state becomes a distinct activity, and when the forms and knowledge and techniques of the human and social sciences become integral to it.[41]

Pat O'Malley, writing for a sociolegal audience, speaks of governmentality as a distinctive 'approach':

> There is a considerable literature exploring and developing this approach ... influenced strongly by the thinking of Michel Foucault ... but ... advanced primarily in recent years by British and Australian scholars. The journal *Economy and Society* has been a principal site for the development of this approach, which is frequently referred to as the 'governmentality' literature. While 'governmentality' refers to a particular technology of government that emerges in the eighteenth century, the term is more generally used to refer to the approach adopted in its study. The approach is characterized by two primary characteristics. The first is a stress on the dispersal of 'government,' that is, on the idea that government is not a preserve of 'the state' but is carried out at all level and sites in societies—including the self government of individuals. ... The second is the deployment of an analytic stance that favors 'how' questions over 'why' questions. In other words it favors accounts in terms of how government of a certain kind becomes possible: in what manner it is thought up by planners, using what concepts; how it is intended to be translated into practice, using what combination of means? Only secondarily is it concerned with accounts that seek to *explain* government—in the sense of understanding the nature of government as the effect of other events.[42]

---

[39] Ibid, 10–16.

[40] Ibid, 16.

[41] *Ibid*, 19.

[42] P O'Malley, 'Imagining Insurance Risk, Thrift and Industrial Life Insurance in Britain' (1988–89) 5 *Connecticut Insurance Law Journal* 676, 679 n 7. For more on the complexities of the governmentality approach, see also A Barry, T Osborne and N Rose (eds), *Foucault and Political Reason: Liberalism, Neo-Liberalism and Rationalities of Government* (London, UCL Press, 1996); G Burchell, C Gordon and P Miller (eds), *The Foucault Effect: Studies in Governmentality* (Brighton, Harvester Wheatsheaf, 1991); M Dean and B Hindess (eds), *Governing Australia* (Melbourne, Cambridge University Press, 1998); P Miller and N Rose, 'Governing Economic Life' (1990) 19 *Economy and Society* 1; N Rose, *Governing the Soul*

These two definitions, taken together, not only capture many features of Foucault's treatment of governmentality (I deal with still other features as this section progresses), they also show the ways in which this treatment builds on his earlier tools and makes use of them, as well as tools developed by others.

In considering how we might think about law in terms of this particular tool, I suggest that governmentality understands law as another means of, and another location for the exercise of, government. Law is not a special 'external force'. As for other objects treated as falling within the ambit of governmentality, legal objects are discrete practices of government: 'Practices of government ... do not form those types of totalities in which the parts are expressions or instances of the whole. Rather, they should be approached as composed of heterogeneous elements having diverse historical trajectories.'[43]

In thinking about law and governmentality we might think of Foucault making something of a shift—from discipline to government.

> It was a matter not of studying the theory of penal law in itself, or the evolution of such and such penal institution, but of analyzing the formation of a certain 'punitive rationality'. ... Instead of seeking the explanation in a general conception of the Law, or in the evolving modes of industrial production ... it seemed to me far wiser to look at ... the refinement, the elaboration and installation since the seventeenth century, of techniques of 'governing' individuals—that is, for 'guiding their conduct'—in domains as different as the school, the army, and the workshop. Accordingly, the analysis does not revolve around the general principle of Law or the myth of Power, but concerns itself with the complex and multiple practices of a 'governmentality' which presupposes, on the one hand, rational forms, technical procedures, instrumentations through which to operate and, on the other hand, strategic games which subject the power relations they are supposed to guarantee to instability and reversal.[44]

The term 'government' in Foucault's hands is, as we have already seen, different from its usual use to describe a combination of legislatures and bureaucracies. In thinking of government as the 'conduct of conduct' Foucault is, again as we have seen, effectively shifting the focus of the study of government away from the notion of the state. In doing so, he is thereby shifting the focus of sociolegal studies away from the nexus between law and state. For Foucault, government is, as it were, a domain of the sociolegal that is much more than law. This means Foucault is, at least in a sense, on the side of sociolegal scholars in their long-running disagreement with 'black letter' lawyers as to the proper scope of the study of the law. Indeed, in the 'On Governmentality' essay referred to earlier, he goes so far as to say that government is,

> not a matter of imposing laws on men, but rather of disposing things, that is to say to employ tactics rather than laws, and if need be to use the laws themselves as tactics ... the instruments of government, instead of being laws, now come to be a range of multiform tactics. Within the perspective of government, law is not what is important.[45]

(London, Routledge, 1989); N Rose and P Miller, 'Political Power beyond the State: Problematics of Government' (1992) 43 *British Journal of Sociology* 173.

[43] Dean, above n 38, 29.
[44] Foucault, above n 6, 337–38.
[45] Foucault, above n 37, 13.

In this essay, Foucault spells out the historical version of the governmentality theme. This features, from roughly the end of the eighteenth century, the emergence of what he calls the concern with 'security', which may be better understood in English by the word 'welfare'. In this period, and well into the twentieth century (and arguably into the twenty-first; see Rose for an argument that this type of 'government of the social' died off in the late twentieth century), a liberal model of government developed that characterised and promoted individuals in a particular way, as bundles of 'interests'. Law's role under this type of liberalism is no longer so negative in Foucault's eyes (though it has to be said that he is oblique here too and I rely on one of his main English interpreters, Colin Gordon, in making this point). Law now becomes a means of setting and regulating the bounds within which individuals can pursue their 'interests', especially, but not exclusively, their economic interests. It is in this context that Foucault discusses the increasing importance of rights. As Gordon puts it: '[D]isrespect of liberty is not simply an illegitimate violation of rights, but an ignorance of how to govern'.[46]

In wrapping up this section, it might be said that this later governmentality work by Foucault suggests a slightly stronger role for law than that indicated by the material considered in the first section. It might be said, but as his discussion of law in the governmentality work is no less oblique than in the earlier work, even such a claim, qualified by the term 'suggests', is, I believe, too strong.

4. CONCLUSION

I have argued that law, for Foucault, is about power, albeit mainly negative power. Law, for Foucault, is about sovereignty and this law-as-sovereignty guarantees a certain truth—the truth of negative power. Law, for Foucault, is about a means of domination. Law, for Foucault, needs to be supported by (or possibly supplanted by) the more subtle notions of disciplines and norms, which he employs to describe institutions that, crucially, do most of the judging in modern societies. In analysing law in society (or, more accurately, the limits of law and the role of disciplines and norms) Foucault makes full use of his toolkit of analysis, featuring archaeology, genealogy, discourse and of course power-knowledge, and anyone studying law who seeks to follow him would do well to come to grips with his use of these tools. The notion of governmentality Foucault developed quite late in his life adds an extra dimension to his approach to law. Inasmuch as this notion is simultaneously a new tool in his toolkit and a more sophisticated description of important aspects of the operation of power from the eighteenth century onwards, it is rich with possibilities for the study of law in society.

I have argued all this, yet I have done so very much on the basis of the concession that when describing Foucault's treatment of law, we largely find ourselves raking through the fallen leaves of his work and picking up a hint here and a suggestion there. This is a somewhat unsatisfactory situation, no doubt, but unavoidable. Foucault simply did not say enough directly about law and its role to allow more

---

[46] C Gordon, 'Governmental Rationality: An Introduction' in Burchell et al (eds), above n 42, at 20.

than this. At very least it is fertile ground for argument. As I hinted above, the 'governmentality approach' seems to me to be the Foucaultian approach most involved in overcoming this limitation, by running hard with what little there is and building what almost amounts to its own 'Foucault and law'.[47] Perhaps this is the best that can be done.[48]

[47] For just some examples, see: D Garland, ' "Governmentality" and the Problem of Crime: Foucault, Criminology, Sociology' (1996) 1 *Theoretical Criminology* 173; B Hudson, 'Punishment and Governance' (1998) 7 *Social and Legal Studies* 553; D Ivison, 'The Technical and the Political: Discourses of Race, Reasons of State' (1998) 7 *Social and Legal Studies* 561; O'Malley, above n 42; P O'Malley, 'Governmentality and the Risk Society' (1999) 28 *Economy and Society* 138; P O'Malley, 'Uncertain Subjects. Risks, Liberalism and Contract' (2000) 29 *Economy and Society* 459; G Pavlich and G Wickham (eds), *Rethinking Law, Society and Governance: Foucault's Bequest* (Oxford, Hart Publishing, 2001); F Pearce and S Tombs, 'Foucault, Governmentality, Marxism' (1998) 7 *Social and Legal Studies* 567; Rose and Valverde, above n 1; L Weir, 'Recent Developments in the Government of Pregnancy' (1996) 25 *Economy and Society* 372.

[48] The editors have been kind enough to judge my chapter worthy of inclusion in their second edition in the same form in which it appeared in the first edition, ten years ago. They have asked me to add just a little by way of references to at least some of the literature on Foucault, law and power that has been published in these ten years.

The most important work on Foucault and law to appear since 2002 is undoubtedly the remarkable publishing project that has made available to a worldwide audience the contents of the different sets of lectures Foucault gave at the Collège de France during the 1970s and into the 1980s. The set of lectures published under the title *'Society Must be Defended': Lectures at the Collège de France 1975–76* (New York, Fontana, 2003) is especially important for those interested in exploring Foucault's thoughts on the role of law in relation to the operation of power. In reading this book, or indeed any of the books published in this series, an invaluable guide is provided by K Tribe 'The Political Economy of Modernity: Foucault's Collège de France Lectures of 1978 and 1979' (2009) 38 *Economy and Society* 679.

More specifically on Foucault and law, I would recommend B Golder and P Fitzpatrick, *Foucault's Law* (Oxford, Routledge Glasshouse, 2009); JM London, *How the Use of Marijuana Was Criminalized and Medicalized, 1906–2004: A Foucaultian History of Legislation in America* (Lewiston, NY, The Edwin Mellon Press, 2009); AN Sharpe, *Foucault's Monsters and the Challenge of Law* (Oxford, Routledge Glasshouse, 2010).

Finally, I turn to the five pieces on Foucault I have published since 2002. I do so because in some of these pieces, but not all, I express views more critical of Foucault than those presented here. The three most critical pieces are: G Wickham, 'Foucault, Law and Power: A Reassessment' (2006) 23 *Journal of Law and Society* 596 (in which I suggest that Foucault's approach to sovereignty and the state is inadequate to understand the post 9/11 West); G Wickham, 'The Social Must Be Limited: Some Problems with Foucault's Approach to Modern Positive Power' (2008) 44 *Journal of Sociology* 29 (in which I argue against Foucault's understanding of society and the way it is governed); G Wickham and G Kendall, 'Critical Discourse Analysis, Description, Explanation, Causes: Foucault's Inspiration Versus Weber's Perspiration' (2008) 33 *Historical Social Research/Historische Sozialforschung* 142 (in which we compare some of Foucault's methods unfavourably with some of Weber's). The two pieces more supportive of Foucault's position are: G Kendall and G Wickham, 'The Foucaultian Framework' in C Seale, G Gobo, JF Gubrium and D Silverman (eds), *Qualitative Research Practice* (London, Sage, 2004) (which is an attempt to condense our thinking about the importance of Foucault's methods); G Wickham, 'Foucault and the Promise of Power without Dogma' in G Delanty and S Turner (eds), *Routledge International Handbook of Contemporary Social and Political Theory* (London, Routledge, 2011) (in which I put my harsher words about Foucault in the context of nearly thirty years of publishing on him, stressing that, while my harsher words are warranted, there is still a great deal to admire about Foucault's thought).

13

Law and Postmodernism

SHAUN MCVEIGH

POSTMODERNISM IS A term born of disputes or polemics between the 'moderns' and the 'postmoderns'. These disputes passed through the humanities and public discourse between the 1960s and the late 1990s. At its peak the dispute emerged as a distinct 'culture war'. For some, postmodernism offered a way of revitalising and moving beyond the modern; for critics, it has been little more than a late flourish of romanticism and irrationalism.

Like an earlier series of disputes waged in France and England between the 'ancients' and 'moderns' at the end of the seventeenth and beginning of the eighteenth century, the debates between the moderns and postmoderns concerned the character of our civilisation and the conduct of our civility compared with those of our past and of our neighbours. The range of the debates between the 'ancients' and 'moderns' is, somewhat surprisingly, comparable to those of our near present. On one reading battle lines were drawn between classical scholarship and modern science, between a past dominated by abstract contemplation and scholastic argument, and a future shaped by the domination of nature and the emancipation of scientific inquiry and critical rational endeavour. For many moderns it was the ability of science and, in a different way, law to create an objective world that creates the 'great divide' of modernity both from the past and from premoderns.[1]

In the arts and humanities the elaboration of the ethos of modern man was shaped by a set of engagements between those humanists who supported models of ethical conduct ordered around the classical forms of life and those who favoured modern virtues shaped by scientific inquiry, commerce and reason.[2] As with contemporary debates these concerns did not simply produce two rival camps. Both 'ancients' and 'moderns', for example, welcomed the rise of science. Many of the 'moderns' advocated not a dismissal of the ancients but the use of modern scholarly practices of history and philology in order to draw out the lessons of the ancients more fully. Resting behind these disputes there was also a concern with the authority of religion and law in public life. What was contested, in short, was what it meant to be modern and the mode and manner of engaging the world. Much the same can be said of

---

[1] E Gellner, *Postmodernism, Reason and Religion* (London, Routledge, 1992).

[2] D Edelstein, *The Enlightenment: A Genealogy* (Chicago, University of Chicago Press, 2010); L Norman, *The Shock of the Ancient* (Chicago, University of Chicago Press, 2011).

contemporary debates that have often turned out to be debates about the inheritance and loss of the modern. Law in this story is viewed as both the noble dream and nightmare of modernity and postmodernism its curse or cure.

The situations in which postmodernism has been invoked have been diffuse. The term postmodern found a home in architecture and the performing arts in the 1950s and 1960s before taking up more general usage in the humanities and later social sciences.[3] Postmodernism arrived mostly in opposition to varieties of modernism and presented itself in terms of new styles of representation and forms of expression. Postmodernism entered the law, or at least law journals, in the 1980s at the same time as it became a distinct form of social theory. However, it is not clearly the case that accounts of the disputes between modernists and postmodernists are capable of being assimilated to one overarching theme, still less a coherent dispute between rival social theories. To name a discourse as modern or postmodern is to enter a polemic rather than to determine a substantive concept.[4]

This chapter presents a relatively restricted range of issues in an attempt to jostle postmodernism into relation with social theory and jurisprudence. While classical social theory has much to say about law and might have much to say about law in a postmodern era, it is not necessarily the case that there is a distinct postmodern social theory or at least one that yields programmatic understanding about the social ordering or understanding of law. In part this is because postmodern theory has been interested in the exploring the end or loss of the 'social', and in part because postmoderns have resisted what has been taken as the deadening effect of treating social theory as the exclusive domain of experts reporting to the public and advising government. The formulation of the key topics of postmodernism in this chapter ties postmodern theory to the inheritance of a set of concerns from German and French philosophy and its reception into Anglophone social or critical theory. While this emphasis is appropriate in a book concerned with law and social theory, it does narrow the engagement with other expressions of postmodernism. In treating postmodernism as 'theory', it is easy to miss the very direct impact of postmodernism as an exuberant (or despairing) rebellion aimed at repeopling and replacing forms of modern life.[5] It might also miss some of the ways in which postmodernism has recast the modes of engaging with the central concerns of social and legal theory: the insistence of the importance of the surface and style, the inevitability of the mixing of genres, and the formation of new conceptual and social personae. The approach taken in this chapter does not directly join the dispute between the moderns and the postmoderns. This polemic, like that of the ancients and moderns, has now largely passed. Postmodernism is presented here as if it engages and continues a number of debates about conducts and politics of life.

1. MODERN

One point of entry into the periodisation, style and ethos of the postmodern is gained

---

[3] T Woods, *Beginning Postmodernism* (Manchester, Manchester University Press, 1999).

[4] The terminology of the postmodern is varied. I have followed a common usage: postmodernity (epoch), postmodernisation (process), postmodernism (a style or idiom) and postmodern theory.

[5] C Jencks *The Story of Post-Modernism: Five Decades of the Ironic, Iconic and Critical in Architecture* (London, Wiley, 2011).

by turning briefly to a number of points of engagement between modern and post-modern social theory. A common formulation of the dispute between the moderns and postmoderns has been phrased in terms of a dispute between those who still adhere to some of the promise of the Enlightenment and those who do not. One result of this within the humanities and social sciences of Anglophone universities is that disputes between moderns and postmoderns have often been elaborated in terms of a series of oppositions and allegiances such those between rationalism and irrationalism, modernism and anti-modernism, foundationalism and anti-foundationalism (in episte-mology), essentialism and anti-essentialism (in ontology), representation and anti-representationalism (in the ability of language and art to present the world), historicism and anti-historicisim (in the determination of the meaning of events), humanism and anti-humanism (in the priority given to the human as universal subject), and so forth. Without entirely letting go of such antagonisms, postmodernism will be addressed here through the inheritance of the enlightenment and the intensification of the criticism of modernisation, modern social theory and modernity.

A significant starting point in elaborating the modern and the postmodern has been made with the inheritance of German philosophy (and legal thought) through the work of Immanuel Kant and his consideration of the status of the enlightenment project. Kant's short public essay 'What Is Enlightenment?' (1784) encapsulates one of the many versions of the 'spirit' of enlightenment: 'Dare to be Wise' or 'Have the courage to make use of your own understanding'.[6] For Kant, such daring is part of what is required for human maturity and freedom.

The way to 'maturity', for Kant, is through linking of autonomy, or will, to public reason. For Kant, the two aspects are held in relation by the moral law, or, rather, it is because there is a moral law that we need to organise our reason in such a way that we can 'act always according to the maxim whose universality as a law you can at the same time will'.[7] The moral law is approached as a matter of individual willing and as a matter of the historical development of public life. As a matter of individual willing, Kant does not ask a direct question such as 'How does one conduct oneself well', instead he examines the conditions of how freedom (or any other human activity) is possible: 'What can I know?', 'What can I do?' With these questions Kant splits reason between two domains: that of theoretical reason conducted in the phenomenal world of appearances, and that of practical reason conducted in the noumenal world of 'things-as-such'. The Kantian person knows him/herself both as a phenomenal (sensible) being and as a free (noumenal) subject. Kant's philosophy, like much ancient philosophy, offers both an account of the proper understanding of existence and a 'training in a life'.[8] For Kant, then, it is through the training for living by the limits of reason alone that we become free. This is how we can join the maturity or wisdom of the philosopher to our historical present.

For many, Kant's philosophy and philosophy of law ('the metaphysics of morals') stands at the pinnacle of Enlightenment reason. Critics, however, have contested most

---

[6] I Kant, 'What Is Enlightenment?' in *Practical Philosophy*, ed M Gregor (Cambridge, Cambridge University Press, 1996) 17.

[7] I Kant, *Foundations of the Metaphysics of Morals* (London, Pearson, Library of Liberal Arts, 1959) 41–42.

[8] P Hadot, *What Is Ancient Philosophy?* (Cambridge, MA, Harvard University Press, 2002) 265–70.

aspects of the forms of life, critical reason and community (or association) that Kant recommended.

The first critical inheritance for modernism and postmodernism shaped in opposition to Kant was established through Georg Hegel and Karl Marx, both of whom questioned the idealism of Kant's thought and of the Enlightenment more generally. For this tradition it is history and, differently, the forces and relations of the production of material life, that give us a proper understanding of existence and possibilities of freedom. For Hegel, what motivated enlightenment was not the work of pure reason but the 'cunning of reason' in the working through of the spirit of a people or state.[9] The inheritance of Marx emphasised the conflict of reason is not one of ideal forms but of conflict to secure the means of production. For many who diagnose our near present as postmodern, it is Marx's political economy that has provided the most trenchant formulations of the character of modern life as understood under the sway of the accumulation of capital and through modes of industrial production. The opening stanzas of *The Communist Manifesto* set out the sense of what is lost and gained:

> The bourgeoisie cannot exist without constantly revolutionizing the instruments of production, and thereby the relations of production, and with them the whole relations of society. ... All fixed, fast frozen relations, with their train of ancient and venerable prejudices and opinions, are swept away, all new-formed ones become antiquated before they can ossify. All that is solid melts into air, all that is holy is profaned, and man is at last compelled to face with sober senses his real condition of life and his relations with his kind.[10]

Marxist scholars, most notably Frederic Jameson and David Harvey, have provided the basic critical and conceptual formulations of the disruptive effects of postmodern relations of commodity exchange and of the reification of human relations.[11]

A second important line of dispute with Kant has emerged through the work of Friedrich Nietzsche and, loosely, the phenomenological. These approaches reshaped Kant's sense of enlightenment and philosophy by questioning both the ways in which reason and appearance are understood and the ways in which morality is taken for granted. Nietzsche attacked Kant's way of ordering his thought according to presuppositions of reason and of morals. If we can only reason on the basis of securing the world of appearances by presupposition, Nietzsche argued, we seem destined to forget that appearances are only appearances. We mistake for truths what are simply appearances that we no longer contest. Once the value of a world legislated by presupposition is brought into question, then so too is morality.[12] Where Kant argues that we are free within the conditions of reason, Nietzsche's work has provided resources for thinking of ethics and conduct by contesting the origins of truth, right and reason. The human world is not one of reason alone but is in constant flux: knowledge is shaped by belief, and truth and truthfulness are the trained expressions of the will to power (control). For Nietzsche, the value and conduct of life should not be shaped by the presupposed existence of God or ordered according to resentment against

[9] T Kochi, *The Other's War: Recognition and the Violence of Ethics* (London, Routledge, 2011).

[10] K Marx and F Engels, *The Communist Manifesto* [1848] (New York, Penguin, 1998) 54; M Berman, *All that Is Solid Melts into Air: The Experience of Modernity* (New York, Simon & Schuster, 1982).

[11] F Jameson, *Postmodernism, or, the Cultural Logic of Late Capitalism* (Durham, NC, Duke University Press, 1991); D Harvey, *The Condition of Postmodernity: An Enquiry into the Origins of Cultural Change* (Oxford, Blackwell, 1991); Z Bauman, *Liquid Modernity* (Cambridge, Polity Press, 2000).

[12] F Nietzsche, *Gay Science* (Cambridge, Cambridge University Press, 2001).

the powerful (an ethic 'beyond good and evil'). It should be shaped by developing a worldly ethic through the sovereign individual that affirms both our subjection to, and will to overcome, fate and suffering.[13] It is Nietzsche who sets the stage for much postmodern theory.

A third response to Kant is made through the phenomenological tradition. It articulates and develops ways of experiencing of the phenomena of the world from the viewpoint of consciousness. The work of Martin Heidegger in particular has been important in shaping the concerns of modernity around questions of ontology (what there is) and the history of the hiding and revelation of Being.[14] Heidegger's work has provided a distinct way of investigating forms of authentic existence and of ways of revealing the condition of being in the world.

A further inheritance of the modern, also, in part, from Kant, comes through the work of sociologists at the end of the nineteenth century who developed critical accounts of society and culture. It is with the emergence of critical accounts of social life in the early twentieth century that most of the themes that characterise postmodern theory take shape. For Max Weber, human life under capitalism should be characterised in relation to two interrelated themes: that of the disenchantment with life and that of the increasing rationalisation of the ordering of the world. We live in a world shaped by the secularisation and systematisation of forms of authority and of intellectual and social life.[15] While Weber's thought has not been important to the French postmoderns, it has been important in the critical reception of postmodern theory in the social sciences in Anglophone universities.[16]

For much contemporary 'social theory' and for the arts and sciences of government, the social has become the theoretical point of the ordering of the understanding of man and society. Kant's 'What is man?' has become 'What is society?' Postmodernism questions this relation. While ordering an account of postmodernism around a Kantian inheritance is only one way of locating modern and postmodern disputes, it gives emphasis to the way in which it is conduct, reason and the world that are in question. It gives emphasis to certain ways of understanding the problems of the modern world and displaces others. In the context of law and social theory, two brief points can be made here. The first is that by placing stress on the critical response to Kant, postmodern social theory is linked to the rivalries of critical theory and a concern with subjectivity—and legal subjectivity. Second, the moderns and postmoderns take up and share many of the criticisms that Kantians make of empirical and positivist social theory. It should be remembered, however, that the discourses of the modern and the postmodern are broader in scope than this suggests.

2. POSTMODERN

If there is a general topic of concern for the postmoderns within social theory, the

---

[13] G Deleuze, *Nietzsche and Philosophy* (New York, Columbia University Press, 2006).

[14] M Heidegger, 'Letter on Humanism' in D Krell (ed), *Basic Writings: from Being and Time (1927) to The Task of Thinking (1964)* (New York, Harper Perennial, 2008).

[15] M Weber, *The Protestant Ethic and the Spirit of Capitalism* [1905] (Oxford, Oxford University Press, 2010).

[16] N Gane, *Weber and Postmodern Theory* (Basingstoke, Palgrave Macmillan, 2001).

most obvious candidate is the way in which human beings inhabit the world and the way in which subjectivity is linked to the understanding of technology. It is the instrumental will to dominate nature and the world that is taken as characteristic of modernity.[17] This 'will to mastery' (or 'technicity') can also be seen in the rationalisation that destroys traditional knowledge and wisdom, as well as the faith in progress that characterised liberalism and the industrial logic of nineteenth-century capitalism and colonialism.[18] For Heidegger, the problem of technicity encompassed all reason and all metaphysics. It marked a primordial turn away from Being. In this light, modernity is, or was, but the latest torsion in a process that has been in the making since the ancient Greeks. What is notable about 'our time' is that the technicity has revealed most starkly the injustice of our understanding of being and subjectivity. In 'our' present condition, technicity and technology can no longer be considered as outside of us: we are, fatally, its subject.[19] The postmoderns have intensified the relation to this 'crisis'.

If only by virtue of the quantity of commentary on their work, Jean Baudrillard, Michel Foucault and Jean-François Lyotard have become exemplary figures in the representation of the contours of a postmodern engagement with social theory within Anglophone humanities, law and social sciences. In somewhat different ways so too have Gilles Deleuze, Felix Guattari and Jacques Derrida. In the United States the work of Robert Venturi and Richard Rorty has provided another set of engagements of postmodernism. This is so despite significant differences between the work of these authors.

For Jean-François Lyotard, two concerns shape the postmodern condition: the significance of the changing understanding of technology since the 1950s and the decline in the authority or legitimacy of scientific reason (and the reason of the university and of experts in general).[20] In *The Postmodern Condition*, Lyotard developed a number of arguments about the status and legitimacy of scientific discourse. Its point of departure was that the 'status of knowledge is altered as societies enter what is the post-industrial age and culture enters what is known as the postmodern age'.[21] Transformations in scientific knowledge and the creation of new 'informational commodities' have changed the way in which science and scientific knowledge relate to ethics and politics and to government and administration.[22] At issue is the ability of ethics and philosophy to legitimate contemporary practices of science. Lyotard's blunt claim was that the 'grand narratives' of modernity—the dialectic of spirit and emancipation of man—are no longer deployed to validate scientific discourse.[23] The new technologies of science, particularly information technologies, have displaced them. In particular, the production of scientific knowledge is no longer closely related to

---

[17] M Heidegger, 'The Question Concerning Technology' in *The Question Concerning Technology and Other Essays* (New York, Harper & Row, 1977).

[18] E Wyschogrod, *Spirit in Ashes: Hegel, Heidegger, and Man-Made Mass Death* (New Haven, Yale University Press, 1985).

[19] No doubt this formulation overemphasises the inheritance of Heidegger. It also points to one of the ways in which questions of gender, race and class are typically given subordinate status within postmodernism.

[20] J-F Lyotard, *The Postmodern Condition: A Report on Knowledge* (Minneapolis, University of Minnesota Press, 1984).

[21] Ibid, 3.

[22] Ibid, 5.

[23] Ibid, 60–61.

the training and conduct of individuals and but is instead shaped around technical means or the efficiency of human action.[24] Kant's ordering of the presuppositions of conduct and reason have ceased to give shape to the world. In a gesture that has become familiar since the 1930s, science has become directed by speed, competiveness and narcissism. These concerns set the stage for the slogans that shape the reception of Lyotard's account of the postmodern condition: the first is incredulity towards metanarratives and the second is the war against totality. The modern unity of knowledge no longer holds.[25] The postmodern, for Lyotard, described a new knowledge and also a new ambivalent attitude to knowledge.

In many ways the writings of Jean Baudrillard have come to represent the tone of postmodernist accounts of the social. From the 1960s to the early 2000s Baudrillard undertook a series of studies in the fields of Marxist social theory, semiotics and the cultural practices of everyday life. In his earlier work Baudrillard analysed the ways in the objects achieve and bestow value as part of the sign systems of contemporary forms of everyday life. Law in this account joined both the order of signs and the ordering of consumption (public law, contract and intellectual property law as well as sumptuary, consumer and media law). In *Symbolic Exchange and Death*, Baudrillard argued for a fundamental break between the modern and the postmodern.[26] Distinctions such as those of status, class, law, economy and social relations no longer explain how everyday life is lived. Where modern social theory has emphasised differentiation, Baudrilliard argued that difference and distinction have collapsed into a general regime of *simulation*. Closely linked to this is Baudrillard's claim that the universe of simulated sign systems has created a *hyperreality* in which new information technologies and forms entertainment create more intense forms of existence than anything possible in everyday life.

In Baudrillard's postmodern world the subject no longer wills or represents the phenomenal world. This situation is not simply concerned with the collapse of social categories, it also affects the subject: there are no longer any critical categories such as judgement, taste or dialectic that can gain purchase on the world. The world has been aestheticised: everything is an image and there is no transcendent position that can be taken in relation to the proliferation of images. Reality is no longer a concern of representation: people live only in a world of appearance.[27]

Others, like Robert Venturi, have been more concerned with the quality of the surface rather than the (exaggerated) 'loss of the real'. In Venturi's account, the postmodern concern with surfaces was not without meaning.[28] For Venturi, the quotation, synthesis and reuse of past forms that characterise postmodern architecture is part of a strategy of resistance to the seduction of universal truths and of their absence and invisibility as the carrier of meaning. It is the surface or form that carries meaning and the living who are to be addressed. Likewise, for postmodern accounts of law, it is not abstract structure that is most important but the creation of visible interiors of law that people can inhabit with pleasure.

If Lyotard is concerned with the formulation of the technologies of knowledge

---

[24] Ibid, 37, 77.
[25] Ibid, 82.
[26] J Baudrillard, *Symbolic Exchange and Death* (London, Sage, 1993).
[27] J Baudrillard, *Impossible Exchange* (London, Verso, 2001).
[28] R Venturi, DS Brown and S Izenour, *Learning from Las Vegas* (Cambridge, MA, MIT Press, 1977).

and Baudrillard with the technologies of representation, then the work of Michel Foucault, in so far as it addresses a concern with the postmodern, might be character-ised in terms of the technologies of government and of the self. The technologies that Foucault investigates are predominantly those concerned with the creation of social relations and the delimitation of modern forms of rationality. (These concerns are addressed in Chapter 12 of this book.)

In the previous two sections of this chapter postmodernism has been presented as part of an engagement with the critical or Kantian tradition of social theory. In doing so, what has been emphasised are the ways in which postmodern theory has recast social theory in the light of the concerns about the subject and the technologies of postmodernisation. Situating these disputes in terms of a contested legacy or inherit-ance from Kant narrows the scope of the disputes between moderns and postmoderns, but it does so by making them more concerned with law and legal theory than they might otherwise be. Thinking about postmodernism in terms of an inheritance from Kant brings into question relations between the form of reason and the form of law. Postmodern theory has been reluctant to engage with modernity and postmodernity through the category of the social. If the arguments made by Baudrillard are accepted (and there are reasons not to do so), there can be no meaningful social theory in the absence of a recognisable social relation. In the analysis of Lyotard (and Foucault) the sense of social is too contingent (and historically situated) to account for all meaning. For many critics, this seems more like a refusal to take seriously the presuppositions and aspirations of social thought.[29] However, what the Kantian inheritance suggests is that the postmoderns continue to engage with the questions of authority and law. What is addressed in the next section are the ethoi and forms of reason of the post-moderns as they engage the social.

3. ETHOS AND REASON

The Kantian inheritance of modernity was framed in terms of the maturity and the authority of reason. The postmoderns have questioned both. In doing so, of course, they have run the risk of both of immaturity and a refusal of genuine political contest. Kant subjected empirical and disciplinary reason to the tribunal of philosophical reason. For the postmoderns, however, Kant's tribunal of reason no longer fulfils its task, and for many, critical reason has become part of the problem of modernity. The postmodern response to this situation has not been so much to produce a sociology or social theory of modern technology but to provide a demonstration of the conse-quences of technology for the thinking of authority, subjectivity and social relations.[30]

Typically postmodern theory has generated responses to the crisis of critical reason across two registers: one in relation to the limits of reason and the other in relation to the elaboration of new conceptual personae, or conducts of life, through which to inhabit the postmodern existence. Lyotard's formulation of postmodernism in terms of ethos—incredulity towards metanarratives—and a mode of engagement within the

---

[29] G Rose, *Dialectic of Nihilism* (Oxford, Blackwell, 1984).
[30] V Descombes, *Modern French Philosophy* (Cambridge, Cambridge University Press, 1980).

modern provides a point of departure. For Lyotard, the postmodern was the avant-garde of modernism:

> [It] would be that which in the modern invokes the unpresentable in presentation itself, which refuses the consolation of correct forms, refuses the consensus of taste permitting a common experience of nostalgia for the impossible, and inquires into new presentations—not to take pleasure in them but to better produce the feeling that there is something unpresentable.[31]

For the French postmoderns, it was necessary to reason against the tyranny of reason in order to escape from both technological nihilism (rationalism) and irrational activism (decisionism). While it is hard to generalise about the forms of reason and life that the postmoderns recommend, one part of postmodernism has pursued a series of heterological and utopian paths that traverse reason. The tone of much of the discourse of postmodernism has been the celebration of the loss of a form of reason and modernity. The affirmative register has been harder to characterise. (The risk, as many counter-polemicists claim, is simply that the postmoderns succumb, with due irony and cynicism, to what they seek to escape or displace.)[32]

For example, the questioning of the philosophical tradition of metaphysics has proceeded by insisting on the 'radical finitude' of metaphysics: a displacement of the way in which metaphysics has produced a closed order of time and place and of the subject.[33] In critical modes, postmodernism has paid attention to the ways in which the systematic forms of modernity are not capable of achieving what they promise. In so doing value is given to what exceeds metaphysical ordering—most notably, the materiality of discourse and things. In an ethical and theological register the postmodern moment or event has been characterised in terms of the recognition of the singularity or otherness of the other. In an aesthetic register the postmodern has been figured as the unassimilable, the unrepresentable or the sublime that characterises the eventfulness of the event.[34] In law, the unassimilable has been related both to injustice that is unmeasurable by law and untouchable by restitution, and to a justice 'yet to come'. Accounts of postmodern reason, especially when inflected through an engagement with postmodernism in the United States, also address the pragmatics of judgement and the contingency of social, legal and political relations.

The displacement of metaphysics has been accompanied by the shaping of new ethical personalities. In order to flourish in a postmodern condition, it is claimed, it is necessary to refashion existing conducts and forms of life.[35] What is striking in this regard is the recasting of the universal subject favoured by Kant in ways that displace or recast the traditions of humanism. In the more apocalyptic strains of postmodernism, the subject is no longer attached to the law (order of being) and life is no longer instituted in terms of an enduring institutional substrate that links conscience, humanity and history. Instead, the subject is instantiated in relation to a variety of

---

[31] J-F Lyotard, *Postmodernism Explained: Correspondence 1982–1985* (Minneapolis, Minnesota University Press, 1993) 15.

[32] J Habermas, *Philosophical Discourse of Modernity* (Cambridge, Polity, 1987).

[33] The metaphysics that is disputed is varied and various. See I Ward, *Kantianism, Postmodernism and Critical Legal Thought* (Amsterdam, Kluwer Academic Publishers, 1997).

[34] C Douzinas and L Nead (eds), *Law and the Image: The Authority of Art and the Aesthetics of Law* (Chicago, University of Chicago Press, 1999); L Moran et al (eds), *Law's Moving Image* (London, Cavendish Publishing, 2004).

[35] W Hennis, *Max Weber, Essays in Reconstruction* (London, Allen & Unwin, 1988).

technical networks: of desire, of power, of language, of media images and so forth. It is in relation to these scapes that the new conceptual personae emerge and conduct themselves.

For example, in *Libidinal Economy*, Lyotard developed the persona (person, mask) of the pagan.[36] The pagan inhabits an economy of libidinal intensities and seeks to affirm life through an 'active passivity'.[37] In contrast to the orders of judgement where every act is used, pagan existence affirms the intensity of every event. The pagan, for Lyotard, practices a sort of unconventional conventionalism fighting against the terror of the 'true' and of mechanical instrumentalism. The pagan conducts his or her life by the liberating power of intensities (even ones of cruelty and violence). In later work, more influenced by Kant, Lyotard elaborated a heterology: the art of judging without the criteria of anthropology or prescriptions (knowledge, obligation and community). Such judgement is ethical in the 'honouring of the name' of the other and in bearing witness to the terror of living in the world. It is political in seeking an ungrounded practice of justice based on the recognition of the agonistic 'incommensurability' of discourses. It resists the improper totalisation of discourses of, say, politics and law in the name of humanity.[38] In this conduct of life, judgement becomes a form of politics. The recognition of the continuing need to judge in situations of incommensurability has become one of the motifs of postmodern and critical jurisprudence.

For Foucault the problem is not so much the technologies of science as that of the governmental relations of power and knowledge. His later work on the formations of the self used aesthetics as a form of self-discipline to shape a persona capable of resisting the indifferent freedoms of rationality. Thematically these postmoderns have attempted to confront technology with personae capable of resisting technicity. They do so by cultivating heterotopic zones beyond 'the law'.

With an extravagant melancholy, Jean Baudrillard has revealed the capacity of contemporary technologies of sign systems to overcome the real through the endless simulation of the media-scape. In return he has proposed a persona impelled by ecstatic mimicry to seduce sign systems into revealing the history of the end of history.[39] In a less apocalyptic tone Jacques Derrida, Luce Irigaray and Jacques Lacan have informed us that the possibilities and impossibilities of full presence—'sensuate' and 'sexuate' being—and subjectivity have been with us for some time.[40] For these writers the postmodern condition is best approached through the aporiae or perplexities of thought; and through rethinking the linkages of law to those of authority and ethics. The personae developed through these lines of thought are less recognisably postmodern.[41] Irigaray has sought to realise the possibility of women within the sphere of civil government. Derrida has mimed and redefined many of the personae of philosophy into the figures of the double and the host.

In the restricted context of postmodernism presented here the personae of the postmoderns might be seen as contributing to the creation of forms of life and an

---

[36] J-F Lyotard, *Libidinal Economy* (London, Athlone Press, 1993).
[37] J Williams, *Lyotard and the Political* (London, Routledge, 2000).
[38] J-F Lyotard, *The Differend* (Manchester, Manchester University Press, 1988) 128–50.
[39] A Kroker, *The Possessed Individual* (London, Macmillan, 1992).
[40] L Irigaray, *Je, Tu, Nous* (London, Routledge, 1993).
[41] D Milovanovic, *Postmodern Law and Disorder* (Liverpool, Deborah Charles Publications, 1992).

ensemble of tools and techniques that enable someone to flourish in a postmodern condition.

Translating from one idiom and genre to another is not without its effects. The results of bringing postmodern conducts or forms of life into relation with those of the common law tradition have been of a distinctly hybrid character.

Two accounts of the 'orders or conducts of life' have dominated the interpretation of legal modernity. They roughly correspond to the two rival 'orders of life' and orders of domination that have flourished in Western Europe: one, secular and political, organised around administration and government; and the other, religious and ethical in origin, concerned with conscience, redemption and transformation. The conduct of life of the secular lawyer and the official was tied to the requirements of office and the state rather than religion. Ethical conduct was determined through reason of state and not directly by any higher ethics. To perform the roles of government it was necessary to practice a certain indifference, or bracketing off, of religious beliefs. By contrast, and often in dispute, the religious and ethical conduct of life has been more concerned with the delimitation of an ethically unified world, peopled with morally unified persons. The conduct of life of the religious order is designed to complete this ethical order.[42]

Reinhart Koselleck has argued that the religious order of life was not defeated in the seventeenth century, but displaced.[43] In their search to restore a fully ethical order, critics of the state and of secular modernity continued the transformative aspirations, and intellectual practices, of both the enlighteners and the religious. They denounce the state as unethical and charge it with stunting the souls of its citizenry and annihilating their enemies in the name of indifference. For them, the officials of the state are capable only of remembering the past and not the possibilities of the future. In short, the conduct of life of the state official refuses life. The counter-arguments in favour of official personae are equally polemical. Far from stunting the souls of its citizens, the conduct of life of the administrative-legal order provides a restricted ethics suitable for the many roles that officials, and citizens, are required to perform for the purposes of security and civil peace.[44]

On their face, the French postmoderns, as heirs of the Enlightenment *philosophes*, and as practitioners of existential dissent, take up their roles within a domain once made available by religious forms of life.[45] Today, perhaps, some or many postmodern personae seem as extravagant and ill-fitted for the accounting of the forms of association that we do maintain (whoever we are) as they do for the accounting of injustices. They do, however, continue to suggest forms of life that do not succumb to false unities of guaranteed progress or development and ones that begin with the honouring of the name and the acknowledgement of the plurality of forms of life.

---

[42] D Saunders, *Anti-Lawyers Religion and the Critics of Law and State* (London, Routledge, 1997) ch 3.

[43] R Koselleck, *Critique and Crisis: Enlightenment and the Pathogenesis of Modern Society* (Oxford, Berg, 1988).

[44] I Hunter, *Rival Enlightenments* (Cambridge, Cambridge University Press, 2001).

[45] P Goodrich, 'Europe in America: Grammatology, Legal Studies, and the Politics of Transmission' (2001) 101 *Columbia Law Review* 2033; P Schlagg, *The Enchantment of Reason* (Durham, NC, Duke University Press, 1998).

4. POSTMODERNISM, JURISPRUDENCE AND JUSTICE

The final section of this chapter turns to postmodernism and justice.[46] In addressing the demands of justice, postmoderns have turned more to the idioms legal theory and jurisprudence than to social theory. In part this reflects an understanding within postmodernism that social theory, particularly as inherited from the Kantian traditions, does not provide a sufficient critical distance from law to assert an independent authority. In part, the domain of law is still seen as an important site for the dispute of justice. Society and the social are considered as a contingent creation rather than a cause or site of explanation.

Postmodern interventions in the reason and conduct of law have steered an uneasy course between showing law as a cynical exercise of power and in contemplating ways of living well before the law. In this postmoderns share a range of concerns associated with critical legal studies and the revival of critical hermeneutics.[47] The postmoderns have taken up the concern with reason and legitimacy and deflated claims to objectivity, meaning, and rationality in the texts and practices of law.[48] At one level these concerns follow that practices of legal interpretation: does or can the text mean what it says? However, as with any critical interpretation (hermeneutics), postmodern theory has tended to question both the internal coherence of law and the ability of the critic to set an uncontested context through which to judge the social meaning of a text.[49]

Since the 1990s postmodern interventions in law have increasingly returned to questions of judgement and ethics as a privileged site from which to consider the responsibilities of law and the engagement with the technicity of law and government. This turn to justice and ethics has been associated with a more general concern with the metaphysical and physical violence of the law. If there is a single text that encapsulates these concerns, it is probably Jacques Derrida's essay 'Force of Law: The "Mystical Foundation of Authority"'.[50] For Derrida the question of the conduct of law and of justice is shaped around the responsibility for the other. Justice is not a symmetrical or reciprocal relation of fairness. It is a relationship shaped around an obligation to respond to the suffering of an other. More extravagantly, the ethical relation gives absolute priority to the other. This may be as simple as welcoming the stranger into your house or a matter of manners ('After you ...'), or it may be an obligation to give your life to another. Justice, for Derrida, is concerned with the ways

---

[46] D Cornell, *The Philosophy of the Limit* (New York, Routledge, 1991). This essay provides an important feminist reformulation of postmodern theory.

[47] See G Minda, *Postmodern Legal Movements* (New York, New York University Press, 1995). For Minda, postmodern jurisprudence emerges as a composite of critical legal studies, critical race theory, feminism, identity jurisprudence, intersectional jurisprudence, law and literature and narrative jurisprudence. Postmodernism is, or is the site of, a 'multiculturalism' of jurisprudence. See also C Douzinas 'Law and Justice in Postmodernity' in S Connor (ed), *The Cambridge Companion to Postmodernism* (Cambridge, Cambridge University Press, 2004).

[48] C Douzinas, R Warrington with S McVeigh, *Postmodern Jurisprudence: The Law of Text in the Texts of Law* (London, Routledge, 1990).

[49] R Cotterrell, *Law, Culture and Society: Legal Ideas in the Mirror of Social Theory* (Aldershot, Ashgate 2006); M Kelman, *A Guide to Critical Legal Studies* (Cambridge, MA, Harvard University Press 1995).

[50] J Derrida, 'Force of Law: The "Mystical Foundation of Authority"' in D Cornell et al (eds), *Deconstruction and the Possibility of Justice* (New York, Routledge, 1992). For a critical reading of this essay, see I Hunter, 'The Desire for Deconstruction: Derrida's Metaphysics of Law' (2008) 41 *Communication, Politics & Culture* 6.

we take up such obligations and the realisation that meeting such obligations is not possible. The demands of justice always exceed what is possible and calculable, if only because there is always more than one obligation to be met.

The centrepiece of Derrida's 'Force of Law' essay is an account of the time of justice. Justice for Derrida (and Lyotard) is 'yet to come': '[T]here is never a moment that we can say *in the present* that a decision *is* just'.[51] Simply to follow a rule is to prejudge the situation. To be just and to attend to the singularity of the other, the judge

> must not only follow a rule of law or a general law but must also assume it, approve it, confirm its value, by a reinstituting act of interpretation, as if ultimately nothing previously existed of the law, as if the judge himself invented the law in every case.[52]

This is not simply a matter of attitude, it is also a concern with the understanding of the nature of judgement and the limits and authority of reason. A just judgement must respond both to the finite and calculable concerns of law and to the exorbitant demands of justice. In practising judgement in relation to that which is beyond measure, there is always the risk of irresponsibility—in failing to attend to justice or law.[53] In this way Derrida, and others, link the analysis of the limits of reason to a training in postmodern conduct.

Finally, in the 'Force of Law' Derrida offers an account of community—albeit one that emphasises hospitality and the asymmetry of the relationship to the other and others: it is the promise and the possibility of a justice and democracy to come rather than authority and legitimacy that gives shape to community. In short, Derrida presents or offers a postmodern conduct of life: to be just it is necessary to remain open and attentive to others for as long as is possible.

5. CONCLUDING COMMENT

In order to hold on to broad contours of postmodernism within the orbit of law and social theory, this chapter has emphasised the continuities of postmodern theory with the critical traditions inherited from Kant.[54] It has been argued that both modern and postmodern theory has been shaped around forms of conduct, reason and association. The critical aspects of postmodern theory have sought to respond to our present condition, the injustices of reason as measure, the ambivalences of the technologies of government, and the possibilities and limits of representations of law. The affirmative aspects shape postmodern conduct around the ethical response to the other.

At the beginning of this chapter it was noted that the dispute between moderns and postmoderns had passed through the humanities. However, it is not the case that the substantive concerns of what has been disputed have been resolved. There is still dispute about the reason and conduct of public and personal life, and the concern

---

[51] Derrida, ibid, 23.
[52] Ibid.
[53] Ibid, 63–66.
[54] P Goodrich, *Languages of Law: From Logics of Memory to Nomadic Masks* (London, Weidenfeld & Nicolson, 1992); D Manderson, *Proximity, Levinas and the Soul of Law* (Montreal and Kingston, McGill Queens University Press, 2007).

with progress, development, domination and the status of the human is no less urgent. The reassertion of the defence of the interests of the sovereign territorial state and the call for technological knowledge to resolve political problems is no less problematic. Against the revolutionary and apocalyptic tone of many of the postmoderns, emphasis in this chapter has been given to the forms of postmodern social theory and jurisprudence that address the care for the conduct of law. It has been argued that the postmoderns have sought ways to dispute and judge with law on grounds that are not altogether there, in the name of a justice that remains, as yet, undetermined, singular—and to come.

14

Postcolonial Theories of Law

EVE DARIAN-SMITH

T HIS CHAPTER EXPLORES postcolonial theories of law that today are more widely recognised than ever before amongst scholars, political theorists and legal practitioners.[1] Concerns with the postcolonial dimensions of legal engagement have been present in some academic circles for over three decades. However, the terms of the conversation have shifted over the years to apply more aptly to current global geopolitical realities. Whereas the language of earlier postcolonial theorists was framed by the parameters of nation-state histories and interests and primarily focused on the dialectic between colonising nations and the colonised, contemporary scholars talk in terms of the relations between what is commonly referred to as the global North and global South. This shift in terminology is important. It expands the lens of analysis from state-centred law in the context of specific national colonial enterprises to a more global post-Westphalian worldview that takes into account the postcolonial dimensions of a range of transnational, regional, state and local legal engagements.[2] It opens up the conversation to include the oppression of all communities historically treated as racially and ethnically inferior to the colonising society, whether or not these communities self-identify as 'indigenous' or think of themselves as colonised. Moreover, it allows for rethinking contemporary legal subjectivities by moving beyond Western versus non-Western binaries and acknowledging new forms of colonialism, such as the colonising of East Timor by Indonesia, Eritrea by Ethiopia, and the occupation of Palestinian territories by Israel.[3] And finally it takes into account neocolonial activities by Western and non-Western nations who exert economic and political power or 'soft imperialism' over sites of

---

[1] For general discussions on postcolonialism and law, see E Darian-Smith and P Fitzpatrick (eds), *Laws of the Postcolonial* (Ann Arbor, University of Michigan Press, 1999); SE Merry, 'Colonial and Postcolonial Law' in A Sarat (ed), *The Blackwell Companion to Law and Society.* (Oxford, Blackwell Publishing, 2004); A Roy, 'Postcolonial Theory and Law: A Critical Introduction' (2008) 29 *Adelaide Law Review* 315–57; BS Chimni (ed), Special Issue: 'Third World Approaches to International Law' (2011) 3(1) *Trade, Law and Development*; P Dann and F Hanschmann (eds), 'Post-colonial Theories and Law' (2012) No 2 *Journal of Law and Politics in Africa, Asia and Latin America* 123–27; N Seuffert and C Coleborne, 'Law, History and Postcolonial Theory and Method' (2003) 7 *Law Text Culture* 1–8.

[2] See R Falk, *Law in an Emerging Global Village: A Post-Westphalian Perspective* (Ardsley, NY, Transnational Publishers, 1998).

[3] See AT Weldemichael, *Third World Colonialism and Strategies of Liberation: Eritrea and East Timor Compared* (Cambridge, Cambridge University Press, 2012).

former colonial control.[4] Hence today's neocolonial activities includes the soft impe-rialism of China's industrial activities in Africa as well as the range of 'new wars' in regions such as the Congo that allow for an economy of extraction and exploitation by Northern capitalists over local communities, often in collusion with local elites.[5]

Given the geopolitical expansion of the postcolonial lens, it is not surprising that contemporary scholars of postcolonial law are interested in a wide variety of issues. Some are concerned with exposing the underlying orientalist assumptions in national and international laws that affirm essentialised constructions of cultural difference,[6] and inform many countries' flawed polices of multiculturalism.[7] Other scholars, many from the global South, are critical of the Eurocentric underpinnings of international law and argue for counterhegemonic forms of resistance.[8] Still others are concerned with the shifting conceptualisation of 'human' in the context of new forms of neo-colonialism and global racial oppression.[9] And many focus on the historical and contemporary oppression of indigenous peoples, be these in former settler nations such as Canada, Australia and the United States,[10] or in former colonies such as Bolivia, Ecuador, Ghana, Kenya and South Africa.[11]

In trying to summarise postcolonial legal studies one is confronted by a variety of problems. Most of the studies are interdisciplinary and present a range of perspec-tives. As a result, postcolonial theories of law do not form a coherent field of inquiry. According to one leading postcolonial scholar, Wes Pue, this is a good thing:

> The spirit of the intellectual encounter between law and colonialism is of necessity interdisciplinary, diverse in perspective, and unbounded. Scholarship in the field does not—should not—fit into overly-neat disciplinary or perspective-bound categories. Individuals drawn to postcolonial legal studies come to the enquiry with a variety of motivations and an array of interests. Some seek primarily theoretical understanding, others encounter the

---

[4] See K Nkrumah, *Neo-Colonialism: The Last Stage of Imperialism* (New York, International Publishers, 1966).

[5] See M Kaldor, *New & Old Wars: Organized Violence in a Globalized World*, 2nd edn (Palo Alto, CA, Stanford University Press, 2006); J Ferguson, *Global Shadows: Africa in the Neoliberal World Order* (Durham, NC and London, Duke University Press, 2006).

[6] See T Ruskola, 'Legal Orientalism' (2002) 101 *Michigan Law Review* 179–234; E Said, *Orientalism* (New York, Vintage, 1978); R Falk, *Achieving Human Rights* (London and New York, Routledge, 2009); S Pahuja, *Decolonizing International Law: Development, Economic Growth and the Politics of Universality* (Cambridge, Cambridge University Press, 2011).

[7] B Bhandar, 'The Ties That Bind: Multiculturalism and Secularism Reconsidered' (2009) 36 *Journal of Law and Society* 301–26; CF Marés, 'Multiculturalism and Collective Rights' in B de Sousa Santos (ed), *Another Knowledge Is Possible: Beyond Northern Epistemologies* (London and New York, Verso, 2007) 75–104.

[8] BS Chimni, 'Third World Approaches to International Law: A Manifesto' (2006) 8 *International Community Law Review* 3–27.

[9] P Cheah, *Inhuman Conditions: On Cosmopolitanism and Human Rights* (Cambridge, MA and London, Harvard University Press, 2006); S Esmeir, *Juridical Humanity: A Colonial History.* (Palo Alto, CA, Stanford University Press, 2012).

[10] See eg R Mawani, *Colonial Proximities: Crossracial Encounters and Juridical Truths in British Columbia, 1871–1921* (Vancouver, University of British Columbia Press, 2009); L Behrendt, *Achieving Social Justice: Indigenous Rights and Australia's Future* (Sydney, The Federation Press,2003); JR Cattelino, *High Stakes: Florida Seminole Gaming and Sovereignty* (Durham, NC, Duke University Press, 2008); G Frank and C Goldberg, *Defying the Odds: The Tule River Tribe's Struggle for Sovereignty in Three Centuries* (New Haven, Yale University Press, 2010); E Darian-Smith, *New Capitalists: Law, Politics and Identity Sur-rounding Casino Gaming on Native American Land* (Belmont, Wadsworth, 2004).

[11] See eg J Comaroff and J Comaroff (eds), *Law and Disorder in the Postcolony* (Chicago, University of Chicago Press, 2006).

postcolonial as a part of sustained historical research, and others still feel a compelling sense of urgency to develop practical strategies by which to confront the legacies of colonialism 'on the ground'. Many pursue a more or less mixed method of enquiry and do so from multiple motivations.[12]

While not a coherent intellectual field, what unites contemporary scholars of post-colonial law—irrespective of their focus or analytical framing—is that they all draw upon an intellectual legacy that emerged among non-Europeans in the decolonisation movement post World War II and subsequently filtered into the Western academy in the 1980s in the movement known as postcolonial studies.[13] Hence underlying all postcolonial legal scholarship is a concern with the endurance of historically struc-tured racial and ethnic divides and correlative asymmetrical power relations between the global North and global South, despite a growing appreciation of their respective regional interdependencies. In other words, postcolonial legal theories are not about legal processes in the time after colonialism, when a former colonised state gains inde-pendence and presumably a measure of self-determination. Rather, postcolonial legal scholarship underscores that even when colonialism has officially ceased to exist, the injustices of material practices endure over time and in many ways frame emergent legalities and legal consciousness. As scholars are only too well aware, the endurance of colonial legal logics is present—albeit perhaps in new forms—in countries formerly colonised in Africa, Latin America, Asia and so on, as well as within former colonial nations such as Britain, Australia, France, the Netherlands and the United States.[14]

Below I discuss two clusters of postcolonial legal scholarship that form theoretical umbrellas under which specific sociolegal studies can be accommodated. These are scholars engaged with the concept of legal orientalism and scholars identifying with 'third world approaches to international law' (TWAIL). I have chosen these two bodies of scholarship because the first underscores the enduring legacy of European legal colonialism, and the second highlights the perspective of the global South in seeking to confront that legacy within subnational, national, international and global contexts. Obviously there exist other lines of inquiry that dovetail into these two clusters of postcolonial legal engagement. For instance, the concept of legal pluralism underpins each in various ways,[15] as does the relationship between law and racism.[16] But legal pluralism and legal racism are not exclusive to colonial/postcolonial contexts and so I treat these concerns as embedded within postcolonial theories of law rather than as the central issue shaping each cluster's theoretical focus.

---

[12] WW Pue, Editorial for special issue (2003) No 1 *Law, Social Justice and Global Development Journal* 2.

[13] The exact date at which postcolonial studies took off is hard to ascertain exactly. Scholars such as WEB Du Bois, Franz Fanon, CLR James and many others were writing decades before postcolonial studies was recognised in the Western academy in the 1980s and 1990s as a distinct intellectual theory and body of literature.

[14] One has only to think of the 2012 presidential election results in the United States to appreciate the extent to which the logics of colonialism and plantation economics endures in contemporary American society. As many commentators noted, those states voting for the Republican candidate, Mitt Romney, cor-related to a large degree with the former southern states who practised slavery in the pre-civil war era, and implemented the harshest Jim Crow laws discriminating against blacks and other minorities up until the civil rights movement of the 1950s and 1960s.

[15] See BZ Tamanaha, C Sage and M Woolcock (eds), *Legal Pluralism and Development: Scholars and Practitioners in Dialogue* (Cambridge, Cambridge University Press, 2012).

[16] See DF Da Silva, *Toward a Global Idea of Race* (Minneapolis, University of Minnesota Press, 2007).

Before engaging with the concept of postcolonialism and the sociolegal theories that it has engendered, I want to mention briefly the shifting landscape of geopolitical power in the current era. These relations of power are very different from that of previous centuries, which were based on the concept of sovereign nation-states operating autonomously in an international arena. This conventional model of state-based power is often referred to as the Westphalian system of governance. This name refers to the German town of Westphalia, where, in 1648, after thirty long years of war, many European nations came together and agreed that each could claim autonomous control over its respective territories and subjects. The modern concepts of 'nation-state', 'nationalism' and 'sovereignty' were inscribed in the Peace of Westphalia and have enjoyed considerable epistemological, ideological and mythical prominence for nearly four hundred years, particularly in the development of modern Euro-American law.[17] Moreover, these concepts historically provided justification for the imperial strategies of European states and these states' overseas oppression and exploitation of colonised peoples.

Today the centre/periphery divide which assumes the West at the center and the third world delegated to the periphery is now no longer seen as an acceptable paradigm for modelling the realities of global economic and political power. Rising powerful global cities and enclaves of extreme wealth contrast with impoverished rural outskirts in many regions around the world. We see this phenomenon happening in Africa, Asia as well as across Europe and the Americas. Today, rich Western nations are experiencing deprivation and poverty formerly only seen in developing nations, and developing nations now have political and economic elites on a par with their Western counterparts. And all countries to varying degrees are experiencing the growth of deluxe shopping malls, office blocks and gated communities alongside shantytowns, refugee camps and impoverished communities.[18] (See Figure 1.) Who are the colonisers and who are the colonised is no longer as clear as it was only sixty years ago in the wake of the decolonialisation movement of the mid-twentieth century.

In addition, since the 1990s there has been an extraordinary proliferation of non-governmental organisations (NGOs), private philanthropic foundations and voluntary, often faith-based, organisations around the world.[19] These non-state actors, in conjunction with global economic bodies such as the International Monetary Fund (IMF) and World Bank, are creating new forms of transnational governance and authority that sometimes work in tandem with state interests and sometimes counter to state interests. Moreover, these non-state actors raise all sorts of issues with respect to accountability, dependency, governmental displacement, and the factors driving coun-

---

[17] J Beard, *The Political Economy of Desire: International Law, Development and the Nation-State* (New York and Abingdon, Routledge/Cavendish, 2006); R Joyce, 'Westphalia: Event, Memory, Myth' in F Johns, R Joyce and S Pahuja (eds), *Events: The Force of International Law* (New York, Routledge, 2011) 55–68.

[18] See JE Stiglitz, The Price of Inequality: How Today's Divided Society Endangers Our Future (New York, WW Norton, 2012); JT Way, The Mayan in the Mall: Globalization, Development, and the Making of Modern Guatemala (Durham, NC and London, Duke University Press, 2012); M Davis, Planet of Slums (Brooklyn, NY, Verso, 2007).

[19] A-M Slaughter, 'Breaking Out: The Proliferation of Actors in the International System' in Y Dezalay and BG Garth (eds), *Global Prescriptions: The Production, Exportation, and Importation of the New Legal Orthodoxy* (Ann Arbor, University of Michigan Press, 2002) 12–36; T Wallace, 'NGO Dilemmas: Trojan Horses for Global Neoliberalism' in L Pantich and C Leys (eds), *The Socialist Register 2004: The New Imperial Challenge* (London, Merlin Press, 2004).

Figure 1. Rochina Favela, Rio de Janerio, Brazil. Photograph by Alicia Nijdam. 21 March 2008. This is one of the largest shantytowns in South America with over 200,000 inhabitants. There are many such slums existing alongside modern high-rise buildings in cities of Brazil. Those who live in these shanty towns prefer its prime location next to the city centre, as they can earn a living being close to the city.

tries' social agendas.[20] According to James Ferguson, 'Social policy and nation-state are, to a very significant degree, decoupled, and we are only beginning to find ways to think about this.'[21] As a result, these contradictory socioeconomic reconfigurations of power have fundamentally altered domestic relations within states, as well as profoundly altering the world of international relations that can no longer be conceived solely in terms of interstate activities.

In the early decades of the twenty-first century, the growing global inequalities between rich and poor (as reflected in the Occupy Movement in 2011), and the new configurations of state and non-state power as demonstrated by the proliferation of NGOs, have dramatically altered global assemblages of power and geopolitical realities.[22] We are, in short, in the process of having to reimagine modernist legal geographies.[23] For the purposes of this discussion, these phenomena suggest that the

[20] See GW Wright, 'NGOs and Western Hegemony: Causes for Concern and Ideas for Change' (2012) 22 *Development in Practice* 123–34; see also SS Silbey, 'Let Them Eat Cake: Globalization, Postmodern Colonialism, and the Possibilities of Justice' (1997) 31 *Law & Society Review* 207–36.

[21] J Ferguson, 'The Uses of Neoliberalism' (2009) 41 *Antipode* 166–84, 168.

[22] S Sassen, 'Neither Global Nor National: Novel Assemblages of Territory, Authority and Rights' (2008) 1 *Ethics & Global Politics* 61–79.

[23] E Darian-Smith, *Laws and Societies in Global Contexts: Contemporary Approaches* (Cambridge, Cambridge University Press, 2013).

implications of postcolonial theories of law are as relevant to the 99% of white people living within wealthy Western nations as to darker-skinned peoples formerly colonised.

1. DEFINING A POSTCOLONIAL PERSPECTIVE

Postcolonial scholarship over the last thirty years has provided enormous insights into understanding contemporary legal processes. A notable contribution to the field is the theoretical insight of Edward Said, who was a leading figure in postcolonial criticism and whose book *Orientalism* (1978) established a long trajectory of critical thinking about the subjugation of non-Western peoples. Specifically, postcolonial theory reveals the violence and the technologies of power involved in understanding concepts such as modernity and capitalism as well as contemporary state, sub-state and trans-state nationalisms.[24] Moreover, postcolonial theory provides the intellectual bridge linking historical colonial injustices to contemporary global asymmetries of economic, political and social power between a global North and global South. In short, postcolonial theory provides the intellectual platform from which to identify, analyse and assess what is encompassed by the term 'postcolonial law' in the twenty-first century.

Postcolonial studies, and postcolonial theory in general, is largely associated with a rethinking of a dominant European historiography that places the 'West' at the centre of the world. Contrary to the assumption of European superiority, postcolonial studies posits a plurality of cultural perspectives, concepts and legalities that do not correlate to a hierarchy dominated by Western Christian values and scientific rationality. Associated with South Asian scholarship, subaltern and literary studies as well as analyses of resistance, postcolonial studies emerged out of the global South in the 1980s and gained an increasing presence in Anglo-European universities.[25] With the proliferation of postcolonial research, there was, and is still, much debate over the meaning and scope of postcolonial terminology and its political agenda.[26] Despite these ongoing deliberations, it is helpful to turn to the most significant implications of a postcolonial perspective which mark it as distinctly different from, yet complementary to, other critical investigations associated with critical race theory, critical legal theory, and poststructuralist and feminist theoretical perspectives. This process will help to flesh out the contours of postcolonial studies and, at the same time, underscore its intellectual lineage and relevance to contemporary legal analyses.

Postcolonial theory acknowledges and recovers the ongoing significance of colonised peoples in shaping the epistemologies, philosophies, practices, and shifting identities

---

[24] U Baxi, 'Postcolonial Legality' in H Schwarz and S Ray (eds), *A Companion to Postcolonial Studies* (Oxford, Blackwell, 2000) 540–55; GC Spivak, *A Critique of Postcolonial Reason* (Cambridge, MA, Harvard University Press, 1999).

[25] G Prakash, 'Writing Post-Orientalist Histories of the Third World: Perspectives from Indian Historiography' (1990) 32 *Comparative Studies in Society and History* 383–408; G Prakash, 'Can the "Subaltern" Ride? A Reply to O'Hanlon and Washbrook' (1992) 32 *Comparative Studies in Society and History* 168–84; R O'Hanlon and D Washbrook, 'After Orientalism: Culture, Criticism, and Politics in the Third World' (1992) 34 *Comparative Studies in Society and History* 141–67; D Chakrabarty, 'Postcoloniality and the Artifice of History: Who Speaks for "Indian" Pasts? (1992) 37 *Representations* 1–26.

[26] P Williams and L Chrisman (eds), *Colonial Discourse and Post-Colonial Theory: A Reader* (New York, Colombia University Press, 1994); H Schwarz and S Ray (eds), *A Companion to Postcolonial Studies* (Oxford, Blackwell, 2000); A Loomba, *Colonialism/Postcolonialism*, 2nd edn (London and New York, Routledge, 2005); P Mongia (ed), *Contemporary Postcolonial Theory: A Reader* (New York, Bloomsbury, 2009).

of dominant and taken-for-granted Western subjects and subjectivities.[27] Postcolonial scholars foreground the cultural and psychological relations between the former colonised and colonisers, whom, they argue, cannot be understood except in conjunction with each other.[28] Postcolonial theorists do not claim that colonialism was experienced in the same way under different regimes, just as they recognise that today neocolonialism operates in very different ways from its earlier configurations. Nonetheless, while paying attention to the details of specific contexts, postcolonial scholars agree that in order to understand all contemporary histories of peoples and places, irrespective of whether there historically existed in any given site an explicit colonial regime, it is important to remain aware of the enduring presence of discourses that posit 'civilised', 'progressive' and 'lawful' Europeans against 'barbaric', 'static' and 'lawless' native populations.

According to these scholars, colonial assumptions of Western superiority endure across time and undermine contemporary attempts to build more inclusive multicultural societies. This is because categories of racial difference were used to varying degrees by colonial governments to gain power and control over locally subjugated peoples.[29] Today, despite claims of increasing acceptance of cultural diversity and policies of multiculturalism, racial categories and racialised differences continue to exist, though often in less overt manifestations.[30] Moreover, according to many postcolonial theorists, these boundaries of difference are insurmountable, because the psychological intersubjectivity between former colonisers and colonised constantly invites re-representations of difference.[31]

Drawing on a variety of theoretical perspectives—including an Hegelian master/slave dialectic, phenomenological essentialism, and psychoanalytical insights gleaned from Franz Fanon and Jacques Lacan—postcolonial theorists such as Homi Bhabha, Gayatri Spivak and Benita Parry bring to the fore complex understandings of how oppressed peoples resist their oppressors and seek empowerment. In recognising processes of mutual desire and negation between the 'master' and 'slave', postcolonial scholars have had to grapple with alternative historical narratives and identities other than those conventionally supplied by the West.[32] The irony is that the process of self-determination by peoples formerly colonised requires the adoption of European knowledge, including concepts such as 'progress', 'development', 'individualism' and what it means to be 'human'. It also means the use of Western forms of government, state-building and, perhaps most importantly of all, European concepts of law. Thus, according to a postcolonial perspective, all assertions of freedom and self-awareness require elements of mimicry and voyeurism. As Douglas Robinson has noted:

---

[27] See de Sousa Santos (ed), above n 7.

[28] L Gandhi, *Postcolonial Theory: A Critical Introduction* (New York, Colombia University Press, 1998).

[29] A Stoler, 'Rethinking Colonial Categories: European Communities and the Boundaries of Rule' (1989) 31 *Contemporary Studies in Society and History* 134–61; NB Dirks, 'From Little King to Landlord: Property Law, and the Gift under the Madras Permanent Settlement' (1986) 28 *Contemporary Studies in Society and History* 307–33.

[30] DT Goldberg, *The Threat of Race: Reflections on Racial Neoliberalism* (Oxford, Wiley-Blackwell, 2008); A Lentin and G Titley, *The Crises of Multiculturalism: Racism in a Neoliberal Age* (London, Zed Books, 2011).

[31] P Fitzpatrick, 'Passions Out of Place: Law, Incommensurability, and Resistance' in Darian-Smith and Fitzpatrick (eds), above n 2, 39–60.

[32] H Trivedi and M Mukherjee (eds), *Interrogating Post-Colonialism: Theory, Text and Context* (Shimla, Indian Institute of Advanced Study, Rashrapati Nivas, 1996).

Postcolonial or subaltern scholars claim it is at once essential and impossible to forge a 'new' postcolonial identity: *essential*, because those colonial constructs were at once alien and negative, because they came from the outside and destroyed much of value in the indigenous cultures, and because an effective postcolonial politics requires the development of more positive indigenous visions: but also *impossible*, because colonial discourse continues to inform even these postcolonial attempts to break free of it, and tends to condition even the imagination of a 'new' (postcolonial) identity along 'old' (colonial) lines.[33]

A prominent postcolonial theorist, Dipesh Chakrabarty, has responded to the ironies of alterity by calling for the 'provincialising' or decentring, of Europe and European epistemological knowledge. Chakrabarty (and others) argue that non-Western knowledge has been historically ignored and precluded from historiographical accounts of humanist understanding and intellectual endeavour.[34] In an effort to critique 'the "Europe" that modern imperialism and (third world) nationalism have, by their collaborative venture and violence, made universal', Chakrabarty urges scholars 'to write into the history of modernity the ambivalences, contradictions, the use of force, and the tragedies and the ironies that attend it'.[35]

Nowhere in the histories of modernity has the 'use of force, and the tragedies and the ironies that attend it' been as obvious as they are in the context of legal engagement. European law, in a variety of ways, was the formal mechanism and institutional frame through which many colonial governments oppressed and controlled indigenous peoples throughout the eighteenth, nineteenth and twentieth centuries. Law, emblematic of Enlightenment rationalism, individual property rights and sovereign state authority, provided the justification for domination and exploitation based on racial, ethnic or religious inferiority. Of course, there were many varieties of legal imposition and not all of these were entirely done through force. In some cases, such as in Africa, the imposition of European law sometimes involved co-opting native chiefs and traditional procedures of arbitration and dispute resolution.[36] In other cases, such as Australia, the British declared upon their arrival there that the continent was *terra nullius* or vacant of other humans. On the basis that native populations were thought to be less than human, with no laws or social rules, they were often systematically annihilated (see Figure 2). As a result, traditional local methods of peacekeeping and legal negotiation were often overlooked or deliberately obliterated.

As postcolonial legal scholars often note, it is impossible to separate the laws set up in colonial outposts from the laws developing back in the European 'motherlands'. Hence it can be said that nineteenth- and twentieth-century metropolises such as New York, Paris, Belgium and London were always connected with and influenced by their nation's colonial peripheries, be these geographically distanced outposts beyond state boundaries such as in the Philippines, Algeria, the Congo or India, or socially and politically isolated enclaves (such as native reservations) within it. Similarly, colonial

---

[33] D Robinson, *Translation and Empire: Postcolonial Theories Explained* (Manchester, St Jerome Publishing, 1997) 19-20.

[34] D Chakrabarty,. *Provincializing Europe: Postcolonial Thought and Historical Difference* (Princeton, NJ, Princeton University Press, 2000).

[35] D Chakrabarty, 'Postcoloniality and the Artiface of History: Who Speaks for 'Indian' Pasts?' (1992) 37 *Representations* 1–26, 20–21.

[36] M Mamdani, Citizen and Subject: Contemporary Africa and the Legacy of Late Colonialism (Princeton, NJ, Princeton University Press, 1996).

Figure 2. *Mounted Police and Blacks* (1852). Godfrey Charles Mundy. Australian War Memorial. This painting depicts the killing of Aboriginals at Slaughterhouse Creek by British troops.

outposts were intimately connected back to their colonising oppressors. Hence colonial legal regimes did not develop as separate isolated entities, but in collaboration the centralised systems of the colonisers.[37] In short, colonies emerged over time as intricately entangled hybrid societies incorporating European and non-European laws, values and sensibilities.[38]

Building upon this understanding of intrinsic legal hybridity, it becomes clear why the decolonised countries of the post-1945 era could not entirely excise their Euro-American colonial legacies. Moreover, these newly independent nations had in many cases little choice but to adopt European forms of state building and the institutions, bureaucracies and constitutions of their former masters. Such formalities were necessary in order for new states to declare themselves 'liberal' and 'modern' and to participate in national and international political and economic organisations such as the United Nations. The rule of law exemplifies the postcolonial dilemma that required—and still requires—self-determining nations to be complicit in the imperial strategies they seek to overcome by copying and adopting Euro-American legal concepts and structures. As a result, many postcolonial states embody the contradictions and pathologies of modern European states whose history of evolving democracy is built upon the oppressive logics of imperialism, colonialism and racism.[39]

---

[37] Merry, above n 1, 569–88.

[38] H Bhabha, *The Location of Culture* (London and New York, Routledge, 1994).

[39] See Comaroff and Comaroff, above n 11; JA Byrd, *The Transit of Empire: Indigenous Critiques of Colonialism* (Minneapolis and London, University of Minnesota Press, 2011); J Reynolds, 'Third World Approaches to International Law and the Ghosts of Apartheid' in D Keane and Y McDermott (eds), *The Challenge of Human Rights: Past, Present, and Future.* (Cheltenham, Edward Elgar, 2012) 194–218.

2. POSTCOLONIAL LAW AND GLOBALISATION

Today's prevailing discussions about law and globalisation epitomise the ironies presented by postcolonial law. For instance, the United Nations, World Bank, IMF and other international legal arrangements all require that in order for a country to participate in the global political economy, it must demonstrate commitment to, and adherence with, the foundational values of Western law.[40] In a postcolonial world, just as in the colonial context of earlier centuries, there are always ongoing modifications and appropriations between all interacting communities and actors. One only has to think of human rights to appreciate the extent to which its apparently universal application has to be constantly translated, modified and 'vernacularised' to fit the social, political and economic values of particular peoples living in localised places.[41] Similarly, Euro-American law is not entirely impervious to the influence of laws emanating from the global South, as illustrated by the adoption of the UN Declaration on the Rights of Indigenous Peoples in 2007. However, despite the legal exchanges and adaptations over time by both colonisers and their former colonies, the global dominance of Euro-American law in the early decades of the twenty-first century is not easily destabilised. And as a result, Euro-American law structurally institutionalises the enduring asymmetries of power between the global South and global North and pervasively fashions and legitimates legal practices, meanings and imaginations that are European in origin.

One consequence of the global hegemony of Euro-American law is that within much Western legal scholarship there lingers a deeply embedded assumption of the global North's legal superiority vis-à-vis the rest of the world. This is evidenced by a majority of US and European scholars continuing to treat the rule of law as a discrete entity and not as a dynamic product of historically contested and culturally informed colonial/postcolonial interactions. Thus well into the twenty-first century, in arguments both for and against the significance of the nation-state amidst the forces of globalisation, the dominance of Western legalism is largely taken as a given. As a result, analysts of domestic and international law tend to look primarily at the privileged domains of legal interaction amongst lawyers, judges, business people and entrepreneurs, and to ignore the perspectives of ordinary people whose culturally informed normative understandings of law may be very different.[42]

One of the central elements of all postcolonial theories of law is the adoption of a bottom-up view that does not ignore the 'contribution of the masses', and in particular the contribution of the masses from the global South.[43] The postcolonial

---

[40] T Halliday and P Osinky, 'Globalization of Law' (2006) 32 *Annual Review of Sociology* 447–70, 455–56.

[41] SE Merry, *Human Rights and Gender Violence: Translating International Law into Local Justice* (Chicago, University of Chicago Press, 2006); A Sarat (ed), Special Issue 'Human Rights: New Possibilities/New Problems' (2001) 56 *Studies in Law, Politics, and Society*; W Twining (ed), *Human Rights, Southern Voices: Francis Deng, Abdullahi An-Na'im, Yash Ghai and Upendra Baxi* (Cambridge, Cambridge University Press, 2009); Keane and McDermott (eds), above n 39; R Banakar (ed), *Rights in Contexts: Law and Justice in Late Modern Society* (Farnham, Ashgate, 2010).

[42] P Ewick and S Silbey *The Common Place of Law: Stories from Everyday Life* (Chicago, University of Chicago Press, 1998).

[43] B Rajagopal, *International Law from Below: Development, Social Movements and Third World Resistance* (Cambridge, Cambridge University Press, 2003) 402.

perspective insists that as scholars, we need to be concerned with how globalisation affects peoples in different ways and hence studies should include both the small cosmopolitan, aeroplane-hopping legal elite *and* the millions of peoples from various classes, cultures, ethnicities and religions whose understanding of law may appear to those embedded in a Western legal heritage as 'traditional', 'backward' or 'inferior'. Postcolonial legal scholars are constantly vigilant against privileging a Euro-American position and are willing to embrace a plurality of legalities that from the perspective of most doctrinal legal scholars may not be easily understood or even initially recognised as law.

3. THEORIES OF LEGAL ORIENTALISM

The presence of postcolonial law requires that scholars and practitioners come to terms with the fact that there is no universal legal code but rather a complex overlapping plurality of legal systems and culturally informed legal meanings.[44] However, given relations between law, capitalism and a global political economy, it is perhaps not surprising that Western legal scholarship has largely ignored (some would argue deliberately) the challenging presence of postcolonial law. In an attempt to move beyond this deadlock, some scholars are coming at the problem of legal plurality by talking about the issue of legal orientalism. These scholars take a long historical view in arguing that legal orientalism has shaped the development of modern Euro-American law from the sixteenth century to the present.[45] This argument forces us to think about how racial and cultural biases continue to inform globally dominant legal concepts and assumptions of Western legal superiority, and may in turn open up ways to challenge or resist these dominant legal understandings of the world.[46]

What is legal orientalism? The concept of legal orientialism draws expressly upon the work of Edward Said, who, as mentioned above, was a leading figure in postcolonial theory. Said coined the word 'Orientalism' to refer to the ways in which European societies throughout the nineteenth century constructed their identity and self-understanding through imagining their difference to the Arab and Muslim world.[47] Essential in this process was the West's stereotyping of the Orient, which included a range of Eastern cultures located in the Middle East as well as China, Japan and South Asia. Orientalist discourses emanating from Europe were not exactly the same as those emanating from the United States because they were usually directed toward the Middle East and China, while in the United States orientalist rhetoric was usually directed to the Philippines and targets closer to home.[48] These differences typically correlated

---

[44] See Tamanaha et al, above n 15.

[45] See Ruskola, above n 6; Falk, above n 6, 39–54; A Anghie, 'The Evolution of International Law: Colonial and Postcolonial Realities' (2006) 27 *Third World Quarterly* 739–53; P Haldar, *Law, Orientalism and Postcolonialism: The Jurisdiction of the Lotus Eaters* (Abingdon, Routledge-Cavendish, 2007).

[46] B de Sousa Santos and C Rodriguez-Gavarito (eds), *Law and Counter-hegemonic Globalization: Toward a Cosmopolitan Legality* (Cambridge, Cambridge University Press, 2005).

[47] See Said, above n 6; id, *Culture and Imperialism* (New York, Alfred A Knopf, 1993).

[48] D Little, *American Orientalism: The United States and the Middle East since 1945* Chapel Hill, University of North Carolina Press, 2008; D Brody, *Visualizing American Empire: Orientalism and Imperialism in the Philippines* (Chicago, University of Chicago Press, 2010; R Francavigilia, *Go East, Young Man: Imagining the America West as the Orient* (Logan, Utah State University Press, 2011).

with a country's imperial and colonial interests and often changed over time. However, what united these various forms of orientalist rhetoric and material practice was the assumed oppositional relations between an exoticised Orient and a civilised Occident.

Typically nineteenth-century orientalist discourses about the East were negative and reinforced a presumed hierarchy of Western superiority and Eastern inferiority. However, this was not always the case, as seventeenth- and eighteenth-century Enlightenment philosophers and missionary Jesuits often praised Chinese people for their ingenuity and skill.[49] However, by the nineteenth century European attitudes about Asian peoples had crystallised into derogatory stereotypes.[50] Europeans promoted themselves as modern, rational, moral and lawful in contrast to a projection of Eastern societies as premodern, irrational, immoral and lawless (see Figure 3). Hence, at the same time that commentators such as Alexis de Toqueville were remarking upon the emphasis given to law in the United States in the 1830s, historians and social theorists were pointing to the lack of law in countries such as China, which was essentially viewed as a backward, 'stagnant' society in which lawlessness reigned.[51] But as insisted upon by Said, this did not mean that the 'Orient was *essentially* an idea, or a creation with no corresponding reality.'[52] Rather, 'The Orient is an integral part of European *material* civilization and culture ... with supporting institutions, vocabulary, scholarship, imagery, doctrines, even colonial bureaucracies and colonial styles.'[53]

Legal orientalism served a variety of purposes. The most obvious of these was that it helped confirm on the world stage the marginality of the East and the centrality of the imperial West. European and American scholars argued that Eastern jurisprudential traditions were based on custom, ritual and religion, in contrast to the so-called rational and scientific legal systems of modern Western nations. Declaring non-Western legal systems inferior helped to justify European law and culture as a superior civilisation, worthy of world leadership and dominance. Orientalist rhetoric also provided the rationale for Western nations to marginalise Asian (and indigenous) peoples within their domestic jurisdictions. For instance, in the United States orientalist rhetoric provided the basis for the Chinese Exclusion Act (1882). This act suspended Chinese immigration into the country and prevented Chinese people already living in the United States from ever being granted citizenship. Under the act, it was argued that Chinese people were non-legal subjects because they were incapable of understanding US law and so deserved to be excluded from the new republic.[54]

Postcolonial legal scholars argue that the oppositional rhetoric between Eastern and Western legal traditions was essential for the development of moden Euro-American law. In other words, European law emerged historically through a perceived difference with non-Western legal concepts. According to the sociolegal scholar Duncan Kennedy, international law must be understood in relation to 'a distinction between the West and the rest of the world, and the role of that distinction in the generation

---

[49] JS Gregory, *The West and China Since 1500* (Basingstoke, Palgrave Macmillan, 2003); DE Mungello, *The Great Encounter of China and the West, 1500–1800 (Critical Issues in World and International History)*, 3rd edn (New York, Rowman & Littlefield, 2009).

[50] Ruskola, above n 6, fn 175.

[51] Ibid, 181–87, 213–15.

[52] Said, above n 6, 5.

[53] Ibid, 2.

[54] JSW Park, *Elusive Citizenship: Immigration, Asian Americans, and the Paradox of Civil Rights* (New York, New York University Press, 2004); Ruskola, above n 6, 15–17.

Figure 3. *Execution Without Trial Under the Moorish Kings of Grenada.* Henri Regnault, 1870. © Musée d'Orsay. The title of this painting situates the image within an orientalist paradigm whereby exoticised 'others' are presented as lacking law and hence deemed intrinsically barbaric.

of doctrines, institutions and state practices'.[55] This perceived difference helped shape the international legal system, which required the 'invention of legal primitivism' to legitimate the West's universal aspirations.[56]

If one accepts this argument, then it follows that Western law has orientalist assumptions historically built into its language, structure and procedures. This suggests that contemporary Euro-American law, and the international legal system on which it is built, remains to this day intrinsically and pervasively cultural and racially biased.[57] In short, legal orientalism endures in twenty-first-century international law

[55] D Kennedy, Review of the *Rights of Conquest* (1997) 91 *American Journal of International Law* 745–48, 748.

[56] See Anghie, above n 45; JT Gathii, 'International Law and Eurocentricity' (1998) 9 *European Journal of International Law* 184–211; B Bowden, 'The Colonial Origins of International Law: European Expansion and the Classical Standard of Civilization' (2005) 7 *Journal of the History of International Law* 1–23; S Wilf, 'The Invention of Legal Primitivism' (2009) 10 *Theoretical Inquiries in Law* 485–509.

[57] See Pahuja, above n 6; L Westra, *Globalization, Violence and World Governance* (Leiden and Boston, Brill 2011).

and global legal relations.[58] Legal orientalism continues to fuel assumptions about the global North's legal superiority over the global South and has been deployed in a range of national and international legal forums such as asylum and refugee claims, as well as indigenous demands for recognition.[59] Moreover, legal orientalism is evident in the ways the global North interprets law in the Middle East, particularly in the wake of the events of 9/11, and how Western nations view legal institutions in China, Africa and Latin America. However, as the international legal scholar Teemu Ruskola remarks, the point of recognising the presence of contemporary legal orientalism is not to overcome ingrained cultural biases—an impossible task—but rather to ask why certain orientalist images of law developed, why they continue to resonate in the contemporary world, and what can be done to dilute these negative stereotypes that undermine international law and prevent sincere global dialogue and creative legal collaboration.[60]

4. THIRD WORLD APPROACHES TO INTERNATIONAL LAW (TWAIL)

There is considerable overlap between scholars who talk about legal orientalism and the intellectual movement associated with TWAIL. TWAIL is linked to a network of critical international legal scholars that first gathered at Harvard Law School in 1997.[61] This network quickly expanded to include a range of practitioners and academics, many of them 'born almost entirely in ex-colonies or part of their diasporas'.[62] The primary objectives of scholars who identify with TWAIL are to critique the uses of international law in perpetuating asymmetrical power relations between Europeans and non-Europeans, 'first' and 'third' worlds. As Gbenga Oduntan and others have argued, the hegemonic forces of the West have operated collectively to underdevelop an inclusive international law regime that empowers non-Western countries and regions.[63] Moreover, TWAIL scholars are concerned with resistance by the oppressed to the normative operation of law, seeking 'to transform international law from being a language of oppression to a language of emancipation—a body of rules and practices that reflect and embody the struggle and aspirations of Third World peoples and which, thereby, promotes truly global justice'.[64] Above all, TWAIL scholars are determined

---

[58] D Otto, 'Subalternity and International Law: The Problems of Global Community and The Incommensurability of Difference' in Darian-Smith and Fitzpatrick, above n 1, 145–80.

[59] SM Akram, 'Orientalism Revisited in Asylum and Refugee Claims' (2000) 12 *International Journal of Refugee Law* 7–40. B Golder, 'Law, History, Colonialism: An Orientalist Reading of Australian Native Title Law' (2004) 9(1) *Deakin Law Review*.

[60] Ruskola, above n 6, 222.

[61] See M Matua, *What Is TWAIL? Proceedings of the 94th Annual Meeting of the American Society of International Law* (2000); JT Gathii, 'TWAIL: A Brief History of its Origins, its Decentralized Network, and a Tentative Bibliography', Special Issue: Third World Approaches to International Law (2011) 3(1) *Trade, Law and Development*; Chimni, above n 1.

[62] L Eslava and S Pahuja, 'Beyond the (Post)Colonial: TWAIL and the Everyday Life of International Law' in P Dann and F Hanschmann, *Post-colonial Theories and Law*, Special Issue (2012) No 2 *Journal of Law and Politics in Africa, Asia and Latin America* 197.

[63] G Oduntan, 'International Law and the Discontented: How the West Underdeveloped International Laws' in A Parashar and A Dhanda (eds), *Decolonization of Legal Knowledge in India* (Routledge, India, 2009) 92–126.

[64] A Anghie and BS Chimni, 'Third World Approaches to International Law and Individual Responsibility in Internal Conflicts' (2003) No 2 *Chinese Journal of International Law* 77; U Baxi, 'What May the "Third

to destabilise a normative legal orthodoxy that assumes the centrality of Western law and as a consequence fails to take into account diverse legal contexts and experiences that inform and constitute the dynamic field of international/transnational/global law.

Among TWAIL scholars there is a divergence of opinion about the meaning and use of the 'third world'.[65] This is, perhaps, not surprising given the vast diversity of ways international law has played out over time across colonies/postcolonies in countries, regions and continents. Nevertheless TWAIL scholars are persistently committed to using the terminology 'third world' because of its explicit political framing of the historical and contemporary oppositional relationship between the West and the non-Western world. In this context, the third world does not refer to a monolithic geographical reality but rather is a contingent referencing of a shared set of experiences and concerns by peoples and nations who share histories of subordination and oppression.[66] Using more vague terminology such as the 'global South' is viewed as diluting this political and ideological critique, in a way not dissimilar to minorities in the United States often rejecting the terminology 'African American' or 'Native American' and preferring instead the politicised terminology of Blacks and Indians.

Among TWAIL scholars there is also divergence on methodologies and priorities, with some focusing on the histories of international law,[67] or the limitations of human rights discourse and its claims to universality.[68] Other scholars are more obviously activist in their leanings and concentrate on resistance to and anti-hegemonic struggles against Western dominance and the development paradigm.[69] And some scholars are involved in all of these areas.[70] However, as Obiora Okafor has argued:

> despite its healthy differences and variegation, TWAIL scholars (or 'TWAILers') are solidly united by a *shared ethical commitment* to the intellectual and practical struggle to expose, reform, or even retrench those features of the international legal system that help create or maintain the generally unequal, unfair, or unjust global order.[71]

Some critics of TWAIL highlight its limitations as a scholarly movement in an effort not to discount its attack upon the hegemony of international law, but to sharpen

World" Expect from International Law?' Special Issue: Reshaping Justice—International Law and the Third World (2006) 27 *Third World Quarterly* 713–26.

[65] R Bachand, 'Les Third world approaches to international law: Perspectives pour une approche subalterniste du droit international' in E Jouannet, H Ruiz-Fabri and M Toufayan (eds), *Droit international et nouvelles approches sur le Tiers Monde*, vol 32 (Paris, Société de législation comparée, 2013).

[66] OC Okafor, 'Globalism, Memory and 9/11: A Critical Third World Perspective' in F Johns, R Joyce and S Pahuja (eds), *Events: The Force of International Law* (New York, Routledge, 2011) 234–45, see 235–36; K Mickelson, 'Rhetoric and Rage: Third World Voices in International Legal Discourse (1998) 16 *Wisconsin International Law Journal* 353.

[67] M Koskenniemi, *The Gentler Civilizer of Nations: The Rise and Fall of International Law 1870–1960* (Cambridge, Cambridge University Press, 2004); A Anghie, *Imperialism, Sovereignty, and the Making of International Law* (Cambridge, Cambridge University Press, 2005). T Mahmud, 'Colonial Cartographies, Postcolonial Borders, and Enduring Failures of International Law: The Unending Wars Along the Afghanistan–Pakistan Frontier' (2011) 36 *Brooklyn Journal of International Law* 1.

[68] MW Matua, 'Savages, Victims and Saviors: The Metaphor of Human Rights' (2001) 42 *Harvard International Law Journal* 201–45.

[69] Chimni, above n 8.

[70] Rajagopal, above n 43.

[71] OC Okafor, 'Newness, Imperialism, and International Legal Reform in our Time: A TWAIL Perspective' (2005) 43 *Osgoode Hall Law Review* 171–91, 176–77. See also OC Okafor, 'Critical Third World Approaches to International Law (TWAIL): Theory, Methodology, or Both?' (2008) 10 *International Community Law Review* 371–78.

its capacity to affect change. So, for instance, Rémi Bachand points to the need to explicitly fold into the analysis of global oppression other categories such as gender, class, race, ethnicity and religion which are too often presumed to be embedded within TWAIL's third/first world framing.[72] As Bachand discusses, complex class, ethnic and cultural interactions are often subsumed or overlooked within this binary model.[73] As a result, Bachand argues, TWAIL scholars fail to fully account for how intersectional forces play out within Western and non-Western states, perhaps altering the terms of the largely taken-for-granted oppositional relationship. For example, little analysis has been done with respect to national elites within many postcolonial states who through active engagement with Western capitalists may be complicit in the oppression of their own peoples.

Other scholars within the TWAIL movement seek to push further the agenda of deconstructing international law by rethinking its universalising potential. This move is driven by the dilemma many TWAIL scholars and practitioners face as critics of international law while at the same time continuing to have faith in its emancipatory and reformist capacities.[74] Against this impasse, Luis Eslava and Sundhya Pahuja argue for a bottom-up ethnographic approach that explores the sites, spaces, performances and things through which the 'international' is constituted, but which are often not recognised as such. 'These other sites of practice we have in mind are not neces-sarily—or even usually—"international" in name, or imagined to be so in terms of their vision, outlook, size or scale.'[75] These sites would be the more obvious sites of courtrooms and customs agencies, as well as less obvious places and practices such as visa processing agencies, border security mechanisms, environmental regulations, urban zoning, and censorship of mobile phone and digital communications. As Eslava and Pahuja go on to say:

> Once we consider this plethora of spaces—or new 'jurisdictions'—in which international law is being materialized today, it becomes clear that we cannot confine our interrogations to only those sites that present themselves as 'international'. The increasing number of jurisdictional forms that are now being created or recreated, in the name of good governance, sustainability or economic competitiveness deserve detailed attention: one capable of linking the existence and operation of these spaces to the ways in which the current global order is unfolding in the everyday lives of people across the world.[76]

Eslava and Pahuja's call for an ethnography of international law that explicitly seeks to engage with the 'regulatory proliferation of international law' in the lives of ordinary people suggests a significant contribution in furthering the political objectives of TWAIL scholarship.[77] First and foremost, it suggests new ways for scholars to appre-ciate the small moments of daily resistance to localised manifestations of international regulatory power. In this sense, Eslava and Pahuja's call for an ethnographic explo-ration of the universality of international law refers to the universality of everyday forms of resistance, revolution and struggle by oppressed peoples against the hege-

---

[72] Bachand, above n 65.
[73] For a notable exception see Otto, above n 58.
[74] See Anghie, above n 45, 752.
[75] Eslava and Pahuja, above n 62, 218.
[76] Ibid, 218–19.
[77] Ibid, 221.

monic power of international law. Significantly, this approach seeks to overcome the contradictory impasse described above by widening and deepening TWAIL critiques of international legality while at the same time retaining optimism about international law's emancipatory potential and capacities to effect change.

Personally, as a scholar deeply sympathetic to TWAIL, it seems to me that both the call for greater intersectionality and for an ethnographic methodology aid critical approaches to international law in dealing with the challenges of the twenty-first century. As discussed briefly in the introduction, the geopolitical realities of our contemporary world have moved beyond a state-centrist system to include a range of non-state actors above and below the level of the nation-state. Unfortunately, much analysis of international law remains stuck in a modernist worldview that speaks more to the second half of the twentieth century than to the current moment. This worldview prioritises a state's legal interrelations with other states and fails to pay sufficient attention to the ever-expanding field of NGOs, volunteer organisations, religious and ethnic regional affiliations, and the mass movement of peoples in search of greater human security. Together these emerging non-state actors and global forces challenge the core principles of international law in profound ways. The calls for greater intersectionality and for an ethnographic methodology provide ways to side-step these challenges by decentring the state and emphasising new sites, locales, objects and processes through which international law is constituted and made meaningful to a diverse range of people.

5. CONCLUDING COMMENTS

One thing that is certain—whether one frames asymmetrical power relations between the global North and South in terms of legal orientalism or critical approaches to international law—is the need to move past a modernist hierarchy of legal authority based on simplistic binaries of rational versus non-rational and civilized versus uncivilized legal systems. Deorientalising and decolonising the twenty-first century's normative global legal order and stereotyped legal divides is seen, by some scholars and analysts at least, as ultimately necessary for the stability and peace of global, international, national, regional and local relations.[78] As the Nigerian legal scholar Ikechi Mgbeoji has eloquently stated, 'the North and South are mutually vulnerable, sharing a common destiny, which cannot be realized unless notions of a civilized self and barbaric other are abandoned'.[79] Moreover, with the deorientalising of law, the naturalised centrality and superiority of a Euro-American legal perspective would be dislodged and necessarily 'provincialised', borrowing Chakrabarty's terminology discussed above.

Postcolonial theorists offer some insights as to how to get past historically structured racialised divides between peoples and communities. The political theorist Duncan Ivison in his book *Postcolonial Liberalism* (2002) argues for the need to

---

[78] See Santos (ed), above n 7; Y Onuma, *A Transcivilizational Perspective on International Law*. Hague Academy of International Law (Leiden and Boston: Martinus Nijhoff Publishers, 2010).

[79] I Mgbeoki, 'The Civilized Self and the Barbaric Other: Imperial Delusions of Order and the Challenges of Human Security' in R Falk, B Rajagopal and J Stevens (eds), *International Law and the Third World: Reshaping Justice* (London and New York: Routledge-Cavendish, 2008) 151–65, 152.

create a 'genuine "multilogue" not just between the state and indigenous peoples, but between them and other cultural and national groups as well'.[80] In his arguing that indigenous peoples can make considerable contributions in the thinking of how to build more inclusive societies, Ivison notes that this will take time and a firm commitment to 'the ideal of a political order in which different national groups, with different modes of belonging and different conceptions of the good and the right, nevertheless share a willingness to live under political arrangements that reflect this plurality'.[81] Ivison's argument underscores the political challenge of a postcolonial perspective with respect to law. In order for there to be 'a context-sensitive and embedded form of public dialogue and deliberation',[82] we must first rethink the prevailing Eurocentric, state-bound understanding of what constitutes law and what processes are deemed legal. In other words, embracing postcolonial legal theories and coming to terms with deeply problematic histories of colonial oppression that endure in today's new geopolitical configurations is perhaps the first step in a process toward building a global legal future that is more responsible, equitable and inclusive of humanity, however defined.

---

[80] D Ivison, *Postcolonial Liberalism* (Cambridge, Cambridge University Press, 2002) 163.
[81] Ibid, 166.
[82] Ibid, 163.

Section 6

Law in a Global Society

REZA BANAKAR and MAX TRAVERS

A S WE SAW in Section 1, the genesis of the sociology of law may be traced back to the turn of the previous century and to the works of Marx, Durkheim and Weber, who explored the development of law as part of their preoccupation with the rise of modernity. Yet, social scientific studies of law, including legal sociology and the law and society movement, first consolidated themselves as fields of research after the Second World War, as industrialisation and urbanisation transformed the social landscape of Western countries, giving rise to a sense of perpetual change and growing social disorder.[1] Social scientific studies of law started to develop in response to this sense of disorder and as part of the attempt by public policy authorities to devise and implement effective forms of social control.[2] The next stage in the development of the sociology of law started in the late 1960s and 1970s as many West European countries developed extensive social welfare programmes which required a better understanding of the social limits of law and regulation. This brings us to the next stage, which is the focus of the final section in this volume and explores the impact of *globalisation* on law and society. Globalisation is a multifaceted phenomenon which may be defined in a number of ways to emphasise its technological, sociocultural and economic consequences.[3] However, in the context of the development of law in society, it marks the transition from the early stage of modernity (characterised by the seemingly 'solid' or enduring institutions of industrial society) to more transitory or fluid forms of social organisation. It also marks the transformation of the state, thus impacting directly on law and legality, which under the early stage of modernity were often defined in terms of the nation-state.

The first three chapters presented in this section, on forms of legal pluralism by Anne Griffiths, on law and globalisation by Ralf Michaels, and on law and regulation in late modernity by Reza Banakar, seek a better understanding of what globalisation entails for contemporary studies of law in society. The fourth chapter, on the legal profession by Ole Hammerslev, provides an overview of the theoretical debates on the legal profession, but it also discusses how the internationalisation of legal practice has

---

[1] For a discussion, see R Banakar, 'Sociology of Law' (2011) *Sociopedia.isa*. E-copy at: http://papers.ssrn.com/sol3/papers.cfm?abstract_id=1761466 .

[2] DM Trubek, 'Back to the Future: The Short, Happy Life of Law and Society Movement' (1990) 18 *Florida State University Law Review* 4–54.

[3] According to Michaels there are three types of globalisation: globalisation as reality, social theory and ideology–see Chapter 16.

impacted upon the formation of the legal profession. The section concludes with a contribution by David Nelken on the comparative sociology of law, which provides a culturally sensitised methodological tool for doing research. Such a tool, we suggest, could also prove effective in studying forms of law in global settings, where various cultures meet and interact.

Social theory has always been mindful of globalisation, but it was in the 1980s that it first engaged earnestly with the social and cultural consequences of globalisation. By the 1990s, globalisation had already become a frequently used catchword in public political debates. In the social sciences it was often discussed in economic, social and cultural terms without reference to law—and this continues to be largely the case even today. Neglecting the role of law is somewhat strange, because many of the economic, commercial and technological developments which facilitated the reproduction of globalisation were dependent on various forms of law.[4] This was not, however, a one-sided relationship: as law facilitated globalisation, helping to create new relationships, networks and spaces, it was transformed by the global forces it was shaping. As Griffiths points out in her chapter, it is more recently that we have become cognisant of what globalisation means for the law; that under global conditions, law becomes 'highly mobile and cuts across local, regional and national boundaries engendering more transnational forms of ordering'. Although this insight requires rethinking the relationship between local, national and transnational law and spheres of legal action, mainstream legal studies continues nonetheless to debate law within a state-centred paradigm. Much of legal thought, and the social theories of modernity for that matter, continues to describe and analyse law and legality within a Westphalian model, which Michaels terms 'methodological nationalism'—'the idea that the state presents the ultimate point of reference for both domestic and international law'.

The contributions in this section show that, notwithstanding the continued dominance of 'methodological nationalism' within much of social and legal theory as well as in legal education, there is a growing awareness among sociolegal scholars that globalisation has created spaces (or specific sites) for action at various national/local, international and global levels. Some of these spaces—whether in cyberspace or at the level of global finance—appear to evade traditional forms of regulation, a contested assumption which also is discussed in this section. There is therefore an emerging sociolegal discourse on the role of non-governmental organisations that gain 'quasi-state status', international development agencies, multinational corporations, elite bankers, stockbrokers and traders, and transnational human rights networks, to mention a few, which operate outside the traditional boundaries of nation-states and generate normative spaces of their own. We should hasten to add that in the literature on globalisation there is a tendency to underline the role of multinational corporations, global law firms, elite lawyers and investment bankers in the production of transnational law. However, Griffiths points out that

> the transnationalisation of law ... is not an exclusive domain of powerful inter- and transnational actors, but also belongs to the domain of ordinary migrants, businessmen and

---

[4] Sociolegal research on the role of law and globalisation started in the 1990s. See eg V Gessner and AC Budak (eds), *Emerging Legal Certainty: Empirical Studies on the Globalisation of Law* (Aldershot, Dartmouth/Ashgate, 1998); V Gessner (ed), *Foreign Courts: Civil Litigation in Foreign Legal Cultures* (Aldershot, Dartmouth, 1996).

traders who do not belong to the political and intellectual elite that feature so prominently in discussions on globalisation.

However, as the global financial crisis of 2007/08 demonstrated, it is not the ordinary migrants and small traders but the investment banks and multinational corporations who have the power to make decisions of significance—decisions which directly impact on the livelihoods of ordinary people at the local levels.

In his chapter, Banakar discusses the role of investment bankers and traders in generating the financial global crisis and asks if it is possible to regulate the behaviour of global actors. Banakar's argument is that to answer this question one has to understand global (elite) actors in the context of 'late modernity' (not to be confused with 'postmodernity'), which is a concept borrowed from Zygmunt Bauman to describe a *new* (postindustrial) form of society, where 'the conditions under which its members act change faster than it takes the ways of acting to consolidate into habits and routines'.[5] Under these 'liquid' conditions, *flexibility*, ie 'a readiness to change tactics and style at short notice, to abandon commitments and royalties without regret', rather than 'conformity to rules', will serve the individual's interest more effectively.[6] This sets a whole new agenda for both law and policy, thus urging us to reconsider our conception of legal regulation. It is also possible that the role of law in a liquid society should not be defined in terms of regulation in the same way as it was understood under 'early modernity'.

A word of warning is necessary, however. Modernity, as Karl Marx and Friedrich Engels observed about a century and a half ago, is the experience of time and space as 'all fixed, fast-frozen relationships ... are swept away, all new-formed ones become obsolete before they can ossify'.[7] Interestingly, Marshall Berman notes that those 'who find themselves in the midst of this maelstrom are apt to feel that they are the first ones, and may be the only ones going through it'.[8] Much of what you read in this section engages with the stage when this experience of modernity transcends all social, cultural and geographical boundaries and subjects humanity to 'a maelstrom of perpetual disintegration and renewal, of struggle and contradiction, of ambiguity and anguish'.[9] It is about the individual and collective experience of 'disembeddedness', that is, when 'culture and norms become loosened from their moorings in time and place: normative borders blur, shift, overlap, detach'.[10] Durkheim did, admittedly, conceptualise the breakdown of social norms, or *anomie* as he called it, and widespread individualism as a consequence of industrialisation,[11] but for him *anomie* was a by-product rather than *the* product of modernity, as it marked a pathological state brought about by exceptional societal developments, resulting in periods of social disruption and severe crisis. In contrast, the experience of disembeddedness we are concerned with in late modernity constitutes a normal rather than an exceptional social condition. It is in this context that Banakar explores how law, which crystallises values and norms by embedding them in institutional settings, thus ensuring durability

---

[5] Z Bauman, *Liquid Life* (Cambridge, Polity, 2005) 1.

[6] Z Bauman, *Liquid Times: Living in an Age of Certainty* (Cambridge, Polity, 2010) 4.

[7] K Marx and F Engels, *The Communist* Manifesto [1848] (Harmondsworth, Penguin, 1967) 224.

[8] M Berman, *All That Is Solid Melts into Air: The Experience of Modernity* (London, Verso, 1991) 15.

[9] Ibid.

[10] J Young, *The Vertigo of Late Modernity* (London, Sage, 2009) 3.

[11] E Durkheim, *The Division of Labour* [1893].

and certitude in social relationships, fares in late modernity's increased liquefaction of social structures.[12]

Law has, admittedly, always been pluralistic and hybrid, but under the normative force of modernity's metanarrative of a universally valid and coherent law, law's diversity and plurality, as well its 'indeterminacy', which we discussed in the previous section, have been overlooked, suppressed and denied. Nevertheless, the spread of globalisation has forced to the surface the social, cultural, religious and legal diversity inherent in the constitution of modern societies and with it compelled many social scientists, and even a few legal theorists, to face up to the practical and intellectual challenges of legal pluralism, on the one hand, and globalisation, on the other. These challenges are not only subverting the 'methodological nationalism' of Western liberal law, but also, as Ole Hammerslev explains in Chapter 18, they are undermining the traditional makeup of the legal profession as a nationally defined group (which has traditionally consisted of men). According to Hammerslev, instead of studying the legal profession as a coherent entity—which was how traditional legal sociology initially approached and viewed the legal profession—we need to 'examine the transnational fields in which institutions and the agents of the institutions play a role'.

This volume ends with a chapter by David Nelken on the comparative sociology of law. Nelken explores what it means to carry out empirical research in different countries—an undertaking that requires methodological sensitivity to the cultural values and conduct of those we study, as well as a critical awareness of our own assumptions and taken-for-granted values and attitudes to our object of study. According to Nelken,

> [O]ne of the most important tasks of the comparative sociologist of law at the present time is to try and capture the process of transnational law-making and to see how far in practice globalisation represents the attempted imposition of one particular legal culture on other societies.

There are, however, other reasons for highlighting the importance of the comparative sociology of law: globalisation as discussed above also entails the interplay of legal orders and assumptions at the local level. It is through the application of a methodology which is, on the one hand, comparatively tuned and, on the other, sensitised to cultural differences that the impact of globalisation on our everyday experiences of legality may be observed and analysed. By giving Nelken the final word in this collection, we suggest that sociolegal research which is conducted under conditions of globalisation would gain from an overall comparative approach to law and culture.[13]

---

[12] D Casey and C Scott, 'Crystallization of Regulatory Norms' (2011) 38 *Journal of Law and Society* 76–95, 77.

[13] For various discussions on the relationship between comparative law and sociology of law, see R Cotterrell, *Law, Culture and Society: Legal Ideas in the Mirror of Social Theory* (Aldershot, Ashgate, 2006); R Banakar, 'Power, Culture and Method in Comparative Law' (2009) 5 *International Journal of Law in Context* 69–85.

15

*Reviewing Legal Pluralism**

ANNE GRIFFITHS

S INCE THE PUBLICATION of *An Introduction to Law and Social Theory*[1] in 2002 legal pluralism is no longer viewed as an arcane area of study, pitting state-centred legal norms against other forms of ordering that are not state centred, but has become an accepted fact of life. For it is now well established that under current conditions of globalisation, law is highly mobile and cuts across local, regional and national boundaries, engendering more transnational forms of law and ordering. Such recognition requires a reappraisal of the relationship that exists between local, national and transnational spheres of action, to take account of a diverse range of actors including transnational corporations, corporate executives, non-governmental organisations (NGOs) and religious movements, as well as refugees, asylum seekers and undocumented migrants whose existence is often precarious due to their illegal status in their host country. These actors are incorporated into global and regional networks of activity, institutions and regimes of governance, as well as transnational social movements and other kinds of transnational association. Such pursuits give rise to conditions where scholars need to 'think ourselves beyond the nation'.[2]

Law forms part of this project because it embodies a complex constellation of relations that create fluid and shifting domains for action that come together to create spaces for action at a whole range of levels. Thus it not only 'serves to produce space yet in turn is shaped by a socio-spatial context'[3] that raises questions about how law is spatialised in the transnationalisation of personal, economic, communicative and reli-

* I am grateful to the Leverhulme Trust, UK, for their funding of this research project during 2009–2010. I would also like to thank the Government of Botswana and all those officials who made the research possible, along with all those who gave interviews, especially those who participated in the life histories. Special thanks must go to my research assistants Phidelia Dintwe, Phenyo Thebe, Kawina Power and Boinelo Baakile for all their hard work and commitment to the field research in 2009–2010. In addition, I would like to thank the Centre for the Study of Work and the Human Life Cycle in Global History, at Humboldt University, Berlin, where I was fortunate enough to have a senior research fellowship during 2011–2012 that enabled me to start analysing my field data. Finally, I would like to thank Daithi Mac Sithigh, a colleague at Edinburgh, Michael Freeman the editor, and the two anonymous reviewers for their comments on the manuscript.

[1] R Banakar and M Travers (eds), *An Introduction to Law and Social Theory* (Oxford, Hart Publishing, 2002).

[2] A Appadurai, 'Disjuncture and Difference in the Global Economy' in M Feathersone (ed), Special Issue: Global Culture, Nationalism, Globalization, and Modernity (1990) 7 *Theory, Culture and Society* 337.

[3] NK Blomley, *Law, Space and the Geographies of Power* (New York, Guilford 1994) 51.

gious relations that give rise to conditions of legal flux. Under these conditions there is a need to acknowledge that space is not conceived of as 'a natural medium outside the way it is conceived',[4] but requires an understanding of the extent to which legal spaces are embedded in broader social and political claims[5] at particular moments in the historical record.[6]

Such claims may involve the negotiation of border disputes, entry to the European Union, sponsoring aid for development, involving participants in antiglobalisation protests and activists promoting the interests and human rights of indigenous or ethnic minorities. They also involve experts creating blueprints for governance of industries such as fisheries, as well as the work of religious and transitional leaders dealing with disputes among their followers. These claims touch on physical, territorial, imagined and symbolic representations of space that are multilayered, embracing horizontal and vertical legal relationships that crosscut one another within and beyond territorial borders. They highlight processes of translocations at different levels of sociopolitical and legal organisation.

In acquiring a better understanding of what these processes entail it is necessary to look at the chains of interaction connecting transnational, national and local domains in multisited arenas of negotiation and at the power relations that structure these interactions and that are reproduced or changed by them. Given the dimensions of what legal pluralism entails it is not possible to give a comprehensive coverage of it in this chapter.[7] What will be highlighted in its place are a number of domains in which the highly mobile and contingent nature of law is revealed under conditions of legal pluralism that are constantly in the making.

1. REFRAMING PARADIGMS; PERSPECTIVES ON GOVERNANCE

In these processes of circulation what is 'local' and what is 'global' becomes open to question, as these categories acquire more flexible dimensions that cannot simply be set apart from, or juxtaposed against, one another, but come to be seen as sets of relations that connect and reconnect, or rupture, in a variety of ways in a number of different places. Nowhere is this more evident than in areas of humanitarian intervention where international law can no longer be seen to 'simply coordinate state interests,

---

[4] M Crang and N Thrift *Thinking Space* (London, Routledge, 2000).

[5] H Lefebvre, *The Production of Space* (Oxford, Blackwell, 1991).

[6] For 'space without time is as improbable as time without space': Crang and Thrift, above n 4, 3.

[7] For some examples, see F and K von Benda-Beckmann and A Griffiths (eds), *Mobile People, Mobile Law: Expanding Legal Relations in a Contracting World* (Aldershot, Ashgate, 2005); F and K von Benda-Beckmann and A Griffiths (eds), *The Power of Law in a Transnational World: Anthropological Enquires.* (New York, Berghahn Books, 2009a); F and K von Benda-Beckmann and A Griffiths (eds), *Spatializing Law: An Anthropological Geography of Law in Society* (Aldershot, Ashgate, 2009b); A Griffiths, 'Legal Pluralism' in Banakar and Travers, above n 1, 289–310; A Griffiths, 'Pursuing Legal Pluralism: The Power of Paradigms in a Global World' (2011) 64 *Journal of Legal Pluralism and Unofficial Law* 173–202; A Hellum, SS Ali and A Griffiths (eds), *From Transnational Relations to Transnational Laws: Northern European Laws at the Crossroads* (Aldershot, Ashgate, 2011); A Stewart, *Gender, Law and Justice in a Global Market* (Cambridge, Cambridge University Press, 2011); W Twining, 'Normative and Legal Pluralism: A Global Perspective' (2009–10) 20 *Duke Journal of Comparative and International Law* 473–517; W Zips and M Weilenmann (eds), *The Governance of Legal Pluralism: Empirical Studies from Africa and Beyond* (Vienna, Lit Verlag, 2011).

but rather must facilitate state and non-state cooperation', [8] paving the way for it to become a form of transnational law that is a subject in its own right[9]. For given the recognition of problems as having a global dimension, in which non-state actors play a significant role, the boundaries between international, foreign and domestic law may become blurred so that it becomes impossible 'to characterize certain concepts as quintessentially local or global in nature'.[10] Take, for example, the position of professionals in the business or legal sphere who may draw selectively on the laws of multiple jurisdictions to create transnational legal constructs designed to undermine public interest to meet their business clients' needs in ways that may subvert national regulations.[11]

Such activities raise questions about the ethics and viability of corporate social responsibility.[12] They also have implications for the delivery of aid through international development agencies and NGOs that acquire 'quasi-state status' and that may undermine the prevailing legal and political orders in recipient countries.[13] Human rights often form part of the agenda of international aid, yet, as Goodale observes, given the diversity and multiple meanings that such rights embody it is important to pay attention to the 'different discursive spaces in which transnational human rights networks are constituted'.[14] In addressing the relationship between law and human rights, a 2009 report by the International Council for Human Rights Policy[15] stresses the need for practitioners and activists in this area to acknowledge that there can be no single paradigm of law that is applicable to the regulation of human rights, as there are no straightforward prescriptions that can be applied on a universal basis.[16] While states may continue to uphold notions of national and legal sovereignty, often for rhetorical or ideological purposes, the reality on the ground requires a reformulation of the type of paradigm through which to capture the relationships between law and space at a number of levels. This is one where the state may feature but in a

---

[8] HH Koh 'Opening Remarks: Transnational Legal Processes Illuminated' in M Likosky (ed), *Transnational Legal Processes: Globalization and Power Disparities* (London, Butterworths, 2002) 327–32, 328.

[9] For challenges posed by humanitarian intervention and the relationship between states, regional organisations and the UN charter, see A Abass *Regional Organisations and the Development of Collective Security: Beyond Chapter VIII of the UN Charter* (Oxford, Hart Publishing, 2004).

[10] Koh, above n 8, 328.

[11] Y Dezalay and BG Garth, *Dealing in Virtue: Commercial Arbitration and the Construction of a Transnational Order* (Chicago, University of Chicago Press, 1996); Y Dezalay and BG Garth, *Lawyers and the Construction of Transnational Justice: Law Development and Globalization* (London, Routledge, 2012).

[12] D McBarnet, A Voiculescu and T Campbell (eds), *New Corporate Accountability: Corporate Social Responsibility and Law* (Cambridge, Cambridge University Press, 2007). See also A Stewart, above n 7, on how plural governance chains are moulding constructions of gender in ways that lead to the unequal distribution of the benefits of globalisation.

[13] M Weilenmann 'Project Law—A Power Instrument of Development Agencies: A Case Study from Burundi' in F and K von Benda-Beckmann and A Griffiths (eds), above n 7 (2009a), 156–75.

[14] M Goodale 'Introduction: Locating Rights, Envisioning Law between the Local and the Global' in M Goodale and SE Merry (eds), *The Practice of Human Rights: Tracking Law Between the Global and the Local* (Cambridge, Cambridge University Press, 2007) 1–38, 24.

[15] International Council on Human Rights Policy (ICHRP), *When Legal Worlds Overlap: State and Non-State Law* (Geneva, ICHRP 2009).

[16] See, for example, the complex decisions that states face with regard to the implementation of human rights in the legal regulation of religious marriages in multi-religious states: A Scolnicov, 'Multi-Religious Societies and State Legal Systems: Religious Marriages, the State and Implications for Human Rights' in T Wilhelmsson, E Paunio and A Pohjolainen (eds), *Private law and the Many Cultures of Europe* (Frederick, MD, Kluwer Law International, 2007) 405–16.

variety of ways that no longer treat them as the central reference point for debates on legal pluralism.

There have long been divergences between juridical and social scientific paradigms of law.[17] These reflect differing questions of scale and projection that revolve round questions about the types of actors involved in the investigation, the purposes for which legal pluralism is being invoked, and the sources and methodological approaches that inform the legal inquiry that is at stake. Making explicit the terms of reference upon which studies in legal pluralism are conducted is crucial, for the sources and theoretical frameworks that are employed in shaping the analysis determine what the scholar 'sees'. Over the years social scientific and anthropological perspectives have expanded to encompass 'multisited' or 'deterritorialised' forms of research and ethnography in their exploration of chains of interaction connecting transnational and local actors. This has opened up new horizons for study, engaging with a landscape that not only encompasses diverging spaces unconfined by territorial or geographic markers,[18] but also includes such areas as 'information flows' emanating from the internet and global conferences[19] or world media[20] in its diaspora.

What has emerged from adopting these approaches to legal pluralism is a less-clear 'top-down' or 'bottom-up' perspective that is linear and monocausal or centric in its orientation, in favour of one that is multidimensional and polycentric in nature, derived from networks or webs of relations. In exploring these dimensions, which some scholars refer to as pathways[21] or trails,[22] there is a recognition that what constitutes knowledge or understanding of these domains is not a given but is always partial and contingent. This standpoint is consonant with an interpretive and reflexive form of anthropology that explores how knowledge is produced and represented.[23] For knowledge 'is not transcendental, but is situated, negotiated and part of an on-going process ... [that] spans personal, professional and cultural domains'.[24] Such reflexivity in relation to the construction of knowledge and its application may be contrasted with law's claims, under models of legal positivism or centralism, to authenticity and exclusivity.

---

[17] Griffiths, 'Legal Pluralism', above n 7.

[18] SG Drummond, *Mapping Marriage Law in Spanish Gitano Communities* (Vanvouver, University of British Columbia Press, 2006).

[19] SE Merry 'Crossing Boundaries: Ethnographies in the Twenty-First Century' (2000) 23 *PoLAR* 127–33, 131.

[20] E Eide, 'Differing Standards of Free Expression; Clashing of Laws during the Cartoon Controversy' in Hellum et al (eds), above n 7, 227–98.

[21] A Griffiths, 'Law, Space and Place: Reframing Comparative Law and Legal Anthropology' (2009) 34 *Law and Social Inquiry* 495–507.

[22] C Greenhouse, 'The Military Order of 13 November 2001: An Ethnographic Reading' in F and K von Benda-Beckmann and A Griffiths (eds), above n 7 (2009a), 33–53.

[23] J Clifford, *The Predicament of Culture: Twentieth Century Ethnography, Literature and the Arts* (Cambridge, MA, Harvard University Press, 1988); J Clifford and GE Marcus (eds), *Writing Culture* (Berkeley, University of California Press, 1986); D Harraway, *Simians, Cyborgs and Women: The Reinvention of Nature* (New York, Routledge, 1991); K Hastrup, 'Writing Ethnography; State of the Art' in J Okely and H Calloway (eds), *Anthropology and Autobiography* (New York, Routledge 1992); A Ong 'Anthropology, China and Modernities: The Geopolitics of Cultural Knowledge' in H Moore (ed), *The Future of Anthropological Knowledge* (New York, Routledge, 1996); E Said 'Representing the Colonized: Anthropology's Interlocutors' (1989) 15 *Critical Inquiry* 205–25.

[24] K Narayan, 'How Native Is the "Native" Anthropoologist' in L Lamphere, H Ragone and P Zavella (eds), *Situated Lives: Gender and Culture in Everyday Life* (New York, Routledge, 1997) 23–41, 37.

2. MULTISITED ARENAS: DEALING WITH MIGRANTS

One area where multisited ethnography is especially pertinent is in addressing research on migration and in following the trajectories of migrants' multisited lives. For the transnationalisation of law across national boundaries is not the exclusive domain of powerful international and transnational actors, but also pertains to ordinary migrants, businessmen and traders who do not belong to the political and intellectual elite that feature so prominently in discussions on globalisation of law. The literature on migration usually describes one aspect of these processes: migrants taking their law to the new country of domicile. This involves the customary or religious law of their place of origin, as well as (to some extent) their national law, which does not lose its relevance for migrants after they have arrived in their new domicile. This law is usually seen as opposing the law of the receiving national state, creating a host of problems for politicians, lawyers and for the migrants.[25] Within Europe, for example, it has sparked great debates on the extent to which polygamy is or should be recognised within host countries that do not themselves permit such a union to be legally constituted.[26] It has also generated heated discussion on the extent to which religious practice and identity should be accommodated within states in acknowledging the need to take multiculturalism seriously.[27] In addressing these issues and the construction of boundaries between 'us' and 'them', scholars have argued for developing a concept of human security that might provide a greater understanding of the processes that are currently taking place across the globe.[28]

In these processes migrants are important actors in the dynamic reconfigurations of law at the different localities with which they are involved. What happens in one of the localities may have important implications for the way law develops in the other localities. However, the changes may occur at different paces and have different results depending on the specifics of the various localities involved. Nuijten,[29] for example

---

[25] MC Foblets, 'Mobility *versus* Law, Mobility *in* the Law? Judges in Europe Are Confronted with the Thorny Queston "Which Law Applies to Litigants of Migrant Origin?"' in F and K von Benda-Beckmann and A Griffiths (eds), above n 7 (2005), 297–315; see also M Rohe, 'The Migration and Settlement of Muslims: The Challenges for European Legal Systems' in P Shah and WF Menski (eds), *Migration, Diasporas and Legal Systems in Europe* (London, Routledge-Cavendish, 2006) 57–71.

[26] P Shah, 'Attitudes to Polygamy in English Law' (2003) 52 *International & Comparative Law Quarterly* 369–400; J Murphy, 'Rationality and Cultural Pluralism in the Non-Recognition of Foreign Marriages' (2000) 49 *International & Comparative Law Quarterly* 643–59.

[27] S Bano, 'In Pursuit of Religious and Legal Diversity: A Response to the Archbishop of Canterbury and the "Sharia Debate" in Britain' (2008) 10 *Ecclesiastical Law Journal* 283–309; M Rohe 'Shari'a in a European Context' in R Grillo, R Ballard, A Ferrari, AJ Hoekma, M Maussen and P Shah (eds), *Legal Practice and Cultural Diversity* (Aldershot, Ashgate, 2009) 93–111; R Freeland and M Lau, 'The Shari'a and English Law: Identity and Justice for British Muslims' in A Quraishi and FE Vogel (eds), *The Islamic Marriage Contract: Case Studies in Islamic Family Law* (Cambridge, Islamic Legal Studies Program and Harvard Law School, Harvard University Press, 2008); P Parkinson 'Taking Multiculturalism Seriously: Marriage Law and the Rights of Minorities' (1994) 16 *Sydney Law Review* 473–505.

[28] See TH Eriksen, E Bal and O Salemink (eds), *A World of Insecurity: Anthropological Perspectives on Human Security* (London, Pluto Press, 2010). In conditions of flux and mobility 'attempts to produce new collective forms of "community security" can produce … ethnic or religious conflict' (119). In these contexts it is important understand the 'way that people define their cultural identity is part and parcel of their subjective sense of human security—first and foremost in terms of cultural security, but eventually also in terms of their physical safety' (129). See E Bartels, KK Nibbe, M de Konig and O Salemink 'Cultural Identity as Key Dimension of Human Security in Western Europe: The Dutch Case' in Eriksen et al (eds), ibid, 116–32.

[29] M Nuitjen, 'Transnational Migration and Re-framing of Normative Values' in F and K von Benda-Beckmann and A Griffiths (eds), above n 7 (2005), 51–68.

focuses on the experience of migrants who move back and forth between La Canoa, a rural village in western Mexico, and the USA. She explores contrasting normative values that migrants are confronted with in their transnational existence and which, in the process of confrontation and reflection, transform their identities. As Rabo observes in her study of Syrian transnational families and family law, exploring inter-sections cannot only be understood in terms of differing legal systems or laws that collide, but requires an understanding of how 'people actually practise family relations across national borders'.[30] From another perspective, that of ethnographic research carried out in Germany, the USA and Haiti, Glick Schiller[31] makes the case for a new category of citizenship for migrants, that of 'transborder citizenship', which explicitly takes account of their multisited lives.

3. PATHWAYS TO KNOWLEDGE: A DETERRITORIALISED PERSPECTIVE

An example of how such an approach challenges state-centred perspectives on law is provided by Drummond.[32] In her investigation of family law in the city of Jerez in Spain, she refers to her research as a 'voyage' that forms part of an 'itinerary'.[33] This represents a conscious strategy on her part to provide the reader with different points of orientation to the material, bringing different perspectives to bear on a set of inter-related themes dealing with state, culture and marriage that form the three chapters of the book. By presenting several perspectives from which law might be viewed the author aims to bring 'various projections of law' more clearly into view, thus allowing for 'some of law's itineraries (in the sense of both agenda and trajectory)' to 'emerge in a place-neutralizing world'.[34] As a result of this type of analysis Drummond challenges the grand narratives of comparative law that adopt a linear overview of legal develop-ment in Europe, emphasising 'the convergence and harmonisation of legal traditions'.[35] This has involved interpreting the spread of secular family law across Europe with no-fault divorce regimes as representing 'the apex of a modernising homogeneity'[36] in which the 'culture and practice of family law in Spain' is seen to be 'in conformity with a single, Western, globally disseminated "modern" model'.[37] Yet, as Drummond points out, 'such a rendering of the history of marriage in Western Europe is one that has been written as though there is one Western family about which a single history can be written'.[38] As a consequence, what is represented as universal in fact represents 'an exclusive and extraordinarily narrow band of the European population'.[39]

By focusing on space and place in the form of the city of Jerez de la Frontera, Drummond explores what constitutes the 'local' or 'locale' through an analysis of

---

[30] A Rabo, 'Syrian Transnational Families and Family Law' in Hellum et al (eds), above n 7, 29–49, 31.
[31] N Glick Schiller, 'Transborder Citizenship: An Outcome of Legal Pluralism' in F and K von Benda-Beckmann and A Griffiths (eds), above n 7 (2005), 27–49.
[32] Drummond, above n 18.
[33] Ibid, 4.
[34] Ibid, 6.
[35] Ibid, 18.
[36] Ibid, 86.
[37] Ibid, 47.
[38] Ibid, 188.
[39] Ibid, 188.

perceptions of locality and community that are discursively and historically constructed, rather than treating it as a given. This perception is one that is not bounded by state notions of territoriality or jurisdiction. This approach is also in keeping with a shift in anthropological perceptions of space in physical or material terms to an interest in the spatial dimensions of culture[40] through the recognition 'that all behaviour is located in and constructed of space'.[41] The locale that forms the subject matter of Drummond's study is not just a place where things happen but represents 'a specific site in which social relations are bounded and locally constituted, while the sense of place relates to the experiences and representational map constructed of a specific place by its occupants'.[42] Thus for her the concept of 'place' is 'the central analytical problematic of the book', which encompasses the actual city as well as the 'metaphorical city of the book's theoretical musings'.[43] Such musings are in keeping with Lefebvre's observations that 'space is not a scientific object removed from ideology or politics, it has always been political and strategic'.[44] In this way Drummond's study, although located in a place that is a physical space, nonetheless represents a form of deterritorialised ethnography.

4. RETHINKING CITIZENSHIP

One area where state-centred views of law have been heavily contested is that of citizenship. Over the years it has been the focus of much attention, given transnational migration discussed earlier and the displacement of persons from countries of origin due to wars or conflicts that have forced individuals to become refugees or asylum seekers. In dealing with the classification of persons, citizenship raises questions about defining who is to be included as a citizen within a state and who is to be excluded from this status. The scope of the concept of citizen is limited by policies implemented in formal laws, leading to a set of criteria applied in making this decision, along with the bureaucratic regulatory institutions that implement them.[45] Those that fail to meet the criteria and who remain in the state acquire an 'illegal' status in law, rendering them liable to expulsion and deportation.[46] The formal criteria for citizenship tend to be somewhat narrow, based on country of birth, marriage, official residence and so on, and have been subject to critique.[47]

Attempts have been made to displace the status quo by framing a category of 'social citizenship' as a step towards challenging and broadening formal, legal definitions of citizenship when it comes to dealing with undocumented persons within a

---

[40] A Gupta and J Ferguson, *Culture, Power, Place: Explorations in Critical Anthropology* (Durham, NC, Duke University Press, 1997) 1.

[41] S Low and D Lawrence-Zuniga (eds), *The Anthropology of Space and Place: Locating Culture* (Oxford, Blackwell Publishing and Carlton, 2003).

[42] Blomley, above n 3, 112.

[43] Drummond, above n 18, 4.

[44] Lefebvre, above n 5, 31.

[45] B Morgan, *Social Citizenship and the Shadow of Competition: The Bureaucratic Politics of Regulatory Justification* (Aldershot, Ashgate, 2003).

[46] NP De Genova, 'Migrant "Illegality" and Deportability in Everyday Life' (2002) 31 *Annual Review of Anthropology* 419–47.

[47] S Coutin, *Legalizing Moves: Salvadoran Immigrants' Struggle for US Residency* (Ann Arbor, University of Michigan Press, 2000).

nation-state. Such new criteria include a period of de facto residence, contributions to and engagement with the local community, birth of children within the country, and so on.[48] It comes as no surprise that many of those constructing categories of social citizenship tend to be anthropologists, sociologists and sociolegal scholars who have a more social-scientific perspective on law and its relationship with society and who seek to apply this perspective to create more inclusive definitions of law.

Other examples include regulatory frameworks that are not formally recognised by state law but that have legitimacy and authority in the eyes of those communities that apply them. This, for example, includes the favellas in Brazil or the barrios of Columbia, which were viewed until recently as illegal, squatter settlements by state law. In recent years attempts have been made in Columbia to recognise and regularise some of these settlements under certain conditions. Another example is that of People's Courts in South Africa that sprang up under the old apartheid regime with no formal legal status but used by local groups to control and regulate life in the townships.

5. CONSTITUTIONAL PLURALISM: THE RECOGNITION OF INDIGENOUS PEOPLE

Another arena of contestation in recent years has been the recognition of indigenous peoples and their laws and rights to self-governance. This has provided an ongoing focus for legal pluralism research and has had ramifications through inquiries into how the concept of indigeneity is constructed within local, national and transnational domains. Merry has long observed that 'indigenous groups often define themselves in terms being developed by the global movement of indigenous peoples human rights and the provision of state law'.[49] This is important because 'the legal provision of the nation in which an indigenous community lives as well as those of the international order affect how a particular indigenous community presents itself and the kinds of identities it assumes'.[50] These represent in part 'accommodations to the shifting global and national frameworks of power and meaning in which the community lives'.[51]

Early strategies for recognition adopted different means. The strategy behind the Mabo case[52] in Australia, for example, was to make the national legal system recognise native title, demonstrating that indigenous laws, customs and traditions could be accommodated within the common law paradigm. While native title could be extinguished in a number of ways, the decision opened up the way for indigenous groups to claim interest in large segments of their traditional lands if they could demonstrate the required continuing connection with those lands. In contrast, the WAI 262 proceedings in New Zealand[53] dealing with the issue of folklore protection alleged, amongst

[48] Ibid.
[49] Merry, above n 19, 127.
[50] Ibid.
[51] Ibid.
[52] *Mabo v Queensland [No 2]* (1992) 175 CLR 1. For discussion, see Justice Ronald Sackville 'The Legal Protection of Indigenous Culture in Australia' (2003) 11 *Journal of International and Comparative Law* 711–45.
[53] For further discussion, see GW Austin, 'Re-treating Intellectual Property? The WAI 262 Proceeding and the Heuristics of Intellectual Property Law' (2003) 11 *Cardozo Journal of International and Comparative Law* 333–63.

other things, that the Crown, by entering into a number of key intellectual property law instruments without proper consultation with the Maori, breached its obligations under the Treaty of Waitangi. The claimants' starting point in these proceedings was not the traditional taxonomy of intellectual property rights and a demonstration of how the concerns of the Maori Iwi could be accommodated within the traditional heuristic structure of intellectual property law, but rather the Treaty of Waitangi and its guarantee of the right to sovereignty which they claimed the Crown had breached.

In responding to claims and rights asserted by indigenous peoples, states such as Australia, New Zealand, Canada and the USA have required such peoples to adopt a written constitution on membership rules. Such rules operate as a condition of official recognition. This requirement has given rise to 'tribal constitutionalism' that generates a new legal and political distinction between indigeneity and tribal membership.[54] This creates 'a jurisdictional split between the category of indigenous persons identified by the state, and the category of tribal members identified by officially recognized tribes'.[55] This is problematic because these classifications create a situation where some 'legally indigenous persons are not tribal members' while 'some tribal members would not qualify as indigenous under public law definitions'.[56] In the settler states she deals with, Gover observes that one of two models are applied to recognition based on race or the nation. The first model, based on race, prioritises indigenous ancestry, while the second, based on the nation, prioritises tribal membership. They operate in opposition to one another with the effect that 'either tribal self-governance is undermined by the State's dealing with non-tribal indigenous people, or a large and growing number of indigenous people are shut out of the State-indigenous relationship by the mediating institutions of tribes'.[57]

Yet, Gover argues, the concept of indigeneity extends beyond that of a narrowly construed emphasis on tribal membership, for many non-tribal persons are recognised by tribes and by other indigenous communities. This is something of which neither model of recognition takes account because 'neither acknowledges the role played by indigenous communities in the construction of indigeneity'.[58] In accommodating this excluded perspective, Gover advocates adopting a concept of 'inter-indigenous' recognition. This would extend the legal category of 'public indigeneity' beyond members of officially recognised tribes to include 'the cultural concept [of indigneity] as it emerges from indigenous practices of recognition'.[59]

6. CHALLENGING EXCLUSIONS: MOBILISING CONSTITUTIONAL REFORM

Mobilising for change within states is not confined to the struggles of indigenous peoples. It can involve widespread political mobilisation for radical legal reform as in

---

[54] K Gover, *Tribal Constitutionalism: States, Tribes and the Governance of Membership* (Oxford, Oxford University Press, 2010).
[55] Gover, ibid, 1.
[56] Ibid.
[57] Ibid, 10.
[58] Ibid.
[59] Ibid.

the case of several Latin American countries. In his study, Houtzager[60] examines the impact of social movements in challenging systemic and durable forms of exclusion; in his case, in the context of the struggle for land engaged in by the Movement of the Landless (MST) in Brazil. He analyses the success of the MST which has made access to land more equitable in parts of Brazil by redefining property rights in practice, in terms of juridical mobilisation through the juridical field. This field is constituted through a wide range of actors and institutions including judges and judicial institutions, private lawyers and law firms, public prosecutors, law school professors, NGOs and professional legal associations. Such mobilisation takes places across multiple fields that 'integrate juridical action into broader political mobilization, politicizing struggles before they become juridified, and mobilizing sophisticated legal skills from diverse actors'.[61] In addition, support was also garnered from other sources that were 'religious (through the progressive wing of the Catholic Church and pastoral organizations), political (through the Workers' Party in particular), labor (through the labor organization *Central Unica dos Trabalhadores)*, academic, and within international advocacy groups and NGOs'.[62] Such support was set in motion because of the transition to democracy.

What Houtzager demonstrates is how substantial legal change may be generated 'when dynamics in the movement field and the political arena converged to alter that of the juridical field'.[63] Even where this does not occur he shows how change on a smaller and more incremental scale can be brought about through mobilisation across multiple fields. In these processes the modalities of legal change may vary. Drawing on the case of land occupation in Pontal do Paranapanema, he demonstrates how MST's land occupation strategy and juridical mobilisation can combine to set in motion different types of modalities of legal change. In Pontal do Paranapanema three modalities were visible, these were '[1] state enforcement of a *de jure* legality that was ignored in practice, [2] a significant procedural innovation that speeded up the judicial clock, and [3] a shift in the sources of law and reinterpretation of substantive legal norms'.[64]

Underpinning these developments is a recognition that ever since the 1990s efforts to constitutionalise law have played a critical role in facilitating judicial modalities of legal change. Such efforts have been strengthened through networks of progressive lawyers, especially the National Network of Popular Lawyers, formally constituted in 1996. Their commitment to the constitutionalisation process within the juridical field 'played an important role in synchronizing the juridical and movement fields'.[65] It has 'played a substantial role in altering a highly exclusionary legality by compelling public authorities to implement existing agrarian reform legislation, by helping to create and institutionalize novel interpretations of the social function of property and an expanded notion of civil disobedience'.[66] What is key in this process is an understanding of the dialectical relationship existing between the movement and juridical

---

[60] P Houtzager, 'Movement of the Landless (MST) and Juridical Modalities of Legal Change in Brazil' in B de Souza Santos (ed), *Law and Globalization from Below: Towards a Constitutional Legality* (Cambridge, Cambridge University Press 2005) 218–40.

[61] Houtzager, ibid, 219.

[62] Ibid, 225.

[63] Ibid, 220.

[64] Ibid, 225

[65] Ibid, 237.

[66] Ibid, 238.

fields that illuminates how 'relations between fields can alter their respective internal logics' to mobilise new perspectives on law.[67]

Turning to other parts of Latin America, Restrepo Amariles draws attention to constitutional change in Colombia (1991), Venezuela (1999) and Bolivia (2009), focused on popular sovereignty as a means of refounding the state.[68] Promoted by the Latin American neoconstitutional movement and its radical wing, constitutional reforms in these countries aim at institutionalising popular sovereignty—based on legitimacy—over legal sovereignty—founded on legality—in the foundation, structure and functioning of the state. What this entails is establishing 'original constituent powers' derived from the people, the promotion of active political participation and a focus on the justiciability of constitutional rights. To this end, and in order to include minorities and historically excluded groups in the process of constitutional reform, Colombia established a constitutional assembly. This was derived out of a national consensus "that claimed for itself the original constituent power" and thus "the legitimate constitutional power of the Colombian State'.[69] According to Restrepo Amariles, the constitutional assembly was characterised by its legitimacy rather than by its legality because it was 'a constituent power and not a constituted power'; it was 'a source of law because it was built upon popular sovereignty'.[70]

Venezuela went further than Colombia in its mechanisms for participation by holding a referendum on whether or not to establish a constitutional assembly, and by presenting the final draft of the constitution prepared by it to the people for approbation in another referendum. The Venezuelan constitution 'established by the sovereign people—in exercise of their constituent power'[71] constructed an institutional arrangement of that state that allows for permanent popular participation through the creation of a new public electoral power. This independent electoral power was established to enable citizens to control state abuses. It does so by guaranteeing the expression of the people's sovereignty 'through vote, referendum, consultation of public opinion, mandate revocation' and other mechanisms as well as 'open forums and meetings of citizens whose decisions are binding'.[72] What is key here is the potential for strengthening civil society organisations and social networks of co-operation without the intermediation of political parties. The electoral power promotes a direct link among citizens, and between citizens and the state.

To strengthen this type of participation the Colombian constitution provides another mechanism for ensuring popular legitimacy in the functioning of the state. This is through provision for the justiciability of constitutional fundamental rights that allow for 'actualizing rather than merely protecting these constitutional rights'.[73] In this process the Constitutional Court 'has used judicial review not only to decide particular cases, but to advance the social agenda of the constitution and promote structural changes that eliminate permanent threats to fundamental rights'.[74] Restrepo

---

[67] Ibid, 223.
[68] D Restrepo Amariles, *Legality and Legitimacy: The Legal and Political Philosophy of Popular Sovereignty in the New Latin American Constitutions* (Saarbrucken, Lambert Academic Publishing, 2010).
[69] Ibid, 89.
[70] Ibid.
[71] Ibid, 95.
[72] Ibid, 98.
[73] Ibid, 104.
[74] Ibid, 110.

Amariles argues further that with the introduction of constitutional actions for the actualisation of fundamental rights 'constitutional review becomes more than an instrument of legality; it becomes a means of achieving popular legitimacy for the state'.[75] This is especially the case given that it is not only negative liberty rights that are protected by the constitutional judges but also positive rights, such as housing, work and social security that increase 'the legitimizing potential of constitutional review'.[76]

These processes underpin broader notions of legitimacy with regard to state policies and actions, as well as providing for greater popular participation in the affairs of state through the development of a concept of popular sovereignty.[77] As such, these developments represent radical changes in the interpretive legal process as well as in the accountability of the state that is expanded through constitutional reform. To be successful they require concerted political action and convergence of interests, as well as the mobilisation of forces that cut across multiple social fields.

7. REACHING BEYOND STATES: APPEALS TO TRANSNATIONAL REGULATION

Defining concepts of indigeneity, involving recognition of membership within social groups and of rights ascribed to their status, entails configuring relations between indigenous peoples and states. This not only involves internal processes of negotiation located within the geographic territories of states but may also involve appeals to transnational forms of governance that may be used to reshape negotiations within these arenas. For example, the UN Declaration on the Rights of Indigenous Peoples (UNDRIP)[78] provides an international instrument that may be utilised by indigenous peoples in the quest for recognition and implementation of international human rights standards to legitimate their claims on states. Framed in terms of international law, UNDRIP refers to international law norms, human rights law, treaties between states and indigenous peoples, state law, and without distinction, to indigenous 'laws, traditions [and] customs'. As such, it marks a significant advance in the recognition of indigenous peoples as subjects of international law, with recognition of their collective rights that may be viewed as separate and distinct from the body of international human rights law (geared to individual rights) and the related rights of minorities. As a resolution, UNDRIP is not a treaty establishing international obligations for those states that consented to its adoption. Nonetheless, it has provided an important mechanism for developing a system of global governance and international human rights law. As Wheatley observes 'applications from indigenous groups have been important in developing the "case law" of the Human Rights Committee on Article 27, Interna-

---

[75] Ibid, 113.

[76] Ibid.

[77] However, he challenges the view put forward by the radical wing of the neoconstitutionalist movement, that popular severiegnty has replaced legal sovereignty underlying the modern political project by producing an alternative refoundation project. He argues that the latter is in face 'essentially a way of recovering the faith in modern ideals ... by creating a new idelogical articact of modern thought aiming to recover faither in itself' (ibid, 124–25).

[78] This was passed by a resolution of the General Assembly, GA Res 61/295, adopted on 13 September 2007.

tional Covenant on Civil and Political Rights (the minority right to a distinctive "way of life")'.[79]

What UNDRIP creates is space for 'political participation in legal regimes outside of the state' that 'allows the possibility of regime capture (or at least influence) with the authority of the international law system then seen to conflict with the state law system'.[80] In appealing to norms developed outside state legal systems, indigenous peoples may challenge legal norms within their own domestic legal systems. This gives rise to a legal pluralism that requires a 'shift in the thinking of public international lawyers'.[81] They must make sense of the 'new complexities' and take account of 'global governance, and the relevance of democracy and democratic legitimacy in the exercise of political authority', including 'a recognition of the social, economic and political life of indigenous peoples'.[82]

Outside of states, bodies that may be used to push the implementation of human rights within states include the Inter-American Commission on Human Rights (IACHR) and the Inter-American Court of Human Rights, which regulate the inter-American human rights system. A recent case, *La Oraya Community v Peru*, pursues the relationship between environmental health and human rights. It seeks to extend the responsibility of a state for the violation of human rights of a non-indigenous community through contamination of the environment. As Spieler observes, the case is significant because it 'has the potential to expand the concept that environmental protection is closely related to human rights promotion and effectiviness'.[83] If the IACHR issues a report in favour of the petitioners, the people of La Oroya, and the state of Peru fails to address the concerns of the IACHR it could remit the case to the Inter-American Court. While the Court has issued judgments dealing with environmental degradation, these have, to date, been confined to dealing with indigenous communities and the protection of their rights and territories. In opening up the scope for recognition of the interrelationship between environmental health and human rights in general, the case has the potential for holding a state accountable for human rights violations in a broader arena. This could include violations of the right to health, life or personal integrity of a community, caused by environmental contamination in a whole range of circumstances, such as pesticide contamination, or air pollution in cities.[84]

8. RE-ENVISIONING SPACE: VIRTUAL WORLDS AND TRANSIENT SPHERES

Rethinking questions of authority and legitimacy with regard to law also arises in spaces that elude conventional approaches to doctrinal analysis. One such arena concerns the internet. Given its global reach there has been much discussion over the

---

[79] S Wheatley 'Indigenous Peoples and the Right of Political Autonomy in an Age of Global Legal Pluralism' in M Freeman and D Napier (eds), *Law and Anthropology*, *Current Legal Issues* 12 (Oxford, Oxford, University Press 2009) 351–384, 383.

[80] Ibid, 383.

[81] Ibid, 384

[82] Ibid.

[83] P Spieler, 'The Le Oroya Case: The Relationship Between Environmental Degradation and Human Rights Violations' (2010) 18 *Human Rights Brief* 19–23, 27.

[84] Ibid, 23.

years as to whom should regulate it, what form this regulation should take and for what purposes. Such deliberations give rise to competing approaches to perceptions of what the 'global commons' entails in a virtual world. Much of the discussion centres on the potential for democratic governance and the ways in which this may be ordered. For Dizon[85] the flaws in popular theories of democracy and information and communications technology (ICT), be they utopian or dystopian, derive from the fact that 'they have a very limited and singular view of what democracy is, where to look for it, and who are involved in its constitution'.[86] For this reason he advocates the need to 'deconstruct and re-imagine the conception of democracy itself beyond the traditionalist state-centred and legal centralist assumptions'.[87] He proposes to do this by expanding the concept 'beyond governmental regulation and political activity' which allows for 'a broader yet more socially-intimate and fine grained experience of democracy' to be comprehended".[88]

Another approach is adopted by Paliwala[89] who explores the way cyberspace's construction of new internet cultures also transforms economic and regulatory cultures that compete with one another. On the one hand, he draws attention to cyberspace's potential for creating a new space for collaborative, non-capitalist, democratic engagement that is emancipatory for its constituents or the 'multitude'. However, he also highlights a competing approach that seeks to defend state and property interests by harnessing the power of capital to develop and control new modes of regulation and production with their inclusionary and exclusionary powers. What emerges are contradictory interpretations of what virtual space embodies. Thus Baxi[90] and others such as Klein[91] and Rajan[92] stress that, far from being emancipatory, the internet represents new technoscientific modes of production that stand for new modes of domination.

From yet another perspective, Ali[93] examines the discourse of internet *fatwa* and how this affects women and gender relations in a transnational sphere. Based on her exploration of selected *fatwas* from three internet sites she asks 'whether this burgeoning field of communication reflects emerging discursive sites for Muslim women within a counter-hegemonic transnational and global "virtual" space'?[94] In addressing this issue her study reveals how these new cyberspace regulation mechanisms serve global Muslim space. As such, they generate an international discourse encompassing a wide spectrum of interacting norms that highlight 'the "irrepressible" plurality of the Islamic tradition'.[95] She demonstrates how these sites have enabled Muslim women to raise questions about their lives that 'they would not have been able to frame in a

---

[85] M Dizon, 'Participatory Democracy and Information and Communications Technology: Legal Pluralist Perspectives' (2010) 1 *European Journal of Law and Technology* 1–36.

[86] Ibid, 7.

[87] Ibid.

[88] Ibid, 9.

[89] A Paliwala, 'Regulating Cyberspace: Modes of Production, Modes of Regulation and Modes of Resistance' in Hellum et al (eds), above n 7, 229–50.

[90] U Baxi, *The Future of Human Rights* (New Delhi, Oxford University Press, 2006).

[91] U Klein, 'Introduction: Techno-Scientific Productivity' (2005) 13 *Perspectives on Sciences* 139–41.

[92] IKS Rajan, *Biocapital: The Constitution of Postgenomic Life* (Durham, NC, Duke University Press, 2006).

[93] SS Ali, 'Behind the Cyberspace Veil: Online Fatwas on Women's Family Rights' in Hellum et al (eds), above n 7, 117–37.

[94] Ibid, 118.

[95] Ibid.

"face to face" encounter due to the sensitive, private and at times challenging nature of the enquiry'.[96] Thus she highlights the transformative potential of internet *fatwas* and the implications that this has for transnational and international family law norms within plural Islamic legal traditions. Her approach challenges existing hegemonies within an Islamic tradition that is predicated upon ethnicity, schools of juristic thought and territorial locations.

Moving in and out of engagements with multisited, transnational arenas poses problems about how to study a world in which all 'is in flux, order is transient, nothing is independent, everything relates to everything else, and no one subsystem is necessarily continuously in charge'.[97] It is a problem at the other end of the scale from deriving law and order from the territorial and sovereign claims of nation-states. While anthropological and/or social-scientific approaches to law have provided alternative visions of legal pluralism from those based on state-centred frameworks, this has generally been accomplished through ethnographic and empirical studies derived from a focus on the 'field' as a locus of study. What this entails has been subject to change over time, from earlier studies of village life to multisited or deterritorialised ethnography discussed earlier. It is constantly undergoing reconceptualisation and adapting to new challenges, as, for example, how to conduct research where there is no easily discernible 'social field'. This is most evident in, but not confined to, moments of political reconstruction and instability.[98]

An example of the challenges this poses is provided by Zabusky's[99] study of space-science mission development in Europe. In examining the worlds of big science and European integration, Zabusky elected to study the Space Science Department (SSD), within the European Space Research and Technology Centre located in the Netherlands, where most of the technical and scientific work is carried out. Zabusky identified what she considered to be a manageable social field for study, one where staff scientists are responsible for co-ordinating the efforts of other scientists, engineers and technicians from across Europe in designing, developing and manufacturing European Space Agency space-science missions. However, it soon became clear that the SSD 'was not a relevant ... even genuine, social field for European scientists',[100] and so she reoriented her focus away from the SSD itself to space-science missions. But this also presented difficulties because there was no central locus of decision-making that could be grasped, or tangible space that presented itself for study.[101]

Instead, she encountered ephemeral virtual networks, such as international review boards that 'did not exist anywhere but appeared only at the moment when called into being by a set of rules and regulations and by ongoing practices of participants'.[102]

---

[96] Ibid.

[97] E Martin, *Flexible Bodies: Tracking Immunity in American Culture from the Days of Polio to the Age of AIDS* (Boston, MA, Beacon Press, 1994).

[98] CJ Greenhouse, E Mertz and KB Warren (eds), *Ethnography in Unstable Places: Everyday Lives in the Contexts of Dramatic Political Change* (Durham, NC, Duke University Press, 2002).

[99] SE Zabusky, 'Ethnography in/of Transnational Processes: Following Gyres in the Worlds of Big Science and European Integration" in Greenhouse et al (eds), ibid, 117–45.

[100] Zabusky, ibid, 125.

[101] For discussion of the 'field' as a site of study, see A Gupta and J Ferguson, 'Discipline and Practice. "The Field" as Site, Method and Location in Anthropology' in A Gupta and J Ferguson (eds), *Anthropological Locations: Boundaries and Grounds of a Field Science* (Berkeley, University of California Press, 1997) 1–46.

[102] Zabusky, above n 99, 129.

For staff participating in mission development this gave rise to a sense of vulnerability and uncertainty in a world where 'networks of people in different locations' working 'toward a common goal' were continually being made and unmade 'in decision-making processes that were constantly taking on different forms, subject to shifting centres of power that in turn dissolved and became reconstituted elsewhere'.[103] The problem for Zabuksy was that these processes 'seemed more defined by constant change than by definitive structures; at every moment, political, economic, and organizational realities shifted'; this challenged Zabusky's ability 'to hone in on a place I could call the field'.[104] These experiences raised questions about where was 'Europe (as opposed to its constituent nation-states)?', along with the problems of identifying 'the international scientific community' since it was, by definition, everywhere.[105] Nonetheless, she continued to grapple with these processes that she viewed as 'widening gyres' where no one is in control of this ongoing 'gyration', which involves 'the making and unmaking of centres'.[106]

In exposing and exploring these dimensions Zabusky reveals how productivity in space-science mission development, far from being the product of political stability, in fact results from 'participants experiences of instability and uncertainty as they improvise moments of clarity in which work can get done'.[107] For participants working at the intersection of two powerful transnational processes, European integration and big science, this is an uphill struggle, as they are faced with constructing missions in the light of forces that are often at odds with one another. They must 'meet their professional or intellectual needs' that are required for their projects 'in the face of constant shifts in political priorities, organisational policies, and economic reallocations over which they have little or no control'.[108] Under such circumstances what becomes apparent is the contingent and highly mobile nature of the world in which space-science missions come into being.[109]

9. REFORMULATING LEGAL PLURALISM: TRANSNATIONAL AND SPATIAL DIMENSIONS OF LAW

This chapter has explored forms of legal pluralism that highlight the multispatial contextualisation of law. It provides a perspective on legal pluralism that highlights the mobile and contingent nature of law, reflecting an ongoing process. In doing so, it has drawn on social scientific and anthropological perspectives on law, especially ethnographic studies. The value of ethnographic fieldwork lies, as Strathern observes, in 'its capacity to contribute to an understanding of how tightly or loosely the compound parts of the large-scale composites are glued together at this particular historical moment, and what the potential is for increasing coherence or for violent, explosive

---

[103] Ibid, 125.
[104] Ibid, 115.
[105] Ibid, 121
[106] Ibid, 113.
[107] Ibid, 114.
[108] Ibid.
[109] See also C Brumann on the importance of engaging in a discursive ethnography of interaction in studying the World Heritage arena in 'Multilateral Ethnography: Entering the World Heritage Arena', Working Paper No 136, Max Planck Institute for Social Anthropology Working Papers, Halle/Saale, 2012.

fragmentation'.[110] Thus it highlights the multiple ways in which international, trans-national, national and local domains intersect with one another in a whole variety of ways that undermine any grand narrative of globalisation and attendant vision of law.

In doing so such ethnographic work provides an analysis that sets out the complex relationships derived from intersections between transnational forms of law, such as human rights and religious law, and local legal orders (such as customary or traditional law) emanating from a plurality of sources within and beyond the state. It also demonstrates the ways in which the effects of globalisation reveal themselves to be highly different in specific contexts, providing an opportunity to observe 'current history in the process of being produced'.[111] This comes about because the ethnographer is 'witness to the active construction and challenging of relationships, meaning, categories, patterns, systems, orders ... and their transformation and undoing as well'.[112] This is because the ethnographer, as positioned subject, has (unlike other researchers) a 'lived experience which enables or inhibits particular kinds of insight'[113] that can be harnessed to provide a more contextualised understanding and analysis of law.

These processes provide an important perspective on law, revealing how it reconstitutes spaces for action and the redrawing of boundaries within an environment in which state sources of law represent only one of a number of elements that may be at work. It also reveals the multistranded composition of state legal pluralism that discloses more shifting alliances and transitory bases for action.[114] In addition, it makes visible the transformative potential for law that derives from the new kinds of political and legal spaces that are in the making, that elude the boundaries of the territorial state and traditional legal scholarship. Such an approach reframes the discussion of institutions and specific practices—both public and private—'away from historically shaped national logics'.[115] Such visibility is critical for acquiring a proper understanding of processes of globalisation that, among other things, are 'taking place inside the national to a far larger extent than is usually recognized'.[116]

In pursuing this form of analysis an understanding of the ways in which law is spatialised becomes apparent. It demonstrates how legal representation of space must be seen 'as constituted by—and in turn, constituted of—complex, normatively charged and often competing visions of social and political life under law'.[117] In struggling to make sense of the complexity and ambiguity of social life, 'legal agents—whether judges, legal theorists, administrative officers or ordinary people—represent and evaluate space in different ways'. What is foregrounded under plural legal conditions are the diverse and often contradictory notions of spaces and boundaries or border-

---

[110] SF Moore, 'The Ethnography of the Present and the Analysis of Process' in R Borofsky (ed), *Assessing Cultural Anthropology* (London, McGraw-Hill, 1994) 365–75, 372.

[111] Ibid, 362.

[112] Ibid.

[113] Hastrup, above n 23, 119.

[114] Merry and Woodman have long called for the need for a more serious investigation into what state legal pluralism involves, to examine the nation-state's ideological claims to legal uniformity and coherence that are used to construct a metanarrative that challenges 'other' forms of ordering. SE Merry, 'Legal Pluralism' (1988) 22 *Law and Society Review* 869–96; GR Woodman, 'Ideological Combat and Social Observations: Recent Debate about Legal Pluralism' (1998) 42 *Journal of Legal Pluralism and Unofficial Law* 61–71.

[115] S Sassen, *Territory, Authority, Rights: From Medieval to Global Assemblages* (Princeton, Princeton University Press, 2008) 2.

[116] Ibid, 1.

[117] Blomley, above n 3, xi.

lands that come to exist. In acknowledging these diverse legal constructions that come into being, what becomes visible are the 'multiple arenas for the exercise of political authority, the localization of rights and obligations, as well as the creation of social relationships and institutions that are characterized by different degrees of abstractions, different temporalities and moral connotations'.[118]

What emerges from these more broadly construed perspectives on law are the different actors who are engaged in contestations over who has the power and authority to generate law and construct its meaning. This is especially pertinent in plural legal constellations where there may be contestation over what is the 'correct' law in particular contexts. The power struggles that emerge under these circumstances often reflect asymmetrical power relations among parties and among legal orders. This affects the ways in which law's legitimacy is constituted and reconstructed. For law plays an important part in creating, producing and enforcing meanings of concepts such as 'justice', 'authority' and 'rights', and in instantiating notions of 'legality' that may be invoked by different social actors in their construction of hegemonic and counter-hegemonic discourses. Such discourses not only operate on a rhetorical or ideological level, but may also serve to underpin the actual use of force or violence to achieve their ends.[119]

The recognition and prioritising of legal orders today continues to create dilemmas and opportunities for contestation. These are ongoing because of a lack of consensus on how relationships between competing legal orders are to be determined. This involves questions about the extent to which such orders can coexist, or the conditions under which one law takes precedence over another. In these negotiations legal pluralism provides a repertoire on which social actors can draw in constructing discourses of legitimacy that may be used to promote and justify multiple forms of intervention, action and policy-making in many different arenas. This is so, whether it is utilised to provide a form of higher legitimacy derived from rhetorical claims or whether it is mobilised for more concrete and instrumental purposes. Comprehending what these dimensions entail engages with the multifaceted nature of law that constitutes legal pluralism. It also underlines the extent to which legal spaces are embedded in broader social and political claims that involve complex negotiations over power that cannot be ignored. In exploring these dimensions the researcher not only acquires a more concrete perspective on the social dynamics of legal pluralism in a transnational world, but acquires the potential to open up new avenues for study. For the practice of fieldwork contains 'the possibility of learning something unexpected',[120] giving 'license to curiosity and to following up paths that at the outset simply could not have got on the map'.[121]

---

[118] F and K von Benda-Beckmann and A Griffiths, 'Space and Legal Pluralism: An Introduction' in F and K von Benda-Beckmann and A Griffiths (eds), above n 7 (2009b), 1–23, 4.

[119] For discussions on the power of legal discourse on the 'war on terror', see U Baxi, 'The Globalization of Fatwas Amidst the Terror Wars Against Pluralism' in F and K von Benda-Beckmann and A Griffiths (eds), above n 7 (2009a), 96–114; Greenhouse, above n 22; L Nader, 'Law and the Frontiers of Illegalities' in F and K von Benda-Beckmann and A Griffiths (eds), above n 7 (2009a), 54–73.

[120] Moore, above n 110, 365.

[121] M Strathern, *Property, Substance and Effect: Anthropological Essays on Persons and Things* (London, Athlone Press, 1999) 8.

16

Globalisation and Law: Law Beyond the State

RALF MICHAELS

1. INTRODUCTION

I F GLOBALISATION IS the main paradigm of our time, then a chapter on globalisation and law could also be entitled, simply, 'The Law of Our Time'. Few, if any, areas of law are not—at least potentially—fundamentally impacted by globalisation. In reality, of course, the impact of globalisation on legal thought has, so far, been more limited. That has various reasons. A first reason is that globalisation, although (or perhaps because) it is generally accepted as the new paradigm of society, has remained a remarkably vague concept in general discourse. The fundamental debates over globalisation of the 1990s more or less petered out, without leading to a clear consensus. A second reason is that legal thought has so far reacted to globalisation not with a true paradigm shift but instead by more and more inapt attempts to adapt the methodological nationalism that has provided its paradigm for the last two hundred years or so. The same can still be said about much of social theory, which also remains within such a state paradigm. Globalisation has not, yet, led to a true paradigm shift.

A third reason, finally, is that globalisation poses interdisciplinary challenges, and interdisciplinarity in law and globalisation is still surprisingly lacking. On the one hand, many of the conceptual and theoretical discussions of globalisation ignore or downplay the law as an important factor (beyond an occasional nod to international law). A widespread understanding of globalisation distinguishes three aspects: economics, culture, politics. Law, in words, is absent. In legal thinking, on the other hand, globalisation is often either purely absent (where discussions are purely doctrinal) or appears as a simple idea of internationalisation that somehow influences the law. Legal theory and doctrine have, until recently, often operated with oversimplified concepts of globalisation.[1]

---

[1] The most impressive theory of legal globalisation, and one that has influenced the thinking behind this chapter, is W Twining, *General Jurisprudence—Understanding Law from a Global Perspective* (Cambridge, Cambridge University Press 2009); summarized in part in W Twining, 'The Implications of "Globalisation" for Law as a Discipline' in A Halpin and V Roeben (eds), *Theorising the Global Legal Order* (Oxford, Hart Publishing) 39–59.

This suggests what this chapter needs to accomplish. In the second section, I try to clarify the meanings of globalisation by introducing three different types of concept: globalisation as reality, as theory, and as ideology. This discussion, just as the rest of the chapter, remains necessarily abstract in two ways. First, it remains abstract from particular areas in which globalisation and law meet—human rights, international economic law, family law, etc. Such areas are used as mere examples. The reason is that globalisation is not confined to these areas of the law; it permeates all of law and thus matters everywhere. Second, the chapter remains abstract from specific theories. Globalisation is not a single theory or even a cluster of theories. Rather, it is the emerging paradigm underlying all current theories of both state and law. Instead of presenting individual theories of globalisation, I present what all of them have in common.

In the third section, I discuss what I consider the core theme of globalisation—the transformation of the state, both empirically and theoretically. The state has long provided the tacit framework for our thinking in both social and legal theory. If, as I argue, globalisation overcomes this focus, then a discussion of the transformation it brings with it must put the state at its centre. My analysis therefore follows along the traditional three elements of the state—territory, citizenship and government—and shows how each of them is transformed.

The fourth section, finally, suggests a theory of globalisation and law, called transnational law. This may look like a legal, not a social theory, so some methodological points should be made here. Although I begin by explaining globalisation and then focus more on the law, in this chapter, social and legal theory are not strictly kept apart. This amalgamation performs one main thesis of the chapter. Globalisation, I argue, is not an external development that comes at the law from the outside. Rather, globalisation and law mutually shape each other—today's globalisation is as much a product of a law as it influences the law. A proper theory of globalization must include the law; a proper theory of the law must have a better idea of globalization. Moreover, just as globalization challenges the distinction between the state and society, so it challenges the distinction between social and legal theory. Legal theories must necessarily not just be influenced by social theory; they must become social theories.[2]

2. THREE TYPES OF GLOBALISATION

There is no universally accepted definition of globalisation, and so this chapter will not offer one. But that does not mean that no clarity can be achieved. Closer analysis of the debates suggests that three different types of concept of globalisation must be distinguished. I call these three types globalisation as reality, globalisation as theory, and globalisation as ideology. Inside each type, fruitful debates can be had. Between the types, however, such debates are less useful because the types are largely independent of each other. All three types are relevant for the law, and I will discuss implica-

---

[2] See R Cotterrell, *Law, Culture and Society. Legal Ideas in the Mirror of Social Theory* (Aldershot, Ashgate, 2007); R Banakar, 'Law Through Sociology's Looking Glass' in A Denis and D Kalekin-Fishman (eds), *The New Handbook in Contemporary International Sociology: Conflict, Competition and Cooperation* (London, Sage, 2009).

tions for the law in each segment. However, I suggest that the last one—globalisation as theory—is the most important for legal thought, because paradigm shifts happen neither in reality nor in ideology but in our ways of understanding the world.

Globalisation as Reality

Globalisation refers, first and foremost, to developments in the real world that are, in some way, global. Many such developments are well known. Some concern the relations between states, in particular the growing interdependence[3]—the increase in global trade and global markets (made possible in part through liberalisation of trade), global communication (due in large part to the internet), global travel and global migration, global networks (from online gamers to terrorists), global environmental destruction and climate change, increased hybridity of cultures and societies, increased influence of US values and culture on the rest of the world. All of these developments are undoubtedly real—even though their extent is sometimes overestimated (for example, most consumption is still domestic). But the question is whether all these events amount to something categorically new that we should call globalisation.

In response to these concerns, the most helpful analytics of globalisation is still one proposed by David Held et al in the late 1990s.[4] They suggest that globalisation is characterized by four elements. The first three of these concerns global transactions, and in particular their *extensity*, *intensity* and *velocity*. Extensity describes the stretching of activities across borders and distances. Intensity describes the magnitude of interconnectedness inherent in these transactions. Velocity describes how these transactions have gained in speed—if a letter from Europe to the USA used to take a week, and a fax ten minutes, an e-mail, today, arrives instantly. The fourth factor concerns what Held et al sometimes call *impact* and sometimes the *enmeshment between the global and the local*—the idea that local events can have global consequences, and that on the other hand global developments materialise locally, often with considerable variations. In this reading, there have been globalisations before our time, but ours is the first that scores high on all four of these factors. The increase of global transactions creates new challenges for legal transactions. The fourth element, the enmeshment between the global and the local, is reflected in the law in the increasingly blurred lines between domestic and international law.

This analytics makes it possible to avoid a number of errors about globalisation. First, globalisation is *not a mere transfer of issues from a local to a supranational sphere*, which could be accompanied by a move from domestic to supranational law (as is the case in the European Union, but not really on an international level). Nor does it seem sufficient to think of the local and the global as distinct spheres that may interconnect—a relation well known in law as the relation between domestic law and international law, to be discussed later. Instead, what we find is that the local and the global mutually constitute each other—Boaventura de Sousa Santos speaks, helpfully,

---

[3] RO Keohane and JS Nye, *Power and Interdependence*, 4th edn (Upper Saddle River, NJ, Pearson, 2011).
[4] D Held, A McGrew, D Goldblatt and J Perraton, *Global Transformations: Politics, Economics, and Culture* (Palo Alto, Stanford University Press 1999) 14–28.

of 'globalized localism' and 'localized globalism'.[5] Global commerce relies, to a large extent, on local laws and domestic enforcement mechanisms—its globalism is localised. Human rights movements, on the other hand, attempt to achieve local policy changes by forming networks—their localism is globalised.

Second, *globalisation is not merely uniformisation*. Although increased communication and competition may sometimes lead towards uniformity—of culture, of policies, and of laws—such uniformity always remains partial. In response to ideas of an 'end of history', scholars have found that there are sustainable 'varieties of capitalism' in different capitalist countries.[6] The same appears to be true in law—different countries can still have different laws, and this may even be beneficial. Even where laws look the same formally, their actual application often differs significantly. The same is true for theses of an 'Americanization'.[7] Even if it is the case that US law has been enormously influential in the world—in contract drafting, in commercial law, in constitutional law—this does not, necessarily, create uniformity: American culture and law in turn have become more diverse—the English language and Caucasian ethnicity, once clearly dominant, are giving way to an ever more hybridised culture.

Third, we can meaningfully compare our current globalisation to *earlier globalisations*. We know that many current developments—internationalisation, liberalisation, universalisation and westernisation—are not new and therefore not sufficient for a definition of globalisation as a new phenomenon.[8] International trade has, relative to domestic trade, only recently surpassed the level of importance it had before the First World War. However, this is a problem only if we think that globalisation describes only our current period and are unwilling to use the title for comparable developments in the past—in particular the nineteenth century.[9]

Globalisation as Theory

Even if the empirics were universally accepted, we would still find different interpretations of these empirics, especially as they relate to law. This leads to a second use of the term globalisation—globalisation as theory. Several theories of globalisation exist. What they have in common is a shift away from the paradigm of *methodological nationalism* that has dominated both social and legal thought over the last two hundred years. Methodological nationalism describes an approach in social theory that takes the nation-state as an assumption. Wimmer and Schiller distinguish, helpfully, three modes in which methodological nationalism occurs.[10] First, they argue, social theories

---

[5] B de Sousa Santos, *Toward a New Common Sense*, 2nd edn (Cambridge, Cambridge University Press, 2002) 179–80.

[6] PA Hall and D Soskice (eds), *Varieties of Capitalism: The Institutional Foundations of Comparative Advantage* (Oxford, Oxford University Press, 2001).

[7] For discussions concerning law, see eg RD Kelemen and EC Sibbett, 'The Globalization of American Law' (2004) 58 *International Organizations* 103.

[8] JA Scholte, *Globalization—A Critical Introduction* (New York, St Martin's Press, 2000) 44–46. For Scholte, the only truly new development is deterritorialisation (ibid, 46–50).

[9] eg J Osterhammel and NP Petersson, *Globalization: A Short History* (Princeton, Princeton University Press, 2009).

[10] A Wimmer and N Glick Schiller, 'Methodological Nationalism and Beyond: Nation-State Building, Migration and the Social Sciences' (2002) 2 *Global Networks* 301.

of modernity have largely ignored that modernity—rationalisation, the transcendence of ethnic, religious and (to some extent) economic differences—took place not just within the nation-state; these theories also went along with a persisting ideological nationalism that must thus be viewed as a constitutive element of modernity, not its opponent. Second, social theory has naturalised the nation-state and thereby made it the framework of its analysis of society, rather than its object. Third, and finally, the analytical focus of social science and theory have been restrained by the boundaries of the nation-state. With regard to the later mode, we can speak of the state as container of social processes.[11]

Regardless of whether or not such methodological nationalism has dominated the social sciences[12] it seems clear that it has been predominant in legal debates. Here, methodological nationalism translates into what is called the *Westphalian model*— the idea that the state presents the ultimate point of reference for both domestic and international law. In this model, all domestic law is the law within one state, whereas in international law, the only actors are states and the supranational institutions that states have set up. We can see the prevalence of this model in all legal disciplines. Discussions in public law assume the existence of one government (unitary or not). Private law has been nationalised—not just formally, as codes (in civil law countries), but also in our understanding of it.[13] Even law that is not national law is understood within such methodological nationalism. Thus, international law, understood as law between states, perpetuates the idea of the state as the only relevant reference point. Even where law is moved to the supranational level—as is the case for the law of the European Union—it remains caught in the perspective of the state.[14] Moreover, even where non-state law is described as law, the concept of law used is typically borrowed from the model of state law.[15] Conflicts between legal systems are, in such a perspective, viewed as an exception; the dominant solution in private international law is to allocate international transactions to one state.

Globalisation as theory explicitly rejects such a nationalism and seeks for new ways to theorise both society and law. There is no space in this chapter to address all of these theories,[16] or even only those that are of relevance for the law. Halliday and Osinsky, who explicitly draw on Held's four factors, distinguish four such interpretations that are, at the same time, models of social theory.[17] The first model is *world polity*, the idea of global convergence. Such convergence encompasses the law, which converges either formally, through increased international and supranational law, or informally, through the diffusion of laws and best practices. The second model is what they call *world system analysis*—the idea of hegemonic states and actors that prevent

---

[11] U Beck, *What Is Globalization?* (Cambridge, Polity Press, 2000).

[12] For doubts, see D Chernilo, 'Social Theory's Methodological Nationalism: Myth and Reality' (2006) 9 *European Journal of Social Theory* 5.

[13] See N Jansen and R Michaels (eds), *Beyond the State? Rethinking Private Law* (Tübingen, Mohr Siebeck, 2008).

[14] JM Smits, 'The Draft-Common Frame of Reference, Methodological Nationalism and the Way Forward' (2008) 4 *European Review of Contract Law* 270.

[15] S Roberts, 'After Government? On Representing Law without the State' (2005) 68 *Modern Law Review* 1.

[16] For a useful overview of theories of globalization, see WI Robinson, 'Theories of Globalization' in G Ritzer (ed), *The Blackwell Companion to Globalization* (Malden, MA, Blackwell, 2007) 125.

[17] TC Halliday and P Osinsky, 'Globalization of Law' (2006) 32 *Annual Review of Sociology* 447.

the development of global norms. In law, we saw this for a long time as the imposition of American laws and institutions on the world, be it in commercial law, or in public international law. Their third model is *postcolonial globalism*, the insight into the power imbalances between powerful and less powerful countries. Its consequence is that law is perceived as neutral and objective in the North, which creates and enforces it, while it often looks fragmented and oppressive for actors in the South. The fourth model is *law and development*, the analysis of law reform in developing countries, influenced (and often imposed) by developed countries.

Globalisation as Ideology

A third understanding of globalisation, finally, is yet distinct from the first and the second one. Understood as an ideology, globalisation (and its flipside, antiglobalisation) are political projects, or ideal, perhaps utopian (or dystopian) views of how the world could be. Globalisation as ideology comes in a number of related variants. One variant is that of a *world community* (or a global village, or cosmopolitanism) in which everyone is connected with everyone. That world would be more homogenised and uniform, resting less on parochial views and instead on values common to humanity. Individuals would no longer be citizens of individual countries but instead citizens of the world—globalisation as cosmopolitanism. In law, we find this reflected in ideas of a world law and a world court that were popular in the beginning of the twentieth century and have more recently become popular again[18] Another variant of globalisation as ideology is *neoliberalisation*: the idea that markets should emancipate from states and their regulation and thereby lead to more freedom and more prosperity. The new *lex mercatoria* in particular is a legal ideal expressing this idea. This is linked to the idea of *individualisation*—in the same way in which the state loses its regulatory appeal, so it is argued, the individual agent is strengthened.

Globalisation as ideology is of course closely related to globalisation as reality and as theory. Ideologies formulated in light of existing empirics and theory. Moreover, both the ever-closer world community and the rise of neoliberalism are often presented as inevitable consequences from the state of the world as it is today. This is so, interestingly, both among proponents and opponents of these ideologies. But it seems fair to say that such necessitarianism is false, or at least too simplistic. This is so not only because the future can never be predicted with accuracy (this is, if anything, even more true today than it ever has been, because of the increased velocity of globalisation). Moreover, such necessitarianism ignores two things.[19] One is the array of alternative developments that are possible, both theoretically and practically—alternative globalisations, alternative constellations. The other is the degree to which globalisation is not just a force of nature but a construct of human agency—even if that agency is decentralised and plural—and thus also, to a large extent, of law.

This does not mean that we need to reject globalisation as ideology. Quite to the contrary, if it is true that we need to rethink radically the role and shape of law in

---

[18] See eg R Domingo, *The New Global Law* (Cambridge, Cambridge University Press, 2011).
[19] See eg RM Unger, *Free Trade Reimagined: The World Division of Labor and the Method of Economics* (Princeton, Princeton University Press, 2010).

our changing society, then we need such ideologies as a normative guidance. What we should reject, however, is the conflating of ideology and empirics.

3. LAW BEYOND THE STATE

For all three concepts of globalisation—reality, theory, ideology—the role of the state is central. This is so especially with regard to law, because the state is so central to our contemporary thinking. Thus, it seems appropriate to look in more detail at how the elements of the state have traditionally been constitutive of the law, and how their transformation under the impact of globalisation has effects on the law as well.

Much debate in the 1990s was dedicated to the question of whether or not globalisation caused the state to decline. For some time, decline seemed more plausible in view of the rise of non-state actors such as multinational enterprises and non-governmental organisations (NGOs), regulatory competition and the ensuing limitations on a state's policy discretion, the rise of neoliberalism. Soon, this literature of the decline of the state spurred a counter-debate that emphasised either that states had remained strong, or that they had even been strengthened by globalisation.[20]

That dichotomy of decline and stability was unsatisfactory for a variety of reasons. First, looking at 'the' state as an abstraction from real states has always been a problem, especially so in international law. It becomes more of a problem in discussions of the impact of globalisation. Whatever we understand globalisation to mean, its effects on countries such as the United States or China are undoubtedly different from those on Somalia or Andorra, and so on.

Second, asking what impact globalisation has on states implies that globalisation is an external factor. The question thus ignores the extent to which states (in large part through their law) are among the institutions that create and shape globalisation.[21] The same is true for many discussions of law and globalisation: law is viewed as a recipient of globalisation, although law is also one of the most important shapers of globalisation. For example, international trade does not occur prior to state regulation; rather, liberalised trade regulations and treaties (first and foremost the World Trade Organization) have made it possible. Similarly, the internet is not external to the state and never has been; it was established with strong support by the US government; its functioning today is guaranteed by a myriad of legal regulations.

Third, the dichotomy of decline/strengthening is much too crude. It makes more sense to speak of transformation of the state[22]—and then to analyse the particular characteristics of this transformation. Of course, transformation is nothing new: the states have always, since their inception, been transformed constantly. What may be new is the specifically global character of current transformations. One such aspect is the so-called 'disaggregation' of the state: the insight that states are not unitary actors but combine a multitude of institutions and actors which may deal with internation-

---

[20] Held et al, above n 4, 3–7 speak, parallelly, of hyperglobalisers and globalisation sceptics.

[21] S Sassen, *Teritory, Authority, Rights: From Medieval to Global Assemblages*, 2nd edn (Princeton, Princeton University Press, 2008).

[22] Held et al, above n 4, 7–9; M Shaw, *Theory of the Global State: Globality as an Unfinished Revolution* (Cambridge, Cambridge University Press, 2000); S Leibfried and M Zürn, *Transformations of the State?* (Cambridge, Cambridge University Press, 2005).

alisation and globalisation in different way.[23] Another aspect is the increased number of informal networks in which states now regulate. A third aspect is the increased regulatory competition that puts pressure on states' abilities to maintain their welfare systems.[24]

With these caveats out of the way, some general findings can nonetheless be described. Although all states undergo different transformations, generalities can be described, using the traditional elements of the state. Traditionally, we understand the state to be constituted by three elements: a territory, a population and an administrative structure.[25] The transformation of the state under conditions of globalisation can most fruitfully be described as a transformation of these three elements.

Territory

We assume that a state's laws apply only within its borders—and that, similarly, no other state's laws apply here. This is unproblematic as long as domestic transactions are at stake. But it has even been true, by and large, for questions of public and private international law. In public international law, the idea of territorial integrity and exclusive jurisdiction remains strong—even though it allows for exceptions, and even though the idea of territoriality has been enhanced to include intraterritorial effects of conduct that took place elsewhere. For example, it is now almost universally accepted that a state has jurisdiction over antitrust violations that have an effect on the state's markets, even if the conduct leading to the violation took place elsewhere. Enforcement actions by the state are traditionally confined by a state's borders. Similarly, territoriality has traditionally played a significant role in private international law (or conflict of laws) even though it does not govern absolutely. Thus, the jurisdiction of courts is mostly based on territorial connections such as the defendant's domicile, or the place of a tort, etc. Territoriality also governs questions of applicable law: the law applicable to a tort, for example, has traditionally been determined by the place where the tort occurred. Such territoriality has never been exclusive, however. Not infrequently, the applicable law is determined on the basis of non-territorial connecting factors such as the parties' nationality.

This great importance of territoriality for the law is not a coincidence. Rather, it reflects the great importance that territoriality has, traditionally, had for sovereignty. Territorial integrity and sovereignty are perhaps the most important characteristics of a state. Globalisation challenges this importance of territoriality in a number of ways. First, globalisation often makes geographical distances less relevant. Travel has become much easier, and accessible to large numbers of people. More importantly, improved means of communication—most importantly the internet—have in many cases made such travel far less necessary: the same document can now be edited at various places

---

[23] A Slaughter, *A New World Order* (Princeton, Princeton University Press, 2005).

[24] N Gilbert, *Transformation of the Welfare State: The Silent Surrender of Public Responsibility* (Oxford University Press, 2002).

[25] G Jellinek, *Allgemeine Staatslehre*, 3rd edn (Berlin, Häring, 1914) 394–434. These three elements, supplemented by a fourth (the capacity to enter into relations with other states) are codified in Art 1 of the Montevideo Convention on Rights and Duties of States (signed at Montevideo 26 December 1933; entered into force 26 December 1934).

at the same time. Global production chains are made possible.[26] And social interaction has undergone a qualitative change.[27] Second, for the same reason, state borders have become less important—and less effective. Previously, it may have been possible to keep unwanted information out by simply closing borders and censoring the press. Today, given the global character of the internet, and the omnipresence of blogs and twitters, this has become much harder.

This has posed challenges for the law's territorial character. The law has reacted in different ways.[28] A first reaction is a declined emphasis on territorial boundaries. Newer theories of sovereignty and of jurisdiction replace territoriality with a state's interests—a state is, more and more, entitled to regulate even extraterritorially when the regulated conduct concerns a justified interest. This has meant that large and powerful countries such as the United States now increasingly apply their laws extraterritorially, or pass laws directly with a view to changing policies elsewhere, for example on minimum wages, press freedom and the persecution of religious groups. A second reaction is enhanced international co-operation to regulate transborder transactions. Such co-operation makes sure that rights acquired in one country will be recognised in other countries; it thereby provides the necessary stability for trade. A third reaction is, ironically, a re-established emphasis on territorial boundaries. Somewhat counter-intuitively, judges have begun to justify territorial approaches to the law precisely with the increase in transborder transactions.[29] In such arguments, borders change their character. They may once have been real physical delimitations between countries; now they have become formal entities to delimit application of the law.

Two issues are important. First, territoriality may have become less central, but it has by no means become irrelevant. Access to water—one of the main challenges facing our overpopulated globe—still requires territorial connections; the internet cannot provide us with water. Distances between large cities with airports may now be bridged easily; small outposts are still hard to reach. Fights over territorial boundaries—military, but also legal—remain regular news topics. Sometimes such fights concern clearly important territories, such as the ongoing disputes over territorial authority in Israel and Palestine. Sometimes they concern seemingly irrelevant territories such as the uninhibited Senkaku Tiaoyu Islands, the source of a fierce dispute between China and Japan.

The last example demonstrates something else. The reason such islands are disputed often lies not in their immediate usefulness, but rather in the legal implications of sovereign authority, in particular a state's ability to claim sovereignty over the sea around the island. This leads to the second important issue: the role and importance of territory remain, to a large extent, a function of the law. The internet is deterritorialised not only because of its technology but also because of how it is (or is

---

[26] F Snyder, 'Governing Economic Globalisation' in F Snyder (ed), *Regional and Global Regulation of International Trade* (Oxford, Hart Publishing, 2001) 1.

[27] LJ Strahilevitz, 'Social Norms from Close-Knit Groups to Loose-Knit Groups' (2003) 70 *University of Chicago Law Review* 359.

[28] R Michaels, 'Territorial Jurisdiction after Territoriality' in PJ Slot and M Bulterman (eds), *Globalisaton and Jurisdiction* (Dordrecht, Kluwer Law International, 2004) 105; G Handl, J Zekoll and P Zumbansen (eds), *Beyond Territoriality: Transnational Authority in an Age of Globalization* (Leiden and Boston, Martinus Nijhoff, 2012).

[29] For two examples from North America, see *Tolofson v Jensen* [1994] 3 SCR 1022 (Canadian Supreme Court); *F Hoffmann-LaRoche Ltd v Empagran SA* (2004) 542 US 155 (US Supreme Court).

not) legally regulated. If states resist this deterritorialisation, they still have means to avoid it, as the example of China shows.[30]

Population/Citizenship

The second traditional element of the state is its population. The romantic ideal-isation of the modern nation-state even suggests that the population, understood as an imagined community (a people, a nation) is prior, logically and historically, to the state—first there was the German people, then there was the German state. In reality, the order is often reversed, as Benedict Anderson has shown: the nation-state, once established, defines its own people.[31] To stay with the German example, there was long the chance that Austria would become part of the newly founded German empire; once it was not, it was also clear that the German people would be defined as excluding the Austrians.

The latter shows already the extent to which citizenship is a function not (at least not primarily) of culture or ethnicity, but instead of the *law*. The designation of citizenship is, traditionally, left to each state (though international law limits the dis-cretion of states to deprive their nationals of citizenship). However, once citizenship is thus established, it creates certain rights and obligations vis-à-vis the state. Rights include in particular civil rights (eg elections); obligations include, in particular, military service. Altogether, citizenship both assumes and creates, traditionally, a bond of allegiance, and defines the most important part of an individual's identity.

Globalisation has an impact on this allegiance and identity as well. A first impact concerns the sharp increase in *global migration*. Migration takes place amongst both sought-after specialists and poor economic refugees. As a consequence, in many coun-tries, large parts of the population are of foreign nationality. The law is an enabler of such migration—by making immigration easy for highly coveted high achievers and enabling the exploitation of unskilled labourers. And the law draws consequences from the increasingly multinational character of its populations. First, most countries have made access to citizenship easier—at least for desirable highly qualified individuals. National identity thus turns from a matter of fate to a matter of choice, shifting also the basis for obligations of allegiance.[32] Second, multiple nationality is increasingly gaining acceptance—the old idea that one could only serve one master is giving way to a recognition of multiple national allegiances. Third, more and more constitutional rights are granted to foreigners and citizens alike. Using Marshall's triad of rights as civil, political and social rights,[33] we can see that more and more civil and social rights are extended to foreign citizens. In the European Union, even the core political right of taking part in elections is now sometimes granted to members of other EU

---

[30] See J Goldsmith and T Wu, *Who Controls the Internet? Illusions of a Borderless World* (Oxford, Oxford University Press, 2006).

[31] B Anderson, *Imagined Communities: Reflections on the Origin and Spread of Nationalism* (London, Verso, 2006,).

[32] E Kofman, 'Citizenship, Migration and the Reassertion of National Citizenship' (2006) 9 *Citizenship Studies* 453.

[33] TH Marshall, *Citizenship and Social Class and Other Essays* (Cambridge, Cambridge University Press, 1950).

countries, at least for local elections. As a consequence, the relative importance of national citizenship declines.[34]

Another impact of globalisation concerns *non-state identities*. Together with the transformation of the state, we find a growing importance of multiple identities and allegiances, of which national identity is only one. Pierre may identify not only as a Frenchman but also as a business consultant, a vegetarian, a conservative, a Catholic, a member of a chess club, a Berber, etc. It is inexact (as is sometimes done) to suggest that such a plurality of identities is a novelty of globalisation. Historically, however, all such identities were considered to be transcended by the national identity. Or, put differently: the national identity served to enable all these identities—*e pluribus unum*. What globalisation increases is the degree to which such identities can be experienced in a transnational fashion. Business consultants now work in multinational firms. Conservatives form international alliances. Chess players meet online to play with counterparts around the world. Ethnic groups are able to communicate around the globe. By their transnational status these identities transcend the state, which remains, relatively, localised. States often recognise such non-state identities through their law with multiculturalism and legal pluralism, but these are topics that will be dealt with in the next section.

Government

The third element of the state, finally, is a government, or a functioning administration. This means, first, that the state, through its government, has the power to lay down binding rules as laws that do not require the specific consent of the governed. It means, secondly, that the state, and only the state, is entitled to enforce its laws—it has the monopoly of violence.

It is important to understand the contingency of this dual monopoly of lawmaking and of enforcement—especially because it is often misrepresented in globalisation literature. First, the *monopoly is a historical, not an analytical finding*. The monopoly is an achievement of the modern state, not a characteristic of every conceivable state. The monopoly did not exist in the Middle Ages, when multiple institutions competed. It did not exist in Germany and Austria after World War II, or in Iraq after the Iraq war, because the occupying powers retained considerable rights.

Second, and importantly, the *monopoly does not mean that state laws are the only binding rules in society*. It has always been known that lots of non-state institutions are able to make binding rules and to have them enforced through the state's courts or through arbitration. What the monopoly implies, here, is merely that such powers of non-state institutions acquire their legally binding force only from delegation or recognition by the state. The state is not the only lawmaker, but it is the only institution that is free to determine whose rules should be recognised as law.

What, then, does globalisation change in this picture? A first important development comes from the increased global *interdependence* of states mentioned earlier. We find more and more delegation of lawmaking powers to supranational institutions, be they global (eg the United Nations) or regional (eg the European Union). We find more

---

[34] R Falk, 'The Decline of Citizenship in an Era of Globalization' (2000) 4 *Citizenship Studies* 1.

and more co-operation between nations, either formally through treaties and executive agreements, or informally through ad hoc international consultations. Sovereignty is thus shared. A state no longer holds absolute discretion on lawmaking. However, such co-operation does not necessarily limit a state's effectiveness. Quite to the contrary, multinational co-operation often seems necessary to deal with transnational issues. Properly, one speaks not of a decline of sovereignty but of the 'new sovereignty'.[35] Much is contested here; in the United States, in particular, a large number of scholars and policymakers are trying to protect US self-determination as provided for in the Constitution against such shared sovereignty.[36] Regardless of whether such a defence is normatively attractive, what is striking from a methodological perspective is how it is based in methodological nationalism: the values of the national constitution are taken as a necessary starting point of the discussion, so the outcome—a prioritisation of national over transnational lawmaking—is almost a logical necessity.

A second important and much-discussed consequence concerns the importance of *non-state norms*. Some of these norms are religious, as in the question of whether Islamic and Jewish divorces should be recognised in England or Canada. Some such norms are based in ethnicity, such as the question of whether we should be more lenient with wifebeaters who come from cultures where beating one's wife is common. Some such norms are economic, such as the alleged privately created law governing relations between global businesses, the so-called new *lex mercatoria*. The state accounts for such rules, typically, without recognising them as law.[37] One such mode is incorporation—the transformation of non-state law into state law, as happened with much of canon law in the emergence of the civil law. Another is deference—the transformation of non-state law into facts for the purpose of adjudication, which is what happens traditionally with commercial customs, but also quite often with customary norms of non-state communities. A third one is delegation—the transformation of non-state law into subordinated law, whereby the rules of non-state communities are simultaneously recognised and subordinated to the laws of the state. Calls that non-state rules have to be recognised as law, for purposes of conflict of laws, have so far largely been rejected.

It has become fashionable to refer to the new state of the law as *global legal pluralism*.[38] This implies, frequently, the suggestion that social realities require us to extend our often exclusive focus on state law and call other things law as well: subnational, national, supranational (international) and non-state law. Such categories are helpful, but they have obvious limits. One such limit is, analytically, that the categorisation still defines every type of legal order by how it relates to the state: subnational law

---

[35] A Chayes and A Handler Chayes, *The New Sovereignty: Compliance with International Regulatory Agreements* (Cambridge, MA, Harvard University Press 1998).

[36] See only JL Goldsmith and EA Posner, *The Limits of International Law* (Oxford, Oxford University Press, 2006); JK and J Yoo, *Taming Globalization: International Law, the US Constitution and the New World Order* (Oxford, Oxford University Press, 2012).

[37] R Michaels, 'The Re-*State*-ment of Non-State Law. The State, Choice of Law, and the Challenge from Global Legal Pluralism' (2005) 51 *Wayne Law Review* 1209.

[38] PS Berman, *Global Legal Pluralism: A Jurisprudence of Law Beyond Borders* (Cambridge, Cambridge University Press, 2012); S Richards, 'Globalization as a Factor in General Jurisprudence' (2012) 41 *Netherlands Journal of Legal Philosophy* 129, but see already eg B de Sousa Santos, *Towards a New Legal Common Sense*, 2nd edn (London, Butterworths, 2002) 85–98; W Twining, *Globalisation and Legal Theory* (Cambridge, Cambridge University Press, 2000) 82–88.

stands below the state; supranational law stands above it; non-state law stands beside it. Instead of overcoming the state paradigm of law, the categorisation thus not only depends on that paradigm, it even expands it by fitting even normative orders into it that were not traditionally its part. Second, and relatedly, some of the categories are not very useful. Non-state law, for example, is a category that must group together such diverse phenomena as the new *lex mercatoria* (to be discussed later), Islamic law and corporate standards of conduct. It is hard to see what holds these laws together, and distinguishes them from state law, other than the fact that they are not state law. Third, theories of global legal pluralism often mesh empirical findings (a lot of rules worldwide are not state laws) with theoretical conceptions (we need to theorise all of these as laws) and ideological positions (we have to grant greater deference to non-state orders, though how much exactly often remains unclear). Altogether, although the phenomena described under the heading of global legal pluralism are immensely relevant, their treatment as legal pluralism seems to be of limited use.[39]

One theoretical challenge, however, emerges without doubt. Traditionally, it was possible to treat a legal system as internally coherent and ultimately founded in some highest rule. In legal theory, Hans Kelsen referred to this highest rule (which for him was a hypothetical one) as basic norm (*Grundnorm*); HLA Hart, in his sociologically inspired theory, called it a rule of recognition.[40] Today's world, with its overlapping laws and claims to regulatory authority, with its forum shopping and regulatory conflicts, cannot so easily be framed as such a system. This does not mean that the old theories, established for the state (and grounded in methodological nationalism), have become useless. It has been suggested, not without plausibility, that the relation between EU law and the law of individual Member States can be conceived of as the relation between two separate rules of recognition.[41] But it seems clear that the state's dual monopoly can no longer be maintained on either empirical or theoretical grounds. New theories of law will be needed.

4. TRANSNATIONAL LAW

It is too early to say whether a new paradigm will replace the methodological nationalism that has shaped our thinking about law over the last centuries, and if so, what this new paradigm might look like. A candidate exists, however, in what is called transnational law. Transnational law, as a theory of law beyond the state, is attractive in particular from the perspective of social theory, because it attempts to combine both doctrine and theory, and both law and social reality. In other words, it promises to fulfil the requirement named in the beginning for an understanding of law and globalisation, namely an approach that views both as deeply interrelated.

The concept of transnational law was originally outlined around the middle of the last century by Philip Jessup.[42] Jessup used the term to describe a body of law 'to include all *law which regulates actions or events that transcend national frontiers.*

---

[39] R Michaels, 'Global Legal Pluralism' (2009) 5 *Annual Review of Law and the Social Sciences* 243.

[40] H Kelsen, *The Pure Theory of Law* trans M Knight (Berkeley, University of California Press, 1960/67); HLA Hart, *The Concept of Law*, 2nd edn (Oxford, Clarendon Press, 1994).

[41] N MacCormick, 'Beyond the Sovereign State' (1993) 56 *Modern Law Review* 1.

[42] P Jessup, *Transnational Law* (New Haven, CT: Yale University Press, 1956) quote at p 2.

Both public and private international law are included, as are other rules which do not wholly fit into such standard categories.' This was, in other words, an understanding of law defined not by its sources or its form but by its object, a functional concept. Although formulated prior to discussions about globalisation, it has thus proved useful under conditions of globalisation. This is so because the very boundaries that transnational law tries to transcend—those between public and private law, but also those between international and domestic law—are precisely those boundaries that are closely tied to the nation-state and have therefore become questionable. An additional boundary was not discussed by Jessup but has become prominent and important under globalisation too—the boundary between (formal) law and non-law.[43] This boundary is of particular importance from the perspective of social theory, because its decline requires us to redefine the relation between law and society. I will discuss these boundaries, and their transformation, in turn.

Domestic/International Law

It was described earlier how the distinction between domestic and international law was representative for the Westphalian model and thus for a methodological nationalism in legal theory and doctrine. In their classical conceptions, international and domestic law dealt with different problems and would thus rarely overlap: international law dealt with the international relations between states; domestic law dealt with relations between the state and the individual (public law) or between individuals (private law).

This dichotomy, always fragile, was broken up in the twentieth century. International law, on the one hand, came to include non-state actors, in particular NGOs and multinational corporations. Moreover, international law began to focus more on individuals—in human rights law on the one hand, in international criminal law on the other. In this way, international law came to reach into what had previously been considered internal matters of sovereign states, and began to break up the idea of absolute state sovereignty. Domestic law, on the other hand, has had to internationalise, the more it has been confronted with situations that cannot be located clearly within one state.

As defined by their objects, then, international and domestic law are no longer as distinct as they once were. Today, this is a direct consequence of globalisation and the decline of the 'state as container'. Nonetheless, international and domestic law remain formally distinct, and a theory of transnational law that ignores this formal distinction would have to be deficient.

Public/Private

A second distinction that is challenged by transnational law is the one between public and private law. Public law is the law that governs relations between the state and the individual; private law governs relations between individuals. In some way, this

---

[43] See P Zumbansen, 'Transnational Legal Pluralism' (2010) 1 *Transnational Legal Theory* 141.

distinction exists in all domestic legal systems, though it has different meanings in different legal systems[44] and is less relevant in some (eg English law) than in others (eg French law).[45] This public/private distinction had been challenged already in the late nineteenth and early twentieth centuries. It appeared to replicate a liberal conception of society, in which neatly distinguished public and private spheres existed, and in which the public (the state) and the private (the market, the family, society) would not interfere with each other.[46] In social theory, antiliberal critique of several variants (feminist, critical, deconstructionist, etc) proclaimed a collapse of the distinction and emphasised the public relevance of the seemingly private spheres of economic and personal relations. In legal theory, similarly, the collapse of the public/private distinction was proclaimed, as well as the public character of private law. The idea behind this argument is this: even private law depends, for its enforcement, on the state and its institutions. Insofar as private plaintiffs enforce their private rights, therefore, they borrow sovereignty from the state.

It should be clear, then, that the critique of the public/private distinction is not specific to globalisation; it is a general element of antiliberal critique. Globalisation, however, challenges the public/private distinction in particular ways. The most important of these has to do, again, with the overcoming of methodological nationalism: once the state loses it privileged position, *public law* (as the law that governs the state's relations with private parties) *loses its special position as well*. Traditional regulatory functions of the state are performed by private actors.[47] The state, on the other hand, sees itself in competition with other states and private parties in a global market for investors; it starts to resemble private actors.

This becomes clear in several constellations. The most obvious one may be the proclaimed confluence of public and private international law.[48] Another of these emerges in *international investment law*, which often pairs states and investors on opposing ends. Here, both parties have asymmetrical powers (the state has sovereignty, the investor has assets), and it is not clear, in terms of either power or law, which is superior.[49]

Another area in which the relations become unclear is party autonomy in private international law. Increasingly, the law applicable to contracts is determined by *party choice* rather than governmental interests; furthermore, commercial parties frequently delegate their disputes to arbitrators instead of state courts. As a result, several of the state's core functions—lawmaking, adjudication—are, in effect, privatised. What remains for the state is to recognise the results of such choices and to enforce choice-

---

[44] R Michaels and N Jansen, 'Private Law Beyond the State. Europeanization, Globalization, Privatization' (2006) 54 *American Journal of Comparative Law* 845.

[45] JWF Allison, *A Continental Distinction in the Common Law—A Historical and Comparative Perspective on English Public Law* (Oxford, Oxford University Press, 1996).

[46] For a more nuanced overview of the multiple meanings, see J Weintraub, 'The Theory and Politics of the Public/Private Distinction' in J Weintraub and K Kumar (eds), *Public and Private in Thought and Practice—Perspectives on a Grand Dichotomy* (Chicago, University of Chicago Press, 1997).

[47] T Büthe and W Mattli, *New Global Rulers: The Privatization of Regulation in the World Economy* (Princeton, Princeton University Press, 2011).

[48] A Mills, *The Confluence of Public and Private International Law* (Cambridge, Cambridge University Press, 2009); H Muir Watt, 'Private International Law Beyond the Schism' (2011) 2 *Transnational Legal Theory* 347.

[49] See JA Maupin, 'Public and Private in International Investment Law: An Integrated Systems Approach' (2013) 54 *Virginia Journal of International Law*.

of-law clauses and arbitral awards. In some ways, therefore, such party choice turns the traditional hierarchy between state and parties on its head. This could be viewed as a consequence of a decline of the state, as described before. But it must be recalled (again) that this growing party autonomy is in effect a creation by the state and its laws.

It is important to see that the international/domestic distinction and the public/ private distinction are transformed simultaneously, with perhaps surprising results. Within the state paradigm it was possible to say that all private law is public law because the state has the power (and discretion) to enforce it. This is true, however, only for domestic law. With only little exaggeration, therefore, we can say that *all international law is private law*. And, indeed, we see such developments. In the same way in which societal institutions (eg markets and families) become transnational while states remain local, so private law is becoming denationalised, while public law remains local. The proclaimed *lex mercatoria*, the alleged autonomous law of international markets, is the most prominent example. In reality, such a reconstitution of the public/private distinction as the domestic/international distinction is nothing new: private law was for most of its history understood as transnational, whereas public law was always tied to the state.[50]

Law/Society

A third distinction is highlighted especially in newer theories of transnational law—that between (formal) law and society and its norms.[51] This distinction has long been important for legal theory and practice, for various reasons: only laws are considered binding; only decisions on law have the force of precedent; questions of law are allocated to judges, whereas questions of fact can sometimes be decided by juries, etc. As a consequence, what counts as law was long based, at least in principle, on the basis of formal criteria—we speak of legal positivism. This is so although the distinction was never clear-cut: the common law, for example, is thought to emerge from custom. But what makes it law is its recognition by the state. Nor was the distinction ever all-encompassing; it was always clear that individuals are restrained not only by law but by multiple other norms.

Now, globalisation challenges this distinction. The reason is not merely, as is sometimes proclaimed, a decline in the importance of the state as regulator. If anything, official laws have become more important than they were in the past: the state regulates more and more affairs. Instead, the distinction begins to collapse because the criteria used in legal positivism to define what should count as law are becoming questionable. Legal positivism requires an unquestioned starting point—a constitution, a sovereign people—and this starting point is, in almost all variants, tied to the state. Once we overcome our methodological nationalism, we are required to justify this very starting

---

[50] See R Michaels, 'Of Islands and the Ocean: The Two Rationalities of European Private Law' in R Brownsword, L Niglia and HW Micklitz (eds), *Foundations of European Private Law* (Oxford, Hart Publishing, 2011) 139.

[51] See eg G Calliess and P Zumbansen, *Rough Consensus and Running Code—A Theory of Transnational Private Law* (Oxford, Hart Publishing, 2010).

point. Moreover, we become aware that the starting point itself is a creation of the law, not just its precursor.

The result is that we must understand law and society as being mutually constitutive: law is created by and in society, but law also creates society in the way in which we find it. Empirically, this may not be a novelty. But such mutual constitution now becomes also theoretically unavoidable. This is so because, after the end of methodological nationalism, the state can no longer be distinguished, analytically and theoretically, from society. It becomes a specific practice within which norms, whether we call them legal or otherwise, is negotiated.

In a sense I have come full circle. I began this chapter describing globalisation as a vague and broad concept. I end with presenting transnational law as an equally vague and broad concept. This parallel vagueness is, of course, no coincidence. At the same time, it may be viewed as unsatisfactory. Transnational law does not seem very helpful: if transnational law encompasses all legal (and non-legal!) rules, it may be thought to lose any distinguishing potential. If everything is transnational law, nothing really is. In this sense, the suggestion made in this chapter is much more cautious. Transnational law is not a theory, just as globalisation is not a theory. If anything, transnational law is an attempt to theorise what we find empirically as law beyond the state, and a theoretical conceptualisation of law after the breakdown of methodological nationalism. Transnational law describes a starting point, not an endpoint, of thinking about law. Most of the actual work of translating globalisation into law, and vice versa, still remains to be done.

17

Law and Regulation in
Late Modernity

REZA BANAKAR

INTRODUCTION

O N THE DAY that the UK government was warned by charities and campaigners against cutting welfare benefits to the poorest—an austerity measure aimed at reducing the country's deficit[1]—a parliamentary report revealed that certain multinational corporations, which generated huge amounts of income by operating in the UK, had used 'secretive jurisdictions, royalties and complex company structures'[2] to avoid paying UK taxes.[3] They had been enjoying the right to operate businesses in the country, unfettered by any sense of responsibility, such as declaring their true taxable income to the UK authorities.[4] They were, however, not breaking any UK laws and had been simply making use of existing domestic rules and international agreements to move their profits to low-tax jurisdictions. Although these companies had not committed any illegal act, the revelation nonetheless provoked a barrage of public criticism followed by demands for new legislation aimed at curbing the tax-avoidance practices of multinational corporations. Some argued that legislative intervention was the only way to ensure that these corporations reported their gross profits as well as their taxable income. Others argued that in order to introduce and enforce a regulatory regime capable of clamping down on this type of tax avoidance, one first needed to ensure international co-operation between various countries. There was therefore no point in the UK government legislating against the tax-avoidance strategies of global companies on its own. Vince Cable, the Business Secretary, summed up the situation in this way:

---

[1] 'Cutting Benefits to Poorest "A Tragedy": Campaigners Warn Chancellor Not to Freeze Welfare Payments to Balance Budget', *The Independent* 3 December 2012.

[2] 'MPs Attack Amazon, Google and Starbucks over Tax Avoidance', *The Guardian* 3 December 2012, see www.guardian.co.uk/business/2012/dec/03/amazon-google-starbucks-tax-avoidance

[3] See 'HM Revenue and Customs, Tax Avoidance by Multinational Companies' at www.publications.parliament.uk/pa/cm201213/cmselect/cmpubacc/716/71605.htm#note19

[4] Although Starbucks briefed its shareholders that its UK business was making a 15% profit, it reported to HM Revenue and Customs that 'it [had] made a loss for 14 of the 15 years it [had] been operating in the UK'. See 'HM Revenue and Customs, Tax Avoidance by Multinational Companies', ibid.

Governments have been very fragmented. They are behind the curve. We operate national systems of business taxation and enforcement in a world where companies operate on a global scale, seeking out low tax jurisdictions. Governments are at a disadvantage.[5]

The news of tax avoidance by global corporations belongs to a long line of recent public scandals—including the irresponsible conduct of 'greedy bankers'[6] and their bonuses, the MPs' expense scandal[7] and more recently the News International hacking scandal[8]—in the UK. These 'scandals' raise a number of questions: why do growing numbers of politicians, journalists, bankers, global corporations and other professional and interest groups, who rely on legal rights to safeguard and promote their ideal and material interests, seem unconcerned with their responsibility towards the society in which they operate? Furthermore, why do governments appear either unwilling or unable to regulate the activities of these groups in a more stringent fashion? These questions can, admittedly, lure us into moralising on the conduct of bankers, politicians, journalists or global corporations. However, they are posed here, firstly, to examine how and why, in a society that is becoming progressively individualised and rights-based, rights are being gradually divorced from a sense of social responsibility; and, secondly, to ask why the traditional forms of regulations have proved inadequate, or simply ineffective, in constraining what appears as socially irresponsible public conduct. Is it because the interests of global capitalism, people of wealth and the political elite coincide to such an extent that governments appear indecisive when regulating corporate activities? Has domestic politics been drained of power, while power has been moved to the global level of transnational organisations and corporations? Have the forces of globalisation created, as some have suggested, new 'law-free spaces' where the global elite and corporations may operate unencumbered by external regulation? Although any attempt to answer these questions would inevitably brush against ethics and politics, in the following pages we shall seek a better understanding of these concerns by exploring the social conditions generated by the unfolding of modernity. Following Zygmunt Bauman, it will be argued that in tandem with the move from industrialisation to late (or reflexive) modernity, social norms, relationships and structures, which were previously considered as enduring and stable over time, have become rapidly unstable—thus giving rise to new, short-lived social formations which do not generate or require ethical commitments. The aim of this chapter is to explore how law fares under these conditions.

Two issues should be stressed at the outset. Firstly, the idea of late modernity will be employed critically to tease out the novelty of ongoing social developments, but without endorsing the idea of liquid society as an adequate description of contemporary society. A point will be made that Bauman underestimates the power of domestic politics and the nation-state—a flaw that is linked to his tendency to underrate the

---

[5] 'Vince Cable Calls for International Efforts on Tax Avoidance', *The Guardian* 12 December 2012.

[6] The banking scandal is discussed in the next section.

[7] In a series of articles published during 2009, the *Daily Telegraph* revealed that a large number of MPs across all parties had exploited their right to a second-home allowance and misused the expense system for personal gains. For a discussion, see R Banakar (ed), 'Law, Rights and Justice in Late Modern Society: A Tentative Theoretical Framework' in *Rights in Context* (Aldershot, Ashgate, 2010).

[8] *News of the World* and other British newspapers published by News International, a subsidiary of News Corporation, were accused of engaging in extensive telephone hacking, police bribery and exercising improper influence as part of their work to obtain stories. See the Leveson Inquiry summary at www.official-documents.gov.uk/document/hc1213/hc07/0779/0779.pdf.

force of existing social structures and the continued 'solidity' of many institutional relationships. Secondly, this chapter will use recent events in the UK to advance its theoretical arguments, and thus it will first of all describe the unfolding of late modernity in a British context. Economic developments in Britain often echo events in the United States, or are influenced by EU policies, regulations and directives, but they do not set the standard for assessing social change in other countries. In the same way that different forms of modernity have emerged in countries with different socio-political histories and economic preconditions,[9] different forms of late modernity will also appear in different parts of the world.

The rest of this chapter is divided into three parts. Part I uses the financial global crisis of 2007–08 as a backdrop against which to formulate a number of concerns regarding the limits of legal regulation in late modernity. Part II explores the formation and operations of the late modern state, asking if power is separated from politics and has moved to the level of global organisations. Part III asks what kind of law is emerging de facto in response to the fluidity of late modernity, and how legal imagination envisages the future of law. The chapter concludes by discussing why late modernity, which marks the agency's heightened powers of reflexivity, appears paradoxically wanting in transcendental imagination and determination.

PART I

When Controlling Risks Generates More Risks

The global financial crisis, which began in 2007–08, was a multidimensional crisis brought on by the unfolding of new social and economic conditions driven by, to borrow from Manuel Castells et al, 'the dynamics of a deregulated global capitalism, anchored in an unfettered financial market made up of global computer networks and fed by a relentless production of synthetic securities as the source of capital accumulation and capital lending'.[10] Howard Davies lists thirty-eight separate macro- and microeconomic factors which have been used to explore the causes of the crisis.[11] These include the build-up of considerable global imbalances that generated a surplus of liquidity in the years before the crisis, growing income inequality among countries, flawed macroeconomic policies which financed the rising consumption trends by borrowing, the undisciplined financial markets which facilitated and encouraged this borrowing, and the failure of regulators to bring these markets under some form of control.[12] Although the crisis was systemic and caused by a combination of these factors, it was initially forced to the surface by 'the accumulation of small, and in themselves relatively harmless, decisions made by individual traders or bankers and banks', who were trying to refine the market.[13] Relatively harmless as these decisions

---

[9] See SN Eisenstadt, 'Modernity and Modernization' (2010) *Sociopedia.isa* 3.

[10] M Castells et al, 'The Culture of Economic Crisis' in M Castells et al (eds), *Aftermath: The Culture of Economic Crisis* (Oxford, Oxford University Press, 2012) 2.

[11] H Davies, *The Financial Crisis: Who Is to blame?* (Cambridge, Polity Press, 2010).

[12] Ibid.

[13] E Engelen et al, *After the Great Complacence: Financial Crisis and the Politics of Reform* (Oxford, Oxford University Press, 2011) 9.

arguably were, they concealed an irresponsible attitude towards excessive risk-taking at the expense of others, illustrated by the subprime mortgage scandal, where mortgages were sold on to another party who had no interest in whether or not they defaulted, and the so-called 'greed game' played out by private equity and hedge funds.[14]

In *Fool's Gold*, Gillian Tett, a social anthropologist working as a financial journalist who was given access to the inner circles of elite bankers, describes how a 'tribe' of young traders at JP Morgan unleashed forces which caused the near collapse of the global financial system.[15] This group of investment bankers, who were fervent believers in the efficiency and superiority of free markets, was largely responsible for engineering a sophisticated financial product known as a 'credit derivative'. This complex financial instrument disembedded and recommodified loan transactions, creating a new and opaque culture of finance, which as Sol Picciotto explains, was 'underpinned by arcane techniques and mathematical modelling based upon calculations of relative volatility'.[16] The young traders combined derivatives[17] with the process of 'securitisation', which involved a lender selling its loans to an investment bank. The amalgam enabled banks to turn the risk attached to their loans, ie repayment risks, into a financial product and sell it as if it were bonds or shares. This innovative use of derivatives reduced the capital reserves the banks required for lending more money to a larger number of investors. Put differently, derivatives allowed them to take risk off their books, package it as 'securities' and sell it on in the market for high fees. When employed conservatively, derivatives, according to Tett, were capable of bringing security to global finance and worked as a means of *controlling* risk. At the same time, Tett admits that there were also many investors who used derivatives to 'make high-risk bets in the hope of windfall profit'.[18] Once used in this way, derivatives not only generated more risk, but also dispersed the risk of investment bankers' excesses across the financial system and around the globe.

As the application of credit derivatives spread across the sector, and other banks such as Citigroup, USB, Deutsche Bank and Merrill Lynch also adopted them, they inevitably fell into the wrong hands and were perverted. The largest application of derivatives was in subprime mortgages, which allowed the repackaging of loans to homeowners, who failed to meet the usual requirements, into bonds for sale on an industrial scale. What had been started by a group of traders at JP Morgan as a financial innovation and an attempt to control risks gradually cascaded into a full-scale crisis of global dimensions, a crisis over which (we were told) no one had any control. The governments of the USA and other countries stepped in only once the international economic crisis was in full bloom to bailout investment banks with

[14] R Peston, 'We Lose in Greed Games', blog posted on the BBC website, 28 March 2008: www.bbc.co.uk/blogs/thereporters/robertpeston/2008/03/we_lose_in_greed_game.html.

[15] G Tett, *Fool's Gold: How Unrestrained Greed Corrupted a Dream, Shattered Global Markets and Unleashed a Catastrophe* (London, Little Brown, 2009).

[16] S Picciotto, 'Dis-embedding and Regulation: The Paradox of International Finance' in C Joerges and J Falke (eds), *Karl Polanyi, Globalisation and Potential of Law in Transnational Markets* (Oxford, Hart Publishing, 2011) 159.

[17] Derivatives are contracts between two parties. Their value 'derives from credit risk attached to an underlying bond, loan or other financial asset' (see Tett, above n 15, 322). According to Alessandrini, this standard definition conceals the speculative properties of derivatives. D Alessandrini, 'Regulating Financial Derivatives: Risks, Contested Values, and Uncertain Futures' (2011) 20 *Social & Legal Studies* 441–62, 445.

[18] Tett, above n 15, 15.

hundreds of billions of dollars of taxpayers' money to avoid a collapse of their national economies.

Tett worked on the assumption that complex derivatives per se were not responsible for the crisis, and if anyone was to be blamed, it was the few 'bad apples' within the banking community who exploited them. There are good reasons for paying attention to the actions and decisions of those individuals who acted recklessly, yet the forces which triggered the financial crisis were, as pointed out above, multilayered, caused by macro- and microeconomic factors, and cannot be reduced to the actions of one group of individuals. One cannot ignore that Tett's 'greedy bankers' operated within a system which lacked transparency and did not allow the external monitoring of the way derivatives were traded. The system was, moreover, driven by an insatiable appetite for profits and paid little heed to warnings about the spread of a speculative economy divorced from production.[19] When examining the financial crisis in terms of the actions of the few 'bad apples', we run the risk of overlooking the role of macroeconomic factors as well as the impact of laissez-faire capitalism that has been spreading in the UK and the USA since the 1980s.

With these points in mind, I use Tett's description of the financial crisis to articulate three sets of concerns at the levels of the individual (human agency or social action), social system (or social structure) and global economy (transnational relations). Focusing on individual bankers and mortgage brokers, the question begging an answer is how they could act in such an *unrestrained* fashion. How could they make highly risky decisions motivated by what appears to be their own short-term interest alone, as well as without a sense of responsibility to their investors, the financial institutions upon which their livelihood depended and the larger society? To repeat, these questions are not meant as an invitation to moralise on the culture of banking, but to explore the limits of formal regulatory regimes under the normative conditions of late modernity. Notwithstanding Tett's attempt to blame 'greedy bankers', the actions of individual actors also need to be assessed in the context of the financial institutions in which they worked and in view of the imperatives of a financial system based on profit-making and speculation. Although banking and finance are regulated domestically (eg the Banking Act in the UK and the Glass–Steagall Act in the USA) and internationally (eg the Basel Accords), the story of the elite traders who manufactured these complex derivatives nevertheless suggests that there are social spaces within which the tribe of bankers may roam free, beyond the reach of the usual forms of regulation and undeterred by external monitoring. Thus, we are led to ask: how can public spaces and networks, such as those of elite bankers, exist beyond the reach of the formal (official) and informal (unofficial/extralegal) regulatory mechanisms of early modernity? Do they exist because they are de facto out of reach of the public authorities, such as central banks and regulatory agencies, with the responsibility for the financial system, or because the liberal state is unwilling to interfere in the operations of the market economy for ideological reasons? Alternatively, could it be that a regulatory system, which has been founded on the market economy's past performance and dysfunctions, is doomed to failure because its formal mechanisms cannot stay abreast of the con-

---

[19] Financial derivatives allow both hedging against risks and speculation in pursuit of windfall profit, and it could be very difficult to differentiate between these two functions of derivatives. See Alessandrini, above n 17, 442.

tinuously changing structures of the capitalist system?[20] These questions will allow us to sharpen our focus on the role of the state, which is responsible for introducing and enforcing formal regulatory regimes, and ask: why were Western governments unable to prevent the crisis and could do so little after the event to redress its consequences?

How Could They Act in such an Unrestrained Fashion?

To understand the constraints exerted on social action in late modern society we need to start with the cultural and political programme of modernity which, as argued by Eisenstadt, has 'entailed a shift in the conception of human agency, of autonomy, and of the place of the individual in the flow of time'.[21] Many forms of modernity have developed in different parts of the world, but despite their differences they share a quest for emancipating human agency from the restraints of tradition. Modernity, liberally paraphrasing Anthony Giddens, replaced the claims of tradition by reason and conferred a durable appearance upon social institutions by transforming their authority from one based on traditional relationships to one based on legal bureaucracy, which facilitated the centralisation of institutional power.[22] The combined power of modern institutions made the expansion of modernity unavoidable; yet this power, which reached its peak under industrialisation, could not totally dominate social developments because 'reflexivity', to borrow again from Giddens, subverted reason, 'where reason [was] understood as the gaining of certain knowledge'.[23]

In its most basic form, reflexivity refers to people's ability to talk to themselves silently in their heads, or as Margaret Archer explains, to have an 'internal conversation'.[24] In its more recent sociological conceptualisation, it indicates a state of self-knowledge through self-dialogue, which allows the individual to reflect on herself in relation to her circumstances and vice versa, to observe herself as subject and object and devise a plan of action accordingly. In this sense, reflexivity links social action and social structures by throwing light on the process through which human agency becomes socially embedded. However, in its radical or late modern form, it highlights the disembeddedness of the agency, or the increasing ability of the agency to reflect on structures in order to emancipate oneself from the constraints of social institutions in a way which, although not new in the context of modernity (for modernity has, admittedly, been partly about the liberation of human agency from the fetters of traditional authority, practices and institutions), is nevertheless unprecedented in its scope and societal consequences.[25]

The reflexivity inherent in modernity has been enhanced by globalisation, accelerating the rate of structural change and causing what Bauman calls the 'liquefaction' of the 'solid' structures and relations of early modernity.[26] Taking this idea to its final

---

[20] See FA Hayek, *The Counter-Revolution of Science: Studies on the Abuse of Reason* (New York, Free Press of Glencoe, 1952).

[21] Eisenstadt, above n 9, 3.

[22] A Giddens, *The Consequences of Modernity* (Cambridge, Polity Press, 1999) 39.

[23] Ibid, 39.

[24] M Archer, 'Reflexivity' (2010) *Sociopedia.isa* 5.

[25] M Archer, *Making Our Way through the World: Human Reflexivity and Social Mobility* (Cambridge, Cambridge University Press, 2007) 2.

[26] Z Bauman, *Liquid Modernity* (Cambridge, Polity, 2000).

conclusion, Bauman describes contemporary society in terms of 'liquid modernity', which refers to a society where 'the conditions under which its members act change faster than it takes the ways of acting to consolidate into habits and routines'.[27] Under these 'liquid' conditions, human agency becomes increasingly *disembedded*, that is, independent of social structures and free from institutional and traditional ties which previously constrained social action at the level of social interaction. This also means that *flexibility*, that is, 'a readiness to change tactics and style at short notice, to abandon commitments and royalties without regret', rather than 'conformity to rules' will serve the individual's interest more effectively.[28] As the reflexivity of the agency is enhanced and disembeddedness spreads across society, the moral contingency of social action grows rapidly, influencing the way social institutions and systems operate. As pointed out by Ulrich Beck, systems such as polity and law become less capable of responding to sociocultural complexity and moral diversity in their environment through further functional differentiation (we shall discuss this point further in Part II).[29] Social forces, which could be evoked by law and polity to reshape society and mould behavioural patterns under the first stage of modernity, either become less effective or redundant, as formal regulation fails to keep pace with continuously evolving social structures.

In short, the apparent solidity and timeless *appearance* of modernity offered an ostensibly durable foundation for building relationships based on trust, certitude and stability, which in turn provided a rational basis for social engineering and reform. These solid structures are now undermined by late modernity's temporary assemblages of shifting and precarious positions, as well as transitory social spaces and forms of community. At the centre of this development we find the increased significance of agency vis-à-vis structures. As Martyn Denscombe points out, this

> does not imply that 'structural' factors cease to exert any influence at all. But it does mean that there is a tendency for them to exert less influence than in the past and for greater significance to attach to individual choices in terms of the creation of self-identities.[30]

This idea can tentatively explain the seemingly unrestrained conduct of the young bankers and other professionals we discussed above. The tribe of young bankers is increasingly 'emancipated' from the general social and moral constraints of the society in which they live and operate, and they belong to the mobile elite of well-to-do professionals who are not constrained by national borders and cannot be pinned down in any one locality or jurisdiction; consequently, their activities cannot be controlled through the traditional means of regulation external to their field of work. Their daily work provides a site (or a rudimentary type of 'habitus',[31] which we shall discuss below as a *technical habitat*) for knowledge-based collaboration, but is largely carried out at

---

[27] Z Bauman, *Liquid Life* (Cambridge, Polity, 2005) 1.

[28] Z Bauman, *Liquid Times: Living in an Age of Certainty* (Cambridge, Polity, 2010) 4.

[29] U Beck, *Risk Society: Towards a New Modernity* (London, Sage, 1992).

[30] M Denscombe, 'Uncertain Identities and Health-Risking Behaviour: The Case of Young People and Smoking in Late Modernity' (2001) 52 *British Journal of Sociology* 157–77, 160.

[31] 'Habitus' refers to 'the habitual, patterned ways of understanding, judging, and acting which arise from our particular position as members of one or several social fields, and from our particular trajectory in the social structure'. See R Terdiman's introduction in P Bourdieu, 'The Force of Law: Toward a Sociology of the Juridical Field' (1987) 38 *Hastings Law Journal* 811.

the global—multijurisdictional[32]—level, where no single external normative system can effectively monitor or regulate individual conduct. For example, as soon as the UK government started considering a supertax to regulate the bonus culture of investment bankers and brokers in the City, the Mayor of London warned that any such measure would only result in them moving to other centres of finance with more liberal tax regimes.[33] The chief executive of one of the state-backed banks warned a few months later that a large number of investment bankers were quitting the UK, causing a 'rapid exodus' as a result of the 'bonus fiasco'.[34]

Tett's use of the word 'tribe' to describe the young group of investment bankers at JP Morgan is significant in itself. In an unrelated study, Ethan Waters also employs the word to portray a group of college-educated young people in California, who being liberated from the structural (economic as well as cultural) pressures to which their parents were subjected choose not to form families, or marry much later than their parents did.[35] At the same time, they are so driven by a culture of hyperindividualism that their lives, as described in Waters' *Urban Tribes*, appear as completely self-absorbed and egoistic.[36] Therefore, their heightened reflexivity, which emancipates them from certain constraining aspects of institutions, does not appear to empower them to look or step beyond modernity's epistemological premises. There is, however, more to this emerging trend than liquefaction. Instead of forming traditional families, the young adults in question are forming their own communities of friends, which Waters calls 'urban tribes'. Tett's tribe is different from that of Waters in that it is created through the knowledge-based practices of traders: it requires of its members shared knowledge of how to trade in derivatives and other financial products, which temporarily joins them together in a collaborative network. However, Tett's and Waters' tribes, different as they are, draw attention not only to the rise of new social formations, but also to the emergence of new forms of inequality and alienation. These tribes consist of well-educated, economically independent and socially successful young professionals, whose privileged backgrounds have granted them access to economic as well as cultural resources required for living flexibly and detached from local concerns and structural pressures. They do not, in other words, represent the whole of society, but a privileged group.

As Hanne Petersen explains, a widening gap is emerging between elite citizens, the successful high-flying global citizens who feel responsible for little more than their own wellbeing and interests, and a local underclass consisting of those who feel socio-economically vulnerable and culturally defenceless.[37] This underclass does not live a liquid life, but takes on more than its share of anxiety and uncertainty, as it is culturally and economically undermined by social processes and political forces beyond its control. In response to late modernity's new forms of inequality, new kinds of social movements, such as the antiglobalisation movement, are born. Occupy Wall Street is

---

[32] They might physically be based in one jurisdiction while operating in other jurisdictions.

[33] Boris Johnson, the Mayor of London, claimed that up to 9,000 bankers would leave London to avoid paying the taxes. *Evening Standard* 1 January 2010.

[34] *Evening Standard* 4 March, 2010.

[35] See E Watters, *Urban Tribes: Are Friends the New Family?* (London, Bloomsbury, 2004).

[36] It should be noted that Watters' journalistic study (ibid) mainly concerns college-educated young people in California. The trend which Watters describes is, nevertheless, familiar to many Western and non-Western societies today (a few of the people Watters interviewed lived in Britain and other countries).

[37] H Petersen, 'Rights and Responsibility' in Banakar, above n 7, 333–47.

an example of a new form of spontaneous social networking, which is organised in cyberspace as well as in urban space. This movement is also known as 'We are the 99%', which refers to the disparity in income and wellbeing between the majority of Americans and the 1% who control the country's wealth.

From Community to Transitory Social Networks

The individual never totally submitted to the normativity of social structures, institutions, customs and traditions. A gap has always existed between injunctive norms, which prescribe what *ought* to be done, and descriptive norms, which reflect empirically ascertainable patterns of behaviour (or how people behave in actual fact).[38] Nonetheless, the growing potential of human agency to free itself from the normative constraints of social structures is decisive for understanding the limits of formal regulation under late modernity. 'The central aspect of regulatory compliance', as Casey and Scott explain, consists of 'institutionalisation and embedding of norms within some wider set of structures.'[39] Employment law, which we shall discuss in Part III, exemplifies how law was employed to embed certain values, such as fairness and equal treatment, in the structures of the labour market. This type of regulation requires the durable structural relations of *early* modernity capable of normatively influencing the agency. In the context of *late* modernity, however, the traditional form of regulation which employs law to ground values and norms in social structures and institutions loses its determinacy, as the agency's reflexivity grows vis-à-vis structures and institutions. Does this therefore mean that the late modern agency exists in a normative vacuum? The fact that Tett considers the young bankers as a 'tribe' suggests that although they might exist as 'nomadic individuals',[40] whose fleeting reality enables them to stay beyond the effective reach of formal (official) and informal (unofficial) regulatory mechanisms of early modernity, they nevertheless exist as a form of community. This late modern form of community is, admittedly, not the same as Ferdinand Tönnies' *Gemeinschaft*,[41] but is instead a temporary *network* created to facilitate collaboration between individual actors.

Gemeinschaft, or the traditional community, is based on tacit mutual understanding, interpersonal trust and care, and as such it has a more or less pronounced ethical dimension. According to Bauman, a traditional community generates inalienable rights, long-term commitments and obligations that bind together the participants of a community.[42] It is therefore, historically speaking, the primary source of law and social order.[43] *Gemeinschaft* may be contrasted with late modern communities or networks

---

[38] For a discussion, see R Banakar and S Nasrolahi Fard, 'Driving Dangerously: Law, Culture and Driving Habits in Iran' (2012) 39 *British Journal of Middle Eastern Studies* 241–57.

[39] D Casey and C Scott, 'Crystallization of Regulatory Norms' (2011) 38 *Journal of Law and Society* 76–95, 77.

[40] RLM Lee, 'On the Origins of Belonging: Confronting Cosmopolitanism in the Late Modern Age' (2010) 46 *Journal of Sociology* 169–86, 170.

[41] F Tönnies (1955) *Community and Association (Gemeinschaft und Gesellschaft)* (London, Routledge and Kegan Paul, 1955).

[42] Z Bauman, *Community: Seeking Safety in an Insecure World* (Cambridge, Polity, 2001) 71.

[43] For a discussion, see R Banakar, 'Can Legal Sociology Account for the Normativity of Law' in M Baiers (ed), *Social and Legal Norms* (Aldershot, Ashgate, 2013).

based on the short-term association of groups of individuals brought together by a common specific interest, which might have been formed 'around "problems" with which individuals are struggling separately and on their own in their daily routine (for example weight-watching or inch-fighting)'.[44] 'Whatever the focal point of these communities', writes Bauman, their common feature is 'the superficial and perfunctory, as well as transient, nature of the bonds emerging between their participants.'[45] Most importantly, these communities do not unite their members by creating 'a web of ethical responsibilities',[46] and they require neither long-term commitment nor geographic locality as their base. Instead, they spread a culture of hyperindividualism which, despite being excessively rights-based, understands rights as entitlements without obligations to others.[47]

If the tribe of bankers, derivative traders and other global elites do not form a *Gemeinschaft* or cultivate long-term webs of ethical responsibility, then what holds them together as a 'tribe'? In her ethnographic study of Japanese derivative traders (which was conducted between 1997 and 2001, ie before the global financial crisis), Annelise Riles provides a tentative answer to this question by focusing on the knowledge-based practices of traders.[48] In Riles' account, derivative traders generate a technical (in contrast to a value-based) context for collaboration through their day-to-day standardised tasks and knowledge practices comprising a 'constellation of both theoretical and doctrinal manoeuvres and material documents'.[49] Riles, who hopes to find a way of making financial regulation more 'stable, effective and democratic',[50] suggests that the daily practices of traders involving the application of legal techniques associated with securing contractual obligations, more specifically collaterals, in the derivative markets provides a possible starting point for regulatory innovation. Her focus is on the *form* of the law itself—the hollow-cored form of regulation such as Japan's 'netting law', the content of which is unspecified—to which she attributes agency. Moreover, Riles contends that in the deployment and application of the law as a form, rather than substantive judgements, resides a commitment to democracy (this is reminiscent of Jürgen Habermas's idea of 'law as a medium', which was discussed in Chapter 4 in this volume, and Gunther Teubner's theory of reflexive law[51]), whilst 'private law doctrines and techniques can stand as a bulwark against the complexity and indeterminacy of the market'.[52] Specialised technical knowledge and the practice of law in derivatives markets do not create a web of ethical commitment—

---

[44] Bauman, above n 42, 71.

[45] Ibid.

[46] Ibid, 72.

[47] For a discussion on the 'colonisation' of rights in late modernity, see C Smith, 'The Sequestration of Experience: Rights, Talk and Moral Thinking in "Late Modernity"' (2002) 36 *Sociology* 43–66; Banakar, above n 7.

[48] A Riles, *Collateral Knowledge: Legal Reasoning in the Global Financial Markets* (Chicago, University of Chicago Press, 2011) 41.

[49] Ibid, 38.

[50] Ibid, 232.

[51] Reflexive law does not require the enforcement of particular substantive rules and does not set particular goals to be achieved in a regulated area. Instead of authoritatively determining the social function of su-systems, or trying to regulate their input and output performances, reflexive law tries to establish norms of procedure, organisation, membership and competence that can 'further the development of reflexive structures within other social sub-systems'. G Teubner, 'Substantive and Reflexive Elements in Modern Law' (1983) 17 *Law and Society Review* 239–85, 275.

[52] Riles, above n 48, 164.

or a 'habitus'—at the transnational level, but they do generate a technical 'habitat' for traders, bankers and other financial actors to collaborate 'according to carefully scripted routines'.[53] Transitory as this space might be, it provides a site for internal self-regulation, which according to Riles lends itself also to state intervention.

There are also forces external to global finance capable of exerting regulatory pressure on transnational corporations. The nation-states remain the most powerful of these—the fact that they chose not to intervene in the markets is, however, another matter which we shall discuss in the next part. States aside, there are other forces in play. The moral condemnation which was triggered by revelations about MPs' expenses, bankers' bonuses or the tax-avoidance strategies adopted by multinational corporations in the UK constitutes a normative force that compels not only corporations but also individual tribe members to take notice of how their actions are viewed from the outside. However, these normative forces, being dependent on the mass media's erratic reporting, lack durability and consistency. Public protests, for instance, against tax avoidance by multinational corporations in the UK lasted for one week and soon abated as new events made the headlines. Moreover, protests have a local dimension (although they are often in part organised in cyberspace, they still require action in urban spaces), while 'nomadic individuals' and the transnational corporations they work for are not committed to local concerns. The burgeoning literature on corporate social responsibility engages with the regulatory challenges that this type of detachment poses by suggesting new forms of self-regulation backed by law.[54] However, their primary assumptions—that through self-regulation norms of social responsibility can be implanted into corporate structures and cultures—appear incompatible with late modernity's postulate that structural conditions can change faster than it takes to consolidate norms of conduct. If true, then what is gained from transplanting norms of social responsibility in corporate structures whose durability is a function of transient networks which do not generate or require ethical commitments? Before we answer this question, we need to consider how the nation-state is influenced by late modernity.

PART II

The Transformation of the State

Within the banking sector and among politicians there were those who knew that the risks to major financial institutions had been dangerously underestimated. For example, as early as 1992, the financier Felix Rohatyn described derivatives as 'financial hydrogen bombs built on personal computers by 26-year-olds with MBAs'.[55] Nevertheless, Western governments chose not to interfere in the way the banks were recasting the financial system. As Alan Greenspan, the former US Federal Reserve Chairman, admitted, they knew that the crisis was growing but did nothing, instead presuming

---

[53] Ibid, 65.

[54] R Shamir, 'Social Responsible Private Regulation: World Culture or World Capitalism?' (2011) 45 *Law and Society Review* 313–36, 315; J Black, 'Paradoxes and Failures: "New Governance" Techniques and the Financial Crisis' (2012) 75 *Modern Law Review* 1037–63.

[55] Quoted in R Manne and D McKnight, *Goodbye to All That? On the Failure of Neo-liberalism and the Urgency of Change* (Melbourne, Black and Agenda, 2010) 24.

that the banks could and would regulate themselves.[56] Greenspan's admission that they decided not to get involved could be described as primarily ideological and an indication of how the logic and representations of markets have been internalised by governments and turned into 'an optimum organizational principle for state and society as a whole'.[57] If true, then we still need to explain why the logic and representations of the market exercise such a hold over late modern states and society. Are states unable to intervene and regulate banks and transnational corporations because, as Vince Cable remarked (see the Introduction), in a world where corporations operated globally, governments had become 'very fragmented' and could act only nationally?[58] Has power been split, as suggested by David Lyon, from local politics, and thus from nation-states, and moved to the level of global relations and transnational corporations?[59]

Here we notice a tendency to underestimate the force of domestic politics. Although it is true that power is exercised globally by, among others, transnational corporations, and, arguably, is outside the reach of national governments, it does not follow that domestic politics has been drained of all power in the way that theorists of late modernity, such as Lyon, argue. The nation-state has not been dissolved by the forces of late modernity, and according to Centeno and Cohen remains 'by far the most powerful force shaping economic life'.[60] The global economy continues to rely on state protection of property rights and 'the supposedly anachronistic notion of territorially defined authority'.[61] The late modern nation-state 'functions with a fundamental governance paradox: policy and enforcement remain within the responsibility of individual states, yet transactions occur in a space policed by none of them'.[62] Following Centeno and Cohen, we may postulate that states and governments were unwilling to intervene when they were warned at an early stage of a pending financial crisis, because they saw the burgeoning global crisis as a problem outside their proper domain of action. This stance was motivated by the ideology of a free market economy and justified by the practical difficulties inherent in regulating private financial activities which take place outside the jurisdiction of the state. Thus, regulators in the USA, the UK and elsewhere relied on—and believed in—the ability and willingness of investment banks to regulate the financial sector's excessive risk-taking. To make matters more complicated, the regulators to whom the regulation of transactions had been delegated—and many regulators such as the credit-rating agencies belonged to private industry bodies—were part of the problem for, as Picciotto points out, they had 'developed a vested interest in encouraging rather than controlling, the growth of markets' in complex financial instruments.[63] Nonetheless, once the collapse of the sector became imminent, states did step in to bail out the banks, demonstrating their ability to act. The policies implemented by national gov-

---

[56] R Neate, 'Financial Crisis: 25 People at the Heart of the Meltdown – Where Are They Now?' *The Guardian* 6 August 2012, www.guardian.co.uk/business/2012/aug/06/financial-crisis-25-people-heart-meltdown.

[57] Shamir, above n 54, 315.

[58] See *The Guardian*, 12 December 2012, above n. 5.

[59] D Lyon, 'Introduction' in Z Bauman and D Lyon, *Liquid Surveillance* (Cambridge, Polity Press, 2013) 5.

[60] MA Centeno and JN Cohen, *Global Capitalism: A Sociological Perspective* (Cambridge, Polity Press, 2010) 8.

[61] Centeno and Cohen, ibid, 16–17.

[62] Ibid.

[63] Piccotto, above n 16, 161.

ernments between 2007 and 2010, according to Davies, were instrumental in avoiding 'the recession turning into a depression', which in turn left many governments with huge fiscal deficits'.[64] It is therefore more accurate to argue that the nation-state has remained an important force under late modernity, although it has redefined its 'mission' in response to the intensification of reflexivity—it has reduced its social role, which required ethical commitment to improved welfare, while continuing to protect and promote the global economy. It is, at the same time, 'widening and strengthening its penal intervention',[65] as well as expanding its powers of surveillance, in order to manage risks more effectively.

A Shift to Risk Management

As the sphere of market economy took shape in the nineteenth and early twentieth centuries, wrote Karl Polanyi in *The Great Transformation*, economic relations which had previously been a function of social organisation—or embedded in social structures—were dislocated from their societal context and turned into an autonomous system.[66] This system possessed its own imperatives and did not exist to serve the society out of which it had been born. Moreover, it had the ability to impose its norms and form of rationality upon other spheres of action and reconstruct law and politics as well as everyday social relationships (a process which Habermas later described as system's colonisation of lifeworld[67]). Much of the 'juridification' of the social sphere that was carried out during the 1960s and 1970s by the welfare state aimed at reversing this disembedding process, that is, was an attempt to re-embed the forces which had been unleashed by the market economy in the social context.[68] The welfare state was in turn overtaken in the 1980s by profound transformative changes in the way economic relations were organised. According to Brendan Edgeworth, these changes, which resulted from the rise of globalisation, included 'the dismantling of welfare safety nets; the greater reliance on markets to restructure regulatory frameworks; and the progressive withdrawal of the states from former areas of responsibility'.[69] The welfare state did not cease to exist and continued its stabilising social role, aimed partly at easing the socially dysfunctional effects of the expanding market economy, albeit with a severely weakened ideological conviction in its own ability to generate lasting social reform.

With the rise of transnational and global forces, we observe a move from the welfare-oriented social and legal policies of the 1960s and 1970s, to forms of regulation more concerned with managing risks than addressing the causes of social problems.

---

[64] Davies, above n 11, 12.

[65] L Wacquant, 'Comment la tolérance zéro vint à l'Europe Sociétés sous contrôle', *Manière de voir*, March–April, quoted in Z Bauman, 'Uncertainty and other Liquid Modern Fears' in J Priban (ed), *Liquid Society and its Law* (Aldershot, Ashgate, 2007) 18.

[66] K Polanyi, *The Great Transformation: The Political and Economic Origins of our Time* [1944] (Boston, MA, Beacon Press, 2001). Also see Joerges and Falke, above n 16.

[67] J Habermas, *Legitimation Crisis* (Boston, Heinemann Education, 1975).

[68] See G Teubner (ed), *Juridification of Social Spheres* (Berlin, de Gruyter, 1987).

[69] B Edgeworth, *Law Modernity, Postmodernity* (Aldershot Ashgate, 2003) vi. Edgeworth contends that postmodernity generates its own specific forms of law. One form is reflected in the development of norms and institutions of global governance—the extension of which is the emergence of law without the state—and, the other, in replacing traditional public law regulations with contractual arrangements for the delivery of public services.

The shift to risk-management strategies is often explained by reference to the inability of late modern social systems and institutions (eg law, economy and polity) to respond fully to and control the increasing complexity of moral conflicts arising out of the 'unforeseen consequences of functional differentiation' through further functional differentiation.[70] This does not imply that early modern social systems responded *fully* to their environment. Instead, it is suggested here that early modern systems operated in a social environment that offered, relatively speaking, prolonged contextual continuity and structural stability, which in turn translated into dispositional durability in patterns of social action. This allowed social systems to respond, if not fully then at least in a seemingly meaningful fashion, to moral conflicts in their environment.

At the local level, late modernity marks the failure of social welfare ideology, which required an omnipotent nation-state to realise its vision of a better society, that is, a welfare society that guaranteed a minimum standard of living, education, healthcare and employment for all its citizens. Put simply, the modern welfare state was characterised by governmental *regulation*, often carried out by introducing legal measures aimed at enhancing *social integration* through a fair allocation of resources, duties and responsibilities. The state was seen as a potential force for good, capable of reorganising social conditions for the better, by legally regulating social and economic relationships. In contrast, late modernity is characterised by governmental *deregulation* (not to be confused with the reduction in the volume of laws and regulations)[71] and system integration through the market economy. In a Western European context in general, but the UK in particular, this is achieved by facilitating two apparently separate, but on closer inspection interrelated, processes at global and local levels by: (i) promoting the rise of transnational networks in production, global finance and trade; and (ii) by passing on responsibility for the general welfare of citizens—for employment (benefits), healthcare, retirement, education, housing, etc—to individual citizens themselves. We also see a move from policies designed to promote social integration through participation and mutual recognition to ones based on cultural *assimilation* (eg in respect to immigrants and ethnic and religious minorities), social *exclusion* (reflected, for example, in the emergence of criminal policies aimed at prevention, preferring to build more prisons to house an ever-growing number of inmates for longer periods instead of attempting to rehabilitate them)[72] and political *neutralisation* (eg in respect to the way moral issues are politically marginalised[73]). Assimilation, exclusion and neutralisation provide the bases for developing forms of social control, which are exercised through an ever-increasing machinery of surveillance, ultimately motivated by the belief that the risk posed by various threats can be calculated and pre-empted.

---

[70] U Beck, *World Risk Society* (Cambridge, Polity, 1999) 2.

[71] The notion of 'deregulation' refers here to the growing privatisation of public services and not to an overall reduction in the number of laws and regulations.

[72] In late modernity, rehabilitation—what Bauman calls the 'recycling of human waste'— is no longer taken seriously. Imprisonment—or 'waste disposal'—is considered too expensive, which means that the public must accept living with an ever-growing threat and fear of crime and must find their own ways of protecting themselves against it. See Bauman, above n 65, 22.

[73] For a discussion see Banakar, above n 7.

PART III

What kind of law and legality can respond to the increasing fluidity of late modernity's social structures? Here we should distinguish between at least three levels of law and regulation.[74] The first level concerns traditional areas such as contract, family, property and criminal justice, which uphold a particular type of social organisation (preserving the status quo). The second concerns public international law, which is of sovereign states but is created to regulate interstate relationships. The third level is that of transnational law of supranational agencies such as the EU, the International Monetary Fund, the World Bank and the United Nations Commission on International Trade Law. Since lack of space does not allow for a discussion on all of these levels separately, in the remaining part of this chapter I shall briefly touch on recent developments within family law and employment law to exemplify how traditional areas of law are influenced by the liquefaction of social structures, before discussing forms of law and regulations which are introduced to bring about social change under late modernity.

When Law Loses a Clear Concept of the Social

The family, once regarded as the bedrock of human society, has been undergoing dramatic transformation in recent decades. Baroness Deech, the Chairwoman of the Bar Standard Board in the UK, warned recently that the 'traditional Christian image of a lifelong marriage is no longer accurate because of the changing nature of relationships and the introduction of legal rights for same-sex couples'.[75] She also warned that human rights law in the UK 'may soon rule that it is discriminatory to ban homosexuals from marrying in the same way that heterosexual couples do'.[76] This not only highlights the changing constitution of the family in Britain, but also shows that local considerations on policy issues are no longer contained by the legal constraints of the national state. Legal deliberations, which are part of any such institutional change, place the national discourse on the family in a broader sociolegal context created by transnational forces. The Human Rights Act 1998, introduced to give further effect in UK law to the rights contained in the European Convention on Human Rights, brings transnational forces to bear on national developments. In addition, in Western Europe, attitudes to marriage, family formation and sexual relationships have changed over the last few decades, leaving their mark on EU law, which in turn influences the legal systems of all Member States.[77]

These changes in attitude and practice can be suggestive of the expansion of a

---

[74] William Twining distinguishes between nine levels of legality, ranging from global and international to transnational, sub-state and non-state law. See W Twining, 'The Implications of "Globalisation" for Law as a Discipline' in A Haplin and V Roeben (eds), *Theorising the Global Legal Order* (Oxford, Hart Publishing, 2009) 39–59.

[75] M Beckford, 'Baroness Deech: English Law No Longer Has Clear Concept of Marriage', *Daily Telegraph* 16 March 2010, at www.telegraph.co.uk/news/uknews/law-and-order/7449696/Baroness-Deech-English-law-no-longer-has-clear-concept-of-marriage.html.

[76] Ibid.

[77] M Antokolskaia, 'Comparative Family Law: Moving with the Times' in E Örücü and D Nelken (eds), *Comparative Law: A Handbook* (Oxford, Hart Publishing, 2007) 241–62, 241.

'liquid society', which the 'solid' traditional bonds of family are melting away. The legal system cannot stay outside social transformations and has to observe, respond to and in many cases accommodate emerging new values, attitudes and practices in the larger society. As a result, traditional institutions of the law can also appear to be losing their solidity and durability. To borrow a phrase from Baroness Deech, the legal system's attempts to accommodate changes in its environment reveal that 'English law has lost any clear concept of marriage'.[78] However, it would be misleading to ignore the fact that traditional family structures also persist, and the majority of families continue to consist of married heterosexual couples. More significantly, as argued by Joanna Wyn et al, the fragmentation of institutional and traditional structures under late modernity does not necessarily lead to the dissolution of the family, but can instead heighten its significance, albeit in a new form.[79] Once new family formations are normalised and allowed to coexist alongside traditional families, they subvert the normativity of traditional structures by constantly reminding us of the existing alternative models of social organisation and our options to act differently. This engenders greater normative uncertainty and institutional fragmentation, but it does not necessarily entail the liquefaction of all solid structures and relationships as Bauman suggests.

Using Law to Generate Uncertainty

Employment law establishes a general legal framework for terms and conditions of employment, which grounds certain legal standards or values—such as fairness, equal treatment and reasonableness—into the structure of a working relationship, thus safeguarding how employees are hired, treated in work and dismissed. In so doing, it regulates the behaviour of employers and their staff as well as their relationship, bringing continuity and certitude into the spheres of work and production. Viewed in this way, employment law helps to solidify the spheres of employment and labour relations, while embedding market relationships in a social context. But social embeddedness, permanence and stability, which were valued highly during early modernity, are no longer regarded as useful organisational qualities by many employers. To meet the challenges of rapidly shifting and perpetually evolving globalised markets, businesses have been increasingly adopting 'non-standard employment relations' based on temporary or short-term contingency work.[80]

According to the UK government, businesses find current employment laws difficult to implement, which deters them from creating new jobs and employing more staff. This in turn, 'slows the growth of businesses and the economy'.[81] Subsequently, the government announced in January 2011 that it planned an overhaul of the law in order to allow employers to 'hire and fire at will'.[82] The 'reform' was heavily criticised by

---

[78] Beckford, above n 75.

[79] See J Wyn et al, 'Beyond Transitions Metaphor: Family Relations and Young People in Late Modernity' (2011) 48 *Journal of Sociology* 3–22, 4.

[80] AL Kalleberg, 'Nonstandard Employment Relations: Part-time, Temporary and Contract Work' (2000) 26 *Annual Review of Sociology* 341–65.

[81] 'Making the Labour Market More Flexible, Efficient and Fair', www.gov.uk/government/policies/making-the-labour-market-more-flexible-efficient-and-fair (accessed 9 January 2013).

[82] 'Employment Law "Will Let Bosses Hire and Fire at Will"' *Evening Standard* 27 January 2011, at www.standard.co.uk/news/employment-law-will-let-bosses-hire-and-fire-at-will-6560471.html,.

unions and the opposition Labour Party, and the government was eventually forced to drop the proposal the following year. Instead, in the Enterprise and Regulatory Reform Bill,[83] the government provided provisions to grant employers new powers, including introducing a cap on unfair dismissal payouts (reducing the amount of compensation for unfair dismissal by two-thirds), making it more difficult to claim unfair dismissal (the employer requires two years' service instead of one before claiming unfair dismissal) and reducing the redundancy consultation time from 90 to 45 days. Finally, the government announced that from April 2013 workers would be able to forfeit some of their employment rights, such as the right to unfair dismissal and redundancy, in return for tax-free shares. This new employment contract is intended to accomplish the initial idea of empowering employers to 'fire at will'.[84]

The public political discourse on employment rights and the way the law is 'reformed' to satisfy the requirements of businesses demonstrate how certain areas of law might fare as the social structures and institutional settings (in this case companies, corporations and firms) which grounded law's normativity (they crystallised the legal standards and values of employment) adopt more flexible and transitory organisational arrangements. As the law struggles to respond to the needs of businesses, employment law starts to melt away, therefore generating flexibility for employers and uncertainty for employees. Employment law is no longer the normative framework for enhancing stability and certainty in the relationship between the employer and the employee; rather, it is an integral part of the organisational fluidity of late modernity.

The Possibility of Social Change

At the height of the welfare state, when legal measures were frequently used to bring about social change, the law showed great regulatory limitations and proved not to be the effective instrument of social control and engineering many had hoped.[85] Under late modern conditions, where law's normativity can no longer find a durable foothold in fleeting social structures, legal measures aimed at generating new patterns of behaviour or social change grow ever more ineffective. In contemporary Britain, law is therefore employed all the more for risk-management purposes, that is, to control the risk of threats which, paradoxically, do not lend themselves to rational assessments or calculations. This is achieved through enhanced methods of surveillance and measures devised to pre-empt threats, the best example of which is to be found in the UK's antiterrorism legislation, which at best generates more and new risks.[86]

Law and surveillance are becoming all the more interwoven. An era of modern surveillance, which began with Jeremy Bentham's 'panopticon', devised as a solid piece of 'moral architecture',[87] is giving way to the 'post-panopticon' era. Lyon main-

---

[83] Enterprise and Regulatory Reform Bill, at http://services.parliament.uk/bills/2012-13/enterpriseandregulatoryreform.html.

[84] 'Workers Can Swap Rights for Company Shares' *The Guardian* 8 October 2012, at www.guardian.co.uk/politics/2012/oct/08/george-osborne-workers-rights-shares .

[85] See R Banakar, 'Sociology of Law' (2011) *Sociopedia*.

[86] See R Banakar, 'Pre-empting Terrorism? Two Case Studies of UK's Anti-Terrorism Legislation' in Banakar, above n 7.

[87] Lyon, above n 59, 11.

tains that the solidity of the panopticon, where neither the prisoners nor the invisible watchers could move physically, has been dissolved and replaced by the liquidity of new surveillance technologies:

> [N]ew surveillance practices, based on information processing rather than the discourse that Foucault had in mind, permit a new transparency in which not just citizens but all of us, across the range of roles we play in everyday life, are constantly checked, monitored, tested, assessed, valued and judged. But the converse is clearly not true. As the details of our daily lives become more transparent to the organizations surveilling us, their own activities become less and less easy to discern.[88]

The Communications Data Bill proposed recently by the UK government exemplifies the rise of the 'post-panopticon' era. The Bill aims at expanding the powers of the police and security services to monitor the websurfing and email activities of all those who live in Britain. This measure is, according to the government, part of a policy to tackle paedophilia, terrorism and other forms of crime.[89] This demonstrates the gradual transformation of law, from an instrument of social change, a mechanism for ensuring continuity and upholding the status quo, into a tool for supporting sophisticated technologies of surveillance.

The description of law as a formal instrument for managing risks does not offer a promising starting point for speculating on the future of the law. Understandably, legal imagination has turned to normative theories, such as those propagating corporate social responsibility and cosmopolitanism, in search of a law which can meet the challenges of contemporary global society. Those who are concerned with the consequences of globalisation, but remain committed to the ideology of a market economy, continue to search for methods of re-embedding the market forces. They either assume, as Riles did,[90] that law enshrines democratic potentials and the agency to realise social goods, or tend to resort to theories of corporate social responsibility in search of a form of law or regulation which can tame the power of transnational corporations and alleviate the dysfunctional consequences of global capitalism.[91] Advocates of one strand of this approach maintain that corporations have to incorporate norms of social responsibility—in effect self-regulate themselves—because they operate in a 'world culture' which expects them to do so, that is, this so-called 'world culture' constrains them normatively.[92] One problem with this approach is that in order for corporations to devise self-regulatory mechanisms, they need durable structures as well as a sense of ethics, whereas they operate in a highly fluid environment that does not lend itself easily to internal or external monitoring and does not foster 'a web of ethical responsibilities'.[93] More importantly, the idea of a 'world culture' as a coherent and normatively forceful global entity is fraught with difficulties, for globalisation interconnects and produces unity as well as fragmentation.[94] Assuming that 'world

---

[88] Ibid, 12.

[89] 'Draft Communication Bill to be Redrafted', 11 December 2012, at www.bbc.co.uk/news/uk-politics-20676284.

[90] Riles, above n 48.

[91] KE Davis et al, 'Indicators as a Technology of Global Governance' (2012) 46 *Law and Society Review* 71–104; Black, above n 54.

[92] See Shamir, above n 54.

[93] Bauman, above n 42, 72.

[94] D Held, 'Democracy: From City States to a Cosmopolitan Order?' in RE Goodin and P Pettit (eds), *Contemporary Political Philosophy*, 2nd edn (Oxford, Blackwells, 2006) 688.

culture' is an empirically discrete unit of analysis, we still have to take into account its interplay with transnational corporations. Moreover, as it interacts with and influences corporations, it is in return shaped normatively by the latter.[95]

There are, however, other universally inclined theories, such as cosmopolitanism, which articulate concerns with globalisation but draw inspiration from natural law by emphasising the moral duty of each person towards the rest of humanity. Cosmopolitanism consists, according to Jeremy Waldron, of several approaches:

> For some it is about the love of mankind, or about duties owed to every person in the world without national or ethnic differentiation. For others, the word 'cosmopolitanism' connotes the fluidity and the evanescence of culture …; and it anticipates a world of fractured and mingled identities. For still others … cosmopolitanism is about order and norms and not just culture and moral sentiment. It envisages a world order, and (in some views) a world government or world polity. According to the cosmopolitan, there are already many norms in the world which operate at a cosmopolitan level, including (for example) the principles that define human rights and crime against humanity, the laws that govern refuge, asylum, travel, and migration.[96]

Whereas Ulrich Beck asserts that cosmopolitanism has left the realm of philosophical castles in the air and has entered reality as 'the defining fixture of reflexive modernity',[97] Robert Fine adopts a more cautious approach by suggesting that it 'should be understood as a research agenda rather than a fixed idea or state to be achieved'.[98] In contrast, Raymond Lee describes it as a 'fragile and incomplete political settlement' and 'a flawed attempt in promoting a new sense of liberal mindedness'.[99] How cosmopolitanism can generate a universal sense of solidarity and belonging in the highly liquid conditions of late modernity remains a contested issue.[100]

Why should we entertain ideas such as corporate social responsibility and cosmopolitanism? The structures and relationships which create corporations are transitory and not disposed to grounding ethical responsibility through the force of law or moral pressure. Cosmopolitanism, on the other hand, appears as the desperate attempt of the liberal-minded intelligentsia to transcend the present impasse by resorting to ideas from the past. In this sense, both approaches arguably reinforce late modernity's sense of stalemate—that there is nothing beyond the culture of consumerism and a legal order based on risk management. In the same vein, late modernity—whether viewed as a theory or an empirically based description of contemporary conditions—lacks imagination and the impetus to break with modernity's order of things. Human agency might be gaining heightened reflexivity vis-à-vis social structures, but individual imagination and transcendental determination remain constrained by the normativity of consumerism and the celebration of hyperindividualism, which is but a form of alienation and translates into a lack of responsibility for others. This should cause neither despair nor nihilism, for in the theoretical and empirical unoriginality of late modernity lies latent the promise of a paradigm shift. Anticapitalist protesters occupying

---

[95] Shamir, above n 54.

[96] J Waldron, 'Cosmopolitan Norms' in S Benhabib (ed), *Another Cosmopolitanism* (Oxford, Oxford University Press, 2008) 83–101.

[97] U Beck, *Cosmopolitanism Vision* (Cambridge, Polity, 2006) 2.

[98] R Fine, *Cosmopolitanism* (London, Routledge, 2007) 133–34.

[99] Lee, above n 40, 172.

[100] Ibid, 40.

the square in front of St Paul's Cathedral, in London in 2011, the Occupy Wall Street Movement in New York and similar movements in Spain, Italy, Portugal, Greece and Israel are examples of late modernity's 'networked social movements' in progress.[101] Theoretical constructs such as corporate social responsibility and cosmopolitanism can potentially contribute to the birth of a new 'state of being' by putting ethical conflicts inherent in the global market economy under the spotlight and demanding solutions. Their potential to generate social change can be preserved by employing them as normative standards for evaluating and challenging existing conditions, claims and disputes. Thus, they carry within them the seeds of future developments.

---

[101] For a discussion on new forms of social movements, see M Castells, *Networks of Outrage and Hope: Social Movements in the Internet Age* (Cambridge, Polity, 2012).

18

Studies of the Legal Profession

OLE HAMMERSLEV

T
HE LEGAL PROFESSION has been a central object of research within
a number of sociological traditions, including mainstream sociology, sociology of law, sociology of professions, political sociology and elite sociology.
Regardless of whether we study the state, the rise of capitalism, elites, comparative
legal systems or transnational institutions, we cannot avoid considering the role of
the legal profession in the development of modernity. Dalberg-Larsen explains that
one reason for the central role professions play in our studies of the law is that their
functions are socially practised and members of the profession share many common
features.[1] The legal profession is also of great interest due to the role it has played in
constructing Western states which were built partly with law by jurists. These states
expressed their norms of organisation and values through law. Such interdependence
between the development of modern law, modern legal institutions and the construction of modern European states has positioned members of the legal profession
as elite agents with state expertise.[2] Thus, the legal profession has been seen as a
vantage point from which we may examine the relationship between power, elites, law
and society in general. More specifically, sociology of law has focused in various ways
on the legal profession, in order to examine its role in creating law, legal institutions
and social organisation, and to explore how it has contributed to the application and
enforcement of the law. As the past works of Karl Marx, Emile Durkheim and Max
Weber demonstrate, classic sociology of law acknowledges the importance of lawyers,
Western formal rational law and modern legal institutions for the development of
industrialisation and capitalism. Talcott Parsons and Niklas Luhmann, among others,
followed Durkheim and Weber when they argued that the legal profession provided
a precondition for the development of modern Western states and formal rational
law. In this sense, a focus on the legal profession provides a point of entry into the
study of law and the construction of states. As Philip Lewis stressed, 'If one is at

---

[1] J Dalberg-Larsen, *Lovene og Livet: En retssociologisk grundbog* (Copenhagen, Jurist- og Økonomfor-
bundets Forlag, 2005) 90.
[2] E Kantorowitz, 'Kingship Under the Impact of Scientific Jurisprudence' in M Clagett, G Post and
R Reynolds (eds), *Twelfth-Century Europe and the Foundation of Modern Society* (Madison, University of
Wisconsin Press, 1961) 89–111; P Bourdieu, 'From the King's House to the Reason of State: A Model of the
Genesis of the Bureaucratic Field' (2004) 11(1) *Constellations*.

all concerned with the sociology of law, one is bound to be concerned with legal professions.'[3]

The purpose of this chapter is to discuss studies of the legal profession while exploring their theoretical and methodological implications for the sociology of law. First, the text focuses on classic convergence studies of legal professions, which examine the function of lawyers in society. Next, it considers conflict studies and discusses the role of lawyers in legitimising and reproducing social structures and the capitalist system. Third, the chapter takes into consideration the more recent studies of women entering into the profession, and finally, it discusses studies which break specifically with the starting point of traditional studies and focus on elite lawyers' resources and strategies as a precondition for the development of transnational law and transnational institutions.

1. DEFINING THE LEGAL PROFESSION

The concept of professions is often used as a term for a specific form of social group with some degree of stability over time. As Dalberg-Larsen notes, the group is not kept together because of close personal relations, as in the case of a family group for instance, yet many studies claim that members of the legal profession have a sense of solidarity through shared values.[4] Professions are often defined as consisting of a group of vocational practitioners with an academic education. They have the monopoly to practice certain tasks and, to a certain degree, have internal control to observe their professional codes of conduct.

Following Lawrence Friedman, we can divide and classify approaches to studies of the legal profession in a number of ways.[5] Firstly, studies which focus on the development of the legal profession and seek to determine which social phenomena generate demand for the legal profession, that is, what is the causal explanation(s) for the existence of the legal profession. Secondly, some studies examine the internal characteristics of the legal profession by enquiring into who lawyers are and how the profession is composed in terms of gender, age, political background, etc. Moreover, such studies examine how the profession is organised, how it is controlled and how autonomous it is from the state. Thirdly, Friedman mentions studies that examine the impact of the legal profession on society—how does its work impact on law, social relations and institutions? Friedman stresses that the latter category of studies is 'the most difficult of all but also the most interesting'.[6]

There are, however, other ways of approaching the legal profession which require focusing on different aspects thereof. For example, several studies have examined the development of law firms and lawyers,[7] whereas others have concentrated on

---

[3] P Lewis, 'Comparison and Change in the Study of Legal Professions' in RL Abel and P Lewis (eds), *Lawyers in Society. Comparative Theories* (Berkeley, University of California Press, 1989) 27–79, 31.

[4] Dalberg-Larsen, above n 1, 89.

[5] LM Friedman, 'Lawyers in Cross-Cultural Perspective' in Abel and Lewis, above n 3, 1–26.

[6] Ibid, 2.

[7] See eg M Galanter and T Palay, *Tournaments of Lawyers: The Transformation of the Big Law Firm* (Chicago, University of Chicago Press, 1991); JP Heinz and EO Laumann, *Chicago Lawyers: The Social Structure of the Bar* (Chicago, Northwestern University Press, 1994); T C Halliday, *Beyond Monopoly: Lawyers, State Crisis, and Professional Empowerment* (Chicago, Chicago University Press, 1987).

judges,[8] yet other studies have taken an interest in comparing different parts of the legal profession or have highlighted its transnationalisation.

One of the difficulties associated with comparing—and writing about—the legal profession is caused by the embeddedness of professional groups in diverse social and historical settings in different countries. Due to different countries' variations in terms of training, function, status, income, entry into the profession, etc, the same English terms often refer to different phenomena. Thus, in English, as Schultz notes:

> '[A]ttorney,' 'barrister' and 'solicitor' designate practicing lawyers in common law countries, while the term 'advocate' tends to be used ... to refer to practising lawyers in civil law countries, signalling the fact that their work comprises both advisory and forensic functions.[9]

The same challenges of definition can be found concerning terms such as 'judges', 'magistrates' and 'notaries', which refer to different legal constructions in different countries. The overarching term of a person with a legal degree who is qualified to work in any branch of the legal profession is a 'jurist' in most civil law countries, whereas it signifies an academic expert in law in common law countries.

2. FUNCTIONAL STUDIES OF THE LEGAL PROFESSION

The functional approach dominated studies of the legal profession throughout the twentieth century. Often these studies had their background in Durkheim's work on how modern society developed towards a greater differentiation of labour,[10] a process that led expert and professional groups to become increasingly specialised and differentiated from each other. Moreover, with a greater differentiation of labour, an altered sense of community occurred whereby solidarity changed from mechanic to organic, which meant that there was greater moral individualisation through which individuals in the different subfunctions or subsystems internalised moral structures differently. Against the backdrop of the division of labour and organic solidarity, Durkheim began to focus on professional ethics, by examining how different occupational groups and professional entities developed. The function of professions and professional ethics was to ensure against anomalies within society by mediating between the state and market, on the one hand, and the individual on the other.[11] This functional approach gave rise to several studies of different professions. The belief in a societal need for professions because of their stabilising function is reflected most explicitly in the following quotation:

> [Professions] inherit, preserve and pass on a tradition ... they engender modes of life, habits of thought and standards of judgement which render them centres of resistance to crude forces which threaten steady and peaceful evolution. ... The family, the church and the

---

[8] See eg B Abel-Smith and R Stevens, *Lawyers and the Courts: A Sociological Study of the English Legal System 1750–1965* (London, Heinemann, 1967); O Hammerslev, *Danish Judges in the 20th Century: A Socio-Legal Study* (Copenhagen, DJØF Publishing, 2003).

[9] U Schultz, 'Introduction: Women in the World's Legal Professions: Overview and Synthesis' in U Schultz and G Shaw (eds), *Women in the World's Legal Professions* (Oxford, Hart Publishing, 2003) xxv–lxii, xxxi. See also RL Abel, 'Comparative Sociology of Legal Professions' in Abel and Lewis, above n 3, 80–153, 101.

[10] E Durkheim, *The Division of Labour in Society* (London, Macmillan, 1984).

[11] E Durkheim, *Professional Ethics and Civic Morals*, 2nd edn (London, Routledge, 1992).

universities, certain associations of intellectuals, and above all the great professions, stand like rocks against which the waves raised by these forces beat in vain.[12]

Talcott Parsons was more nuanced in his approach, even though it followed the same direction. Like Durkheim, Parsons focused on the specific 'third power' modern professions hold in society due to their positions within the state. He claimed that it is not primarily profit or self-interest that makes professional agents act, nor is it the political power to dominate others,[13] because professionals are carriers of altruistic virtues in the sense that they serve others. He also acknowledged that many of the organisations of modern society are dependent on how the professions function, and thus the professions are important power bases in society.[14] Furthermore, Parsons focused on the legal profession when he recognised the importance of the professions for the development of the capitalistic economy and the rise of modern Western states. Parsons noted that professions as groups with specific roles have a certain collective orientation and their members are usually

> trained in that tradition, usually by a formally organized educational process, so that only those with the proper training are considered qualified to practice the profession. Furthermore only members of the profession are treated as qualified to interpret the tradition authoritatively and, if it admits of this, to develop and improve it. Finally, though there usually is considerable division of labour within such a group, a substantial proportion of the members of the profession will be concerned largely with the 'practical application' of the tradition to a variety of situations where it can be useful to others than the members of the profession itself.[15]

Despite the fact that each profession is divided in different subgroups with different roles, these groups have often been examined as a unit. Professionals are the carriers of traditions and professional knowledge, which are transmitted to them through education. Parsons saw professions as important in the modern state, because their power provides certain functions which society demands. Social systems have normative expectations vis-à-vis social roles, which are related to introjected values that become motivating factors for social action. In order for systems to survive, they are coherent and relatively closed, and they can be delimited as systems from other systems by their norms and roles.

This functional approach, inspired by Parsons, has guided a number of studies about the legal profession from various angles and approaches. In his early work, Luhmann examined the West German legal profession and found that the legal system developed its own distinct set of legal codes as the profession established itself. When a system has differentiated, its framework of communication follows specific patterns and logic that are different from other forms of communication in other systems. As the legal profession gained a monopoly over interpreting legal codes, it became a point of coupling between the legal system and other social systems.[16] Disputes that arise

---

[12] AM Carr-Saunders and PA Wilson, *The Professions* (Oxford, Clarendon Press, 1933) 497.

[13] T Parsons, 'Professions' (1968) 12 *International Encyclopaedia of the Social Sciences* 536–47.

[14] T Parsons, 'The Professions and Social Structure' in *Essays in Sociological Theory* (New York, The Free Press, 1954) 39–49; T Parsons, 'A Sociologist Looks at the Legal Profession' in *Essays in Sociological Theory* (New York, The Free Press, 1954) 370–85; T Parsons, 'The Law and Social Control' in WM Evan (ed), *The Sociology of Law* (New York, The Free Press, 1962) 60–68.

[15] Parsons, ibid (1952), 372.

[16] N Luhmann, *Rechtssoziologie* (Opladen, Westdeutscher Verlag, 1987) 105.

outside the legal system are transformed into legal disputes when they enter the legal system, and are then handled according to legal codes. It is here that the legal profession provides a link between the legal system and its surroundings. According to Luhmann, the function of the legal profession in modern society is to create normative expectations between different kinds of social systems.[17] Nonetheless, Luhmann was worried that the cohesiveness of the profession was decreasing as the number of jurists increased significantly and because many jurists specialised following the development of the welfare state. He found that the law was differentiating and that the 'power base of law' was changing 'from central to local pressures and from written instructions to face-to-face interaction'.[18] Disputes are resolved in other systems, which means that dispute resolution is moving out of the legal system and into systems with codes other than legal—in other words, disputes are being solved by extralegal means.

The studies of Vilhelm Aubert on the Norwegian legal profession are nuanced exemplifications of the functional approach. Aubert examined the role of the legal profession and the law in the development of the modern Norwegian state. Like Luhmann, he applied statistics to a number of members from different professions in order to examine how society was organised and how it solved its conflicts. The number of jurists in different parts of the profession—seen relationally and in relation to other professions—indicates, according to Aubert, which types of expert and expertise society needs in order to maintain social order.[19] Against this statistical background, and a large body of biographical material about jurists, Aubert found that the legal profession was one of the largest occupational groups in Norwegian society in the nineteenth century. Members were employed in the most important positions in society: in the central administration and in commerce, they took part in developing infrastructure and the finance sector just as they were well represented in politics—a lot of jurists sat in parliament. Thus, by counting jurists in relation to other professions and examining in which areas of society they were engaged, Aubert could conclude that the legal profession had a crucial impact on the development of the modern Norwegian state and its economy. In addition, Aubert stressed that the reason for the crucial role of the legal profession was a societal need for jurists because the function of the legal profession was to create trust between different individuals and parts of society in their interactions, trade and transactions. Aubert drew implicitly on a Durkheimian framework:

> In a rural society the population will trust their kin, their neighbours and a few figures of authority. However, there are few social bonds capable of creating a basis for trust beyond this limited circle. From this derive a large number of difficulties when new economic enterprises are going to be established. Credit, commerce, loyal payment of taxes, contracts of work, establishment of banks and limited liability companies, presuppose that it is possible to

---

[17] N Luhmann, 'Die Profession der Juristen: Kommentare zur Situation in der Bundesrepublik Deutschland' in *Ausdifferenzierung des Rechts. Beiträge zur Rechtssoziologie und Rechtstheorie* (Frankfurt am Main, Suhrkamp Verlag, 1981) 173–90; N Luhmann, *Das Recht der Gesellschaft* (Frankfurt am Main, Suhrkamp Verlag, 1993).

[18] N Luhmann, 'The Self-Reproduction of Law and its Limits' in G Teubner (ed), *Dilemmas of Law in the Welfare State* (Berlin, Walter de Gruyter 1985) 111–27, 123.

[19] V Aubert, 'The Changing Role of Law and Lawyers in Nineteenth- and Twentieth-Century Norwegian Society' in DN MacCormick (ed), *Lawyers in Their Social Setting* (Edinburgh, Green, 1976) 1–17; V Aubert, *Continuity and Development in Law and Society* (Oslo, Scandinavian University Press, 1989) 338; V Aubert et al, *The Professions in Norwegian Social Structure 1720–1955* (Oslo, Institute for Social Research, 1961).

establish trust between people who have not been capable of trying out each other's reliability through personal contact over a period of years. The preconditions for the growth of trust, which can make the nation into a common market, are many. However, I venture to propose the hypothesis that the growth of a fairly large legal profession in Norway contributed to establish this trust on certain points in the social structure where this was a critical precondition. This took place in part as a consequence of the participation of lawyers in the establishment and development of the governmental apparatus itself, including the judiciary.[20]

Having been the most important profession during the nineteenth century, or—in Aubert's words—'the midwives' of the modern state, a change happened following the development of the welfare state. During the twentieth century, and especially in the 1960s and 1970s, other professions entered into central state and market positions and removed legal entities from their important positions. According to Aubert, this meant that society needed forms of expertise other than what the legal profession could provide. At the same time jurists specialised and became more—in line with Weber's idiom—technocratic.

3. FUNCTIONAL STUDIES IN GENERAL: COUNTING MEMBERS OF THE LEGAL PROFESSION

By examining where the legal profession occupies positions, the functional approach examines its role and that of law in society. Law is analysed through the legal profession, as professionals are seen as the 'carriers' of law, while its members are actors who hold the authority or even monopoly to resolve conflicts through the correct interpretation of legal sources. In general, studies inspired by functionalism discuss the role of the legal profession—based on numbers of professionals—in the development of the modern state. The state transfers the monopoly of certain societal functions to the professions, which in turn can be seen in relation to the development of the state.

By means of statistical sources, these studies—inspired by functionalism—examine the legal profession by counting the overall number of members of different branches of the legal profession, by using the same kind of data. The studies are based primarily on statistics and information about the number of jurists, the transformation of career patterns, places of occupation and jurist backgrounds. By measuring the legal profession in this way and relating the material to the development of the modern state, all the studies agree that jurists have played a central role in the emergence of the modern state.

Several comparative studies, which emerged against this background, tended to assume that societies at similar stages of differentiation would have similar professions. According to this view, if society reaches a specific stage of development, it needs specific forms of expertise to handle certain social duties. This is the generative mechanism behind the development of the professions, which means, as Friedman notes, that 'if one starts from the notion that lawyers perform certain functions, one expects convergence between societies that otherwise resemble each other'.[21] Accordingly,

---

[20] Aubert, ibid (1976), 3.
[21] Friedman, above n 5, 2. See also M Bertilsson (ed), *Rätten i Förvandling. Jurister mellan stat och marknad* (Stockholm, Nerenius & Santerus Förlag, 1995).

countries such as Japan, the USA and European countries would resemble each other structurally in a number of ways in relation to the functions which need to be carried out in society, while the ratio of legal professionals to the population should be more or less equal, or at least other expert groups should perform some of the tasks carried out by jurists, since society needs certain functions to obtain a certain level. However, as demonstrated, jurist ratios are very different in countries such as France, the USA and Japan.[22] Therefore, it would be easy to conclude that the functional approach is more interested in social functions than with which forms of experts perform them. Friedman notes that the functional approach

> rejects a view of the profession that emphasizes historical or traditional similarities or differences. It downplays the specifically 'legal' aspects of the legal profession. The functionalist is not (initially, at least) terrible interested in whether lawyers learn civil law, common law, or something else. Function and social structure are crucial, not the technical basis of professional life or its roots in a given legal past.[23]

Moreover, functional approaches tend to ignore competition between different expert groups to perform certain tasks. Many tasks that lawyers perform do not necessarily belong to the legal sphere, but could be performed by other expert groups such as accountants,[24] so it is not a necessity that lawyers should have a monopoly over certain tasks.

4. THE CONFLICT PERSPECTIVE: NEO-MARXISM AND NEO-WEBERIAN STUDIES

In the 1970s, attention was drawn to power, interests and conflicts within concrete historical settings, rather than to consensus, social functions and systemic balances.[25] Anthony Giddens summarised the critique of functionalist studies as follows:

> In such a perspective, power cannot become treated as a problematic component of divergent group interests embodied in social action, since the meshing of interests is treated first and foremost as a question of the relation between 'the individual' and 'society'.[26]

Within the functional approach, this emphasis on power became clear when jurists' backgrounds and elite statuses became the primary object of research. The focus was not on different power interests but on a frictionless function of the legal system and on how individuals with different social backgrounds can ensure social order. The system is open to everyone as long as they adapt to the values and requirements therein. In contrast, conflict studies focused on issues such as the elite positions of the legal

---

[22] RL Abel and PSCE Lewis (eds), *Lawyers in Society. The Civil Law World* (Berkeley, University of California Press, 1988a); RL Abel and PSCE Lewis (eds), *Lawyers in Society. The Common Law World* (Berkeley, University of California Press, 1988b).

[23] Friedman, above n 5, 3.

[24] See eg Y Dezalay and B Garth, 'The Big Five versus Big Law: Confrontational Rhetoric in the Service of Legitimating Shifting Relationships Between Business and Law' in J Drolshammer and M Pfeifer (eds), *The Internationalization of the Practice of Law* (The Hague, Kluwer Law International, 2001) 513–35.

[25] M Bertilsson, *On the role of the Professions and Professional Knowledge in Global Development* (Stockholm, Forskningsrådsnämnden 99:5, 1999) 80; KM Macdonald, *The Sociology of the Professions* (London, Sage, 1995).

[26] A Giddens, *New Rules of Sociological Method*, 2nd edn (Cambridge, Polity Press, 1993) 104.

profession, which were seen in relation to power and interest structures, state building and social stratification. The neo-Marxian perspectives took up questions such as the entrance of the middle classes into the professions,[27] the division of labour that occurred with the increasing number and diversification of members,[28] how legal elites were reproducing capitalist society and law,[29] and how professionalisation was related to the formation of the state.[30] Marxist studies made class relations central, since they were the driving forces for societal developments and hence for the movement towards a classless society. However, one problem for orthodox Marxists was how to place professions within a Marxist understanding of class structures. Marx had seen the social space as a division between the bourgeois and the proletariat, between owners and workers, so the question was how the professions could be placed within this distinction.[31] Nevertheless, based on the biographies of legal elites, the legal profession was seen simultaneously as being part of the upper classes and taking part in the reproduction of capitalist structures. By enforcing the law from state institutions and by sitting on different legislative committees and boards through which law was made, Marxism found that the legal profession, like other professions, preserved relations of production and thus relations of power by both inventing and legitimising ideas and discourses and by occupying important positions in society through which they could ensure the reproduction of existing capitalist structures. The approach goes back to Marx's studies, in which he stressed that because of its objectifying character law seemed to be just, but in reality it legitimised and preserved capitalistic social structures—and thus the ownership of capital. Marx distinguished between what Alan Hunt called 'coercive and ideological domination'. The former is especially notable when the legal system protects and reinforces dominant capitalistic structures, while the latter occurs when the legal system 'conveys or transmits a complex set of attitudes, values, and theories about aspects of society. Its ideological content forms part of the dominant ideology because these attitudes, values, etc are ones that reinforce and legitimize the existing social order.'[32]

Other studies took a Weberian approach and focused on how actors pursue and achieve relative control within a market structured by the state but dominated by professional producers of services. Agents compete over social status and economic rewards.[33] In order to create a demand for professional services, consumers have to acknowledge—or even believe—that they need the services of the professions, since consumers cannot perform certain tasks themselves. From this notion follows the specialisation and functional division of labour among different occupations, and the professions are distinguished by various strategies of social closure through which they try to improve and safeguard their market share.[34] One seminal study inspired

---

[27] Macdonald, above n 25, 41.

[28] J Goldthorpe, *The Affluent Worker: Political Attitudes and Behaviour* (Cambridge, Cambridge University Press, 1963); EO Wright, 'Intellectuals and the Class Structure of Capitalist Society' in P Walker (ed), *Between Labor and Capital* (Boston, South End Press, 1979) 191–212.

[29] T Mathiesen, *Ideologi og motstand* (Oslo, Pax Forlag, 1979).

[30] TJ Johnson, 'The State and the Professions: Peculiarities of the British' in A Giddens and G Mackenzie (eds), *Social Class and the Division of Labour* (Cambridge, Cambridge University Press, 1982).

[31] RL Abel, *The Legal Profession in England and Wales* (Oxford, Basil Blackwell, 1988) 22.

[32] A Hunt, *Explorations in Law and Society* (London and New York, Routledge, 1993) 25.

[33] Abel, above n 31, 4.

[34] TJ Johnson, *Professions and Power* (London, Macmillan, 1972) 41; F Parkin, *Marxism and Class Theory: A Bourgeois Critique* (London, Tavistock, 1979).

by the Weberian approach was Dietrich Rueschmeyer's comparative study of German and American lawyers, in which the different powerbases of lawyers in the two countries were examined.[35] On the European continent it was the early bureaucratic state, founded on rational principles, which was the base for an increasing use of expert services. In contrast to common law countries, continental states were important for the early development of professionalisation. In the US, however, professionalisation developed in close relation with the development of the market. Another important study is Magali Sarfatti Larson's *The Rise of Professionalism*, which examined the rise and development of the classical professions from early capitalism to modern times. Larson argued that social mobility and market control are outcomes of a professional project, that is, a more or less deliberate, coherent and consistent course of action.[36] In England and the USA, jurists' exclusive privileges ensured the bourgeoisie's interests. In contrast to Parsons, who saw professions as a link between the state and the market, Larson drew attention to their involvement in class struggles. Professions, including the legal, took part in the continuous development of capitalism.

In conflict studies, the empirical material that is used to illustrate the legal profession's powerbases consists of information on activities in which members are involved and on their relation to the other main actors and systems. By examining their engagement in different activities, it is possible to interrogate their relationship to other elite groups. Thus, these studies use data, such as biographical material, to explore the relationship between members of the legal profession and market forces. As such, their empirical material resembles that used by the functional approach.

5. FEMINISATION OF THE LEGAL PROFESSION

Along with a host of socioeconomic changes in many Western states in the 1960s and 1970s, legal education was introduced into many new Western universities, and legal programmes were opened up to students who came from families with no academic background. Consequently, legal education in many Western states became part of mass education. Changes in how people were recruited into the profession led to different forms of studies, some of which concerned social closure to the highest positions in the field, such as the studies described above. Other studies focused on legal education, law students and their background, etc,[37] how they learn to think as a lawyer,[38] and the power structures of higher education, including transnational educational strategies and the export of legal education.[39]

---

[35] D Rueschemeyer, *Lawyers and Their Society: A Comparative Study of the Legal Profession in Germany and in the United States* (Cambridge, MA, Harvard University Press, 1973); D Rueschemeyer, 'Professional Autonomy and the Social Control of Expertise' in R Dingwall and P Lewis (eds), *The Sociology of the Professions: Lawyers, Doctors and Others* (London, Macmillan, 1983) 38–58.

[36] MS Larson, *The Rise of Professionalism: A Sociological Analysis* (Berkeley, University of California Press, 1977) 6.

[37] See eg G Neave, 'From the Other End of the Telescope: Deprofessionalization, Reprofessionalization, and the Development of Higher Education, 1950-1986' in Abel and Lewis, above n 3, 154–95; A Bradney and F Cownie, 'Transformative Visions of Legal Education' [1998] *Journal of Law and Society* 1.

[38] E Mertz, *The Language of Law School: Learning to 'Think Like a Lawyer'* (Oxford, Oxford University Press, 2007).

[39] M Börjesson and D Broady 'The Social Profile of Swedish Law Students: National Divisions and Transnational Strategies' (2006) 29(3/114) *Retfærd. Nordic Journal of Law and Justice* 80–107; Y Dezalay and

However, one of the most striking features of the legal profession has been its femi-nisation. In many countries, especially in the West, there has been a dramatic rise in the overall number of women in the legal profession,[40] which in turn has attracted the attention of researchers. *Women in Law*, by Cynthia Fuchs Epstein, was one of the first comprehensive studies in this area, and used biographical material to investigate why women entered the legal profession relatively late and to monitor how they pro-gressed within the profession.[41] Another was Carrie Menkel-Meadow's comparative study, which asked whether the access of women to the legal profession had trans-formed its social status, income, tasks, etc, or if the women changed their behaviour, visions and so on when they entered the profession.[42]

Ulrike Schultz and Gisela Shaw's *Women in the World's Legal Professions* surveyed women in several countries around the world, and noted that elements such as the legal family of civil law or common law, the legal cultures of different countries and the language used in relation to lawyers had an impact on the categorisation of women.[43] Schultz and Shaw presented a general overview of the history and quantita-tive status of women in the legal profession. One of the findings of their book was that the time when a women could enter the legal profession varied a lot; thus, in Italy, the first female law student graduated in 1777, while in many European coun-tries and North America the first female law students graduated late in the nineteenth century. In Korea, the first female law student graduated as late as 1951. Women's position in the legal profession varies considerably in different countries. In civil law countries, more women are employed in the judicial branch than in common law countries (with the exception of Israel). However, the figures show that the lower the court in the judicial hierarchy, the higher the number of female judges. The proportion of practising female lawyers seems to be between one-quarter and one-third of the total cohort, but with just a few exceptions, eg France and Finland have more than 40% female lawyers, whereas Japan and South Korea only have 5.9% and 1.9% female lawyers, respectively. On the basis of the comparative data available, Schultz and Shaw assume that a higher percentage of women than men work in public administration or in industry, and they note that job security represents a comparatively significant criterion in women's choice of profession.

Regarding the number of women in legal education, equality between the genders has been reached in most countries. Schultz discusses different hidden mechanisms that subject female law students to male dominance, one example of which is in relation to exams. In most countries, women's academic qualifications tend to be equal to or even better than those of their male counterparts (Germany presents an exception). Yet, based partly on the case of Germany, where male students in general show better qualifications than female students measured on the exam results, Schultz notes:

B Garth, *The Internationalization of Palaces War: Lawyers, Economists, and the Contest to Transform Latin American States* (Chicago, University of Chicago Press, 2002); JA Gardner, *Legal Imperialism: American Lawyers and Foreign Aid in Latin America* (Madison, University of Wisconsin Press, 1980).

[40] Schultz and Shaw, above n 9.
[41] C Funchs Epstein, *Women in Law* (New York, Basic Books, 1981).
[42] C Menkel-Meadow, 'Feminization of the Legal Profession: The Comparative Sociology of Woman Lawyers' in Abel and Lewis, above n 3, 196–255.
[43] Schultz, above n 9, xxviii.

It is not unreasonable to regard as at least a partial explanation of men's superior examination success the fact that oral examinations, which produce an important component of the overall results, are conducted mainly by male examiners and according to male standards. In these oral examinations, what counts is the candidate's general *habitus*, that is the degree to which her appearance and behaviour meet traditional expectations. Not surprisingly, women experience them as an initiation test into professional conformity.[44]

Inequalities between men and women can also be found in the later stages of women's careers, both when it concerns entrance to a certain part of the profession and when it regards their specialisation, duties and tasks in the later stages of their career in various parts of the legal profession. In several countries, entrance qualifications to private practice are not only academic but also have to be complemented with social capital, that is, a social network, respect and reputation.[45] In general, women have less social and cultural capital than men, so they 'try to set up their own mentoring systems and networks as a counterstrategy, but their slight representation at the higher echelons makes this a less effective process'.[46] Some studies focusing on social stratification even claim that women represent the working class of the legal service market[47] because they are more likely to get—in the words of Mossman—'pink files' than men, who in general get 'blue files'.[48] In other words, women in general receive cases that are less visible, less prestigious and have lower financial reward. In contrast, men are more likely to get high-prestige cases and greater client contact, which is an important factor in gaining more clients.[49] As Sommerlad notes, this pattern is followed due to women's lack of participation in male socialisation activities, such as pub visits, drinking, dining and discussing sports. All these subtle forms of male domination can also be seen in forms of payment, long working hours, concerns for the family and children, and how women tend to be more mobile than their male counterparts, although they have a 'sideways, downward, or out' mobility.

One problem with studies of the feminisation of the legal profession is that it is difficult to cope with the broad categories of women (and men for that matter; see Chapter 7 on feminism),[50] which hide great differences that actually exist between them in terms of status, lifestyles, income, visions, context, etc. The methodologies used to study this subject differ to a certain extent. One of the first objectives was to show that differences between men and women existed as regards status, income, position, etc. As was the case with several of the previously mentioned studies, statistics was one core source of information. However, more qualitative approaches have been used as well.

---

[44] Ibid, xxxix.

[45] See A Boigeol, 'Male Strategies in the Face of the Feminisation of a Profession: The Case of the French Judiciary' in Schultz and Shaw, above n 9, 401–18

[46] Schultz, above n 9, xli.

[47] H Sommerlad, 'Can Women Lawyer Differently? A Perspective from the UK' in Schultz and Shaw, above n 9, 191–224.

[48] MJ Mossman, 'Engendering the Legal Profession: The Education Strategy' in Schultz and Shaw, above n 9, 77–86.

[49] Sommerlad, above n 47; Menkel-Meadow, above n 42.

[50] Menkel-Meadow, above n 42, 196.

6. INTERNATIONALISATION OF THE LEGAL PROFESSION

With the intensification of transnational markets and the construction of transnational institutions such as the World Trade Organization, arbitration institutions and the European Union, a number of studies began to emphasise the role and function of the legal profession in such construction. It appeared that the legal profession, as with other professions, if not directly involved in creating internationalisation, was at least engaged at a transnational level.[51]

One approach which tries to explain the concept of 'the international' takes its point of departure from Bourdieu's criticism of the very notion of profession, which he criticised because it gives an impression of a coherent and fraternal group. According to Bourdieu, using the term 'profession'

> is to fasten on a true reality, onto a set of people who bear the same name (they are all 'lawyers' for instance); they are endowed with a roughly equivalent economic status and, more importantly, they are organised into 'professional associations' endowed with a code of ethics, collective bodies that define rules for admission, etc. 'Profession' is a folk concept which has been uncritically smuggled into scientific language and which imports into it a whole social unconscious. It is the *social product* of a historical work of construction of a group and of a *representation* of groups that has surreptitiously slipped into the science of this very group.[52]

Bourdieu problematises the scientific manoeuvre, which uncritically adopts this kind of conceptualisation inherited in a struggle, by a group of different persons to achieve a goal. Bourdieu notes that the notion is created from the name of a group in its struggle for a better position in society. Seen from such a perspective, the notion hides the objective differences between different members within the profession in relation to financial and cultural resources, sex, social backgrounds, etc. Utilising the Bourdieusian scientific tools of 'field' and 'capital' (discussed in Chapter 6) and taking Bourdieu's studies of the state to a transnational level,[53] Yves Dezalay and Bryant Garth have stressed in several studies that law and legal development are, to a large extent, related to social capital and to the relative strengths of different positions in the very fields they have examined. In relation to this point, they have showed how legal ideas and transnational institutions are exported from dominant centres, primarily in the USA, and taken up and imported to various fields and jurisdictions by brokers in various countries. Law and legal institutions cannot, however, just be transferred from one country to another—the very implementation process is dependent on the relative strengths of the importing agents in the fields and countries.[54] Bourdieu emphasises

---

[51] See eg Galanter and Palay, above n 7; DM Trubek et al, 'Global Restructuring and the Law: Studies of the Internationalization of Legal Fields and the Creation of Transnational Arenas' (1994) 44 *Case Western Reserve Law Review* 407–98; TC Halliday and L Karpik (eds), *Lawyers and the Rise of Western Political Liberalism: Europe and North America from the Eighteenth to Twentieth Centuries* (Oxford, Clarendon Press, 1997).

[52] P Bourdieu and LJD Wacquant, *An Invitation to Reflexive Sociology* (Chicago, University of Chicago Press, 1992) 242.

[53] For an overview of Bourdieu's engagement with the state, see J Arnholtz and O Hammerslev, 'Transcended Power of the State: The Role of Actors in Pierre Bourdieu's Sociology of the State' [2013] *Distinktion: Scandinavian Journal of Social Theory* 42–64.

[54] Y Dezalay and B Garth, *Dealing in Virtue: International Commercial Arbitration and the Construction of a Transnational Legal Field* (Chicago, University of Chicago Press 1996); Dezalay and Garth, above n 39.

how they use the tool of the field to replace spontaneous and preconstructed notions such as 'globalisation' with systematised and empirical studies of internationalisation processes.[55] Through interviews with the key agents in various fields such as international commercial law and human rights, Dezalay and Garth show how different disciplines emerge and develop just as they illustrate how the importation and exportation of different forms of expertise and law happen. Thus, they examine which agents manage, through various forms of resources, to be in a position to create and develop certain logics and practices. By writing a 'collective relational biography' of the development of fields, they show how different agents with significant forms of social and cultural capital promote different ideas, practices and state models. Law is thus related closely to the persons who create it and to the resources and surroundings of the agents. Internationalisation and globalisation happen by importing and exporting such practices, institutions and symbolic forms.

Rather than focusing on institutions and the legal profession as a coherent entity, as traditional professional studies of the legal profession have a tendency to do, Bourdieusian studies examine the transnational fields in which institutions and the agents of the institutions play a role.

In their exploration of the genesis of international arbitration, these studies showed how an international field of arbitration was developed first by *legal honoratiores* legitimising decisions in a field with limited law. When the field had been structured to a certain degree, the old men were ousted by younger and more specialised lawyers. Through historical sociology focusing on different agents involved in the field, Dezalay and Garth managed to show how various agents compete and use different forms of resources in developing legal institutions, legal expertise, power hierarchies and, to a certain degree, the law.[56]

7. CONCLUSION AND CURRENT CHALLENGES

As Schultz notes, studies of legal professionals have recently developed from studies with a theoretical framework mediating grand narratives to more specific and particular forms of analysis.[57] Moreover, different foci have developed, whereby a number of studies examine the legal profession from a comparative perspective reflecting national contexts, while others study gender dimensions and yet others draw attention mostly to how lawyers belonging to different jurisdictions participate in developing transnational institutions and laws. Whereas national studies have often examined the entire population of lawyers in order to show differences and similarities, feminist studies have most often focused on gender differences and similarities. Instead of examining the entire population of lawyers in different countries by counting the entire

---

[55] P Bourdieu, 'Foreword' in Dezalay and Garth, above n 54, vii–viii.

[56] Following Dezalay and Garth, other studies have taken up different sites of how the EU is constructed, see eg A Cohen, 'Bourdieu Hits Brussels: The Genesis and Structure of the European Field of Power' (2011) 5 *International Political Sociology* 335–39; O Hammerslev, 'The US and the EU in East European Legal Reform' in Y Dezalay and B Garth (eds), *Lawyers and the Rule of Law in an Era of Globalization* (New York, Routledge, 2010); MR Madsen, 'From Cold War Instrument to Supreme European Court: The European Court of Human Rights at the Crossroads of International and National Law and Politics' (2007) 32 *Law & Social Inquiry* 137–60.

[57] Schultz, above n 9.

member populations, transnational studies have 'counted lawyers that count',[58] that is, they have shown how different national systems are related closely to the development of other national systems as well as a transnational agenda through legal elites. The latter studies, in particular, have deconstructed the notion of profession and related it instead to various turf battles in international domains. They stress, as in the case of some feminist studies and conflict studies in general, that the legal profession consists of different individuals with different goals and resources. Nevertheless, these studies employ relational collective biographies and thus link struggles between individuals to legal and institutional changes. Moreover, they underline that developments in law and legal institutions are related closely to social and cultural capital, and they also illustrate that the creation of international institutions, fields and state-building depends to a large extent on the transnational circulation of legal ideas, expertise and models of legal institutions. Even though national studies have not recognised it, lawyers have always operated within a transnational context.

The questions that remain—besides the question about how studies of the legal profession progress—pertain to current challenges for the legal profession. One issue which has attracted attention is how information and computing technology, as well as the current recession, will change legal work and the legal profession. Richard Susskind has argued that information and computing technology will reform legal work and its organisation in a number of ways.[59] He describes how different 'legal pioneers' have advanced different sorts of online advice systems, auctions for procuring legal services, virtual case rooms and electronic case management systems.[60] Yet, one of the most striking ways in which information and computing technology has had an impact is on outsourcing and/or offshoring legal services to places such as India and the Philippines. Outsourcing refers to using a third party to provide services previously provided by the firm itself, while offshoring denotes outsourcing to a non-domestic provider. With the latest recession, competition between law firms has increased, and clients are more likely than before the recession to replace their legal service provider in order to reduce the costs. Therefore, the largest European and US law firms, as well as in-house departments servicing large and multinational corporations, have already outsourced and/or offshored back-office functions, such as finance and administration, to reduce costs and thus be more competitive. However, it should be noted that Susskind moderates his presumptions by referring to an estimated percentage of outsourced legal services on a global level as being a mere 0.1% of the total value of legal services, estimated at $460 billion.[61] According to Susskind, one of the challenges for legal service providers is to limit those costs dictated by clients, which may ultimately restructure work processes in and the organisation of law firms.

Another challenge to the established part of the legal field, ie especially law firms, is the effort to liberalise the legal market in Europe, illustrated by the British Legal

---

[58] The phrase is taken from C Marchand and A Vauchez, 'Counting Lawyers that Count: A Sociology of EU Lawyers Pleading to the European Court of Justice', paper presented at the annual meeting of the Law and Society Association, Berlin, 2007.

[59] R Susskind, *The End of Lawyers? Rethinking the Nature of Legal Services* (Oxford, Oxford University Press, 2010); see also R Susskind, *Tomorrow's Lawyers: An Introduction to your Future* (Oxford, Oxford University Press, 2013).

[60] Ibid (2013), 21.

[61] Ibid, xxxv.

Services Act 2007, which made it possible for non-lawyers, such as insurance companies, banks or supermarkets, to offer legal services and to own law firms. The Act was issued in order to encourage competition and to provide a new path for consumer complaints.

Regarding judiciaries in Europe, the European Commission strives to harmonise judicial training within the EU. In 2011, the Commission stressed the need to train judges and legal practitioners in EU law, 'to empower citizens and businesses to stand up for their rights and to ensure the effectiveness of the Single Market'.[62] Based on Mario Monti's report, the Commission combines the development of EU law with the effective implementation of this law, hence guaranteeing legal predictability, security and uniform interpretation of law throughout EU Member States. A key issue in order to have a more effective single market is, according to Monti, to pay more attention to law enforcement.[63] Monti notes that

> national judges play a key role in interpreting and applying EU law next to national law. The Commission, in partnership with Member States, should step up its support for training programmes and structures to ensure that national judges and legal professionals have a solid knowledge of the Single Market rules they are most often required to apply.[64]

Against this background, the EU Commission's objective is to enable half of the estimated 1.4 million legal practitioners in the EU to participate in European judicial training activities by 2020.[65]

Increasing competition between legal professionals on an international scale is supported by the presumably increasing transnationalisation of legal degrees, either through the exportation of legal faculties from the West to other parts of the world or by distance learning. It could be argued that global power balances between different legal service providers will partially follow the direction of the old production industries to other and cheaper parts of the world. This will, of course, have many knock-on effects on a number of issues in the West, not least on the welfare state. These developments may lead to increasing segmentation regarding gender, financial and cultural resources of different parts of the legal profession, both nationally and internationally. Although following the emergence of Western industrial nation-states and later the welfare state, the research questions of classical legal profession studies are still relevant to a certain degree, as they focus on functional necessities and power structures alike. Nevertheless, new changes challenge traditional studies which concentrated merely on national legal professions without examining them from an international perspective.

---

[62] COM(2011) 551, 3.

[63] M Monti, 'A New Strategy for the Single Market: At the Service of Europe's Economy and Society', Report to the President of the European Commission, 2010.

[64] Ibid, 102.

[65] COM(2011) 551.

19

Comparative Sociology of Law

DAVID NELKEN

APPRECIATING HOW LAW works in other countries can be a matter of life and death. One well-travelled colleague who teaches legal theory likes to tell a story of the way crossing the road when abroad requires good knowledge of the local customs. In England, let us assume, you are relatively safe on pedestrian crossings, but rather less secure if you try to cross elsewhere. In Italy, he argued, you need to show almost the same caution in both places; but at least motorists will do their best to avoid actually hitting you. In Germany, on the other hand, or so he alleged, you are totally safe on the zebra crossing. You do not even need to look out for traffic. But if you dare to cross elsewhere, you will simply not be seen. Whatever elements of truth this comparison may contain, the example also illustrates the dangers of oversimplification and stereotyping that makes writing about and learning from other societies so complicated. In this chapter I shall first indicate the type of questions studied by comparative sociology of law and then describe some of the ways it can be pursued. I then introduce the concept of legal culture and consider the influence of starting points in grasping other cultures. Finally, I ask how far it is appropriate to continue to focus on variation in national legal cultures at a time of globalisation.

1. RETHINKING COMPARATIVE SOCIOLOGY OF LAW

The sociological study of law from a comparative perspective can number such distinguished predecessors as Montesquieu, Maine or Weber. In attempting to throw light on how things are elsewhere, empirical research on law in different societies can be extremely intellectually stimulating because it raises many of the most puzzling questions about the relationship between law and society. Why do the UK and Denmark complain most about the imposition of EU law but maintain the best records of implementation? And what does this tell us about the centrality of enforcement as an aspect of law in different societies? Why in the USA and the UK does it often take a sex scandal to create official interest in doing something about corruption, whereas in Latin countries it takes a major corruption scandal to excite interest in marital unfaithfulness? What does this tell us about the way culture conditions the boundaries of law and the way law helps shape those same boundaries?

Comparative sociology of law cannot go it alone. Progress in this field requires learning from and collaborating with many other disciplines including comparative law, history, international relations, political science, anthropology, cultural studies, comparative psychology and comparative economics. But, as is most obvious in the case of much comparative law scholarship, it may also be necessary to contest other approaches.[1] There is much to be learned from the attention which comparative lawyers give to legal elites, to doctrine and to history. Such matters are often an essential element in explaining which legal ideas and institutions are adopted and the logic of their internal evolution. Comparative sociology of law, however, also aims to get to the parts that comparative law cannot reach. In part it does this by studying the 'law in action', alternatives to law and the avoidance of law, and the way legal developments interrelate with wider social and political trends. As a social science perspective, however, it also works with different categories: no longer merely rules, procedures and institutions, but disputes, 'trouble cases' and scandals, law as social control and social regulation, law as an aspect of social and cultural order, law as producer and product of social change, and law as shaper and controller of cultural flows. Instead of focusing only on legal systems or legal traditions it is likely to employ unfamiliar concepts borrowed from social and political theory such as regimes of 'power-knowledge', the 'symbolic capital' of different professional groups, or the autopoiesis of legal systems under modern conditions of social system differentiation.

Within the social sciences, some argue that *all* sociological research is inherently comparative: the aim is always to explain variation.[2] But where data is drawn from foreign societies there are further complications of understanding other languages, practices and world views which make it more difficult to know whether we are comparing like with like (indeed often it is that which becomes the problem). Others claim that for these and other reasons comparative work is actually impossible. It faces the allegedly unavoidable dangers of Occidentalism, thinking that other societies are necessarily like ours, or Orientalism, assuming that they are inherently different from us.[3] In a period of globalisation, it has been suggested, the links between societies and individuals have been so extended that it makes little sense to look for independent legal cultures.[4] But comparisons continue to be made, and need to be made, and the extent to which societies and cultures have become homogenised is an empirical question.

Comparative sociology of law has a long way to go to realise its potential. Some work is too closely linked to the more practical questions raised by comparative lawyers, for example the much discussed problem of whether Continental legal

---

[1] E Orucu and D Nelken (eds), *Comparative Law: A Handbook* (Oxford, Hart Publishing, 2007); V Gessner and D Nelken (eds), *European Ways of Law* (Oxford, Hart Publishing, 2007).

[2] M Feeley, 'Comparative Criminal Law: Comparison for What Purpose?' in D Nelken (ed), *Comparing Legal Cultures* (Aldershot, Dartmouth, 1997) 93–104.

[3] M Cain, 'Orientalism, Occidentalism and the Sociology of Crime' (2000) 40 *British Journal of Criminology* 239–60; D Nelken, 'Comparative Criminal Justice: Beyond Ethnocentrism and Relativism' (2009) 6 *European Journal of Criminology* 291–311.

[4] RJ Coombe, 'Contingent Articulations: Critical Studies of Law' in A Sarat and T Kearns (eds), *Law in the Domains of Culture* (Ann Arbor, University of Michigan Press, 2000); D Nelken, 'Globalisation and crime' in P Kennett (ed), *Handbook of Comparative Social Policy* (Cheltenham, Edward Elgar, 2004) 373–87; D Nelken (ed), *Comparative Criminal Justice and Globalisation* (Aldershot, Ashgate, 2011).

systems control their police forces better than is done in Anglo-American systems.[5] Much of the more theoretical work in English is about Japan, and there is relatively little written, for example, about the countries of Continental Europe. It is particularly important not to ghettoise this type of work (as in the way comparative law leads a somewhat fugitive existence in the law schools). Comparative research should be seen as a way of testing any claims made by the sociology of law and as an essential means of helping this discipline fulfil its promise. By helping us appreciate the fit (or lack of fit) between law and society in different social contexts it brings into view those aspects of the relationship which are usually hidden from the scholar who is, after all, also part of his or her own society.[6]

2. DOING COMPARATIVE RESEARCH

All comparative work is demanding and difficult. We should not underestimate what is entailed merely in trying to describe carefully how similar processes, for example criminal procedures, actually work in other societies.[7] But we should beware of using the challenges of comparative research merely as occasions for 're-enacting' past theoretical battles such as those between positivists and interpretivists, or between the search for explanation and the enterprise of translation.[8] A wide range of theoretical approaches may all have something to contribute, even though, of course, our ideas as to what comparison is and can be about will condition what we look for and how we look for it. Likewise, our choice of empirical research methods will depend on and further our chosen theoretical approach. For example, different types of data are likely to be gathered through exercises in 'virtual comparison' which rely on collaboration between foreign scholars, the method of 'researching there' which entails short research visits, and the process of actually 'living there' associated with ethnography.[9]

Some current approaches, however, are unlikely to be productive. A common form of extensive collective comparative work proceeds on the basis of what we might describe as comparison 'by juxtaposition': 'This is how we do it in Denmark; how do you do it in your country?' Usually this is policy-driven research on the look out for new ideas, and almost always it fails to get to grips with the questions of comparability which should be the object of any comparative exercise. What are we trying to understand? Why are *these* societies being compared? What needs to be made explicit is the theoretical justification for and point of any comparison. The number of countries being compared does not matter as such. Even one foreign society, if examined

---

[5] JH Langbein and LL Weinreb, 'Continental Criminal Procedure: Myth and Reality' (1978) 87 *Yale Law Journal* 1549–69.

[6] D Nelken, 'The Meaning of Success in Transnational Legal Transfers' (2001) 19 *Windsor Yearbook of Access to Justice* 349–66.

[7] See eg D Nelken (ed), *Contrasting Criminal Justice* (Aldershot, Ashgate, 2000); D Nelken 'When is a Society Non-punitive? A Case-Study of Italy' in J Pratt et al (eds), *The New Punitiveness: Current Trends, Theories, Perspectives* (Cullompton, Willan Publishing, 2005) 218–38; D Nelken, 'Theorising the Embeddedness of Punishment' in D Melossi, M Sozzo and R Sparks (eds), *Travels of the Criminal Question: Cultural Embeddedness and Diffusion* (Oxford, Hart Publishing, 2011) 65–94.

[8] D Nelken, 'Whom Can You Trust? The Future of Comparative Criminology' in D Nelken (ed), *The Futures of Criminology* (London, Sage, 1994) 220–44.

[9] D Nelken, 'Virtually There, Researching There, Living There' in Nelken, above n 7 (2000), 23–48.

with reference to a theoretical problem, can furnish important findings. Thus Haley treats 'law as a window on Japan and Japan as a window on law', so as to show what happens in a society where the cultural ideal is to make legal enforcement depend to the maximum extent on existing social consensus.[10]

All comparative research involves the search for social, cultural and other similarities and differences. Whilst it is common to find entrenched arguments in favour of one or other of these strategies, neither should be embraced dogmatically. Both are important and at the end of the day inseparable. Careful comparison requires avoiding the assumption of similarity at all costs, whilst also taking care not to be deceived by what may turn out to be only apparent differences. Assuming as an universal that criminal behaviour is essentially associated with young men is simply ethnocentric presumption.[11] But setting out to demonstrate that all higher courts have an essential role in governmental social control becomes a provocative argument if the cultures surveyed are as different as Muslim, Chinese, French and British.[12] Arguing that 'legal epistemes' are incommensurable paralyses comparison.[13] But it can be very fruitful to try to explain patterned differences in legal ideas and behaviour, for example in attitudes to mediation in the penal system, against a background of otherwise similar social and economic political conditions.[14] In looking for similarities and differences we will need to examine both action and words, and their interrelationship. In the face of current immigration influxes into the European Union some EU Member States have strong ideals about integration but weak social provisions for assistance with employment and housing; for others it is the reverse. In general, in many legal cultures what is of most importance may often be found more in words than in practice;[15] it does not (yet) have a place in the world of practice and hence represents an ideal of what the society would like to become.

The idea of 'functional equivalence', the claim that all societies face similar problems, even if they solve them in somewhat different ways, is a heuristic tool which should be handled with care. It may be the case that other societies meet a given social problem by using unfamiliar types of law and legal techniques.[16] But it will also be worth extending our analysis to the role of other legal and non-legal institutions, alternatives to law, competing professional expertises as well as other groupings within civil society such as the family or patron–client network. There may also simply be no 'solution', especially if the 'problem' is not conceived as such. We should be prepared to find that cultures have the power to produce relatively circular definitions of what is worth fighting for and against, and that institutions and practices express genuinely different histories and distinct priorities.

Societies construct the role, boundaries and meaning of law in very different ways.

---

[10] J Haley, *Authority without Power: Law and the Japanese Paradox* (New York, Oxford University Press, 1991); D Nelken, *Comparative Criminal Justice: Making Sense of Difference* (London, Sage, 2010).

[11] M Gottfredson and T Hirschi, *A General Theory of Crime* (Stanford, CA, Stanford University Press, 1990).

[12] M Shapiro, *Courts* (Chicago, Chicago University Press, 1981).

[13] P Legrand, 'What Legal Transplants?' in D Nelken and J Feest (eds), *Adapting Legal Cultures* (Oxford, Hart Publishing, 2001).

[14] A Crawford, 'Contrasts in Victim–Offender Mediation and Appeals to Community in France and England' in Nelken, supra n 7 (2000).

[15] D Nelken (ed), *Law as Communication* (Aldershot, Dartmouth, 1996).

[16] K Zweigert and H Kotz, *An Introduction to Comparative Law*, trans T Weir, 2nd edn (Oxford, Oxford University Press, 1987).

Sometimes even subtle differences can be important, for example whether diversion from criminal justice is seen as intrinsic to the criminal process, as in Holland, or somehow extrinsic to it, as in the UK.[17] The often unexpected social consequences of such definitions need to be examined empirically. Attempts in Italy to deny prosecutors any discretion actually ended up strengthening their hands against corrupt politicians.[18] Conversely, Weber's Muslim *kadi* judges can make little of their apparently unlimited discretion because it has to be exercised in accordance with community norms.[19]

3. THE CONCEPT OF LEGAL CULTURE

There is a great dearth of concepts which can be deployed in comparative sociology of law. Apart from terms borrowed from theorising within the master social science disciplines, something can and needs to be done to rework the categories used in comparative law. The idea of legal culture, in its more sociological versions,[20] represents one such possible conceptual tool.[21] But it is not without its detractors. And the problems in employing it illustrate many of the disagreements about how to do comparative work which we have mentioned so far.

Legal culture points to differences in the way aspects of law are themselves embedded in larger frameworks of social structure and culture which constitute and reveal the place of law in society. These may concern the extent to which law is party or state directed (bottom up or top down). It has to do with the number, role and power of courts and legal professions, the role and importance of the judiciary, the nature of legal education and legal training.[22] It draws attention to ideas of what is meant by 'law' (and what law is 'for'), of where and how it is to be found (types of legal reasoning, the role of case law and precedent, of general clauses as compared to detailed drafting, of the place of law and fact). It can be found in different approaches to regulation, administration and dispute resolution.[23] There may be important con-

---

[17] C Brants and S Field, 'Legal Cultures, Political Cultures and Procedural Traditions' in Nelken, above n 7 (2000), 77–116.

[18] D Nelken, 'Comparing Criminal Justice' in M Maguire, R Morgan and R Reiner (eds), *The Oxford Handbook of Criminology*, 3rd edn (Oxford, Oxford University Press, 2002) 175–202.

[19] L Rosen, *The Anthropology of Justice* (Cambridge, Cambridge University Press, 1989).

[20] Contrast V Gessner et al (eds), *European Legal Cultures* (Dartmouth, Aldershot, 1996) and C Varga (ed), *Comparative Legal Cultures* (Aldershot, Dartmouth, 1992).

[21] See eg D Nelken, 'Understanding/Invoking Legal Culture' in D Nelken (ed), *Legal Culture, Diversity and Globalization* (1995) 4 *Social and Legal Studies* 435–52; D Nelken, 'Using the Concept of Legal Culture' (2004) 29 *Australian Journal of Legal Philosophy* 1–28; D Nelken, 'Comparing Legal Cultures' in A Sarat (ed), *Blackwell Companion to Law and Society* (Oxford, Blackwell, 2004) 113–28; F Bruinsma and D Nelken (eds), *Exploring Legal Cultures*, *Recht der Werkelijkheid* Special Issue (Amsterdam, 2007); D Nelken, 'Defining and Using the Concept of Legal Culture' in E Orucu and D Nelken (eds), *Comparative Law: A Handbook* (Oxford, Hart Publishing, 2007) 109–32; D Nelken (ed), *Using Legal Culture* (2012) 5 *Journal of Comparative Law* Special Issue.

[22] See eg P Polak and D Nelken, 'Polish Prosecutors, Corruption and Legal Culture' in A Febbrajo and W Sadurski (eds), *East-Central Europe After Transition: Towards a New Socio-legal Semantics* (Aldershot, Ashgate, 2011) 219–54; R Montana and D Nelken, 'The Ambivalent Role of Italian Prosecutors and their Resistance to "Moral Panics" about Crime' in C Smith et al (eds), *Handbook of International Criminology* (London, Routledge, 2010) 286–96.

[23] See eg D Nelken, 'Law, Liability and Culture' in D Engel and M McCann (eds), *Fault Lines: Tort Law as Cultural Practice* (Stanford, CA, Stanford University Press, 2009) 10–24; D Nelken, 'Human Trafficking and Legal Culture' (2011) 43 *Israel Law Review* 479–513.

trasts in the degree to which given controversies are subject to law, the role of other expertises, the part played by 'alternatives' to law, including not only arbitration and mediation but also the many 'infrastructural' ways of discouraging or resolving disputes.[24] Attention must be given to the role of other religious or ethical norms and the ambit of the informal. Accompanying and concretising such differences, explaining and attempting to justify them, there are likely to be contrasting attitudes to the role of law, formal and substantive ideas of legitimacy, or the need for public participation.

How, then, should legal culture be distinguished from other aspects of society and culture? On this there is no unanimity. For different purposes, or in line with competing approaches to social theory, legal culture can be seen as manifested through institutional behaviour, or as a factor shaping and shaped by differences in individual legal consciousness, as a pattern of ideas which lie behind behaviour, or as another name for politicolegal discourse itself. Sometimes legal culture is identified independently from political culture, at other times it is categorised as an inseparable aspect of political culture. It may be sought in 'high culture' and 'low culture'. When treated as constitutive of cultural consciousness generally, this may be examined through structured interviews about the sense of justice,[25] contextualised as part of everyday narratives, as in the work of the Amherst school of interpretative sociology of law, or distilled from the ideology behind legal doctrine, as in the writings of American critical legal scholars.

The diversity in ways of thinking about how to draw the line between legal culture and other phenomena is not necessarily unproductive. It can be useful for reminding us that in many societies there is a wide gulf between legal culture and general culture, as where the criminal law purports to maintain principles of impersonal equality before the law in societies where clientilistic and other particularistic practices are widespread. Indeed, there is need for more attention to be given to the way past and present work in the sociology of law assumes and mobilises a (local) vision of legal culture even (or even especially) where the problem of legal culture is left unexplicated rather than being squarely addressed. It forces the sociologist of law to confront the problem of reflexivity, the way her framing of problems for discussion reproduces rather than questions the taken-for-granted assumptions of her own legal—and academic—culture about the role and the rule of law.

Disagreements over how to define the term help produce lively disputes over the usefulness of this concept and of over how it should be studied. Lawrence Friedman, who has made extensive use of the term in his writings, introduced the useful distinction between the 'internal legal culture' of legal professionals and academics and the 'external legal culture' representing the opinions and pressures brought to bear by wider social groups. On the other hand, Roger Cotterrell criticises Friedman's broad-brush use of the concept, claiming that it is too vague and impressionistic.[26] He argues instead for the study of the way professionally managed legal ideology shapes wider consciousness. Friedman replies that even a vague concept can subsume other less vague and more measurable categories. Legal culture determines when, why and

---

[24] E Blankenburg, 'Civil Litigation Rates as Indicators for Legal Culture' in Nelken, above n 2, 41–68.

[25] V Hamilton and J Sanders, *Everyday Justice: Responsibility and the Individual in Japan and the United States* (New Haven, Yale University Press, 1992).

[26] R Cotterrell, 'The Concept of Legal Culture' in Nelken, above n 2, 13–32.

where people turn for help to law or to other institutions, or choose to 'lump it'. For example, it would be a finding about legal culture if French but not Italian women were reluctant to call police to complain about sexual harassment. As a step in explanation, our accounts of legal culture serve to capture an essential intervening variable in influencing the type of legal changes which follow on large social transformations such as those following technological breakthroughs.[27]

In line with the different methodologies which compete in the social sciences there is an important divide between those scholars who look for 'indicators' of legal culture in the activity of courts and other legal institutions, and those who insist instead on the need to interpret cultural meaning. The first approach uses culture (or deliberately simplified aspects of it) to explain variation in levels and types of litigation or social control; the second approach seeks to use legally related behaviour by institutions or individuals as an 'index' of culture. The first strategy seeks a sort of sociolegal esperanto which abstracts from the language used by members of different cultures, preferring for example to talk of 'decision-making' rather than 'discretion'. The rival approach aims at providing 'thick descriptions of law as local knowledge';[28] it is concerned precisely with grasping linguistic nuance and cultural packaging and with the problems this poses of faithfully translating another system's ideas of fairness and justice and making proper sense of its web of meanings.

Some authors draw a contrast, not unrelated to Friedman's typology, between the factors conditioning the 'supply side' of law as embodied in the activities of legal and paralegal institutions, and the 'demand side' representing social patterns of use of legal institutions. In what he calls a sort of 'natural experiment' Erhard Blankenburg asks why Germany has one of the highest litigation rates in Europe, and Holland one of the lowest when both countries are socially and culturally so similar and economically interdependent. (In respect of our example of traffic accidents, Germany brings sixteen such cases per thousand population to court for every two brought to trial in Holland.) His answer, carefully documented with respect to different types of legal controversy, is that in Holland there are a series of 'infrastructural' alternatives to litigation. This is said to demonstrate the determinant role played by the 'supply side' even where the 'demand' for law is assumed to be similar.

Blankenburg's argument is not free from the ambiguities identified by Cotterrell. It is not always clear whether his aim is to find a way of characterising differences in (national) legal cultures or instead to use the concept of legal culture itself as a tool for explaining the behaviour of legal institutions. Sometimes legal culture seems to be the explanation for the filters and alternatives which Blankenburg sees as characterising Dutch 'law in action', at other times it is only the name we give to such patterns of litigation and avoidance (in which case it would be tautologous to use this as part of any explanation). Any clear-cut distinction between supply and demand is also questionable (are lawyers' strategies one or the other?). Demand is shaped by supply, and vice versa. Assumptions of 'functional equivalence' across cultures are always questionable; what counts as an alternative or 'supplement' is itself culturally

---

[27] L Friedman, 'The Concept of Legal Culture: A Reply' in Nelken, above n 2, 34.

[28] C Geertz, 'Thick Description: Towards an Interpretive Theory of Culture' in C Geertz, *The Interpretation of Culture* (London, Fontana, 1973); C Geertz, *Local Knowledge: Further Essays in Interpretive Anthropology* (New York, Basic Books, 1983).

contingent. We could just as well say that it is the different function of the courts in Holland which means that the ready availability of paralegals and other intermediaries leads to less litigation. In another society (including Germany) the alternatives which Blankenburg uses to explain the low rate of litigation in Holland could easily lead to still greater litigation.[29]

However, the main drawback of such an approach is its insistence that rates of social behaviour can be understood independently of the meanings that actors themselves attach to them. Interpretative approaches, by contrast, try to grasp the secrets of culture by focusing on key local terms, which are sometimes admitted to be almost but not quite untranslatable. Blankenburg himself explores the meaning of the term 'beleid' in Holland which refers to the often explicit policy guidelines followed by government, criminal justice personnel and complex (public) organisations in general.[30] Other scholars have examined the idea of the state in common law and Continental countries and have sought to understand, for example, why litigation is seen as essentially democratic in the USA and as antidemocratic in France. They contrast the different meanings of the 'rule of law', the 'Rechtstaat', or the 'stato di diritto', the Italian term 'garantismo' versus 'due process', or 'law and order' as compared to the German 'innere Sicherheit'; they unpack the meaning of 'lokale Justiz' as compared to 'community crime control'.[31] This strategy explores how concepts both reflect and constitute culture; as in the changes undergone by the meaning of 'contract' in a society where the individual is seen as necessarily embodied in wider relationships,[32] or the way that the Japanese ideogram for the new concept of 'rights' came to settle on a sign associated with 'self-interest' rather than morality.[33]

4. WE AND THE OTHER

But who uses such terms, when and for what purposes? The problem besetting the interpretative approach is deciding whose ideas we should be trying to understand. For different purposes we may be interested in the views and behaviour of politicians, legal officials, legal and other professionals, or legal scholars, in the powerful or the powerless. Is it safe to expect practitioners or academics necessarily to know the answers to our questions? Although we will always want to know what the natives think, it does not follow that we actually want to think like a native. We may want to know more or less than they do, and for certain purposes we may even come to know more. But if we do not look to them for corroboration of our ideas, there is always the risk of imposing our own interpretations.

The ability to look at a culture with new eyes is the great strength of the outside

---

[29] D Nelken, 'Puzzling Out Legal Culture: A Comment on Blankenburg' in Nelken, above n 2, 58–88; see now also M Hertogh 'The Curious Case of Dutch Legal Culture: A Reassessment of Survey Evidence' in Nelken, above n 21 (2012).

[30] E Blankenburg and F Bruinsma, *Dutch Legal Culture*, 2nd edn (Deventer, Kluwer, 1994).

[31] L Zedner, 'In Pursuit of the Vernacular; Comparing Law and Order Discourse in Britain and Germany' (1995) 4 *Social and Legal Studies* 517–34.

[32] JK Winn, 'Relational Practices and the Marginalization of Law: Informal Practices of Small Businesses in Taiwan' (1994) 28 *Law and Society Review* 193–232.

[33] E Feldman, 'Patients Rights, Citizen Movements and Japanese Legal Culture' in Nelken, above n 2, 215–36.

scholar. However, the observer's questions may often have more relevance to the country of origin than that under observation. Similarities and differences, for example, often come to life for an observer when they are exemplified by 'significant absences', such as the lack of any reference to 'community' in discourse about crime prevention in Germany.[34] This obliges us to interrogate the way our own cultural assumptions shape the questions we ask and the answers we find convincing. Do we want to understand why Italy has apparently high rates of political corruption or why the UK has apparently low ones?[35] Do we seek to explain why the Italian system of criminal justice has relatively more built-in leniency than the Anglo-American system or the opposite?[36] Why did Blankenburg find the unusually low rate of litigation in Holland more puzzling than the exceptionally high rate of litigation in Germany?

This question of starting points is often left begging because of the implicit collusion between the writer and her audience which privileges what the audience wants to know as if it is what it *should want to know*. What therefore tends to be highlighted are those aspects of the society under investigation which seem especially relevant in confirming or disconfirming previous audience expectations. One result of this is that it can often be instructive to read comparative work, whatever its purported aims, not for what it says about the country or culture being observed, but for what it reveals about the cultural viewpoint of the observer and her home audience (as if we were looking through the other end of the telescope). It is easy for us to see that what an Italian scholar finds strange and problematic about law in the USA is likely to tell us at least as much about Italian assumptions about the role and rule of law as it is does about how things are organised in the USA.[37] We are less quick to appreciate that the same is true in reverse. Much of the voluminous American research on the specificity of Japanese criminal and civil justice, for example, can be criticised for attempting to explain as distinctive features of Japanese legal culture matters which should rather be attributed to the Continental European models which shaped and still shape legal institutions in Japan.

Sometimes the natives whose views we are trying to understand make judgements which are themselves explicitly comparative. Take, for example, the claim by an Italian from Palermo that northern Europeans 'have the state in their hearts'.[38] It is important to see how this judgement tells us something *both* about the observer's own preconceptions and about those he is observing. This accusation (which is more likely, I think, to leave northern Europeans puzzled rather than offended) expresses all the contradictory feelings of someone brought up in the south of Italy and in Sicily, parts of Italy which have, on the one hand, regularly experienced external and internal colonisation, and on the other hand, can with reason lament continued neglect and abandonment by an absentee state. Hence such strong feelings about the state as an object of love and

---

[34] N Lacey and L Zedner, 'Discourses of Community in Criminal Justice' (1995) 22 *Journal of Law and Society* 301–320.

[35] D Nelken, 'Judicial Politics and Corruption in Italy' in M Levi and D Nelken (eds), *The Corruption of Politics and the Politics of Corruption* (Oxford, Blackwell, 1996) 95–113.

[36] D Melossi, 'The Economy of Illegalities: Normal Crimes, Elites and Social Control in Comparative Analysis' in Nelken, above n 8, 202–19.

[37] MR Ferrarese, 'An Entrepreneurial Conception of the Law? The American Model Through Italian Eyes' in Nelken, above n 2, 157–81.

[38] D Nelken, 'Telling Difference: Of Crime and Criminal Justice in Italy' in Nelken, above n 7 (2000) 233–64.

hate: to have *such* a state in our hearts would indeed be worthy of reproach. But most northern Europeans, and especially those used to Anglo-American political discourse in which the term 'the state' hardly appears, do not think of their relationship with government in these terms. Still less would they accept that it is this background sentiment—which they are unaware of having— which both explains their relative law abidingness and permits their individualistic expressions of non-conformity. Perhaps, however, 'we' have indeed internalised the state at such a deep level of our hearts and minds that we simply can no longer recognise this (as Foucault would well have agreed).

As this suggests, cultures are themselves reflexive. Indeed, they often define themselves in part through and against encounters with other cultures (or more specifically, their 'idea' of other cultures.) The formation of identity is usually in part also a product of denial. Faced with legal developments to protect copyright on the continent, Britain in the nineteenth century reinvented its law of copyright so that it became possible to claim that a specific British approach had always existed.[39] In the 1980s the appearance of league tables of relative levels of incarceration induced elites in Finland to change policies so as to move towards the Scandinavian norm by reducing the Finnish prison population. Whether East European cultures can come to resemble Western legal cultures, assuming this to be desirable, depends on whether their citizens believe they can escape the patterns inherited from the past.[40] Conversely, for some scholars rooted in Chinese traditions, what others describe as the welcome spread of 'the rule of law' is criticised as the marginalisation of the importance of 'quing', or the appeal to others' feelings, towards an overemphasis on 'li' or reasonableness.[41]

5. NATIONAL LEGAL CULTURES, AND BEYOND

The search to explain or interpret legal culture at the level of the nation-state (as in the 'Japanese approach to law', 'Dutch legal culture', 'French criminal justice', etc) continues to be an important ambition of comparative law and comparative sociology of law. Ingenious efforts have been made to unsettle stereotypes of which nations are supposedly most or least litigious.[42] But is national legal culture a valid unit for comparison? It is undeniable that legal culture is tied in many ways to its own past, and that national authorities deliberately use law to impose institutional and procedural distinctions, for all sorts of political and legal reasons. Differences between legal cultures may also mobilise or reflect wider social and cultural similarities which roughly coincide with political boundaries. But any direct experience of the myriad differences *within* another society soon demonstrates how unwise it is to talk in stereotypes. Crossing the road in Trento in north Italy is a much safer enterprise than doing so in Naples!

[39] B Sherman, 'Remembering and Forgetting: The Birth of Modern Copyright Law' in Nelken, above n 2, 237–66.

[40] M Krygier, 'Is there Constitutionalism after Communism? Institutional Optimism, Cultural Pessimism, and the Rule of Law' (1997) 26 *International Journal of Sociology* 17–47.

[41] SW Man and CY Wai, 'Whose Rule of Law? Rethinking (Post) Colonial Legal Culture in Hong Kong' (1999) 8 *Social and Legal Studies* 147–70.

[42] E Feldman, 'Blood Justice, Courts, Conflict and Compensation in Japan, France and the United States' (2000) 34 *Law and Society Review* 651–702.

And, if the worst actually happens, there are also important differences in the time it takes to get accident damages from the tribunals in these cities. Nor is legal culture necessarily uniform (either organisationally or meaningfully) across different branches of law. The purported uniformity, coherence or stability of given national cultures will often be no more than an ideological projection or rhetorical device.[43]

National legal cultures do not remain the same over time. The Italian legal system currently suffers from extensive legal delays for which it is routinely condemned by the Strasbourg Court of Human Rights.[44] But two generations before this, judges were getting through more work than was coming in. What has mainly changed is the number of cases they were asked to handle. Likewise, relying on ideas of national character would make it difficult to understand the level of defiance of law in Weimar Germany as compared to the over-deference to law of the Fascist period. Political changes are often the key factor. The Dutch penal system was rightly celebrated for its 'tolerance' from the 1960s onwards in keeping its proportionate prison population well below that of its European neighbours.[45] However, shortly after receiving such praise, Holland engaged in a massive programme of prison building which took it back towards the levels of the 1950s, when its relative level of incarceration was comparable to that of the rest of Europe. The criminal justice elite who pioneered the 'Utrecht' approach were sidelined by the pressures of gaining popular political consensus in the face of Holland's growing drug problem. But if cultures are always changing, they also often show important continuities. To take one of the previous illustrations. Recent years have seen both increasing numbers of prosecutions for political corruption in the UK as well as an effort in Italy to bring down the Berlusconi government through the exposure of sex scandals. Yet the corruption scandals in the UK mainly concerned personal greed by MPs rather than any overlap between business and politics. And the Berluscoi government was not in fact brought down even by accusations of sex with an underaged prostitute—but rather by the larger financial crisis linked to the unsustainable level of national debt.

Rather than limiting ourselves to national legal cultures, both a narrower and larger focus will often be more appropriate. At the level below that of the nation-state it may be fruitful to study the culture of the local courthouse, of different social and interest groups and professional associations, as well as the roles and relationships of individuals in engaging or avoiding disputes. Law will have a different, and changing, role and significance in different social arenas, settings, and for different groups and classes. On the other hand, we may also want to explore wider cultural entities; not only the civil law and common law (or 'Anglo-American') worlds long identified by comparative lawyers, but also more idiosyncratic categories such as the so-called 'Latin legal culture',[46] or even 'modern legal culture' with its alleged converging tendencies.[47] It is also increasingly important to explore so-called 'third cultures' of international

---

[43] Coombe, above n 4.

[44] D Nelken, 'Normalising Time: European Integration and Court Delays in Italy' in H Petersen, H Krunke, A-L Kjær and MR Madsen (eds), *Paradoxes of European Integration* (Aldershot, Ashgate, 2008) 299–323.

[45] D Downes, *Contrasts in Tolerance: Post War Penal Policy in the Netherlands and England and Wales* (Oxford, Oxford University Press, 1988).

[46] A Garapon, 'French Legal Culture and the Shock of "Globalization"' in Nelken, above n 21 (2012), 493–506.

[47] L Friedman, 'Is there a Modern Legal Culture?' (1994) *Ratio Juris* 117.

trade, communication networks and other transnational processes.[48] Recent developments in opening up the world to trade and communication mean that many people increasingly have the sense of living in an interdependent global system marked by borrowing and lending across porous cultural boundaries which are saturated with inequality, power and domination. On the other hand, 'increasing homogenisation of social and cultural forms seems to be accompanied by a proliferation of claims to specific authenticities and identities'.[49]

Nation-states are increasingly interdependent. Indeed, with the advance of globalisation, the pre-eminence of the positive law of the nation-state could be seen as no more than a temporal fusion of law's globalising and localising elements. Different legal systems participate in world or regional bodies and in common projects or trends such as the attempt to construct a 'Fortress Europe' or combat political corruption or money laundering. Each respond in their own way to Europeanisation, Americanisation and globalisation, and each are affected by the culture of modernity (or postmodernity).[50] Thus the boundaries between units of legal culture(s) are fluid and they intersect at the macrolevel and microlevel in ways that are often far from harmonious. In spite of what critics allege, however, this untidiness, as well as the attempts to conceal or resolve it, are all part of the phenomenon of living legal cultures rather than evidence that the concept is otiose.

A problem that is ever more relevant is the question of in what sense a national legal culture can be considered the product of the nation-state in which it is found rather than the outcome of contingent processes of legal transfer. Transplants which derive from other places and other times can range from single laws and legal institutions to entire codes or borrowed systems of law.[51] Many non-European countries have mixed or pluralistic legal systems which testify to waves of colonial invasions as well as imitation.[52] Nearer to home, some of the disputing institutions, which people in Holland think of as most typically Dutch, are in fact a result of German imposition during the occupation and have been abandoned in Germany itself.[53] Law may (or may not) be remade by wider national culture, but it can also itself help mould

---

[48] Y Dezalay and B Garth, *Dealing in Virtue* (Chicago, University of Chicago Press, 1996); F Snyder, 'Governing Economic Globalisation: Global Legal Pluralism and European Law' (1999) 5 *European Law Journal* 334–74; G Teubner, 'Global Bukowina: Legal Pluralism in the World Society' in G Teubner (ed), *Global Law without a State* (Aldershot, Dartmouth, 1997) 3–38; G Teubner, 'Legal Irritants: Good Faith in British Law or How Unifying Law Ends up in New Divergences' (1998) 61 *Modern Law Review* 11–32.

[49] M Strathern (ed), 'Introduction' in *Shifting contexts: Transformations in Anthropological Knowledge* (London, Routledge, 1995) 3.

[50] See eg D Nelken, 'Signaling Conformity: Changing Norms in Japan and China' (2006) 27 *Michigan Journal of International Law* 933-72; D Nelken, 'Corruption as governance', in F von Benda Beckmann and K von Benda Beckmann (eds) *Rules of Law, Laws of Ruling* (Aldershot, Ashgate, 2009) 275–95.

[51] D Nelken, 'Towards a Sociology of Legal Adaptation' in Nelken and Feest, above n 13, 4–55; D Nelken, 'Beyond the Metaphor of Legal Transplants? Consequences of Autopoietic Theory for the study of Cross-Cultural Legal Adaptation' in J Priban and D Nelken (eds), *Law's New Boundaries: The Consequences of Legal Autopoiesis* (Dartmouth, Aldershot, 2001); D Nelken, 'Rethinking Legal Transfers' in P Legrand and RJC Munday (eds), *Comparative Legal Studies: Traditions and Transitions* (Cambridge, Cambridge University Press, 2002).

[52] A Harding, 'Comparative Law and Legal Transplantation in South East Asia' in Nelken and Feest, above n 13.

[53] A Jettinghoff, 'State Formation and Legal Change: On the Impact of International Politics' in Nelken and Feest, above n 13.

that culture. In advance of empirical investigation it would be wrong to assume any particular 'fit' between law and its immediate social and cultural context.

The implications of these processes for theory and practice in the sociology of law emerge most clearly once we recognise that most legal transfers must be seen as attempts to bring about an imagined and different *future*, rather than to conserve the present (as the transplant metaphor might suggest). Hence ex-communist countries try to become more like selected examples of the more successful market societies; South Africa models its new constitution on the best that Western regimes have to offer rather than on constitutional arrangements found in its nearer neighbours in Africa. The hope is that law may be a means of resolving current problems by transforming their society into one more like the source of such borrowed law; legal transfer becomes part of the effort to become more democratic, more economically successful, more secular or more religious. In what is almost a species of sympathetic magic, borrowed law is deemed capable of bringing about the same conditions of a flourishing economy or a healthy civil society that are found in the social context from which the borrowed law has been taken.

The adoption of dissimilar legal models is perhaps most likely where the legal transfer is imposed by third parties as part of a colonial project and/or insisted on as a condition of trade, aid, alliance or diplomatic recognition. But it has also often been sought by elites concerned to 'modernise' their society or otherwise bring it into the wider family of 'civilised' nations. Japan and Turkey are the most obvious examples. There is much discussion of whether or not such transfers can succeed. But even when they do succeed to all apparent purposes, this may be at a high price. There is, for example, continuing controversy in Japan about the significance of the 1890 reception of Western law. Some indigenous scholars say Japan has an underlying culture which is incompatible with modern Western law, others reject this argument, alleging that it is an invention of the power elite by which the people are led to believe in their non-litigiousness (and lack of interest in rights) in order to leave the power holders undisturbed.[54] But, more subtly, because Japan achieved its incredible modernisation not by Western law but through bureaucratic authoritarianism, there are some who feel that Japan has 'not yet achieved the modern'.

Thus, according to one leading Japanese scholar,

> Japan is experienced by the Japanese as a kind of double layered society. On the surface it is an industrialised society with necessary modern paraphernalia, while at bottom, or I would rather say, at the core, it is a hollow yet to be filled by the modern substance.[55]

Having achieved modernisation without 'the modern', which they were told was necessary, the Japanese have a sense of guilt, and engage in a compulsive search for the modern that only leaves them frustrated. As examples of the consequent ambivalent approach to law, Tanase points to the stigma attached to using legal remedies amongst neighbours as well as to a special concern with deciding what source of legitimacy other than law itself can make something count as legal. Interestingly, however, Tanase's conclusion is not that Japanese culture is irreducibly different but that post-

---

[54] T Tanase, 'The Empty Space of the Modern in Japanese Law Discourse' in Nelken and Feest, above n 13.

[55] Ibid.

modern man will increasingly come to resemble the Japanese, 'the decentred man with a hollow core inside who negotiates flexibly his relation with others and improvises workable arrangements ad hoc'.[56]

Many of those participating in the new law and development movement focus on the techniques appropriate for transferring legal and political institutions as if these can be abstracted from culture and from wider social change: '[T]oday's development policy assumes that a country must adapt the proper institutions to facilitate growth and that institutions can be transferred across borders'.[57] Currently many international organisations, such as the International Monetary Fund, are seeking to reshape societies according to a supposedly universal pattern of political and financial integrity. Some of these reforms have or are intended to lead to important changes. Others may be mainly symbolic, a way of marking willingness to accept the 'rules of the game' of the wider global economy. This explains the adhesion to intellectual property or anti-trust provisions of the World Trade Organization by countries who have few ways of enforcing such rules or little need to do so.

But some scholars return from missions abroad all the more convinced that law only makes sense in terms of its own (national) environment. One leading constitutional scholar reports that his experience in China confirmed him in the view that the type of administrative law used in the USA would not be currently workable there. This is because of its interdependence with wider features of American society, above all the presence of a litigious culture and the presumption that party involvement by numerous interest groups can be counted on to comment on and improve bureaucratic regulations. He argues that recommendations for change must rather draw on identifiable features of existing Chinese society.

> [B]y a sort of double reflection, the characterisation of American law that China's distance illuminates, becomes a way of perceiving what the underlying characterisation of a Chinese law would be. That law draws upon the hierarchy, centralisation and governmental prestige in the Chinese system. It would create governmental supervisory agencies, independent of other agencies, but possessing the full power and prestige of government, to enforce statutorily and required procedures.[58]

The current so-called globalisation of law is a complex process that is likely to produce increasing social and economic differentiation as much as harmony.[59] Assumptions of necessary convergence risks underestimating the continuing importance of culture and resistance (even if such resistance itself increasingly comes to be organised globally).[60] Nevertheless, one of the most important tasks of the comparative sociologist of law

---

[56] Ibid.

[57] T Ginsburg, 'Does Law Matter for Economic Development? Evidence from East Asia' (2000) *Law and Society Review* 829–56, 833.

[58] E Rubin, 'Administrative Law and the Complexity of Culture' in A Seidman, R Seidman and J Payne (eds), *Legislative Drafting for Market Reform: Some Lessons from China* (Basingstoke, Macmillian, 2000) 108.

[59] B de Sousa Santos, *Towards a New Common Sense* (London, Routledge, 1995); D Nelken, 'The Globalization of Crime and Criminal Justice: Prospects and Problems' in M Freeman (ed), *Law and Opinion at the End of the 20th Century* (Oxford, Oxford University Press, 1997) 251–79; W Heyderbrand, 'Globalization and the Rule of Law at the End of the 20th Century' in A Febbrajo, D Nelken and V Olgiati (eds), *Social Processes and Patterns of Legal Control: European Yearbook of Sociology of Law 2000* (Milan, Giuffrè, 2001) 25–127.

[60] Friedman, above n 47.

at the present time is to try and capture the process of transnational lawmaking[61] and to see how far in practice globalisation represents the attempted imposition of one particular legal culture on other societies. Importing countries are offered both the Anglo-American model whose prestige is spread by trade and the media, and national versions of the Continental legal system embodied in ready-packaged codes. The Anglo-American model is seen to be characterised by its emphasis on the care taken to link law and economics (rather than law and the state), procedures which rely on orality, party initiative, negotiation inside law or more broad cultural features such as individualism and the search for 'total justice'. Only some of these elements are actually on offer in legal transfers and much of this model does not accurately describe how the law operates at home (much of the American legal and regulatory system relies on inquisitorial methods). Much of what was represented by the 'rule of law' itself, as a way of providing certainty and keeping the state within bounds, seems increasingly outdated for the regulation of international commercial exchange by computers between multinationals more powerful than many of the governments of the countries in which they trade.[62]

More than any particular feature of legal culture, however, what does seem to be spreading is the common law ideology of 'pragmatic legal instrumentalism', *the very idea that law is something which does or should 'work'*, together with the claim that this is something which can or should be assessed in ways which are separable from wider political debates. Only time will tell what consequences this may have. How far, for example, has the North American Free Trade Agreement succeeded in transforming a legal culture such as Mexico where, according to one insider, 'law institutes without regulating'?[63]

---

[61] S Merry, *Human Rights and Gender Violence* (Chicago, University of Chicago Press 2006); D Nelken 'Transnational Legal Processes and the (Re)Construction of the "Social": The Case of Human Trafficking' in D Feenan (ed), *The 'Social' in Social-Legal Studies* (London, Routledge, 2012).

[62] WE Scheuerman, 'Globalization and the Fate of Law' in D Dyzenhaus (ed), *Recrafting the Rule of Law: The Limits of Legal Order* (Oxford, Hart Publishing, 1999) 243–66.

[63] S Lopez-Ayllon, 'Notes on Mexican Legal Culture' in Nelken, above n. 21 (1995), 477–492.

Index